The World [illegible]

Volume I

TITLES IN THE BLOOMSBURY REVELATIONS SERIES

Aesthetic Theory, Theodor W. Adorno

The Oresteia, Aeschylus

Being and Event, Alain Badiou

Infinite Thought, Alain Badiou

On Religion, Karl Barth

The Language of Fashion, Roland Barthes

The Intelligence of Evil, Jean Baudrillard

Key Writings, Henri Bergson

I and Thou, Martin Buber

The Tomb of Tutankhamun: Volumes 1-3, Howard Carter

A History of the English-Speaking Peoples: Volumes 1-4,
Sir Winston S. Churchill

Never Give In! Sir Winston S. Churchill

The Boer War, Sir Winston S. Churchill

The Second World War, Sir Winston S. Churchill

The World Crisis: Volumes 1-5, Sir Winston S. Churchill

In Defence of Politics, Bernard Crick

Intensive Science and Virtual Philosophy, Manuel DeLanda

Cinema I, Gilles Deleuze

Cinema II, Gilles Deleuze

Difference and Repetition, Gilles Deleuze

A Thousand Plateaus, Gilles Deleuze and Félix Guattari

Anti-Oedipus, Gilles Deleuze and Félix Guattari

Origins of Analytical Philosophy, Michael Dummett

Taking Rights Seriously, Ronald Dworkin

Discourse on Free Will, Desiderius Erasmus and Martin Luther

The Theatre of the Absurd, Martin Esslin

Education for Critical Consciousness, Paulo Freire
Pedagogy of Hope, Paulo Freire
Marx's Concept of Man, Erich Fromm
To Have or To Be?, Erich Fromm
Truth and Method, Hans Georg Gadamer
All Men Are Brothers, Mohandas K. Gandhi
Violence and the Sacred, René Girard
Among the Dead Cities, A.C. Grayling
Towards the Light, A.C. Grayling
The Three Ecologies, Félix Guattari
The Essence of Truth, Martin Heidegger
The Odyssey, Homer
Eclipse of Reason, Max Horkheimer
Language of the Third Reich, Victor Klemperer
Rhythmanalysis, Henri Lefebvre
After Virtue, Alasdair MacIntyre
Time for Revolution, Antonio Negri
Apologia Pro Vita Sua, John Henry Newman
The Politics of Aesthetics, Jacques Rancière
Course in General Linguistics, Ferdinand de Saussure
An Actor Prepares, Constantin Stanislavski
Building A Character, Constantin Stanislavski
Creating A Role, Constantin Stanislavski
Interrogating the Real, Slavoj Žižek
The Universal Exception, Slavoj Žižek

Some titles are not available in North America.

The World Crisis

Volume I: 1911–1914

Winston S. Churchill

Bloomsbury Academic
An imprint of Bloomsbury Publishing Plc

B L O O M S B U R Y
LONDON • NEW DELHI • NEW YORK • SYDNEY

Bloomsbury Academic
An imprint of Bloomsbury Publishing Plc

50 Bedford Square
London
WC1B 3DP
UK

1385 Broadway
New York
NY 10018
USA

www.bloomsbury.com

BLOOMSBURY and the Diana logo are trademarks of Bloomsbury Publishing Plc

First published by Odhams Press 1950

Bloomsbury Revelations edition first published in 2015 by Bloomsbury Academic

British Library Cataloguing-in-Publication Data
A catalogue record for this book is available from the British Library.

ISBN: HB: 978-1-4742-2337-9
PB: 978-1-4725-8640-7
ePDF: 978-1-4725-8642-1
ePub: 978-1-4725-8641-4

Library of Congress Cataloging-in-Publication Data
A catalog record for this book is available from the Library of Congress.

Series: Bloomsbury Revelations

Typeset by Deanta Global Publishing Services, Chennai, India
Printed and bound in India

Contents

Maps and Illustrations

PREFACE*

I

With regard to the first section of this book, it is essential to state that from October 25, 1911, to May 28, 1915, I was, in the words of the Royal Letters Patent and Orders in Council, 'responsible to Crown and Parliament for all the business of the Admiralty.' This period comprised the final stage in the preparation against a war with Germany; the mobilization and concentration of the Fleet before the outbreak; the organization of the Blockade; the gathering in 1914 of the Imperial forces from all over the world; the clearance from the oceans of all the German cruisers and commerce destroyers; the reinforcement of the Fleet by new construction in 1914 and 1915; the frustration and defeat of the first German submarine attack upon merchant shipping in 1915; and the initiation of the enterprise against the Dardanelles. It was marked before the war by a complete revision of British naval war plans; by the building of a fast division of battleships armed with 15-inch guns and driven by oil fuel; by the proposals, rejected by Germany, for a naval holiday; and by the largest supplies till then ever voted by Parliament for the British Fleet. It was distinguished during the war for the victories of the Heligoland Bight, of the Falkland Islands, and the Dogger Bank; and for the attempt to succour Antwerp. It was memorable for the disaster to the three cruisers off the Dutch Coast; the loss of Admiral Cradock's squadron at Coronel; and the failure of the Navy to force the Dardanelles.

Eight years had passed since I quitted the Admiralty, and I felt it both my right and my duty to set forth the manner in which I endeavoured to discharge my share in these hazardous responsibilities. In doing so I adhered to certain strict rules. I made no important statement of fact relating to naval operations or Admiralty business, on which I did not possess unimpeachable documentary proof. I made or implied no criticism of any decision or action taken or neglected by others, unless I could prove that I had expressed the same opinion in writing *before the event*.

In every case where the interests of the State allowed, I printed the actual memoranda, directions, minutes, telegrams or letters written by me at the time, irrespective of whether these documents had been vindicated or falsified by the march of history and of time. The only excisions of relevant matter from the documents were made to avoid needlessly hurting the feelings of individuals, or the pride of friendly nations. For such reasons here and there sentences were softened or suppressed. But the whole story is recorded as it happened, by the actual counsels offered and orders given in the fierce turmoil of

*This Preface is the result of the merging of the Prefaces to the three Parts of the original edition.

each day. The principal minutes by which Admiralty business was conducted embody in every case decisions for which, as the highest executive authority in the department, I was directly responsible, and are in all cases expressed in my own words. I am equally accountable, together with the First Sea Lord at the time, for the principal telegrams which moved fleets, squadrons and individual ships, all of which (unless the contrary appears) bear my initials as their final sanction.

If in the great number of decisions and orders which these pages recount and which deal with so many violent and controversial affairs, mistakes can be found which led to mishap, the fault is mine. If, on the other hand, favourable results were achieved, that should be counted to some extent as an offset. Where the decision lay outside my powers and was taken contrary to my advice, I rest on the written record of my warning. Should it be objected that in any of these matters, many of them so highly technical, a landsman and layman could form no valuable opinion, I point to the documents themselves. They can be judged as they stand. But lest, on the other hand, it should be thought that I am seeking to claim credit which is not mine, it must be remembered that throughout this period I enjoyed the assistance, loyal, spontaneous and unstinted, of the best brains of the Royal Navy, that every treasure of every branch of the Admiralty and the Fleet was lavished upon my instruction, and that I had only to apply my own reason and instinct to the arguments of those who I believe stood in the foremost rank of the naval experts of the world.

II

In the first section of this Account I had a long and varied tale to tell: nor was it possible to avoid dealing with many episodes of peace and war necessarily exciting dispute. Still the broad and enduring results were crowned with success, and there was praise and honour for all concerned in their achievement. The second section deals with a year of ill-fortune to the cause of the Allies. Brilliant opportunities presented themselves in vain; grave mistakes were made, and losses were incurred measureless in their pain. The assignment and the division of the responsibility for these events is a task at once difficult and invidious. Moreover I was for a time an actor exercising an influence or even an authority, sometimes decisive and often potent, upon the unfolding of the tragedy. I was brought by the convictions I held and the course I took into unyielding conflict with two of the most honoured and famous war-figures of our national life—Lord Fisher and Lord Kitchener. Both are now silent for ever. Yet my contention persists, nor could I without insincerity, without concealment, without a woeful surrender of the truth as I see it, fail to make that contention good.

I disclaimed in my original Preface the position of the historian. It is not for me with my record and special point of view to pronounce a final conclusion. That must be left to others and to other times. But I have set forth what I believe to be fair and true; and I present it once more as a contribution to history of which note should be taken together with other accounts. I cannot expect to alter the fixed and prevailing opinions of the war generation. They lived and fought their way through the awful struggle in the light of the knowledge given to them at the time, and their minds are stamped with its imprint. All I ask is that this Account shall also be placed on record and shall survive as one of the factors upon which the judgment of our children will be founded.

It is absurd to argue that the facts should not be fully published, or that obligations of secrecy are violated by their disclosure in good faith. Thousands of facts have been made public and hundreds of secret matters exposed. A whole library, for instance, has sprung into existence about the Dardanelles Campaign and the circumstances which led to it. All the principal actors have told their stories, and many minor ones. Lord Fisher has published two volumes in which may be read not only his official memoranda, but even the full record of his personal interventions in the secret discussion of the War Committee. Lord Kitchener's biographer has printed whatever documents he considered necessary to the case he was unfolding, including even extracts from my own Cabinet papers. Sir Ian Hamilton has published in the fullest detail his records and diaries. Major-General C. E. Callwell, Director of Military Operations at the time, has written what purports to be a history of the Dardanelles. The Official Naval Historian and the Official Historian of the Commonwealth of Australia, with access to every form of secret information, have traversed the whole ground, dealing with every episode and quoting or summarizing every important order or telegram for which I was answerable, and all other confidential papers which they considered relevant. The Royal Commission on the Dardanelles has issued its lengthy and searching report. There are many other works of importance and repute in the English language alone, professing to deal authoritatively with the whole subject.

Upon me more than any other person the responsibility tor the Dardanelles and all that it involved was cast. Upon me fell almost exclusively the fierce war-time censures of Press and Public. Upon me alone among the high authorities concerned was the penalty inflicted—not of loss of office, for that is a petty thing—but of interruption and deprivation of control while the fate of the enterprise was still in suspense. In these circumstances it was my intention to set forth the facts as they were known to me without bitterness, but without compunction, seeking no offence, but concealing no essential.

It was certainly not my purpose to shift or shirk my responsibility, or to set upon other shoulders burdens which are my own. On the contrary, as will be seen, I accepted the fullest responsibility for all that I did and had the power to do. I took also my share for the unforeseeable consequences of these actions. But I wished to define and recount exactly what that share was, and what those actions were, and to do this not in the easily turned language of the aftertime, but as far as possible in the actual operation orders and counsels given by me at the time and *before* the event.

Concerning the more general aspects of the war on which this second section touches, I was equally conscious of running counter to many established opinions, to the dominant military doctrines of those days, and to some extent to the naval performance. I never therefore expected to do more than submit the convictions by which I was actuated, and in which I still reside, to the consideration of my countrymen. I could not ask them to share my views. I was content that they should know them.

III

Turning now to the final section of this work, I wish to point out that in dealing with a field so wide as that of the last three years of the World War, a highly selective process was necessary. I tried to find and follow the stepping-stones of Fate. I set myself at each stage to answer the questions 'What happened, and Why?' I sought to guide the reader to those points where the course of events was being decided, whether on a battlefield, in a conning-tower, in Council, in Parliament, in a lobby, a laboratory or a workshop. Such a method is no substitute for history, but it may be an aid both to the writing and to the study of history.

I had many and varied opportunities of learning about the war. During the first five months of the period which this section covers, till May, 1916, I commanded a battalion in the line at 'Plugstreet.' Thereafter, until July, 1917, I was occupied in Parliament, and also in defending my conduct as First Lord of the Admiralty before the Statutory Commission of Inquiry into the Dardanelles Expedition. In both these periods I was closely in touch with some of the leading personalities, military and civil, who were conducting British affairs, and also to a lesser extent with those similarly placed in France. I was therefore able though in a private station to follow with attention political and military incidents. In July, 1917, I became Minister of Munitions in Mr. Lloyd George's administration, and thus for the last seventeen months of the war I was responsible for supplying the Army and Air Force with all their war material.

I deemed it of interest to record before they faded the impression and emphasis of various episodes, so far as I was personally able to appreciate them.

Many years have elapsed since the events in this account were ended. Almost all the actors—Admirals, Generals, Prime Ministers, Foreign Secretaries, Chancellors, even Sovereigns and Presidents in the victorious or vanquished states have told their tale, and a gigantic library upon the Great War is already in existence. The official histories of the leading powers march out steadily volume after volume. There is therefore no lack of materials to check and amplify personal recollection.

I have been greatly struck in my reading during recent years with the enormous superiority of French war literature and criticism to anything that has appeared in England. Not only is the quantity of authoritative works far greater, but their quality and knowledge are incomparably higher. An immense number of brilliantly written books by responsible persons have enabled the French public to form an instructed view upon the whole inner conduct of the war in its military and political aspects. As far as I can judge, an even greater activity of publication and discussion has taken place in Germany. And here again all the material facts and documents have been disclosed through one channel or another. The time is surely coming when the British public should receive in the form of a series of official publications a full supply of authentic documents in order that a true judgment may be formed of this tremendous epoch. In the meanwhile, I confined myself to printing textually only documents which I had written myself and for which I was personally responsible, or those which had already been published by others here or abroad.

My last section was far advanced when I read for the first time Defoe's *Memoirs of a Cavalier*. In this delightful work the author hangs the chronicle and discussion of great military and political events upon the thread of the personal experiences of an individual. I was immensely encouraged to find that I had been unconsciously following with halting steps the example of so great a master of narrative. In this last section I tried to present the reader at once with a comprehensive view of the mighty panorama and with a selection of its dominating features; but I also told my own story and surveyed the scene from my own subordinate though responsible station. My own doctrines on the methods of waging war, and the action or advice for which I was accountable, have been the target for many criticisms set forth in books by writers of high professional authority. I was glad to be able to unfold my ideas by means of authentic documents written by me during or before the event. I hope that the result will stimulate yet further reflection upon the prodigious cataclysm which has shattered and re-shaped our life and the world we live in.

I desire once again to express my thanks to those who assisted me by reading the proofs and advising on technical matters, and I respect their wish for anonymity.

Finally, I have made it plain—though it was scarcely necessary—that for all the expressions of opinion and statements of fact which this work contains, I am alone responsible. They do not profess to represent the official views of the military departments; and they in no way committed the Government of which I was a member to endorsement or agreement. They constitute a personal judgment and record of events which now belong to History.

W. S. C.

FOREWORD TO NEW EDITION

This book was originally published in four large volumes which appeared at intervals and at a cost that was necessarily beyond the means of many whom I would have been glad to reach. It is therefore particularly gratifying to me to know that arrangements have been made for its appearance in a form that will appeal to the large public of average means who could never have put the earlier edition upon their shelves.

Since the publication of that issue I have submitted the work to considerable revision, and in doing so I have been able to profit by not a little new knowledge. In especial I have been able to give a more correct account of the circumstances attending Lord Fisher's resignation and a much fuller narrative of the great opening battles in France. All this new matter, which includes all the pages devoted to the Battle of the Marne, has hitherto only appeared in a one-volume edition which was of necessity very considerably abridged. In the present edition, therefore, it takes its place for the first time in the complete work. The reader thus obtains a narrative that not only appears in a form far less costly than its earlier issues, but is also fuller and more correct.

This book, as I have elsewhere pointed out, strives to follow throughout the methods and balance of Defoe's *Memoirs of a Cavalier*. It is a contribution to history strung upon a fairly strong thread of personal reminiscence. It does not pretend to be a comprehensive record; but it aims at helping to disentangle from an immense mass of material the crucial issues and cardinal decisions. Throughout I have set myself to explain faithfully and to the best of my ability what happened and why.

I write this new Preface in a day of extraordinary difficulty and danger. So strange indeed is the present international situation that it passes the wit of man to say what new portent will have appeared in the European sky by the time these words see the light. Armed to the teeth and feverishly adding to their armaments, the nations of Europe are asking themselves, "Is this the peace for which we fought? What have all our sacrifices brought us? What is coming next?" Is it possible that the appalling drama with which this book is concerned was enacted in vain? Is it conceivable that in our own day the hand of Destiny will raise the curtain on a tragedy of even greater horror?

These are gloomy questions, but History's answer need not be gloomy. The attainment of a genuine peace should not be beyond the reach of human wisdom inspired by human goodwill. But if we are to escape a cataclysm fatal to civilization itself let us lay to heart before it is too late the lesson, writ large in these pages, of the tragic years 1914–18, a lesson that the events of this Autumn have only too bitterly emphasized—the paramount necessity of preparedness.

WINSTON S. CHURCHILL. *November* 22, 1938.

FOREWORD TO NEW EDITION

CHAPTER I
THE VIALS OF WRATH: 1870–1904

'To put on record what were their grounds of feud.'

—Herodotus.

The Unending Task—Ruthless War—The Victorian Age—National Pride—National Accountability—The Franco-German Feud—Bismarck's Apprehension—His Precautions and Alliances—The Bismarckian Period and System—The Young Emperor and Caprivi—The Franco-Russian Alliance, 1892—The Balance of Power—Anglo-German Ties—Anglo-German Estrangement—Germany and the South African War—The Beginnings of the German Navy—The Birth of a Challenge—The Anglo-Japanese Alliance—The Russo-Japanese War—Consequences—The Anglo-French Agreement of 1904—Lord Rosebery's Comment—The Triple Entente—Degeneration in Turkey and Austria—The Long Descent—The Sinister Hypothesis.

It was the custom in the palmy days of Queen Victoria for statesmen to expatiate upon the glories of the British Empire, and to rejoice in that protecting Providence which had preserved us through so many dangers and brought us at length into a secure and prosperous age. Little did they know that the worst perils had still to be encountered and that the greatest triumphs were yet to be won.

Children were taught of the Great War against Napoleon as the culminating effort in the history of the British peoples, and they looked on Waterloo and Trafalgar as the supreme achievements of British arms by land and sea. These prodigious victories, eclipsing all that had gone before, seemed the fit and predestined ending to the long drama of our island race, which had advanced over a thousand years from small and weak beginnings to a foremost position in the world. Three separate times in three different centuries had the British people rescued Europe from a military domination. Thrice had the Low Countries been assailed: by Spain, by the French Monarchy, by the French Empire. Thrice had British war and policy, often maintained single-handed, overthrown the aggressor. Always at the outset the strength of the enemy had seemed overwhelming, always the struggle had been prolonged through many years and across awful hazards, always the victory had at last been won: and the last of all the victories had been the greatest of all, gained after the most ruinous struggle and over the most formidable foe.

Surely that was the end of the tale as it was so often the end of the book. History showed the rise, culmination, splendour, transition and decline of States and Empires. It seemed inconceivable that the same series of tremendous events through which since the days of Queen Elizabeth we had three times made our way successfully, should be repeated a fourth time and on an immeasurably larger scale. Yet that is what has happened, and what we have lived to see.

* * * * *

The Great War through which we have passed differed from all ancient wars in the immense power of the combatants and their fearful agencies of destruction, and from all modern wars in the utter ruthlessness with which it was fought. All the horrors of all the ages were brought together, and not only armies but whole populations were thrust into the midst of them. The mighty educated States involved conceived with reason that their very existence was at stake. Germany having let Hell loose kept well in the van of terror; but she was followed step by step by the desperate and ultimately avenging nations she had assailed. Every outrage against humanity or international law was repaid by reprisals often on a greater scale and of longer duration. No truce or parley mitigated the strife of the armies. The wounded died between the lines: the dead mouldered into the soil. Merchant ships and neutral ships and hospital ships were sunk on the seas and all on board left to their fate, or killed as they swam. Every effort was made to starve whole nations into submission without regard to age or sex. Cities and monuments were smashed by artillery. Bombs from the air were cast down indiscriminately. Poison gas in many forms stifled or seared the soldiers. Liquid fire was projected upon their bodies. Men fell from the air in flames, or were smothered, often slowly, in the dark recesses of the sea. The fighting strength of armies was limited only by the manhood of their countries. Europe and large parts of Asia and Africa became one vast battlefield on which after years of struggle not armies but nations broke and ran. When all was over, Torture and Cannibalism were the only two expedients that the civilized, scientific, Christian States had been able to deny themselves: and these were of doubtful utility.

But nothing daunted the valiant heart of man. Son of the Stone Age, vanquisher of nature with all her trials and monsters, he met the awful and self-inflicted agony with new reserves of fortitude. Freed in the main by his intelligence from mediæval fears, he marched to death with sombre dignity. His nervous system was found in the twentieth century capable of enduring physical and moral stresses before which the simpler natures of primeval times would have collapsed. Again and again to the hideous bombardment, again and again from the hospital to the front, again and again to the hungry submarines, he strode unflinching. And withal, as an individual, preserved through these torments the glories of a reasonable and compassionate mind.

* * * * *

In the beginning of the twentieth century men were everywhere unconscious of the rate at which the world was growing. It required the convulsion of the war to awaken the nations to the knowledge of their strength. For a year after the war had begun hardly anyone understood how terrific, how almost inexhaustible were the resources in force, in substance, in virtue, behind every one of the combatants. The vials of wrath were full: but so were the reservoirs of power. From the end of the Napoleonic Wars, and still more after 1870, the accumulation of wealth and health by every civilized community had been practically unchecked. Here and there a retarding episode had occurred. The waves had recoiled after advancing: but the mounting tides still flowed. And when the dread signal of Armageddon was made, mankind was found to be many times stronger in valour, in endurance, in brains, in science, in apparatus, in organization, not only than it had ever been before, but than even its most audacious optimists had dared to dream.

The Victorian Age was the age of accumulation; not of a mere piling up of material wealth, but of the growth and gathering in every land of all those elements and factors which go to make up the power of States. Education spread itself over the broad surface of the millions. Science had opened the limitless treasure-house of nature. Door after door had been unlocked. One dim mysterious gallery after another had been lighted up, explored, made free for all: and every gallery entered gave access to at least two more. Every morning when the world woke up, some new machinery had started running. Every night while the world had supper, it was running still. It ran on while all men slept.

And the advance of the collective mind was at a similar pace. Disraeli said of the early years of the nineteenth century, 'In those days England was for the few—and for the very few.' Every year of Queen Victoria's reign saw those limits broken and extended. Every year brought in new thousands of people in private stations who thought about their own country and its story and its duties towards other countries, to the world and to the future, and understood the greatness of the responsibilities of which they were the heirs. Every year diffused a wider measure of material comfort among the higher ranks of labour. Substantial progress was made in mitigating the hard lot of the mass. Their health improved, their lives and the lives of their children were brightened, their stature grew, their securities against some of their gravest misfortunes were multiplied, their numbers greatly increased.

Thus when all the trumpets sounded, every class and rank had something to give to the need of the State. Some gave their science and some their wealth, some gave their business energy and drive, and some their wonderful personal prowess, and some their patient strength or patient weakness. But none gave more, or gave more readily, than the common man or woman who had nothing but a precarious week's wages between them and poverty, and owned little more than the slender equipment of a cottage, and the garments in which they stood upright. Their love and pride of country, their loyalty to the symbols with which they were familiar, their keen sense of right and wrong as they saw it, led them to outface and endure perils and ordeals the like of which men had not known on earth.

But these developments, these virtues, were no monopoly of any one nation. In every free country, great or small, the spirit of patriotism and nationality grew steadily; and in every country, bond or free, the organization and structure into which men were fitted by the laws, gathered and armed this sentiment. Far more than their vices, the virtues of nations ill-directed or mis-directed by their rulers, became the cause of their own undoing and of the general catastrophe. And these rulers, in Germany, Austria, and Italy; in France, Russia or Britain, how far were they to blame? Was there any man of real eminence and responsibility whose devil heart conceived and willed this awful thing? One rises from the study of the causes of the Great War with a prevailing sense of the defective control of individuals upon world fortunes. It has been well said, 'there is always more error than design in human affairs.' The limited minds even of the ablest men, their disputed authority, the climate of opinion in which they dwell, their transient and partial contributions to the mighty problem, that problem itself so far beyond their compass, so vast in scale and detail, so changing in its aspect—all this must surely be considered before the complete condemnation of the vanquished or the complete acquittal of the victors can be pronounced. Events also got on to certain lines, and no one could get them off again. Germany clanked obstinately, recklessly, awkwardly towards the crater and dragged us all in with her. But fierce resentments dwelt in France, and in Russia there were wheels within wheels. Could we in England perhaps by some effort, by some sacrifice of our material interests, by some compulsive gesture, at once of friendship and command, have reconciled France and Germany in time and formed that grand association on which alone the peace and glory of Europe would be safe? I cannot tell. I only know that we tried our best to steer our country through the gathering dangers of the armed peace without bringing her to war or others to war, and when these efforts failed, we drove through the tempest without bringing her to destruction.

* * * * *

There is no need here to trace the ancient causes of quarrel between the Germans and the French, to catalogue the conflicts with which they have scarred the centuries, nor to appraise the balance of injury or of provocation on one side or the other. When on the 18th of January, 1871, the triumph of the Germans was consolidated by the Proclamation of the German Empire in the Palace of Versailles, a new volume of European history was opened. 'Europe,' it was said, 'has lost a mistress and has gained a master.' A new and mighty State had come into being, sustained by an overflowing population, equipped with science and learning, organized for war and crowned with victory. France, stripped of Alsace and Lorraine, beaten, impoverished, divided and alone, condemned to a decisive and increasing numerical inferiority, fell back to ponder in shade and isolation on her departed glories.

But the chiefs of the German Empire were under no illusions as to the formidable character and implacable resolves of their prostrate antagonist. 'What we gained by arms in half a year,' said Moltke, 'we must protect by arms for half a century, if it is not to be torn from us again.' Bismarck, more prudent still, would never have taken Lorraine. Forced by military pressure to assume the double burden against his better judgment, he exhibited from the outset and in every act of his policy an extreme apprehension. Restrained by the opinion of the world, and the decided attitude of Great Britain, from striking down a reviving France in 1875, he devoted his whole power and genius to the construction of an elaborate system of alliances designed to secure the continued ascendancy of Germany and the maintenance of her conquests. He knew the quarrel with France was irreconcilable except at a price which Germany would never consent to pay. He understood that the abiding enmity of a terrific people would be fixed on his new-built Empire. Everything else must be subordinated to that central fact. Germany could afford no other antagonisms. In 1879 he formed an alliance with Austria. Four years later this was expanded into the Triple Alliance between Germany, Austria and Italy. Roumania was brought into the system by a secret alliance in 1883. Not only must there be Insurance; there must be Reinsurance. What he feared most was a counter-alliance between France and Russia; and none of these extending arrangements met this danger. His alliance with Austria indeed, if left by itself, would naturally tend to draw France and Russia together. Could he not make a league of the three Emperors—Germany, Austria, and Russia united? There at last was overwhelming strength and enduring safety. When in 1887, after six years, this supreme ideal of Bismarck was ruptured by the clash of Russian and Austrian interests in the Balkans, he turned—as the best means still open to him—to his Reinsurance Treaty with Russia. Germany, by this arrangement, secured herself against becoming the object of an aggressive combination by France and Russia. Russia on the other hand was reassured that the Austro-German alliance would not be used to undermine her position in the Balkans.

All these cautious and sapient measures were designed with the object of enabling Germany to enjoy her victory in peace. The Bismarckian system, further, always included the principle of good relations with Great Britain. This was necessary, for it was well known that Italy would never willingly commit herself to anything that would bring her into war with Great Britain, and had, as the world now knows, required this fact to be specifically stated in the original and secret text of the Triple Alliance. To this Alliance in its early years Great Britain had been wholly favourable. Thus France was left to nurse her scars alone; and Germany, assured in her predominance on the Continent, was able to take the fullest advantage of the immense industrial developments which characterized the close of the nineteenth century. The policy of Germany further encouraged France as a consolation to develop her colonial possessions in order to take her thoughts off Europe, and incidentally to promote a convenient rivalry and friction with Great Britain.

This arrangement, under which Europe lived rigidly but peacefully for twenty years, and Germany waxed in power and splendour, was ended in 1890 with the fall of Bismarck. The Iron Chancellor was gone, and new forces began to assail the system he had maintained with consummate ability so long. There was a constant danger of conflagration in the Balkans and in the Near East through Turkish misgovernment. The rising tides of pan-Slavism and the strong anti-German currents in Russia began to wash against the structure of the Reinsurance Treaty. Lastly, German ambitions grew with German prosperity. Not content with the hegemony of Europe, she sought a colonial domain. Already the greatest of military Empires, she began increasingly to turn her thoughts to the sea. The young Emperor, freed from Bismarck and finding in Count Caprivi, and the lesser men who succeeded him, complacent coadjutors, began gaily to dispense with the safeguards and precautions by which the safety of Germany had been buttressed. While the quarrel with France remained open and undying, the Reinsurance Treaty with Russia was dropped, and later on the naval rivalry with Britain was begun. These two sombre decisions rolled forward slowly as the years unfolded. Their consequences became apparent in due season. In 1892 the event against which the whole policy of Bismarck had been directed came to pass. The Dual Alliance was signed between Russia and France. Although the effects were not immediately visible, the European situation was in fact transformed. Henceforward for the undisputed but soberly exercised predominance of Germany, there was substituted a balance of power. Two vast combinations, each disposing of enormous military resources, dwelt together at first side by side, but gradually face to face.

* * * * *

Although the groupings of the great Powers had thus been altered sensibly to the disadvantage of Germany, there was in this alteration nothing that threatened her with war. The abiding spirit of France had never abandoned the dream of recovering the lost provinces, but the prevailing temper of the French nation was pacific, and all classes remained under the impression of the might of Germany and of the terrible consequences likely to result from war.

Moreover, the French were never sure of Russia in a purely Franco-German quarrel. True, there was the Treaty; but the Treaty to become operative required aggression on the part of Germany. What constitutes aggression? At what point in a dispute between two heavily armed parties, does one side or the other become the aggressor? At any rate there was a wide field for discretionary action on the part of Russia. Of all these matters she would be the judge, and she would be the judge at a moment when it might be said that the Russian people would be sent to die in millions over a quarrel between France and Germany in which they had no direct interest. The word of the Tsar was indeed a great assurance. But Tsars who tried to lead their nations, however honourably, into unpopular wars might disappear. The policy of a great people, if hung too directly upon the person of a single individual, was liable to be changed by his disappearance. France, therefore, could never feel certain that if on any occasion she resisted German pressure and war resulted, Russia would march.

Such was the ponderous balance which had succeeded the unquestioned ascendancy of Germany. Outside both systems rested England, secure in an overwhelming, and as yet unchallenged, naval supremacy. It was evident that the position of the British Empire received added importance from the fact that adhesion to either Alliance would decide the predominance of strength. But Lord Salisbury showed no wish to exploit this favourable situation. He maintained steadily the traditional friendly attitude towards Germany combined with a cool detachment from Continental entanglements.

* * * * *

It had been easy for Germany to lose touch with Russia, but the alienation of England was a far longer process. So many props and ties had successively to be demolished. British suspicions of Russia in Asia, the historic antagonism to France, memories of Blenheim, of Minden and of Waterloo, the continued disputes with France in Egypt and in the Colonial sphere, the intimate business connexions between Germany and England, the relationship of the Royal Families—all these constituted a profound association between the British Empire and the leading State in the Triple Alliance. It was no part of British policy to obstruct the new-born Colonial aspirations of Germany, and in more than one instance, as at Samoa, we actively assisted them. With a complete detachment from strategic considerations, Lord Salisbury exchanged Heligoland for Zanzibar. Still even before the fall of Bismarck the Germans did not seem pleasant diplomatic comrades. They appeared always to be seeking to enlist our aid and reminding us that they were our only friend. To emphasize this they went even farther. They sought in minor ways to embroil us with France and Russia. Each year the Wilhelmstrasse looked inquiringly to the Court of St. James's for some new service or concession which should keep Germany's diplomatic goodwill alive for a further period. Each year they made mischief for us with France and Russia, and pointed the moral of how unpopular Great Britain was, what powerful enemies she had, and how lucky she was to find a friend in Germany. Where would she be in the councils of Europe if German assistance were withdrawn, or if Germany threw her influence into the opposing combination? These manifestations, prolonged for nearly twenty years, produced very definite sensations of estrangement in the minds of the rising generation at the British Foreign Office.

But none of these woes of diplomatists deflected the steady course of British policy. The Colonial expansion of Germany was viewed with easy indifference by the British Empire. In spite of their rivalry in trade, there grew up a far more important commercial connexion between Britain and Germany. In Europe we were each other's best customers. Even the German Emperor's telegram to President Kruger on the Jameson Raid in 1896, which we now know to have been no personal act but a decision of the German Government, produced only a temporary ebullition of anger. All the German outburst of rage against England during the Boer War, and such attempts as were made to form a European coalition against us, did not prevent Mr. Chamberlain in 1901 from advocating an alliance with Germany, or the British Foreign Office from proposing in the same year to make the Alliance between Britain and Japan into a Triple Alliance including Germany. During this period we had at least as serious differences with France as with Germany, and sufficient naval superiority not to be seriously disquieted by either. We stood equally clear of the Triple and of the Dual Alliance. We had no intention of being drawn into a Continental quarrel. No effort by France to regain her lost provinces appealed to the British public or to any political party. The idea of a British Army fighting in Europe amid the mighty hosts of the Continent was by all dismissed as utterly absurd. Only a menace to the very life of the British nation would stir the British Empire from its placid and tolerant detachment from Continental affairs. But that menace Germany was destined to supply.

* * * * *

'Among the Great Powers,' said Moltke in his Military Testament, 'England necessarily requires a strong ally on the Continent. She would not find one which corresponds better to all her interests than a United Germany, that can never make claim to the command of the sea.'

From 1873 to 1900 the German Navy was avowedly not intended to provide for the possibility of 'a naval war against great naval Powers.' Now in 1900 came a Fleet Law of a very different kind. 'For the protection of trade and the Colonies,' declared the preamble of this document, 'there is only one thing that will suffice, namely, a strong Battle Fleet.'

> 'In order to protect German trade and commerce under existing conditions, only one thing will suffice, namely, Germany must possess a battle fleet of such a strength that, even for the most powerful naval adversary, a war would involve such risks as to make that Power's own supremacy doubtful.
>
> 'For this purpose it is not absolutely necessary that the German Fleet should be as strong as that of the greatest naval Power, for, as a rule, a great naval Power will not be in a position to concentrate all its forces against us. Even if it were successful in bringing against us a much superior force, the defeat of a strong German fleet would so considerably weaken the enemy that, in spite of the victory that might be achieved, his own supremacy would no longer be assured by a fleet of sufficient strength.
>
> 'For the attainment of this object, viz., protection of our trade and colonies by assuring peace with honour, Germany requires, according to the strength of the great naval Powers and with regard to our tactical formations, two double squadrons of first-class battleships, with the necessary attendant cruisers, torpedo boats, etc. Since the Fleet Law provides for only two squadrons, the construction of third and fourth squadrons is proposed. Two of these four squadrons will form one fleet. The tactical formation of the second fleet should be similar to that of the first as provided for in the Fleet Law.'

And again:—

> 'In addition to the increase of the Home Fleet an increase of the foreign service ships is also necessary. . . . In order to estimate the importance of an increase in our foreign service ships, it must be realized that they represent the German Navy abroad, and that to them often falls the task of gathering fruits which have ripened as a result of the naval strength of the Empire embodied in the Home Battle Fleet.'

And again:—

> 'If the necessity for so strong a Fleet for Germany be recognized, it cannot be denied that the honour and welfare of the Fatherland authoritatively demand that the Home Fleet be brought up to the requisite strength as soon as possible.'

* * * * *

The determination of the greatest military Power on the Continent to become at the same time at least the second naval Power was an event of first magnitude in world affairs. It would, if carried into full effect, undoubtedly reproduce those situations which at previous periods in history had proved of such awful significance to the Islanders of Britain.

Hitherto all British naval arrangements had proceeded on the basis of the two-Power standard, namely, an adequate superiority over the next two strongest Powers, in those days France and Russia. The possible addition of a third European Fleet more powerful than either of these two would profoundly affect the life of Britain. If Germany was going to create a Navy avowedly measured against our own, we could not afford to remain 'in splendid isolation' from the European systems. We must in these circumstances find a trustworthy friend. We found one in another island Empire situated on the other side of the globe and also in danger. In 1901 the Alliance was signed between Great Britain and Japan. Still less could we afford to have dangerous causes of quarrel open both with France and Russia. In 1902 the British Government, under Mr. Balfour and Lord Lansdowne, definitely embarked upon the policy of settling up our differences with France. Still, before either of these steps was taken the hand was held out to Germany. She was invited to join with us in the alliance with Japan. She was invited to make a joint effort to solve the Moroccan problem. Both offers were declined.

In 1903, the war between Russia and Japan broke out. Germany sympathized mainly with Russia; England stood ready to fulfil her Treaty engagements with Japan, while at the same time cultivating good relations with France. In this posture the Powers awaited the result of the Far Eastern struggle. It brought a surprise to all but one. The military and naval overthrow of Russia by Japan and the internal convulsions of the Russian State produced profound changes in the European situation. Although German influence had leaned against Japan, she felt herself enormously strengthened by the Russian collapse. Her Continental predominance was restored. Her self-assertion in every sphere became sensibly and immediately pronounced. France, on the other hand, weakened and once again, for the time being, isolated and in real danger, became increasingly anxious for an Entente with England. England, whose statesmen with penetrating eye alone in Europe had truly measured the martial power of Japan, gained remarkably in strength and security. Japan, her new ally, was triumphant: France, her ancient enemy, sought her friendship: the German Fleet was still only a-building, and meanwhile all the British battleships in China seas could now be safely brought home.

* * * * *

The settlement of outstanding differences between England and France proceeded, and at last in 1904 the Anglo-French Agreement was signed. There were various clauses; but the essence of the compact was that the French desisted from opposition to British interests in Egypt, and Britain gave a general support to the French views about Morocco. This agreement was acclaimed by the Conservative forces in England, among whom the idea of the German menace had already taken root. It was also hailed somewhat shortsightedly by Liberal statesmen as a step to secure general peace by clearing away misunderstandings and differences with our traditional enemy. It was therefore almost universally welcomed. Only one profound observer raised his voice against it. 'My mournful and supreme conviction,' said Lord Rosebery, 'is that this agreement is much more likely to lead to complications than to peace.' This unwelcome comment was indignantly spurned from widely different standpoints by both British parties, and general censure fell upon its author.

Still, England and all that she stood for had left her isolation, and had reappeared in Europe on the opposite side to Germany. For the first time since 1870, Germany had to take into consideration a Power outside her system which was in no way amenable to threats, and was not unable if need be to encounter her single-handed. The gesture which was to sweep Delcassé from power in 1905, the apparition 'in shining armour' which was to quell Russia in 1908, could procure no such compliance from the independent Island girt with her Fleet and mistress of the seas.

Up to this moment the Triple Alliance had on the whole been stronger than France and Russia. Although war against these two Powers would have been a formidable undertaking for Germany, Austria and Italy, its ultimate issue did not seem doubtful. But if the weight of Britain were thrown into the adverse scale and that of Italy withdrawn from the other, then for the first time since 1870 Germany could not feel certain that she was on the stronger side. Would she submit to it? Would the growing, bounding ambitions and assertions of the new German Empire consent to a situation in which, very politely no doubt, very gradually perhaps, but still very surely, the impression would be conveyed that her will was no longer the final law of Europe? If Germany and her Emperor would accept the same sort of restraint that France, Russia and England had long been accustomed to, and would live within her rights as an equal in a freer and easier world, all would be well. But would she? Would she tolerate the gathering under an independent standard of nations outside her system, strong enough to examine her claims only as the merits appealed to them, and to resist aggression without fear? The history of the next ten years was to supply the answer.

Side by side with these slowly marshalling and steadily arming antagonisms between the greatest Powers, processes of degeneration were at work in weaker Empires almost equally dangerous to peace. Forces were alive in Turkey which threatened with destruction the old regime and its abuses on which Germany had chosen to lean. The Christian States of the Balkans, growing stronger year by year, awaited an opportunity to liberate their compatriots still writhing under Turkish misrule. The growth of national sentiment in every country created fierce strains and stresses in the uneasily knit and crumbling Austro-Hungarian Empire. The Balkan States saw also in this direction kinsmen to rescue, territory to recover, and unities to achieve. Italy watched with ardent eyes the decay of Turkey and the unrest of Austria. It was certain that from all these regions of the South and of the East there would come a succession of events deeply agitating both to Russia and to Germany.

To create the unfavourable conditions for herself in which Germany afterwards brought about the war, many acts of supreme unwisdom on the part of her rulers were nevertheless still necessary. France must be kept in a state of continued apprehension. The Russian nation, not the Russian Court alone, must be stung by some violent affront inflicted in their hour of weakness. The slow, deep, restrained antagonism of the British Empire must be roused by the continuous and repeated challenge to the sea power by which it lived. Then and then only could those conditions be created under which Germany by an act of aggression would bring into being against her, a combination strong enough to resist and ultimately to overcome her might. There was still a long road to travel before the Vials of Wrath were full. For ten years we were to journey anxiously along that road.

* * * * *

It was for a time the fashion to write as if the British Government during these ten years were either entirely unconscious of the approaching danger or had a load of secret matters and deep forebodings on their minds hidden altogether from the thoughtless nation. In fact, however, neither of these alternatives, taken separately, was true; and there is a measure of truth in both of them taken together.

The British Government and the Parliament out of which it sprang, did not believe in the approach of a great war, and were determined to prevent it; but at the same time the sinister hypothesis was continually present in their thoughts, and was repeatedly brought to the attention of Ministers by disquieting incidents and tendencies.

During the whole of those ten years this duality and discordance were the keynote of British politics; and those whose duty it was to watch over the safety of the country lived simultaneously in two different worlds of thought. There was the actual visible world with its peaceful activities and cosmopolitan aims; and there was a hypothetical world, a world 'beneath the threshold,' as it were, a world at one moment utterly fantastic, at the next seeming about to leap into reality—a world of monstrous shadows moving in convulsive combinations through vistas of fathomless catastrophe.

CHAPTER II
MILESTONES TO ARMAGEDDON: 1905–1910

'Enmities which are unspoken and hidden are more to be feared than those which are outspoken and open.'

—Cicero.

A Narrower Stage—The Victorian Calm—The Chain of Strife—Lord Salisbury Retires—Mr. Balfour and the End of an Epoch—Fall of the Conservative Government—The General Election of 1906—The Algeciras Conference—Anglo-French Military Conversations—Mr. Asquith's Administration—The Austrian Annexations—The German Threat to Russia—The Admiralty Programme of 1909—The Growth of the German Navy—German Finance and its Implications—The Inheritance of the New German Chancellor.

If the reader is to understand this tale and the point of view from which it is told, he should follow the author's mind in each principal sphere of causation. He must not only be acquainted with the military and naval situations as they existed at the outbreak of war, but with the events which led up to them. He must be introduced to the Admirals and to the Generals; he must study the organization of the Fleets and Armies and the outlines of their strategy by sea and land; he must not shrink even from the design of ships and cannon; he must extend his view to the groupings and slow-growing antagonisms of modern States; he must contract it to the humbler but unavoidable warfare of parties and the interplay of political forces and personalities.

The *dramatis personæ* of the previous chapter have been great States and Empires and its theme their world-wide balance and combinations. Now the stage must for a while be narrowed to the limits of these islands and occupied by the political personages and factions of the time and of the hour.

In the year 1895 I had the privilege, as a young officer, of being invited to lunch with Sir William Harcourt. In the course of a conversation in which I took, I fear, none too modest a share, I asked the question, 'What will happen then?' 'My dear Winston,' replied the old Victorian statesman, 'the experiences of a long life have convinced me that nothing ever happens.' Since that moment, as it seems to me, nothing has ever ceased happening. The growth of the great antagonisms abroad was accompanied by the progressive aggravation of party strife at home. The scale on which events have shaped themselves, has dwarfed the episodes of the Victorian Era. Its small wars between great nations, its earnest disputes about superficial issues, the high, keen intellectualism of its personages, the sober, frugal, narrow limitations of their action, belong to a vanished period. The smooth river with its eddies and ripples along which we then sailed, seems inconceivably remote from the cataract down which we have been hurled and the rapids in whose turbulence we are now struggling.

I date the beginning of these violent times in our country from the Jameson Raid, in 1896. This was the herald, if not indeed the progenitor, of the South African War. From the South African War was born the Khaki Election, the Protectionist Movement, the Chinese Labour cry and the consequent furious reaction and Liberal triumph of 1906. From this sprang the violent inroads of the House of Lords upon popular Government, which by the end of 1908 had reduced the immense Liberal majority to virtual impotence, from which condition they were rescued by the Lloyd George Budget in 1909. This measure became, in its turn, on both sides, the cause of still greater provocations, and its rejection by the Lords was a constitutional outrage and political blunder almost beyond compare. It led directly to the two General Elections of 1910, to the Parliament Act, and to the Irish struggle, in which our country was brought to the very threshold of civil war. Thus we see a succession of partisan actions continuing without intermission for nearly twenty years, each injury repeated with interest, each oscillation more violent, each risk more grave, until at last it seemed that the sabre itself must be invoked to cool the blood and the passions that were rife.

* * * * *

In July, 1902, Lord Salisbury retired. With what seems now to have been only a brief interlude, he had been Prime Minister and Foreign Secretary since 1885. In all those seventeen years the Liberal Party had never exercised any effective control upon affairs. Their brief spell in office had only been obtained by a majority of forty Irish Nationalist votes. During thirteen years the Conservatives had enjoyed homogeneous majorities of 100 to 150, and in addition there was the House of Lords. This long reign of power had now come to an end. The desire for change, the feeling that change was impending, was widespread. It was the end of an epoch.

Lord Salisbury was followed by Mr. Balfour. The new Prime Minister never had a fair chance. He succeeded only to an exhausted inheritance. Indeed, his wisest course would have been to get out of office as decently, as quietly, and, above all, as quickly as possible. He could with great propriety have declared that the 1900 Parliament had been elected on war conditions and on a war issue; that the war was now finished successfully; that the mandate was exhausted and that he must recur to the sense of the electors before proceeding farther with his task. No doubt the Liberals would have come into power, but not by a large majority; and they would have been faced by a strong, united Conservative Opposition, which in four or five years, about 1907, would have resumed effective control of the State. The solid ranks of Conservative members who acclaimed Mr. Balfour's accession as First Minister were however in no mood to be dismissed to their constituencies when the Parliament was only two years old and had still four or five years more to run. Mr. Balfour therefore addressed himself to the duties of Government with a serene indifference to the vast alienation of public opinion and consolidation of hostile forces which were proceeding all around him.

Mr. Chamberlain, his almost all-powerful lieutenant, was under no illusions. He felt, with an acute political sensitiveness, the ever-growing strength of the tide setting against the ruling combination. But instead of pursuing courses of moderation and prudence, he was impelled by the ardour of his nature to a desperate remedy. The Government was reproached with being reactionary. The moderate Conservatives and the younger Conservatives were all urging Liberal and conciliatory processes. The Opposition was advancing hopefully towards power, heralded by a storm of angry outcry. He would show them, and show doubting or weary friends as well, how it was possible to quell indignation by violence, and from the very heart of reaction to draw the means of popular victory. He unfurled the flag of Protection.

Time, adversity and the recent Education Act had united the Liberals; Protection, or Tariff Reform as it was called, split the Conservatives. Ultimately, six Ministers resigned and fifty Conservative or Unionist members definitely withdrew their support from the Government. Among them were a number of those younger men from whom a Party should derive new force and driving power, and who are specially necessary to it during a period of opposition. The action of the Free Trade Unionists was endorsed indirectly by Lord Salisbury himself from his retirement, and was actively sustained by such pillars of the Unionist Party as Sir Michael Hicks-Beach and the Duke of Devonshire. No such formidable loss had been sustained by the Conservative Party since the expulsion of the Peelites.

But if Mr. Balfour had not felt inclined to begin his reign by an act of abdication, he was still less disposed to have power wrested from his grasp. Moreover, he regarded a Party split as the worst of domestic catastrophes, and responsibility for it as the unforgivable sin. He therefore laboured with amazing patience and coolness to preserve a semblance of unity, to calm the tempest, and to hold on as long as possible in the hope of its subsiding. With the highest subtlety and ingenuity he devised a succession of formulas designed to enable people who differed profoundly, to persuade themselves they were in agreement. When it came to the resignation of Ministers, he was careful to shed Free Trade and Protectionist blood as far as possible in equal quantities. Like Henry VIII, he decapitated Papists and burned hot Gospellers on the same day for their respective divergencies in opposite directions from his central, personal and artificial compromise.

In this unpleasant situation Mr. Balfour maintained himself for two whole years. Vain the clamour for a General Election, vain the taunts of clinging to office, vain the solicitations of friends and the attempts of foes to force a crucial issue. The Prime Minister remained immovable, inexhaustible, imperturbable; and he remained Prime Minister. His clear, just mind, detached from small things, stood indifferent to the clamour about him. He pursued, as has been related, through the critical period of the Russo-Japanese War, a policy in support of Japan of the utmost firmness. He resisted all temptations, on the other hand, to make the sinking of our trawlers on the Dogger Bank by the Russian Fleet an occasion of war with Russia. He formed the Committee of Imperial Defence—the instrument of our preparedness. He carried through the agreement with France of

1904, the momentous significance of which the last chapter has explained. But in 1905 political Britain cared for none of these things. The credit of the Government fell steadily. The process of degeneration in the Conservative Party was continuous. The storm of opposition grew unceasingly, and so did the unification of all the forces opposed to the dying regime.

Late in November, 1905, Mr. Balfour tendered his resignation as Prime Minister to the King. The Government of Sir Henry Campbell-Bannerman was formed, and proceeded in January to appeal to the constituencies. This Government represented both the wings into which the Liberal Party had been divided by the Boer War. The Liberal Imperialists, so distinguished by their talents, filled some of the greatest offices. Mr. Asquith went to the Exchequer; Sir Edward Grey to the Foreign Office; Mr. Haldane became Secretary of State for War. On the other hand, the Prime Minister, who himself represented the main stream of Liberal opinion, appointed Sir Robert Reid, Lord Chancellor, and Mr. John Morley, Secretary of State for India. Both these statesmen, while not opposing actual war measures in South Africa, had unceasingly condemned the war; and in Mr. Lloyd George and Mr. John Burns, both of whom entered the Cabinet, were found democratic politicians who had gone even farther. The dignity of the Administration was enhanced by the venerable figures of Lord Ripon, Sir Henry Fowler, and the newly returned Viceroy of India, Lord Elgin.

The result of the polls in January, 1906, was a Conservative landslide. Never since the election following the great Reform Bill, had anything comparable occurred in British parliamentary history. In Manchester, for instance, which was one of the principal battle-grounds, Mr. Balfour and eight Conservative colleagues were dismissed and replaced by nine Liberals or Labour men. The Conservatives, after nearly twenty years of power, crept back to the House of Commons barely a hundred and fifty strong. The Liberals had gained a majority of more than one hundred over all other parties combined. Both great parties harboured deep grievances against the other; and against the wrong of the Khaki Election and its misuse, was set the counter-claim of an unfair Chinese Labour cry.

* * * * *

Sir Henry Campbell-Bannerman was still receiving the resounding acclamations of Liberals, peace-lovers, anti-jingoes, and anti-militarists, in every part of the country, when he was summoned by Sir Edward Grey to attend to business of a very different character. The Algeciras Conference was in its throes. When the Anglo-French Agreement on Egypt and Morocco had first been made known, the German Government accepted the situation without protest or complaint. The German Chancellor, Prince Bülow, had even declared in 1904 that there was nothing in the Agreement to which Germany could take exception. 'What appears to be before us is the attempt by the method of friendly understanding to eliminate a number of points of difference which exist between England and France. We have no objection to make against this from the standpoint of German interest. A serious agitation most embarrassing to the German Government was, however, set on foot by the Pan-German and Colonial parties. Under this pressure the attitude of the Government changed, and a year later Germany openly challenged the

Agreement and looked about for an opportunity to assert her claims in Morocco. This opportunity was not long delayed.

Early in 1905 a French mission arrived in Fez. Their language and actions seemed to show an intention of treating Morocco as a French Protectorate, thereby ignoring the international obligations of the Treaty of Madrid. The Sultan of Morocco appealed to Germany, asking if France was authorized to speak in the name of Europe. Germany was now enabled to advance as the champion of an international agreement, which she suggested France was violating. Behind this lay the clear intention to show France that she could not afford in consequence of her agreement with Britain, to offend Germany. The action taken was of the most drastic character. The German Emperor was persuaded to go to Tangiers, and there, against his better judgment, on March 31, 1905, he delivered, in very uncompromising language chosen by his ministers, an open challenge to France. To this speech the widest circulation was given by the German Foreign Office. Hot-foot upon it (April 11 and 12) two very threatening despatches were sent to Paris and London, demanding a conference of all the Signatory Powers to the Treaty of Madrid. Every means was used by Germany to make France understand that if she refused the conference there would be war; and to make assurance doubly sure a special envoy[1] was sent from Berlin to Paris for that express purpose.

France was quite unprepared for war; the army was in a bad state; Russia was incapacitated; moreover, France had not a good case. The French Foreign Minister, Monsieur Delcassé, was, however, unwilling to give way. The German attitude became still more threatening; and on June 6 the French Cabinet of Monsieur Rouvier unanimously, almost at the cannon's mouth, accepted the principle of a conference, and Monsieur Delcassé at once resigned.

So far Germany had been very successful. Under a direct threat of war she had compelled France to bow to her will, and to sacrifice the Minister who had negotiated the Agreement with Great Britain. The Rouvier Cabinet sought earnestly for some friendly solution which, while sparing France the humiliation of a conference dictated in such circumstances, would secure substantial concessions to Germany. The German Government were, however, determined to exploit their victory to the full, and not to make the situation easier for France either before or during the conference. The conference accordingly assembled at Algeciras in January, 1906.

Great Britain now appeared on the scene, apparently quite unchanged and unperturbed by her domestic convulsions. She had in no way encouraged France to refuse the conference. But if a war was to be fastened on France by Germany as the direct result of an agreement made recently in the full light of day between France and Great Britain, it was held that Great Britain could not remain indifferent. Sir Henry Campbell-Bannerman therefore authorized Sir Edward Grey to support France strongly at Algeciras. He also authorized, almost as the first act of what was to be an era of Peace, Retrenchment, and Reform, the beginning of military conversations between the British

[1]Prince Henckel von Donnesmarck.

and French General Staffs with a view to concerted action in the event of war. This was a step of profound significance and of far-reaching reactions. Henceforward the relations of the two Staffs became increasingly intimate and confidential. The minds of our military men were definitely turned into a particular channel. Mutual trust grew continually in one set of military relationships, mutual precautions in the other. However explicitly the two Governments might agree and affirm to each other that no national or political engagement was involved in these technical discussions, the fact remained that they constituted an exceedingly potent tie.

The attitude of Great Britain at Algeciras turned the scale against Germany. Russia, Spain and other signatory Powers associated themselves with France and England. Austria revealed to Germany the limits beyond which she would not go. Thus Germany found herself isolated, and what she had gained by her threats of war evaporated at the Council Board. In the end a compromise suggested by Austria, enabled Germany to withdraw without open loss of dignity. From these events, however, serious consequences flowed. Both the two systems into which Europe was divided, were crystallized and consolidated. Germany felt the need of binding Austria more closely to her. Her open attempt to terrorize France had produced a deep impression upon French public opinion. An immediate and thorough reform of the French Army was carried out, and the *Entente* with England was strengthened and confirmed. Algeciras was a milestone on the road to Armageddon.

* * * * *

The illness and death of Sir Henry Campbell-Bannerman at the beginning of 1908 opened a way for Mr. Asquith. The Chancellor of the Exchequer had been the First Lieutenant of the late Prime Minister, and, as his chief's strength failed, had more and more assumed the burden. He had charged himself with the conduct of the new Licensing Bill which was to be the staple of the Session of 1908, and in virtue of this task he could command the allegiance of an extreme and doctrinaire section of his Party from whom his Imperialism had previously alienated him. He resolved to ally to himself the democratic gifts and rising reputation of Mr. Lloyd George. Thus the succession passed smoothly from hand to hand. Mr. Asquith became Prime Minister; Mr. Lloyd George became Chancellor of the Exchequer and the second man in the Government. The new Cabinet, like the old, was a veiled coalition. A very distinct line of cleavage was maintained between the Radical-Pacifist elements who had followed Sir Henry Campbell-Bannerman and constituted the bulk both of the Cabinet and the Party on the one hand, and the Liberal Imperialist wing on the other. Mr. Asquith, as Prime Minister, had now to take an impartial position; but his heart and sympathies were always with Sir Edward Grey, the War Office and the Admiralty, and on every important occasion when he was forced to reveal himself, he definitely sided with them. He was not, however, able to give Sir Edward Grey the same effectual countenance, much as he might wish to do so, that Sir Henry Campbell-Bannerman had done. The old chief's word was law to the extremists of his Party. They would accept almost anything from him. They were quite sure he would do nothing more in matters of foreign policy and defence than was absolutely necessary, and that he would do it in the manner least calculated to give satisfaction to jingo sentiments. Mr. Asquith, however, had been far from 'sound' about the Boer War, and was the lifelong friend of the Foreign Secretary, who had wandered even further from the strait path into patriotic pastures. He was therefore in a certain sense suspect, and every step he took in external affairs was watched with prim vigilance by the Elders. If the military conversations with France had not been authorized by Sir Henry Campbell-Bannerman, and if his political virtue could not be cited in their justification, I doubt whether they could have been begun or continued by Mr. Asquith.

Since I had crossed the Floor of the House in 1904 on the Free Trade issue, I had worked in close political association with Mr. Lloyd George. He was the first to welcome me. We sat and acted together in the period of opposition preceding Mr. Balfour's fall, and we had been in close accord during Sir Henry Campbell-Bannerman's administration, in which I had served as Under-Secretary of State for the Colonies. This association continued when I entered the new Cabinet as President of the Board of Trade, and in general, though from different angles, we leaned to the side of those who would restrain the forward both in foreign policy and in armaments. It must be understood that these differences of attitude and complexion, which in varying forms reproduce themselves in every great and powerful British Administration, in no way prevented harmonious and agreeable relations between the principal personages, and our affairs proceeded amid many amenities in an atmosphere of courtesy, friendliness and goodwill.

* * * * *

It was not long before the next European crisis arrived. On October 5, 1908, Austria, without warning or parley proclaimed the annexation of Bosnia and Herzegovina. These provinces of the Turkish Empire had been administered by her under the Treaty of Berlin, 1878; and the annexation only declared in form what already existed in fact. The Young Turk Revolution which had occurred in the summer, seemed to Austria likely to lead to a reassertion of Turkish sovereignty over Bosnia and Herzegovina, and this she was concerned to forestall. A reasonable and patient diplomacy would probably have secured for Austria the easements which she needed. Indeed, negotiations with Russia, the Great Power most interested, had made favourable progress. But suddenly and abruptly Count Aerenthal, the Austrian Foreign Minister, interrupted the discussions by the announcement of the annexation, before the arrangements for a suitable concession to Russia had been concluded. By this essentially violent act a public affront was put upon Russia, and a personal slight upon the Russian negotiator, Monsieur Isvolsky.

A storm of anger and protest arose on all sides. England, basing herself on the words of the London Conference in 1871, 'That it is an essential principle of the law of nations that no Power can free itself from the engagements of a Treaty, nor modify its stipulations except by consent of the contracting parties,' refused to recognize either the annexation of Bosnia and Herzegovina or the declaration of Bulgarian independence which had synchronized with it. Turkey protested loudly against a lawless act. An effective boycott of Austrian merchandise was organized by the Turkish Government. The Serbians mobilized their army. But it was the effect on Russia which was most serious. The bitter animosity excited against Austria throughout Russia became a penultimate cause of the Great War. In this national quarrel the personal differences of Aerenthal and Isvolsky played also their part.

Great Britain and Russia now demanded a conference, declining meanwhile to countenance what had been done. Austria, supported by Germany, refused. The danger of some violent action on the part of Serbia became acute. Sir Edward Grey, after making it clear that Great Britain would not be drawn into a war on a Balkan quarrel, laboured to restrain Serbia, to pacify Turkey, and to give full diplomatic support to Russia. The controversy dragged on till April, 1909, when it was ended in the following remarkable manner. The Austrians had determined, unless Serbia recognized the annexation of Bosnia and Herzegovina, to send an ultimatum and to declare war upon her. At this point the German Chancellor, Prince von Bülow, intervened. Russia, he insisted, should herself advise Serbia to give way. The Powers should officially recognize the annexation without a conference being summoned and without any kind of compensation to Serbia. Russia was to give her consent to this action, without previously informing the British or French Governments. If Russia did not consent, Austria would declare war on Serbia *with the full and complete support of Germany*. Russia, thus nakedly confronted by war both with Austria and Germany, collapsed under the threat, as France had done three years before. England was left an isolated defender of the sanctity of Treaties and the law of nations. The Teutonic triumph was complete. But it was a victory gained at a perilous cost. France, after her treatment in 1905, had begun a thorough military reorganization. Now Russia, in 1910, made an enormous increase in her already vast army; and both Russia and France, smarting under similar experiences, closed their ranks, cemented their alliance, and set to work to construct with Russian labour and French money the new strategic railway systems of which Russia's western frontier stood in need.

* * * * *

It was next the turn of Great Britain to feel the pressure of the German power.

In the spring of 1909, the First Lord of the Admiralty, Mr. McKenna, suddenly demanded the construction of no less than six Dreadnought battleships. He based this claim on the rapid growth of the German Fleet and its expansion and acceleration under the new naval law of 1908, which was causing the Admiralty the greatest anxiety. I was still a sceptic about the danger of the European situation, and not convinced by the Admiralty case. In conjunction with the Chancellor of the Exchequer, I proceeded at once to canvass this scheme and to examine the reason by which it was supported. The conclusions which we both reached were that a programme of four ships would sufficiently meet our needs. In this process I was led to analyse minutely the character and composition of the British and German Navies, actual and prospective. I could not agree with the Admiralty contention that a dangerous situation would be reached in the year 1912. I found the Admiralty figures on this subject were exaggerated. I did not believe that the Germans were building Dreadnoughts secretly in excess of their published Fleet Laws. I held that our margin in pre-Dreadnought ships would, added to a new programme of four Dreadnoughts, assure us an adequate superiority in 1912, 'the danger year' as it was then called. In any case, as the Admiralty only claimed to lay down the fifth and sixth ships in the last month of the financial year, i.e. March, 1910, these could not affect the calculations. The Chancellor of the Exchequer and I therefore proposed that four ships should be sanctioned for 1909, and that the additional two should be considered in relation to the programme of 1910.

Looking back on the voluminous papers of this controversy in the light of what actually happened, there can be no doubt whatever that, so far as facts and figures were concerned, we were strictly right. The gloomy Admiralty anticipations were in no respect fulfilled in the year 1912. The British margin was found to be ample in that year. There were no secret German Dreadnoughts, nor had Admiral von Tirpitz made any untrue statement in respect of major construction.

The dispute in the Cabinet gave rise to a fierce agitation outside. The process of the controversy led to a sharp rise of temperature. The actual points in dispute never came to an issue. Genuine alarm was excited throughout the country by what was for the first time widely recognized as a German menace. In the end a curious and characteristic solution was reached. The Admiralty had demanded six ships: the economists offered four: and we finally compromised on eight. However, five out of the eight were not ready before 'the danger year' of 1912 had passed peacefully away.

But although the Chancellor of the Exchequer and I were right in the narrow sense, we were absolutely wrong in relation to the deep tides of destiny. The greatest credit is due to the First Lord of the Admiralty, Mr. McKenna, for the resolute and courageous manner in which he fought his case and withstood his Party on this occasion. Little did I think, as this dispute proceeded, that when the next Cabinet crisis about the Navy arose our rôles would be reversed; and little did he think that the ships for which he contended so stoutly would eventually, when they arrived, be welcomed with open arms by me.

Whatever differences might be entertained about the exact number of ships required in a particular year, the British nation in general became conscious of the undoubted fact that Germany proposed to reinforce her unequalled army by a navy which in 1920 would be far stronger than anything up to the present possessed by Great Britain. To the Navy Law of 1900 had succeeded the amending measure of 1906; and upon the increases of 1906 had followed those of 1908. In a flamboyant speech at Reval in 1904 the German Emperor had already styled himself 'The Admiral of the Atlantic.' All sorts of sober-minded people in England began to be profoundly disquieted. What did Germany want this great navy for? Against whom, except us, could she measure it, match it, or use it? There was a deep and growing feeling, no longer confined to political and diplomatic circles, that the Prussians meant mischief, that they envied the splendour of the British Empire, and that if they saw a good chance at our expense, they would take full advantage of it. Moreover, it began to be realized that it was no use trying to turn Germany from her course by abstaining from counter measures. Reluctance on our part to build ships was attributed in Germany to want of national spirit, and as another proof that the virile race should advance to replace the effete over-civilized and pacifist society which was no longer capable of sustaining its great place in the world's affairs. No one could run his eyes down the series of figures of British and German construction for the first three years of the Liberal Administration, without feeling in presence of a dangerous, if not a malignant, design.

In 1905 Britain built 4 ships, and Germany 2.

In 1906 Britain *decreased* her programme to 3 ships, and Germany *increased* her programme to 3 ships.

In 1907 Britain *further decreased* her programme to 2 ships, and Germany *further increased* her programme to 4 ships.

These figures are monumental.

It was impossible to resist the conclusion, gradually forced on nearly everyone, that if the British Navy lagged behind, the gap would be very speedily filled.

* * * * *

As President of the Board of Trade I was able to obtain a general view of the structure of German finance. In 1909 a most careful report was prepared by my direction on the whole of this subject. Its study was not reassuring. I circulated it to the Cabinet with the following covering minute:—

November 3, 1909.

> Believing that there are practically no checks upon German naval expansion except those imposed by the increasing difficulties of getting money, I have had the enclosed report prepared with a view to showing how far those limitations are becoming effective. It is clear that they are becoming terribly effective. The overflowing expenditure of the German Empire strains and threatens every dyke by which the social and political unity of Germany is maintained. The high customs duties have been largely rendered inelastic through commercial treaties, and cannot meet the demand. The heavy duties upon food-stuffs, from which the main proportion of the customs revenue is raised, have produced a deep cleavage between the agrarians and the industrials, and the latter deem themselves quite uncompensated for the high price of food-stuffs by the most elaborate devices of protection for manufactures. The splendid possession of the State railways is under pressure being continually degraded to a mere instrument of taxation. The field of direct taxation is already largely occupied by State and local systems. The prospective inroad by the universal suffrage Parliament of the Empire upon this depleted field unites the propertied classes, whether Imperialists or State-right men, in a common apprehension, with which the governing authorities are not unsympathetic. On the other hand, the new or increased taxation on every form of popular indulgence powerfully strengthens the parties of the Left, who are themselves the opponents of expenditure on armaments and much else besides.
>
> Meanwhile the German Imperial debt has more than doubled in the last thirteen years of unbroken peace, has risen since the foundation of the Empire to about £220,000,000, has increased in the last ten years by £105,000,000, and practically no attempt to reduce it has been made between 1880 and the present year. The effect of recurrent borrowings to meet ordinary annual expenditure has checked

the beneficial process of foreign investment, and dissipated the illusion, cherished during the South African War, that Berlin might supplant London as the lending centre of the world. The credit of the German Empire has fallen to the level of that of Italy. It is unlikely that the new taxes which have been imposed with so much difficulty this year will meet the annual deficit.

These circumstances force the conclusion that a period of severe internal strain approaches in Germany. Will the tension be relieved by moderation or snapped by calculated violence? Will the policy of the German Government be to soothe the internal situation, or to find an escape from it in external adventure? There can be no doubt that both courses are open. Low as the credit of Germany has fallen, her borrowing powers are practically unlimited. But one of the two courses must be taken soon, and from that point of view it is of the greatest importance to gauge the spirit of the new administration from the outset. If it be pacific, it must soon become markedly pacific, and conversely.

W. S. C.

That is, I think, the first sinister impression that I was ever led to record.

* * * * *

We have now seen how within the space of five years Germany's policy and the growth of her armaments led her to arouse and alarm most profoundly three of the greatest Powers in the world. Two of them, France and Russia, had been forced to bow to the German will by the plain threat of war. Each had been quelled by the open intention of a neighbour to use force against them to the utmost limit without compunction. Both felt they had escaped a bloody ordeal and probable disaster only by submission. The sense of past humiliation was aggravated by the fear of future affronts. The third Power—unorganized for war, but inaccessible and not to be neglected in the world's affairs—Britain, had also been made to feel that hands were being laid upon the very foundation of her existence. Swiftly, surely, methodically, a German Navy was coming into being at our doors which must expose us to dangers only to be warded off by strenuous exertions, and by a vigilance almost as tense as that of actual war. As France and Russia increased their armies, so Britain under the same pressure increased her fleet. Henceforward the three disquieted nations will act more closely together and will not be taken by their adversary one by one. Henceforward their military arrangements will be gradually concerted. Henceforward they will consciously be facing a common danger.

Ah! foolish-diligent Germans, working so hard, thinking so deeply, marching and counter-marching on the parade grounds of the Fatherland, poring over long calculations, fuming in new-found prosperity, discontented amid the splendour of mundane success, how many bulwarks to your peace and glory did you not, with your own hands, successively tear down!

'In the year 1909,' writes von Bethmann-Hollweg, then the successor of Prince von Bülow, 'the situation was based on the fact that England had firmly taken its stand on the side of France and Russia in pursuit of its traditional policy of opposing whatever

Continental Power for the time being was the strongest; and that Germany held fast to its naval programme, had given a definite direction to its Eastern policy, and had moreover to guard against a French antagonism that had in no wise been mitigated by its policy in later years. And if Germany saw a formidable aggravation of all the aggressive tendencies of Franco-Russian policy in England's pronounced friendship with this Dual Alliance, England on its side had grown to see a menace in the strengthening of the German Fleet and a violation of its ancient rights in our Eastern policy. Words had already passed on both sides. The atmosphere was chilly and clouded with distrust.' Such, in his own words, was the inheritance of the new German Chancellor.

He was now to make his own contribution to the anxieties of the world.

CHAPTER III
THE CRISIS OF AGADIR: 1911

'On the idle hill of summer,
Sleepy with the sound of streams,
Far I hear the steady drummer
Drumming like a noise in dreams.

Far and near and low and louder,
On the roads of earth go by,
Dear to friends and food for powder,
Soldiers marching, all to die.'

The Shropshire Lad, XXXV.

Agadir—The *Panther*—The Alarm Bells of Europe—Sir Edward Grey's Warning—The Period of Silence—Situation in the Cabinet—Decision of the Chancellor of the Exchequer—His Mansion House Speech—The German Rejoinder—Naval Precautions—Effect of the Mansion House Speech on German Policy—British Apprehensions of Attack—The Naval Magazines—Vulnerable Points—The Military Situation—Sir Henry Wilson—A Talk with the German Ambassador—Count Metternich—The Old Diplomacy—Meeting of the Committee of Imperial Defence, August 23—Sir Henry Wilson's Forecast—Admiralty Views—Divergences between the Generals and Admirals—My Memorandum of August 13—The Twentieth Day—The Fortieth Day—Plans for Army Expansion—Continued Anxiety—My Letter to Sir Edward Grey, August 30—End of the Crisis—Consequences in Germany—The Prime Minister invites me to go to the Admiralty—The Ninth Chapter of Deuteronomy.

In the spring of 1911 a French expedition occupied Fez. This action, added to the growing discontent in Germany over the Moroccan question, tempted the German Government at the beginning of July to an abrupt act. The Brothers Mannesmann, a German firm at that time very active in European financial circles, claimed that they had large interests in a harbour on the Atlantic seaboard of the Moroccan Coast and in the hinterland behind it. This harbour bore the name of Agadir. Herr von Kiderlen-Wächter, the German Foreign Minister, raised this point with the French. The French Government fully realized that the advantages they were gaining in Morocco, justified Germany in seeking certain colonial compensations in the Congo area. The German press, on the other hand, was indignant at exchanging German interests in the moderate climate of Morocco for unhealthy tropical regions of which they had already more than enough. The questions involved were complicated and intrinsically extremely unimportant. The French prepared themselves for a prolonged negotiation. So far as the harbour and hinterland of Agadir were concerned, there seemed to be no difficulty. They denied altogether the existence of any German interests there. They said there was only a sandy bay untouched by the hand of man; there was no German property on the shore, not a trading establishment, not a house; there were no German interests in the interior. But these facts could easily be ascertained by a visit of accredited representatives of both countries. Such a visit to ascertain the facts they professed themselves quite ready to arrange. They also courted a discussion of the frontier of the Congo territories.

Suddenly and unexpectedly, on the morning of July 1, without more ado, it was announced that His Imperial Majesty the German Emperor had sent his gunboat *Panther* to Agadir to maintain and protect German interests. This small ship was already on its way. All the alarm bells throughout Europe began immediately to quiver. France found herself in the presence of an act which could not be explained, the purpose behind which could not be measured. Great Britain, having consulted the atlas, began to wonder what bearing a German naval base on the Atlantic coast of Africa would have upon her maritime security, 'observing,' as the sailors say when they have to write official letters to each other, that such a fact must be taken in conjunction with German activities at Madeira and in the Canaries and with the food routes and trade routes from South America and South Africa which converged and passed through these waters. Europe was uneasy. France was genuinely alarmed. When Count Metternich apprised Sir Edward Grey of the German action, he was informed that the situation was so important that it must be considered by the Cabinet. On July 5, after the Cabinet, he was told that the British Government could not disinterest themselves in Morocco, and that until Germany's intentions were made known their attitude must remain one of reserve. From that date until July 21 not one word was spoken by the German Government. There is no doubt that the decided posture of Great Britain was a great surprise to the German Foreign Office. There ensued between the Governments what was called at the time 'the period of silence.' Meanwhile the French and German newspapers carried on a lively controversy, and the British press wore a very sombre air.

It was difficult to divine from the long strings of telegrams which day after day flowed in from all the European Chancelleries, what was the real purpose behind the German action. I followed attentively the repeated discussions on the subject in the British Cabinet. Was Germany looking for a pretext of war with France, or was she merely trying by pressure and uncertainty to improve her colonial position? In the latter case the dispute would no doubt be adjusted after a period of tension, as so many had been before. The great Powers marshalled on either side, preceded and protected by an elaborate cushion of diplomatic courtesies and formalities, would display to each other their respective arrays. In the forefront would be the two principal disputants, Germany and France, and echeloned back on either side at varying distances and under veils of reserves and qualifications of different density, would be drawn up the other parties to the Triple Alliance and to what was already now beginning to be called the Triple Entente. At the proper moment these seconds or supporters would utter certain cryptic words indicative of their state of mind, as a consequence of which France or Germany would step back or forward a very small distance or perhaps move slightly to the right or to the left. When these delicate rectifications in the great balance of Europe, and indeed of the world, had been made, the formidable assembly would withdraw to their own apartments with ceremony and salutations and congratulate or condole with each other in whispers on the result. We had seen it several times before.

But even this process was not free from danger. One must think of the intercourse of the nations in those days not as if they were chessmen on the board, or puppets dressed in finery and frillings grimacing at each other in a quadrille, but as prodigious organizations of forces active or latent which, like planetary bodies, could not approach each other in space without giving rise to profound magnetic reactions. If they got too near, the lightnings would begin to flash, and beyond a certain point they might be attracted altogether from the orbits in which they were restrained and draw each other into dire collision. The task of diplomacy was to prevent such disasters; and as long as there was no conscious or subconscious purpose of war in the mind of any Power or race, diplomacy would probably succeed. But in such grave and delicate conjunctions one violent move by any party, would rupture and derange the restraints upon all, and plunge Cosmos into Chaos.

I thought myself that the Germans had a certain grievance about the original Anglo-French agreement. We had received many conveniences in Egypt. France had gained great advantages in Morocco. If Germany felt her relative position prejudiced by these arrangements, there was no reason why patiently and amicably she should not advance and press her own point of view. And it seemed to me that Britain, the most withdrawn, the least committed of the Great Powers, might exercise a mitigating and a modifying influence and procure an accommodation; and that of course was what we tried to do. But if Germany's intention were malignant, no such process would be of the slightest use. In that event a very decided word would have to be spoken, and spoken before it was too late. Nor would our withdrawing altogether from the scene have helped matters. Had we done so all our restraining influence would have vanished, and an intenser aggravation of the antagonistic forces must have occurred. Therefore I read all the papers and telegrams which began to pass with a suspicion, and I could see beneath the calm of Sir Edward Grey a growing and at some moments a grave anxiety.

The sultry obscurity of the European situation was complicated by the uncertain play of forces within our own council chamber. There again in miniature were reproduced the balances and reserves of the external diplomatic situation. The Ministers who were conducting the foreign policy of Britain, with the ponderous trident of sea power towering up behind them, were drawn entirely from the Liberal Imperialist section of the Government. They were narrowly watched and kept in equipoise by the Radical element, which included the venerable figures of Lord Morley and Lord Loreburn, on whose side the Chancellor of the Exchequer and I had usually leaned. It was clear that this equipoise might easily make it impossible for Great Britain to speak with a decided voice either on one side or the other if certain dangerous conditions supervened. We should not, therefore, either keep clear ourselves by withdrawing from the danger nor be able by resolute action to ward it off in time. In these circumstances the attitude of the Chancellor of the Exchequer became of peculiar importance.

For some weeks he offered no indication of what his line would be, and in our numerous conversations he gave me the impression of being sometimes on one side and sometimes on the other. But on the morning of July 21, when I visited him before the Cabinet, I found a different man. His mind was made up. He saw quite clearly the course to take. He knew what to do and how and when to do it. The tenor of his statement to me was that we were drifting into war. He dwelt on the oppressive silence of Germany so far as we were concerned. He pointed out that Germany was acting as if England did not count in the matter in any way; that she had completely ignored our strong representation; that she was proceeding to put the most severe pressure on France; that a catastrophe might ensue; and that if it was to be averted we must speak with great decision, and we must speak at once. He told me that he was to address the Bankers at their Annual Dinner that evening, and that he intended to make it clear that if Germany meant war, she would find Britain against her. He showed me what he had prepared, and told me that he would show it to the Prime Minister and Sir Edward Grey after the Cabinet. What would they say? I said that of course they would be very much relieved; and so they were, and so was I.

The accession of Mr. Lloyd George in foreign policy to the opposite wing of the Government was decisive. We were able immediately to pursue a firm and coherent policy. That night at the Bankers' Association the Chancellor of the Exchequer used the following words:—

> 'I believe it is essential in the highest interests not merely of this country, but of the world, that Britain should at all hazards maintain her place and her prestige amongst the Great Powers of the world. Her potent influence has many a time been in the past, and may yet be in the future, invaluable to the cause of human liberty. It has more than once in the past redeemed continental nations, who are sometimes too apt to forget that service, from overwhelming disaster and even from national extinction. I would make great sacrifices to preserve peace. I conceive that nothing would justify a disturbance of international goodwill except questions of the gravest national moment. But if a situation were to be forced upon us in which peace could only be preserved by the surrender of the great and beneficent position Britain has won by centuries of heroism and achievement, by allowing Britain to be treated where her interests were vitally affected as if she were of no account in the Cabinet of nations, then I say emphatically that peace at that price would be a humiliation intolerable for a great country like ours to endure.'

His City audience, whose minds were obsessed with the iniquities of the Lloyd George Budget and the fearful hardships it had inflicted upon property and wealth—little did they dream of the future—did not comprehend in any way the significance or the importance of what they heard. They took it as if it had been one of the ordinary platitudes of ministerial pronouncements upon foreign affairs. But the Chancelleries of Europe bounded together.

Four days later, at about 5.30 in the afternoon, the Chancellor of the Exchequer and I were walking by the fountains of Buckingham Palace. Hot-foot on our track came a messenger. Will the Chancellor of the Exchequer go at once to Sir Edward Grey? Mr. Lloyd George stopped abruptly and turning to me said, 'That's my speech. The Germans may demand my resignation as they did Delcassé's.' I said, 'That will make you the most popular man in England' (he was not actually the most popular at that time). We returned as fast as we could and found Sir Edward Grey in his room at the House of Commons. His first words were: 'I have just received a communication from the German Ambassador so stiff that the Fleet might be attacked at any moment. I have sent for McKenna to warn him!' He then told us briefly of the conversation he had just had with Count Metternich. The Ambassador had said that after the speech of the Chancellor of the Exchequer no explanation could be made by Germany. In acrid terms he had stated that if France should repel the hand offered her by the Emperor's Government, the dignity of Germany would compel her to secure by all means full respect by France for German treaty rights. He had then read a long complaint about Mr. Lloyd George's speech, 'which to say the least could have been interpreted as a warning to Germany's address and which as a matter of fact had been interpreted by the presses of Great Britain and France as a warning bordering on menace.' Sir Edward Grey had thought it right to reply that the tone of the communication which had just been read to him, rendered it inconsistent with the dignity of His Majesty's Government to give explanations with regard to the speech of the Chancellor of the Exchequer. The First Lord arrived while we were talking, and a few minutes later hurried off to send the warning orders.

They sound so very cautious and correct, these deadly words. Soft, quiet voices purring, courteous, grave, exactly-measured phrases in large peaceful rooms. But with less warning cannons had opened fire and nations had been struck down by this same Germany. So now the Admiralty wireless whispers through the ether to the tall masts of ships, and captains pace their decks absorbed in thought. It is nothing. It is less than nothing. It is too foolish, too fantastic to be thought of in the twentieth century. Or is it fire and murder leaping out of the darkness at our throats, torpedoes ripping the bellies of half-awakened ships, a sunrise on a vanished naval supremacy, and an island well-guarded hitherto, at last defenceless? No, it is nothing. No one would do such things. Civilization has climbed above such perils. The interdependence of nations in trade and traffic, the sense of public law, the Hague Convention, Liberal principles, the Labour Party, high finance, Christian charity, common sense have rendered such nightmares impossible. Are you quite sure? It would be a pity to be wrong. Such a mistake could only be made once—once for all.

The Mansion House speech was a surprise to all countries: it was a thunder-clap to the German Government. All their information had led them to believe that

Mr. Lloyd George would head the peace party and that British action would be neutralized. Jumping from one extreme to another, they now assumed that the British Cabinet was absolutely united, and that the Chancellor of the Exchequer of all others had been deliberately selected as the most Radical Minister by the British Government to make this pronouncement.[1] They could not understand how their representatives and agents in Great Britain could have been so profoundly misled. Their vexation proved fatal to Count Metternich, and at the first convenient opportunity he was recalled. Here was an Ambassador who, after ten years' residence in London, could not even forecast the action of one of the most powerful Ministers on a question of this character. It will be seen from what has been written that this view was hard on Count Metternich. How could he know what Mr. Lloyd George was going to do? Until a few hours before, his colleagues did not know. Working with him in close association, I did not know. No one knew. Until his mind was definitely made up, he did not know himself.

It seems probable now that the Germans did not mean war on this occasion. But they meant to test the ground; and in so doing they were prepared to go to the very edge of the precipice. It is so easy to lose one's balance there: a touch, a gust of wind, a momentary dizziness, and all is precipitated into the abyss. But whether in the heart of the German State there was or was not a war purpose before England's part had been publicly declared, there was no such intention afterwards.

After the speech of the Chancellor of the Exchequer and its sequel the German Government could not doubt that Great Britain would be against them if a war was forced upon France at this juncture. They did not immediately recede from their position, but they were most careful to avoid any fresh act of provocation; and all their further conduct of the negotiations with France tended to open in one direction or another paths of accommodation and of retreat. It remained extremely difficult for us to gauge the exact significance of the various points at issue, and throughout the months of July, August and September the situation continued obscure and oppressive. The slight yet decisive change which came over the character of German diplomacy, was scarcely perceptible, and at the same time certain precautionary military measures which were taken behind the German frontiers, so far as they were known to us, had the effect of greatly increasing our anxiety. In consequence the atmosphere in England became constantly more heavily charged with electricity as one hot summer's day succeeded another.

Hitherto as Home Secretary I had not had any special part to play in this affair, though I had followed it with the utmost attention as a Member of the Cabinet. I was now to receive a rude shock. On the afternoon of July 27, I attended a garden party at 10, Downing Street. There I met the Chief Commissioner of Police, Sir Edward Henry. We talked about the European situation, and I told him that it was serious. He then

---

[1]Von Tirpitz's account (p. 169) is quite direct. At his [von Kiderlen-Wächter's] suggestion the Chancellor dispatched the gunboat *Panther* to the Moroccan port Agadir on July 1, 1911, and left the British Government, when it asked the reason, completely in the dark and without a reply for many weeks. The result was that on July 21 Lloyd George delivered a speech which had been drawn up in the British Cabinet, in which he warned Germany that she would find British power on the side of France in the event of a challenge.

remarked that by an odd arrangement the Home Office was responsible, through the Metropolitan Police, for guarding the magazines at Chattenden and Lodge Hill, in which all the reserves of naval cordite were stored. For many years these magazines had been protected without misadventure by a few constables. I asked what would happen if twenty determined Germans in two or three motor cars arrived well armed upon the scene one night. He said they would be able to do what they liked. I quitted the garden party.

A few minutes later I was telephoning from my room in the Home Office to the Admiralty. Who was in charge? The First Lord was with the Fleet at Cromarty; the First Sea Lord was inspecting. Both were, of course, quickly accessible by wireless or wire. In the meantime an Admiral (he shall be nameless) was in control. I demanded Marines at once to guard these magazines, vital to the Royal Navy. I knew there were plenty of Marines in the depôts at Chatham and Portsmouth. The Admiral replied over the telephone that the Admiralty had no responsibility and had no intention of assuming any; and it was clear from his manner that he resented the intrusion of an alarmist civilian Minister. 'You refuse then to send the Marines?' After some hesitation he replied, 'I refuse.' I replaced the receiver and rang up the War Office. Mr. Haldane was there. I told him that I was reinforcing and arming the police that night, and asked for a company of infantry for each magazine in addition. In a few minutes the orders were given: in a few hours the troops had moved. By the next day the cordite reserves of the Navy were safe.

The incident was a small one, and perhaps my fears were unfounded. But once one had begun to view the situation in this light, it became impossible to think of anything else. All around flowed the busy life of peaceful, unsuspecting, easy-going Britain. The streets were thronged with men and women utterly devoid of any sense of danger from abroad. For nearly a thousand years no foreign army had landed on British soil. For a hundred years the safety of the homeland had never been threatened. They went about their business, their sport, their class and party fights year after year, generation after generation, in perfect confidence and considerable ignorance. All their ideas were derived from conditions of peace. All their arrangements were the result of long peace. Most of them would have been incredulous, many would have been very angry if they had been told that we might be near a tremendous war, and that perhaps within this City of London, which harboured confidingly visitors from every land, resolute foreigners might be aiming a deadly blow at the strength of the one great weapon and shield in which we trusted.

I began to make inquiries about vulnerable points. I found the far-seeing Captain Hankey, then Assistant Secretary to the Committee of Imperial Defence, already on the move classifying them for the War Book, which project had actually been launched.[2] I inquired further about sabotage and espionage and counter-espionage. I came in touch with other officers working very quietly and very earnestly, but in a small way and with small means. I was told about German spies and agents in the various British ports. Hitherto the Home Secretary had to sign a warrant when it was necessary to examine

[2]The work had been begun by Lieutenant-Colonel Adrian Grant-Duff, afterwards killed on the Aisne.

any particular letter passing through the Royal Mails. I now signed general warrants authorizing the examination of all the correspondence of particular people upon a list, to which additions were continually made. This soon disclosed a regular and extensive system of German-paid British agents. It was only in a very small part of the field of preparation that the Home Secretary had any official duty of interference, but once I got drawn in, it dominated all other interests in my mind. For seven years I was to think of little else. Liberal politics, the People's Budget, Free Trade, Peace, Retrenchment and Reform—all the war cries of our election struggles began to seem unreal in the presence of this new pre-occupation. Only Ireland held her place among the grim realities which came one after another into view. No doubt other Ministers had similar mental experiences. I am telling my own tale.

I now began to make an intensive study of the military position in Europe. I read everything with which I was supplied. I spent many hours in argument and discussion. The Secretary of State for War told his officers to tell me everything I wanted to know. The Chief of the General Staff, Sir William Nicholson, was an old friend of mine. I had served with him as a young officer on Sir William Lockhart's staff at the end of the Tirah Expedition in 1898. He wrote fine broad appreciations and preached a clear and steady doctrine. But the man from whom I learned most was the Director of Military Operations, General Wilson (afterwards Field-Marshal Sir Henry Wilson). This officer had extraordinary vision and faith. He had acquired an immense and, I expect, an unequalled volume of knowledge about the Continent. He knew the French Army thoroughly. He was deeply in the secrets of the French General Staff. He had been Head of the British Staff College. For years he had been labouring with one object, that if war came we should act immediately on the side of France. He was sure that war would come sooner or later. All the threads of military information were in his hands. The whole wall of his small room was covered by a gigantic map of Belgium, across which every practicable road by which the German armies could march for the invasion of France, was painted clearly. All his holidays he spent examining these roads and the surrounding country. He could not do much in Germany: the Germans knew him too well.

One night the German ambassador, still Count Metternich, whom I had known for ten years, asked me to dine with him. We were alone, and a famous hock from the Emperor's cellars was produced. We had a long talk about Germany and how she had grown great; about Napoleon and the part he had played in uniting her; about the Franco-German War and how it began and how it ended. I said what a pity it was that Bismarck had allowed himself to be forced by the soldiers into taking Lorraine, and how Alsace-Lorraine lay at the root of all the European armaments and rival combinations. He said these had been German provinces from remote antiquity until one day in profound peace Louis XIV had pranced over the frontier and seized them. I said their sympathies were French: he said they were mixed. I said that anyhow it kept the whole thing alive. France could never forget her lost provinces, and they never ceased to call to her. The conversation passed to a kindred but more critical subject. Was he anxious about the present situation? He said people were trying to ring Germany round and put her in a net, and that she was a strong animal to put in a net. I said, how could she be netted when she had an alliance with two other first-class Powers, Austria-Hungary and Italy? *We* had often stood quite alone for years at a time without getting flustered. He said it was a very different business for an island. But when you had been marched through and pillaged and oppressed so often and had only the breasts of your soldiers to stand between you and invasion, it ate into your soul. I said that Germany was frightened of nobody, and that everybody was frightened of her.

Then we came to the Navy. Surely, I said, it was a great mistake for Germany to try to rival Britain on the seas. She would never catch us up. We should build two to one or more if necessary, and at every stage antagonism would grow between the countries. Radicals and Tories, whatever they might say about each other, were all agreed on that. No British Government which jeopardized our naval supremacy could live. He said Mr. Lloyd George had told him very much the same thing, but the Germans had no thought of naval supremacy. All they wanted was a Fleet to protect their commerce and their colonies. I asked what was the use of having a weaker Fleet? It was only another hostage to fortune. He said that the Emperor was profoundly attached to his Fleet, and that it was his own creation. I could not resist saying that Moltke had pronounced a very different opinion of Germany's true interest.

I have recorded these notes of a pleasant though careful conversation, not because they are of any importance, but because they help to show the different points of view. I learned afterwards that the Chancellor of the Exchequer in similar circumstances had spoken more explicitly, saying that he would raise a hundred millions in a single year for the British Navy if its supremacy were really challenged.

Count Metternich was a very honourable man, serving his master faithfully but labouring to preserve peace, especially peace between England and Germany. I have heard that on one occasion at Berlin in a throng of generals and princes, someone had said that the British Fleet would one day make a surprise and unprovoked attack upon Germany. Whereupon the Ambassador had replied that he had lived in England for nearly ten years, and he knew that such a thing was absolutely impossible. On this remark being received with obvious incredulity, he had drawn himself up and observed that he made it on the honour of a German officer and that he would answer for its truth with his honour. This for a moment had quelled the company.

It is customary for thoughtless people to jeer at the old diplomacy and to pretend that wars arise out of its secret machinations. When one looks at the petty subjects which have led to wars between great countries and to so many disputes, it is easy to be misled in this way. Of course such small matters are only the symptoms of the dangerous disease, and are only important for that reason. Behind them lie the interests, the passions and the destiny of mighty races of men; and long antagonisms express themselves in trifles. 'Great commotions,' it was said of old, 'arise out of small things, but not concerning small things.' The old diplomacy did its best to render harmless the small things: it could not do more. Nevertheless, a war postponed may be a war averted. Circumstances change, combinations change, new groupings arise, old interests are superseded by new. Many quarrels that might have led to war have been adjusted by the old diplomacy of Europe and have, in Lord Melbourne's phrase, 'blown over.' If the nations of the world, while the sense of their awful experiences is still fresh upon them, are able to devise broader and deeper guarantees of peace and build their houses on a surer foundation of brotherhood and interdependence, they will still require the courtly manners, the polite and measured phrases, the imperturbable demeanour, the secrecy and discretion of the old diplomatists of Europe. This is, however, a digression.

On August 23, after Parliament had risen and Ministers had dispersed, the Prime Minister convened very secretly a special meeting of the Committee of Imperial Defence. He summoned the Ministers specially concerned with the foreign situation and with the fighting services, including of course the Chancellor of the Exchequer. There were also the principal officers of the Army and the Navy. I was invited to attend, though the Home Office was not directly concerned. We sat all day. In the morning the Army told its tale: in the afternoon, the Navy.

General Wilson, as Director of Military Operations, stated the views of the General Staff. Standing by his enormous map, specially transported for the purpose, he unfolded, with what proved afterwards to be extreme accuracy, the German plan for attacking France in the event of a war between Germany and Austria on the one hand and France and Russia on the other. It was briefly as follows:—

In the first place, the Germans would turn nearly four-fifths of their strength against France and leave only one-fifth to contain Russia. The German armies would draw up on a line from the Swiss frontier to Aix-la-Chapelle. They would then swing their right wing through Belgium, thus turning the line of fortresses by which the eastern frontiers of France were protected. This enormous swinging movement of the German right arm would require every road which led through Belgium from Luxembourg to the Belgian Meuse. There were fifteen of these roads, and three divisions would probably march along each. The Belgian Meuse flowed parallel to the march of these divisions and protected their right flank. Along this river were three important fortified passages or bridgeheads. First, nearest Germany, Liège; the last, nearest France, Namur; and midway between the two, the fort of Huy. Now arose the question, Would the Germans after seizing these bridgeheads confine themselves to the eastern side of the Belgian Meuse and use the river for their protection, or would they be able to spare and bring a large body of troops to prolong their turning movement west of the Belgian Meuse and thus advance beyond it instead of inside it? This was the only part of their plan which could not be foreseen. Would they avoid the west side of the Belgian Meuse altogether? Would they skim along it with a cavalry force only, or would they march infantry divisions or even army corps west of that river? When the time came, as we now know, they marched two whole armies. At that date, however, the most sombre apprehension did not exceed one, or at the outside two, army corps.

Overwhelming detailed evidence was adduced to show that the Germans had made every preparation for marching through Belgium. The great military camps in close proximity to the frontier, the enormous depots, the reticulation of railways, the endless sidings, revealed with the utmost clearness and beyond all doubt their design. Liège would be taken within a few hours of the declaration of war, possibly even before it, by a rush of motor cars and cyclists from the camp at Elsenborn. That camp was now

(August, 1911) crowded with troops, and inquisitive persons and ordinary countryfolk were already being roughly turned back and prevented from approaching it.

What would Belgium do in the face of such an onslaught? Nothing could save Liège, but French troops might reach Namur in time to aid in its defence. For the rest the Belgian Army, assuming that Belgium resisted the invader, would withdraw into the great entrenched camp and fortress of Antwerp. This extensive area, intersected by a tangle of rivers and canals and defended by three circles of forts, would become the last refuge of the Belgian monarchy and people.

The position of Holland was also examined. It was not thought that the Germans would over-run Holland as they would Belgium, but they might find it very convenient to march across the curiously shaped projection of Holland which lay between Germany and Belgium, and which in the British General Staff parlance of that time was called 'the Maestricht Appendix.' They would certainly do this if any considerable body of their troops was thrown west of the Belgian Meuse.

The French plans for meeting this formidable situation were not told in detail to us; but it was clear that they hoped to forestall and rupture the German enveloping movement by a counter-offensive of their own on the greatest scale.

The numbers of divisions available on both sides and on all fronts when mobilization was completed were estimated as follows:—

French	85
German	110

It was asserted that if the six British divisions were sent to take position on the extreme French left, immediately war was declared, the chances of repulsing the Germans in the first great shock of battle were favourable. Every French soldier would fight with double confidence if he knew he was not fighting alone. Upon the strength of Russia General Wilson spoke with great foresight, and the account which he gave of the slow mobilization of the Russian Army swept away many illusions. It seemed incredible that Germany should be content to leave scarcely a score of divisions to make head against the might of Russia. But the British General Staff considered that such a decision would be well-founded. We shall see presently how the loyalty of Russia and of the Tsar found the means by prodigious sacrifices to call back to the East vital portions of the German Army at the supreme moment. Such action could not be foreseen then, and most people have forgotten it now.

There was of course a considerable discussion and much questioning before we adjourned at 2 o'clock. When we began again at three, it was the turn of the Admiralty, and the First Sea Lord, Sir Arthur Wilson, with another map expounded his views of the policy we should pursue in the event of our being involved in such a war. He did not reveal the Admiralty war plans. Those he kept locked away in his own brain, but he indicated that they embodied the principle of a close blockade of the enemy's ports. It was very soon apparent that a profound difference existed between the War Office and the Admiralty view. In the main the Admiralty thought that we should confine our efforts to the sea; that if our small Army were sent to the Continent it would be swallowed up among the immense hosts conflicting there, whereas if kept in ships or ready to embark for counter-strokes upon the German coast, it would draw off more than its own weight of numbers from the German fighting line. This view, which was violently combated by the Generals, did not commend itself to the bulk of those present, and on many points of detail connected with the landings of these troops the military and naval authorities were found in complete discord. The serious disagreement between the military and naval staffs in such critical times upon fundamental issues was the immediate cause of my going to the Admiralty. After the Council had separated, Mr. Haldane intimated to the Prime Minister that he would not continue to be responsible for the War Office unless a Board of Admiralty was called into being which would work in full harmony with the War Office plans, and would begin the organization of a proper Naval War Staff. Of course I knew nothing of this, but it was destined soon to affect my fortunes in a definite manner.

I thought that the General Staff took too sanguine a view of the French Army. Knowing their partisanship for France, I feared the wish was father to the thought. It was inevitable that British military men, ardently desirous of seeing their country intervene on the side of France, and convinced that the destruction of France by Germany would imperil the whole future of Great Britain, should be inclined to overrate the relative power of the French Army and accord it brighter prospects than were actually justified. The bulk of their information was derived from French sources. The French General Staff were resolute and hopeful. The principle of the offensive was the foundation of their military art and the mainspring of the French soldier. Although according to the best information, the French pre-war Army when fully mobilized was only three-fourths as strong as the German pre-war Army, the French mobilization from the ninth to the thirteenth day yielded a superior strength on the fighting front. High hopes were entertained by the French Generals that a daring seizure of the initiative and a vigorous offensive into Alsace-Lorraine would have the effect of rupturing the carefully thought out German plans of marching through Belgium on to Paris. These hopes were reflected in the British General Staff appreciations.

I could not share them. I had therefore prepared a memorandum for the Committee of Imperial Defence which embodied my own conclusions upon all I had learned from the General Staff. It was dated August 13, 1911. It was, of course, only an attempt to pierce the veil of the future; to conjure up in the mind a vast imaginary situation; to balance the incalculable; to weigh the imponderable. It will be seen that I named the *twentieth* day of mobilization as the date by which 'the French armies will have been driven from the line of the Meuse and will be falling back on Paris and the South,' and the *fortieth* day as that by which 'Germany should be extended at full strain both internally and on her war fronts,' and that 'opportunities for the decisive trial of strength may then occur.' I am quite free to admit that these were not intended to be precise dates, but as guides to show what would probably happen. In fact, however, both these forecasts were almost literally verified three years later by the event.

I reprinted this memorandum on the 2nd of September, 1914, in order to encourage my colleagues with the hope that if the unfavourable prediction about the twentieth day had been borne out, so also would be the favourable prediction about the fortieth day. And so indeed it was.

MILITARY ASPECTS OF THE CONTINENTAL PROBLEM

Memorandum by Mr. Churchill

August 13, 1911.

The following notes have been written on the assumption. . . that a decision has been arrived at to employ a British military force on the Continent of Europe. It does not prejudge that decision in any way.

It is assumed that an alliance exists between Great Britain, France, and Russia, and that these Powers are attacked by Germany and Austria.

1. The decisive military operations will be those between France and Germany. The German army is at least equal in quality to the French, and mobilizes 2,200,000 against 1,700,000. The French must therefore seek for a situation of more equality. This can be found either before the full strength of the Germans has been brought to bear or after the German army has become extended. The first might be reached between the ninth and thirteenth days; the latter about the fortieth.

2. The fact that during a few days in the mobilization period the French are equal or temporarily superior on the frontiers is of no significance, except on the assumption that France contemplates adopting a strategic offensive. The Germans will not choose the days when they themselves have least superiority for a general advance; and if the French advance, they lose at once all the advantages of their own internal communications, and by moving towards the advancing German reinforcements annul any numerical advantage they may for the moment possess. The French have therefore, at the beginning of the war, no option but to remain on the defensive, both upon their own fortress line and behind the Belgian frontier; and the choice of the day when the first main collision will commence rests with the Germans, who must be credited with the wisdom of choosing the best possible day, and cannot be forced into decisive action against their will, except by some reckless and unjustifiable movement on the part of the French.

3. A prudent survey of chances from the British point of view ought to contemplate that, when the German advance decisively begins, it will be backed by sufficient preponderance of force, and developed on a sufficiently wide front to compel the French armies to retreat from their positions behind the Belgian frontier, even though they may hold the gaps between the fortresses on the Verdun-Belfort front. No doubt a series of great battles will have been fought with varying local fortunes, and there is always a possibility of a heavy German check. But, even if the Germans were brought to a standstill, the French would not be strong

enough to advance in their turn; and in any case we ought not to count on this. The balance of probability is that by the twentieth day the French armies will have been driven from the line of the Meuse and will be falling back on Paris and the south. All plans based upon the opposite assumption ask too much of fortune.

4. This is not to exclude the plan of using four or six British divisions in these great initial operations. Such a force is a material factor of significance. Its value to the French would be out of all proportion to its numerical strength. It would encourage every French soldier and make the task of the Germans in forcing the frontier much more costly. But the question which is of most practical consequence to us, is what is to happen after the frontier has been forced and the invasion of France has begun. France will not be able to end the war successfully by any action on the frontiers. She will not be strong enough to invade Germany. Her only chance is to conquer Germany in France. It is this problem which should be studied before any final decision is taken.

5. The German armies in advancing through Belgium and onwards into France will be relatively weakened by all or any of the following causes:—

By the greater losses incidental to the offensive (especially if they have tested unsuccessfully the French fortress lines);

By the greater employment of soldiers necessitated by acting on exterior lines;

By having to guard their communications through Belgium and France (especially from the sea flank);

By having to invest Paris (requiring at least 500,000 men against 100,000) and to besiege or mask other places, especially along the sea-board;

By the arrival of the British army;

By the growing pressure of Russia from the thirtieth day;

And generally by the bad strategic situation to which their right-handed advance will commit them as it becomes pronounced.

All these factors will operate increasingly in proportion as the German advance continues and every day that passes.

6. Time is also required for the naval blockade to make itself felt on German commerce, industry, and food prices, as described in the Admiralty Memorandum, and for these again to react on German credit and finances already burdened with the prodigious daily cost of the war. All these pressures will develop simultaneously and progressively. [The Chancellor of the Exchequer has drawn special attention to this and to the very light structure of German industry and economic organizations.]

7. By the fortieth day Germany should be extended at full strain both internally and on her war fronts, and this strain will become daily more severe and ultimately overwhelming, unless it is relieved by decisive victories in France. If the French army has not been squandered by precipitate or desperate action, the balance of

forces should be favourable after the fortieth day, and will improve steadily as time passes. For the German armies will be confronted with a situation which combines an ever-growing need for a successful offensive, with a battle-front which tends continually towards numerical equality. Opportunities for the decisive trial of strength may then occur.

8. Such a policy demands heavy and hard sacrifices from France, who must, with great constancy, expose herself to invasion, to having her provinces occupied by the enemy, and to the investment of Paris, and whose armies may be committed to retrograde or defensive operations. Whether her rulers could contemplate or her soldiers endure this trial may depend upon the military support which Great Britain can give; and this must be known beforehand, so that the French war-plans can be adjusted accordingly, and so that we may know, before we decide, what they would be prepared to do.

9. The following measures would appear to be required to enable Great Britain to take an effective part in the decisive theatre of the war:—

	Men (Approximate).
The four divisions of the expeditionary army, with their auxiliary troops, should be sent on the outbreak of war to France	107,000
To these should be added the two remaining divisions as soon as the naval blockade is effectively established	53,000
And the 7th Division from South Africa and the Mediterranean (as soon as the colonial forces in South Africa can be embodied)	15,000
And 5,000 additional Yeomanry cavalry or light horse, with 10,000 volunteer cyclist Territorials	15,000
As we should be allies of Russia, the Anglo-Indian Army could be drawn upon so long as two native regiments were moved out of India for every British regiment. Lord Kitchener has stated that it would be possible in so grave a need, to withdraw six out of the nine field divisions from India, and this should be done immediately. This force could be brought into France by Marseilles by the fortieth day	100,000
Thus making a total force of	290,000

This fine army, almost entirely composed of professional soldiers, could be assembled around (say) Tours by the fortieth day, in rear of the French left (instead of being frittered into action piecemeal), and would then become a very important factor in events. The Russian army would also by then be engaged in full force on the eastern frontiers of Germany and Austria, and the power of the three allies should then be sufficient either to hold the Germans in a position of growing difficulty or, if desirable, to assume the offensive in concert.

10. To provide meanwhile for the security of Great Britain, for unforeseeable contingencies, and for sustaining the expeditionary army with a continuous supply of volunteer drafts, it would be necessary on the outbreak:—

(*a*) To embody the whole Territorial force.

(*b*) To call for volunteers for Home defence from all persons possessing military experience.

(*c*) To raise a compulsory levy of 500,000 men for Home defence.

This levy should be formed upon the cadres of the Territorial divisions, so as to enable a proportion of the Territorial army to be released at the end of the sixth month. The question of sending any part of the compulsory levy *by compulsion* to the Continent would not arise until after this force had been trained. The steady augmentation of British military strength during the progress of the war would, however, put us in a position by the end of the twelfth month to secure or re-establish British interests outside Europe, even if, through the defeat or desertion of allies, we were forced to continue the war alone.

No lesser steps would seem adequate to the scale of events.

W. S. C.

* * * * *

The Conference separated. Apprehension lay heavy on the minds of all who had participated in it.

The War Office hummed with secrets in those days. Not the slightest overt action could be taken. But every preparation by forethought was made and every detail was worked out on paper. The railway time-tables, or graphics as they were called, of the movement of every battalion—even where they were to drink their coffee—were prepared and settled. Thousands of maps of Northern France and Belgium were printed. The cavalry manœuvres were postponed 'on account of the scarcity of water in Wiltshire and the neighbouring counties.' The press, fiercely divided on party lines, overwhelmingly pacific in tendency, without censorship, without compulsion, observed a steady universal reticence. Not a word broke the long-drawn oppressive silence. The great railway strike came to an end with mysterious suddenness. Mutual concessions were made by masters and men after hearing a confidential statement from the Chancellor of the Exchequer.

In the middle of August I went to the country for a few days. I could not think of anything else but the peril of war. I did my other work as it came along, but there was only one field of interest fiercely illuminated in my mind. Sitting on a hilltop in the smiling country which stretches round Mells, the lines I have copied at the top of this chapter kept running through my mind. Whenever I recall them, they bring back to me the anxieties of those Agadir days.

From Mells I wrote the following letter to Sir Edward Grey It speaks for itself.

Mr. Churchill to Sir Edward Grey.

30 *August*, 1911.

Perhaps the time is coming when decisive action will be necessary. Please consider the following policy for use if and when the Morocco negotiations fail.

Propose to France and Russia a triple alliance to safeguard (*inter alia*) the independence of Belgium, Holland, and Denmark.

Tell Belgium that, if her neutrality is violated, we are prepared to come to her aid and to make an alliance with France and Russia to guarantee her independence. Tell her that we will take whatever military steps will be most effective for that purpose. But the Belgian Army must take the field in concert with the British and French Armies, and Belgium must immediately garrison properly Liège and Namur. Otherwise we cannot be responsible for her fate.

Offer the same guarantee both to Holland and to Denmark contingent upon their making their utmost exertions.

We should, if necessary, aid Belgium to defend Antwerp and to feed that fortress and any army based on it. We should be prepared at the proper moment to put extreme pressure on the Dutch to keep the Scheldt open for *all* purposes. If the Dutch close the Scheldt, we should retaliate by a blockade of the Rhine.

It is very important to us to be able to blockade the Rhine, and it gets more important as the war goes on. On the other hand, if the Germans do not use the 'Maestricht Appendix' in the first days of the war, they will not want it at all.

Let me add that I am not at all convinced about the wisdom of a close blockade, and I did not like the Admiralty statement. If the French send cruisers to Mogador and Saffi, I am of opinion that we should (for our part) move our main fleet to the north of Scotland into its war station. Our interests are European, and not Moroccan. The significance of the movement would be just as great as if we sent our two ships with the French.

Please let me know when you will be in London; and will you kindly send this letter on to the Prime Minister.

My views underwent no change in the three years of peace that followed. On the contrary they were confirmed and amplified by everything I learned. In some respects, as in the abolition of the plan of close blockade and the sending of the Fleet to its war station, I was able to carry them out. In other cases, such as the defence of Antwerp, I had not the power to do in time what I believed to be equally necessary. But I tried my best, not, as has frequently been proclaimed, upon a foolish impulse, but in pursuance of convictions reached by pondering and study. I could not help feeling a strong confidence in the truth of these convictions, when I saw how several of them were justified one after the other in that terrible and unparalleled period of convulsion. I had no doubts whatever what ought to be done in certain matters, and my only difficulty was to persuade or induce others.

* * * * *

The Agadir crisis came however peacefully to an end. It terminated in the diplomatic rebuff of Germany. Once more she had disturbed all Europe by a sudden and menacing gesture. Once more she had used the harshest threats towards France. For the first time she had made British statesmen feel that sense of direct contact with the war peril which was never absent from Continental minds. The French, however, offered concessions and compensations. An intricate negotiation about the frontiers of French and German territory in West Africa, in which the 'Bec de Canard' played an important part, had resulted in an agreement between the two principals. To us it seemed that France had won a considerable advantage. She was not, however, particularly pleased. Her Prime Minister, Monsieur Caillaux, who had presided during those anxious days, was dismissed from office on grounds which at the time it was very difficult to appreciate here, but which viewed in the light of subsequent events can more easily be understood. The tension in German governing circles must have been very great. The German Colonial Secretary, von Lindequist, resigned rather than sign the agreement. There is no doubt that deep and violent passions of humiliation and resentment were coursing beneath the glittering uniforms which thronged the palaces through which the Kaiser moved. And of those passions the Crown Prince made himself the exponent. The world has heaped unbounded execrations upon this unlucky being. He was probably in fact no better and no worse than the average young cavalry subaltern who had not been through the ordinary mill at a public school nor had to think about earning his living. He had a considerable personal charm, which he lavished principally upon the fair sex, but which in darker days has captivated the juvenile population of Wieringen. His flattered head was turned by the burning eyes and guttural words of great captains and statesmen and party leaders. He therefore threw himself forward into this strong favouring current, and became a power, or rather the focus of a power, with which the Kaiser was forced to reckon. Germany once more proceeded to increase her armaments by land and sea.

'It was a question,' writes von Tirpitz (*Memories vol. I*, p. 191), 'of our keeping our nerve, *continuing to arm on a grand scale*, avoiding all provocation, and waiting without anxiety *until our sea power was established*[3] and forced the English to let us breathe in peace.' Only to breathe in peace! What fearful apparatus was required to secure this simple act of respiration!

Early in October Mr. Asquith invited me to stay with him in Scotland. The day after I had arrived there, on our way home from the links, he asked me quite abruptly whether I would like to go to the Admiralty. He had put the same question to me when he first became Prime Minister. This time I had no doubt what to answer. All my mind was full of the dangers of war. I accepted with alacrity. I said, 'Indeed I would.' He said that Mr. Haldane was coming to see him the next day and we would talk it over together. But I saw that his mind was made up. The fading light of evening disclosed in the far distance

[3]The italics are mine.

the silhouettes of two battleships steaming slowly out of the Firth of Forth. They seemed invested with a new significance to me.

That night when I went to bed, I saw a large Bible lying on a table in my bedroom. My mind was dominated by the news I had received of the complete change in my station and of the task entrusted to me. I thought of the peril of Britain, peace-loving, unthinking, little prepared, of her power and virtue, and of her mission of good sense and fairplay. I thought of mighty Germany, towering up in the splendour of her Imperial State and delving down in her profound, cold, patient, ruthless calculations. I thought of the army corps I had watched tramp past, wave after wave of valiant manhood, at the Breslau manœuvres in 1907; of the thousands of strong horses dragging cannon and great howitzers up the ridges and along the roads around Wurzburg in 1910. I thought of German education and thoroughness and all that their triumphs in science and philosophy implied. I thought of the sudden and successful wars by which her power had been set up. I opened the Book at random, and in the 9th Chapter of Deuteronomy I read:—

Hear, O Israel: Thou art to pass over Jordan this day, to go in to possess nations greater and mightier than thyself, cities great, and fenced up to heaven;

2. A people great and tall, the children of the Anakims, whom thou knowest, and of whom thou hast heard say, Who can stand before the children of Anak!

3. Understand therefore this day, that the Lord thy God is he which goeth over before thee; as a consuming fire he shall destroy them, and he shall bring them down before thy face: so shalt thou drive them out, and destroy them quickly, as the Lord hath said unto thee.

4. Speak not thou in thine heart, after that the Lord thy God hath cast them out from before thee, saying, For my righteousness the Lord hath brought me in to possess this land; but for the wickedness of these nations the Lord doth drive them out from before thee.

5. Not for thy righteousness, or for the uprightness of thine heart, dost thou go to possess their land; but for the wickedness of these nations the Lord thy God doth drive them out from before thee, and that he may perform the word which the Lord sware unto thy fathers, Abraham, Isaac and Jacob.

It seemed a message full of reassurance.

CHAPTER IV
ADMIRALS ALL

'Concerning brave Captains
Our age hath made known.'

Rudyard Kipling.

At the Admiralty—The State of Business—Immediate Measures—The Two Leading Sailors—Lord Fisher of Kilverstone—His Great Reforms—His Violent Methods—The Schism in the Fleet—Difficulties of His Task—The Bacon Letters—Our Conference at Reigate Priory—A Fateful Decision—Lord Fisher's Correspondence—Sir Arthur Wilson, the First Sea Lord—Deadlock concerning the War Staff Policy—Formation of a New Board of Admiralty—The Command of the Home Fleets—Sir Arthur Wilson's Retirement—A Digression Forward—Captain Pakenham's Sea-going Record—Rear-Admiral Beatty—The Naval Secretary—Prince Louis of Battenberg becomes Second Sea Lord—The War Staff—Military Education and Staff Training—Captains of Ships and Captains of War—Fifteen Years and only Thirty Months.

Mr. McKenna and I changed guard with strict punctilio. In the morning he came over to the Home Office and I introduced him to the officials there. In the afternoon I went over to the Admiralty; he presented his Board and principal officers and departmental heads to me, and then took his leave. I knew he felt greatly his change of office, but no one would have divined it from his manner. As soon as he had gone, I convened a formal meeting of the Board, at which the Secretary read the new Letters Patent constituting me its head, and I thereupon in the words of the Order-in-Council became 'responsible to Crown and Parliament for all the business of the Admiralty.' I was to endeavour to discharge this responsibility for the four most memorable years of my life.

The state of Admiralty business was as follows:—The Estimates and plans for the financial year 1912–13 were far advanced: the programme had been settled and the designs of the vessels only awaited final approval. We were to lay down three battleships, one battle-cruiser, two light cruisers ('Dartmouths'), one smaller light cruiser (a 'Blonde'), the usual flotilla of twenty destroyers and a number of submarines and ancillary craft. The Estimates embodying this policy had to be passed by the Cabinet at the latest by the end of February, and presented to the House of Commons in the utmost detail in March.

But a great uncertainty hung over all these plans. A continued succession of rumours and reports from many sources, and of hints and allusions in the German Press, foreshadowed a further German naval increase. This, following upon all that had gone before and coming at a moment when relations were so tense, must certainly aggravate the situation. It would inevitably compel us to take important additional counter-measures. What these counter-measures would have to be, could not be decided till the text of the new German Navy Law was known to us. It was clear, however, from the information received, that it was not only to be an increase in new construction but in the number of squadrons or vessels maintained in a state of instant and constant readiness.

In addition to these complications were a number of naval questions of prime importance which I conceived required new treatment. First, the War Plans of the Fleet, which up to that moment had been based upon the principle of close blockade. Second, the organization of the fleets with a view to increasing their instantly ready strength. Third, measures to guard against all aspects of surprise in the event of a sudden attack. Fourth, the formation of a Naval War Staff. Fifth, the concerting of the War Plans of the Navy and the Army by close co-operation of the two departments. Sixth, further developments in design to increase the gun power of our new ships in all classes. Seventh, changes in the high commands of the Fleet and in the composition of the Board of Admiralty.

To all these matters I addressed myself in constant secret consultations with the principal persons concerned in each. For the the present, however, I arrived at no important decisions, but laboured continually to check and correct the opinions with which I had arrived at the Admiralty by the expert information which on every subject was now at my disposal.

With the agreement of the Sea Lords I gave certain directions on minor points immediately. The flotilla of destroyers sanctioned in the 1911–12 Estimates would not have been let out to contract till the very end of the financial year. We now accelerated these twenty boats (the 'L's') by four months, and thus, though we could not possibly foresee it, they were almost all fully commissioned just in time for the great review and mobilization of the Fleet which preceded the outbreak of war. I gave, moreover, certain personal directions to enable me 'to sleep quietly in my bed.' The naval magazines were to be effectively guarded under the direct charge of the Admiralty. The continuous attendance of naval officers, additional to that of the resident clerks, was provided at the Admiralty, so that at any hour of the day or night, weekdays, Sundays, or holidays, there would never be a moment lost in giving the alarm; and one of the Sea Lords was always to be on duty in or near the Admiralty building to receive it. Upon the wall behind my chair I had an open case fitted, within whose folding doors spread a large chart of the North Sea. On this chart every day a Staff Officer marked with flags the position of the German Fleet. Never once was this ceremony omitted until the War broke out, and the great maps, covering the whole of one side of the War Room, began to function. I made a rule to look at my chart once every day when I first entered my room. I did this less to keep myself informed, for there were many other channels of information, than in order to inculcate in myself and those working with me a sense of ever-present danger. In this spirit we all worked.

I must now introduce the reader to the two great Admirals-of-the-Fleet, Lord Fisher and Sir Arthur Wilson, whose outstanding qualities and life's work, afloat and at the

Admiralty, added to and reacted upon by the energies and patriotism of Lord Charles Beresford, had largely made the Royal Navy what it was at this time. The names of both Fisher and Wilson must often recur in these pages, for they played decisive parts in the tale I have to tell.

I first met Lord Fisher at Biarritz in 1907. We stayed for a fortnight as the guests of a common friend. He was then First Sea Lord and in the height of his reign. We talked all day long and far into the nights. He told me wonderful stories of the Navy and of his plans—all about Dreadnoughts, all about submarines, all about the new education scheme for every branch of the Navy, all about big guns, and splendid Admirals and foolish miserable ones, and Nelson and the Bible, and finally the island of Borkum. I remembered it all. I reflected on it often. I even remembered the island of Borkum when my teacher had ceased to think so much of it. At any rate, when I returned to my duties at the Colonial Office I could have passed an examination on the policy of the then Board of Admiralty.

For at least ten years all the most important steps taken to enlarge, improve or modernize the Navy had been due to Fisher. The water-tube boiler, the 'all big gun ship,' the introduction of the submarine ('Fisher's toys,' as Lord Charles Beresford called them), the common education scheme, the system of nucleus crews for ships in reserve, and latterly—to meet the German rivalry—the concentration of the Fleets in Home Waters, the scrapping of great quantities of ships of little fighting power, the great naval programmes of 1908 and 1909, the advance from the 12-inch to the 13.5-inch gun—all in the main were his.

In carrying through these far-reaching changes he had created violent oppositions to himself in the Navy, and his own methods, in which he gloried, were of a kind to excite bitter animosities, which he returned and was eager to repay. He made it known, indeed he proclaimed, that officers of whatever rank who opposed his policies would have their professional careers ruined. As for traitors, i.e. those who struck at him openly or secretly, 'their wives should be widows, their children fatherless, their homes a dunghill.' This he repeated again and again. 'Ruthless, relentless and remorseless' were words always on his lips, and many grisly examples of Admirals and Captains eating out their hearts 'on the beach' showed that he meant what he said. He did not hesitate to express his policy in the most unfavourable terms, as if to challenge and defy his enemies and critics. 'Favouritism.' he wrote in the log of Dartmouth College, 'is the secret of efficiency.' What he meant by 'favouritism' was selection without regard to seniority by a discerning genius in the interests of the public; but the word 'favouritism' stuck. Officers were said to be 'in the fish-pond'—unlucky for them if they were not. He poured contempt upon the opinions and arguments of those who did not agree with his schemes, and abused them at all times both by word and letter.

In the Royal Navy, however, there were a considerable number of officers of social influence and independent means, many of whom became hostile to Fisher. They had access to Parliament and to the Press. In sympathy with them, though not with all their methods, was a much larger body of good and proved sea officers. At the head of the whole opposition stood Lord Charles Beresford, at that time Commander-in-Chief of the Channel or principal Fleet. A deplorable schism was introduced into the Royal Navy, which spread to every squadron and to every ship. There were Fisher's men and Beresford's men. Whatever the First Sea Lord proposed the Commander-in-Chief opposed, and through the whole of the Service Captains and Lieutenants were encouraged to take one side or the other. The argument was conducted with technicalities and with personalities. Neither side was strong enough to crush the other. The Admiralty had its backers in the Fleet, and the Fleet had its friends in the Admiralty: both sides therefore had good information as to what was passing in the other camp. The lamentable situation thus created might easily have ruined the discipline of the Navy but for the fact that a third large body of officers resolutely refused, at whatever cost to themselves, to participate in the struggle. Silently and steadfastly they went about their work till the storms of partisanship were past. To these officers a debt is due.

There is no doubt whatever that Fisher was right in nine-tenths of what he fought for. His great reforms sustained the power of the Royal Navy at the most critical period in its history. He gave the Navy the kind of shock which the British Army received at the time of the South African War. After a long period of serene and unchallenged complacency, the mutter of distant thunder could be heard. It was Fisher who hoisted the storm-signal and beat all hands to quarters. He forced every department of the Naval Service to review its position and question its own existence. He shook them and beat them and cajoled them out of slumber into intense activity. But the Navy was not a pleasant place while this was going on. The 'Band of Brothers' tradition which Nelson had handed down, was for the time, but only for the time, discarded; and behind the open hostility of chieftains flourished the venomous intrigues of their followers.

I have asked myself whether all this could not have been avoided; whether we could not have had the Fisher reforms without the Fisher methods? My conviction is that Fisher was maddened by the difficulties and obstructions which he encountered, and became violent in the process of fighting so hard at every step. In the government of a great fighting service there must always be the combination of the political and professional authorities. A strong First Sea Lord, to carry out a vigorous policy, needs the assistance of a Minister, who alone can support him and defend him. The authority of both is more than doubled by their union. Each can render the other services of supreme importance when they are both effective factors. Working in harmony, they multiply each other. By the resultant concentration of combined power, no room or chance is given to faction. For good or for ill what they decide together in the interests of the Service must be loyally accepted. Unhappily, the later years of Fisher's efforts were years in which the Admiralty was ruled by two Ministers, both of whom were desperately and even mortally ill. Although most able and most upright public men, both Lord Cawdor and Lord Tweedmouth, First Lords from 1904 to 1908, were afflicted with extreme ill-health. Moreover, neither was in the House of Commons and able himself, by exposition in the responsible Chamber, to proclaim in unquestioned accents the policy which the Admiralty would follow and which the House of Commons should ratify. When in 1908 Mr. McKenna became First Lord, there was a change. Gifted with remarkable clearness of mind and resolute courage, enjoying in the prime of life the fullest vigour of his faculties, and having acquired a strong political position in the House of Commons, he was able to supply an immediate steadying influence. But it was too late for Fisher. The Furies were upon his track. The opposition and hatreds had already grown too strong. The schism in the Navy continued, fierce and open.

The incident which is most commonly associated with the end of this part of his career is that of the 'Bacon letters.' Captain Bacon was one of the ablest officers in the Navy and a strong Fisherite. In 1906 he had been serving in the Mediterranean under Lord Charles Beresford. Fisher had asked him to write to him from time to time and keep him informed of all that passed. This he did in letters in themselves of much force and value, but open to the reproach of containing criticisms of his immediate commander. This in itself might have escaped unnoticed; but the First Sea Lord used to print in beautiful and carefully considered type, letters, notes and memoranda on technical subjects for the instruction and encouragement of the faithful. Delighted at the cogency of the arguments in the Bacon letters, he had them printed in 1909 and circulated fairly widely throughout the Admiralty. A copy fell at length into hostile hands and was swiftly conveyed to a London evening newspaper. The First Sea Lord was accused of encouraging subordinates in disloyalty to their immediate commanders. The episode was fatal, and at the beginning of 1910 Sir John Fisher quitted the Admiralty and passed, as every one believed, finally into retirement and the House of Lords, crowned with achievements, loaded with honours, but pursued by much obloquy, amid the triumph of his foes.

As soon as I knew for certain that I was to go to the Admiralty I sent for Fisher: he was abroad in sunshine. We had not seen each other since the dispute about the Naval Estimates of 1909. He conceived himself bound in loyalty to Mr. McKenna, but as soon as he learned that I had had nothing to do with the decision which had led to our changing offices, he hastened home. We passed three days together in the comfort of Reigate Priory.

Although my education had been mainly military, I had followed closely every detail of the naval controversies of the previous five years in the Cabinet, in Parliament, and latterly in the Committee of Imperial Defence; and I had certain main ideas of what I was going to do and what, indeed, I was sent to the Admiralty to do. I intended to prepare for an attack by Germany as if it might come next day. I intended to raise the Fleet to the highest possible strength and secure that all that strength was immediately ready. I was pledged to create a War Staff. I was resolved to have all arrangements made at once in the closest concert with the military to provide for the transportation of a British Army to France should war come. I had strong support from the War Office and the Foreign Office: I had the Prime Minister and the Chancellor of the Exchequer at my back. Moreover, every one who knew the crisis through which we had passed had been profoundly alarmed. In these circumstances it only remained to study the methods, and to choose the men.

I found Fisher a veritable volcano of knowledge and of inspiration; and as soon as he learnt what my main purpose was, he passed into a state of vehement eruption. It must indeed have been an agony to him to wait and idly watch from the calm Lake of Lucerne through the anxious weeks of the long-drawn Agadir crisis, with his life's work, his beloved Navy, liable at any moment to be put to the supreme test. Once he began, he could hardly stop. I plied him with questions, and he poured out ideas. It was always a joy to me to talk to him on these great matters, but most of all was he stimulating in all that related to the design of ships. He also talked brilliantly about Admirals, but here one had to make a heavy discount on account of the feuds. My intention was to hold the balance even, and while adopting in the main the Fisher policy, to insist upon an absolute cessation of the vendetta.

Knowing pretty well all that has been written in the preceding pages, I began our conversations with no thought of Fisher's recall. But by the Sunday night the power of the man was deeply borne in upon me, and I had almost made up my mind to do what I did three years later, and place him again at the head of the Naval Service. It was not the outcry that I feared; that I felt strong enough at this time to face. But it was the revival and continuance of the feuds; and it was clear from his temper that this would be inevitable. Then, too, I was apprehensive of his age. I could not feel complete confidence in the poise of the mind at 71. All the way up to London the next morning I was on the brink of saying 'Come and help me,' and had he by a word seemed to wish to return, I would surely have spoken. But he maintained a proper dignity, and in an hour we were in London. Other reflections supervened, adverse counsels were not lacking, and in a few days I had definitely made up my mind to look elsewhere for a First Sea Lord.

I wonder whether I was right or wrong.

For a man who for so many years filled great official positions and was charged with so much secret and deadly business, Lord Fisher appeared amazingly voluminous and reckless in correspondence. When for the purposes of this work and for the satisfaction of his biographers I collected all the letters I had received from the Admiral in his own hand, they amounted when copied to upwards of 300 closely typewritten pages. In the main they repeat again and again the principal naval conceptions and doctrines with which his life had been associated. Although it would be easy to show many inconsistencies and apparent contradictions, the general message is unchanging. The letters are also presented in an entertaining guise, interspersed with felicitous and sometimes recondite quotations, with flashing phrases and images, with mordant jokes and corrosive personalities. All were dashed off red-hot as they left his mind, his strong pen galloping along in the wake of the imperious thought. He would often audaciously fling out on paper thoughts which other people would hardly admit to their own minds. It is small wonder that his turbulent passage left so many foes foaming in his wake. The wonder is that he did not shipwreck himself a score of times. The buoyancy of his genius alone supported the burden. Indeed, in the process of years the profuse and imprudent violence of his letters became, in a sense, its own protection. People came to believe that this was the breezy style appropriate to our guardians of the deep, and the old Admiral swept forward on his stormy course.

To me, in this period of preparation, the arrival of his letters was always a source of lively interest and pleasure. I was regaled with eight or ten closely-written double pages, fastened together with a little pearl pin or scrap of silken ribbon, and containing every kind of news and counsel, varying from blistering reproach to the highest forms of inspiration and encouragement. From the very beginning his letters were couched in an affectionate and paternal style. 'My beloved Winston,' they began, ending usually with a variation of 'Yours to a cinder,' 'Yours till Hell freezes,' or 'Till charcoal sprouts,' followed by a P.S. and two or three more pages of pregnant and brilliant matter. I have found it impossible to re-read these letters without sentiments of strong regard for him, his fiery soul, his volcanic energy, his deep creative mind, his fierce outspoken hatreds, his love of England. Alas, there was a day when Hell froze and charcoal sprouted and friendship was reduced to cinders; when 'My beloved Winston' had given place to 'First Lord: I can no longer be your colleague.' I am glad to be able to chronicle that this was not the end of our long and intimate relationship.

* * * * *

Sir Arthur Wilson, the First Sea Lord, received me with his customary dignified simplicity. He could not, of course, be wholly unaware of the main causes which had brought me to the Admiralty. In conversation with the other Sea Lords when the well-kept secret of my appointment first reached the Admiralty, he said: 'We are to have new masters: if they wish us to serve them, we will do so, and if not, they will find others to carry on the work.' I had only met him hitherto at the conferences of the Committee of Imperial Defence, and my opinions were divided between an admiration for all I heard of his character and a total disagreement with what I understood to be his strategic views. He considered the creation of a War Staff quite unnecessary: I had come to set one up. He did not approve of the War Office plans for sending an army to France in the event of war: I considered it my duty to perfect these arrangements to the smallest detail. He was, as I believed, still an advocate of a close blockade of the German ports, which to my lay or military mind the torpedo seemed already to have rendered impossible.[1] These were large and vital differences. He on his side probably thought we had got into an unnecessary panic over the Agadir crisis, and that we did not properly understand the strength and mobility of the British Fleet nor the true character of British strategic power. He was due to retire for age from the Service in three or four months, unless his tenure had been extended, while I, for my part, came to the Admiralty with a very clear intention to have an entirely new Board of my own choosing. In these circumstances our association was bound to be bleak.

This is, however, the moment for me to give an impression of this striking naval personality. He was, without any exception, the most selfless man I have ever met or even read of. He wanted nothing, and he feared nothing—absolutely nothing. Whether he was commanding the British Fleet or repairing an old motor car, he was equally keen, equally interested, equally content. To step from a great office into absolute retirement, to return from retirement to the pinnacle of naval power, were transitions which produced no change in the beat of that constant heart. Everything was duty. It was not merely that nothing else mattered. There was nothing else. One did one's duty as well as one possibly could, be it great or small, and naturally one deserved no reward. This had been the

[1]The close blockade of the German ports was prescribed in the war orders of 1909, during Lord Fisher's term of office. Sir Arthur Wilson did not reveal any modification which he had made in consequence of new conditions to anyone.

spirit in which he had lived his long life afloat, and which by his example he had spread far and wide through the ranks of the Navy. It made him seem very unsympathetic on many occasions, both to officers and men. Orders were orders, whether they terminated an officer's professional career or led him on to fame, whether they involved the most pleasant or the most disagreeable work; and he would snap his teeth, and smile his wintry smile to all complaints and to sentiment and emotion in every form. Never once did I see his composure disturbed. He never opened up, never unbent. Never once, until a very dark day for me, did I learn that my work had met with favour in his eyes.

All the same, for all his unsympathetic methods, 'Tug,' as he was generally called (because he was always working, i.e. pulling, hauling, tugging), or alternatively 'old' Ard 'Art,' was greatly loved in the Fleet. Men would do hard and unpleasant work even when they doubted its necessity, because he had ordered it and it was 'his way.' He had served as a midshipman in the Crimean War. Every one knew the story of his V.C., when the square broke at Tamai in the Soudan, and when he was seen, with the ammunition of his Gatling exhausted, knocking the Dervish spearmen over one after another with his fists, using the broken hilt of his sword as a sort of knuckle-duster. Stories were told of his apparent insensibility to weather and climate. He would wear a thin monkey-jacket in mid-winter in the North Sea with apparent comfort while every one else was shivering in great-coats. He would stand bareheaded under a tropical sun without ill-effects. He had a strong inventive turn of mind, and considerable mechanical knowledge. The system of counter-mining in use for forty years in the Navy, and the masthead semaphore which continued till displaced by wireless telegraphy, were both products of his ingenuity. He was an experienced and masterly commander of a Fleet at sea. In addition to this, he expressed himself with great clearness and thoroughness on paper, many of his documents being extended arguments of exact detail and widely comprehensive scope. He impressed me from the first as a man of the highest quality and stature, but, as I thought, dwelling too much in the past of naval science, not sufficiently receptive of new ideas when conditions were changing so rapidly, and, of course, tenacious and unyielding in the last degree.

After we had had several preliminary talks and I found we were not likely to reach an agreement, I sent him a minute about the creation of a Naval War Staff, which raised an unmistakable issue. He met it by a powerfully reasoned and unqualified refusal, and I then determined to form a new Board of Admiralty without delay. The Lords of the Admiralty hold quasi-ministerial appointments, and it was of course necessary to put my proposals before the Prime Minister and obtain his assent.

Mr. Churchill to the Prime Minister.

H.M.S. *Enchantress*,
Portsmouth.
November 5, 1911.

The enclosed memorandum from Sir A. Wilson is decisive in its opposition, not only to any particular scheme, but against the whole principle of a War Staff for the Navy. Ottley's[2] rejoinder, which I also send you, shows that it would not be difficult to continue the argument. But I feel that this might easily degenerate into personal controversy, and would, in any case, be quite unavailing. I like Sir A. Wilson personally, and should be very sorry to run the risk of embittering relations which are now pleasant. I therefore propose to take no public action during his tenure.

If Wilson retires in the ordinary course in March, I shall be left without a First Sea Lord in the middle of the passage of the Estimates, and his successor will not be able to take any real responsibility for them. It is necessary, therefore, that the change should be made in January at the latest.

I could, if it were imperative, propose to you a new Board for submission to the King at once. The field of selection for the first place is narrow; and since I have, with a good deal of reluctance, abandoned the idea of bringing Fisher back, no striking appointment is possible. I may, however, just as well enjoy the advantage of reserving a final choice for another month. At present, therefore, I will only say that Prince Louis is certainly the best man to be Second Sea Lord, that I find myself in cordial agreement with him on nearly every important question of naval policy, and that he will accept the appointment gladly.... I should thus hope to start in the New Year with a united and progressive Board, and with the goodwill of both the factions whose animosities have done so much harm.

Meanwhile I am elaborating the scheme of a War Staff.

Mr. Churchill to the Prime Minister.

November 16, 1911.

I have now to put before you my proposals for a new Board of Admiralty, and the changes consequent thereupon. Having now seen all the principal officers who might be considered candidates for such a post, I pronounce decidedly in favour of Sir Francis Bridgeman as First Sea Lord. He is a fine sailor, with the full confidence of the Service afloat, and with the aptitude for working with and through a staff, well developed. If, as would no doubt be the case, he should bring Captain de Bartolomé as his Naval Assistant, I am satisfied that the work of this office would proceed smoothly and with despatch. I have discussed the principal questions of strategy, administration and finance with him, and believe that we are in general agreement on fundamental principles. If you approve, I will write to Sir Francis and enter more fully into these matters in connection with an assumption by him of these new duties.

This appointment harmonizes, personally and administratively, with that of the new Second Sea Lord, Prince Louis of Battenberg, of whom I have already written to you, and of whose assistance I have the highest expectations. Rear-Admiral Briggs, the Controller and Third Sea Lord, has, after a year, just begun to acquire a complete knowledge of his very extensive department, and I do not think it necessary to transfer him at the present

[2]Sir Charles Ottley: at that time Secretary to the Committee of Imperial Defence.

time. He will be the only naval member of the old Board to remain. Rear-Admiral Madden is, in any case, leaving on January 5, and I am advised from all quarters, including both the proposed First and Second Sea Lords, that the best man to fill his place is Captain Pakenham. This officer, who is very highly thought of for his intellectual attainments, has also the rare distinction of having served throughout the Russo-Japanese War, including the battle of the Tsushima.

> The Home Fleet, which becomes vacant, has not, unhappily, any candidate of clear and pre-eminent qualifications. Admiral Jellicoe is not yet sufficiently in command of the confidence of the Sea Service, to justify what would necessarily be a very startling promotion. I shall, however, be taking the perfectly straightforward and unexceptionable course in placing Vice-Admiral Sir George Callaghan, the present Second in Command, who has been in almost daily control of the largest manœuvres of the Home Fleet, and who has previously been Second in Command in the Mediterranean, in the place of Sir F. Bridgeman. Sir John Jellicoe will be his Second in Command, and we shall thus be able to see what fitness he will develop for the succession.
>
> It appears to me not merely important but necessary that these changes should operate without delay. The draft Estimates have all arrived for discussion, and a month of the most severe work, governing the whole future policy of the next two years, awaits the Board of Admiralty. This task can only be satisfactorily discharged if it is undertaken by men who come together with consenting minds, and who will find themselves responsible to the Cabinet and to Parliament for the immediate consequences of their decisions. I would therefore ask you to authorize me to approach all parties concerned without delay, and unless some unexpected hitch occurs I shall hope to submit the list to the King not later than Wednesday next. The New Board would thus be fully constituted before the end of the present month.

Afloat the decisive appointment was that of Sir John Jellicoe to be second in command of the Home Fleet. He thus in effect passed over the heads of four or five of the most important senior Admirals on the active list and became virtually designated for the supreme command in the near future.

The announcement of these changes (November 28) created a considerable sensation in the House of Commons when, late at night, they became known. All the Sea Lords, except one, had been replaced by new men. I was immediately interrogated, 'Had they resigned, or been told to go?' and so on. I gave briefly such explanations as were necessary. At this time I was very strong, because most of those who knew the inner history of the Agadir crisis were troubled about the Fleet, and it was well known that I had been sent to the Admiralty to make a new and a vehement effort.

Sir Arthur Wilson and I parted on friendly, civil, but at the same time cool terms. He showed not the least resentment at the short curtailment of his tenure. He was as good-tempered and as distant as ever. Only once did he show the slightest sign of vehemence. That was when I told him that the Prime Minister was willing to submit his name to the

King for a Peerage. He disengaged himself from this with much vigour. What would he do with such a thing? It would be ridiculous. However, His Majesty resolved to confer upon him the Order of Merit, and this he was finally persuaded to accept. On his last night in office he gave a dinner to the new Sea Lords in the true 'band of brothers' style, and then retired to Norfolk. I could not help thinking uncomfortably of the famous Tenniel cartoon, 'Dropping the Pilot,' where the inexperienced and impulsive German Emperor is depicted carelessly watching the venerable figure of Bismarck descending the ladder. Nevertheless I had acted on high public grounds and on those alone, and I fortified myself with them.

As will be seen in its proper place, Sir Arthur Wilson came back to the Admiralty three years later, and worked with Lord Fisher and me during the six months of our association in the war. When Lord Fisher resigned in May 1915, I invited Sir Arthur to take up the duties of First Sea Lord and he consented to do so. On learning, however, a few days later that I was to leave the Admiralty, he wrote to Mr. Asquith refusing to undertake the task under any other First Lord but me. Here is his letter:—

May 19, 1915.

Dear Mr. Asquith,—

In view of the reports in the papers this morning as to the probable reconstruction of the Government, I think I ought to tell you that although I agreed to undertake the office of First Sea Lord under Mr. Churchill because it appeared to be the best means of maintaining continuity of policy under the unfortunate circumstances that have arisen, I am not prepared to undertake the duties under any new First Lord, as the strain under such circumstances would be far beyond my strength.

Believe me,
Yours truly,
A. K. Wilson.

At that time I hardly seemed to have a friend in the official or Parliamentary world. All the press were throwing the blame of the Dardanelles entanglement and of many other things upon me, and I was everywhere represented as a rash, presumptuous person with whom no Board of Admiralty could work. Sir Arthur had never previously given me any sign of approval, though, of course, we had laboured together day after day. I was, therefore, astounded to learn what he had done. It came as an absolute surprise to me: and I do not mind saying that I felt as proud as a young officer mentioned for the first time in despatches. I thought it my duty, however, to try to overcome his objections, as I knew the Prime Minister wanted him to take the post. But it was all in vain. He stuck to his opinion that he could do it with me and with nobody else. I felt deeply touched. There was nothing to be touched about, he observed, 'You know all the moves on the board. I should only have to put the brake on from time to time. I could not possibly manage with anyone else.' And that was the end of it. He continued working in a subordinate position at the Admiralty till the end of the war. I hardly ever saw him afterwards; but I have preserved a memory which is very precious to me.

The new Fourth Sea Lord was an officer of singular firmness of character. He possessed a unique experience of naval war. Since Nelson himself, no British naval officer had been so long at sea in time of war on a ship of war without setting foot on land. Captain Pakenham had been fourteen months afloat in the battleship *Asahi* during the war between Russia and Japan. Although this vessel was frequently in harbour, he would not leave it for fear she might sail without him; and there alone, the sole European in a great ship's company of valiant, reticent, inscrutable Japanese, he had gone through the long vigil outside Port Arthur, with its repeated episodes of minefields and bombardments, till the final battle in the Sea of Japan. Always faultlessly attired, he matched the Japanese with a punctilio and reserve the equal of their own, and finally captivated their martial spirit and won their unstinted and outspoken admiration. Admiral Togo has related how the English officer, as the *Asahi* was going into action at the last great battle, when the heavy shells had already begun to strike the ship, remained impassive alone on the open after-bridge making his notes and taking his observations of the developing action for the reports which he was to send to his Government; and acclaiming him, with Japanese chivalry, recommended him to the Emperor for the highest honour this war-like and knightly people could bestow.

The unique sea-going record in time of war on a ship of war which Captain Pakenham brought to the Admiralty has been maintained by him to this day, and to fourteen months of sea-going service with the Japanese Fleet, he may now add fifty-two months constant service with the Battle-Cruisers, during which time it is credibly reported that he never on any occasion at sea lay down to rest otherwise than fully dressed, collared and booted, ready at any moment of the night or day.

A few weeks after my arrival at the Admiralty I was told that among several officers of Flag rank who wished to see me was Rear-Admiral Beatty. I had never met him before, but I had the following impressions about him. First, that he was the youngest Flag Officer in the Fleet. Second, that he had commanded the white gunboat which had come up the Nile as close as possible to support the 21st Lancers when we made the charge at Omdurman. Third, that he had seen a lot of fighting on land with the army, and that consequently he had military as well as naval experience. Fourth, that he came of a hard-riding stock; his father had been in my own regiment, the 4th Hussars, and I had often heard him talked of when I first joined. The Admiral, I knew, was a very fine horseman, with what is called 'an eye for country.' Fifth, that there was much talk in naval circles of his having been pushed on too fast. Such were the impressions aroused in my mind by the name of this officer, and I record them with minuteness because the decisions which I had the honour of taking in regard to him were most serviceable to the Royal Navy and to the British arms.

I was, however, advised about him at the Admiralty in a decisively adverse sense. He had got on too fast, he had many interests ashore. His heart it was said was not wholly in the Service. He had been offered an appointment in the Atlantic Fleet suited to his rank as Rear-Admiral. He had declined this appointment—a very serious step for a Naval Officer to take when appointments were few in proportion to candidates—and he should in consequence not be offered any further employment. It would be contrary to precedent to make a further offer. He had already been unemployed for eighteen months, and would probably be retired in the ordinary course at the expiration of the full three years' unemployment.

But my first meeting with the Admiral induced me immediately to disregard this unfortunate advice. He became at once my Naval Secretary (or Private Secretary, as the appointment was then styled). Working thus side by side in rooms which communicated, we perpetually discussed during the next fifteen months the problems of a naval war with Germany. It became increasingly clear to me that he viewed questions of naval strategy and tactics in a different light from the average naval officer: he approached them, as it seemed to me, much more as a soldier would. His war experiences on land had illuminated the facts he had acquired in his naval training. He was no mere instrumentalist. He did not think of *matériel* as an end in itself but only as a means. He thought of war problems in their unity by land, sea and air. His mind had been rendered quick and supple by the situations of polo and the hunting-field, and enriched by varied experiences against the enemy on Nile gunboats, and ashore. It was with equal pleasure and profit that I discussed with him our naval problem, now from this angle, now from that; and I was increasingly struck with the shrewd and profound sagacity of his comments expressed in language singularly free from technical jargon.

I had no doubts whatever when the command of the Battle-Cruiser Squadron fell vacant in the spring of 1913, in appointing him over the heads of all to this incomparable command, the nucleus as it proved to be of the famous Battle-Cruiser Fleet—the strategic cavalry of the Royal Navy, that supreme combination of speed and power to which the thoughts of the Admiralty were continuously directed. And when two years later (February 3, 1915) I visited him on board the *Lion*, with the scars of victorious battle fresh upon her from the action of the Dogger Bank, I heard from his Captains and his Admirals the expression of their respectful but intense enthusiasm for their leader. Well do I remember how, as I was leaving the ship, the usually imperturbable Admiral Pakenham caught me by the sleeve, 'First Lord, I wish to speak to you in private,' and the intense conviction in his voice as he said, 'Nelson has come again.' Those words often recurred to my mind.

So much of my work in endeavouring to prepare the Fleet for war was dependent upon the guidance and help I received from Prince Louis of Battenberg, who, taking it as a whole, was my principal counsellor, as Second Sea Lord from January, 1912, to March, 1913 (when Sir Francis Bridgeman's health temporarily failed), and as First Sea Lord thenceforward to the end of October, 1914, that it is necessary to give some description of this remarkable Prince and British sailor. All the more is this necessary since the accident of his parentage struck him down in the opening months of the Great War and terminated his long professional career.

Prince Louis was a child of the Royal Navy. From his earliest years he had been bred to the sea. The deck of a British warship was his home. All his interest was centred in the British Fleet. So far from his exalted rank having helped him, it had hindered his career: up to a certain point no doubt it had been of assistance, but after that it had been a positive drawback. In consequence he had spent an exceptionally large proportion of his forty years' service afloat usually in the less agreeable commands. One had heard at Malta how he used to bring his Cruiser Squadron into that small, crowded harbour at speed and then in the nick of time, with scarcely a hundred yards to spare, by dropping his anchors, checking on his cables and going full speed astern, bring it safely into station. He had a far wider knowledge of war by land and sea and of the Continent of Europe than most of the other Admirals I have known. His brother, as King of Bulgaria, had shown military aptitudes of a very high order at the Battle of Slivnitza, and he himself was deeply versed in every detail, practical and theoretic, of the British Naval Service. It was not without good reason that he had been appointed under Lord Fisher to be Head of the British Naval Intelligence Department, that vital ganglion of our organization. He was a thoroughly trained and accomplished Staff Officer, with a gift of clear and lucid statement and all that thoroughness and patient industry which we have never underestimated in the German race.

It was recounted of him that on one occasion, when he visited Kiel with King Edward, a German Admiral in high command had reproached him with serving in the British Fleet, whereat Prince Louis, stiffening, had replied 'Sir, when I joined the Royal Navy in the year 1868, the German Empire did not exist.'

The part which he played in the events with which I am dealing, will be recorded as the story unfolds.

Our first labour was the creation of the War Staff. All the details of this were worked out by Prince Louis and approved by the First Sea Lord. I also resorted to Sir Douglas Haig, at that time in command at Aldershot. The general furnished me with a masterly paper setting forth the military doctrine of Staff organization and constituting in many respects a formidable commentary on existing naval methods. Armed with these various opinions, I presented my conclusions to the public in January, 1912, in a document of which the first two paragraphs may be repeated here. They were, as will be seen, designed so far as possible to disarm the prejudices of the naval service.

> '1. In establishing a War Staff for the Navy it is necessary to observe the broad differences of character and circumstances which distinguish naval from military problems. War on land varies in every country according to numberless local conditions, and each new theatre, like each separate battle-field, requires a special study. A whole series of intricate arrangements must be thought out and got ready for each particular case; and these are expanded and refined continuously by every increase in the size of armies, and by every step towards the perfection of military science. The means by which superior forces can be brought to decisive points in good condition and at the right time are no whit less vital, and involve far more elaborate processes than the strategic choice of those points, or the actual conduct of the fighting. The sea, on the other hand, is all one, and, though ever changing, always the same. Every ship is self-contained and self-propelled. The problems of transport and supply, the infinite peculiarities of topography which are the increasing study of the general staffs of Europe, do not affect the naval service except in an occasional and limited degree. The main part of the British Fleet in

sufficient strength to seek a general battle is always ready to proceed to sea without any mobilization of reserves as soon as steam is raised. Ships or fleets of ships are capable of free and continuous movement for many days and nights together, and travel at least as far in an hour as an army can march in a day. Every vessel is in instant communication with its fleet and with the Admiralty, and all can be directed from the ports where they are stationed on any sea points chosen for massing, by a short and simple order. Unit efficiency, that is to say, the individual fighting power of each vessel and each man, is in the sea service for considerable periods entirely independent of all external arrangements, and unit efficiency at sea, far more even than on land, is the prime and final factor, without which the combinations of strategy and tactics are only the preliminaries of defeat, but with which even faulty dispositions can be swiftly and decisively retrieved. For these and other similar reasons a Naval War Staff does not require to be designed on the same scale or in the same form as the General Staff of the Army.

'2. Naval war is at once more simple and more intense than war on land. The executive action and control of fleet and squadron Commanders is direct and personal in a far stronger degree than that of Generals in the field, especially under modern conditions. The art of handling a great fleet on important occasions with deft and sure judgment is the supreme gift of the Admiral, and practical seamanship must never be displaced from its position as the first qualification of every sailor. The formation of a War Staff does not mean the setting up of new standards of professional merit or the opening of a road of advancement to a different class of officers. It is to be the means of preparing and training those officers who arrive, or are likely to arrive, by the excellence of their sea service at stations of high responsibility, for dealing with the more extended problems which await them there. It is to be the means of sifting, developing, and applying the results of actual experience in history and present practice, and of preserving them as a general stock of reasoned opinion available as an aid and as a guide for all who are called upon to determine, in peace or war, the naval policy of the country. It is to be a brain far more comprehensive than that of any single man, however gifted, and tireless and unceasing in its action, applied continuously to the scientific and speculative study of naval strategy and preparation. It is to be an instrument capable of formulating any decision which has been taken, or may be taken, by the Executive in terms of precise and exhaustive detail.'

I never ceased to labour at the formation of a true General Staff for the Navy. In May, 1914, basing myself on the report of a Committee which I had set up a year before, I drafted a fairly complete scheme for the further development of Staff training. I quote a salient passage:[3]

[3]The memorandum, abridged, can be read in Appendix A.

> 'It is necessary to draw a distinction between the measures required to secure a general diffusion of military knowledge among naval officers and the definite processes by which Staff Officers are trained. The first may be called "Military Education," and the second "War Staff Training." They require to be treated separately and not mixed together as in the report of the Committee. Both must again be distinguished from all questions of administration, of material, and of non-military education and training. The *application* of fighting power can thus be separated from its development. We are not now concerned with the forging of the weapon, but only with its use.
>
> 'As early as possible in his service the mind of the young officer must be turned to the broad principles of war by sea and land. His interest must be awakened. He must be put in touch with the right books and must be made to feel the importance of the military aspect of his profession. . . .'

But it takes a generation to form a General Staff. No wave of the wand can create those habits of mind in seniors on which the efficiency and even the reality of a Staff depends. Young officers can be trained, but thereafter they have to rise step by step in the passage of time to positions of authority in the Service. The dead weight of professional opinion was adverse. They had got on well enough without it before. They did not want a special class of officer professing to be more brainy than the rest. Sea time should be the main qualification, and next to that technical aptitudes. Thus when I went to the Admiralty I found that there was no moment in the career and training of a naval officer, when he was obliged to read a single book about naval war, or pass even the most rudimentary examination in naval history. The Royal Navy had made no important contribution to Naval literature. The standard work on Sea Power was written by an American Admiral.[4] The best accounts of British sea fighting and naval strategy were compiled by an English civilian.[5] 'The Silent Service' was not mute because it was absorbed in thought and study, but because it was weighted down by its daily routine and by its ever-complicating and diversifying technique. We had competent administrators, brilliant experts of every description, unequalled navigators, good disciplinarians, fine sea-officers, brave and devoted hearts: but at the outset of the conflict we had more captains of ships than captains of war. In this will be found the explanation of many untoward events. At least fifteen years of consistent policy were required to give the Royal Navy that widely extended outlook upon war problems and of war situations without which seamanship, gunnery, instrumentalisms of every kind, devotion of the highest order, could not achieve their due reward.

Fifteen years! And we were only to have thirty months!

---

[4]Admiral Mahan.

[5]Sir Julian Corbett.

CHAPTER V
THE GERMAN NAVY LAW

'The young disease, that must subdue at length,
Grows with his growth, and strengthens with his strength.'

Pope, *Essay on Man*.

The Morrow of Agadir—Mission of Sir Ernest Cassel—The New German Navy Law—The Haldane Visit to Berlin—An Imperial Mare's Nest—The Opening of the Reichstag—A Speech at Glasgow—The *Luxus Flotte*—Mr. Haldane Returns—Attempt to Reach a Settlement—Correspondence with Lord Fisher—Fisher's Vision—The Navy Estimates—The Navy Holiday—Efforts at Goodwill—Consequences of German Naval Power—Von Tirpitz' Illusions—Anglo-French Naval Conversations—The Entente Strengthened—Von Tirpitz' Unwisdom—Organization of the Navy—The New Structure—With the Fleet—The *Enchantress* in Portland Harbour—The Safeguard of Freedom

I have shown how forward the Chancellor of the Exchequer was during the crisis of Agadir in every matter that could add to the strength of the British attitude. But as soon as the danger was passed he adopted a different demeanour. He felt that an effort should be made to heal any smart from which Germany might be suffering, and to arrive at a common understanding on naval strength. We knew that a formidable new Navy Law was in preparation and would shortly be declared. If Germany had definitely made up her mind to antagonize Great Britain, we must take up the challenge; but it might be possible by friendly, sincere and intimate conversation to avert this perilous development. We were no enemies to German colonial expansion, and we would even have taken active steps to further her wishes in this respect. Surely something could be done to break the chain of blind causation. If aiding Germany in the Colonial sphere was a means of procuring a stable situation, it was a price we were well prepared to pay. I was in full accord with this view. Apart from wider reasons, I felt I should be all the stronger in asking the Cabinet and the House of Commons for the necessary monies, if I could go hand in hand with the Chancellor of the Exchequer and testify that we had tried our best to secure a mitigation of the naval rivalry and failed. We therefore jointly consulted Sir Edward Grey, and then with the Prime Minister's concurrence we invited Sir Ernest Cassel to go to Berlin and get into direct touch with the Emperor. Sir Ernest was qualified for this task, as he knew the Emperor well and was at the same time devoted to British interests. We armed him with a brief but pregnant memorandum, which cannot be more tersely summarized than in von Bethmann-Hollweg's own words[1]: 'Acceptance of English superiority at sea—no augmentation of the German naval programme—a reduction as far as possible of that programme—and on the part of England, no impediment to our Colonial expansion—discussion and promotion of our Colonial ambitions—proposals for mutual declarations that the two Powers would not take part in aggressive plans or combinations against one another.' Cassel accepted the charge and started at once. He remained only two days in Berlin and came at once to me on his return. He brought with him a cordial letter from the Emperor and a fairly full statement by von Bethmann-Hollweg of the new German Navy Law. We devoured this invaluable document all night long in the Admiralty, and in the morning I wrote as follows to Sir Edward Grey:—

January 31, 1912.

Cassel returned last night, having travelled continuously from Berlin. At 10 a.m. on Monday he saw Ballin, who went forthwith to the German Chancellor, and in the afternoon he saw Ballin, Bethmann-Hollweg and the Emperor together. They all appeared deeply pleased by the overture. Bethmann-Hollweg earnest and cordial, the Emperor 'enchanted, almost childishly so.' The Emperor talked a great deal on naval matters to Cassel, the details of which he was unable to follow. After much consultation the Emperor wrote out with Bethmann-Hollweg paper 'A,' which Ballin transcribed. The second paper, 'B,' is Bethmann-Hollweg's statement of the impending naval increases, translated by Cassel. Cassel says they did not seem to know what they wanted in regard to colonies. They did not seem to be greatly concerned about expansion. 'There were ten large companies in Berlin importing labour *into* Germany.' Overpopulation was not their problem. They were delighted with Cassel's rough notes of our ideas. They are most anxious to hear from us soon. . . .

Such is my report.

Observations

It seems certain that the new Navy Law will be presented to the Reichstag, and that it will be agreed to, even the Socialists not resisting. The naval increases are serious, and will require new and vigorous measures on our part. The spirit may be good, but the facts are grim. I had been thinking that if the old German programme had been adhered to, we should have built 4, 3, 4, 3, 4, 3, against their six years' programme of 2, 2, 2, 2, 2, 2. If their new programme stands, as I fear it must, and they build 3, 2, 3, 2, 3, 2, we cannot build less than 5, 4, 5, 4, 5, 4. This maintains 60 per cent superiority in Dreadnoughts and Dreadnought Cruisers over Germany only. It will also be 2 keels to 1 on their additional 3 ships.

The creation of a third squadron in full commission is also a serious and formidable provision. At present, owing to the fact that in the six winter months the first and second squadrons of the High Sea Fleet are congested with recruits, there

[1] *Reflections on the World War*, v. Bethmann-Hollweg p. 48.

is a great relief to us from the strain to which we are put by German naval power. The addition of the third squadron will make that strain continual throughout the year. The maintenance in full commission of 25 battleships, which after the next four or five years will all be Dreadnoughts, exposes us to constant danger, only to be warded off by vigilance approximating to war conditions. A further assurance against attack is at present found in the fact that several of the German Dreadnoughts are very often the wrong side of the Kiel Canal, which they cannot pass through and must therefore make a long *détour*. The deepening of the Canal by 1913 will extinguish this safety signal.[2] The fact that the defenders are always liable to be attacked while only at their ordinary average strength by an enemy at his selected moment and consequent maximum strength, means that our margins would have to be very large. Against 25 battleships we could not keep less than 40 available within twenty-four hours. This will involve additional expense.

The German increase in personnel must also be met. I had intended to ask Parliament for 2,000 more men this year and 2,000 next. I expect to have to double these quotas. On the whole the addition to our estimates consequent upon German increases will not be less than three millions a year. This is certainly not dropping the naval challenge.

I agree with you that caution is necessary. In order to meet the new German squadron, we are contemplating bringing home the Mediterranean battleships. This means relying on France in the Mediterranean,[3] and certainly no exchange of system[4] would be possible, even if desired by you.

The only chance I see is roughly this. They will announce their new programme, and we will make an immediate and effective reply. Then if they care to slow down the 'tempo' so that their Fleet Law is accomplished in twelve and not in six years, friendly relations would ensue, and we, though I should be reluctant to bargain about it, could slow down too. All they would have to do, would be to make their quotas biennial instead of annual. Nothing would be deranged in their plan. Twelve years of tranquillity would be assured in naval policy. The attempt ought to be made.

We laid these matters before the Cabinet, who decided that a British Cabinet Minister should go to Berlin and selected Mr. Haldane for that purpose. The ex-Emperor in his Memoirs makes a ridiculous story out of this:—

'. . . a keen dispute had arisen among Ministers—especially between Churchill and Grey—as to who should go to Berlin, in the event of the achievement of the object of making Germany abandon the further development of her fleet, and affix his name to this great historical document. Churchill considered himself the right man for the job, seeing that he was the head of the Navy, but Grey and Asquith

---

[2]It was not in fact completed till August, 1914.

[3]By later decisions a squadron of British Battle-Cruisers was stationed in the Mediterranean.

[4]i.e., The Entente.

would not allow their colleague to reap the glory. Thus for a time, Grey stood in the foreground—another proof that some political purpose rather than the number of ships was the leading factor. After a while, however, it was decided that it was more fitting to Grey's personal and official importance that he should appear only at the termination of the negotiations, to affix his name to the agreement, and. . . "to get his dinner from the Emperor and to come in for his part of the festivities and fireworks," which, in good German, means to enjoy the "Bengal light illumination." As it had been decided that in any event Churchill was not to get this, it was necessary to choose somebody for the negotiations who was in close accord with Asquith and Grey and who, possessing their complete confidence, was willing to conduct the negotiations as far as the beginning of the "fireworks"; one, moreover, who was already known at Berlin and not a stranger to Germany. Churchill certainly qualified to this extent, for he had attended the Imperial manœuvres in Silesia and Würtemberg on several occasions as a guest of the Emperor.'

On this it may be observed that there never was any question of my going to Berlin to negotiate about the Navy; nor did I at this time wish to go. All the British ministers concerned worked together in the utmost accord. After full discussions we authorized Sir Ernest Cassel to send the following telegram:—

Sir E. Cassel to Herr Ballin (drafted by Sir E. Cassel, the First Lord, Mr. Haldane, Sir Edward Grey).

February 3, 1912.

Spirit in which statements of German Government have been made is most cordially appreciated here. New German programme would entail serious and immediate increase of British naval expenditure which was based on assumption that existing German naval programme would be adhered to.

If the British Government are compelled to make such increase, it would make negotiations difficult if not impossible.

If, on the other hand, German naval expenditure can be adapted by an alteration of the tempo or otherwise so as to render any serious increase unnecessary to meet German programme, British Government will be prepared at once to pursue negotiations on the understanding that the point of naval expenditure is open to discussion and that there is a fair prospect of settling it favourably.

If this understanding is acceptable, the British Government will forthwith suggest the next step, as they think that the visit of a British Minister to Berlin should in the first instance be private and unofficial.

All being acceptable, the Secretary of State for War, accompanied by Sir Ernest Cassel, started accordingly on February 6 for Berlin.

I had undertaken some weeks earlier to make a speech in support of the Home Rule Bill in Belfast. Violent hostility to this project developed in the inflammable capital of Ulster. Being publicly committed, I had no choice but to fulfil my engagement, though to avoid unnecessary provocation the meeting-place was changed from the Ulster Hall to a large tent which was erected in the outskirts of the city. Threats of violence and riot were loudly proclaimed on every side and nearly 10,000 troops were concentrated in the area to keep the peace. I had planned, if all went well at Belfast, to go on the next day to Glasgow to inspect some of the shipbuilding works along the Clyde, and to make a speech on the Naval position, which should state very plainly our root intentions and be the necessary counterpart of the Haldane mission. As I was waiting for the train for Ireland to leave the London railway station, I read in the late edition of the evening papers the German Emperor's speech on the opening of the Reichstag announcing Bills for the increase both of the Army and the Navy. The new Navy Law was still a secret to the British and German nations alike, but knowing as I did its scope and character and viewing it in conjunction with the Army Bill, I sustained a strong impression at this moment of the approaching danger. One sentence, full of German self-revelation, stood out vividly. 'It is my constant duty and care to maintain and to strengthen on land and water, the power of defence of the German people, *which has no lack of young men fit to bear arms*.' It was indeed true. One thought of France with her declining birth-rate peering out across her fortresses into the wide German lands and silently reflecting on these 'young men fit to bear arms' of whom there was indeed 'no lack.' My mind, skipping over the day of Irish turmoil and the worry of the speech that lay before me, fixed upon Glasgow as the place where some answer to this threat of continental domination might perhaps be provided. Once again Europe might find a safeguard against military overlordship in an island which had never been and never would be 'lacking in trained and hardy mariners bred from their boyhood up to the service of the sea.'

Accordingly, after the Irish ordeal was over, I said at Glasgow:—

> 'The purposes of British naval power are essentially defensive. We have no thoughts, and we have never had any thoughts of aggression, and we attribute no such thoughts to other great Powers. There is, however, this difference between the British naval power and the naval power of the great and friendly Empire—and I trust it may long remain the great and friendly Empire—of Germany. The British Navy is to us a necessity and, from some points of view, the German Navy is to them more in the nature of a luxury. Our naval power involves British existence. It is existence to us; it is expansion to them. We cannot menace the peace of a single Continental hamlet, no matter how great and supreme our Navy may become. But, on the other hand, the whole fortunes of our race and Empire, the whole treasure accumulated during so many centuries of sacrifice and achievement, would perish and be swept utterly away if our naval supremacy were to be impaired. It is the British Navy which makes Great Britain a great Power. But Germany was a great Power respected and honoured all over the world, before she had a single ship. . . .
>
> 'If to-day our position is eminently satisfactory we owe much to the foresight and resolution of Mr. McKenna. . . . Whatever is needed for the safety of the country will be asked for by the Government, and granted by the representatives of the nation with universal assent. There is no need for anxiety in regard to our

shipbuilding capacity. There is no chance whatever of our being overtaken in naval strength unless we want to be. . . .

'But what of the men? We have to-day 135,000 men in the active service ratings of the Navy. The great bulk of them are long-service men who have begun as boys and have been trained as a life-long profession to the naval service. We have no difficulty in recruiting for the Navy. . . and there is no doubt whatever of our ability to make any increases which may be necessary, and which I think will be necessary, in the *personnel* of the Navy. We have great reserves of seamen in this country. There are measures which may be taken to make a greater use of our reserves than has hitherto been found possible, and I have given directions for that part of the subject to be carefully studied by the naval experts upon whom I rely. Our reserves, both from the Royal Navy and from the Mercantile Marine, are a great resource, *and this island has never been, and never will be, lacking in trained and hardy mariners bred from their boyhood up to the service of the sea.*

'Whatever may happen abroad there will be no whining here, no signals of distress will be hoisted, no cries for help or succour will go up. We will face the future as our ancestors would have faced it, without disquiet, without arrogance, but in stolid and inflexible determination. We should be the first Power to welcome any retardation or slackening of naval rivalry. We should meet any such slackening not by words but by deeds.... If there are to be increases upon the Continent of Europe, we shall have no difficulty in meeting them to the satisfaction of the country. *As naval competition becomes more acute, we shall have not only to increase the number of the ships we build, but the ratio which our naval strength will have to bear to other great naval Powers*, so that our margin of superiority will become larger and not smaller as the strain grows greater. Thus we shall make it clear that other naval Powers, instead of overtaking us by additional efforts, will only be more outdistanced in consequence of the measures which we ourselves shall take.'

This speech created a considerable outcry in Germany, which was immediately re-echoed by a very large proportion of our own Liberal press. It appeared that the word 'luxury' had a bad significance when translated into German. The '*Luxus Flotte*' became an expression passed angrily from lip to lip in Germany. As I expected, on my return to London I found my colleagues offended. Their congratulations upon Belfast were silenced by their reproaches about Glasgow. Mr. Haldane returned two days later from Berlin, and the Cabinet was summoned to receive an account of his mission. Contrary to general expectation, however, the Secretary of State for War declared that so far from being a hindrance to him in his negotiations, the Glasgow speech had been the greatest possible help. He had in fact used almost identical arguments to von Bethmann-Hollweg the day before. He had told the Chancellor that if Germany added a third squadron we should have 'to maintain five or even six squadrons in home waters, perhaps bringing ships from the Mediterranean to strengthen them'; that if ships were added to the existing programme we should 'proceed at once to lay down two keels to each of the new German additions'; and that for the sake of the Navy 'people would not complain of the addition of another shilling to the income tax.' He described how he had read the operative passages in my speech himself to the Emperor and von Tirpitz in proof and confirmation of what he had himself been saying during their previous discussions. This settled the matter so far as I was concerned. It was only another instance of the very manly and loyal part which Mr. Haldane took at all times and on every question connected with the preparedness of this country for war with Germany.

Mr. Haldane brought back with him the actual text of the new German Navy Law, or 'Novelle' as it was called. This had been handed to him by the Emperor during the course of the discussion. It was an elaborate technical document. Mr. Haldane had had the prudence to refuse to express any opinion upon it till it had been examined by the Admiralty experts. We now subjected this document to a rigorous scrutiny. The result more than confirmed my first unfavourable impression.

> 'The main feature in the new law,' I reported to the Cabinet on February 14, 'is the extraordinary increase in the striking force of ships of all classes immediately available throughout the year. Whereas formerly we reckoned against 17 battleships, 4 battle cruisers, and 12 small cruisers in the active battle fleet, demobilized to a great extent during the winter months, we must in future prepare against 25, 12 and 18, which are not to be subject to anything like the same degree of temporary demobilization.... Full permanent crews are to be provided for all, or nearly all, torpedo boat destroyers, now aggregating 115, and working up to an authorized total of 144, instead of for half the number as at present. There is to be an increase on the already large provision of £750,000 in this year's Estimates for submarines. The numbers are not stated, but from the fact that 121 additional executive officers are required for this service alone by 1920, we may infer that between 50 and 60 submarines are to be added.[5] We know nothing of the rate at which this construction is to be achieved. The increases in personnel are also important. Under their existing law, the Germans are working to a total of 86,500 in 1917 by annual increments of 3,500. The new law adds 15,000 officers and men, and raises the total in 1920 to 101,500.'

On March 9 I pointed out that the fundamental proposition of the negotiations from the Admiralty point of view had been that the existing German Navy Law should not be increased, but, if possible, reduced, whereas on the contrary a new law was certainly to be enacted providing for large and progressive increases not only in 1912 but in the five following years. Practically four-fifths of the German Navy were to be placed permanently upon a war footing. The German Government would be able to have available at all seasons of the year twenty-five, or perhaps twenty-nine, fully commissioned battleships, 'whereas at the present time the British Government have in full commission in Home Waters only twenty-two, even counting the Atlantic Fleet.'

---

[5]The final published text of the law provided for 72.

Thus on the fundamental proposition we encountered an unyielding attitude. Nevertheless we persevered and the discussion was transferred to the question of a mutual declaration against aggressive plans. Here Sir Edward Grey offered the following formula: 'England will make no unprovoked attack upon Germany, and pursue no aggressive policy towards her. Aggression upon Germany is not the subject, and forms no part of any treaty, understanding, or combination to which England is now a party, nor will she become a party to anything that has such an object.' The German Government considered this formula inadequate and suggested through their Ambassador the following additional clause: 'England will therefore observe at least a benevolent neutrality should war be forced upon Germany'; or, 'England will therefore, as a matter of course, remain neutral if a war is forced upon Germany.'

This last condition would have carried us far beyond our original intention, and might well have been held to deprive us of the power to come to the aid of France in a war 'forced,' or alleged to be 'forced,' upon Germany as the result of a quarrel between Austria and Russia. It would certainly have been regarded as terminating the Entente. Moreover, even if we had taken this step the new German Navy Law was not to be withdrawn. At the most it was to be modified. Thus a complete deadlock was reached at an early stage. Still, so important did we think it to create at least a friendly spirit, and so desirous were we of placating Germany and gratifying her aspirations, that we still persisted in an endeavour to come to an arrangement beneficial to Germany in the colonial sphere. These negotiations were still progressing and had almost reached a conclusion definitely advantageous to Germany, when the war broke out.

* * * * *

Lord Fisher did not like the idea of a naval programme. On February 13, 1912, he wrote:—

> 'I can't support you at all in any way whatever for any two years' or more programme. Some d——d fool has got hold of you to have made you say that! THE GREAT SECRET IS TO PUT OFF TO THE VERY LAST HOUR THE SHIP (big or little) *that you mean to build* (or PERHAPS NOT TO BUILD HER AT ALL!). You see all your rival's plans fully developed, their vessels started beyond recall, and then in each individual answer to each such rival vessel you plunge with a design 50 per cent better! knowing that your rapid shipbuilding and command of money will enable you to have your vessel fit to fight as soon if not sooner than the rival vessel. Sometimes, as in one famous year, you can drop an armoured ship and put the money into acceleration of those building because you have a new design coming along, so don't be a d——d ass and deliberately lay down a ship which you know is obsolete by some sudden vast step in old Watts' brain! "*Sufficient for the year is the programme thereof.*" For God's sake get that written up somewhere for you to look at when you get out of bed in the morning! and do please tell me the name of the born fool who hoaxed you. Is it. . . ? He has just got a gold medal in America for advocating smaller battleships I believe. . . . You know Archbishop Whately proved that Napoleon Bonaparte never existed! . . .

'We are asses now for not building a 16-inch gun as Sir E. Wilmot told you in the letter I sent you—but you can't help yourself any more than you can help deliberately laying down ships for the Line of Battle that go less than 30 knots—there are certain things my beloved Winston that even God Almighty can't help! (let alone you!). He for instance can't help two added to two being four! …

'*The most damnable thing in the world is a servile copyist!* One of the four Nelsonic attributes is "*Power of Initiative*"! and "*Plunge*" is the watchword of "*Progress*"! but I sicken you with my reiteration, so good-bye.'

I replied on February 19:—

'I am delighted to see your handwriting again. I had begun to fear the well of truth and inspiration was running dry. Do not, however, shut your mind against a programme. The Chancellor of the Exchequer and I have been agreed on this policy ever since 1909, and I am quite certain that it can be developed so as to secure the greatest advantages without any sacrifice of elasticity. Such a programme as I have in mind will cover the whole period of the existing German Navy Law. It will deal only with the numbers of capital ships. It will be framed on certain clearly defined assumptions. It will be capable both of expansion and of diminution, of retardation and acceleration. It will not necessarily be embodied in an Act of Parliament. It will probably have to be revised after four years. It will recite certain definite facts of the existing shipbuilding situation, particularly in relation to Germany and Austria. It will be measured in relation to these facts so as to secure ample margins of superiority both in new construction and in establishment over those Powers. Unforeseen contingencies will be met by additions, but it would always be open within certain limits for England and Germany to agree upon proportionate reductions. The programme of minor construction will be entirely flexible and expressed only in terms of money.

'At present we suffer every disadvantage: a panic and a row every year, spasmodic building, hopeless finance, total lack of foresight in regard to the labour market, and no means of bargaining with our competitors. At present we have nothing to put against their threats. Nothing, in my opinion, would more surely dishearten Germany, than the certain proof that as the result of all her present and prospective efforts she will only be more hopelessly behindhand in 1920. She would know it was not bluff because if a Liberal Government could propose it, a Tory Government would *a fortiori* carry it farther. The vast financial reserves of which John Bull can dispose would come into view, and would weigh in the balance with a direct and real weight. It is the uncertainty as to whether we shall throw up the sponge or not, on which the German Navy has lived and fattened. The standard will be 60 per cent preponderance in new construction against the present law, and two keels to one for all increases above it. Sixty per cent preponderance in men, 20 to 12 in destroyers, at least 2 to 1 in armoured cruisers, protected cruisers and their equivalents, submarines and small fry generally. This is no new idea of mine. I have been working it out ever since I came to the Admiralty, and am absolutely convinced that it is the only way of securing economy, efficiency and moral effect. Whether the plan when made should be published is a political question. How Navy Estimates should be financed is for the Treasury and the House of Commons to decide. What the Admiralty are concerned with is the maintenance of proper margins of superiority, the power to look ahead, and the power within certain prescribed limits to manœuvre.

'Hopwood[6] and Sir Marcus Samuel are hard at it over oil.'

This letter mollified the Admiral. On the 25th February, 1912, he wrote:—

'I hasten to reply to your letter of February 19 just arrived, because if your Programme (which has my enthusiastic admiration) *is not embodied in an Act of Parliament* then all my objections vanish! An Act of Parliament (The Naval Defence Act) *made* us build 20 cruisers that had only 48 hours coal supply. *Can I ever forget that!* but Providence came along and made them useful as "*Minelayers*." However ocean "tramps" at £10 a ton would have been cheaper and more effective. Sir W. White built the "*County Class*" and forgot the guns, but Providence came along and has made them useful for commerce protectors with their 6-inch guns and big coal supply and good speed—however a few "Mauretanias" would be far more effective than a hundred "Countys"![7]

'I can only pray that your Programme will be officially published—for *it is sure to leak out*! It will add immensely to your reputation and influence and the moral effect will be prodigious! 'The *Key Note* is 2 keels to 1 for all increases above the present German Law! 2 *to* 1 *in Armoured Cruisers is also vital!*

'You don't say a word of your visit to Jellicoe—*but he does*! He is "*much impressed with your grasp of the whole business*," and as Jellicoe very seldom indeed gives praise I think you must have talked well! as well as that night we stumbled over the dockyard stores at Devonport returning from the *Lion* and the *Monarch*! (It's a pity we didn't have a shorthand writer!)

'*Don't make any mistake about big submarines being obligatory!* …

'Big risks bring big success! (it was Napoleon, wasn't it? "*Risk nothing, get nothing!*") Increased surface speed is *above all* a necessity, and broadside torpedo discharges and the bigger gun will come automatically with the above two essentials, and they (*the Big Submarines*) will be Destroyers with all the advantages of the present Destroyers and—as well—the power of submergence during daylight attacks. Battle tactics will be revolutionized and England's power will be multiplied not sevenfold but manifold! and with a radius of action of 6,000 miles… but it wants an Isaiah to proclaim this vision!

'For God's sake trample on and stamp out protected Cruisers and hurry up Aviation. . . .'

---

[6]Sir Francis Hopwood, now Lord Southborough, the Additional Civil Lord.

[7]A doubtful gem! They could have coaled only in a few ports with special appliances.

For a specimen of Fisher's genius I commend these last few lines. Ten years of submarine development, spurred on by war on the greatest scale, were required to overtake in exact sequence the processes of that amazing vision in technical affairs. The consequences to Great Britain were, however, not so satisfactory as he forecasted.

Early in March, while the new German Navy Law was still unannounced, it was necessary to present our Estimates to the House of Commons. It would of course have been a breach of faith with the German Emperor to let any suggestion pass my lips that we already knew what the text of the Navy Law was. I was therefore obliged to make my first speech on naval matters on a purely hypothetical basis: 'This is what we are going to do if no further increases are made in the German Fleet. Should unhappily the rumours which we hear prove true, I shall have to present a Supplementary Estimate to the House, etc.'

In this speech I laid down clearly, with the assent of the Cabinet, the principles which should govern our naval construction in the next five years, and the standards of strength we should follow in capital ships. This standard was as follows: Sixty per cent in Dreadnoughts over Germany as long as she adhered to her present declared programme, and two keels to one for every additional ship laid down by her. Two complications of these clear principles were unavoidable. First, the two 'Lord Nelsons' although not Dreadnoughts were stronger in many ways, particularly in armour and subdivision, than the original *Dreadnought* herself. Although projected earlier, they had actually been completed later. Acting on the advice of the Naval Staff, I counted these throughout as 'Dreadnoughts.' On the other hand, any ships provided by the Dominions were to be additional to anything we might build ourselves. Otherwise the efforts of the Dominions would not have resulted in any accession to our naval strength, and consequently these efforts might have been discouraged. Proceeding on these lines I set out the six years of British construction at 4, 3, 4, 3, 4, 3, against a uniform German construction of 2. These numbers were well received by the House of Commons. We were not sure whether the Germans would adhere to an offer made to Mr. Haldane to drop one of the three extra ships embodied in their new Navy Law. This, however, proved ultimately to be the case and was at any rate a tangible result of the Haldane mission. In Tirpitz' words: 'He (Haldane) next came out with a proposal of a certain delay in the building of the three ships; could we not distribute them over twelve years? . . .He only wanted a token of our readiness to meet England, more for the sake of form. . . . Haldane himself proposed that we should retard the rate of our increase "in order to lubricate the negotiations," or that we should at least cancel the first of the three ships. He outlined in writing of his own accord the same principle which I had previously fixed upon in my own mind as a possible concession. I *therefore sacrificed the ship*.'

We therefore 'sacrificed' two hypothetical ships, and our programmes, which would have been increased to 5, 4, 5, 4, 5, 4, were ultimately declared at 4, 5, 4, 4, 4, 4. The splendid gift of the *Malaya* by the Federated Malay States raised the figure of the first year from 4 to 5.

In announcing these decisions to Parliament later in the same month I made publicly and definitely those proposals for a Naval Holiday which were fruitless so far as Britain and Germany were concerned, but the principle of which has since been adopted by the English-speaking peoples of the world:—

> 'Take, as an instance of this proposition I am putting forward for general consideration, the year 1913. In that year, as I apprehend, Germany will build three capital ships, and it will be necessary for us to build five in consequence.
>
> 'Supposing we were both to take a holiday for that year and introduce a blank page into the book of misunderstanding; supposing that Germany were to build no ships that year, she would save herself between six and seven millions sterling. But that is not all. In ordinary circumstances we should not begin our ships until Germany had started hers. The three ships that she did not build would therefore automatically wipe out no fewer than five British potential super-Dreadnoughts. That is more than I expect they could hope to do in a brilliant naval action. As to the indirect results within a single year, they simply cannot be measured, not only between our two great brother nations, but to all the world. They are results immeasurable in their hope and brightness. This then is the position which we take up—that the Germans will be no gainers over us so far as naval power is concerned by any increases they may make, and no losers, on the basis I have laid down by any diminution.'

By the beginning of April it became certain that no general arrangement for a naval holiday could be effected with Germany. The Emperor sent me a courteous message through Sir Ernest Cassel expressing his great regret, but adding that such arrangements would only be possible between allies. Herr Ballin wrote at this same time to Sir Ernest:—

> 'I entirely share your opinion of C.'s (Churchill's) speech, and believe that it is simply the unusual feature of frankness and honesty which flustered the whole world, and especially the leading parties here, and has caused a torrent of indignation in the Press. It is not easy to become all at once accustomed to such a complete change from the mystery mongering hitherto prevalent; up to now, it was thought that language was given to British and German Navy Ministers to conceal their thoughts. Suddenly, some one makes a new departure, and everybody asks disconcertedly, "What does this man want?"
>
> 'A few friendly lines addressed to you about the report I sent would have a happy effect. [A complaint which we were reputed to have made about an alleged clandestine visit of certain German ships to the Shetland Islands.] . . . If he wishes it, C. can make use of this opportunity in a few quite unofficial lines addressed to you, to brush away the shadows which were created in high quarters here by the "luxury fleet" (luxus flotte) and the absence of warmth in his last speech. This will be a great help in the political negotiations. It would be too pitiful if, owing to misunderstanding and sentiment, the great work of arrangement were to be hindered. . . etc., etc.'

In compliance I therefore wrote the following letter for the Emperor's eye:—

Mr. Churchill to Sir Ernest Cassel, April 14, 1912.

I am deeply impressed by the Emperor's great consideration. I only mentioned the incident to Ballin as an example to show the kind of anxieties and the strain to which the naval situation gives rise. I am very glad to know that it was free from all sinister significance: and I take this opportunity of saying again that we have been throughout equally innocent of any offensive design. I suppose it is difficult for either country to realize how formidable it appears to the eyes of the other. Certainly it must be almost impossible for Germany, with her splendid armies and warlike population capable of holding their native soil against all comers, and situated inland with road and railway communications on every side, to appreciate the sentiments with which an island State like Britain views the steady and remorseless development of a rival naval power of the very highest efficiency. The more we admire the wonderful work that has been done in the swift creation of German naval strength, the stronger, the deeper and the more preoccupying those sentiments become. Patience, however, and good temper accomplish much; and as the years pass many difficulties and dangers seem to settle themselves peacefully. Meanwhile there is an anxious defile to be traversed, and what will help more perhaps than anything else to make the journey safe for us all, is the sincere desire for goodwill and confidence of which Ballin's letter and its enclosure are a powerful testimony.

* * * * *

The growth of the German Navy produced its inevitable consequences. The British Fleet for safety's sake had to be concentrated in Home Waters. The first concentration had been made by Lord Fisher in 1904. This had effected the reduction of very large numbers of small old vessels which were scattered about the world 'showing the flag' and the formation in their place of stronger, better, more homogeneous squadrons at home. This measure was also a great and wise economy of money. A few months later the British battleships were recalled from China. The more distant oceans had thus been abandoned. But now a further measure of concentration was required. We saw ourselves compelled to withdraw the battleships from the Mediterranean. Only by this measure could the trained men be obtained to form the Third Battle Squadron in full commission in Home Waters. It was decided by the Cabinet that we must still maintain a powerful force in the Mediterranean, and ultimately, four battle cruisers and an armoured cruiser squadron were accordingly based on Malta. It was further decided that a Dreadnought battle squadron should also be developed in the Mediterranean by the year 1916 equal in strength to that of the growing Austrian battle fleet. These decisions were taken with the deliberate object of regaining our complete independence. But the withdrawal—even if only for a few years—of the battleships from the Mediterranean was a noteworthy event. It made us appear to be dependent upon the French Fleet in those waters. The French also at the same time redisposed their forces. Under the growing pressure of German armaments Britain transferred her whole Battle Fleet to the North Sea, and France moved all her heavy ships into the Mediterranean. And the sense of mutual reliance grew swiftly between both navies.

It is astonishing that Admiral von Tirpitz should never have comprehended what the consequences of his policy must be. Even after the war he could write:—

> 'In order to estimate the strength of the trump card which our fleet put in the hands of an energetic diplomacy at this time, one must remember that in consequence of the concentration of the English forces which we had caused in the North Sea, the English control of the Mediterranean and Far-Eastern waters had practically ceased.'

The only 'trump card' which Germany secured by this policy was the driving of Britain and France closer and closer together. From the moment that the Fleets of France and Britain were disposed in this new way our common naval interests became very important. And the moral claims which France could make upon Great Britain if attacked by Germany, whatever we had stipulated to the contrary, were enormously extended. Indeed my anxiety was aroused to try to prevent this necessary recall of our ships from tying us up too tightly with France and depriving us of that liberty of choice on which our power to stop a war might well depend.

When in August, 1912, the Cabinet decided that naval conversations should take place between the French and British Admiralties, similar to those which had been held since 1906 between the General Staffs, I set forth this point as clearly as possible in a minute which I addressed to the Prime Minister and the Foreign Secretary, and we did our utmost to safeguard ourselves.

> *Sir Edward Grey,* *August* 23, 1912.
> *Prime Minister.*
>
> The point I am anxious to safeguard is our freedom of choice if the occasion arises, and consequent power to influence French policy beforehand. That freedom will be sensibly impaired if the French can say that they have denuded their Atlantic seaboard, and concentrated in the Mediterranean on the faith of naval arrangements made with us. This will not be true. If we did not exist, the French could not make better dispositions than at present. They are not strong enough to face Germany alone, still less to maintain themselves in two theatres. They therefore rightly concentrate their Navy in the Mediterranean where it can be safe and superior and can assure their African communications. Neither is it true that we are relying on France to maintain our position in the Mediterranean. . . . If France did not exist, we should make no other disposition of our forces.
>
> Circumstances might arise which in my judgment would make it desirable and right for us to come to the aid of France with all our force by land and sea. But we ask nothing in return. If we were attacked by Germany, we should not make it a charge of bad faith against the French that they left us to fight it out alone; and nothing in naval and military arrangements ought to have the effect of exposing us to such a charge if, when the time comes, we decide to stand out.

> This is my view, and I am sure I am in line with you on the principle. I am not at all particular how it is to be given effect to, and I make no point about what document it is set forth in. But [consider] how tremendous would be the weapon which France would possess to compel our intervention, if she could say, 'On the advice of and by arrangement with your naval authorities we have left our Northern coasts defenceless. We cannot possibly come back in time.' Indeed [I added somewhat inconsequently], it would probably be decisive whatever is written down now. Every one must feel who knows the facts that we have the obligations of an alliance without its advantages, and above all without its precise definitions. W. S. C.

The difficulty proved a real one. The technical naval discussions could only be conducted on the basis that the French Fleet should be concentrated in the Mediterranean, and that in case of a war in which both countries took part, it would fall to the British fleet to defend the Northern and Western coasts of France. The French, as I had foreseen, naturally raised the point that if Great Britain did not take part in the war, their Northern and Western coasts would be completely exposed. We however, while recognizing the difficulty, steadfastly declined to allow the naval arrangements to bind us in any political sense. It was eventually agreed that if there was a menace of war, the two Governments should consult together and concert beforehand what common action, if any, they should take. The French were obliged to accept this position and to affirm definitely that the naval conversations did not involve any obligation of common action. This was the best we could do for ourselves and for them. When the time came there was no doubt as to what England wished to do.

I commend these discussions and the document I have printed above to German eyes. The German Naval Minister exults in a policy which has had the effect of uniting in common defence against Germany, in spite of themselves, two powerful Fleets till then rivals. The British Ministers so far from welcoming this consolidation of forces in the opposite balance to Germany, are anxious to preserve their freedom of action and reluctant to become entangled with continental Powers. Germany was, in fact, forging a coalition against herself, and Britain was seeking to save her from the consequences of her unwisdom. It is not often that one can show so plainly the workings of events. But all was lost on Admiral von Tirpitz.

This sincere, wrongheaded, purblind old Prussian firmly believed that the growth of his beloved navy was inducing in British minds an increasing fear of war, whereas it simply produced naval rejoinders and diplomatic reactions which strengthened the forces and closed the ranks of the Entente. It is almost pathetic to read the foolish sentences in which on page after page of his Memoirs he describes how much Anglo-German relations were improved in 1912, 1913 and 1914 through the realization by the British people of Germany's great and growing naval power. He notices that the violent agitations against German naval expansion which swept England in 1904 and again in 1908 were succeeded by a comparatively calm period in which both Powers were building peacefully and politely against each other. This he thinks was a proof that his treatment was succeeding, and that all friction was passing away—another dose or two and it would be gone altogether. The violent agitations in England were, however, the symptom of doubt and differences of opinion in our national life about whether the German menace was real or not, and whether the right measures were being taken to meet it. As doubts and differences on these points were gradually replaced by general agreement among the leading men in all parties to meet a grave danger, the agitations subsided. The excitement in the Press and in Parliament, the warning speeches and counter-speeches, were not intended for foreign consumption. England was not trying to make an impression upon Germany. She was trying to make up her own mind: and in proportion as this mind arrived at solid and final conclusions, silence was again restored. But it was not the silence of sleep. With every rivet that von Tirpitz drove into his ships of war, he united British opinion throughout wide circles of the most powerful people in every walk of life and in every part of the Empire. The hammers that clanged at Kiel and Wilhelmshaven were forging the coalition of nations by which Germany was to be resisted and finally overthrown. Every threatening gesture that she made, every attempt to shock or shake the loosely knit structure of the Entente, made it close and fit together more tightly. Thus Tirpitz:—

> 'British statesmen naturally did not stress the fact in their conversations with Germans that it was mainly the presence of our nearly completed fleet in the North Sea that had produced their respectful tone, and had lessened the probability of a British attack. Of course they only spoke of their peaceful inclinations and not so much of the facts which strengthened these inclinations.' And again (*Memories vol. I*, p. 192): 'Seventeen years of fleet-building had, it is true, improved the prospects of an acceptable peace with England.'

Is it possible to be further from the truth than this? There never had been any probability or possibility of a British attack on Germany. Why should we attack Germany for building ships when we could ourselves build more ships quicker and cheaper? Why incur the guilt, cost and hazard of war, when a complete remedy was obvious and easy? But the 'respectful tone' was that of men who felt how serious the position had become, and were anxious to avoid any responsibility for causing a crisis. It was not restraint imposed by fear of the 'nearly completed fleet in the North Sea,' but the calm resulting from resolve to be prepared.

* * * * *

The organization of a Fleet differs throughout from that of an Army. Armies only keep a small proportion of their soldiers in regular service. These form the framework of the battalions, train the recruits and keep guard in times of peace. When the order is given to mobilize, all the men who have been already trained but are living at home in civil life are called up as they are wanted: and then and not till then the Army is ready to fight.

Navies on the other hand were in the main always ready. The British Navy had all its best ships fully and permanently manned with whole-time men (called active service ratings). Measured by quality nearly the whole of its power was therefore constantly available. Measured even by numbers nearly three-quarters of the ships could go into action without calling out the Reserves. Only the oldest and most obsolete ships were manned in time of war by the Naval Reserve, i.e., men who had left the Navy and had returned to civil life. These obsolete vessels were the only part of the Fleet which had to be 'mobilized' like the armies of Europe.

Thus mobilization, which is the foundation of all great armies, plays only a very small part in fleets. Every ship that really counted was always ready to steam and fight as soon as an order reached her.

The organization of the British Home Fleets when I came to the Admiralty seemed to a mind accustomed to military symmetry, to leave much to be desired. The terminology was misleading and confused. The word 'Division' was used in three different senses, sometimes tactical and sometimes administrative. The battle units were uneven in numbers. The degree of readiness and efficiency of the different squadrons was not apparent from the classes in which they were grouped. In consultation with Sir Francis Bridgeman, Prince Louis and Rear-Admiral Troubridge, the first Chief of the new War Staff, I designed a new and symmetrical organization for the Fleets.

All the ships available for Home Defence were divided into the First, Second and Third Fleets, comprising eight battle squadrons of eight battleships each, together with their attendant cruiser squadrons, flotillas and auxiliaries. The First Fleet comprised a Fleet Flagship and four battle squadrons of ships 'in full commission' manned entirely with active service ratings, and therefore *always ready*. To form this Fleet it was necessary to base the former 'Atlantic Fleet' on Home Ports instead of on Gibraltar, and to base the battleships hitherto in the Mediterranean on Gibraltar instead of Malta. By this concentration an additional battle squadron of strong ships *(King Edwards)* was *always ready* in Home waters. The Second Fleet consisted of two battle squadrons, also fully manned with active service ratings, but having about 40 per cent of these learning and requalifying in the gunnery, torpedo and other schools. This Fleet was termed 'in active commission' because it could fight at any moment; but to realize its highest efficiency, it required to touch at its Home Ports, and march on board its balance crews from the schools. In all these six battle squadrons, containing with their cruiser squadrons every modern and middle-aged ship in the Navy, there was not to be found a single reservist. No mobilization was therefore necessary to bring the whole of this force into action. The Third Fleet also consisted of two battle squadrons and five cruiser squadrons of our oldest ships. These were only manned by care and maintenance parties and required the Reserves to be called out before they could put to sea. In order to accelerate the mobilization of the leading battle squadrons and certain cruisers of the Third Fleet, a special class of the Reserve was now formed called the 'Immediate Reserve,' who received higher pay and periodical training, and were liable to be called up in advance of general mobilization.

Germany was adding a third squadron to the High Sea Fleet, thus increasing her *always ready* strength from 17 to 25. We in reply, by the measures set out above and various others too technical for description here, raised our *always ready* Fleet from

33 battleships to 49, and other forces in like proportion. On mobilization the German figures would rise to 38, and the British at first to 57, and ultimately, as the new organization was completed, to 65.

The reader will not be able to understand the issues involved in the completion and mobilization of the Fleets on the eve of the war unless this organization as explained above is mastered.

* * * * *

We made a great assembly of the Navy this spring of 1912 at Portland. The flags of a dozen admirals, the broad pennants of as many commodores and the pennants of a hundred and fifty ships were flying together. The King came in the Royal Yacht, the Admiralty flag at the fore, the Standard at the main and the Jack at the mizzen, and bided among his sailors for four days. One day there is a long cruise out into mist, dense, utterly baffling—the whole Fleet steaming together all invisible, keeping station by weird siren screamings and hootings. It seemed incredible that no harm would befall. And then suddenly the fog lifted and the distant targets could be distinguished and the whole long line of battleships, coming one after another into view, burst into tremendous flares of flame and hurled their shells with deafening detonations while the water rose in tall fountains. The Fleet returns—three battle squadrons abreast, cruisers and flotillas disposed ahead and astern. The speed is raised to twenty knots. Streaks of white foam appear at the bows of every vessel. The land draws near. The broad bay already embraces this swiftly moving gigantic armada. The ships in their formation already fill the bay. The foreign officers I have with me on the *Enchantress* bridge stare anxiously. We still steam fast. Five minutes more and the van of the Fleet will be aground. Four minutes, three minutes. There! At last. The signal! A string of bright flags is hauled down from the *Neptune's* halyards. Every anchor falls together; their cables roar through the hawser holes; every propeller whirls astern. In a hundred and fifty yards, it seems every ship is stationary. Look along the lines, miles this way and miles that, they might have been drawn with a ruler. The foreign observers gasped.

These were great days. From dawn to midnight, day after day, one's whole mind was absorbed by the fascination and novelty of the problems which came crowding forward. And all the time there was a sense of power to act, to form, to organize: all the ablest officers in the Navy standing ready, loyal and eager, with argument, guidance, information; every one feeling a sense that a great danger had passed very near us; that there was a breathing space before it would return; that we must be better prepared next time. Saturdays, Sundays and any other spare day I spent always with the Fleets at Portsmouth or at Portland or Devonport, or with the Flotillas at Harwich. Officers of every rank came on board to lunch or dine and discussion proceeded without ceasing on every aspect of naval war and administration.

The Admiralty yacht *Enchantress* was now to become largely my office, almost my home; and my work my sole occupation and amusement. In all, I spent eight months afloat in the three years before the war. I visited every dockyard, shipyard and naval establishment in the British Isles and in the Mediterranean and every important ship.

I examined for myself every point of strategic consequence and every piece of Admiralty property. I got to know what everything looked like and where everything was, and how one thing fitted into another. In the end I could put my hand on anything that was wanted and knew thoroughly the current state of our naval affairs.

I recall vividly my first voyage from Portsmouth to Portland where the Fleet lay. A grey afternoon was drawing to a close. As I saw the Fleet for the first time drawing out of the haze a friend reminded me of 'that far-off line of storm-beaten ships on which the eyes of the grand Army had never looked,' but which had in their day' stood between Napoleon and the dominion of the world.' In Portland Harbour the yacht lay surrounded by the great ships; the whole harbour was alive with the goings and comings of launches and small craft of every kind, and as night fell ten thousand lights from sea and shore sprang into being and every masthead twinkled as the ships and squadrons conversed with one another. Who could fail to work for such a service? Who could fail when the very darkness seemed loaded with the menace of approaching war?

For consider these ships, so vast in themselves, yet so small, so easily lost to sight on the surface of the waters. Sufficient at the moment, we trusted, for their task, but yet only a score or so. They were all we had. On them, as we conceived, floated the might, majesty, dominion and power of the British Empire. All our long history built up century after century, all our great affairs in every part of the globe, all the means of livelihood and safety of our faithful, industrious, active population depended upon them. Open the sea-cocks and let them sink beneath the surface, as another Fleet was one day to do in another British harbour far to the North, and in a few minutes—half an hour at the most—the whole outlook of the world would be changed. The British Empire would dissolve like a dream; each isolated community struggling forward by itself; the central power of union broken; mighty provinces, whole Empires in themselves, drifting hopelessly out of control, and falling a prey to strangers; and Europe after one sudden convulsion passing into the iron grip and rule of the Teuton and of all that the Teutonic system meant. There would only be left far off across the Atlantic unarmed, unready, and as yet uninstructed America, to maintain, single-handed, law and freedom among men.

Guard them well, admirals and captains, hardy tars and tall marines; guard them well and guide them true.

CHAPTER VI
THE ROMANCE OF DESIGN

'For a scrutiny so minute as to bring an object under an untrue angle of vision, is a poorer guide to a man's judgment, than the most rapid and sweeping glance which sees things in their true proportions.'

—Kinglake.

The Big Punch—The 15-inch Gun—An Anxious Decision—The Design of a Battleship—Gun-power and Speed—The Argument for the Fast Division—The Fifth Turret—Liquid Fuel—The Oil Problem—Financial Entanglements—The Royal Commission on Oil Supplies—The Anglo-Persian Convention—A Golden Reward—The Fast Division at Jutland—Swifter Destroyers—Cruiser Design—Correspondence with Lord Fisher—The Light Armoured Cruisers—The *Arethusa*.

Until I got to the Admiralty I had never properly appreciated the service which Mr. McKenna and Lord Fisher had rendered to the Fleet in 1909 by their big leap forward from the 12-inch to the 13.5-inch gun. To illustrate this I set out the weight of the shell fired by the principal guns in the British and German Navies:—

The 1-inch gun fires a		1-pound shot.
The 2-inch	"	6-pound shot.
The 3-inch	"	12 or 15-pound shot.
The 4-inch	"	28 to 32-pound shot.
The 5-inch	"	50-pound shot.
The 6-inch[1]	"	100-pound shot.
The 7.5-inch	"	200-pound shot.
The 9.2-inch	"	380-pound shot.
The 10-inch	"	500-pound shot.

The British 12-inch gun fires a 850-pound shot.

The German 12-inch gun fires approximately a 1,000-pound shot, but this is asking a lot of the gun.

The 13.5-inch gun fired a 1,250-pound shot; and its later marks fired a 1,400-pound shot.

[1]This is the biggest gun which can be completely worked by hand, the shot being lifted by a single man.

The increase of 1½ inch in the calibre of the gun was enough to raise the British shell from 850 pounds to 1,400 pounds. No fewer than twelve ships were actually building on the slips for the Royal Navy armed with these splendid weapons, quite unsurpassed at that time in the world, and firing a projectile nearly half as heavy again as the biggest fired by the German Fleet.

I immediately sought to go one size better. I mentioned this to Lord Fisher at Reigate, and he hurled himself into its advocacy with tremendous passion. 'Nothing less than the 15-inch gun could be looked at for all the battleships and battle-cruisers of the new programme. To achieve the supply of this gun was the equivalent of a great victory at sea; to shrink from the endeavour was treason to the Empire. What was it that enabled Jack Johnson to knock out his opponents? It was the big punch. And where were those miserable men with bevies of futile popguns crowding up their ships?' No one who has not experienced it has any idea of the passion and eloquence of this old lion when thoroughly roused on a technical question. I resolved to make a great effort to secure the prize, but the difficulties and the risks were very great, and looking back upon it, one feels that they were only justified by success. Enlarging the gun meant enlarging the ships, and enlarging the ships meant increasing the cost. Moreover, the redesign must cause no delay and the guns must be ready as soon as the turrets were ready. No such thing as a modern 15-inch gun existed. None had ever been made. The advance to the 13.5-inch had in itself been a great stride. Its power was greater; its accuracy was greater; its life was much longer. Could the British designers repeat this triumph on a still larger scale and in a still more intense form? The Ordnance Board were set to work and they rapidly produced a design. Armstrongs were consulted in deadly secrecy, and they undertook to execute it. I had anxious conferences with these experts, with whose science I was of course wholly unacquainted, to see what sort of men they were and how they really felt about it. They were all for it. One did not need to be an expert in ballistics to discern that. The Director of Naval Ordnance, Rear-Admiral Moore, was ready to stake his professional existence upon it. But after all there could not be absolute certainty. We knew the 13.5-inch well. All sorts of new stresses might develop in the 15-inch model. If only we could make a trial gun and test it thoroughly before giving the orders for the whole of the guns of all the five ships, there would be no risk; but then we should lose an entire year, and five great vessels would go into the line of battle carrying an inferior weapon to that which we had it in our power to give them. Several there were of the responsible authorities consulted who thought it would be more prudent to lose the year. For, after all, if the guns had failed, the ships would have been fearfully marred. I hardly remember ever to have had more anxiety about any administrative decision than this.

I went back to Lord Fisher. He was steadfast and even violent. So I hardened my heart and took the plunge. The whole outfit of guns was ordered forthwith. We arranged that one gun should be hurried on four months in front of the others by exceptional efforts so as to be able to test it for range and accuracy and to get out the range tables and other complex devices which depended upon actual firing results. From this moment we were irrevocably committed to the whole armament, and every detail in these vessels, extending to thousands of parts, was redesigned to fit them. Fancy if they failed. What a disaster. What an exposure. No excuse would be accepted. It would all be brought home to me—'rash, inexperienced,' 'before he had been there a month,' 'altering all the plans of his predecessors' and producing 'this ghastly fiasco,' 'the mutilation of all the ships of the year.' What could I have said? Moreover, although the decision, once taken, was irrevocable, a long period of suspense—fourteen or fifteen months at least—was unavoidable. However, I dissembled my misgivings. I wrote to the First Sea Lord that 'Risks have to be run in peace as well as in war, and courage in design now may win a battle later on.'

But everything turned out all right. British gunnery science proved exact and true, and British workmanship as sound as a bell and punctual to the day. The first gun was known in the Elswick shops as 'the hush and push gun,' and was invariably described in all official documents as 'the 14-inch experimental.' It proved a brilliant success. It hurled a 1,920-pound projectile 35,000 yards; it achieved remarkable accuracy at all ranges without shortening its existence by straining itself in any way. No doubt I was unduly anxious; but when I saw the gun fired for the first time a year later and knew that all was well, I felt as if I had been delivered from a great peril.

In one of those nightmare novels that used to appear from time to time before the war, I read in 1913 of a great battle in which, to the amazement of the defeated British Fleet, the German new vessels opened fire with a terrible, unheard-of 15-inch gun. There was a real satisfaction in feeling that anyhow this boot was on the other leg.

The gun dominated the ship, and was the decisive cause of all the changes we then made in design. The following was in those days the recipe in very unexpert language for making a battleship:—

You take the largest possible number of the best possible guns that can be fired in combination from one vessel as a single battery. You group them conveniently by pairs in turrets. You put the turrets so that there is the widest possible arc of fire for every gun and the least possible blast interference. This regulates the position of the turrets and the spacing between them. You draw a line around the arrangement of turrets thus arrived at, which gives you the deck of the ship. You then build a hull to carry this deck or great gun platform. It must be very big and very long. Next you see what room you have got inside this hull for engines to drive it, and from this and from the length you get the speed. Last of all you decide on the armour.

All these calculations and considerations act and react upon one another at every stage, and the manner in which the Royal Corps of Constructors can juggle with these factors, and the facility with which the great chiefs and masters of battleship design like Sir Philip Watts and Sir Eustace Tennyson-D'Eyncourt and their faithful confederate Sir Henry Oram, the Chief Engineer, were able to speak on these matters were marvellous beyond belief. In a few hours, or at most in a few days, one could be told the effect of an alteration in any one set of conditions upon every other set of conditions. On this vast process of juggling and higgling we now embarked.

From the beginning there appeared a ship carrying ten 15-inch guns, and therefore at least 600 feet long with room inside her for engines which would drive her 21 knots and capacity to carry armour which on the armoured belt, the turrets and the conning tower would reach the thickness unprecedented in the British Service of 13 inches. For less armour you could have more speed: for less speed you could have more armour, and so on within very considerable limits. But now a new idea began to dawn. Eight 15-inch guns would fire a simultaneous broadside of approximately 16,000 lb. Ten of the latest 13.5-inch would only fire 14,000 lb. Therefore, we could get for eight 15-inch guns a punch substantially greater than that of ten 13.5-inch. Nor did the superiority end there. With the increased size of the shell came a far greater increase in the capacity of the bursting charge. It was not quite a geometric progression, because other considerations intervened; but it was in that order of ideas. There was no doubt about the punch. On the other hand, look at the speed. Twenty-one knots was all very well in its way, but suppose we could get a much greater speed. Suppose we could cram into the hull a horse-power sufficient to drive these terrific vessels, already possessing guns and armour superior to that of the heaviest battleship, at speeds hitherto only obtained by the lightly armoured 12-inch gun battle-cruisers, should we not have introduced a new element into naval war?

And here we leave the region of material. I have built the process up stage by stage as it was argued out, but of course all the processes proceeded in simultaneous relation, and the result was to show a great possibility. Something like the ship described above could be made if it were wanted. Was it wanted? Was it the right thing to make? Was its tactical value sufficient to justify the increase in cost and all the changes in design? We must turn for the answer to the tactical sphere.

Here I felt able to see a little more clearly. As cannot be too often repeated, war is all one; and the same principles of thought which are true in any form are true *mutatis mutandis* in every other form. Obviously in creating an Army or an Air Force or a squadron of battleships you must first of all have regard to their highest tactical employment, namely, decisive battle. Let us therefore, first of all, visualize the battle. Let us try to imagine what its conditions will be; what we shall have to meet and what would help us most to win. The first naval idea of our supreme battle at this time was that it would be fought about something: somebody would want to be going somewhere and somebody else would try to stop him. One of the Fleets would be proceeding in a certain direction and the other Fleet would come along and try to prevent it. However they might approach, the battle would soon resolve itself into two lines of ships steaming along parallel and bringing all their broadsides to bear upon each other. Of course if one Fleet is much stronger than the other, has heavier guns and shoots better, the opposite line begins to get the worst of it. Ships begin to burn and blow up and fall out of the line, and every one that falls out increases the burden of fire upon the remainder. The Fleet which has more ships in it also has a tail which overlaps the enemy, and a good many ships in this tail can concentrate their fire upon the rear ships of the enemy, so that these unlucky vessels have not only to fight the ships opposite to them, but have to bear the fire of a number of others firing obliquely at them from behind. But smashing up the tail of an enemy's Fleet is a poor way of preventing him from achieving his objective, i.e. going where he wants to go. It is not comparable to smashing up his head. Injuries at the head of the line tend to throw the whole line into confusion, whereas injuries at the tail only result in the ships dropping astern without causing other complications. Therefore the Admiralissimo will always try to draw a little ahead if he possibly can and bring his van nearer and nearer to the enemy and gradually, if he can, force that enemy to turn off, so that he can then curl round him. This well-known manœuvre is called 'Crossing the T,' and Admiral Togo had used it in the battle of the Sea of Japan.

If the speeds of the Fleets are equal, how can this be done? The heads of both lines will be abreast and the fire will only be given and returned ship for ship.

But suppose you have a division of ships in your Fleet which go much faster than any of your other ships or of your enemy's ships. These ships will be certainly able to draw ahead and curl round the head of the enemy's line. More than that, as they draw ahead they will repeat in a much more effective fashion the advantage of an overlapping tail, because the ships at the head of the enemy's line will have to bear the fire of the overlapping ships as well as the fire of those which are lying opposite to them, and therefore two or three ships might be firing on every one of the leading ships of the enemy, thus smashing to pieces the head of the enemy's line and throwing his whole formation into confusion.

Here then in simple outline is the famous argument for the Fast Division. A squadron of ships possessing a definite superiority of speed could be so disposed in the approaching formation of your own Fleet as to enable you, whichever way the enemy might deploy, to double the fire after a certain interval upon the head of his line, and also to envelop it and cross it and so force him into a circular movement and bring him to bay once and for all without hope of escape.

Hitherto in all our battle plans this rôle had been assigned to the battle-cruisers. Their speed would certainly enable them to get there. But we must imagine that they would also be met by the enemy's battle-cruisers, whereupon, as they say in the reports of the House of Commons, 'debate arising,' they might easily fight a separate action of their own without relation to the supreme conflict. Further, the battle-cruisers, our beautiful 'Cats,' as their squadron was irreverently called,[2] had thin skins compared to the enemy's strongest battleships, which presumably would head his line. It is a rough game to pit battle-cruisers against battleships with only seven or nine inches of armour against twelve or thirteen, and probably with a weaker gun-power as well.[3]

Suppose, however, we could make a division of ships fast enough to seize the advantageous position and yet as strong in gun-power and armour as any battleship afloat. Should we not have scored almost with certainty an inestimable and a decisive advantage? The First Sea Lord, Sir Francis Bridgeman, fresh from the command of the

---

[2]*Lion, Tiger, Queen Mary, Princess Royal.*

[3]Contrary to common opinion and, as many will think, to the proved lessons of the war, I do not believe in the wisdom of the battle-cruiser type. If it is worth while to spend far more than the price of your best battleship upon a fast heavily-gunned vessel, it is better at the same time to give it the heaviest armour as well. You then have a ship which may indeed cost half as much again as a battleship, but which at any rate can do everything. To put the value of a first-class battleship into a vessel which cannot stand the pounding of a heavy action is false policy. It is far better to spend the extra money and have what you really want. The battle-cruiser, in other words, should be superseded by the fast battleship, i.e. fast strongest ship, in spite of her cost.—W.S.C.

Home Fleet, and most of his principal officers, certainly thought so. The Fast Division was the dream of their battle plans. But could we get such ships? Could they be designed and constructed? And here we came back again to Sir Philip Watts and Sir Henry Oram and the Ordnance Board and the Royal Corps of Naval Constructors.

At this stage the War College were asked to work out on the tactical board the number of knots superiority in speed required in a Fast Division in order to ensure this Division being able to manœuvre around the German Fleet as it would be in the years 1914 and 1915.

The answer was that if the Fast Division could steam in company 25 knots or better, they could do all that was necessary. We therefore wanted 4 or 5 knots additional speed. How were we to get it? With every knot the amount of horse-power required is progressively greater. Our new ship would steam 21 knots, but to steam 25 to 26 she wanted 50,000 horse-power. Fifty thousand horse-power meant more boilers, and where could they be put? Why, obviously they could be put where the fifth turret would go, and having regard to the increased punch of the 15-inch gun we could spare the fifth turret.

But even this would not suffice. We could not get the power required to drive these ships at 25 knots except by the use of oil fuel.

The advantages conferred by liquid fuel were inestimable. First, speed. In equal ships oil gave a large excess of speed over coal. It enabled that speed to be attained with far greater rapidity. It gave forty per cent greater radius of action for the same weight of coal. It enabled a fleet to re-fuel at sea with great facility. An oil-burning fleet can, if need be and in calm weather, keep its station at sea, nourishing itself from tankers without having to send a quarter of its strength continually into harbour to coal, wasting fuel on the homeward and outward journey. The ordeal of coaling ship exhausted the whole ship's company. In wartime it robbed them of their brief period of rest; it subjected everyone to extreme discomfort. With oil, a few pipes were connected with the shore or with a tanker and the ship sucked in its fuel with hardly a man having to lift a finger. Less than half the number of stokers was needed to tend and clean the oil furnaces. Oil could be stowed in spare places in a ship from which it would be impossible to bring coal. As a coal ship used up her coal, increasingly large numbers of men had to be taken, if necessary from the guns, to shovel the coal from remote and inconvenient bunkers to bunkers nearer to the furnaces or to the furnaces themselves, thus weakening the fighting efficiency of the ship perhaps at the most critical moment in the battle. For instance, nearly a hundred men were continually occupied in the *Lion* shovelling coal from one steel chamber to another without ever seeing the light either of day or of the furnace fires. The use of oil made it possible in every type of vessel to have more gun-power and more speed for less size or less cost. It alone made it possible to realize the high speeds in certain types which were vital to their tactical purpose. All these advantages were obtained simply by burning oil instead of coal under the boilers. Should it at any time become possible to abolish boilers altogether and explode the oil in the cylinders of internal combustion engines, every advantage would be multiplied tenfold.

On my arrival at the Admiralty we had already built or were building 56 destroyers solely dependent on oil and 74 submarines which could only be driven by oil; and a proportion of oil was used to spray the coal furnaces of nearly all ships. We were not, however, dependent upon oil to such an extent as to make its supply a serious naval problem. To build any large additional number of oil-burning ships meant basing our naval supremacy upon oil. But oil was not found in appreciable quantities in our islands. If we required it, we must carry it by sea in peace or war from distant countries. We had, on the other hand, the finest supply of the best steam coal in the world, safe in our mines under our own hand.

To change the foundation of the Navy from British coal to foreign oil was a formidable decision in itself. If it were taken it must raise a whole series of intricate problems all requiring heavy initial expense. First there must be accumulated in Great Britain an enormous oil reserve large enough to enable us to fight for many months if necessary, without bringing in a single cargo of oil. To contain this reserve enormous installations of tanks must be erected near the various naval ports. Would they not be very vulnerable? Could they be protected? Could they be concealed or disguised? The word '*Camouflage*' was not then known. Fleets of tankers had to be built to convey the oil from the distant oilfields across the oceans to the British Isles, and others of a different pattern to take it from our naval harbours to the fleets at sea.

Owing to the systems of finance by which we had bound ourselves, we were not allowed to borrow even for capital or 'once for all' expenditure. Every penny must be won from Parliament year by year, and constituted a definite addition to the inevitably rising and already fiercely challenged Naval Estimates. And beyond these difficulties loomed up the more intangible problems of markets and monopolies. The oil supplies of the world were in the hands of vast oil trusts under foreign control. To commit the Navy irrevocably to oil was indeed 'to take arms against a sea of troubles.' Wave after wave, dark with storm, crested with foam, surged towards the harbour in which we still sheltered. Should we drive out into the teeth of the gale, or should we bide contented where we were? Yet beyond the breakers was a great hope. If we overcame the difficulties and surmounted the risks, we should be able to raise the whole power and efficiency of the Navy to a definitely higher level; better ships, better crews, higher economies, more intense forms of war-power—in a word, mastery itself was the prize of the venture. A year gained over a rival might make the difference. Forward, then!

The three programmes of 1912, 1913 and 1914 comprised the greatest additions in power and cost ever made to the Royal Navy. With the lamentable exception of the battleships of 1913—and these were afterwards corrected—they did not contain a coal-burning ship. Submarines, destroyers, light cruisers, fast battleships—all were based irrevocably on oil. The fateful plunge was taken when it was decided to create the Fast Division. Then, for the first time, the supreme ships of the Navy, on which our life depended, were fed by oil and could only be fed by oil. The decision to drive the smaller craft by oil followed naturally upon this. The camel once swallowed, the gnats went down easily enough.

A decision like this involved our national safety as much as a battle at sea. It was as anxious and as harassing as any hazard in war. It *was* war in a certain sense raging under a surface of unbroken peace. Compare it with the decision to attempt to force the Dardanelles with the old surplus vessels of a fleet which had already proved its supremacy. The oil decision was vital; the Dardanelles decision was subsidiary. The first touched our existence; the second our superfluities. Having succeeded in the first, it did not seem difficult when the time came to attempt the second. I did not understand that in war the power of a civilian Minister to carry through a plan or policy is greatly diminished. He cannot draw his strength year by year from Parliament. He cannot be sure of being allowed to finish what he has begun. The loyalties of peace are replaced by the jealous passions of war. The Parliamentary safeguards are in abeyance. Explanation and debate may be impossible or may be denied. I learnt this later on.

I shall show presently the difficulties into which these decisions to create a fast division of battleships and to rely upon oil led me into during the years 1913 and 1914. Nor can I deny that colleagues who could not foresee the extra expense which they involved had grounds of complaint. Battleships were at that time assumed to cost 2¼ millions each. The *Queen Elizabeth* class of fast battleships cost over three millions each. The expenditure of upwards of 10 millions was required to create the oil reserve, with its tanks and its tankers, though a proportion of this would have been needed in any case. On more than one occasion I feared I should succumb. I had, however, the unfailing support of the Prime Minister. The Chancellor of the Exchequer whose duty it was to be my most severe critic, was also my most friendly colleague. And so it all went through. Fortune rewarded the continuous and steadfast facing of these difficulties by the Board of Admiralty and brought us a prize from fairyland far beyond our brightest hopes.

An unbroken series of consequences conducted us to the Anglo-Persian Oil Convention. The first step was to set up a Royal Commission on Oil Supply. Lord Fisher was invited and induced to preside over this by the following letter:—

Mr. Churchill to Lord Fisher.

June 11, 1912.

We are too good friends (I hope) and the matters with which we are concerned are too serious (I'm sure) for anything but plain language.

This liquid fuel problem has got to be solved, and the natural, inherent, unavoidable difficulties are such that they require the drive and enthusiasm of a big man. I want you for this, viz. to crack the nut. No one else can do it so well. Perhaps no one else can do it at all. I will put you in a position where you can crack the nut, if indeed it is crackable. But this means that you will have to give your life and strength, and I don't know what I have to give in exchange or in return. You have got to find the oil: to show how it can be stored cheaply: how it can be purchased regularly and cheaply in peace; and with absolute certainty in war. Then by all means develop its application in the best possible way to existing and prospective ships. But on the other hand, your Royal Commission will be advisory and not executive. It will assemble facts and state conclusions. It cannot touch *policy* or action. That would not be fair to those on whom I must now rely.

Nor would you wish it. Its report must be secret from the public, and its work separate from the Admiralty. I cannot have Moore's position[4] eclipsed by a kind of Committee of Public Safety on Designs. The field of practical policy must be reserved for the immediately responsible officers. Research however authoritative lies outside. All this I know you will concur in.

Then as to *personnel*. I do not care a d__n whom you choose to assist you, so long as (1) the representative character of the Committee is maintained, and (2) the old controversies are not needlessly revived. Let us then go into names specifically.

Further, 'Step by step' is a valuable precept. When you have solved the riddle, you will find a very hushed attentive audience. But the riddle will not be solved unless you are willing—for the glory of God—to expend yourself upon its toils.

I recognize it is little enough I can offer you. But your gifts, your force, your hopes, belong to the Navy, with or without return; and as your most sincere admirer, and as the head of the Naval Service, I claim them now, knowing well you will not grudge them. You need a plough to draw. Your propellers are racing in air.

Simultaneously with the setting up of this Commission we pursued our own Admiralty search for oil. On the advice of Sir Francis Hopwood and Sir Frederick Black,[5] I sent Admiral Slade with an expert Committee to the Persian Gulf to examine the oil fields on the spot. These gentlemen were also the Admiralty representatives on the Royal Commission. To them the principal credit for the achievement is due. At the later financial stage the Governor of the Bank of England, afterwards Lord Cunliffe, and the directors of the Anglo-Persian and the Royal Burmah Oil Companies were most serviceable. All through 1912 and 1913 our efforts were unceasing.

Thus each link forged the next. From the original desire to enlarge the gun we were led on step by step to the Fast Division, and in order to get the Fast Division we were forced to rely for vital units of the Fleet upon oil fuel. This led to the general adoption of oil fuel and to all the provisions which were needed to build up a great oil reserve. This led to enormous expense and to tremendous opposition on the Naval Estimates. Yet it was absolutely impossible to turn back. We could only fight our way forward, and finally we found our way to the Anglo-Persian Oil agreement and contract, which for an initial investment of two millions of public money (subsequently increased to five millions) has not only secured to the Navy a very substantial proportion of its oil supply, but has led to the acquisition by the Government of a controlling share in oil properties and interests which are at present valued at scores of millions sterling, and also to very considerable economies, which are still continuing, in the purchase price of Admiralty oil.

---

[4]The Third Sea Lord.

[5]Director of Admiralty Contracts.

All forecasts in this speculative market are subject to revision. The figures set out below are recent and authoritative.[6]

On this basis it may be said that the aggregate profits, realized and potential, of this investment may be estimated at a sum not merely sufficient to pay for all the programme of ships, great and small of that year and for the whole pre-war oil fuel installation, but are such that we may not unreasonably expect that one day we shall be entitled also to claim that the mighty fleets laid down in 1912, 1913 and 1914, the greatest ever built by any Power in an equal period, were added to the British Navy without costing a single penny to the taxpayer.

Such is the story of the creation of a Fast Division of five famous battleships, the *Queen Elizabeth*, *Warspite*, *Barham*, *Valiant* and *Malaya*, all oil-driven, each capable of steaming a minimum of 25 knots, mounting eight 15-inch guns and protected by 13 inches of armour. It is permissible to look ahead and see what happened to these ships in the Battle of Jutland. Let us take the accounts of the enemy.

Says Tirpitz (*Memories vol. II*, p. 284): 'In the further course of the fight,' i.e. after the destruction of the *Indefatigable* and *Queen Mary*, 'the English were strongly reinforced by five[7] of their newest ships of the Queen Elizabeth class, only completed during the war; these vessels, driven exclusively by oil-fuel, possessed such a high speed that they were able to take part in the cruiser engagement—they attached themselves to the English cruisers and joined in the battle at long range.'

The First Gunnery Officer of the *Derfflinger* is more explicit:[8]

> 'Meanwhile we saw that the enemy were being reinforced. Behind the battle cruiser line approached four big ships. We soon identified these as of the *Queen Elizabeth* class. There had been much talk in our fleet of these ships. They were ships of the line with the colossal armament of eight 15-inch guns, 28,000 tons displacement and a speed of twenty-five knots. Their speed, therefore, was scarcely inferior to

---

[6]An approximate estimate of the return obtained by His Majesty's Government on their original investment of £2,200,000, in the Anglo-Persian Oil Co., Ltd.:

(1)	The original Government investment of £2,200,200 in £1 Ordinary Shares has become one of five millions shares, and the Appreciation in value of these at current prices represents approximately some	16,000,000
(2)	The Government has received in dividends, interest, Income Tax, Excess Profits' Duty and Corporation Tax, over	6,500,000
(3)	The supply contract has enabled the Government Departments to save on the purchase price of oil as compared with current prices, about........	7,500,000
(4)	It may also be claimed that the prices of oil supplied by other companies have been brought down by the competition of the Anglo-Persian Company, though to what extent must be a matter of opinion: and further, that the saving on oil prices under the supply contract may be expected to continue throughout the currency of the contract. It would not be unfair to estimate the effect of the last two factors at an additional.......	10,000,000
	Total	£40,000,000

[7]Actually four.

[8]*Kiel and Jutland*, by Commander Georg von Hase.

ours (twenty-six knots), but they fired a shell more than twice as heavy as ours. They engaged at portentous range …' (p. 164).

'As we were altering course to N.N.W. we caught sight of the head of our Third Squadron, the proud ships of the *König* class. Everyone now breathed more freely. While we had been engaged by the English Fifth Battle Squadron with its 15-inch guns in addition to the Battle Cruiser Squadron we had felt rather uncomfortable.' (p. 167).

'After the gradual disappearance of the four battle cruisers we were still faced with the four powerful ships of the Fifth Battle Squadron, *Malaya*, *Valiant*, *Barham* and *Warspite*.

'These ships cannot have developed very high speed in this phase of the battle, for they soon came within range of our Third Squadron, and were engaged by the ships at the head of the line, particularly the flagship, the *König*. In this way the four English battleships at one time and another came under the fire of at least nine German ships, five battle cruisers and from four to five battleships. According to my gunnery log, we were firing after 7.16 p.m. at the second battleship from the right, the one immediately astern of the leader. At these great ranges I fired armour-piercing shell.

'The second phase passed without any important events as far as we were concerned. In a sense this part of the action, fought against a numerically inferior but more powerfully armed enemy, who kept us under fire at ranges at which we were helpless, was highly depressing, nerve-racking and exasperating. Our only means of defence was to leave the line for a short time when we saw that the enemy had our range. As this manœuvre was imperceptible to the enemy, we extricated ourselves at regular intervals from the hail of fire.' (p. 173).

* * * * *

We may now turn to the smaller vessels.

There was no difficulty whatever in settling the design of the destroyers. The Admiralty had vacillated about destroyers in previous years. In 1908 they built large fast 33-knot *Tribals* burning oil, and then, worried by the oil problem and shocked at the expense, reverted for two years to 27-knot coal-burning flotillas (*Acastas* and *Acherons*). I was too late to stop the last bevy of these inferior vessels, but I gave directions to design the new flotilla to realize 35 knots speed without giving up anything in gun-power, torpedoes or seaworthiness. I proposed to the Board that if money ran short we should take sixteen of these rather than twenty of the others. Building slow destroyers! One might as well breed slow racehorses.

The cruisers were much more difficult. The duties of a British cruiser are very varied: now scouting for the Battle Fleet; now convoying merchantmen; now fighting an action with another cruiser squadron; now showing the flag in distant or tropical oceans. In an effort to produce a type which would combine all these requirements, the purity of design had been lost and a number of compromise ships, whose types melted into one another, were afloat or building. They ranged from the strong, heavily-gunned and well-armoured vessels like the *Minotaur* through lighter but still armoured variants of the 'County' class cruisers down to unarmoured but large ships like the *Dartmouths* (the 'Town' class), and the little vessels of 3,350 tons like the *Blonde*. Altogether there were nine distinct classes. It was time to classify and clarify thought and simplify nomenclature on this subject. The large armoured cruisers were already superseded by the battle-cruiser. They still remained a very powerful force, numbering no less than thirty-five vessels. We would call them 'Cruisers.' All the rest should be called 'Light Cruisers.' For the future we would build only battle-cruisers (or fast battleships) and light cruisers. The future evolution of the battle-cruiser was well defined and depended on the numbers and character of any that might be laid down by Germany. Our lead in battle-cruisers (9 to 4) and the creation of the fast division of battleships made it possible to delay decision on this type; but the light cruiser was urgent and even vital. We required a very large number of small fast vessels to protect the Battle Fleet from torpedo attack, to screen it and within certain limits to scout for it. After hearing many arguments, I proposed to the Board that we should concentrate on this type, to exclude all consideration of the requirements of the distant seas, and to build vessels for attendance on the Battle Fleets in home waters and for that duty alone.

Now arose the question of design. Should the new light cruiser be the smallest of the cruisers or the biggest of the destroyers? We had already in existence a few unarmoured light cruisers carrying 4-inch guns called the *Blondes*. We had also an experimental destroyer of enormous size, nearly 2,000 tons and about 36 knots speed, called the *Swift*. In between these were eight hybrid vessels called 'Scouts,' representing weakness and confusion of thought: they had neither speed to run nor guns to fight; they steamed only 24 knots and mounted only a litter of 12-pounders; they carried no armour, but they ate up men and money. Whatever happened we must avoid a feeble compromise like that. I therefore called for designs of an improved *Swift* and an improved *Blonde*. The main object of both these types was to rupture a torpedo attack on the Battle Fleet, scout for it, and otherwise protect it. But destroyers were now being freely armed with 4-inch guns firing a 32-lb. shell capable of inflicting very serious injury on an unarmoured vessel. We must therefore have some protection, if not to keep out the shell, at any rate to keep the bulk of the explosion outside the vessel. We must also have high speed and guns sufficient to punish even the biggest destroyers cruelly.

The constructors and engineers toiled and schemed, and in a few weeks Sir Philip Watts and Sir Henry Oram, *par nobile fratrum*, produced two joint alternative designs, the super-*Blonde* and the super-*Swift*. Both these vessels showed far higher qualities than anything previously achieved for their size and cost; but both were dependent upon oil only. I remitted these designs to a conference of Cruiser Admirals. I could feel opinion turning to the super-*Blonde*. I wrote to Fisher on the 12th January, 1912:—

January 12, 1912.

In sustained rumination about super-*Swifts*, two types emerging.

(1) The super-*Swift*. 37 knots. Six 4-inch—600 tons of oil. £250,000. I want her to be superior at every point to all T.B.D.'s. Speed she has, and stronger armament,

and superior stability. But it is alleged by Briggs[9] (*Advocatus Diaboli*—a very necessary functionary) that she will be as flimsy as the destroyers, and a bigger target. So I have tried to find her a thicker skin—not much, but enough to flash off a 12-pounder or even a 4-inch shell. I can get from Admirable Watts 2-inch tensile steel round all vitals with great strengthening of the general structure of the vessel for 160 tons, £2,200, and three-quarters of a knot speed. The speed would come back as the oil was used up. I think it is a great advance. What do you feel?

(2) Do you know the *Active*? She is a *Blonde*. The super-*Active*, or *Frenzy*, *Mania*, and *Delirium* type, now in question, will be 3,500 tons, 30 knots, 40,000 h.p., ten 4-inch guns and 290 tons of armour distributed in 2-inch plates round vitals. She is therefore much smaller than the *Dartmouths*, £65,000 cheaper (£285,000 as against £350,000), about the same price or size as the *Actives*, but 4.7 knots faster (? in smooth water) and with 2-inch protection as against nothing.

Now if all this bears test, how about chucking the two *Dartmouths* and the *Blonde* in the programme, and substituting four *Frenzies*, all of a kind, the gain being one additional ship, four 30-knot cruiscrlets or cruiserkins, and the cost being an extra £170,000. What is your view?

Fisher wrote on the 16th January:—

'Of course there can be no moment's doubt that you ought to chuck the two *Dartmouths* and the *Blonde* and take four *Frenzies* in lieu. I hope you won't hesitate!'

He did not approve of them, however.

'You are forced,' he said, 'by the general consensus of opinion to have these useless warships and this therefore is your wisest choice. I say to you deliberately that *aviation* has entirely dispensed with the necessity for this type. What you DO want is the super-*Swift*—all oil—and don't fiddle about armour; it really is so VERY silly! There is only ONE defence and that is SPEED! for all small vessels (*except those who go under water*).

'The super-*Swift* is MAINLY wanted for the submarine. The submarine has no horizon. The *Swift* tells her where the enemy is and then flees for her life with 40 knots speed!

'The super-*Lion*, the super-*Swift* and the super-Submarine—*all else is wasted money*!

'The luxuries of the present are the necessities of the future. Our grandfathers never had a bath-room. . . . *You have got to plunge for three years ahead!* And *THE ONE* thing is to keep Foreign Admiralties running after you! It's Hell for *them*!

---

[9]Rear-Admiral Briggs was at this time, January, 1912, still Controller or Third Sea Lord.

'The Germans are going to have a motor battleship before us and a cruiser that will make the circuit of the world without having to replenish her fuel!

'*What an Alabama!*

'The most damnable person for you to have any dealings with is a Naval Expert! Sea fighting is pure common sense. The first of all its necessities is *SPEED*, so as to be able to fight—

When you like
Where you like
and *How* you like.

Therefore the super-*Lion*, the super-*Swift* and the super-*Submarine* are the only three types for fighting (*speed* being THE characteristic of each of these types). AVIATION has wiped out the intermediate types. No armour for anything but the super-*Lion and there restricted*! Cost £1,995,000; speed *over* 30 *knots*; all oil; 10 "*improved*" guns; and you'll make the Germans "*squirm!*" '

And again:—

'*You had better adopt* 2 *keels to* 1! *You have it now*. It will be safe; it will be popular; it will head off the approaching German naval increase. Above all remember Keble in *The Christian Year.*

'"The dusky hues of glorious War!"

'There is always the risk of a [bad Admiral] before a second A. K. Wilson comes along to supersede him! How that picture of old *'ard 'eart* (as the sailors call him) rises before me now! . . . Three big fleets that had never seen each other came from three different quarters to meet him off Cape St. Vincent—in sight of Trafalgar. When each was many hundreds of miles away from him he ordered them by "wireless" exactly what to do, and that huge phalanx met together at his prescribed second of time without a signal or a sound and steamed a solid mass at 14 knots and dropped their anchors with one splash! Are we going to look at his like again?

'So you had better have 2 keels to 1!

'"The dusky hues of glorious War." What a hymn for *The Christian Year* by a Saint like Keble!'

On the 14th January he wrote:—

'I yesterday had an illuminating letter from Jellicoe.... He has all the Nelsonic attributes. . . . He writes to me of new designs. His *one, one, one* cry is SPEED! *Do lay that to heart!* Do remember the receipt for jugged hare in Mrs. Glasse's Cookery Book! "*First catch your hare*!" . . . Also he advocates the "improved" gun and the far bigger ship and (it) will COST LESS.

'"*It's your money we want,*" as those Tariff Reform asses say! . . . Take my advice—2 *keels to* 1!'

The Cruiser Admirals however plumped for the Super-*Blonde*. Meanwhile, between the hammer and the anvil, Sir Philip Watts had scraped together another inch of armour, making 3 inches in all, and Sir Henry Oram guaranteed 30 or even 31 knots of speed.

Now for the guns. The proverbial three alternatives presented themselves. We could have ten 4-inch (32-lb. shell) or five 6-inch (100-lb. shell), or we could compromise on a blend of the two. The Cruiser Admirals' Committee finally agreed on a compromise. Six 4-inch guns were to be mounted on the superstructure forward and two 6-inch on the main deck aft. It was denied that this arrangement was a compromise. It must be judged in relation to what the ship would have to do. When advancing to attack destroyers she could fire a large number of 32-lb. shots, each sufficient to wound them grievously; when retreating from a larger cruiser she could strike back with her two 6-inch guns. I personally insisted upon the two 6-inch. The Navy would never recognize these vessels as cruisers if they did not carry metal of that weight. The ultimate evolution of this type in subsequent years was to a uniform armament of five 6-inch.

We must now admit that this was right, but they were big guns to put in so small a ship, and many doubted whether the platform would be sufficiently stable. For the value then of the two *Dartmouths* and one *Blonde* which had been previously proposed, plus something scraped from other incidentals of the programme, plus a hope that the Chancellor of the Exchequer would not be too severe, we were able to lay down no less than eight of these new vessels. I presented them to Parliament in the following words:—

'They are described as Light Armoured Cruisers, and they will in fact be the smallest, cheapest and fastest vessels protected by vertical armour ever projected for the British Navy. They are designed for attendance on the Battle Fleet. They are designed to be its eyes and ears by night and day; to watch over it in movement and at rest. They will be strong enough and fast enough to overhaul and cut down any torpedo boat destroyer afloat, and generally they will be available for the purposes of observation and reconnaissance.'

Judged by its popularity in peace and war this type may claim success. In the three programmes of 1912, 1913 and 1914, 8, 8, and 6 of them were built respectively, and after the war began no fewer than 18 more were built. The first eight fired their torpedoes from the deck as if they were destroyers. I put the greatest pressure on the constructors to give them underwater torpedo tubes, but they could not manage it in 1912. In 1913 this had been achieved, and was continued in all other vessels of this class. Such were the advantages of speed in Light Cruisers that not one of these vessels, nor the C Class, nor D Class which were their successors, although frequently engaged with the enemy, was ever sunk by gunfire. The first of them from which the class was named was the *Arethusa*, and under the broad pennant of Commodore Tyrwhitt she established, this time on an unchallengeable foundation, the glories claimed of old for that ship.

> 'Come, all you gallant seamen bold,
> Whose hearts are cast in honour's mould;
> I will to you a tale unfold
> Of the saucy *Arethusa*.'

Such were the characteristics of the new vessels with which we proceeded to equip the Royal Navy in the programme of 1912.

CHAPTER VII
THE NORTH SEA FRONT

'The great impediment to action is not discussion, but the want of that knowledge which is gained by discussion preparatory to action.'

—Pericles.

Our First Line of Defence—The Great Change of Front—Close Blockade and an Oversea Base—The New War-Plans: Distant Blockade—Manœuvre Experiments, 1912 and 1913—Cordons—Prowling Squadrons—The Perils of Surprise—The Limits of Precaution—A Bolt from the Blue—The Limits of German Morality—The Invasion Problem and the Expeditionary Force—The Invasion Committee—First Lord's Notes—The South and East Fronts Compared—Raid or Invasion—Impossibility of Close Blockade—The Patrol Flotillas—The Coastal Watch—Bolt from the Grey—Possible German Objectives for Raids—Assumptions and Conclusions—Difficulties of Preparation—The Initial Dangers the Greatest—Letter to a Friend—The Other Side.

The traditional war policy of the Admiralty grew up during the prolonged wars and antagonisms with France. It consisted in establishing immediately upon the outbreak of war a close blockade of the enemy's ports and naval bases by means of flotillas of strong small craft supported by cruisers with superior battle fleets in reserve. The experience of 200 years had led all naval strategists to agree on this fundamental principle, 'Our first line of defence is the enemy's ports.'

When the torpedo was invented, the French tried to frustrate this well-known British policy by building large numbers of torpedo-boats, and the Admiralty, after some years, retorted by building torpedo-boat destroyers. These destroyers fulfilled two conditions: first, they were large enough to keep the seas in most weathers and to operate across the Channel for sufficient periods; secondly, their guns were heavy enough to destroy or dominate the French torpedo-boats. Thus, in spite of the advent of the torpedo, we preserved our power to maintain stronger flotillas in close proximity to the enemy's naval bases. Meanwhile, all along the South Coast of England a series of fortified torpedo-proof harbours in the neighbourhood of our great naval establishments afforded safe, close, and convenient stations for our battle fleets and other supporting vessels when not actually at sea.

When early in the present century our potential enemy for the first time became not France, but Germany, our naval strategic front shifted from the South to the East Coast and from the Channel to the North Sea.[1] But although the enemy, the front, and the theatre had changed, the sound principle of British naval strategy still held good. Our first line of defence was considered to be the enemy's ports. The Admiralty policy was still a close blockade of those ports by means of stronger flotillas properly supported by cruisers and ultimately by the battle fleets.

It was not to be expected that our arrangements on this new front could rapidly reach the same degree of perfection as the conflicts of so many generations had evolved in the Channel; and so far as our naval bases were concerned, we were still in the process of transition when the great war began. More serious, however, was the effect of the change on the utility of our destroyers. Instead of operating at distances of from 20 or 60 miles across the Channel with their supporting ships close at hand in safe harbours, they were now called upon to operate in the Heligoland Bight, across 240 miles of sea, and with no suitable bases for their supporting battle fleet nearer than the Thames or the Forth. Nevertheless, the Admiralty continued to adhere to their traditional strategic principle, and their war plans up till 1911 contemplated the close blockade of the enemy's ports immediately upon the declaration of war. Our destroyers were constructed with ever-increasing sea-keeping qualities and with a great superiority of gun-power. The Germans, on the other hand, adhered rather to the French conception of the torpedo-boat as a means of attack upon our large ships. While we relied in our destroyer construction principally on gun-power and sea-keeping qualities, they relied upon the torpedo and high speed in fair weather opportunities. But the much greater distances over which our destroyers had now to operate across the North Sea immensely reduced their effectiveness. Whereas across the Channel they could work in two reliefs, they required three across the North Sea. Therefore only one-third instead of one-half of our fighting flotillas could be available at any given moment. Against this third the enemy could at any moment bring his whole force. In order to carry out our old strategic policy from our Home bases we should have required flotillas at least three and probably four times as numerous as those of Germany. This superiority we had not got and were not likely to get.

Therefore from shortly before 1905 when the French agreement was signed, down to the Agadir crisis in 1911, the Admiralty made plans to capture one or other of the German islands. On this it was intended to establish an oversea base at which from the beginning of the war our blockade flotillas could be replenished and could rest, and which as war progressed would have developed into an advanced citadel of our sea-power. In this way, therefore, the Admiralty would still have carried out their traditional war policy of beating the enemy's flotillas and light craft into his ports and maintaining a constant close blockade.

These considerations were not lost upon the Germans. They greatly increased the fortifications of Heligoland, and they proceeded to fortify one after another such of the Frisian Islands as were in any way suitable for our purposes. At the same time a new

---

[1]See general map of the North Sea on pages 242, 243.

and potent factor appeared upon the scene—the submarine. The submarine not only rendered the capture and maintenance of an oversea base or bases far more difficult and, as some authorities have steadfastly held, impossible, but it threatened with destruction our cruisers and battleships without whose constant support our flotillas would easily have been destroyed by the enemy's cruisers.

This was the situation in October, 1911, when immediately after the Agadir crisis I became First Lord and proceeded to form a new Board of Admiralty. Seeing that we had not for the time being the numerical force of destroyers able to master the destroyers of the potential enemy in his home waters, nor the power to support our flotillas with heavy ships, and having regard also to the difficulty and hazard in all the circumstances of storming and capturing one of his now fortified islands, we proceeded forthwith to revise altogether the War Plans and substitute, with the full concurrence of our principal commanders afloat, the policy of distant blockade set out in the Admiralty War Orders of 1912.

The policy of distant blockade was not adopted from choice, but from necessity. It implied no repudiations on the part of the Admiralty of their fundamental principle of aggressive naval strategy, but only a temporary abandonment of it in the face of unsolved practical difficulties; and it was intended that every effort should be made, both before and after a declaration of war, to overcome those difficulties. It was rightly foreseen that by closing the exits from the North Sea into the Atlantic Ocean, German commerce would be almost completely cut off from the world. It was expected that the economic and financial pressure resulting from such a blockade would fatally injure the German power to carry on a war. It was hoped that this pressure would compel the German fleet to come out and fight, not in his own defended waters, but at a great numerical disadvantage in the open sea. It was believed that we could continue meanwhile to enjoy the full command of the seas without danger to our sea communications or to the movement of our armies, and that the British Isles could be kept safe from invasion. There was at that time no reason to suppose that these conditions would not continue indefinitely with undiminished advantage to ourselves and increasing pressure upon the enemy. So far as all surface vessels are concerned, and certainly for the first three years of the war, these expectations were confirmed by experience.

Under these orders the Fleet was disposed strategically so as to block the exits from the North Sea by placing the Grand Fleet at Scapa Flow and drawing a cordon of destroyers across the Straits of Dover supported by the older battle-ships and protected by certain minefields. These conclusions stood the test of the war. They were never departed from in any important respect by any of the Boards of Admiralty which held office. By this means the British Navy seized and kept the effective control of all the oceans of the world.

They did not, however, secure the command of the Baltic, nor the absolute control of the North Sea. We could no longer hope to prevent the enemy from sallying out of his harbours whenever he chose. What use would he make of this liberty, at the outset or during the progress of a war? By what means could we restrict him most effectually?

We sought to probe these questions in the naval manœuvres of 1912 and 1913.

In 1912 the newly-formed Admiralty War Staff prepared, as an experiment, a plan for an immense cordon of cruisers and destroyers, supported by the Battle Fleet, from the Coast of Norway to a point on the East Coast of England. To a military eye this system appeared unsound, and indeed outside the Admiralty it was generally condemned by naval opinion. I quoted Napoleon's scathing comment in 1808: 'Est-ce qu'on a adopté le système des cordons? Est-ce qu'on veut empêcher la contrebande de passer ou l'ennemi? Qui est-ce qui peut conseiller au Roi de faire des cordons? Après dix années de guerre doit-on revenir à ces bêtises-la?' The cordon system was however tried, and was completely exposed and broken down. We then fell back upon a system of what I may call 'prowling squadrons and occasional drives,' that is to say, we recognized that we could not maintain any continuous control of the North Sea. The best we could do was to sweep it in strength at irregular intervals and for the rest await the action of the enemy. This clearly involved a considerable risk of raiding forces which might amount to ten or twenty thousand men slipping through and disembarking on our coast. I therefore called for careful individual study to be made of all the different points where such forces could be landed, and what would be the best plans for the Germans to make in each case. At the manœuvres of 1913 Sir John Jellicoe adopted several of these plans for raiding the British coast and put them into execution. He achieved so considerable a measure of success that I thought it necessary to stop the manœuvres on the third day lest we might teach the Germans as well as ourselves.

But before there could be any question of employing the war policy on which the Admiralty had decided, there was a preliminary period to be traversed of the most momentous and critical character. This period raised another set of problems before which the inconveniences of raids, or even an attempt at serious invasion, paled in gravity. Of all the dangers that menaced the British Empire, none was comparable to a surprise of the Fleet. If the Fleet or any vital part of it were caught unawares or unready and our naval preponderance destroyed, we had lost the war, and there was no limit to the evils which might have been inflicted upon us, except the mercy of an all-powerful conqueror. We have seen in recent years how little completely victorious nations can be trusted to restrain their passions against a prostrate foe. Great Britain, deprived of its naval defence, could be speedily starved into utter submission to the will of the conqueror. Her Empire would be dismembered; the Dominions, India, and her immense African and island possessions would be shorn off or transferred to the victors. Ireland would be erected into a hostile well-armed republic on the flank of Great Britain; and the British people, reduced to a helpless condition, would be loaded with overwhelming indemnities calculated to shatter their social system, if, indeed, they were not actually reduced, in Sir Edward Grey's mordant phrase, to the position of 'the conscript appendage of a stronger Power.' Less severe conditions than have since been meted out to Germany would certainly have sufficed to destroy the British Empire at a stroke for ever. The stakes were very high. If our naval defence were maintained we were safe and sure beyond the lot of any other European nation; if it failed, our doom was certain and final.

To what lengths, therefore, would the Germans go to compass the destruction of the British Fleet? Taking the demonic view of their character which it was necessary to assume for the purposes of considering a war problem, what forms of attack ought we to reckon with? Of course, if Germany had no will to war, all these speculations were mere nightmares. But if she had the will and intention of making war, it was evident that there would be no difficulty in finding a pretext arising out of a dispute with France or Russia, to create a situation in which war was inevitable, and create it at the most opportune moment for herself. The wars of Frederick and of Bismarck had shown with what extraordinary rapidity and suddenness the Prussian nation was accustomed to fall upon its enemy. The Continent was a powder magazine from end to end. One single hellish spark and the vast explosion might ensue. We had seen what had happened to France in 1870. We had seen what neglect to take precautions had brought upon the Russian fleet off Port Arthur in 1904. We know now what happened to Belgium in 1914, and, not less remarkable, the demand Germany decided to make upon France on August 1, 1914, that if she wished to remain neutral while Germany attacked Russia, she must as a guarantee hand over to German garrisons her fortresses of Verdun and Toul.

Obviously, therefore, the danger of a 'bolt from the blue' was by no means fantastic. Still, might one not reasonably expect certain warnings? There would probably be some kind of dispute in progress between the great Powers enjoining particular vigilance upon the Admiralty. We might hope to get information of military and naval movements. It was almost certain that there would be financial perturbations in the Exchanges of the world indicating a rise of temperature. Could we therefore rely upon a week's notice, or three days' notice, or at least twenty-four hours' notice before any blow actually fell?

In Europe, where great nations faced each other with enormous armies, there was an automatic safeguard against surprise. Decisive events could not occur till the armies were mobilized, and that took at least a fortnight. The supreme defence of France, for instance, could not therefore be overcome without a great battle in which the main strength of the French nation could be brought to bear. But no such assurance was enjoyed by the British Fleet. No naval mobilization was necessary on either side to enable all the modern ships to attack one another. They had only to raise steam and bring the ammunition to the guns. But beyond this grim fact grew the torpedo menace. So far as gunfire alone was concerned, our principal danger was for our Fleet to be caught divided and to have one vital part destroyed without inflicting proportionate damage on the enemy. This danger was greatly reduced by wireless, which enabled the divided portions to be instantly directed to a common rendezvous and to avoid action till concentration was effected. Besides, gunfire was a game that two could play at. One could not contemplate that the main strength of the fleets would ever be allowed to come within range of each other without taking proper precautions. But the torpedo was essentially a weapon of surprise, or even treachery; and all that was true of the torpedo in a surface vessel applied with tenfold force to the torpedo of a submarine.

Obviously there were limits beyond which it was impossible to safeguard oneself. It was not simply a case of a few weeks of special precautions. The British Navy had to live its ordinary life in time of peace. It had to have its cruises and its exercises, its periods of leave and refit. Our harbours were open to the commerce of the world. Absolute security against the worst conceivable treachery was physically impossible. On the other hand, even treachery, which required the co-operation of very large numbers of people in different stations and the setting in motion of an immense and complicated apparatus, is not easy to bring about. It was ruled by the Committee of Imperial Defence, after grave debate, that the Admiralty must not assume that if it made the difference between victory and defeat, Germany would stop short of an attack on the Fleet in full peace without warning or pretext. We had to do our best to live up to this standard, and in the main I believe we succeeded. Certainly the position and condition of the British Fleet was every day considered in relation to that of Germany. I was accustomed to check our dispositions by asking the Staff from time to time, unexpectedly, 'What happens if war with Germany begins to-day?' I never found them without an answer which showed that we had the power to effect our main concentration before any portion of the Fleet could be brought to battle. Our Fleet did not go for its cruises to the coast of Spain until we knew that the German High Seas Fleet was having its winter refits. When we held Grand Manœuvres we were very careful to arrange the coaling and leave which followed in such a way as to secure us the power of meeting any blow which could possibly reach us in a given time. I know of no moment in the period of which I am writing up to the declaration of war in which it was physically possible for the main British Fleet to have been surprised or caught dispersed and divided by any serious German force of surface vessels. An attempt in full peace to make a submarine attack upon a British squadron in harbour or exercising, or to lay mines in an area in which they might be expected to exercise, could not wholly be provided against; but in all human probability its success would only have been partial. Further, I do not believe that such treachery was ever contemplated by the German Admiralty, Government or Emperor. While trying as far as possible to guard against even the worst possibilities, my own conviction was that there would be a cause of quarrel accompanied by a crisis and a fall in markets, and followed very rapidly by a declaration of war, or by acts of war intended to be simultaneous with the declaration, but possibly occurring slightly before. What actually did happen was not unlike what I thought would happen.

Early in 1912, the Prime Minister set up again, under his own chairmanship, the Invasion Committee of the Committee of Imperial Defence. This was virtually the Committee which had assembled during the Agadir crisis in the previous August, and henceforth down to the outbreak of the war it continued to meet not infrequently. I asked that Mr. Balfour, who had retired from the leadership of the Unionist party, should be added to the Committee. This was effected.

The main question before us was the possibility of the invasion of Great Britain by Germany; but incidentally many other aspects of a war with Germany were patiently and searchingly examined. The position which I stated on behalf of the Admiralty was briefly as follows:—

Once the Fleet was concentrated in its war station, no large army could be landed in the British Isles. 'Large Army' was defined for this purpose as anything over 70,000 men. More than that we guaranteed to intercept or break up while landing. Less than that could be dealt with by the British Regular Army provided it had not left the country.

But the War Office proposed to send the whole Expeditionary Force of six Divisions out of the country immediately upon the declaration of war, and to have it all in France by the thirteenth or fourteenth day. The Admiralty were unable to guarantee—though we thought it very unlikely—that smaller bodies of perhaps twenty or thirty thousand Germans might not slip across the North Sea. These would have to be met at once by well-trained troops. The Territorial Force would not be capable in the very early days of their embodiment of coping with the invaders. Some regular troops ought, therefore, to be left in the country till we saw how matters went at sea, and could measure our real position with more certainty. It would be a disastrous mistake to begin sending six Divisions, and then because of a successful raid have to interrupt the whole process and disentangle two or more Divisions from the troops in transit to make head against the raiders. We therefore argued that four Divisions only should be sent in the first instance, and that two should be left behind till we knew how we stood at sea. The presence of these two Divisions at home, together with the Territorial Force, would make it not worth while for the Germans to invade, except with an army large enough to be certainly caught in transit by the Fleet. Only an army of a certain size at home could give the Navy a sufficiently big target on salt water. 'You could not,' as Sir Arthur Wilson pithily observed, 'expect the Navy to play international football without a goalkeeper.' The War Office, on the other hand, continued to demand the immediate dispatch of the whole six Divisions.

This controversy was never finally settled till the war began. It certainly afforded the means of exploring every imaginable aspect of the conditions which would arise in the first few weeks of war. Further than that no man could see. When the actual test came, both the War Office and the Admiralty abandoned their respective contentions simultaneously. Lord Kitchener decided to send only four Divisions immediately to France, while I on behalf of the Admiralty announced at the great War Council on the 5th August that as we were fully mobilized and had every ship at its war station, we would take the responsibility of guarding the island in the absence of the whole six Divisions. We thus completely changed places. The Admiralty were better than their word when it came to the point, and the War Office more cautious than the intentions. Surveying it all in retrospect, I believe Lord Kitchener's decision was right. But it was taken freely and not under duress from the Admiralty.

While the discussions of the Invasion Committee were at their height during the spring and summer of 1913, I prepared a series of papers in support of the Admiralty view, but also designed to explore and illuminate the situations that might arise. They show the hopes and fears we felt before the event, what we thought the enemy might do against us, and the dangers we hoped to avoid ourselves. They show the kind of mental picture I was able to summon up in imagination of the tremendous period which was so soon to rush upon us. My intention also was to stimulate thought in the Admiralty War Staff, and to expose weak points in our arrangements. For this purpose I entered into an active discussion and correspondence with several of the ablest Admirals (notably Admiral Beatty, Admiral Lewis Bayly, and Sir Reginald Custance), seeking to have the whole matter argued out to the utmost limit possible. I caused war games to be played at the War College in which, aided by one or the other of my naval advisers, I took one side, usually the German and forced certain situations. I also forecasted the political data necessary to a study of military and naval action on the outbreak of war.

Various papers which I prepared in 1913 were the result of this process of study and discussion. The first, entitled 'Notes by the First Lord of the Admiralty,' deals with the problem of raid and invasion in general terms, and shows the conditions which would prevail in a war with Germany. The second propounds the issues to be faced by the War Staff. The third records my written discussion of the problem with the First Sea Lord, while the sittings of the Invasion Committee were proceeding. The fourth and fifth entitled 'The Time-Table of a Nightmare' and 'A Bolt from the Grey,' were imaginative exercises couched in a half-serious vein, but designed to disturb complacency by suggesting weak points in our arrangements and perilous possibilities. Space forbids the inclusion of these last. The first three have been subjected to a certain compression.

NOTES BY THE FIRST LORD OF THE ADMIRALTY.

It is much harder for the British Navy to stop raids or an invasion from Germany to-day than it was fifteen years ago from France. The tension between England and France had in the course of successive generations led to the development of a sea front opposite to France of great military strength. The line Berehaven, Queenstown, Pembroke, Falmouth, Plymouth, Portland, Portsmouth, Newhaven, Dover, Sheerness and Chatham, covers with suitable defences every point of strategic significance, comprises three great naval bases and dockyards and two torpedoproof war harbours (Portland and Dover). In close proximity to this line are our three principal military establishments, the Curragh, Salisbury, and Aldershot.

From the British military harbours and bases on this line close observation of all French Channel ports where transports could be assembled can be maintained by a superior British naval force. Cherbourg and Havre can be controlled from Portland, and Calais and Boulogne from Dover. Flotillas and light craft employed on this service of observation would have their own home base close at hand and a high proportion could be constantly maintained on duty. The proximity of the battle fleets in the numerous well-protected harbours, where every necessity is supplied, ensures the effective support of the flotillas against any serious attempt to drive them off.

Very different is the situation on the sea front against Germany. With the exception of Chatham, no naval base or military harbour exists. Chatham itself has no graving docks for the later Dreadnoughts, and the depth of the Medway imposes serious limitations of tides and seasons upon great vessels using the dockyard. Harwich affords anchorage only to torpedo-craft [and light cruisers], and is lightly defended. The Humber and the Tyne are unsuitable for large battle fleets and are but lightly defended. Rosyth will not be ready even as a war repairing-base till 1916 at the earliest. Defences are being erected at Cromarty, and a temporary floating base is in process of creation at that point.[2] Only improvised emergency arrangements are contemplated for Scapa Flow, and the Shetlands are quite unprotected. The only war bases available for the fleet along the whole of this front are Rosyth, Cromarty, and Scapa—the more remote being preferred, although the least defended. The landing places along the coast are numerous, extensive, and evenly distributed; the strategic objectives open to an enemy are numerous and important. The Shetlands are a strategic position of the highest consequence, totally undefended and ungarrisoned. The same is true of the Orkneys. Edinburgh and Glasgow, Newcastle, Hull, and Harwich are all points of primary importance. No large military garrisons comparable to those on the southern front exist.

But the comparison of the new conditions with the old becomes most unfavourable when we extend our view from the British to the German coast. It is difficult to find any sea front of greater natural defensive strength than the German North Sea coast. Intricate navigation, shifting and extensive sandbanks and currents, strong tides, frequent mists and storms, make the Heligoland Bight a very difficult theatre for oversea operations. The deep re-entrant widening into a broad debouch, flanked at each side by lines of islands and sustained in the centre by Heligoland, confers the greatest possible natural advantages upon the defence. To these have been added, and are being added, everything that military art can devise. Heligoland is an almost impregnable fortress and an advanced torpedo and airship station. Borkum and Sylt are both heavily defended by batteries, mine-fields, and strong garrisons, and both can be commanded by fire from the mainland. Into this great defended area, with its wide debouch facing towards us, access is given from the Ems, the Elbe, the Weser, the Jade and from the Kiel Canal communicating with the Baltic, and open for Dreadnoughts at the present year. Within this area are all the naval establishments of Germany. A fleet or transports assembled at either end of the Kiel Canal have the widely separated alternatives of emerging either from the Heligoland Bight or from the Baltic for offensive purposes. There would be no difficulty on the declaration of war in assembling unperceived at Hamburg, Kiel, Wilhelmshaven, and other ports, the shipping necessary to transport at least 20,000 men; enough to transport 10,000 men is always in those ports. Large garrisons exist in the neighbourhood, amply sufficient to supply whatever military force was required. The Germans possess to-day large ships of the liner class suitable for transport in a way which the French never did. The rigour with which agents suspected of sending information have been pursued

[2]No one can form any idea of the difficulties the Admiralty encountered in securing adequate defences for Eastern harbours. Coast Defence was in the province of the War Office and paid for on their estimates. They needed every penny for their Field Army and Expeditionary Force, and naturally marshalled all their experts against expenditure on fortifications in Great Britain. In consequence expert opinion was always divided. The discussions evaporated in technicalities, and the lay members of the Committee were rarely convinced of the unwelcome need of spending money. To such a point was the dispute carried, that Prince Louis and I undertook in desperation to fortify Cromarty ourselves, arm it with naval guns and man it with marines. And this was the only new work completed when the war broke out.

during the last five or six years has made it difficult to arrange for the transmission of intelligence. Consular officers are marked men; and it is to be expected that their communications by the usual postal and telegraphic channels will be delayed if hostilities are imminent. Although the sources from which information may be obtained have been increased in numbers during recent years, and are still being increased as opportunity offers, yet the Admiralty are not prepared to make any confident assertion that a force of upwards of 20,000 men could not be collected in time of peace, and embarked without their knowledge. As a matter of fact, very considerable embarkations of a test character have been carried out without our having any knowledge until some days after the event.

The continuous development of the mine and the torpedo makes it impossible to establish a close watch with heavy ships on the exits from the Heligoland Bight. To do so for a long period of time would mean a steady and serious wastage of valuable units from the above causes, and, if prolonged, would effectually alter the balance of naval power. On the other hand, torpedo craft, which cannot keep at sea like great vessels, and must every three or four days return to port for rest and replenishment, have no base nearer than Harwich, 240 miles away. The operation of controlling the debouches from the Heligoland Bight by means of flotillas would require twice the number of oversea torpedo craft that we now possess. The watch would have to be maintained in three reliefs: one on duty, one in transit, and one at rest, and therefore only a third of the existing vessels would be available at any given time. Such a force could be overwhelmed by a sudden attack of two or three times their numbers by a well-chosen blow, opportunities for which would frequently recur. Unless, therefore, we were to take by storm some fortified German island which could be held as a base, or were permitted to use Dutch or Danish territory, the closing of the debouches of the Heligoland Bight by a close flotilla cordon is, in the opinion of the Admiralty, impracticable at present.

The development of submarines of ocean-going capacity may be expected to modify this situation in our favour.

The problem of controlling the alternative debouches from the Baltic by watching over the Skaw or the Belts presents many of the features that have been found so unfavourable in regard to the Heligoland Bight. Nothing effective could be done, or still less maintained, with our present forces without using the territory of Norway or Denmark, or both. It must be borne in mind that the enemy have the option of striking with their whole force on either line.

* * * * *

On the assumption that a close blockade, either of the Heligoland Bight or of the exits from the Baltic, is not possible, the Admiralty cannot guarantee that individual vessels will not frequently slip through the cruiser squadrons patrolling the wide area of the North Sea. The North Sea comprises an area of more than 125,000 square miles. The number of cruisers available is less than 30, of which a large proportion will always be recoaling. The aid that can be given at a distance from the British shore by torpedo craft would be partial and fleeting. The weather is frequently thick; on a third of the days in the year the visibility is not more than 4 miles; on a quarter of the days in the year it is not more than 2 miles. There are about five days fog per month during the year. April averages ten days fog. At night it is frequently impossible to see a ship without lights at more than a few hundred yards distance, and often not at that. It is no exaggeration to say that the main risk which a single fast ship would run, steaming at night without lights, would be that of collision, which chance may be very well accepted. It will be easy to demonstrate this by experiments at the forthcoming manœuvres. If, therefore, close and certain observation becomes impossible, there is a very good chance of an indefinite succession of individual transports reaching the British coasts without being intercepted by the controlling cruiser squadrons.

Let us now consider what arrangements exist or are possible along the line of the British coasts to detect and attack such vessels.

Four flotilla cruisers, seventy-four destroyers and torpedoboats, and eighteen submarines are placed under the command of the Admiral of Patrols for the defence of the East Coast from the Shetlands to Dover; less than 100 vessels and more than 600 miles of sea front. It is quite impossible with such a small force to maintain a regular patrol, or still less a line of observation. These flotillas are not intended for observation, but to attack. To employ them on the former service, for which their numbers are wholly insufficient, would speedily exhaust them: at least half would have to be resting and refuelling. It is not possible with the forces available for the patrol flotillas to prevent enemy vessels from reaching the British coast. Our dispositions are intended to make it certain that they will be attacked in force with the least possible delay.

A curious distinction attaches to the work of naval coast defence. Usually the line of observation lies in advance of the line of resistance. In coast defence the line of observation is in rear of the line of resistance. So far as the patrol flotillas are concerned, the British coasts are themselves the only true and certain line of observation. The approach of an enemy may be undetected by the cruising squadrons or by the patrolling flotillas. But it ought to be certain that his first contact with the coast at any point is reported to the Admiral of Patrols, and that that officer will have his available forces massed at convenient points from which an attack can be at once delivered. The Admiral of Patrols must treat his problems selectively and recognize that absolute certainty is out of reach, that his flotillas are for fighting purposes, and that their rôle of scouting is secondary. It is of very little use reporting the approach of an enemy when one has not the forces with which to strike him. The patrol flotillas are therefore kept in hand at the best strategic points, neither scattered nor exhausted, and a system of land observation by outposts, cyclists, aircraft and signal stations, all connected by telephone, ought to be perfected, from which accurate information can be transmitted to the points where the patrol flotillas are massed.

Dalesvoe (Shetlands), Fort Ross, Firth of Forth, North Shields, Grimsby, and Yarmouth are the bases of the patrol flotillas, and a force of fourteen or fifteen vessels would, on the average, be available for each. It is upon this disposition that the

Admiralty rely to interrupt the disembarkation of any considerable force. It is of vital importance that the watching of the coast-line from the shore should be taken up from the earliest moment and in advance of general mobilization. The effectiveness of the work of the patrol flotillas and consequently the restriction of possible landings depend upon early information being received of any disembarkation. The size of any raiding party that could be landed will, of course, be accurately proportionate to the delay. It would no doubt be impossible or undesirable to put the whole system of coast watches into operation in the precautionary period. No doubt the arrangements made after war had actually begun would be much more thorough, and larger numbers of cyclists and watchers would be available. But a system of watching likely landing-places ought to be devised which could be brought silently into operation as soon as the precautionary period is declared or, if necessary, immediately before, just in the same way as the watch over the magazines and other vital points can unostentatiously be improved.

It may well be, therefore, that the coast watch should be set up in two stages; the first secret, and the second open. For the first the police and selected cyclists from the Territorial Force would appear to be the only resources. It ought to be possible to organize a pretty effective watch with these, and to make arrangements which could be actually rehearsed in time of peace in connection with the work of the patrol flotillas. It is not so much armed force which is required as vigilant watching by persons who know what to look for and where to report their information. Aerial squadrons along the coast-line or airships would appear to be of the greatest value. The new naval aeroplane stations which are being constructed will be of service for this purpose. After war has been declared, or general mobilization ordered, the full arrangements devised by the War Office could come into force in their entirety, but it is imperative that the precautionary period in advance of mobilization should be provided for.

March 29, 1913.

NOTES BY THE FIRST LORD OF THE ADMIRALTY

(*Addressed to the Admiralty War Staff*)

The problem of oversea attack requires to be examined under three heads:—

1. Absolute surprise to-morrow (19th April): everything going on as usual—Bolt from the Blue.

Objectives to raiders—to prevent the Expeditionary Force being sent to help France, and incidentally, if possible, to damage naval arsenals and dockyards.

2. The whole expeditionary army has gone to India or some other distant theatre of war. The war has been going on some time: the Territorials have been embodied, but great numbers have been allowed to proceed on leave. The Second Fleet has been completed to full strength by the closing of the schools. The Immediate Reserve has been called out; and the whole of the First and Second Fleets are in

those harbours which enable them to reach their actual war stations as quickly as possible. The patrol flotillas are mobilized in their war stations. The forts are manned, and the coastal look-out is active. But this has been going on for several months while complete peace continues in Europe. The tension has begun to be somewhat relaxed, and we have settled down to our ordinary way of life, while at the same time taking special precautions and having our forces so disposed that they are easily and readily available on the slightest sign of danger. This may be called 'Bolt from the Grey.' The only adequate objective of the enemy in this case would be invasion in such force as to overcome the comparatively feeble military establishment on foot in the United Kingdom.

3. War with Germany has begun. All the fleets are fully mobilized and in active operation against the enemy according to the war plans of the Admiralty. The objectives open to the enemy would be minor raids to destroy naval arsenals and dockyards: the seizure of bases for flotilla action (this last may occur also in 1 and 2), and threats or attempts to invade in force to distract or divide the British fleet simultaneously with bringing about a great fleet action.

All these three situations with their variants deserve patient examination.

4. The first condition governing the dimensions of oversea attack from Germany is the number of troops available—

(i.) Instantly;
(ii.) In twenty-four hours; and
(iii.) At any time after a general mobilization is complete.

* * * * *

5. A second great limiting condition is the shipping available in German ports. For all phases after the war has become open, whether under 1, 2, or 3, ample shipping is available of every class required, and the matter need not be further considered. But in case 1, the invading force is limited by the amount of suitable shipping available instantly at the right ports, and secondly, by what is available after 24 hours: in case 2 by the amount of shipping available instantly. After that, when war has actually begun, there is no difficulty in finding the ships or the men; the only difficulty is to get them across.

6. The third condition is the time taken to embark, transport, and land the various forces at different points concurrently and alternatively. This requires separate calculations in every case. These are complicated by the hours of daylight and darkness, the tides, the weather, and other uncertain features. Each case must be worked out separately, and risked on its merits.

7. The last consideration is the distance of the practicable objective from the landing-point. Here again each case must be considered individually:—

Harwich is invaluable because it threatens London, and is unquestionably the best place for so doing. In no other way could you react so instantaneously upon

British public opinion. On the other hand, once the invaders were turned out, the actual damage done would be small.

Immingham is a purely local injury not worth touching before war breaks out, and afterwards belonging to the 'driblets' phase.

Blyth or the Tyne are striking places for Newcastle, involving considerable moral effect and immense permanent damage, not of a vital character.

The Tay (Dundee) is valuable as affording a good landing-place and ample supplies for a large army (if it could get there), within effective striking distance of Glasgow and the Clyde.

Cromarty, as long as it is undefended by land and if undefended by ships, would be a good place of disembarkation for a large force, but they would be isolated in barren country with great natural difficulties between them and any real vulnerable point. Cromarty and the Invergordon oil tanks might, however, be the object of a minor raid in the 'driblets' phase, if undefended.

Balta Sound, in the Shetlands, and those islands generally would be of the greatest value as a flotilla base to the Germans. Until they were expelled from them, which would be costly both in ships and men, all attempts to blockade the North Sea would be rendered futile.

On the West Coast there are numerous undefended landing-places in sheltered waters suitable for the disembarkation of a large force (if it could get there). Oban, 60 miles away from the Clyde, deserves special attention. The mouth of the Clyde itself, which is lightly defended by land and has only three submarines at Lamlash, is suitable both for the landing of a large force and also for a raid on an arsenal. The same may be said of Barrow.

This would seem to exhaust the principal serviceable landing-places which should be considered, but there may be others.

April 18, 1913. W. S. C.

NOTES BY THE FIRST LORD OF THE ADMIRALTY

(*Addressed to the First Sea Lord.*)

(**Marginal Notes by First Sea Lord.**)

A.

The following assumptions appear to me, as at present advised, to be justified:—

Should like to limit this to two or three ports at most.

1. That not more than 20,000 men could be collected and embarked in German North Sea Ports without our knowing it before the expedition actually sailed; but that up to that number might actually put to sea before we were warned.

3b answers this, otherwise the assumption is risky.

2. That no military expedition of upwards of 10,000 men could reach the British coast before the general alarm was given.

3. That the intention of the German Government to attack us would either (*a*) be discovered or (*b*), more probably, formally declared while the expedition was in transit.

(b) The latter should, I think, be assumed.

4. That, having regard to the time taken in transit, three to six hours' warning would have been given throughout the country, along the coasts, and at all ports, and preparations advanced accordingly.

Yes.

5. That any expedition arriving at a port must expect to encounter resistance from whatever forces or defences are on the spot after three hours' alarm notice; but that no one place can be considered more certain than another, and that only the ordinary preparations prescribed under our existing mobilization arrangements have been made at each particular place.

Yes.

6. That any German expedition seeking to seize a port defended or otherwise must be provided with an escort sufficient to overcome the local defences and to beat off the British torpedo craft or cruisers known to be in the vicinity.

Yes.

7. That the moment chosen will be one when the British Battle Fleet is on the south-west or west coasts of Great Britain or Ireland.

Assuming that some kind of diplomatic discussion had preceded the Declaration of War it is to be hoped that Admiralty will have begun concentrating, but we cannot be sure.

8. That the return of the Battle Fleet to the North Sea will be obstructed by mines and submarines, and at night by flotilla attacks.

Our own flotillas should be able to clear the road.

9. That pending the return of the Battle Fleet the German Navy will have the command of the North Sea, and that so long as it holds the command of the North Sea it can continue, though at considerable risk to pass individual vessels, in addition to the original 20,000 men, into the defended harbour which has been seized. The maximum time which in the most unfavourable circumstances would elapse before the return of the British Fleet to the North Sea and consequent resumption of British naval superiority is therefore a vital matter, and should be worked out in as many variants as possible by the staff.

Attempt may be made, but in the case of Harwich (the most probable) there will be 2nd Fleet ships from Nore, also Nore Flotilla, besides patrol vessels to deal with.

The time-table given in your 'Bolt from the Blue' is quite sufficient, and cannot be varied to any appreciable extent.

It is almost hopeless to forecast what may happen during this critical time. No escorts could then be spared.

10. That the British Fleet when it has returned to the North Sea, whether northabout or through the Straits of Dover, may have to fight a general battle at once with the whole strength of the enemy; and that during the preliminaries, the progress, and the aftermath of this battle attempts may be made either to reinforce the original landing or to make further landings at other points on the British coasts.

Resident Germans may certainly be expected to cooperate locally. There are always a number of officers over here map-making.

11. That sabotage, i.e. acts of treachery before a declaration of war, are improbable, but that they may occur simultaneously with the first military hostilities, and that in any case they are not included in the present phase of the inquiry which deals essentially with military operations.

April 26, 1913. W.S.C.

B.

Carefully.

It is useless labour to work out in detail a series of *conventional* operations. It is only necessary to work out real operations, i.e. the sort of operations an enemy might be expected to attempt. The numbers of these are limited: there are only four types.

Except local co-operation (see A. 11).

2. First, sabotage, by which is meant acts of treachery perpetrated by persons or vessels in disguise before any declaration of war. Instances of these acts are given by Captain Hankey in his paper. They are an important study, but they do not touch the problems we are now examining, and they are therefore excluded for the present.

Yes.

3. Secondly, a military raid on Blyth for the purpose of destroying Elswick.

We have hitherto assumed 10,000 men for Blyth-Newcastle; either more or less may be required. The force must be numerous enough to make its way in the face of sporadic opposition by unmobilized territorials and by the population, from Blyth to Elswick; to seize and destroy effectively the Elswick Works and the ships in the Tyne. It seems improbable that less than 10,000 men would be sufficient.

Yes.

4. Thirdly, a raid of not less than 20,000 men on Harwich, with the object of stopping the regular army from going to France.

* * * * *

The Harwich operation is essentially—

(*a*) The secret concentration and embarkation of 20,000 men.

(*b*) The destruction of the floating and land defences of Harwich by the escorting hostile squadron.

(*c*) The disembarkation of 20,000 men with a proportion of artillery before the British Fleet can arrive in sufficient force to give battle.

5. Fourthly, a landing in the Firth of Tay. This is not worth doing unless the force landed is at least 35,000 men. It is assumed that war has begun before the enemy actually completed their embarkation; that the British Fleet has been forced to concentrate to the southward* in order to fight a general battle with the German Fleet; that in consequence the northern waters of the North Sea are denuded of ships; and that the passage of fifteen or twenty independent transports to a fixed rendezvous, as suggested, will not be obstructed by any naval force which could not be overcome by the German warship escort.† In this case the forts are fully manned and the whole coast is alarmed and vigilant. The enemy's transports must be escorted and protected by cruisers or old battleships; the opposition of the forts must be beaten down, and any resistance by local territorials on land must be overcome and quelled. The objective of the invaders is Glasgow and the Clyde. The whole six divisions of the expeditionary force have left England for a distant war.‡

**The transports are not likely to sail before some certainty as to whereabouts of our Fleet has been obtained. Every delay adds to the number of cruisers, etc., which would be in the way.*

†I doubt if much in the way of escort could be spared. The enemy must be prepared to meet our entire superior force in the North Sea.

‡On the whole this seems a very risky undertaking, but by no means impossible, and on the assumption above, quite worth trying.

The question to be resolved is whether these are all the operations which need be considered at the present time. Are they practicable?[§] And if so, to what extent?[||] How could they be achieved?[#] What are the circumstances most favourable to their success? What are the measures which should be taken in each case?[**]

[§] First three certainly.
[||] With limitations.
[#] As described.

[**] Navy—

Provide sea defences for Blyth.

Strengthen existing ones (notably Harwich) on East Coast.

Man them on the principle of a ship in commission with nucleus crew.

Provide local *submarine defence flotillas at the principal East Coast ports.*

Army—

Adhere rigidly to the Committee of Imperial Defence recommendations (1008), as accepted by His Majesty's Government [*i.e., retain two divisions at home*].

The times and conditions which I have prescribed are illustrative of the problem; and before any attempt is made to work out these cases in detail the conditions should be formulated exactly.

W.S.C.

April 24, 1913.

These papers are sufficient to show that we did not ignore the dangers that lay before us or neglect the attempt to penetrate their mysteries. It it easy to underrate the difficulty of such work in days of peace.

In time of war there is great uncertainty as to what the enemy will do and what will happen next. But still, once you are at war the task is definite and all-dominating. Whatever may be your surmises about the enemy or the future, your own action is circumscribed within practical limits. There are only a certain number of alternatives open. Also, you live in a world of reality where theories are constantly being corrected and curbed by experiment. Resultant facts accumulate and govern to a very large extent the next decision.

But suppose the whole process of war is transported out of the region of reality into that of imagination. Suppose you have to assume to begin with that there will be a war at all: secondly, that your country will be in it when it comes: thirdly, that you will go in as a united nation and that the nation will be united and convinced *in time*, and that the necessary measures will be taken before it is *too late*,—then the processes of thought become speculative indeed. Every set of assumptions which it is necessary to make, draws new veils of varying density in front of the dark curtain of the future. The life of the thoughtful soldier or sailor in time of peace is made up of these experiences—intense effort, amid every conceivable distraction, to pick out across and among a swarm of confusing hypotheses what actually will happen on a given day and what actually must be done to meet it before that day is ended. Meanwhile all around people, greatly superior in authority and often in intelligence, regard him as a plotting knave, or at the best an overgrown child playing with toys, and dangerous toys at that.

Therefore the most we could do in the days before the war was to attempt to measure and forecast what would happen to England on the outbreak and in the first few weeks of a war with Germany. To look farther was beyond the power of man. To try to do so was to complicate the task beyond mental endurance. The paths of thought bifurcated too rapidly. Would there be a great sea battle or not? What would happen then? Who would win the great land battle? No one could tell. Obviously the first thing was to be ready; not to be taken unawares: to be concentrated: not to be caught divided: to have the strongest Fleet possible in the best stations under the best conditions, and in good time, and then if the battle came one could await its result with a steady heart. Everything, therefore, to guard against surprise; everything, therefore, to guard against division: everything, therefore, to increase the strength of the forces available for the supreme sea battle.

But suppose the enemy did not fight a battle at sea. And suppose the battle on land was indeterminate in its results. And suppose the war went on not for weeks or months, but for years. Well, then it would be far easier to judge those matters at the time, and far easier then, when everybody was alarmed and awake and active, to secure the taking of the necessary steps; and there would be time to take them. No stage would be so difficult or so dangerous as the first stage. The problems of the second year of war must be dealt with by the experience of the first year of war. The problems of the third year of war must be met by results observed and understood in the second, and so on.

I repulse, therefore, on behalf of the Boards of Admiralty over which I presided down to the end of May, 1915, all reproaches directed to what occurred in 1917 and 1918. I cannot be stultified by any lessons arising out of those years. It is vain to tell me that if the Germans had built in the three years before the war, the submarines they built in the three years after it had begun, Britain would have been undone; or that if England had had in August, 1914, the Army which we possessed a year later, there would have been no war. Every set of circumstances involved every other set of circumstances. Would Germany in profound peace have been allowed by Great Britain to build an enormous fleet of submarines which could have no other object than the starvation and ruin of this island through the sinking of unarmed merchant ships? Would Germany have waited to attack France while England raised a powerful conscript army to go to her aid?

Every event must be judged in fair relation to the circumstances of the time, and only in such relation.

In examining the questions with which this chapter has been concerned, I was accustomed to dwell upon the dangers and the darker side of things. I did this to some extent intentionally, in order to create anxiety which would lead to timely precautions. Every danger set forth we tried to meet. Many we met. More never matured, either because they were prevented by proper measures, or because the Germans were less enterprising than I thought it prudent to assume. I will end on a more robust note.

The following letter was written by me on November 1, 1913, to a friend—a high naval authority—who had delivered a pessimistic lecture at the War College:—

> Do you not think you are looking at the problem from a weak and one-sided point of view which sees only the dangers which menace us and is blind to all the far greater dangers which surround the weaker fleet?
>
> Taking your hypothesis that the German Fleet come out to fight with every unit they can bring into line, why should it be supposed that we should not be able to defeat them? A study of the comparative fleet strength in the line of battle will be found reassuring.
>
> Why are our Second Fleet ships, which do not require a single reservist, to be considered less ready than German ships dependent on mobilized men?
>
> Why should it be supposed that a British Fleet is bound to fight the German Fleet at the exact time and place the German Fleet desires?

Why should we not, if we wish, refuse battle until any detached division has joined up?

Why should we be forced to follow the enemy on to his selected ground (presumably, from your paper, off our coasts) when a movement across his communications would not only place us in healthy waters, but cut him from his only hope of retreat and fuel?

Why should the British Battle Fleets have to fly the North Sea when the Germans apparently can move about in perfect safety?

All this drift of mind is pusillanimous. Put yourself for a few moments in the position of the Admiral Commanding the weaker fleet. If he goes out to fight 'with every unit,' he knows he must expect to be attacked by a force at least three to two superior in numbers, superior in addition in strength, and superior by far ship for ship, and squadron for squadron, in quality.

He knows he will have to move with his weaker force into waters which (to him) will appear 'infested' by 70 or 80 British submarines and over 200 sea-going torpedo craft. He knows that he must sooner or later, and sooner much rather than later, return to German ports to coal; and that if he is cut off either by the British Fleet or by the British submarines, or preferably by both, he runs the gravest risk of being not merely defeated but destroyed. If he tries to reduce his inferiority in the line of battle by attempting diversions in the shape of landings, he knows he will have to send transports crowded with men through waters commanded by an unfought superior enemy and swarming with torpedo craft, any one of which will send 5,000 or 6,000 men to the bottom.

If he succeeds by great good fortune, probably at a heavy sacrifice, in landing 15,000 or 20,000 men, he knows that is perfectly useless unless it can be reinforced by three or four times as many.

He knows that if his raid is not successfully supported within a very few days those already on shore will have been killed or captured, and he will have to begin all over again.

Lastly, he knows what people at manœuvres so often forget, viz., that cannons kill men and smash ships and that battles produce decisions against which there is no appeal.

He knows that it will pay his enemy to lose ship for ship with him in every class, and that when this melancholy process has run its full course, that enemy would still have on the water a fleet in being not less numerous than that with which Germany had begun the war.

If, knowing all this, the 'naturally offensive character of the German' leads him to come out and stake everything on a pitched battle, surely that ought to be a cause to us of profound satisfaction.

The second hypothesis—the war of harassments—is more indeterminate, and both sides may look about for some means of waiting on each other without undue risk, till decisive periods supervene. For after all a ship can only fight another ship when she meets her.

CHAPTER VIII
IRELAND AND THE EUROPEAN BALANCE

The Oil Reserves and Supply—The Anglo-Persian Agreement—The 1914 Estimates—The Rise of Naval Expenditure—The Canadian Ships—The Conflict over the Estimates—The Admiralty Case—A New Year's Declaration—Final Stage of the Estimates—The European Calm and the Anglo-German Détente—Renewed Efforts for an Anglo-German Naval Agreement—British Party Strife and Irish Feuds—Aggravation of the Irish Struggle—Faction—The Curragh Episode—Parliamentary Fury—Appeals to Reason—The Buckingham Palace Conference—Visits of the British Squadrons to Kiel and Kronstadt—The Crime of Sarajevo—The Sunlit World—Origin of the Test Mobilization—The Great Review.

During the whole of 1913 I was subjected to an evergrowing difficulty about the oil supply. We were now fully committed to oil as the sole motive power for a large proportion of the Fleet, including all the newest and most vital units. There was great anxiety on the Board of Admiralty and in the War Staff about our oil-fuel reserves. The Second Sea Lord, Sir John Jellicoe, vehemently pressed for very large increases in the scales contemplated. The Chief of the War Staff was concerned not only about the amount of the reserves, but about the alleged danger of using so explosive a fuel in ships of war. Lastly, Lord Fisher's Royal Commission, actuated by Admiralty disquietude, showed themselves inclined to press for a reserve equal to four year's expected war consumption. The war consumption itself had been estimated on the most liberal scale by the Naval Staff. The expense of creating the oil reserve was however enormous. Not only had the oil to be bought in a monopoly-ridden market, but large installations of oil tanks had to be erected and land purchased for the purpose. Although this oil-fuel reserve when created was clearly, whether for peace or war, as much an asset of the State as the gold reserve in the Bank of England, we were not allowed to treat it as capital expenditure: all must be found out of the current Estimates. At the same time, the Treasury and my colleagues in the Cabinet were becoming increasingly indignant at the naval expense, which it might be contended was largely due to my precipitancy in embarking on oil-burning battleships and also in wantonly increasing the size of the guns and the speed and armour of these vessels. On the one hand, therefore, I was subjected to this ever-growing naval pressure, and on the other to a solid wall of resistance to expense. In the midst of all lay the existence of our naval power.

I had thus to fight all the year on two fronts: on one to repulse the excessive and, as I thought, extravagant demands of the Royal Commission and of my naval advisers, and on the other to wrest the necessary supplies from the Treasury and the Cabinet. I had to be very careful that arguments intended for one front did not become known to my antagonists on the other. I wrote to Lord Fisher that to prescribe a four years' standard of reserves would be the deathblow to the oil policy of which he was the champion. I was forced to enter into arguments of extreme technical detail with the Second Sea Lord and the War Staff both as to the probable consumption per month of oil in the opening phases of a naval war, and secondly upon the number of months' supply that should be in the country in each individual month. I had extreme difficulties with the Board of Admiralty in regard to the reductions which I thought necessary in both scales, and I feared for some time that I should lose the services of the Second Sea Lord. This, however, was happily averted, and we finally agreed upon reduced scales which were in the end accepted by all concerned. These conclusions stood the test of war.

The reduced scales estimated a total consumption in the first ten months of war of 1,000,000 tons. The actual consumption was 800,000. At the end of the ten months we held 1,000,000 tons in reserve, or another twelve months' supply at the current rate of expenditure, apart from further purchases which proceeded ceaselessly on the greatest scale.

During this year (1913) also I carried through the House of Commons the Bill authorizing the Anglo-Persian Oil Convention. This encountered a confusing variety of oppositions—economists deprecating naval expenditure; members for mining constituencies who were especially sensible of the danger of departing from the sound basis of British coal; oil magnates who objected to a national inroad upon their monopolies; Conservatives who disapproved of State trading; partisan opponents who denounced the project as an unwarrantable gamble with public money and did not hesitate to impute actual corruption. There was always a danger of these divergent forces combining on some particular stage or point. However, we gradually threaded our way through these difficulties and by the Autumn the Convention was the law of the land. We now at any rate had an oil supply of our own.

All our financial commitments, fomented by rising prices and the ever-increasing complexity and refinement of naval appliances, came remorselessly to a head at the end of 1913 when the Estimates for the new year had to be presented first to the Treasury and then to the Cabinet. Knowing that the conflict would be most severe, I warned all Admiralty departments to be well ahead with their financial work and to prepare justification for the unprecedented demands we were obliged to make. We set forth our case in a volume of some eighty pages in which we analysed minutely each vote and marshalled our reasons. The main burden of this task fell upon the Financial Secretary, Dr. Macnamara, whose long experience of Admiralty business was invaluable.

We failed to reach any agreement with the Treasury in the preliminary discussions, and the whole issue was remitted to the Cabinet at the end of November. There followed nearly five months of extreme dispute and tension, during which Naval Estimates formed the main and often the sole topic of conversation at no less than fourteen full and prolonged meetings of the Cabinet. At the outset I found myself almost in a minority of one. I was not in a position to give way on any of the essentials, especially in regard to the Battleship programme, without departing from the calculated and declared standards of strength on which the whole of our policy towards Germany depended. The Cabinet had decided in 1912 to maintain equality in the Mediterranean with the Austrian Fleet, four Dreadnoughts of which were steadily building. Moreover, the issue was complicated by the promised three Canadian Dreadnoughts. The Canadian Government had stipulated that these should be additional to the 60 per cent, standard. We had formally declared that they were indispensable, and on this assurance Sir Robert Borden was committed to a fierce party fight in Canada. As it was now clear, owing to the action of the Canadian Senate, that these 'additional' 'indispensable' ships would not be laid down in the ensuing year, I was forced to demand the earlier laying down of three at least of the battleships of the 1914–15 programme. This was a very hard matter for the Cabinet to sanction. By the middle of December it seemed to me certain that I should have to resign. The very foundations of naval policy were challenged, and the controversy was maintained by Ministerial critics specially acquainted with Admiralty business, versed in every detail of the problem and entitled to be exactly informed on every point. The Prime Minister, however, while appearing to remain impartial, so handled matters that no actual breach occurred. On several occasions when it seemed that disagreement was total and final, he prevented a decision adverse to the Admiralty by terminating the discussion; and in the middle of December, when this process could go on no longer, he adjourned the whole matter till the middle of January.

I wrote to him on December 18:—

'Your letter is very kind, and I appreciate *fully* all the difficulties of the situation. But there is no chance whatever of my being able to go on, if the quota of capital ships for 1914–15 is reduced below four. Even the *Daily News* does not expect that. I base myself on (1) my public declarations in Parliament; (2) the 60 per cent, standard (see Minute of the Sea Lords); (3) the Cabinet decision on the Mediterranean; and (4) my obligations towards Mr. Borden. You must in this last aspect consider broad effects.

'If on a general *révirement* of Naval Policy the Cabinet decide to reduce the quota, it would be indispensable that a new exponent should be chosen. I have no doubts at all about my duty.

'My loyalty to you, my conviction of your superior judgment and superior record on naval matters, prompt me to go all possible lengths to prevent disagreement in the Cabinet. But no reduction or postponement beyond the year of the four ships is possible to me.

'I gathered that the final decision was to stand over till we reassemble in January. But there is no hope of any alteration in my view on this cardinal point, or of the view of my naval advisers.'

To the First Sea Lord I wrote on December 26:—

'I could not in any circumstances remain responsible if the declared programme of four ships were cut down. But my responsibility is greater than anyone else's, and I hold my naval colleagues perfectly free to review the situation without regard to the action which I should take in the circumstances which may now be apprehended.'

Prince Louis, however, assured me that he and the other Sea Lords would not remain in their appointments in the situation described. My two political colleagues, Dr. Macnamara and Mr. Lambert, the Civil Lord, were both stalwart Radicals, but there was no doubt that they also would have declined responsibility. They had both been at the Admiralty for six or seven years, and their devotion to the interests of the Navy and of the National Defence was unquestionable. We thus all stood together.

During the interval of the Christmas holidays, which I spent in the south of France, I restated the Admiralty case in the light of all the discussions which had taken place. The closing passages of this document may be reproduced.

The General Situation

No survey of British naval expenditure and no controversy arising out of it can be confined to our naval strength. It must also have regard to our military weakness compared to all the other European States that are building Navies. Even the modest establishments which Parliament has regarded as necessary have not been and are not being maintained. In 1913, when the five Great Powers of Europe have added over 50 millions to their military expenditure, when every Power in the world is increasing the numbers and efficiency of its soldiers, our regular army has dropped by 6,200 men. The Special Reserve is 20,000 short, and the Territorials are 65,000 short. Only the belief that the naval strength of the country is being effectively maintained prevents a widespread, and in important respects a well-justified, alarm. If at any time we lose the confidence which the country has given to our naval administration in the last 5 years, the public attention cannot fail to be turned into channels which, apart from raising awkward questions, will lead directly to largely increased expenditure.

Our naval standards and the programmes which give effect to them must also be examined in relation not only to Germany but to the rest of the world. We must begin by recognizing how different the part played by our Navy is from that of the Navies of every other country. Alone among the great modern States we can neither defend the soil upon which we live nor subsist upon its produce. Our whole regular army is liable to be ordered abroad for the defence of India. The food of our people, the raw material of their industries, the commerce which constitutes our wealth, has to be protected as it traverses thousands of miles of sea and ocean from every quarter of the globe. Our necessary insistence upon the right of capture of private property at sea exposes British merchant ships to the danger of attack not only by enemy warships but by converted armed-merchantmen. The burden of responsibility laid upon the British Navy is heavy, and its weight increases year by year.

All the world is building ships of the greatest power, training officers and men, creating arsenals, and laying broad and deep the foundations of future permanent naval development and expansion. In every country powerful interests and huge industries are growing up which will render any check or cessation in the growth of Navies increasingly difficult as time passes. Besides the Great Powers, there are many small States who are buying or building great ships of war and whose vessels may by purchase, by some diplomatic combination, or by duress, be brought into the line against us. None of these Powers need, like us, Navies to defend their actual safety or independence. They build them so as to play a part in the world's affairs. It is sport to them. It is death to us.

These possibilities were described by Lord Crewe in the House of Lords last year. It is not suggested that the whole world will turn upon us, or that our preparations should contemplate such a monstrous contingency. By a sober and modest conduct, by a skilful diplomacy, we can in part disarm and in part divide the elements of potential danger. But two things must be remembered. First, that our diplomacy depends in a great part for its effectiveness upon our naval position, and that our naval strength is the one great balancing force which we can contribute to our own safety and to the peace of the world. Secondly, we are not a young people with a scanty inheritance. We have engrossed to ourselves, in times when other powerful nations were paralysed by barbarism or internal war, an immense share of the wealth and traffic of the world. We have got all we want in territory, and our claim to be left in the unmolested enjoyment of vast and splendid possessions, often seems less reasonable to others than to us.

Further, we do not always play the humble rôle of passive unassertiveness. We have intervened regularly—as it was our duty to do, and as we could not help doing—in the affairs of Europe and of the world. We are now deeply involved in the European situation. We have responsibilities in many quarters. It is only two years ago that the Chancellor of the Exchequer went to the Mansion House and delivered a speech which to save Europe from war, brought us to the very verge of it. I have myself heard the Foreign Secretary say to my predecessor that he had received so stiff a communication from the German Ambassador, that the Fleet must be placed in a condition of readiness to be attacked at any moment. The impression which those events produced in my mind is ineffaceable. I saw that even a Liberal Government, whose first and most profound resolve must always be to preserve peace, might be compelled to face the gravest and most hateful possibilities. All Governments in England will not be Liberal Governments; all Foreign Secretaries will not have the success of Sir Edward Grey. We have passed through a year of continuous anxiety and, although I believe the foundations of peace among the Great Powers have been strengthened, the causes which might lead to a general war have not been removed and often remind us of their presence. There has not been the slightest abatement of naval and military preparation. On the contrary, we are witnessing this year increases of expenditure by the Continental Powers beyond all previous experience. The world is arming as it has never armed before. Every suggestion of arrest or limitation has been brushed aside. From time to time awkward things happen, and situations occur which make it necessary that the

> naval force at our immediate disposal, now in this quarter now in that, should be rapidly counted up. On such occasions the responsibilities which rest on the Admiralty come home with brutal reality to the Minister at its head, and unless our naval strength is solidly, amply and unswervingly maintained, with due and fair regard to the opinions of the professional advisers of the Government, I could not feel that I was doing my duty if I did not warn the country of its danger.

The memorandum and the interval for reflection produced a certain change in the situation, and on my return to England in the middle of January, I was informed by several of my most important colleagues that they considered the Admiralty case on main essentials had been made good. The conflict, however, renewed itself with the utmost vigour. We continued to pump out documents and arguments from the Admiralty in a ceaseless stream, dealing with each new point as it was challenged. I telegraphed to Sir Robert Borden acquainting him with the crisis that was developing about the three ships to be accelerated in lieu of the Canadian Dreadnoughts, informing him of my intention to resign if unsuccessful, and invoking his aid by a full exposition of the Canadian point of view. This he most readily gave, setting forth in a masterly telegram the embarrassed position in which his Government would stand in their naval effort if no additional measure were taken by us to cover their interim default.

Meanwhile, echoes of the controversy had found their way into the newspapers. As early as January 3, the Chancellor of the Exchequer, in an interview with the *Daily Chronicle*, had deplored the folly of expenditure upon armaments, had pointedly referred to the resignation of Lord Randolph Churchill on the subject of economy, and had expressed the opinion that the state and prospects of the world were never more peaceful. The Liberal and Radical press were loud in their economy chorus, and a very strong movement against the Admiralty developed among our most influential supporters in the House of Commons. However, Parliament soon reassembled. The Irish question began to dominate attention. Eager partisans of the Home Rule cause were by no means anxious to see the Government weakened by the resignation of the entire Board of Admiralty. We were already so hard pressed in the party struggle that the defection even of a single Minister might have produced a serious effect. No one expected me to pass away in sweet silence. The prospect of a formidable naval agitation added to the Irish tension was recognized as uninviting. In order to strengthen myself with my party, I mingled actively in the Irish controversy; and in this precarious situation the whole of February and part of March passed without any ground given or taken on either side.

At last, thanks to the unwearying patience of the Prime Minister, and to his solid, silent support, the Naval Estimates were accepted practically as they stood. In all these months of bickering we had only lost three small cruisers and twelve torpedo-boats for harbour defence. Estimates were presented to Parliament for 52½ millions. We had not secured this victory without being compelled to give certain general assurances with regard to the future. I agreed, under proper reserves, to promise a substantial reduction on the Estimates of the following year.

But when the time came, I was not pressed to redeem this undertaking.

* * * * *

The spring and summer of 1914 were marked in Europe by an exceptional tranquillity. Ever since Agadir the policy of Germany towards Great Britain had not only been correct, but considerate. All through the tangle of the Balkan Conferences British and German diplomacy laboured in harmony. The long distrust which had grown up in the Foreign Office, though not removed, was sensibly modified. Some at least of those who were accustomed to utter warnings began to feel the need of revising their judgment. The personalities who expressed the foreign policy of Germany, seemed for the first time to be men to whom we could talk and with whom common action was possible. The peaceful solution of the Balkan difficulties afforded justification for the feeling of confidence. For months we had negotiated upon the most delicate questions on the brink of local rupture, and no rupture had come. There had been a score of opportunities had any Power wished to make war. Germany seemed, with us, to be set on peace. Although abroad the increase of armaments was proceeding with constant acceleration, although the fifty million capital tax had been levied in Germany, and that alarm bell was ringing for those that had ears to hear, a distinct feeling of optimism passed over the mind of the British Government and the House of Commons. There seemed also to be a prospect that the personal goodwill and mutual respect which had grown up between the principal people on both sides might play a useful part in the future; and some there were who looked forward to a wider combination in which Great Britain and Germany, without prejudice to their respective friendships or alliances, might together bring the two opposing European systems into harmony and give to all the anxious nations solid assurances of safety and fair-play.

Naval rivalry had at the moment ceased to be a cause of friction. We were proceeding inflexibly for the third year in succession with our series of programmes according to scale and declaration. Germany had made no further increases since the beginning of 1912. It was certain that we could not be overtaken as far as capital ships were concerned. I thought that the moment was opportune to renew by another method the conversations about a naval agreement if not a naval holiday, which had been interrupted in 1912. I therefore suggested to the Foreign Secretary that I should meet Admiral von Tirpitz if a convenient opportunity presented itself, and I set out in the following minute some of the points which I thought might be discussed and which, though small, if agreed upon, would make for easement and stability.

May 20, 1914.

Prime Minister.
Sir Edward Grey.

In Madrid at Easter, Sir Ernest Cassel told me that he had received from Herr Ballin a statement to this effect: 'How I wish that I could get Churchill here during the Kiel Week. Tirpitz will never allow the Chancellor to settle any naval questions, but I know he would like to have a talk with his English colleague on naval matters, and I am sure that if the subject of limiting naval armaments were ever approached in a businesslike way, some agreement would be reached.' On the same day I received a telegram from the Admiralty, saying that the Foreign Office particularly wished a British squadron to visit German ports simultaneously with other naval visits. Personally I should like to meet Tirpitz, and I think a non-committal, friendly conversation, if it arose naturally and freely, might do good, and could not possibly do any harm. Indeed, after all I have said about a Naval Holiday, it would be difficult for me to repulse any genuine desire on his part for such a conversation. The points I wish to discuss are these:—

1st. My own Naval Holiday proposals and to show him, as I can easily do, the good faith and sound reasons on which they are based. I do not expect any agreement on these, but I would like to strip the subject of the misrepresentation and misunderstanding with which it has been surrounded, and put it on a clear basis in case circumstances should ever render it admissible.

2nd. I wish to take up with him the suggestion which he made in his last speech on Naval Estimates of a limitation in the size of capital ships. Even if numbers could not be touched, a limitation in the size would be a great saving, and is on every ground to be desired. This subject could only be satisfactorily explored by direct personal discussion in the first instance.

3rd. I wish to encourage him to send German ships to foreign stations by showing him how much we wish to do the same, and how readily we shall conform to any dispositions which have the effect of reducing the unwholesome concentration of fleets in Home Waters. Quite apart from the diplomatic aspect, it is bad for the discipline and organization of both navies, and the Germans fully recognize this.

4th. I wish to discuss the abandonment of secrecy in regard to the numbers and general characteristics (apart from special inventions) of the ships, built and building, in British and German dockyards. This policy of secrecy was instituted by the British Admiralty a few years ago with the worst results for us, for we have been much less successful in keeping our secrets than the Germans. I should propose to him in principle that we give the Naval Attachés equal and reciprocal facilities to visit the dockyards and see what was going on just as they used to do in the past. If this could be agreed upon it would go a long way to stopping the espionage on both sides which is a continued cause of suspicion and ill-feeling.

I hope, in view of the very strong feeling there is about naval expenditure and the great difficulties I have to face, my wish to put these points to Admiral von Tirpitz if a good opportunity arises, and if it is clear that he would not resent it, may not be dismissed. On the other hand, I do not wish to go to Germany for the purpose of initiating such a discussion. I would rather go for some other reason satisfactory in itself, and let the discussion of these serious questions come about only if it is clearly appropriate. . . .

For the present I suggest that nothing should be done until the Emperor's invitation arrives; and, secondly, until we hear what Tirpitz's real wish is.

W. S. C.

Sir Edward Grey was apprehensive that more harm than good might result from such a discussion, and I do not myself pronounce upon the point; but I am anxious to place the letter on record as a proof of my desire, while maintaining our naval position, to do all that could be done to mitigate asperity between the British and German Empires.

* * * * *

The strange calm of the European situation contrasted with the rising fury of party conflict at home. The quarrel between Liberals and Conservatives had taken on much of that tense bitterness and hatred belonging to Irish affairs. As it became certain that the Home Rule Bill would pass into law under the machinery of the Parliament Act, the Protestant counties of Ulster openly developed their preparations for armed resistance. In this they were supported and encouraged by the whole Conservative party. The Irish Nationalist leaders—Mr. Redmond, Mr. Dillon, Mr. Devlin and others—watched the increasing gravity of the situation in Ulster with apprehension. But there were elements behind them whose fierceness and whose violence were indescribable; and every step or gesture of moderation on the part of the Irish Parliamentary Party excited passionate anger. Between these difficulties Mr. Asquith's Government sought to thread their way.

From the earliest discussions on the Home Rule Bill in 1909 the Chancellor of the Exchequer and I had always advocated the exclusion of Ulster on a basis of county option or some similar process. We had been met by the baffling argument that such a concession might well be made as the final means of securing a settlement, but would be fruitless till then. The time had now arrived when the Home Rule issue had reached its supreme climax, and the Cabinet was generally agreed that we could not go farther without providing effectually for the exclusion of Ulster. In March, therefore, the Irish leaders were informed that the Government had so resolved. They resisted vehemently. They had it in their power at any time to turn out the Government, and they would have been powerfully reinforced from within the Liberal Party itself. There is no doubt that the Irish leaders feared, and even expected, that any weakening of the Bill would lead to its and their repudiation by the Irish people. Confronted, however, with the undoubted fact that the Government would not shrink from being defeated and broken up on the point, they yielded. Amendments were framed which secured to any Ulster county the right to vote itself out of the Home Rule Bill until after two successive General Elections had taken place in the United Kingdom. There could be no greater practical safeguard than this. It preserved the principle of Irish unity, but it made certain that unity could never be achieved except by the free consent of the Protestant North after seeing a Dublin Parliament actually on trial for a period of at least five years.

These proposals were no sooner announced to Parliament than they were rejected with contumely by the Conservative opposition. We, however, embodied them in the text of the Bill and compelled the Irish Party to vote for their inclusion. We now felt that we could go forward with a clear conscience and enforce the law against all who challenged it. My own personal view had always been that I would never coerce Ulster to make her come under a Dublin Parliament, but I would do all that was necessary to prevent her stopping the rest of Ireland having the Parliament they desired. I believe this was sound and right, and in support of it I was certainly prepared to maintain the authority of Crown and Parliament under the Constitution by whatever means were necessary. I spoke in this sense at Bradford on March 14.

It is greatly to be hoped that British political leaders will never again allow themselves to be goaded and spurred and driven by each other or by their followers into the excesses of partisanship which on both sides disgraced the year 1914, and which were themselves only the culmination of that long succession of biddings and counter-biddings for mastery to which a previous chapter has alluded. No one who has not been involved in such contentions can understand the intensity of the pressures to which public men are subjected, or the way in which every motive in their nature, good, bad and indifferent, is marshalled in the direction of further effort to secure victory. The vehemence with which great masses of men yield themselves to partisanship and follow the struggle as if it were a prize fight, their ardent enthusiasm, their glistening eyes, their swift anger, their distrust and contempt if they think they are to be baulked of their prey; the sense of wrongs mutually interchanged, the extortion and enforcement of pledges, the infectious loyalties, the praise that waits on violence; the chilling disdain, the honest disappointment, the cries of 'treachery' with which every proposal of compromise is hailed; the desire to keep good faith with those who follow, the sense of right being on one's side, the harsh unreasonable actions of opponents—all these acting and reacting reciprocally upon one another tend towards the perilous climax. To fall behind is to be a laggard or a weakling, not sincere, not courageous; to get in front of the crowd, if only to command them and to deflect them, prompts often very violent action. And at a certain stage it is hardly possible to keep the contention within the limits of words or laws. Force, that final arbiter, that last soberer, may break upon the scene.

The preparations of the Ulstermen continued. They declared their intention of setting up a provisional Government. They continued to develop and train their forces. They imported arms unlawfully and even by violence. It need scarcely be said that the same kind of symptoms began to manifest themselves among the Nationalists. Volunteers were enrolled by thousands, and efforts were made to procure arms.

As all this peril grew, the small military posts in the North of Ireland, particularly those containing stores of arms, became a source of preoccupation to the War Office. So also did the position of the troops in Belfast. The Orangemen would never have harmed the Royal forces. It was more than probable that the troops would fraternize with them. But the Government saw themselves confronted with a complete overturn of their authority throughout North-East Ulster. In these circumstances, military and naval precautions were indispensable. On 14th March it was determined to protect the military stores at Carrickfergus and certain other places by small reinforcements, and as it was expected that the Great Northern Railway of Ireland would refuse to carry the troops, preparations were made to send them by sea. It was also decided to move a battle squadron and a flotilla from Arosa Bay, where they were cruising, to Lamlash, whence they could rapidly reach Belfast. It was thought that the popularity and influence of the Royal Navy might produce a peaceable solution, even if the Army had failed. Beyond this nothing was authorized; but the Military Commanders, seeing themselves confronted with what might well be the opening movements in a civil war, began to study plans of a much more serious character on what was the inherently improbable assumption that the British troops would be forcibly resisted and fired upon by the Orange army.

These military measures, limited though they were, and the possible consequences that might follow them, produced the greatest distress among the officers of the Army, and when on 20th March the Commander-in-Chief in Ireland and other Generals made sensational appeals to gatherings of officers at the Curragh to discharge their constitutional duty in all circumstances, they encountered very general refusals.

These shocking events caused an explosion of unparalleled fury in Parliament and shook the State to its foundations. The Conservatives accused the Government of having plotted the massacre of the loyalists of Ulster, in which design they had been frustrated only by the patriotism of the Army. The Liberals replied that the Opposition were seeking to subvert the Constitution by openly committing themselves to preparations for rebellion, and had seduced not the Army but its officers from their allegiance by propaganda. We cannot read the debates that continued at intervals through April, May and June, without wondering that our Parliamentary institutions were strong enough to survive the passions by which they were convulsed. Was it astonishing that German agents reported and German statesmen believed, that England was paralysed by faction and drifting into civil war, and need not be taken into account as a factor in the European situation? How could they discern or measure the deep unspoken understandings which lay far beneath the froth and foam and fury of the storm?

In all these scenes I played a prominent and vehement part, but I never doubted for a moment the strength of the foundation on which we rested. I felt sure in my own mind that, now that the sting was out of the Home Rule Bill, nothing in the nature of civil war would arise. On the contrary I hoped for a settlement with the Conservative Party not only upon the Home Rule Bill with Ulster excluded, but also on other topics which ever since 1909 had been common ground between some of those who were disputing so angrily. I felt, however, that the Irish crisis must move forward to its climax, and that a reasonable settlement could only be reached in the recoil.

On the 28th April I closed a partisan reply to a violent attack with the following direct appeal to Sir Edward Carson:—

> 'I adhere to my Bradford speech. . . but I will venture to ask the House once more at this moment in our differences and quarrels to consider whither it is we may find ourselves going. . . . Apart from the dangers which this controversy and this Debate clearly show exist at home, look at the consequences abroad.
>
> 'Anxiety is caused in every friendly country by the belief that for the time being Great Britain cannot act. The high mission of this country is thought to be in abeyance, and the balance of Europe appears in many quarters for the time being to be deranged. Of course, foreign countries never really understand us in these islands. They do not know what we know, that at a touch of external difficulties or menace all these fierce internal controversies would disappear for the time being,

and we should be brought into line and into tune. But why is it that men are so constituted that they can only lay aside their own domestic quarrels under the impulse of what I will call a higher principle of hatred? . . .

'Why cannot the right hon. and learned Gentleman (Sir Edward Carson) say boldly, "Give me the Amendments to this Home Rule Bill which I ask for, to safeguard the dignity and the interests of Protestant Ulster, and I in return will use all my influence and goodwill to make Ireland an integral unit in a federal system"?'

These words gave the debate an entirely new turn. The Prime Minister said the next day, 'The First Lord's proposal was made on his own account, but I am heartily in sympathy with it.' Mr. Balfour declared that it had 'the promise and the potency of a settlement which would avoid this final and irreparable catastrophe of civil war.' Later, Sir Edward Carson, after laying stress on the gravity of the crisis and the weakening it entailed of the position of Great Britain abroad, declared that he would not quarrel with the matter or the manner of my proposal, and that 'he was not very far from the First Lord.' If Home Rule passed, his most earnest hope would be that it might be such a success that Ulster might come under it, and that mutual confidence and goodwill might arise in Ireland, rendering Ulster a stronger unit in the federal scheme.

These potent indications were not comprehended on the Continent.

During the whole of May and June the party warfare proceeded in its most strident form, but underneath the surface, negotiations for a settlement between the two great parties were steadily persisted in. Thesc eventuated on the 20th July in a summons by the King to the leaders of the Conservative, Liberal and Irish parties to meet in conference at Buckingham Palace. When this conference was in its most critical stage I wrote the following letter to Sir Edward Grey: the wording is curious in view of the fact that I had then no idea of what the next forty-eight hours was to produce. On this I am content to rest so far as the Irish question before the war is concerned.

Mr. Churchill to Sir Edward Grey.

July 22, 1914.

. . . Failing an Irish agreement there ought to be a British decision. Carson and Redmond, whatever their wishes, may be unable to agree about Tyrone; they may think it worth a war; and from their point of view it may be worth a war. But that is hardly the position of the forty millions who dwell in Great Britain; and their interests must, when all is said and done, be our chief and final care. In foreign affairs you would proceed by two stages. First you would labour to stop Austria and Russia going to war; second, if that failed, you would try to prevent England, France, Germany and Italy being drawn in. Exactly what you would do in Europe, is right in this domestic danger, with the difference that in Europe the second step would only hope to limit and localize the conflict, whereas at home the second step—if practicable and adopted—would prevent the local conflict.

The conference therefore should labour to reduce the difference to the smallest definite limits possible. At that point, if no agreement had been reached, the Speaker should be asked to propose a partition; and we should offer the Unionist leaders to accept it if *they* will. . . .

I want peace by splitting the outstanding differences, if possible with Irish acquiescence, but if necessary over the heads of both Irish parties.

* * * * *

At the end of June the simultaneous British naval visits to Kronstadt and Kiel took place. For the first time for several years some of the finest ships of the British and German Navies lay at their moorings at Kiel side by side surrounded by liners, yachts and pleasure craft of every kind. Undue curiosity in technical matters was banned by mutual agreement. There were races, there were banquets, there were speeches. There was sunshine, there was the Emperor. Officers and men fraternized and entertained each other afloat and ashore. Together they strolled arm in arm through the hospitable town, or dined with all goodwill in mess and wardroom. Together they stood bareheaded at the funeral of a German officer killed in flying an English seaplane.

In the midst of these festivities, on June 28, arrived the news of the murder of the Archduke Charles at Sarajevo. The Emperor was out sailing when he received it. He came on shore in noticeable agitation, and that same evening, cancelling his other arrangements, quitted Kiel.

Like many others, I often summon up in my memory the impression of those July days. The world on the verge of its catastrophe was very brilliant. Nations and Empires crowned with princes and potentates rose majestically on every side, lapped in the accumulated treasures of the long peace. All were fitted and fastened—it seemed securely—into an immense cantilever. The two mighty European systems faced each other glittering and clanking in their panoply, but with a tranquil gaze. A polite, discreet, pacific, and on the whole sincere diplomacy spread its web of connections over both. A sentence in a despatch, an observation by an ambassador, a cryptic phrase in a Parliament seemed sufficient to adjust from day to day the balance of the prodigious structure. Words counted, and even whispers. A nod could be made to tell. Were we after all to achieve world security and universal peace by a marvellous system of combinations in equipoise and of armaments in equation, of checks and counter-checks on violent action ever more complex and more delicate? Would Europe thus marshalled, thus grouped, thus related, unite into one universal and glorious organism capable of receiving and enjoying in undreamed of abundance the bounty which nature and science stood hand in hand to give? The old world in its sunset was fair to see.

But there was a strange temper in the air. Unsatisfied by material prosperity the nations turned restlessly towards strife internal or external. National passions, unduly exalted in the decline of religion, burned beneath the surface of nearly every land with fierce, if shrouded, fires. Almost one might think the world wished to suffer. Certainly men were everywhere eager to dare. On all sides the military preparations, precautions and counter precautions had reached their height. France had her Three Years' military service; Russia her growing strategic Railways. The Ancient Empire of the Hapsburgs, newly smitten by the bombs of Sarajevo, was a prey to intolerable racial stresses and profound processes of decay. Italy faced Turkey; Turkey confronted Greece; Greece, Serbia and Roumania stood against Bulgaria. Britain was rent by faction and seemed almost negligible. America was three thousand miles away. Germany, her fifty million capital tax expended on munitions, her army increases completed, the Kiel Canal open for Dreadnought battleships that very month, looked fixedly upon the scene and her gaze became suddenly a glare.

* * * * *

In the autumn of 1913, when I was revolving the next year's Admiralty policy in the light of the coming Estimates, I had sent the following minute to the First Sea Lord:—

October 22, 1913.

First Sea Lord.
Second Sea Lord.
Secretary

We have now had manœuvres in the North Sea on the largest scale for two years running, and we have obtained a great deal of valuable data which requires to be studied. It does not therefore seem necessary to supplement the ordinary tactical exercises of the year 1914–15 by Grand Manœuvres. A saving of nearly £200,000 could apparently be effected in coal and oil consumption, and a certain measure of relief would be accorded to the Estimates in an exceptionally heavy year.

In these circumstances I am drawn to the conclusion that it would be better to have no Grand Manœuvres in 1914–15, but to substitute instead a mobilization of the Third Fleet. The whole of the Royal Fleet Reserve, and the whole of the Reserve officers could be mobilized and trained together for a week or ten days. The Third Fleet ships would be given the exact complements they would have in war, and the whole mobilization system would be subjected to a real test. The balance Fleet Reservists could be carefully tested as to quality, and trained either afloat or ashore. I should anticipate that this would not cost more than £100,000, in which case there would still be a saving on the fuel of the manœuvres. While the Third Fleet ships were mobilized the First Fleet ships would rest, and thus plenty of officers would be available for the training of the reservists on shore, and possibly, if need be, for their peace training afloat. This last would, of course, reveal what shortage exists. A very large staff would be employed at all the mobilizing centres to report upon the whole workings of the mobilization. The schools and training establishments would be closed temporarily according to the mobilization orders, and the whole process of putting the Navy on a war footing, so far as the Third Fleet was concerned, would be carried out. I should not propose to complete the Second Fleet, as we know all about that.

At another time in the year I should desire to see mobilized the whole of the Royal Naval Volunteer Reserve, and put them afloat on First Fleet ships for a week as additional to complements.

Please put forward definite proposals, with estimates, for carrying out the above policy, and at the same time let me have your opinion upon it.

W. S. C.

Prince Louis agreed. The necessary measures were taken and the project was mentioned to Parliament on the 18th March, 1914. In pursuance of these orders and without connection of any kind with the European situation, the Test Mobilization began on the 15th July. Although there was no legal authority to compel the reservists to come up, the response was general, upwards of 20,000 men presenting themselves at the naval depôts. The whole of our mobilization arrangements were thus subjected for the first time in naval history to a practical test and thorough overhaul. Officers specially detached from the Admiralty watched the process of mobilization at every port in order that every defect, shortage or hitch in the system might be reported and remedied. Prince Louis and I personally inspected the process at Chatham. All the reservists drew their kits and proceeded to their assigned ships. All the Third Fleet ships coaled and raised steam and sailed for the general concentration at Spithead. Here on the 17th and 18th of July was held the grand review of the Navy. It constituted incomparably the greatest assemblage of naval power ever witnessed in the history of the world. The King himself was present and inspected ships of every class. On the morning of the 19th the whole Fleet put to sea for exercises of various kinds. It took more than six hours for this armada, every ship decked with flags and crowded with bluejackets and marines, to pass, with bands playing and at 15 knots, before the Royal Yacht, while overhead the naval seaplanes and aeroplanes circled continuously. Yet it is probable that the uppermost thought in the minds both of the Sovereign and those of his Ministers there present, was not the imposing spectacle of British majesty and might defiling before their eyes, not the oppressive and even sultry atmosphere of continental politics, but the haggard, squalid, tragic Irish quarrel which threatened to divide the British nation into two hostile camps.

One after another the ships melted out of sight beyond the Nab. They were going on a longer voyage than any of us could know.

CHAPTER IX
THE CRISIS: JULY 24–JULY 30

'Prepare, prepare the iron helm of war,
Bring forth the lots, cast in the spacious orb;
The Angel of Fate turns them with mighty hands,
And casts them out upon the darkened earth!
Prepare, prepare!'

Blake.

Cabinet of Friday, July 24—Fermanagh and Tyrone—The Austrian Ultimatum to Serbia—Seventeen Points to remember—The Naval Position—The Mission of Herr Ballin—Sunday, July 26—The Fleet held together—The Admiralty Communiqué—The Cabinet and the Crisis—The Policy of Sir Edward Grey: Cardinal Points—Belgium and France—Was there an Alternative?—Justice to France—Naval Preparations of July 27 and 28—The Precautionary Period—The Turkish Battleships—What the German Admiralty knew—German Agents—The Decisive Step—Passage of the Straits of Dover by the Fleet, July 30—The Fleet in its War Station—The King's Ships at Sea.

The Cabinet on Friday afternoon sat long revolving the Irish problem. The Buckingham Palace Conference had broken down. The disagreements and antagonisms seemed as fierce and as hopeless as ever, yet the margin in dispute, upon which such fateful issues hung, was inconceivably petty. The discussion turned principally upon the boundaries of Fermanagh and Tyrone. To this pass had the Irish factions in their insensate warfare been able to drive their respective British champions. Upon the disposition of these clusters of humble parishes turned at that moment the political future of Great Britain. The North would not agree to this, and the South would not agree to that. Both the leaders wished to settle; both had dragged their followers forward to the utmost point they dared. Neither seemed able to give an inch. Meanwhile, the settlement of Ireland must carry with it an immediate and decisive abatement of party strife in Britain, and those schemes of unity and co-operation which had so intensely appealed to the leading men on both sides, ever since Mr. Lloyd George had mooted them in 1910, must necessarily have come forward into the light of day. Failure to settle on the other hand meant something very like civil war and the plunge into depths of which no one could make any measure. And so, turning this way and that in search of an exit from toe deadlock, the Cabinet toiled around the muddy byways of Fermanagh and Tyrone. One had hoped that the events of April at the Curragh and in Belfast would have shocked British public opinion, and formed a unity sufficient to impose a settlement on the Irish factions. Apparently they had been insufficient. Apparently the conflict would be carried one stage further by both sides with incalculable consequences before there would be a recoil. Since the days of the Blues and the Greens in the Byzantine Empire, partisanship had rarely been carried to more absurd extremes. An all-sufficient shock was, however, at hand.

The discussion had reached its inconclusive end, and the Cabinet was about to separate, when the quiet grave tones of Sir Edward Grey's voice were heard reading a document which had just been brought to him from the Foreign Office. It was the Austrian note to Serbia. He had been reading or speaking for several minutes before I could disengage my mind from the tedious and bewildering debate which had just closed. We were all very tired, but gradually as the phrases and sentences followed one another, impressions of a wholly different character began to form in my mind. This note was clearly an ultimatum; but it was an ultimatum such as had never been penned in modern times. As the reading proceeded it seemed absolutely impossible that any State in the world could accept it, or that any acceptance, however abject, would satisfy the aggressor. The parishes of Fermanagh and Tyrone faded back into the mists and squalls of Ireland, and a strange light began immediately, but by perceptible gradations, to fall and grow upon the map of Europe.

I always take the greatest interest in reading accounts of how the war came upon different people; where they were, and what they were doing, when the first impression broke on their mind, and they first began to feel this overwhelming event laying its fingers on their lives. I never tire of the smallest detail, and I believe that so long as they are true and unstudied they will have a definite value and an enduring interest for posterity; so I shall briefly record exactly what happened to me.

I went back to the Admiralty at about 6 o'clock. I said to my friends who have helped me so many years in my work[1] that there was real danger and that it might be war.

I took stock of the position, and wrote out to focus them in my mind a series of points which would have to be attended to if matters did not mend. My friends kept these as a check during the days that followed and ticked them off one by one as they were settled.[2]

1. First and Second Fleets. Leave and disposition.
2. Third Fleet. Replenish coal and stores.
3. Mediterranean movements.
4. China dispositions.
5. Shadowing cruisers abroad.
6. Ammunition for self-defensive merchantmen.

---

[1]Mr Marsh and Mr. (now Sir James) Masterton Smith.

[2]See p. 136.

7. Patrol Flotillas. Disposition.
   Leave.
   Complete.
   35 ex-Coastals.
8. Immediate Reserve.
9. Old Battleships for Humber. Flotilla for Humber.
10. Ships at emergency dates. Ships building for Foreign Powers.
11. Coastal Watch.
12. Anti-aircraft guns at Oil Depôts.
13. Aircraft to Sheerness. Airships and Seaplanes.
14. K. Espionage.
15. Magazines and other vulnerable points.
16. Irish ships.
17. Submarine dispositions.

I discussed the situation at length the next morning (Saturday) with the First Sea Lord. For the moment, however, there was nothing to do. At no time in all these last three years were we more completely ready.

The test mobilization had been completed, and with the exception of the Immediate Reserve, all the reservists were already paid off and journeying to their homes. But the whole of the 1st and 2nd Fleets were complete in every way for battle and were concentrated at Portland, where they were to remain till Monday morning at 7 o'clock, when the 1st Fleet would disperse by squadrons for various exercises and when the ships of the 2nd Fleet would proceed to their Home Ports to discharge their balance crews. Up till Monday morning therefore, a word instantaneously transmitted from the wireless masts of the Admiralty to the *Iron Duke* would suffice to keep our main force together. If the word were not spoken before that hour, they would begin to separate. During the first twenty-four hours after their separation they could be reconcentrated in an equal period; but if no word were spoken for forty-eight hours (i.e. by Wednesday morning), then the ships of the 2nd Fleet would have begun dismissing their balance crews to the shore at Portsmouth, Plymouth and Chatham, and the various gunnery and torpedo schools would have recommenced their instruction. If another forty-eight hours had gone before the word was spoken, i.e. by Friday morning, a certain number of vessels would have gone into dock for refit, repairs or laying up. Thus on the Saturday morning we had the Fleet in hand for at least four days.

The night before (Friday), at dinner, I had met Herr Ballin. He had just arrived from Germany. We sat next to each other, and I asked him what he thought about the situation. With the first few words he spoke, it became clear that he had not come here on any mission of pleasure. He said the situation was grave. 'I remember,' he said, 'old Bismarck telling me the year before he died that one day the great European War would come out of some damned foolish thing in the Balkans.' These words, he said, might come true.

Points

1. [illegible]
2. [illegible]
3. [illegible]
4. [illegible]
5. [illegible] abroad.
6. Ammunition for Self Defensive Merchantmen.
7. [illegible]
8. [illegible]
9. [illegible]
10. [illegible]
11. [illegible]
12. [illegible]
13. [illegible]
14. K. espionage
15. [illegible]
16. Irish ships
17. Submarine dispositions

Seventeen Points to Remember

It all depended on the Tsar. What would he do if Austria chastised Serbia? A few years before there would have been no danger, as the Tsar was too frightened for his throne, but now again he was feeling himself more secure upon his throne, and the Russian people besides would feel very hardly anything done against Serbia. Then he said, 'If Russia marches against Austria, we must march; and if we march, France must march, and what would England do?' I was not in a position to say more than that it would be a great mistake to assume that England would necessarily do nothing, and I added that she would judge events as they arose. He replied, speaking with very great earnestness. 'Suppose we had to go to war with Russia and France, and suppose we defeated France and yet took nothing from her in Europe, not an inch of her territory, only some colonies to indemnify us. Would that make a difference to England's attitude? Suppose we gave a guarantee beforehand.' I stuck to my formula that England would judge events as they arose, and that it would be a mistake to assume that we should stand out of it whatever happened.

I reported this conversation to Sir Edward Grey in due course, and early in the following week I repeated it to the Cabinet. On the Wednesday following the exact proposal mooted to me by Herr Ballin, about Germany not taking any territorial conquests in France but seeking indemnities only in the colonies, was officially telegraphed to us from Berlin and immediately rejected. I have no doubt that Herr Ballin was directly charged by the Emperor with the mission to find out what England would do.

Herr Ballin has left on record his impression of his visit to England at this juncture. 'Even a moderately skilled German diplomatist,' he wrote, 'could easily have come to an understanding with England and France, who could have made peace certain and prevented Russia from beginning war.' The editor of his memoirs adds: 'The people in London were certainly seriously concerned at-the Austrian Note, but the extent to which the Cabinet desired the maintenance of peace may be seen (as an example) from the remark which Churchill, almost with tears in his eyes, made to Ballin as they parted: "My dear friend, don't let us go to war."'

I had planned to spend the Sunday with my family at Cromer, and I decided not to alter my plans. I arranged to have a special operator placed in the telegraph office so as to ensure a continuous night and day service. On Saturday afternoon the news came in that Serbia had accepted the ultimatum. I went to bed with a feeling things might blow over. We had had, as this account has shown, so many scares before. Time after time the clouds had loomed up vague, menacing, constantly changing; time after time they had dispersed. We were still a long way, as it seemed, from any danger of war. Serbia had accepted the ultimatum, could Austria demand more? And if war came, could it not be confined to the East of Europe? Could not France and Germany, for instance, stand aside and leave Russia and Austria to settle their quarrel? And then, one step further removed, was our own case. Clearly there would be a chance of a conference, there would be time for Sir Edward Grey to get to work with conciliatory processes such as had proved so effective in the Balkan difficulties the year before. Anyhow, whatever happened, the British Navy had never been in a better condition or in greater strength. Probably the call would not come, but if it did, it could not come in a better hour. Reassured by these reflections I slept peacefully, and no summons disturbed the silence of the night.

At 9 o'clock the next morning I called up the First Sea Lord by telephone. He told me that there was a rumour that Austria was not satisfied with the Serbian acceptance of the ultimatum, but otherwise there were no new developments. I asked him to call me up again at twelve. I went down to the beach and played with the children. We dammed the little rivulets which trickled down to the sea as the tide went out. It was a very beautiful day. The North Sea shone and sparkled to a far horizon. What was there beyond that line where sea and sky melted into one another? All along the East Coast, from Cromarty to Dover, in their various sally-ports, lay our patrol flotillas of destroyers and submarines. In the Channel behind the torpedo-proof moles of Portland Harbour waited all the great ships of the British Navy. Away to the north-east, across the sea that stretched before me, the German High Sea Fleet, squadron by, squadron, was cruising off the Norwegian coast.

At 12 o'clock I spoke to the First Sea Lord again. He told me various items of news that had come in from different capitals, none however of decisive importance, but all tending to a rise of temperature. I asked him whether all the reservists had already been dismissed. He told me they had. I decided to return to London. I told him I would be with him at nine, and that meanwhile he should do whatever was necessary.

Prince Louis awaited me at the Admiralty. The situation was evidently degenerating. Special editions of the Sunday papers showed intense excitement in nearly every European capital. The First Sea Lord told me that in accordance with our conversation he had told the Fleet not to disperse. I took occasion to refer to this four months later in my letter accepting his resignation. I was very glad publicly to testify at that moment of great grief and pain for him that his loyal hand had sent the first order which began our vast naval mobilization.

I then went round to Sir Edward Grey, who had rented my house at 33 Eccleston Square. No one was with him except Sir William Tyrrell of the Foreign Office. I told him that we were holding the Fleet together. I learned from him that he viewed the situation very gravely. He said there was a great deal yet to be done before a leally dangerous crisis was reached, but that he did not at all like the way in which this business had begun. I asked whether it would be helpful or the reverse if we stated in public that we were keeping the Fleet together. Both he and Tyrrell were most insistent that we should proclaim it at the earliest possible moment: it might have the effect of sobering the Central Powers and steadying Europe. I went back to the Admiralty, sent for the First Sea Lord, and drafted the necessary communiqué.

The next morning the following notice appeared in all the papers:—

BRITISH NAVAL MEASURES

ORDERS TO FIRST AND SECOND FLEETS

NO MANŒUVRE LEAVE

We received the following statement from the Secretary of the Admiralty at an early hour this morning:—

> Orders have been given to the First Fleet, which is concentrated at Portland, not to disperse for manœuvre leave for the present. All vessels of the Second Fleet are remaining at their home ports in proximity to their balance crews.

On Monday began the first of the Cabinets on the European situation, which thereafter continued daily or twice a day. It is to be hoped that sooner or later a detailed account of the movement of opinion in the Cabinet during this period will be compiled and given to the world. There is certainly no reason for anyone to be ashamed of honest and sincere counsel given either to preserve peace or to enter upon a just and necessary war. Meanwhile it is only possible, without breach of constitutional propriety, to deal in the most general terms with what took place.

The Cabinet was overwhelmingly pacific. At least three-quarters of its members were determined not to be drawn into a European quarrel, unless Great Britain were herself attacked, which was not likely. Those who were in this mood were inclined to believe first of all that Austria and Serbia would not come to blows; secondly, that if they did, Russia would not intervene; thirdly, if Russia intervened, that Germany would not strike; fourthly, they hoped that if Germany struck at Russia, it ought to be possible for France and Germany mutually to neutralize each other without fighting. They did not believe that if Germany attacked France, she would attack her through Belgium or that if she did the Belgians would forcibly resist; and it must be remembered, that during the whole course of this week Belgium not only never asked for assistance from the guaranteeing Powers but pointedly indicated that she wished to be left alone. So here were six or seven positions, all of which could be wrangled over and about none of which any final proof could be offered except the proof of events. It was not until Monday, August 3, that the direct appeal from the King of the Belgians for French and British aid raised an issue which united the overwhelming majority of Ministers and enabled Sir Edward Grey to make his speech on that afternoon to the House of Commons.

My own part in these events was a very simple one. It was first of all to make sure that the diplomatic situation did not get ahead of the naval situation, and that the Grand Fleet should be in its War Station before Germany could know whether or not we should be in the war, *and therefore if possible before we had decided ourselves.* Secondly, it was to point out that if Germany attacked France, she would do so through Belgium, that all her preparations had been made to this end, and that she neither could nor would adopt any different strategy or go round any other way. To these two tasks I steadfastly adhered.

Every day there were long Cabinets from eleven onwards. Streams of telegrams poured in from every capital in Europe. Sir Edward Grey was plunged in his immense double struggle (*a*) to prevent war and (*b*) not to desert France should it come. I watched with admiration his activities at the Foreign Office and cool skill in Council. Both these tasks acted and reacted on one another from hour to hour. He had to try to make the Germans realize that we were to be reckoned with, without making the French or Russians feel they had us in their pockets. He had to carry the Cabinet with him in all he did. During the many years we acted together in the Cabinet, and the earlier years in which I read his

Foreign Office telegrams, I thought I had learnt to understand his methods of discussion and controversy, and perhaps without offence I might describe them.

After what must have been profound reflection and study, the Foreign Secretary was accustomed to select one or two points in any important controversy which he defended with all his resources and tenacity. They were his fortified villages. All around in the open field the battle ebbed and flowed, but if at nightfall these points were still in his possession, his battle was won. All other arguments had expended themselves, and these key positions alone survived. The points which he selected over and over again proved to be inexpugnable. They were particularly adapted to defence. They commended themselves to sensible and fair-minded men. The sentiments of the patriotic Whig, the English gentleman, the public school boy all came into the line for their defence, and if they were held, the whole front was held, including much debatable ground.

As soon as the crisis had begun he had fastened upon the plan of a European conference, and to this end every conceivable endeavour was made by him. To get the Great Powers together round a table in any capital that was agreeable, with Britain there to struggle for peace, and if necessary to threaten war against those who broke it, was his plan. Had such a conference taken place, there could have been no war. Mere acceptance of the principle of a conference by the Central Powers would have instantly relieved the tension. A will to peace at Berlin and Vienna would have found no difficulties in escaping from the terrible net which was drawing in upon us all hour by hour. But underneath the diplomatic communications and manœuvres, the baffling proposals and counter-proposals, the agitated interventions of Tsar and Kaiser, flowed a deep tide of calculated military purpose. As the ill-fated nations approached the verge, the sinister machines of war began to develop their own momentum and eventually to take control themselves.

The Foreign Secretary's second cardinal point was the English Channel. Whatever happened, if war came, we could not allow the German Fleet to come down the Channel to attack the French ports. Such a situation would be insupportable for Great Britain. Every one who counted was agreed on that from a very early stage in our discussions. But in addition we were, in a sense, morally committed to France to that extent. No bargain had been entered into. All arrangements that had been concerted were, as has been explained, specifically preluded with a declaration that neither party was committed to anything further than consultation together if danger threatened. But still the fact remained that the whole French Fleet was in the Mediterranean. Only a few cruisers and flotillas remained to guard the Northern and Atlantic Coasts of France; and simultaneously with that redisposition of forces, though not contingent upon it or dependent upon it, we had concentrated all our battleships at home, and only cruisers and battle-cruisers maintained British interests in the Mediterranean. The French had taken their decision on their own responsibility without prompting from us, and we had profited by their action to strengthen our margin in the Line of Battle at home. Whatever disclaimers we had made about not being committed, could we, when it came to the point, honourably stand by and see the naked French coasts ravaged and bombarded by German Dreadnoughts under the eyes and within gunshot of our Main Fleet?

It seemed to me, however, very early in the discussion that the Germans would concede this point to keep us out of the war, at any rate till the first battles on land had been fought without us; and sure enough they did. Believing as I did and do, that we could not, for our own safety and independence, allow France to be crushed as the result of aggressive action by Germany, I always from the very earliest moment concentrated upon our obligations to Belgium, through which I was convinced the Germans must inevitably march to invade France. Belgium did not count so largely in my sentiments at this stage. I thought it very unlikely that she would resist. I thought, and Lord Kitchener, who lunched with me on the Tuesday (28th), agreed, that Belgium would make some formal protest and submit. A few shots might be fired outside Liège or Namur, and then this unfortunate State would bow its head before overwhelming might. Perhaps, even, there was a secret agreement allowing free passage to the Germans through Belgium. How otherwise would all these preparations of Germany, the great camps along the Belgian Frontier, the miles and miles of sidings, the intricate network of railways have been developed? Was it possible that German thoroughness could be astray on so important a factor as the attitude of Belgium?

Those wonderful events which took place in Belgium on Sunday and Monday and in the week that followed could not be foreseen by us. I saw in Belgium a country with whom we had had many differences over the Congo and other subjects. I had not discerned in the Belgium of the late King Leopold the heroic nation of King Albert. But whatever happened to Belgium, there was France whose very life was at stake, whose armies in my judgment were definitely weaker than those by whom they would be assailed, whose ruin would leave us face to face alone with triumphant Germany: France, in those days schooled by adversity to peace and caution, thoroughly democratic, already stripped of two fair provinces, about to receive the final smashing blow from overwhelming brutal force. Only Britain could redress the balance, could defend the fair-play of the world. Whatever else failed, we must be there, and we must be there in time. A week later every British heart burned for little Belgium. From every cottage labouring men, untrained to war but with the blood of an unconquered people in their veins, were hurrying to the recruiting stations with intent to rescue Belgium. But at this time it was not Belgium one thought of, but France. Still, Belgium and the Treaties were indisputably an obligation of honour binding upon the British State such as British Governments have always accepted; and it was on that ground that I personally, with others, took my stand.

I will now examine the alternative question of whether more decided action by Sir Edward Grey at an early stage would have prevented the war. We must first ask, At what early stage? Suppose after Agadir or on the announcement of the new German Navy Law in 1912 the Foreign Secretary had, in cold blood, proposed a formal alliance with France and Russia, and in execution of military conventions consequential upon the alliance had begun to raise by compulsion an army adequate to our responsibilities and to the part we were playing in the world's affairs; and suppose we had taken this action as a united nation; who shall say whether that would have prevented or precipitated the war? But what chance was there of such action being unitedly taken? The Cabinet of the day would never have agreed to it. I doubt if four Ministers would have agreed to it. But if the

Cabinet had been united upon it, the House of Commons would not have accepted their guidance. Therefore the Foreign Minister would have had to resign. The policy which he had advocated would have stood condemned and perhaps violently repudiated; and with that repudiation would have come an absolute veto upon all those informal preparations and noncommittal discussions on which the defensive power of the Triple Entente was erected. Therefore, by taking such a course in 1912, Sir Edward Grey would only have paralysed Britain, isolated France, and increased the preponderant and growing power of Germany.

Suppose again, that now after the Austrian ultimatum to Serbia, the Foreign Secretary had proposed to the Cabinet that if matters were so handled that Germany attacked France or violated Belgian territory, Great Britain would declare war upon her. Would the Cabinet have assented to such a communication? I cannot believe it. If Sir Edward Grey could have said on Monday that if Germany attacked France or Belgium, England would declare war upon her, might there not still have been time to ward off the catastrophe? The question is certainly arguable. But the knowledge which we now have of events in Berlin tends to show that even then the German Government were too deeply committed by their previous action. They had before their eyes the deliberate British announcement that the Fleet was being held together. That at least was a serious if silent warning. Under its impression the German Emperor, as soon as he returned to Berlin, made on this same Monday and succeeding days strong efforts to bring Austria to reason and so to prevent war. But he could never overtake events or withstand the contagion of ideas. However this may be, I am certain that if Sir Edward Grey had sent the kind of ultimatum suggested, the Cabinet would have broken up, and it is also my belief that up till Wednesday or Thursday at least, the House of Commons would have repudiated his action. Nothing less than the deeds of Germany would have converted the British nation to war. To act in advance of those deeds would have led to an exposure of division worse than the guarded attitude which we maintained, which brought our country into the war united. After Wednesday or Thursday it was too late. By the time we could speak decisive words of warning, the hour of words had certainly passed for ever.

It is true to say that our Entente with France and the military and naval conversations that had taken place since 1900, had led us into a position where we had the obligations of an alliance without its advantages. An open alliance, if it could have been peacefully brought about at an earlier date, would have exercised a deterring effect upon the German mind, or at the least would have altered their military calculations. Whereas now we were morally bound to come to the aid of France and it was our interest to do so, and yet the fact that we should come in appeared so uncertain that it did not weigh as it should have done with the Germans. Moreover, as things were, if France had been in an aggressive mood, we should not have had the unquestioned right of an ally to influence her action in a pacific sense: and if as the result of her aggressive mood war had broken out and we had stood aside, we should have been accused of deserting her, and in any case would have been ourselves grievously endangered by her defeat.

However, in the event there was no need to moderate the French attitude. Justice to France requires the explicit statement that the conduct of her Government at this awful juncture was faultless. She assented instantly to every proposal that could make for peace. She abstained from every form of provocative action. She even compromised her own safety, holding back her covering troops at a considerable distance behind her frontier, and delaying her mobilization in the face of continually gathering German forces till the latest moment. Not until she was confronted with the direct demand of Germany to break her Treaty and abandon Russia, did France take up the challenge; and even had she acceded to the German demand, she would only, as we now know, have been faced with a further ultimatum to surrender to German military occupation as a guarantee for her neutrality the fortresses of Toul and Verdun. Thus there never was any chance of France being allowed to escape the ordeal. Even cowardice and dishonour would not have saved her. The Germans had resolved that if war came from any cause, they would take and break France forthwith as its first operation. The German military chiefs burned to give the signal, and were sure of the result. She would have begged for mercy in vain. She did not beg.

The more I reflect upon this situation, the more convinced I am that we took the only practical course that was open to us or to any British Cabinet; and that the objections which may be urged against it were less than those which would have attended any other sequence of action.

* * * * *

After hearing the discussions at Monday's Cabinet and studying the telegrams, I sent that night to all our Commanders-in-Chief the following very secret warning:—

July 27, 1914.

> This is not the Warning Telegram, but European political situation makes war between Triple Entente and Triple Alliance Powers by no means impossible. Be prepared to shadow possible hostile men-of-war and consider dispositions of H.M. ships under your command from this point of view. Measure is purely precautionary. No unnecessary person is to be informed. The utmost secrecy is to be observed.

On Tuesday morning I sent the following minute to the First Sea Lord, to which he replied marginally the same day:—

July 28, 1914.

Will go North with Fleet.	1. It would appear that the minesweepers should be quietly collected at some suitable point for attendance on the Battle Fleet, should it move.
Done.	2. Let me have a short statement on the coal position and what measures you propose.
Yes.	3. I presume *Firedrake* and *Lurcher* will now join their proper flotilla.

Have been ordered away.

4. All the vessels engaged on the coast of Ireland should be considered as available on mobilization, and on receipt of the warning telegram should move to their war stations without the slightest delay.

Will be done as soon as F.O. concur.

5. It would certainly be desirable that *Triumph* should be quietly mobilized and that she should be ready to close [i.e. join] the China flagship with available destroyers. The position of the German heavy cruisers in China waters makes it clear that this can be done. Please examine and report what disadvantages this mobilization would entail. We can then discuss whether it is worth while taking them in the present circumstances. The China Squadron must be capable of concentrating as soon as the warning telegram is sent and before a main action is necessary. Without the *Triumph* the margin of superiority is small and any reinforcement from other stations would be slow.

Should concentrate at Hong Kong at once.

Decided 'No' at Conference.

6. You should consider whether the position of the *Goeben*[3] at Pola does not justify the detachment of the *New Zealand* to join the Mediterranean flag.

Settled personally with C. of I.G.S.

7. Yesterday, after consultation with the Prime Minister, I arranged personally with the Chief of the Imperial General Staff for the better guarding of magazines and oil tanks against evilly-disposed persons and attacks by aircraft. These measures have now been taken. See attached letter from the Chief of the Imperial General Staff and my reply. You should direct the Director of Operations Division to obtain full detailed information from the War Office of what has been done, and in the event of any place being overlooked, to make the necessary representations.

Done.

8. Director of the Air Division should be asked to report the exact positions of the aircraft which were concentrated yesterday in the neighbourhood of the Thames Estuary, and further to state what is being done to reach a complete understanding between the aircraft and the military authorities in charge of the aerial gun defences at various points. This is of the utmost importance if accidents are to be avoided.

W. S. C.

---

[3]I have adopted the familiar spelling of this ship's name instead of *Göben*.

The official 'warning telegram' was dispatched from the Admiralty on Wednesday, the 29th. On this same day I obtained from the Cabinet the authority to put into force the 'Precautionary Period' regulations. The work of Ottley and of Hankey and generally of the Committee of Imperial Defence, was now put to the proof. It was found in every respect thorough and comprehensive, and all over the country emergency measures began to astonish the public. Naval harbours were cleared, bridges were guarded, steamers were boarded and examined, watchers lined the coasts.

First Sea Lord.
Fourth Sea Lord.
Director of Air Department.

July 29, 1914.

In the present stage of aeronautics, the primary duty of British aircraft is to fight enemy aircraft, and thus afford protection against aerial attack. This should be made clear to air officers, Commander-in-Chief, Nore, and Admiral of Patrols, in order that machines may not be needlessly used up in ordinary scouting duties. After the primary requirement is well provided for, whatever aid is possible for coastal watch and extended defence scouting should be organized. But the naval aircraft are to regard the defence against attack from the air as their first and main responsibility. They must be carefully husbanded.

W. S. C.

And the day before:—

July 28, 1914.

Director Intelligence Division.

Please mark off on my 'Table of Battleship Strength' all British and German Dreadnought battleships available for war (*a*) in the next month, and (*b*) at the end of three months. You should include the two Turkish ships in your calculation. Let me also have a similar table about battle-cruisers.

W. S. C.

Our war arrangements comprised an elaborate scheme for dealing with vessels under construction. In 1912 measures had been taken to keep it perpetually up to date. The principle was that for the first three months of a war all efforts should be concentrated on finishing ships that could be ready in the first six months, other vessels whose dates of completion were more remote being somewhat retarded. This ensured the greatest possible superiority in the early months, and would give us time to see what kind of a war it was and how it went, before dealing with more distant contingencies. The plan of course covered all ships building in Great Britain for foreign Powers. Of these there were two battleships building for Turkey, three flotilla leaders for Chili, four destroyers for Greece, and three monitors for Brazil. There were also other important ships, including a Chilian and a Brazilian battleship and a Dutch cruiser, which would not be ready till much later. The Turkish battleships were vital to us. With a margin of only seven Dreadnoughts we could not afford to do without these two fine ships. Still less could we afford to see them fall into bad hands and possibly be used against us. Had we delivered them to Turkey, they would, as the event turned out, have formed with the *Goeben* a hostile force which would have required a force of not less than four British Dreadnought battleships or battle-cruisers to watch them. Thus the British numbers would have been reduced by two instead of being increased by two. One of the Turkish battleships (the *Reshadieh*) which Armstrongs were building on the Tyne when the crisis began, was actually complete. The Turkish crew, over 500 strong, had already arrived to take her over and were lying in their steamer in the river. There seemed to be a great danger of their coming on board, brushing aside Messrs. Armstrongs' workmen and hoisting the Turkish flag, in which case a very difficult diplomatic situation would have been created. I determined to run no risks, and on July 31 I sent written instructions that adequate military guards were to be placed on board this vessel and that in no circumstances was she to be boarded by the Turks. It has sometimes been made a ground for reproach against me that the requisition of these ships was one of the causes which brought Turkey into the war three months later. We now know that negotiations were taking place from July 24 onwards between the Germans and the leaders of the Committee of Union and Progress for an alliance between Germany and Turkey, and that such Alliance was actually signed on August 2.

It is interesting to read in the German Official History what they knew about our preparations at this time.

> 'At 6.20 p.m. on July 28 the following telegram was received in Berlin from the German Naval Attaché:—
>
> ' "Admiralty are not publishing ships' movements. 2nd Fleet remains fully manned. Schools closed in naval bases; preliminary measures taken for recall from leave. According to unconfirmed news 1st Fleet still at Portland, one submarine flotilla left Portsmouth. It is to be assumed that Admiralty is preparing for mobilization on the quiet."
>
> 'He telegraphed later on the same day as follows:—
>
> ' "As already reported by telegram, the British Fleet is preparing for all eventualities. In broad outline the present distribution is as follows: 1st Fleet is assembled at Portland. The battleship *Bellerophon* which was proceeding to Gibraltar for refit has been recalled. The ships of the 2nd Fleet are at their bases: they are fully manned. The schools on shore have not reopened. Ships of the 2nd and 3rd Fleets have coaled, completed with ammunition and supplies, and are at their bases. In consequence of the training of reservists, just completed, latter can be manned more quickly than usual and with more or less practised personnel, the *Times* says, within 48 hours. The destroyer and patrol flotillas and the submarines are either at

or *en route* for their stations. No leave is being granted, officers and men already on leave have been recalled.

'"In the naval bases and dockyards great activity reigns; in addition special measures of precaution have been adopted, all dockyards, magazines, oil tanks, etc., being put under guard. Repairs of ships in dockyard hands are being speeded up. A great deal of night work is being done.

'"The Press reports that the Mediterranean squadron had left Alexandria; it is said that it will remain at Malta.

'"All ships and squadrons have orders to remain ready for sea.

'"Outwardly complete calm is preserved, in order not to cause anxiety by alarming reports about the Fleet.

'"Movements of ships, which are generally published daily by the Admiralty, have been withheld since yesterday. . . .

'"The above preparations have been made on the Admiralty's independent initiative. The result is the same, whoever gave the orders."'

The German Naval Attaché thus showed himself extremely well informed. As I have already mentioned in an earlier chapter, the general warrants to open the letters of certain persons which I had signed three years before as Home Secretary, had brought to light a regular network of minor agents, mostly British, in German pay in all our naval ports. Had we arrested them, others of whom we might not have known, would have taken their place. We therefore thought it better, having detected them, to leave them at large. In this way one saw regularly from their communications, which we carefully forwarded, what they were saying to their paymasters in Berlin during these years, and we knew exactly how to put our hands upon them at the proper moment. Up to this point we had no objection to the German Government knowing that exceptional precautions were being taken throughout the Navy. Indeed, apart from details, it was desirable that they should know how seriously we viewed the situation. But the moment had now come to draw down the curtain. We no longer forwarded the letters and a few days later, on a word from me to the Home Secretary, all these petty traitors, who for a few pounds a month were seeking to sell their country, were laid by the heels. Nor was it easy for the Germans to organize on the spur of the moment others in their places.

The most important step remains to be recounted. As early as Tuesday, July 28, I felt that the Fleet should go to its War Station. It must go there at once, and secretly; it must be steaming to the north while every German authority, naval or military, had the greatest possible interest in avoiding a collision with us. If it went thus early it need not go by the Irish Channel and north-about. It could go through the Straits of Dover and through the North Sea, and therefore the island would not be uncovered even for a single day. Moreover, it would arrive sooner and with less expenditure of fuel.

At about 10 o'clock, therefore, on the Tuesday morning I proposed this step to the First Sea Lord and the Chief of the Staff and found them whole-heartedly in favour of it. We decided that the Fleet should leave Portland at such an hour on the morning of the 29th as to pass the Straits of Dover during the hours of darkness, that it should traverse these waters at high speed and without lights, and with the utmost precaution proceed to Scapa Flow. I feared to bring this matter before the Cabinet, lest it should mistakenly be considered a provocative action likely to damage the chances of peace. It would be unusual to bring movements of the British Fleet in Home Waters from one British port to another before the Cabinet. I only therefore informed the Prime Minister, who at once gave his approval. Orders were accordingly sent to Sir George Callaghan, who was told incidentally to send the Fleet up under his second-in-command and to travel himself by land through London in order that we might have an opportunity of consultation with him.

Admiralty to Commander-in-Chief Home Fleets.

July 28, 1914. *Sent* 5 p.m.

> To-morrow, Wednesday, the First Fleet is to leave Portland for Scapa Flow. Destination is to be kept secret except to flag and commanding officers. As you are required at the Admiralty, Vice-Admiral 2nd Battle Squadron is to take command. Course from Portland is to be shaped to southward, then a middle Channel course to the Straits of Dover. The Squadrons are to pass through the Straits without lights during the night and to pass outside the shoals on their way north. *Agamemnon* is to remain at Portland, where the Second Fleet will assemble.

We may now picture this great Fleet, with its flotillas and cruisers, steaming slowly out of Portland Harbour, squadron by squadron, scores of gigantic castles of steel wending their way across the misty, shining sea, like giants bowed in anxious thought. We may picture them again as darkness fell, eighteen miles of warships running at high speed and in absolute blackness through the narrow Straits, bearing with them into the broad waters of the North the safeguard of considerable affairs.

Although there seemed to be no conceivable motive, chance or mischance, which could lead a rational German Admiralty to lay a trap of submarines or mines or have given them the knowledge and the time to do so, we looked at each other with much satisfaction when on Thursday morning (the 30th) at our daily Staff Meeting the Flagship reported herself and the whole Fleet well out in the center of the North Sea.[4]

The German Ambassador lost no time in complaining of the movement of the Fleet to the Foreign Office. According to the German Official Naval History, he reported to

---

[4]Later in the morning I learnt that Lord Fisher was in the office and I invited him into my room. I told him what we had done and his delight was wonderful to see.

Foolish statements have been made from time to time that this sending of the Fleet to the North was done at Lord Fisher's suggestion. The interview with me which Lord Fisher records in his book is correctly given by him as having taken place on the 30th. The Fleet had actually passed the Straits of Dover the night before. I think it necessary to place on record the fact that my sole naval adviser on every measure taken prior to the declaration of war was the First Sea Lord.

his Government on the evening of the 30th that Sir Edward Grey had answered him in the following words:—

> 'The movements of the Fleet are free of all offensive character, and the Fleet will not approach German waters.'

'But,' adds the German historian, 'the strategic concentration of the Fleet had actually been accomplished with its transfer to Scottish ports.' This was true. We were now in a position, whatever happened, to control events, and it was not easy to see how this advantage could be taken from us. A surprise torpedo attack before or simultaneous with the declaration of war was at any rate one nightmare gone for ever. We could at least see for ten days ahead. If war should come no one would know where to look for the British Fleet. Somewhere in that enormous waste of waters to the north of our islands, cruising now this way, now that, shrouded in storms and mists, dwelt this mighty organization. Yet from the Admiralty building we could speak to them at any moment if need arose. The king's ships were at sea.

CHAPTER X
THE MOBILIZATION OF THE NAVY: JULY 31—AUGUST 4

'The meteor flag of England
  Shall yet terrific burn;
Till danger's troubled night depart,
  And the star of peace return.'

Campbell.

Cabinet Tension—The Opposition Leaders—The Naval Reserves—British Decision to Close the Channel to German Warships—Germany declares War upon Russia—General Mobilization of the Navy—Sir John Jellicoe appointed Commander-in-Chief—German Invasion of Luxemburg and Belgium—Monday, August 3, in the House of Commons—British Ultimatum to Germany—Nation and Empire—Situation in the Mediterranean—Menace of the *Goeben*—Admiralty Instructions to Sir Berkeley Milne—August 4. The *Goeben* Found—Cabinet Veto on Hostilities—Italian Declaration of Neutrality—First Escape of the *Goeben*—Awaiting the Signal—'Commence Hostilities against Germany.'

There was complete agreement in the Cabinet upon every telegram sent by Sir Edward Grey and in his handling of the crisis. But there was also an invincible refusal on the part of the majority to contemplate British intervention by force of arms should the Foreign Secretary's efforts fail and a European war begin. Thus, as the terrific week wore on and the explosion became inevitable, it seemed probable that a rupture of the political organism by which the country had so long been governed was also rapidly approaching. I lived this week entirely in the official circle, seeing scarcely anyone but my colleagues of the Cabinet or of the Admiralty, and moving only to and fro across the Horse Guards between Admiralty House and Downing Street. Each day as the telegrams arrived showing the darkening scene of Europe, and the Cabinets ended in growing tension, I pulled over the various levers which successively brought our naval organization into full preparedness. It was always necessary to remember that if Peace was preserved every one of these measures, alarmist in their character and involving much expense, would have to be justified to a Liberal House of Commons. That assembly once delivered from the peril, would certainly proceed upon the assumption that British participation in a continental struggle would have been criminal madness. Yet it was not practicable often to divert the main discussions of the Cabinet into purely technical channels. It was therefore necessary for me to take a peculiar and invidious personal responsibility for many things that had to be done when their turn came. I had also to contemplate a break-up of the governing instrument. Judged by reports and letters from members, the attitude of the House of Commons appeared most uncertain.

On Thursday evening I entered into communication with the Unionist leaders through Mr. F. E. Smith.[1] I informed him of the increasing gravity of the European situation and of the military preparations which were everywhere in progress in Europe. I stated that no decision had been reached by the Cabinet, and that I had received letters from one or two Unionists of influence protesting vehemently against our being drawn into a Continental war. I asked him to let me know where he and his friends stood on the supreme issue. He replied at once that he himself was unreservedly for standing by France and Belgium. After consulting with Mr. Bonar Law, Sir Edward Carson and others who were gathered at Sir Edward Goulding's house at Wargrave, he sent me the following written assurance, which I showed to Mr. Asquith the next morning (Saturday):—

Mr. F. E. Smith to Mr. Churchill.

July 31, 1914.

I have spoken to my friends of whom you know and I have no doubt that on the facts as we understand them—and more particularly on the assumption (which we understand to be certain) that Germany contemplates a violation of Belgian neutrality—the Government can rely upon the support of the Unionist Party in whatever manner that support can be most effectively given.

* * * * *

Secretary, Saturday, *August* 1, 1914.
First Sea Lord.

It seems certain that the order to mobilize will be issued after Cabinet this morning. Have everything in readiness.

Examination service should be put into force simultaneously.

W. S. C.

At the Cabinet I demanded the immediate calling out of the Fleet Reserves and the completion of our naval preparations. I based this claim on the fact that the German Navy was mobilizing, and that we must do the same. The Cabinet, who were by no means ill-informed on matters of naval organization, took the view after a sharp discussion that this step was not necessary to our safety, as mobilization only affected the oldest ships in the Fleet, and that our main naval power was already in full preparedness for war and the Fleet in its war station. I replied that though this was true, we needed the Third Fleet ships, particularly the older cruisers, to fulfil the rôles assigned to them in our war plan. However, I did not succeed in procuring their assent.

---

[1]Afterwards Lord Birkenhead.

On Saturday evening I dined alone at the Admiralty. The foreign telegrams came in at short intervals in red boxes which already bore the special label 'Sub-Committee,' denoting the precautionary period. The flow was quite continuous, and the impression produced on my mind after reading for nearly an hour was that there was still a chance of peace. Austria had accepted the conference, and intimate personal appeals were passing between the Tsar and the Kaiser. It seemed to me, from the order in which I read the series of telegrams, that at the very last moment Sir Edward Grey might succeed in saving the situation. So far no shot had been fired between the Great Powers. I wondered whether armies and fleets could remain mobilized for a space without fighting and then demobilize.

I had hardly achieved this thought when another Foreign Office box came in. I opened it and read 'Germany has declared war on Russia.' There was no more to be said. I walked across the Horse Guards Parade and entered 10, Downing Street, by the garden gate. I found the Prime Minister upstairs in his drawing-room: with him were Sir Edward Grey, Lord Haldane and Lord Crewe; there may have been other Ministers. I said that I intended instantly to mobilize the Fleet notwithstanding the Cabinet decision, and that I would take full personal responsibility to the Cabinet the next morning. The Prime Minister, who felt himself bound to the Cabinet, said not a single word, but I was clear from his look that he was quite content. As I walked down the steps of Downing Street with Sir Edward Grey, he said to me, 'You should know I have just done a very important thing. I have told Cambon that we shall not allow the German fleet to come into the Channel.' I went back to the Admiralty and gave forthwith the order to mobilize. We had no legal authority for calling up the Naval Reserves, as no proclamation had been submitted to His Majesty in view of the Cabinet decision, but we were quite sure that the Fleet men would unquestioningly obey the summons. This action was ratified by the Cabinet on Sunday morning, and the Royal Proclamation was issued some hours later.

Another decision and a painful one was required. Sir George Callaghan's command of the Home Fleets had been extended by a year, and was now due to end on October 1. It had been announced that he would then be succeeded by Sir John Jellicoe. Further, our arrangements prescribed that Sir John Jellicoe should act as second-in-command in the event of war. The First Sea Lord and I had a conference with Sir George Callaghan, on his way through London to the North on the 30th. As the result of this conference we decided that if war came, it would be necessary to appoint Sir John Jellicoe immediately to the chief command. We were doubtful as to Sir George Callaghan's health and physical strength being equal to the immense strain that would be cast upon him; and in the crash of Europe it was no time to consider individuals. Sir John Jellicoe left London for the Fleet with sealed instructions, directing him on the seals being broken to take over the command. On the night of August 2, when we considered war certain, we telegraphed to both Admirals apprising them of the Admiralty decision. It was naturally a cruel blow to Sir George Callaghan to have to lay down his charge at such a moment, and his protests were re-echoed by practically all the principal Admirals who had served under him and by Sir John Jellicoe himself. It was also a grave matter to make a change in the command of the Fleets at this juncture. However, we did what we thought right, and that without an hour's delay. To Sir John Jellicoe I telegraphed: "Your feelings do you credit, and we understand them. But the responsibility rests with us, and we have given our decision. Take up your great task in buoyancy and hope. We are sure that all will be well." Sir John Jellicoe assumed command on the evening of August 3, and received almost immediately an order from the Admiralty to proceed to sea at daylight on the 4th.[2]

The Cabinet sat almost continuously throughout the Sunday, and up till luncheon-time it looked as if the majority would resign. The grief and horror of so many able colleagues were painful to witness. But what could any one do? In the luncheon interval I saw Mr. Balfour, a veritable rock in times like these, and learned that the Unionist leaders had tendered formally in writing to the Prime Minister their unqualified assurances of support.

I returned to the Admiralty. We telegraphed to our Commanders-in-Chief:—

> 'To-day, August 2, at 2.20 the following note was handed to the French and German Ambassadors. [*Begins*] The British Government would not allow the passage of German ships through the English Channel or the North Sea in order to attack the coasts or shipping of France [*ends*].
>
> 'Be prepared to meet surprise attacks.'

The French Naval Attaché, the Comte de Saint-Seine, had been summoned. The following is the précis of our conversation:—

> *August* 2, 1914.
>
> The First Lord in the presence of the First Sea Lord and Chief of the War Staff, informed the French Naval Attaché of the Cabinet's decision and the note on naval matters handed to M. Cambon at 2.20 p.m., August 2.
>
> In order to prepare for the possibility of an alliance being concluded between the Governments, but without prejudging the question, the following preliminary steps are to be taken:—
>
> The package containing the secret signal books to be distributed and opened but not used. Mutual regulations for the entry of allied ships into each other's ports to be issued now. The officers in command of the Mediterranean and China Stations will be given permission to enter into communication with the French Senior Officers in command on their stations.
>
> Certain staff questions were discussed, but the First Lord clearly pointed out that these involved no question of policy which would have to be decided by Parliament.
>
> The general direction of the naval war to rest with the British Admiralty. The direction of the allied fleets in the Mediterranean to rest with the French, the British Admiral being junior.

[2]Sir George Callaghan was immediately appointed to the very important command of the Nore, which he filled with distinction throughout the war.

> In the event of the neutrality of Italy being assured, France would undertake to deal with Austria assisted only by such British ships as would be required to cover German ships in that sea, and secure a satisfactory composition of the allied fleet. . . . .
>
> British naval bases would be at the disposal of the French.
>
> Should any portion of the German main fleet make its way South towards the Mediterranean, it would be followed by a superior British force.

Meanwhile events were influencing opinion hour by hour. When the Cabinet met on Sunday morning we were in presence of the violation of the Grand Duchy of Luxemburg by the German troops. In the evening the German ultimatum to Belgium was delivered. The next day arrived the appeal of the King of the Belgians that the guaranteeing Powers should uphold the sanctity of the Treaty regarding the neutrality of Belgium. This last was decisive. By Monday the majority of Mr. Asquith's colleagues regarded war as inevitable. Discussion was resumed on Monday morning in a different atmosphere, though it seemed certain that there would be numerous resignations.

Before the Cabinet separated on Monday morning, Sir Edward Grey had procured a predominant assent to the principal points and general tone of his statement to Parliament that afternoon. Formal sanction had been given to the already completed mobilization of the Fleet and to the immediate mobilization of the Army. No decision had been taken to send an ultimatum to Germany or to declare war upon Germany, still less to send an army to France. These supreme decisions were never taken at any Cabinet. They were compelled by the force of events, and rest on the authority of the Prime Minister. We repaired to the House of Commons to hear the statement of the Foreign Secretary. I did not know which of our colleagues had resigned or what the composition of a War Government would be. The aspect of the assembly was awed but resolute. No one could mistake its intention. Sir Edward Grey made his statement with the utmost moderation. In order that there should be no ground for future reproaches, he informed the House that the Germans were willing to comply with the British demand that no German warships should be sent into the English Channel. The sombre march of his argument carried this weighty admission forward in its stride. When he sat down he was possessed in an overwhelming measure of the support of the assembly. Neither he nor I could remain long in the House. Outside, I asked him 'What happens now?' 'Now,' he said, 'we shall send them an ultimatum to stop the invasion of Belgium within 24 hours.'

Some of the Ministers still clung to the hope that Germany would comply with the British ultimatum and would arrest the onrush of her armies upon Belgium. As well recall the avalanche, as easily suspend in mid-career the great ship that has been launched and is sliding down the ways. Germany was already at war with Russia and France. It was certain that in 24 hours she would be at war with the British Empire also.

All through the tense discussions of the Cabinet one had in mind another greater debate which must begin when these were concluded. Parliament, the nation, the Dominions, would have to be convinced. That the cause was good, that the argument was overwhelming, that the response would be worthy, I did not for a moment doubt. But it seemed that an enormous political task awaited us, and I saw in the mind's eye not only the crowded House of Commons, but formidable assemblies of the people throughout the land requiring full and swift justification of the flaming action taken in their name. But such cares were soon dispersed. When the Council doors had opened and ministers had come into the outer air, the British nation was already surging forward in its ancient valour, and the Empire had sprung to arms.

'Men met each other with erected look,
The steps were higher that they took,
Friends to congratulate their friends made haste,
And long-inveterate foes saluted as they passed.'[3]

* * * * *

Meanwhile in the Mediterranean a drama of intense interest, and as it ultimately proved of fateful consequence, was being enacted.

The event which would dominate all others, if war broke out, was the main shock of battle between the French and German armies. We knew that the French were counting on placing in the line a whole army corps of their best troops from North Africa, and that every man was needed. We were informed also that they intended to transport these troops across the Mediterranean as fast as ships could be loaded, under the general protection of the French Fleet, but without any individual escort or system of convoys. The French General Staff calculated that whatever happened, most of the troops would get across. The French Fleet disposed between this stream of transports and the Austrian Fleet afforded a good guarantee. But there was one ship in the Mediterranean which far outstripped in speed every vessel in the French Navy. She was the *Goeben*. The only heavy ships in the Mediterranean that could attempt to compete with the *Goeben* in speed were the three battle-cruisers. It seemed that the *Goeben*, being free to choose any point on a front of three or four hundred miles, would easily be able to avoid the French Battle Squadrons and, brushing aside or outstripping their cruisers, break in upon the transports and sink one after another of these vessels crammed with soldiers. It occurred to me at this time that perhaps that was the task she had been sent to the Mediterranean to perform. For this reason as a further precaution I had suggested to the First Sea Lord as early as July 28 that an additional battle-cruiser, the *New Zealand*, should be sent to reinforce our squadron. When it came to the pinch a few days later, Admiral Boué de Lapeyrère, the French Commander-in-Chief, adopted a system of convoys; and on August 4 he prudently delayed the embarkation of the troops until he could organize adequate escorts. But of this change of plan the Admiralty was not advised.

On July 30 I called for the war orders of the Mediterranean command and discussed them fully with the First Sea Lord. These orders, issued in August, 1913, had had to

[3]Dryden, *Threnodia Augustalis*.

take into consideration a variety of political contingencies, viz. Great Britain at war with Germany only, with Germany and Austria only, or with Germany, Austria and Italy; and Great Britain and France allied together against each or any of the three aforesaid opponents. The course to be followed differed somewhat in each case. Briefly, if Britain found herself single-handed against the whole Triple Alliance, we should temporarily have to abandon the Mediterranean and concentrate at Gibraltar. In all other cases the concentration would be at Malta, and if the French were allies our squadrons would join them for a general battle. It now seemed necessary to give the Commander-in-Chief in the Mediterranean some more specific information and directions.

Admiralty to Commander-in-Chief, Mediterranean.

July 30, 1914.

> It now seems probable should war break out and England and France engage in it, that Italy will remain neutral and that Greece can be made an ally. Spain also will be friendly and possibly an ally. The attitude of Italy is however uncertain, and it is especially important that your Squadron should not be seriously engaged with Austrian ships before we know what Italy will do. Your first task should be to aid the French in the transportation of their African army by covering and if possible bringing to action individual fast German ships, particularly *Goeben*, which may interfere with that transportation. You will be notified by telegraph when you may consult with the French Admiral. Except in combination with the French as part of a general battle, do not at this stage be brought to action against superior forces. The speed of your Squadrons is sufficient to enable you to choose your moment. You must husband your force at the outset and we shall hope later to reinforce the Mediterranean.

These directions on which the First Sea Lord and I were completely in accord, gave the Commander-in-Chief guidance in the general conduct of the naval campaign; they warned him against fighting a premature single-handed battle with the Austrian Fleet in which our battle-cruisers and cruisers would be confronted with Austrian Dreadnought battleships; they told him to aid the French in transporting their African forces, and they told him how to do it, viz., 'by covering and, if possible, bringing to action individual fast German ships, particularly *Goeben*.' So far as the English language may serve as a vehicle of thought, the words employed appear to express the intentions we had formed.

Sir Berkeley Milne accordingly replied on July 31 that he would keep his forces concentrated in readiness to assist the French Fleet to protect the transports, and he rightly left our trade in the Eastern Mediterranean to shift for itself. In this posture he awaited permission to consult with the French Admiral. This permission could not be given him till August 2 at 7.6 p.m., when I telegraphed as follows to our Commanders-in-Chief all over the world:—

> 'Situation very critical. Be prepared to meet surprise attacks. You can enter into communication with the French Senior Officer on your station for combined

> action in case Great Britain should decide to become ally of France against Germany.'

Earlier that same day the following, initialled both by the First Sea Lord and myself, was also sent to Sir Berkeley Milne from the Admiralty:—

> '*Goeben* must be shadowed by two battle-cruisers. Approaches to Adriatic must be watched by cruisers and destroyers. Remain near Malta yourself. It is believed that Italy will remain neutral, but you cannot yet count absolutely on this.'

At 12.50 a.m. on August 3, I emphasized the importance of the *Goeben* compared with all other objectives by a further telegram, which I drafted myself, to Sir Berkeley Milne:—

> 'Watch on mouth of Adriatic should be maintained, but *Goeben* is your objective. Follow her and shadow her wherever she goes and be ready to act on declaration of war, which appears probable and imminent.'

Early on the morning of August 4 we were delighted by the following news from the Commander-in-Chief, Mediterranean, to the Admiralty:—

> '*Indomitable*, *Indefatigable* shadowing *Goeben* and *Breslau* 37° 44′ North 7° 56′ East.'
>
> We replied:—
>
> 'Very good. Hold her. War imminent.'
>
> (This to go now.)
>
> '*Goeben* is to be prevented by force from interfering with French transports.'
>
> (This to await early confirmation.)

I then sent the following minute to the Prime Minister and Sir Edward Grey:—

MEMORANDUM

> (*Most Urgent.*)
> Prime Minister.
> Sir Edward Grey.
>
> German battle-cruiser *Goeben* and fast light cruiser *Breslau* have been found west of Sicily and are being shadowed by British battle-cruisers *Indomitable* and *Indefatigable*. It would be a great misfortune to lose these vessels as is possible in the dark hours. She is evidently going to interfere with the French transports which are crossing to-day.

The following telegram has already been sent:—

'Good. Hold her. War imminent.'

We wish to add this:—

'If *Goeben* attacks French transports you should at once engage her.'

An immediate decision is required.

W. S. C.

Sir Edward Grey agreed to this and so did the Prime Minister, but the latter asked that it should be mentioned to the Cabinet, which was meeting almost immediately, for their confirmation. On this I sent, before going to the Cabinet, the following:—

'If *Goeben* attacks French transports you should at once engage her. You should give her fair warning of this beforehand.'

The Cabinet, however, adhered formally to the view that no act of war should be committed by us before the expiration of the ultimatum. The moral integrity of the British Empire must not be compromised at this solemn moment for the sake of sinking a single ship.

The *Goeben* of course did not attack the French transports. In fact, though this we did not know at the time, she was steaming away from the French transport routes when sighted by the *Indomitable* and *Indefatigable*. Even if, however, she had attacked transports, the decision of the British Cabinet would have prevented our battle-cruisers from interfering. This decision obviously carried with it the still more imperative veto against opening fire on the *Goeben*, if she did not attack French transports, during the hours when we had her in our power. I cannot impeach the decision. It is right that the world should know of it. But little did we imagine how much this spirit of honourable restraint was to cost us and all the world.

In consequence of the Cabinet decision, the First Sea Lord sent by my directions the following telegram from the Admiralty:—

Admiralty to all ships, August 4, 2.5 p.m.

The British ultimatum to Germany will expire at midnight Greenwich Mean Time, August 4. No act of war should be committed before that hour, at which time the telegram to commence hostilities against Germany will be dispatched from the Admiralty.

Special addition to Mediterranean, *Indomitable*, *Indefatigable*.

This cancels the authorization to *Indomitable* and *Indefatigable* to engage *Goeben* if she attacks French transports.

At about the same time I received the following minute from the First Sea Lord:—

First Lord. *August* 4.

> In view of the Italian declaration of neutrality, propose to telegraph to Commander-in-Chief, Mediterranean, acquainting him and enjoining him to respect this rigidly and not to allow a ship to come within six miles of the Italian coast.
>
> B.

Bearing in mind how disastrous it would be if any petty incident occurred which could cause trouble at this fateful moment with Italy and approving of the First Sea Lord's precaution, I replied in writing:—

> *August* 4.
>
> So proceed. Foreign Office should intimate this to Italian Government.
>
> W. S. C.

Thereupon at 12.55 p.m. the following telegram was sent by the Admiralty to the Commander-in-Chief in the Mediterranean:—

> Italian Government have declared neutrality. You are to respect this neutrality rigidly and should not allow any of His Majesty's ships to come within six miles of Italian coast.

This certainly as it turned out was destined to complicate the task of catching the *Goeben*; but not, as it will appear, in a decisive manner.

During the afternoon I sent the following minute to the Chief of the Staff and the First Sea Lord:—

> *August* 4, 1914.
>
> I presume you have fully informed French Admiralty of our intentions and that the closest co-operation has been established at all points with the French Fleet. If not, this should be done immediately.
>
> W. S. C.

On this the Chief of the Staff sent the following telegram to all stations: 'You can enter into the closest co-operation with the French officers on your station.'

Throughout this long summer afternoon three great ships, hunted and hunters, were cleaving the clear waters of the Mediterranean in tense and oppressive calm. At any moment the *Goeben* could have been smitten at under 10,000 yards range by sixteen 12-inch guns firing nearly treble her own weight of metal. At the Admiralty we suffered the tortures of Tantalus.

At about 5 o'clock Prince Louis observed that there was still time to sink the *Goeben* before dark. In the face of the Cabinet decision I was unable to utter a word. Nothing less than the vital safety of Great Britain could have justified so complete an overriding of the authority of the Cabinet. We hoped to sink her the next day. Where could she go? Pola seemed her only refuge throughout the Mediterranean. According to international law nothing but internment awaited her elsewhere. The Turks had kept their secret well. As the shadows of night fell over the Mediterranean the *Goeben* increased her speed to twenty-four knots, which was the utmost that our two battle-cruisers could steam. She increased her speed still further. We have since learned that she was capable for a very short time of an exceptional speed, rising even to twenty-six or twenty-seven knots. Aided by this, she shook off her unwelcome companions and vanished gradually in the gathering gloom.

We shall return to this story in due course.

* * * * *

At 5.50 p.m. we sent the following message:—

Admiralty to all ships.

> General message. The war telegram will be issued at midnight authorizing you to commence hostilities against Germany, but in view of our ultimatum they may decide to open fire at any moment. You must be ready for this.

Now, after all the stress and convulsion of the preceding ten days, there came to us at the Admiralty a strange interlude of calm. All the decisions had been taken. The ultimatum to Germany had gone: it must certainly be rejected. War would be declared at midnight. As far as we had been able to foresee the event, all our preparations were made. Mobilization was complete. Every ship was in its station: every man at his post. All over the world, every British captain and admiral was on guard. It only remained to give the signal. What would happen then? It seemed that the next move lay with the enemy. What would he do? Had he some deadly surprise in store? Some awful design, long planned and perfected, ready to explode upon us at any moment NOW? Would our ships in foreign waters have been able to mark down their German antagonists? If so, morning would witness half a dozen cruiser actions in the outer seas. Telegrams flowed in from the different naval stations round our coasts reporting the movements of vessels and rumours of sighting of enemies. Telegrams still flowed in from the Chancelleries of Europe as the last futile appeals of reason were overtaken by the cannonade. In the War Room of the Admiralty, where I sat waiting, one could hear the clock tick. From Parliament Street came the murmurs of the crowd; but they sounded distant and the world seemed very still. The tumult of the struggle for life was over: it was succeeded by the silence of ruin and death. We were to awake in Pandemonium.

I had the odd sense that it was like waiting for an election result. The turmoil of the contest seemed finished: the votes were being counted, and in a few hours the announcement would be made. One could only wait; but for what a result! Although the special duties of my office made it imperative that I, of all others, should be vigilant and forward in all that related to preparation for war, I claim, as these pages show, that in my subordinate station I had in these years before the war done nothing wittingly or willingly to impair the chances of a peaceable solution, and had tried my best as opportunity offered to make good relations possible between England and Germany.

I thank God I could feel also in that hour that our country was guiltless of all intended purpose of war. Even if we had made some mistakes in the handling of this awful crisis, though I do not know them, from the bottom of our hearts we could say that we had not willed it. Germany it seemed had rushed with head down and settled resolve to her own undoing. And if this were what she had meant all along, if this was the danger which had really menaced us hour by hour during the last ten years, and would have hung over us hour by hour until the crash eventually came, was it not better that it should happen now: now that she had put herself so hopelessly in the wrong, now that we were ready beyond the reach of surprise, now that France and Russia and Great Britain were all in the line together?

The First Sea Lord and the Chief of the Staff came in with French Admirals who had hurried over to concert in detail arrangements for the co-operation of the two Fleets in the Channel and in the Mediterranean. They were fine figures in uniform, and very grave. One felt in actual contact with these French officers how truly the crisis was life or death for France. They spoke of basing the French Fleet on Malta—that same Malta for which we had fought Napoleon for so many years, which was indeed the very pretext of the renewal of the war in 1803. '*Malte ou la guerre!*' Little did the Napoleon of St. Helena dream that in her most desperate need France would have at her disposal the great Mediterranean base which his strategic instinct had deemed vital. I said to the Admirals, 'Use Malta as if it were Toulon.'

The minutes passed slowly.

Once more now in the march of centuries Old England was to stand forth in battle against the mightiest thrones and dominations. Once more in defence of the liberties of Europe and the common right must she enter upon a voyage of great toil and hazard across waters uncharted, towards coasts unknown, guided only by the stars. Once more 'the far-off line of storm-beaten ships' was to stand between the Continental Tyrant and the dominion of the world.

It was 11o'clock at night—12 by German time—when the ultimatum expired. The windows of the Admiralty were thrown wide open in the warm night air. Under the roof from which Nelson had received his orders were gathered a small group of Admirals and Captains and a cluster of clerks, pencil in hand, waiting. Along the Mall from the direction of the Palace the sound of an immense concourse singing 'God save the King' floated in. On this deep wave there broke the chimes of Big Ben; and, as the first stroke of the hour boomed out, a rustle of movement swept across the room. The war telegram, which meant 'Commence hostilities against Germany,' was flashed to the ships and establishments under the White Ensign all over the world.

I walked across the Horse Guards Parade to the Cabinet room and reported to the Prime Minister and the Ministers who were assembled there that the deed was done.

CHAPTER XI

WAR: THE PASSAGE OF THE ARMY: AUGUST 4—AUGUST 22, 1914

'The Time to visualize what will fall under the harrow of war is before the harrow is set in motion. Afterwards comes in Inevitableness with iron lips, and Fatalism with unscrutinizing gaze, and Use with filmed eyes, and Instinct with her cry, "Do not look too closely, seeing one must keep one's senses!"'

Mary Johnston, '*Cease Firing*,' Chapter XXIX.

British Strategy—The Great War Council, August 5—Four Divisions or Six—Changes in the Cabinet—Lord Kitchener: Secretary of State for War—Organization of the British Armies—Lord Kitchener's Task—The Royal Naval Division—Departure of the German and Austrian Ambassadors—The Board of Admiralty in War—Responsibilities of the First Lord—Procedure—The German Method—Relative Naval Strength—The Prospects of Battle—British Command of the Sea—Paralysis of the German Mercantile Marine—Frustration of the German Attack on Trade—The *Goeben* at Messina on August 5—Knowledge and Dispositions of Sir Berkeley Milne—Orders to the *Indomitable*—The Southern Exit—No Contact with the French—The *Goeben* and *Breslau* leave Messina—Rear-Admiral Troubridge's Successive Decisions—Second Escape of the *Goeben*—Explanations—A Sinister Fatality—Final Abandonment of the Pursuit—Transportation of the British Army to France—Instructions to Sir John Jellicoe—Covering Movements of the Fleet—Safe Passage of the Army—The Deadly Hush.

The entry of Great Britain into war with the most powerful military Empire which has ever existed was strategically impressive. Her large Fleets vanished into the mists at one end of the island. Her small Army hurried out of the country at the other. By this double gesture she might seem to uninstructed eyes to divest herself of all her means of defence, and to expose her coasts nakedly to the hostile thrust. Yet these two movements, dictated by the truest strategy, secured at once our own safety and the salvation of our Allies. The Grand Fleet gained the station whence the control of the seas could be irresistibly asserted. The Regular Army reached in the nick of time the vital post on the flank of the French line. Had all our action been upon this level, we should to-day be living in an easier world.

* * * * *

The differences which had prevailed about entering the war were aggravated by a strong cross-current of opinion, by no means operative only in the Cabinet, that if we participated it should be by naval action alone. Men of great power and influence, who throughout the struggle laboured tirelessly and rendered undoubted services, were found at this time resolutely opposed to the landing of a single soldier on the Continent. And, if everything had not been prepared, if the plan had not been perfected, if it had not been the only plan, and if all military opinion had not been industriously marshalled round it—who shall say what fatal hesitancy might not have intervened?

On the afternoon of August 5 the Prime Minister convened an extraordinary Council of War at Downing Street. I do not remember any gathering like it. It consisted of the Ministers most prominently associated with the policy of our entering the war, the chiefs of the Navy and the Army, all the high military commanders, and in addition Lord Kitchener and Lord Roberts. Decision was required upon the question, How should we wage the war that had just begun? Those who spoke for the War Office knew their own minds and were united. The whole British Army should be sent at once to France, according to what may justly be called the Haldane Plan. Everything in that Minister's eight years' tenure of the War Office had led up to this and had been sacrificed for this. To place an army of four or six divisions of infantry thoroughly equipped with their necessary cavalry on the left of the French line within twelve or fourteen days of the order to mobilize, and to guard the home island meanwhile by the fourteen Territorial Divisions he had organized, was the scheme upon which, aided by Field-Marshals Nicholson and French, he had concentrated all his efforts and his stinted resources. It was a simple plan, but it was a practical plan. It had been persistently pursued and laboriously and minutely studied. It represented approximately the maximum war effort that the voluntary system would yield applied in the most effective and daring manner to the decisive spot; and mobilization schemes, railway graphics, timetables, the organization of bases, depôts, supply arrangements, etc., filling many volumes, regulated and ensured a thorough and concerted execution. A commander whose whole life led up to this point had been chosen. All that remained to be done was to take the decision and give the signal.

At this point I reported on behalf of the Admiralty that our mobilization being in every respect complete and all our ships in their war stations, we would waive the claim we had hitherto made in all the discussions of the Committee of Imperial Defence that two Regular Divisions should be retained in Great Britain as a safeguard against invasion, and that so far as the Admiralty was concerned, not four but the whole six divisions could go at once; that we would provide for their transportation and for the security of the island in their absence. This considerable undertaking was made good by the Royal Navy.

Discussion then turned upon the place to which they should be dispatched. Lord Roberts inquired whether it was not possible to base the British Army on Antwerp so as to strike, in conjunction with the Belgian armies, at the flank and rear of the invading

German hosts. We were not able from an Admiralty point of view to guarantee the sea communications of so large a force on the enemy side of the Straits of Dover, but only inside the Anglo-French flotilla cordon which had already taken up its station. Moreover, no plans had been worked out by the War Office for such a contingency. They had concentrated all their thought upon integral co-operation with the French left wherever it might be. It was that or nothing.

Another discussion took place upon how far forward the British Expeditionary Force should be concentrated. Some high authorities, dwelling on the fact that the mobilization of the British army had begun three days later than the French, were for concentrating it around Amiens for intervention after the first shock of battle had been taken. But in the end Sir John French and the forward school had their way, and it was felt that we must help France in the way the French Staff thought would be most effective.

* * * * *

When I next went to the Cabinet after the declaration of war, I found myself with new companions. During the previous seven years Lord Morley had always sat on the left of the Prime Minister, and I had always sat next to Lord Morley. Many a wise and witty admonition had I received pencilled in scholarly phrase from my veteran neighbour, and many a charming courtesy such as he excelled in had graced the toilsome path of business. He had said to me on the Sunday of Resolve, 'If it has to be, I am not the man to do it. I should only hamper those like you who have to bear the burden.' Now he was gone. In his place sat Lord Kitchener. On my left also there was a fresh figure—the new Minister of Agriculture, Lord Lucas. I had known him since South African War days, when he lost his leg: and to know him was to delight in him. His open, gay, responsive nature, his witty, ironical, but never unchivalrous tongue, his pleasing presence, his compulsive smile, made him much courted by his friends, of whom he had many and of whom I was one. Young for the Cabinet, heir to splendid possessions, happy in all that surrounded him, he seemed to have captivated Fortune with the rest.

Both these two men were marked for death at the hands of the enemy, the young Minister grappling with his adversary in the high air, the old Field-Marshal choking in the icy sea. I wonder what the twenty politicians round the table would have felt if they had been told that the prosaic British Cabinet was itself to be decimated in the war they had just declared. I think they would have felt a sense of pride and of relief in sharing to some extent the perils to which they were to send their countrymen, their friends, their sons.

* * * * *

At the Council of War on August 5, Lord Kitchener had not yet become Secretary of State for War, but I knew that his appointment was impending. The Prime Minister, then also Secretary of State for War, could not possibly be burdened with the continuous flow of inter-departmental work proceeding between the War Office and the Admiralty and requiring to be transacted between Ministers. He therefore invited Lord Kitchener to undertake ministerial charge of the War Office, and the Field-Marshal, who had certainly not sought this post in any way, had no choice but to accept.

My relations with Lord Kitchener had been limited. Our first meeting had been on the field of Omdurman, when as a lieutenant in the 21st Lancers I had been sent back to report verbally to the Commander-in-Chief the position of the advancing Dervish Army. He had disapproved of me severely in my youth, had endeavoured to prevent me from coming to the Soudan Campaign, and was indignant that I had succeeded in getting there. It was a case of dislike before first sight. On my side, I had dealt with his character and campaigns in two bulky volumes conceived throughout in a faithful spirit of critical impartiality. It was twelve years before I saw him again, when we were formally introduced to each other and had a brief talk at the Army Manœuvres in 1910. I got to know him a little at the Malta Conference in 1912, and thenceforward we used to talk over Imperial Defence topics when from time to time we met. On these occasions I had found him much more affable than I had been led to expect from my early impressions or from all I had heard about him. In the week before the war we had lunched and dined together two or three times, and we had discussed all the possibilities so far as we could foresee them. I was glad when he was appointed Secretary of State for War, and in those early days we worked together on close and cordial terms. He consulted me constantly on the political aspects of his work, and increasingly gave me his confidence in military matters. Admiralty and War Office business were so interlaced that during the whole of the first ten months we were in almost daily personal consultation. I cannot forget that when I left the Admiralty in May, 1915, the first and, with one exception, the only one of my colleagues who paid me a visit of ceremony was the over-burdened Titan whose disapprobation had been one of the disconcerting experiences of my youth.

* * * * *

As is well known, the British armies on mobilization consisted of a highly organized expeditionary force of six Regular Divisions of Infantry and a Cavalry Division. In addition there were two Regular Infantry Divisions, the 7th and 8th, which had to be collected from their garrisons all over the Empire or formed out of troops surplus to the Expeditionary Force at home; and it was decided also to employ two divisions, half British and half native, from India. Behind these trained forces, unquestionably of a very high order, stood fourteen Territorial Divisions and thirteen mounted Brigades to whom the defence of Britain must be confided. These were little trained, lightly equipped with artillery, but composed of far-sighted and intelligent men who had not waited for the hour of danger to make their country's cause their own. In six months or, as some thought, in a shorter period, such troops could be made to play their part.

Lord Kitchener now came forward to the Cabinet, on almost the first occasion after he joined us, and in soldierly sentences proclaimed a series of inspiring and prophetic truths. Every one expected that the war would be short; but wars took unexpected courses, and we must now prepare for a long struggle. Such a conflict could not be ended on the sea or by sea-power alone. It could be ended only by great battles on the Continent. In these the British Empire must bear its part on a scale proportionate to its magnitude and power.

We must be prepared to put armies of millions in the field and maintain them for several years. In no other way could we discharge our duty to our allies or to the world.

These words were received by the Cabinet in silent assent; and it is my belief that had Lord Kitchener proceeded to demand universal national service to be applied as it might be required, his request would have been acceded to. He, however, proposed to content himself with calling for volunteers, and in the first instance to form six new regular divisions. It would have been far better to have formed the new volunteers upon the cadres of the Territorial Army, each of which could have been duplicated or quadruplicated in successive stages. But the new Secretary of State had little knowledge of and no faith in the British territorial system. The name itself was to him a stumbling-block. In the war of 1870 he had been present at a battle on the Loire, probably Le Mans, in which the key of the position, confided to French Territorial troops, had been cast away, entailing the defeat of the whole army. He dwelt on this incident to me on several occasions, and I know it had created fixed impressions in his mind. Vain to explain how entirely different were the characters of the troops forming the French and British Territorial forces—the former aged conscripts in their last periods of service; the latter keen and ardent youths of strong military predilections. They were Territorials, and that was the end of it.

This at the very outset aggravated the difficulties of his already gigantic task. He set himself to create the cadres first of six, then of twelve, and ultimately of twenty-four 'Kitchener Army' divisions, at the same time that the recruits were pouring in upon him by the hundred thousand. That this vast feat of improvisation was accomplished must certainly rank among the wonders of the time.

The arguments against compulsory service, cogent as they no doubt were, were soon reinforced by the double event of overwhelming numbers of volunteers and of a total lack of arms and equipment. Apart from the exiguous stores held by the Regular Army, there was literally nothing. The small scale of our military forces had led to equally small factories for war material. There were no spare rifles, there were no extra guns; and the modest supplies of shells and ammunition began immediately to flash away with what seemed appalling rapidity. Many months must elapse, even if the best measures were taken, before new sources of supply even on a moderate scale could be opened up. One was now to learn for the first time that it took longer to make a rifle than a gun; and rifles were the cruellest need of all. We had nothing but staves to put in the hands of the eager men who thronged the recruiting stations. I ransacked the Fleet and the Admiralty stores and scraped together another 30,000 rifles, which literally meant another 30,000 men in the field. Afloat only the Marines would have their rifles; Jack must, in the last resort, trust to his cutlass as of old.

At the moment when Lord Kitchener began the formation of his first six new army divisions and before the great rush of, recruits had begun, I offered him the Royal Naval Division, which he gladly accepted. Before the war we had foreseen the fact that the Navy would on mobilization have many thousands of men in their depots for whom there would be no room in any ship of war that we could send to sea. I had therefore proposed to the Committee of Imperial Defence in 1913 the formation of three brigades, one composed of Marines and the other two of men of the Royal Naval

Volunteer Reserve and of the Royal Fleet Reserve. These brigades it was intended to use to assist in home defence in the early stages of a war. The cadres were therefore easily formed from the available resources. The Marine Brigade was already virtually in existence, and it was clear that all three would be ready for action long before any of the new troops that were being raised. The Naval Volunteers, who longed to serve afloat, accepted the new task with many heartburnings but with boundless loyalty. Alas, for most of them it proved a fateful decision. Few there were of that gallant company that survived unscathed. As for their deeds, they will not be forgotten in the history even of these crowded times.[1]

* * * * *

It fell to my lot to prescribe the arrangements for the departure of the German Ambassador and, eight days later, of his Austrian colleague. Accordingly on the morning of August 5, I sent my Naval Secretary Admiral Hood in uniform to the German Embassy desiring to know in what manner we might facilitate Prince Lichnowsky's wishes and convenience. While the German mob were insulting and even pelting the departing French and British Ambassadors, we set ourselves to work with meticulous care to secure the observance of every propriety and courtesy towards those for whom we were responsible. Prince Lichnowsky has given his own record of his ceremonious treatment, which appeared to make a marked impression upon his mind.

To Count Mensdorf, the Austrian Ambassador, I wrote as follows:—

August 13, 1914.

> My Naval Secretary Admiral Hood, who brings this letter, is instructed to put himself at your disposal in arranging for the comfort and convenience of your journey by sea. If there is any way in which I can be of service to you at this time, you will not I hope fail to command me.
>
> Although the terrible march of events has swept aside the ancient friendship between our countries, the respect and regard which spring from so many years of personal association cannot pass from the hearts of your English friends.

The Austrian Ambassador asked that a ship might be provided to take him direct to Trieste, and that consideration might be shown to a number of unhappy Austrian noncombatants long resident in London who now had to fly the country. I therefore arranged that upwards of 200 persons should embark in the Ambassador's ship. I felt sure that in taking these measures I was acting in accord with what British dignity required.

* * * * *

The position of the Admiralty in relation to the Fleet, and of the First Lord in relation to his naval colleagues under conditions of war, requires explanation. The control of

[1]The minute constituting the Division is printed in Appendix E.

the main armies was divided between the War Office and General Headquarters, but in the Admiralty these functions were inevitably combined to a far larger extent. The Naval Commander-in-Chief, living with his actual fighting Fleet and always ready at a few hours' notice to lead it personally into full battle, stood much nearer to the event than his military counterpart. The staff which he could accommodate upon his flagship, the volume of business which he could transact, were necessarily limited by physical conditions. Everything must be ready to move at the shortest notice into extreme danger, and Staff, office, organization, Commander-in-Chief, might vanish out of existence in an instant. The first duty of the Commander-in-Chief was to keep his mind and body fit for the supreme task of personally commanding the mighty array of ships when in contact with the enemy. The vigilant guarding of the Fleet from danger, its training for battle, its organization, its efficiency and the direct personal conduct of individual operations were all concentrated in one man. But this was enough. It was the duty of the Admiralty so far as possible to shield him from all further responsibilities or anxieties, to lap him round with securities and assistance and to bear all other parts of the great load of war themselves.

The Admiralty itself was also in direct contact with the event. It not only exercised administrative control over the Navy and over the whole of the preparations for strengthening and developing the Fleet; it not only determined the strategic distribution of our naval power in every theatre; but from its wireless masts or by cable it issued information often of a vital character to ships in many instances actually in contact with the enemy. It was the only place from which the supreme view of the naval scene could be obtained. It was the intelligence centre where all information was received, where alone it could be digested, and whence it was transmitted wherever required. It moved the fleets, squadrons and flotillas out of harbour when information pointed to enemy's activities being probable. It specified the minimum forces which should be employed in any operation, while leaving the Commander-in-Chief free to add to them at his discretion. Apart from actual battle or the tactical conduct of particular operations, in which the Admiralty never interfered, it decided every important question arising out of the conduct of the naval war. Robed in the august authority of centuries of naval tradition and armed with the fullest knowledge available, the Board of Admiralty wielded unchallenged power.

As these conditions arose naturally and inevitably and will certainly be reproduced in one form or another should there be a future war, it is of high importance to pierce beneath the corporate responsibility of this organism and lay bare how the machine actually worked. In practice it resolved itself, and could only resolve itself, into the intimate comradeship and co-operation of the First Lord and the First Sea Lord with the Chief of the Staff, not at this time a member of the Board, standing at their side. By the Letters Patent and Orders in Council constituting his office, the First Lord is responsible to Crown and Parliament for all the business of the Admiralty. In virtue of this he delegates to an eminent sailor the responsibility for its technical and professional conduct. But he cannot thus relieve himself either in theory or in fact. He is held strictly accountable for all that takes place; for every disaster he must bear the blame. The credit of victories rightly goes to the commanders who gain them; the burden of defeat or miscarriage must be shouldered by the Admiralty, and the censures of the nation fall primarily upon its Head.

How then is a civilian Minister appointed for political or parliamentary reasons and devoid of authoritative expert knowledge, to acquit himself of his duty? Clearly it depends upon the character, temperament and capacity both of the First Lord and the First Sea Lord. They must settle it between themselves, and if they cannot agree whole-heartedly on the momentous problems with which they are confronted in swift succession, another combination must be chosen by the Sovereign on the advice of the Prime Minister. I interpreted my duty in the following way: I accepted full responsibility for bringing about successful results, and in that spirit I exercised a close general supervision over everything that was done or proposed. Further, I claimed and exercised an unlimited power of suggestion and initiative over the whole field, subject only to the approval and agreement of the First Sea Lord on all operative orders. Right or wrong, that is what I did, and it is on that basis that I wish to be judged.

In practice the difficulties were less than would be imagined. Indeed, over long periods of unending crisis and tension the machine worked very smoothly. The Second, Third and Fourth Sea Lords dropped back upon the outbreak of war into the positions the 'Supply Boards' had occupied in the great naval wars of the past. They were the providers of men, of ships and of stores. They took no part, or only a very occasional part, in strategic decisions. It was the responsibility of the First Sea Lord to keep the Second Sea Lord fully informed of what was in progress in order that the latter could replace him temporarily at a moment's notice. In practice, however, both Prince Louis and Lord Fisher worked more closely with the Chief of the Staff, and these two presented themselves to me always in full accord.

The constitutional authority of the Board of Admiralty was exercised at that time in accordance with long custom by two Members of the Board, sitting together with the Secretary of the Admiralty. Thus the Admiralty War Group at the beginning of the struggle consisted of the First Lord, the First Sea Lord, the Chief of the Staff and the Secretary. To these were added, when the First Sea Lord wished and on particular occasions, the Second Sea Lord and certain special advisers, of whom more anon. We met every day and sometimes twice a day, reviewed the whole position and arrived at a united decision on every matter of consequence. The execution was confided to the Chief of the Staff. The Secretary registered, recorded, and, apart from the orders given by the War Staff, took the consequential action. Besides our regular meetings the First Sea Lord and I consulted together constantly at all hours. Within the limits of our agreed policy either he or I gave in writing authority for telegrams and decisions which the Chief of the Staff might from hour to hour require. Moreover, it happened in a large number of cases that seeing what ought to be done and confident of the agreement of the First Sea Lord, I myself drafted the telegrams and decisions in accordance with our policy, and the Chief of the Staff took them personally to the First Sea Lord for his concurrence before dispatch. In addition to these urgent executive matters, the regular flow of Admiralty papers passed upwards from the First Sea Lord or other Lords to me for decision by minute; and I further, by minutes and memoranda, initiated discussion and action over the whole area of naval business.

The advantages and disadvantages of these methods must be judged by their general results; but it is instructive to compare them with those which we now know prevailed at the German Admiralty. On the outbreak of war, the Naval Secretary of State von Tirpitz, himself an admiral, found himself cut off entirely from the strategical and quasi-tactical control of the fleets, to such an extent that he declares, 'he did not know the naval war plans.' He was confined to purely administrative business, and thus charged, he was carried off as an adjunct to the Emperor's suite at Great Headquarters. The Naval Staff, headed in the first instance by von Pohl, alone had the ear of the Emperor and received from the lips of the All-Highest indications of his Imperial pleasure. The position of Admiral von Tirpitz was therefore most unhappy. The Naval Staff warded him off the Emperor as much as possible, and persuaded the Emperor to repulse his efforts to break in. The Emperor, oppressed with the whole burden of the State, gave to the Staff from time to time directions and uttered passing expressions which thereafter operated with irresistible authority. It is to this state of affairs that Admiral von Tirpitz ascribes the paralysis which gripped the German Fleet through the first critical months of the naval war. This it was, according to him, that lost the opportunity of fighting the supreme battle under the least unfavourable conditions, enabled the control of the seas to pass into our hands practically without a struggle, and secured the uninterrupted transport of our armies to the Continent. If our solution of the difficult problem of naval war direction was imperfect, so also was that of our enemy.

* * * * *

A study of the tables and diagrams set out in the Appendix[2] shows that our known margin of superiority in Home Waters was smaller then than at any subsequent moment in the war. The Grand Fleet as concentrated in its Northern war station on August 1, 1914, comprised 24 vessels classified as 'Dreadnoughts' or better. In addition the battle-cruiser *Invincible* was at Queenstown watching the Atlantic, the two *Lord Nelsons* were with the Channel Fleet, and three battle-cruisers were in the Mediterranean. The Germans actually mobilized 16 ships similarly classed.[3] We could not be absolutely certain, though we thought it unlikely, that they might not have ready two, or even three, more; and these of the greatest power. Happily, every British ship was ready and in perfect order. None was under repair. Our strength for an immediate fleet action was 24 to a certain 16 and a possible 19. These figures do not, as the tables in the Appendix reveal, do justice to the full material strength of the British Fleets as a whole, still less to the gun-power of the British Line of Battle, which after the Dreadnoughts comprised eight King Edwards markedly superior to the next eight Germans. But apart from all that may be said on this, and of the confidence which it inspired, the fact remains that from five to eight Dreadnoughts was all the certain numerical superiority we had. There was not much margin here for

---

[2]Appendix B.

[3]Admiral Scheer, p. 13.

mischance, nor for the percentage of mechanical defects which in so large a Fleet has to be expected, and no margin whatever for a disaster occasioned by surprise had we been unready. To a superficial observer who from the cliffs of Dover or Portland had looked down upon a Battle Squadron of six or seven ships, lying in distant miniature below, the foundation upon which the British world floated would have presented itself in a painfully definite form. If the intelligence and courage of British seamen were not all that we believed them to be; if the workmanship which had built these great vessels were not honest and thorough; if our seamanship or our gunnery had turned out to be inferior; if some ghastly novelty or blunder supervened—the battle might be very even.

It is easy to understand how tense were the British naval expectations. If the German Navy was ever to fight a battle, now at the beginning was its best chance. The German Admiralty knew, of course, what ships we had available, and that we were mobilized, concentrated and at sea. Even if they assumed the extraordinary fact that every one of our Dreadnoughts was ready and that not one of them had developed a defect, they could fight to German eyes a battle of 16 against a maximum 27—heavy odds from their point of view, still heavier when the survey was extended to the whole of the Fleets, but yet odds far less heavy than they would have to face after six months, after twelve months or at any later period. For look at the reinforcements which were approaching these two opposing Fleets. They must assume that, in addition to completing our own vessels, we should requisition every battleship building for a foreign Power in our yards, and on this basis seven great ships must join the Grand Fleet within three months, and twelve great ships within six months, against which only three in three months and five in six months could be reckoned on their side, leaving the balance in three months at 34 to 19 and in six months at 39 to 21; and this took no account of three battle-cruisers in the Mediterranean and one (*Australia*) in the Pacific which obviously we could bring home if necessary.

Here then, was the least unfavourable moment for Germany; here was the best chance they would ever see. Was it not also the strategic moment? Might they not assume that the transportation of the British Army to France would be a grave preoccupation for the Admiralty? Was it not clear that a victory, even a partial victory, would be more fruitful at this juncture than at any other? Forty-two fast German merchant cruisers needed only a breathing space to get loose and to arm upon the seas, requiring afterwards to be hunted down one by one. Might not above all the interruption and delay in the transportation of the Army be of real effect in the supreme trial of strength on land? The German Staff believed in a short war. They were staking everything upon a supreme trial of strength on land. Why should not the German Fleet be hurled in too and play its part for what it was worth in the supreme decision? To what other equal use could it ever be put?

We therefore looked for open battle on the sea. We expected it and we courted it. The news that the two Navies were approaching each other to take a decision in blue water would have been received in the Fleet with unaffected satisfaction, and at the Admiralty with composure. We could not send our Grand Fleet into the minefields and submarine-infested areas of the Heligoland Bight. But had battle been offered by the enemy under any conditions which did not put us at a serious disadvantage, it would have been at once accepted.

In fact, however, the sober confidence of the Admiralty was based upon calculations of relative naval strength, the soundness of which was not disputed by the German Naval Staff. Even von Tirpitz, the advocate of action, writes (*Memories vol. II*, p. 356): 'Against an immediate fight was the fact that the whole English Fleet was ready for battle when the war broke out owing to the test mobilization, whereas only our active squadrons were ready.' 'Great Britain,' says the Official German Naval History, '. . . had secured extensive military advantages by her test mobilization and her subsequent measures, regardless of the uneasiness necessarily provoked thereby. . . which advantage Germany could not counter or overtake.' The German Staff felt that even if this was the best chance for a trial of strength, it was still a chance so hazardous and even so forlorn that it was not worth taking; and their Battle Fleet remained hoarded up in harbour for an ignominious day, imposing upon the British, no doubt, a continued and serious expenditure of our resources for naval purposes, gaining for Germany substantial advantages of a secondary character, but not exercising any decisive influence upon the whole course of the war.

So we waited; and nothing happened. No great event immediately occurred. No battle was fought. The Grand Fleet remained at sea: the German Fleet did not quit the shelter of its harbours. There were no cruiser actions. A German minelayer sowing a minefield off Harwich was chased and sunk by a flotilla of destroyers led by the *Amphion*; and the *Amphion* returning, was blown up on the German minefield. Otherwise silence unbroken by cannon brooded over the broad and narrow waters. But during that silence and from its first moment the sea-power of Great Britain ruled unchallenged throughout the world. Every German cruiser in foreign waters vanished into the immense spaces of the sea; every German merchant ship, from the earliest moment when the entry of Britain into the war became apparent, fled for neutral harbours. Seven out of eight potential commerce destroyers were bottled up without ever a shot being fired. German seaborne trade outside the Baltic ceased to exist from the night of August 4. On the other hand, after a few days of hesitation the swarming mercantile marine of Britain, encouraged by a Government insurance of no more than six per cent., began to put to sea; and even before the main armies had met in battle on the Continent, the whole vast ocean traffic of the British Empire was proceeding with the utmost activity. By the end of August the rate of insurance had already fallen to 3 per cent., and the Admiralty was able to announce that of the forty-two German liners from whom attacks on trade were to be apprehended, eleven were tied up unarmed in harbours of the United States watched outside territorial limits by British cruisers, six had taken refuge in other neutral harbours, where they were either dismantled or observed, fourteen were in German ports gripped by the blockade, six were held as prizes in British hands, and only five remained unaccounted for and unlocated. The fate of these five will be recounted later.

All fell out in these respects, therefore, in broad accordance with the views set forth in my memorandum on commerce protection of August 23, 1913, revised in April, 1914, which is printed in full in the Appendix for the benefit of the thorough.[4] None of those

[4]Appendix C. I hope it may be read.—W.S.C.

gloomy prophecies which had formed the staple of so many debates and articles, that our merchant ships would be hunted from the seas by German raiders, that scores of additional British cruisers would be required for commerce protection, that British merchant ships once safe in harbour would not venture to sea, materialized; and they might be relegated to the limbo of exploded alarms. The three great naval dangers which had bulked most largely in our minds in the years before the war—first, the danger of surprise of the Fleet; second, the Mine danger; third, the paralysis of our seaborne trade—rolled away behind us like giant waves which a ship has finally surmounted.

More than a hundred years had passed since the British Navy had been called upon to face an emergency of the first magnitude. If a hundred years hence, in similar circumstances, it is found equally ready, we shall have no more reason to complain of our descendants than they will find in the history of this convulsion, reason to complain of us.

* * * * *

It is time to return to the Mediterranean.

Admiral Souchon, the German Commander, having outdistanced our shadowing cruisers in the darkness of the night, pursued his course to Messina, where he arrived with the *Goeben* and *Breslau* on the morning of August 5. He had already received, as we now know, a telegram sent from Nauen at 1.35 a.m. on the preceding day by the German Admiralty. This message gave him all-important information. It stated that an alliance had been concluded between Germany and Turkey, and directed him to proceed to Constantinople immediately. Of this treaty we knew nothing. All our reports were of an entirely different tenor; nor was it till long afterwards that we learnt the true attitude of Turkey at this hour.

On arrival at Messina the *Goeben* and *Breslau* began to coal from German colliers. This occupied the whole of the day, the whole of the night and the greater part of the next day, the 6th. Exactly thirty-six hours elapsed before the *Goeben* moved. Meanwhile the light cruiser *Gloucester*, watching off the Southern exit of the Straits of Messina, reported at 3.35 p.m. on August 5 to Sir Berkeley Milne that the strength of the wireless signals she was taking in indicated that the *Goeben* must be at Messina.

The British Commander-in-Chief had left the Malta Channel in his flagship the *Inflexible* after midnight of August 4, and at about 11 a.m. on August 5 he had assembled all his three battle-cruisers and two light cruisers off Pantellaria island, midway between Sicily and the African coast.[5] According to his own published account,[6] he had learned on the 4th that the German mail steamer *General* was remaining at Messina at the disposition of the *Goeben*. He therefore believed throughout the whole of the 5th that 'the *Goeben*, *Breslau* and *General* were all at Messina.' His belief was correct.

One of his battle-cruisers, the *Indomitable*, had to coal. He sent her to Biserta. This was an important decision. Considering that he believed that the *Goeben* was at Messina,

---

[5]See map on pages 178–9.

[6]*The Flight of the Goeben*, Admiral Sir Berkeley Milne.

and that he intended himself to watch to the Northward with two battle-cruisers, some authorities have held that it would have been a sensible precaution to let his third ship coal at Malta, where facilities were certain and instant, and whence she could so easily move to close the Southern exit from Messina, or join Rear-Admiral Troubridge in the mouth of the Adriatic, as that officer had been led to expect.[7] By sending the *Indomitable* to coal at Malta, he could have placed two battle-cruisers watching the Northern exit and one at the Southern. But the Commander-in-Chief decided to keep all three battle-cruisers together in his own hand and to patrol off the Western end of Sicily between Sardinia and Biserta. The Southern exit was therefore left completely open to the *Goeben:* and a severe action was reserved for Rear-Admiral Troubridge if, as seemed likely, she ran up the Adriatic.

At 5 p.m. on the 5th, Sir Berkeley Milne received the signal sent by the *Gloucester* at 3.35 p.m. reporting the presence of the *Goeben* at Messina. Here was certain confirmation of his belief. He was at this moment about 100 miles West of Sicily. He continued however to cruise with his two ships between Sicily and Sardinia, and as late as the evening of August 6, his orders to the *Indomitable* were still to join him thereabouts. He did this because he considered that placing all three battle-cruisers in this position was his surest way of carrying out the instructions of the Admiralty telegram of July 30 about aiding the French in the transport of their African army. That it was one method of carrying out these orders cannot be disputed, and the Admiral has set out in his book the reasons which led him to adopt it. The superior speed of the *Goeben* made it necessary, he states, if he were to intercept her, that he should stand a long way off and have timely notice of her approach. To place his whole force in this way between her and the French transports was, he argues, the best chance of catching the *Goeben* if she tried to attack them. He reported his intended dispositions late on the 4th to the Admiralty, whose only comment upon them was, 'Watch over the Adriatic should be maintained for the double purpose of preventing the Austrians from coming out or the Germans from entering.' The exceedingly prompt manner in which the *Goeben* had been found, although in the open sea, on the 4th had given the Admiralty the feeling that the Admiral on the spot had a grip of the situation and needed no further directions.

Sir Berkeley Milne had not, however, succeeded in communicating with the French Admiral, although he had made repeated attempts by wireless and had sent the *Dublin* to Biserta with a letter. He did not know where the French Fleet or the French transports were. He did not tell the Admiralty this. The Admiralty for their part, after the general telegram of August 4 enjoining immediate consultation with the French, assumed that the two Commanders-in-Chief in the Mediterranean were acting in concert. They did not therefore ask the French for any information, nor was any volunteered by the French Admiralty. Any inquiry addressed to Paris would have elicited the fact that the French had changed their plans and that no transports were yet at sea. All parties were on this point to some extent in fault.

---

[7]See Official Naval History, pages 60, 61.

Meanwhile the British Ambassador in Rome was endeavouring to tell the Admiralty as soon as the pressure on the wires allowed, that the *Goeben* was at Messina. The news did not reach London till 6 p.m. on August 5. The Admiralty passed it without comment, though with some delay, to Sir Berkeley Milne, who already knew from other sources. It is a fair criticism on the Admiralty that they did not immediately they knew the *Goeben* was at Messina authorize the British ships to follow her into the Straits. The point was not put to me either by the First Sea Lord or the Chief of the Staff, and as I had not myself been concerned in initiating or drafting the telegram about rigidly respecting Italian neutrality, it was not specially in my mind. Had it been put to me I should at once have consented. This was no petty incident and the prize was well worth the risk of vexing the Italians. In fact, permission to chase through the Straits was given by the Admiralty unasked to Sir Berkeley Milne, as soon as it was realized that the *Goeben* was escaping unblocked to the Southward. It was then too late.

In pursuance of the orders he had received from Germany, Admiral Souchon with the *Goeben* and *Breslau*, having at length completed coaling and made his will, steamed out of Messina harbour at 5 p.m. on August 6, cleared for action and with his bands playing. He no doubt expected to encounter at least one and possibly two of the British battle-cruisers as soon as he was outside territorial waters. In view of the fact that, as he was aware, his position must have been accurately known to the British Commander-in-Chief for many hours, this assumption was not unreasonable. Unhappily, as has been described, every one of the three British battle-cruisers was otherwise engaged. Thus when the German Admiral rounded the Southern point of Italy and turned Eastward, the only three antagonists whose combination of power and speed he had to dread were already far astern.

Still there was the British armoured cruiser squadron watching the Adriatic. This squadron consisted of four good ships, viz. *Defence*, *Warrior*, *Duke of Edinburgh* and *Black Prince*. It was commanded by Rear-Admiral Troubridge, who had also under his orders eight destroyers, and was being joined by the light cruiser *Dublin* and two more destroyers from Malta. It is necessary to restate the facts of this officer's action.

On the assumption—which was dominant—that the *Goeben* would make for Pola, Admiral Troubridge was well placed for meeting her. It was not until he heard from the *Gloucester* that she had turned South and was persistently steering on a South-Easterly course that any new decision was required from him. He received no orders to quit his station from Sir Berkeley Milne. He was in constant hope of receiving a battle-cruiser. But Admiral Troubridge decided to act on his own responsibility. Eight minutes after midnight of August 6 (i.e. 0.08, August 7) he gave orders to his four cruisers and his eight destroyers to steam Southward at full speed for the purpose of intercepting the *Goeben*. He also signalled to the *Dublin* (Captain John Kelly), at that moment coming from Malta to join him with the two extra destroyers, to head her off. He reported his decision to the Commander-in-Chief. Thus at midnight August 6–7 sixteen British vessels were converging upon the *Goeben* and *Breslau* and were in positions from which they could hardly fail to intercept the enemy shortly after daylight. At 3.50 a.m., however, after further reflection and having received no orders or reply from Sir Berkeley Milne,

Admiral Troubridge became convinced that he could not hope to engage the *Goeben* under the advantageous conditions of the half light of dawn, and that in an action fought in broad waters in full daylight, his four ships would be sunk one after another by the *Goeben*, who all the time would keep outside the range—16,000 yards—of the British 9.2-inch guns. This is thought by some naval officers to be an extreme view. The limited ammunition of the *Goeben* would have had to have been wonderfully employed to have sunk all four British armoured cruisers *seriatim* at this long range.[8] Moreover, if the *Goeben* and *Breslau* had become involved in an action, it is hard to believe that none of the sixteen British cruisers and destroyers which were available could have closed in upon them and attacked them with gun or torpedo. All the destroyers were capable of reaching the enemy and could have found their opportunity to attack. It would have been indeed a prodigious feat on the part of the Germans to dispose of so many antagonists at once. However, the Admiral came to the conclusion that the *Goeben* was 'a superior force' which by his instructions, passed to him by the Commander-in-Chief, he was not to engage. And in this conclusion he has been sustained by a British naval court-martial.

He thereupon desisted from his attempt to intercept the *Goeben*, turned his ships and destroyers and entered the harbour of Zante about 10 a.m. preparatory to resuming his watch in the Adriatic. The *Dublin* and her two destroyers having asked and been refused permission to make a daylight attack, had attempted to intercept the *Goeben* before dawn, but did not succeed in finding her in the darkness.

By 6 o'clock therefore on the morning of August 7 the *Goeben*, already the fastest capital unit in the Mediterranean, was steaming on an unobstructed course for the Dardanelles, carrying with her for the peoples of the East and Middle East more slaughter, more misery and more ruin than has ever before been borne within the compass of a ship.

Thus of all the British vessels which were or could have been brought within effective distance, none did anything useful excepting only the two light cruisers *Dublin* and *Gloucester*, commanded, as it happened, by two brothers. The *Dublin* (Captain John Kelly) as we have seen did all in her power to place herself and her two destroyers athwart the enemy's course and to fight him by night or day; and the *Gloucester* (Captain W. A. Howard Kelly) hung on to the heels of the *Goeben* till late in the afternoon, in extreme danger and with the utmost tenacity, and only relinquished the chase under the direct orders of the Commander-in-Chief.

Various explanations have been offered for the failure to bring the *Goeben* to action after the declaration of war, and every telegram sent by the Admiralty was searched to find phrases which could justify or palliate what had occurred. For instance, it was pleaded that the sentence in the Admiralty telegram to the Commander-in-Chief of July 30, 'Do not at this stage be brought to action against superior forces except in combination with the French as part of a general battle,' justified Admiral Troubridge in refraining from attacking the *Goeben* with his four armoured cruisers. On this it may be

---

[8]At the Falklands the two British battle-cruisers used up nearly three-quarters of their ammunition to sink only two weaker antagonists, using 12-inch guns against 8.8 inch. The *Goeben* single-handed would have had to have sunk four, using 11-inch guns against 9.2 inch.

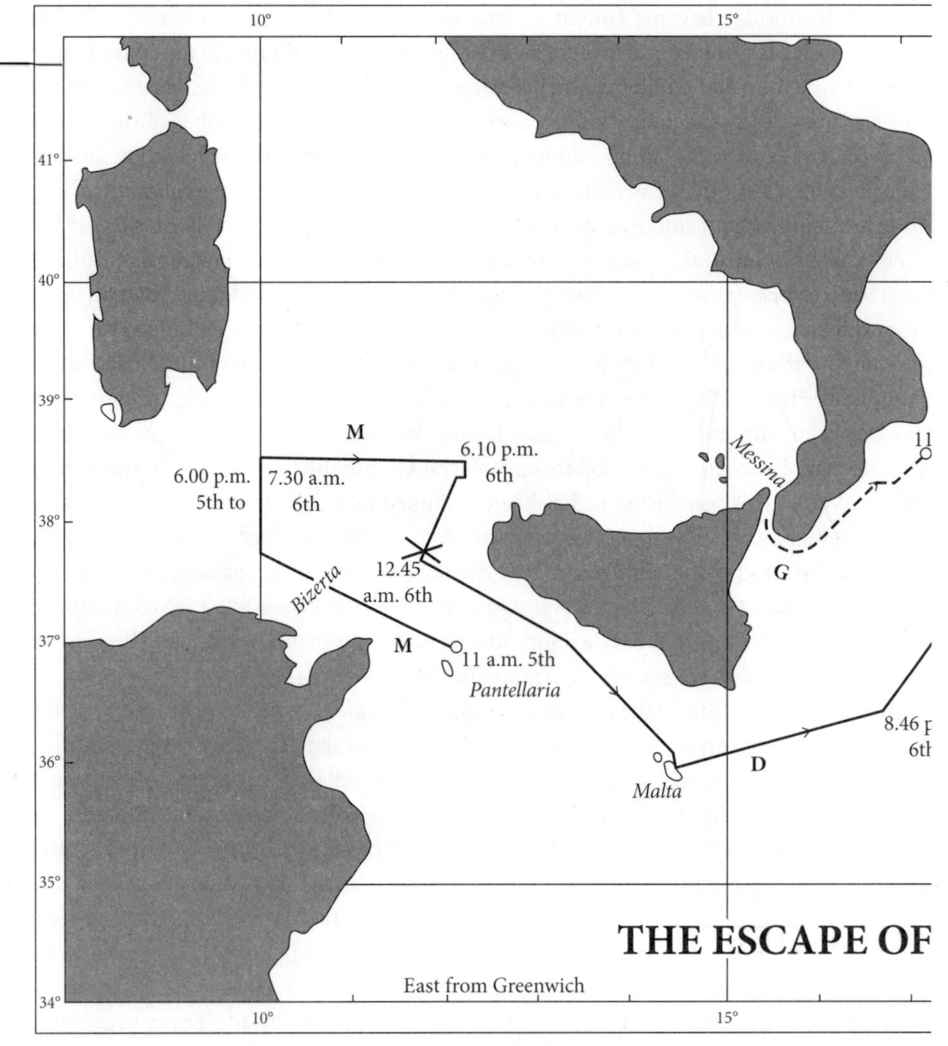

EXPLANATION.

M MILNE WITH TWO BATTLE CRUISERS, TWO LIGHT CRUISERS.
T TROUBRIDGE WITH FOUR ARMOURED CRUISERS, EIGHT DESTROYERS.
D LIGHT CRUISER DUBLIN AND TWO DESTROYERS JOINING TROUBRIDGE.
G GOEBEN AND BRESLAU SHADOWED BY GLOUCESTER.
X POSITIONS AT MIDNIGHT, AUGUST 6th, 7th.

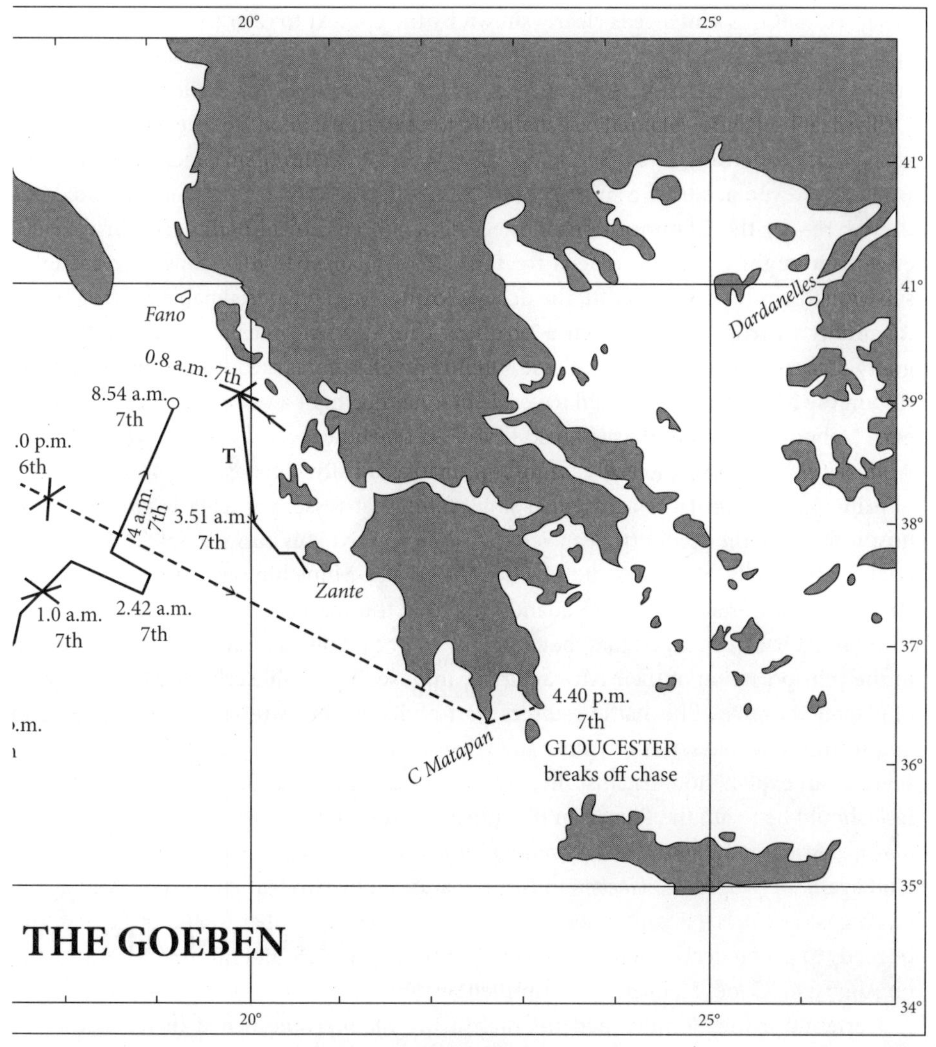

TIME TABLE.

0.8 A.M.,	5th.	MILNE LEAVES MALTA FOR MERIDIAN OF 10°E.
1.15 A.M.,	5th.	ORDERS RECEIVED TO COMMENCE HOSTILITIES AGAINST GERMANY.
5.0 A.M.,	*5th.*	*GOEBEN ARRIVED MESSINA.*
11.0 A.M.,	5th.	INFLEXIBLE, INDEFATIGABLE, INDOMITABLE, DUBLIN, WEYMOUTH, CHATHAM RENDEZVOUS OFF PANTELLARIA. DUBLIN SENT TO MALTA TO COAL AND THEN TAKE TWO DESTROYERS TO TROUBRIDGE, INDOMITABLE SENT TO BIZERTA TO COAL. MILNE WITH INFLEXIBLE, INDEFATIGABLE, WEYMOUTH AND CHATHAM STEERS FOR MERIDIAN 10°E.
3.35 P.M.,	5th.	GLOUCESTER REPORTS GOEBEN AT MESSINA.
7.30 A.M.,	6th.	MILNE LEAVES HIS PATROL LINE AND STEAMS EAST.
5.0 P.M.,	*6th.*	*GOEBEN LEAVES MESSINA.*
10.45 P.M.,	*6th.*	*GOEBEN TURNS SOUTH-EAST.*
0.8 A.M.,	7th.	TROUBRIDGE RESOLVES TO INTERCEPT HER AND STEERS SOUTH.
3.51 A.M.,	7th.	TROUBRIDGE TURNS INTO ZANTE.
NOON,	7th.	MILNE ARRIVES MALTA.
4.40 P.M.,	7th.	GLOUCESTER OFF MATAPAN, GIVES UP, BY ORDERS, HER TENACIOUS CHASE.

observed that this sentence is clearly shown by the context to refer to the Austrian Fleet against whose battleships it was not desirable that our three battle-cruisers should be engaged without battleship support. Secondly, it was contained in a telegram giving the Commander-in-Chief general directions for the strategic conduct of the naval campaign in the Mediterranean. It was not intended by the Admiralty to govern tactical action. The words, however, acquired a more particular significance when they were repeated—as they were—by the Commander-in-Chief to his subordinate, Admiral Troubridge. But even so it ought not to have been treated as a veto upon British ships ever engaging superior forces however needful the occasion. This was an unreasonable reading of the Admiralty instructions. On such a reading both the *Gloucester* and the *Dublin* were guilty of disobedience. On such a reading, pedantically construed, no individual British ship in the Mediterranean would have been allowed to fight a vessel stronger by a single gun. Nobody ever honestly supposed that such doctrines were being laid down by the Admiralty. Moreover, the self-same telegram specifically emphasized the importance of bringing the *Goeben* to action and singled out that vessel particularly among all the hostile forces in the Mediterranean. No such conception of his duty was taken by either of the Captains Kelly. Nor was it the view of Sir Berkeley Milne himself; for he disapproved strongly of Admiral Troubridge's abandonment of the chase.

Again, it has been urged that the sentence, 'Your first task should be to aid the French in the transportation of their African army,' imposed upon Sir Berkeley Milne the duty of placing *all three* of his battle-cruisers west of Sicily. Thus wrested from their context and from the whole series of Admiralty telegrams, these directions have been made to serve as an explanation. Against them must be read the full text. On July 30,'Your first task should be to aid the French in the transportation of their African army *by covering and if possible bringing to action individual fast German ships, particularly* "*Goeben*."'[9] And again, on August 2, '*Goeben* must be shadowed by two battle-cruisers.' And again, on August 3, '*Goeben* is your objective. Follow her and shadow her *wherever she goes*, and be ready to act on declaration of war, which appears probable and imminent.' And again, on August 4, 'Good. Hold er. War imminent.'

Certainly if the Commander-in-Chief in the Mediterranean had in reliance upon these dominant and reiterated instructions managed to put one battle-cruiser each side of the Straits of Messina, instead of all on one side, and if in consequence he had brought the *Goeben* to action, as would have been inevitable, and if he had thus protected the French transports in the most effectual manner by fighting the *Goeben*, no one could have found fault with him on the score that he had exceeded his orders.

The reader is now in a position to form his own judgment on this affair. I have indicated plainly the point on which the Admiralty was in fault, namely, in not spontaneously lifting the prohibition to enter Italian waters the moment we learned the *Goeben* was at Messina. The conduct of Rear-Admiral Troubridge was subsequently investigated by a Court of Inquiry composed of the three Commanders-in-Chief of Portsmouth,

[9]The italics are mine.—W.S.C.

Devonport and Chatham. As the result of their report, he was tried by court-martial at Portland in September and honourably acquitted of all blame. His career in the Navy was, however, at an end, the general feeling of the service not accepting the view that the four armoured cruisers and other vessels at his disposal ought not to have fought the *Goeben*. In view of his acquittal he was appointed to take charge of the naval guns which we sent with a mission to Serbia. In this capacity his work was distinguished and successful. He gained the confidence and respect of the Serbians and their Government, and he proved on various occasions that whatever might be thought of his reasons for not attacking the *Goeben*, want of personal courage was not among them.

After studying the reports of Sir Berkeley Milne and other officers concerned, the First Sea Lord recorded the opinion that Admiral Milne had taken the best measures with the force at his disposal, that his dispositions were the proper ones, and that they were successful inasmuch as they prevented the Germans from carrying out their primary rôle of interrupting French troops crossing from Africa. On this I find that my sole comment was (August 27): 'The explanation is satisfactory; the result unsatisfactory.' Thereafter on August 30, 1914, the Admiralty issued a statement that: 'The conduct and dispositions of Sir Berkeley Milne in regard to the German vessels *Goeben* and *Breslau* have been the subject of the careful examination of the Board of Admiralty, with the result that their Lordships have approved the measures taken by him in all respects.'

In all this story of the escape of the *Goeben* one seems to see the influence of that sinister fatality which at a later stage and on a far larger scale was to dog the enterprise against the Dardanelles. The terrible 'If's' accumulate. If my first thoughts on July 27 of sending the *New Zealand* to the Mediterranean had materialized; if we could have opened fire on the *Goeben* during the afternoon of August 4; if we had been less solicitous for Italian neutrality; if Sir Berkeley Milne had sent the *Indomitable* to coal at Malta instead of Biserta; if the Admiralty had sent him direct instructions when on the night of the 5th they learned where the *Goeben* was; if Rear-Admiral Troubridge in the small hours of August 7 had not changed his mind; if the *Dublin* and her two destroyers had intercepted the enemy during the night of the 6th–7th—the story of the *Goeben* would have ended here. There was, however, as it turned out, one more chance of annulling the doom of which she was the bearer. That chance, remote though it was, the Fates were vigilant to destroy.

At 1 a.m. on August 8 Sir Berkeley Milne, having collected and coaled his three battle-cruisers at Malta, set out at a moderate speed on an Easterly course in pursuit of the *Goeben*. At this juncture, the Fates moved a blameless and punctilious Admiralty clerk to declare war upon Austria. The code telegram ordering hostilities to be commenced against Austria was inadvertently released without any authority whatever. The mistake was repaired a few hours later; but the first message reached Sir Berkeley Milne at 2 p.m. on August 8 when he was half-way between Sicily and Greece. His original war orders had prescribed that in the event of a war with Austria he should in the first instance concentrate his fleet near Malta, and faithful to these instructions he turned his ships about and desisted from the pursuit of the *Goeben*. Twenty-four hours were thus lost before orders could reach him to resume it. But the *Goeben* herself had come to a standstill. Admiral Souchon was cruising irresolutely about the Greek islands endeavouring to make sure that he would be admitted by the Turks to the Dardanelles. He dallied thirty-six hours at Denusa and was forced to use his tell-tale wireless on several occasions. It was not till the evening of the 10th that he entered the Dardanelles and the Curse descended irrevocably upon Turkey and the East.

* * * * *

From the 9th to the 22nd of August the Army was crossing the Channel.[10] This was a period of great anxiety to us. All the most fateful possibilities were open. We were bound to expect a military descent upon our coasts with the intention of arresting or recalling our Army, or a naval raid into the Channel to cut down the transports, or a concentrated submarine attack upon these vessels crowded with our troops. The great naval battle might begin at any moment, either independently or in connection with any of these operations. It was a period of extreme psychological tension.

In continued anxiety lest some capital mistake should be made through a different sense of proportion prevailing in the Fleet and at the Admiralty, I drew up the following appreciation which with the concurrence of the First Sea Lord was sent officially to Sir John Jellicoe.

Admiralty to Commander-in-Chief, Home Fleets.

August 8, 1914. *Sent* 10.15 p.m.

1. To-morrow, Sunday, the Expeditionary Force begins to cross the Channel. During that week the Germans have the strongest incentives to action. They know that the Expeditionary Force is leaving, and that the mobilization and training of the Territorial Army is incomplete. They may well argue that a raid or raids now upon the East Coast would interrupt, confuse and probably delay the departure of the Army, and further that it might draw the Grand Fleet rapidly South to interfere with the landing.

2. Alternatively, or simultaneously, they may attempt to rush the Straits and interrupt the passage of the Army. It seems in the last degree improbable that if they did so they would use their modern Battle Fleet. Their principle has been, according to all we know about them, to aim at a general battle with the British Fleet when by attrition and accident our margin of superiority has been reduced. They may be assumed to know our general dispositions in the South, and the strong and numerous Submarine flotillas of which we and the French dispose. They must apprehend that the Straits are mined. Since the distance across the Channel can be covered in 6 to 8 hours, 3 hours' notice of their approach would enable every transport to reach safety. To force the Straits and enter the Channel with their best ships means the certain loss of units which it is vital to them to preserve

[10]See general map of the North Sea on pages 242–3.

if they are ever to fight a general battle. And this sacrifice, with all its hazards, would lead them only into an Anglo-French lake, lined with fortified harbours and infested with torpedo craft, at the end of which lies the Atlantic Ocean, and the Grand Fleet—wherever it is—certainly between them and home. If this plan were followed by the Germans, we should mine the Straits of Dover heavily behind them, and leave you to engage them at your convenience.

3. A far more probable German plan would be (A) to send a last division to rush the Straits and attack the transports, while at the same time (B) making raids on the East Coast to create a diversion. Our dispositions in the Channel and its approaches provide fully for (A). With regard to (B), it is not considered that more than 10,000 men can be spared from Germany at present for raids. Such raid or raids would inconvenience the military arrangements, but the Army is ready to meet the raiders if they land. Their Lordships would wish to emphasize that *it is not part of the Grand Fleet's duty to prevent such raids, but to deal with the enemy's Battle Fleet.* The enemy's older ships will possibly be used to cover either one or more raids. Their main Battle Fleet may be in rear to support them. They may expect you to come direct to prevent the raid, and therefore may lay one or more lines of mines across your expected course, or use their Submarines for the same purpose. Whereas if you approach from an Easterly or North-Easterly direction, i.e. behind them, you would cut the German Battle Fleet from its base, the landed raiders from all reinforcements, and you would approach by a path along which the chance of meeting mines would be sensibly reduced. In our view therefore you should ignore the raid or raids, and work by a circuitous route so as to get between the enemy's fleet, or covering force, and home. It would seem undesirable to come South of latitude 57° until news of a raid has been actually received; and even then the possibility of the German Battle Fleet being still in the Heligoland Bight, i.e. behind you, cannot be excluded.

This appreciation of the situation is not intended to hamper your discretion to act according to circumstances.

The naval dispositions by which the passage of the Army was covered have been fully described in the Official History of the War and in other Service works. The northern approaches to the Straits of Dover were patrolled by cruiser squadrons and by flotillas from Harwich and the Thames. The Straits of Dover were minutely watched by the British and French Destroyer flotillas of the Dover cordon and by the Submarine flotillas of Commodore Keyes. Behind these there was constituted on August 7 the Channel Fleet, comprising nineteen battleships of the 5th 7th and 8th Battle Squadrons, now all fully mobilized. This fleet, having assembled under the command of Admiral Burney at Portland, cruised in readiness for battle at the western end of the Channel at such distances from the Dover cordon as its commander might judge convenient. The western entrance to the Channel was guarded by other cruiser squadrons.

During the first few days of the transportation no great numbers of troops were crossing the Channel, but from the 12th to the 17th the bulk of the Army was in transit, and the strategic tension reached its climax. Until this period was reached the Grand Fleet was kept in its northern station and was even permitted to cruise northwards of the Orkneys, but on August 12 Admiral Jellicoe was directed to re-enter the North Sea and to cruise southward into a position of effective proximity.

Admiralty to Commander-in-Chief, Home Fleets.

August 12, 1914.

> We cannot wholly exclude the chance of an attempt at a landing during this week on a large scale supported by High Sea Fleet. In addition to the possibilities explained in Admiralty appreciation of situation sent you 8th, extraordinary silence and inertia of enemy may be prelude to serious enterprises. Our view remains as expressed in appreciation, and even if larger landing forces were employed the general principles of action would remain unaltered except that the urgency of interrupting the landing would of course be greater. You ought however to be nearer the theatre of decisive action, as we originally contemplated, and now that you have shaken off the submarine menace, or as soon as you can do so, it would appear necessary to bring the Fleet to the Eastward of the Orkneys passing either N. or S. of the Shetlands keeping well out of sight of land and stopping traffic if necessary. Cruiser sweeps to the South and South-east should be made as convenient. Acknowledge this immediately on receipt.

During the three days of heaviest transportation, August 15, 16 and 17, the Heligoland Bight was closely blockaded by submarines and destroyers, supported between the Horn Reef and the Dogger Bank by the whole of the Grand Fleet. Thus battle in open water was offered to the German Navy during the three days when their inducements to fight were at their maximum. But except for an occasional submarine, no sign betrayed the existence of the enemy's naval power.

All went well. Not a ship was sunk, not a man was drowned: all arrangements worked with the utmost smoothness and punctuality. The Army concentration was completed three days in advance of Sir John French's original undertaking to General Lanrezac;[11] and with such secrecy was the whole of this vast operation enshrouded, that on the evening of August 21, only a few hours before the British cavalry patrols were in contact with the Germans, General von Kluck, commanding the First German Army in Belgium, received from the Supreme Command no better information than the following:—

> 'A landing of British troops at Boulogne and their advance from about Lille must be reckoned with. It is believed that no landing of British troops on a big scale has yet taken place.'[12]

Three days later the whole British Army was fighting the battle of Mons.

---

[11]General Lanrezac: *Le Plan de Campagne Française*.
[12]General von Kluck: *The March on Paris*.

Since August 1 the armies of Europe had been mobilizing. Millions of men pouring along the roads and railroads, flowing across the Rhine bridges, entraining from the farthest provinces of the Russian Empire, streaming northwards from Southern France and Northern Africa, were forming in immense masses of manœuvre or in the line of battle. Yet the silence at sea was accompanied by suspense on land. There was a long stifling pause before the breaking of the storm. The combatants were taking up their stations with every precaution and strictest secrecy; and apart from the splutters of cannon fire at Liège and Belgrade—in the little countries first to be attacked—and a French raid into Alsace, only the covering troops of the great armies were in contact. There was plenty to fill the newspapers; but to those who understood what was coming, the fortnight with which this chapter is concerned—the first fortnight of Armageddon—seemed oppressed by a deathly hush.

CHAPTER 12
THE BATTLE IN FRANCE: AUGUST 20—SEPTEMBER 6, 1914

'For while the dagger gleam'd on high
Reel'd soul and sense, reel'd brain and eye.'

Scott, 'The Lady of the Lake,' Canto V, xvi.

The Schlieffen Plan—The French Offensive School—One View of French Strategy—Plan XVII—Its Complete Failure—The Dispatch of the Sixth Division—The Morrow of Mons—Fears for the Channel Ports—The Lloyd George of Agadir—The British Base shifted to St. Nazaire—Some Expedients—The Retreat—A Press Communiqué—The Eve of the Marne—The Russian Pressure—Lord Kitchener's Journey to Paris—Correspondence with Sir John French—A Day on the Aisne—The Sea Flank Project—Lord Kitchener's Wise Restraint.

The opening was not only the first, but incomparably the greatest, crisis of the war. From August 18 to the middle of September all the best-trained troops of the seven warring states were continuously hurled against one another in open warfare with ample ammunition and in all the ardour of warlike inexperience arising from what, for most, had been a generation of peace. In this awful month more divisions fought on more days, and more men were killed and wounded that in any whole year of the struggle. There were in fact two crises—one in the West and one in the East—each surpassing in scale and intensity anything subsequently endured, and each reacting reciprocally upon the other.

There had arisen for Germany the long foreseen and profoundly studied case of the War on Two Fronts. For this she had prepared the Schlieffen plan. The main German effort was directed against France. More than seven-eighths of the German armies was employed in the West. Out of 40 German Army Corps less than five were left to defend the eastern provinces of Germany against the onslaught of the Russian Empire. The Schlieffen plan staked everything upon the invasion of France and the destruction of the French armies by means of an enormous turning march through Belgium. In order to strengthen this movement by every means, General von Schlieffen was resolved to run all risks and make all sacrifices in every other quarter. He was prepared to let the Austrians bear the brunt of the Russian attack from the east, and to let all East Prussia be overrun by the Russian armies, even if need be to the Vistula. He was ready to have Alsace and Lorraine successfully invaded by the French. The violation and trampling down of Belgium, even if it forced England to declare war, was to him only a corollary of his main theme. In his conception nothing could resist the advance of Germany from the north into the heart of France, and the consequent destruction of the French armies, together with the incidental capture of Paris and the final total defeat of France within six weeks. Nothing, as he saw it, would happen anywhere else in those six weeks to prevent this supreme event from dominating the problem and ending the war in victory.

To this day no one can say that the Schlieffen plan was wrong. However, Schlieffen was dead. His successors on the German General Staff applied his plan faithfully, resolutely, solidly—but with certain reservations enjoined by prudence. These reservations were fatal. Moltke, the nephew of the great Commander, assigned 20 per cent. more troops to the defence of the German western frontier and 20 per cent less troops to the invasion of northern France than Schlieffen had prescribed. Confronted with the Russian invasion of East Prussia he still further weakened the Great Right Wheel into France. Thus as will be seen the Schlieffen plan applied at four-fifths of its intensity just failed, and we survive to this day.

* * * * *

We have seen how accurately General Wilson was able to forecast to the British Cabinet in August, 1911, the true German Schlieffen plan, and how he measured almost exactly the number of German divisions which would be used in the great turning movement.

I had throughout the greatest misgivings of an impulsive offensive by the French based, not on calm calculations of numbers, distances and times, but upon 'the psychology of the French nation,' 'the best traditions of the French Army,' 'the natural *élan* of the *poilu*.' I knew, of course, that the offensive school held the dominance in France. One could see its reflection in the language of our military men, though these were strongly anchored to modern realities by unpleasant recollections of the Boer War. Without knowing with any certainty or exactness the French plan, I dreaded, whenever I reflected on the problem, an impetuous onset followed by a shattering shock.

As between the two nations, France and Germany, it would be natural for the stronger to be left to take the offensive and invade the weaker. Four or five marches from the frontier the task of the invader becomes very difficult and may be made more difficult still. The defenders have superior communications from flank to flank and from front to rear; they fall back on carefully-chosen, well-prepared positions and on ample magazines of munitions and supplies. The invader finds himself in a hostile country, surrounded by spies, with bridges and roads, especially lateral roads, broken and disorganized, and important junctions defended by fortresses still in the hands of the enemy. He is thus forced to deliver the first great battle on ground selected and prepared by his opponent. It is surely at this moment, and after this first shock has been sustained under the best conditions, that the opportunity for the offensive energy of the weaker Power presents itself.

If the Germans invaded France it seemed to me in those days that the French would be wise to act as follows:—

They should entrench themselves conveniently along or near their frontier, constructing a vast system of field fortifications, open and concealed, sham and real, according to every device known at that time; and in these positions they should await the first shock of the Germans. I believed that the Germans did not appreciate the tremendous power of modern weapons, particularly the rifle. I based this on what I had seen of their methods in their manœuvres of 1906 and 1909 and on what I had learned about rifle fire in the South African War. The Germans were the challengers; they were the stronger, but not, in my opinion, strong enough for the continuous storming and reduction of well-fortified positions held by French regular armies or by British troops. I did not, of course, contemplate that the French would dig one uniform line along the whole length of their frontier. They would naturally treat the problem selectively, here resisting with their utmost strength, there allowing the enemy to penetrate and bulge into unpromising country or into some well-considered tactical area only to be brought up by lines fifteen to twenty miles in rear. They would not hesitate to sell the Germans piece by piece a certain amount of ground for disproportionate losses. The universal tactical object to be pursued in this first phase should be to force the Germans to expose themselves in the open to the rifle and artillery fire of well-trained Frenchmen.

It would be reasonable to hope that a process of this kind, continued for three or four days along the whole front, would have resulted in far heavier losses to the Germans than to the French, and that a larger proportion of the German than of the French armies would have been deployed and extended. One hoped in this way to see the French take toll of the manhood of the German nation at the outset of the war, as the British Army did on a small scale at Mons and Le Cateau. This would in no way have excluded tactical action by means of counter-attacks wherever opportunities presented themselves. Meanwhile at least two-fifths of the French armies should have been held back in a great mass of manœuvre, north-east of Paris. With this mass of manœuvre I hoped the British Army would have been associated. This general disposition should not have been compromised by any effort to proceed to the relief of Belgium, except with cavalry and small detachments to encourage the Belgians and to gain time. I was, of course, firmly persuaded, in common with the British General Staff, that the main German encircling movement would take place through Belgium and would comprise considerable forces west of the Belgian Meuse. I hoped that if this movement eventuated and prolonged itself in great strength, the French would find an opportunity of using the greater part of their armies of manœuvre against it after the Germans had been well punished along the whole front. At any rate, that is the sort of way in which I thought then, before the event, and think still, the French Command might best have safeguarded the vital interests of France.

The accession of General Joffre to the chief command had led, however, to a complete recasting of the French ideas. Under the Joffre régime the French General Staff had made a new plan of which they darkly nursed the secret. They called it 'Plan XVII.' The famous 'Plan XVII' consisted in a general offensive in an easterly and north-easterly direction by four French armies, with the last remaining army in reserve behind their centre. It was based upon an ardent faith that the French right would penetrate deeply into Alsace and Lorraine and an obstinate disbelief that the French left would be turned by a German movement west of the Meuse through Belgium. Both these calculations were to be completely falsified by the first events of the war. From the very earliest days it was clear that the views which the British General Staff had consistently held since 1911, of a great German turning movement through Belgium, probably on both sides of the Belgian Meuse, were correct. Why should the Germans with their eyes open throw first Belgium and then the British Empire into the scales against them unless for an operation of supreme magnitude? Besides, there were the evidences of their long preparations—camps, railways and railway sidings—which the British Staff under Sir John French and Sir Henry Wilson had so minutely studied. Lastly, reported with much accuracy from day to day, there came the enormous troop movements on the German right, towards and into Belgium on both sides of the Meuse. Before the end of the first week in August, General Lanrezac, the Commander of the left French Army (the Fifth), was raising loud cries of warning and alarm about the menace to his left, and indeed his rear, if he carried out the rôle assigned to him and attacked as ordered in a north-easterly direction. By the end of the second week the presence of the accumulating masses of the German right could no longer be denied by the French High Command, and certain measures, tardy and inadequate, were taken to cope with it. Nevertheless, after the raid of a corps and a cavalry division into Alsace on the 13th August, General Joffre began his offensive into Lorraine with the two armies of the French right, the centre armies conforming a few days later; and up till the evening of the 18th General Lanrezac and the left French army were still under orders to advance north-east. Three days later this same army was defending itself in full battle from an attack from the north and north-west. It had been compelled to make a complete left wheel.

The Germans, as General Michel and Sir Henry Wilson had predicted three years before, made their vast turning movement through Belgium. They brought into action almost immediately 34 Army Corps, of which 13 or their equivalent were reserve formations. Of the 2,000,000 men who marched to invade France and Belgium 700,000 only were serving conscripts and 1,300,000 were reservists. Against these General Joffre could muster only 1,300,000, of whom also 700,000 were serving conscripts but only 600,000 were reservists. 1,200,000 additional French reservists responded immediately to the national call, encumbering the depots without equipment, without arms, without cadres, without officers. In consequence the Germans outnumbered the French at the outbreak by 3 to 2 along the whole line of battle, and as they economized the forces on their left they were able to deliver the turning movement on their right in overwhelming strength. At Charleroi they were 3 to 1.

It was for the tactical sphere that General Joffre and his school of 'Young Turks,' as they came to be called in France, had reserved their crowning mistakes. The French infantry marched to battle conspicuous on the landscape in blue breeches and red coats. Their artillery officers in black and gold were even more specially defined targets. Their cavalry gloried in ludicrous armour. The doctrine of the offensive raised to the height of a religious frenzy animated all ranks, and in no rank was restricted by the foreknowledge of the modern rifle and machine gun. A cruel surprise lay before them.

The battle began on the 20th when the two armies of the French right advanced to the south of Metz. They were resisted on the front by strongly prepared German defences and violently attacked upon their left by the Bavarian Army issuing from the radial roads and railways of the fortress. The Third French Army marching north towards Arlon blundered into the Germans in the morning mist of August 22, four or five of its divisions having their heads shorn away while they were still close to their camping grounds. Everywhere along the battle front, whenever Germans were seen, the signal was given to charge. 'Vive la France!' 'A la baïonnette,' 'En Avant'—and the brave troops, nobly led by their regimental officers, who sacrificed themselves in even greater proportion, responded in all the magnificent fighting fury for which the French nation has been traditionally renowned. Sometimes these hopeless onslaughts were delivered to the strains of the Marseillaise, six, seven or even eight hundred yards from the German positions. Though the Germans invaded, it was more often the French who attacked. Long swathes of red and blue corpses littered the stubble fields. The collision was general along the whole battle front, and there was a universal recoil. In the mighty battle of the Frontiers, the magnitude and terror of which is scarcely now known to British consciousness, more than 300,000 Frenchmen were killed, wounded or made prisoners.

These disasters heralded the enormous perils to which the French and British armies on the left or northern flank were now to be exposed. The Fifth French Army had no sooner completed with severe exertions its deployment on the Sambre, and the British Army advancing by forced marches had no sooner reached the neighbourhood of Mons, when the overwhelming force of the German turning movement through Belgium fell upon them. Both General Lanrezac and Sir John French were about to be launched in a vehement offensive which the French Headquarters believed would hurl back the wheeling German right. The British Command accepted this guidance with implicit faith. Lanrezac, sure that Joffre was utterly adrift from facts, watched with insolent distrust the impending disaster. But even he never imagined the weight and sweep of the German enveloping swing. The two armies of the left only escaped disaster by the timely retreat which Lanrezac and Sir John French each executed independently and on his own initiative. And also by the most stubborn resistance and rifle fire of the highly trained professional British infantry. Many faults of temperament and indeed of loyalty to the British Army on his left are urged against General Lanrezac. Nevertheless his grasp of the situation and stern decision to retreat while the time remained has earned the gratitude of France. It was a pity he forgot to tell his British allies about it.

* * * * *

The utmost secrecy had naturally been maintained by the French about their general plan. The existence of their nation was at stake. Neither the British Cabinet nor what was left of the War Office were in a position to understand what was passing. I do not know how far Lord Kitchener was specially informed. I think it very improbable that he shared the secrets of the French Headquarters to the extent of being able to measure what was happening on the front as a whole. If he shared them, he did not show it by any remark which escaped him. He knew, of course, all there was to be known about the situation of our own army, and a good deal about the forces contiguous to it.

As the shock drew near, Prince Louis and I felt it our duty at the Admiralty to free Lord Kitchener's hands in every respect and to bear to the full our burden of responsibility. I therefore wrote to him on the 22nd August as follows:—

> 'The Admiralty are confident of their ability to secure this country against invasion or any serious raid. If you wish to send the 6th Division abroad at once, we should not raise any objection from the naval standpoint. The situation, now that both the Navy and the Territorials are mobilized and organized, is entirely different from those which have been discussed in the Invasion Committee of the C.I.D.[1]; and if you want to send the last Regular Division, the First Sea Lord and I are quite ready to agree, and so far as possible to accept responsibility.'

He replied:—

> 'It is very doubtful if the division now crossing[2] will get up in time to take part in the battle now impending on the Sambre. As soon as I can I will let you know about the 6th Division going over. If I send it we have practically nothing left.'

Late on the evening of August 23 I had a talk with Lord Kitchener. We knew the main battle had been joined and that our men had been fighting all day; but he had received no news. He was darkly hopeful. The map was produced. The dense massing of German divisions west of the Belgian Meuse and curling round the left flank of the Anglo-French line was visible as a broad effect. So was the pivot of Namur, in front of which this whole vast turning movement seemed precariously to be hinged. He had in his mind a great French counterstroke—a thrust at the shoulder, as it were, of the long, straining, encircling arm which should lop it off or cripple it fatally. He said of the Germans, 'They are running a grave risk. No one can set limits to what a well-disciplined army can do; but if the French were able to cut in here,' he made a vigorous arrow N.W. from Namur, 'the Germans might easily have a Sedan of their own on a larger scale.' I had a pleasing vision of the first phase of Austerlitz, with the Austrians stretching and spreading their left far out to the villages of Tellnitz and Sokolnitz. while Napoleon remained crouched for his spring at the Pratzen plateau. But had France a Napoleon? One had marched through Charleroi ninety-nine years before. Was there another? And were the Germans like the Austrians and Russians of Austerlitz? However, we went anxiously but hopefully to our slumbers.

At 7 o'clock the next morning I was sitting up in bed in Admiralty House working at my boxes, when the door of my bedroom opened and Lord Kitchener appeared. These were the days before he took to uniform, and my recollection is that he had a bowler

---

[1]Committee of Imperial Defence.

[2]The Fourth Division (the fifth to go).

hat on his head, which he took off with a hand which also held a slip of paper. He paused in the doorway and I knew in a flash and before ever he spoke that the event had gone wrong. Though his manner was quite calm, his face was different. I had the subconscious feeling that it was distorted and discoloured as if it had been punched with a fist. His eyes rolled more than ever. His voice, too, was hoarse. He looked gigantic. 'Bad news,' he said heavily and laid the slip of paper on my bed. I read the telegram. It was from Sir John French.

> 'My troops have been engaged all day with the enemy on a line roughly east and west through Mons. The attack was renewed after dark, but we held our ground tenaciously. I have just received a message from G.O.C. 5th French Army that his troops have been driven back, that Namur has fallen, and that he is taking up a line from Maubeuge to Rocroi. I have therefore ordered a retirement to the line Valenciennes-Longueville-Maubeuge, which is being carried out now. It will prove a difficult operation, if the enemy remains in contact. I remember your precise instructions as to method and direction of retirement if necessity arises.
>
> 'I think that immediate attention should be directed to the defence of Havre.'

I did not mind it much till I got to Namur. Namur fallen! Namur taken in a single day—although a French brigade had joined the Belgians in its defence. We were evidently in the presence of new facts and of a new standard of values. If strong fortresses were to melt like wisps of vapour in a morning sun, many judgments would have to be revised. The foundations of thought were quaking. As for the strategic position, it was clear that the encircling arm was not going to be hacked off at the shoulder, but would close in a crushing grip. Where would it stop? What of the naked Channel ports? Dunkirk, Calais, Boulogne! 'Fortify Havre,' said Sir John French. One day's general battle and the sanguine advance and hoped-for counter-stroke had been converted into 'Fortify Havre.' 'It will be difficult to withdraw the troops if the enemy remains in contact'—a disquieting observation. I forget much of what passed between us. But the apparition of Kitchener *Agonistes* in my doorway will dwell with me as long as I live. It was like seeing old John Bull on the rack!

When I met the Admirals later, at ten, they were deeply perturbed about these Channel ports. They had never taken the War Office view of the superiority of the French Army. They saw in this first decisive shock the confirmation of their misgivings. Some one suggested we should at any rate make sure of the Cotentin peninsula, as an ample place of arms, girt on three sides by the sea, from which the British armies of the future might proceed to the rescue of France. Fortify Havre indeed! Already we looked to Cherbourg and St. Nazaire.

British Admiralty to French Admiralty.

August 24th, 1914.

> Admiralty think it most important to naval interests to defend Dunkirk, Calais and Boulogne as long as possible. We release Admiral Rouyer's armoured cruiser

squadron to co-operate in the land defences of these three places. We will reinforce him if necessary with a battle squadron. French flotilla bases and naval stores at Calais and Boulogne can be transferred to Dover, and all preparations for that should be immediately worked out. . . . We wish also to receive without delay French views about land defences of Dunkirk, Boulogne, Calais and Havre and what the military prospects are of holding on to all of them. We will, of course, assist in any way in our power.

Lastly, we are considering shifting all military stores of British Expeditionary Force now at Boulogne to Cherbourg. We wish to know French views on the necessity for this as the result of the present battle becomes more clear. . . .

First Lord to Commander-in-Chief Grand Fleet.

August 24*th*, 1914.

Personal. News from France is disappointing and serious results of battle cannot yet be measured, as it still continues over enormous front.

I have had the telegrams about it repeated to you.

We have not entered the business without resolve to see it through and you may be assured that our action will be proportioned to the gravity of the need.

I have absolute confidence in final result.

No special action is required from you at present, but you should address your mind to a naval situation which may arise where Germans control Calais and French coasts and what ought to be the position of Grand Fleet in that event.

I had not seen the Chancellor of the Exchequer, except at Cabinets, since the fateful Sunday before the war. I had been buried in the Admiralty and he in the Treasury. I sustained vague general impressions of a tremendous financial crisis—panic, bankruptcies, suspension of the Bank Act, moratoriums, paper money—like a distant tumult. I realized that he, aided by the Lord Chief Justice, Lord Reading, was riding the storm and regaining effective control of events. But I did not attempt to follow and appreciate the remarkable sequence of decisions by which an unprecedented, unimaginable situation was met. Now, however, with this fateful news, I felt intensely the need of contact with him, and I wanted to know how it would strike him and how he would face it. So I walked across the Horse Guards Parade and made my way to the tunnel entrance of the Treasury Board Room. It must have been about 10 o'clock in the morning and, as I opened the door, I saw the room was crowded. One of that endless series of conferences with all the great business and financial authorities of Britain, by means of which the corner was turned, was in progress. He saw me at once: I beckoned with my finger and he came out. We went into a little room scarcely bigger than a cupboard which adjoined, and I told him what had happened. I was relieved and overjoyed at his response. He was once again the Lloyd George of Agadir. Not since the morning of the Mansion House speech, three years before, had I seen him so strong and resolute for our country or so sure of its might.

First Lord to Commander-in-Chief Grand Fleet.

August 25th, 1914.

British retirement on French frontier successfully and skilfully effected. Army now in strong position, well supported. Our casualties reported not severe considering continued engagement with two German corps and two cavalry divisions. Enemy was well punished and lost heavily. Main battle has still to be fought. General impression better this morning. Hope all is well with you.

Then came the days of retreat. We saw that the French armies of the right were holding their own, but all the centre and left was marching southwards towards Paris as fast as possible, while our own five divisions[3] were for several days plainly in the very jaws of destruction. At the Admiralty we received requests to shift the base of the whole army from Havre to St. Nazaire; and with this complicated business we had to cope. The process of retreat continued day after day. A seemingly irresistible compulsion was pressing and forcing backwards the brave armies of France. Why should it stop? Would they ever be able to turn? If France could not save herself, nothing could save her.

Casting about for help in this bitter time, I ventured to make the suggestions which follow. But it was not found possible, in view of all the difficulties, to give effect to them.

Mr. Churchill to Lord Kitchener.

August 28th, 1914.

Here is an idea which deserves examination. The Siberian troops would, if used against Germany and Austria, have to come south at an awkward moment and derange the communications (so I am told). On the other hand, it would probably be easy to send them to Archangel, and it is (roughly) only six days from Archangel to Ostend.

If a couple of Russian Corps d'Armée were transported round this route, it would be possible to strike at the German communications in a very effective manner.

It is an interesting idea, though I dare say it would not greatly commend itself to the Russians. Don't trouble to answer.

Prime Minister.
Sir Edward Grey.
Lord Kitchener.

September 5, 1914.

I hear from many sources of the keen and widespread desire of individual Americans to take part in the war on our side. It has been stated that 50,000 or

---

[3]The Fourth Division (fifth in order of embarkation) arrived on the field at the beginning of the battle of Le Cateau.

60,000 Americans have volunteered, including a number of Virginians. I also hear that wealthy Americans are anxious to subscribe to the equipment of a force. There is no doubt that a large number of American citizens of quality and character are anxious to fight on our side. The value and advantage of such aid cannot be overrated from any point of view. I am ignorant of the law on these subjects: but Foreign Legions have played their part in many wars. It ought to be possible to organize in Canada an American volunteer force amounting to at least a Division, which could go into action as such. Nothing will bring American sympathy along with us so much as American blood shed in the field. What is wanted now is that there should be an announcement made that we will accept the services of Americans who come to Canada or England and volunteer; that they will be formed into units in which they can serve together with their friends and comrades; that they will be able to choose their own regimental officers; that the British Government will bear the whole expense of equipment and transportation; and that they shall share in every way the perils and fortunes of our troops.

I believe there is a source of fighting manhood here of the highest possible quality, whose very employment would produce beneficial reactions in every direction. The problem is how to set up the rallying flag in Canada, and so indicate where those who wish to help us can go to join.

W. S. C.

Personally, I was hopeful that the wave of invasion would spend its fury, and as I had indicated in my memorandum of three years before, I believed that if the French forces had not been squandered by precipitate action on the frontiers, an opportunity of striking the decisive blow would occur about the fortieth day. In order to encourage my colleagues I reprinted this memorandum and circulated it to the whole Cabinet on September 2, pointing out that I had never counted upon a victorious issue at the frontiers, had always expected that the French armies would be driven into retreat by the twentieth day, but that, in spite of this, there were good hopes of success. But I had no means of measuring the forces by which this result would be achieved, except by the most general processes.

Meanwhile the impression of an overwhelming disaster was conveyed to England through a hundred channels. Newspaper correspondents made their way in the confusion to the very fringe of the German advance. Stragglers by the thousand, and even detachments from the British Army, appeared in a desperate condition behind it and far out on its flanks. In spite of the censorship, the reports in the papers were alarming, while rumour much exceeded anything that was printed. Acute distress was manifested. In these circumstances, at the request of Lord Kitchener and the Prime Minister, I drafted on Sunday, September 4, the following communiqué, which was universally accepted as coming from the Army, and I hope and believe gave comfort without concealing the truth.

It is now possible to make another general survey, in continuation of that issued on August 30, of the operations of the British Army during the last week.

No new main trial of strength has taken place. There have indeed been battles in various parts of the immense front which in other wars would have been considered operations of the first magnitude, but in this war they are merely the incidents of the strategic withdrawal and contraction of the allied forces necessitated by the initial shock on the frontiers and in Belgium, and by the enormous strength which the Germans have thrown into the western theatre while suffering heavily through weakness in the eastern.

The British Expeditionary Army has conformed to the general movement of the French forces and acted in harmony with the strategic conceptions of the French General Staff. Since the battle at Cambrai [Le Cateau] on August 26, where the British troops successfully guarded the left flank of the whole line of French Armies from a deadly turning attack supported by enormous force, the 7th French Army[4] has come into operation on our left, and this, in conjunction with the 5th Army on our right, has greatly taken the strain and pressure off our men. The 5th French Army in particular on August 29 advanced from the line of the Oise River to meet and counter the German forward movement, and a considerable battle developed to the south of Guise. In this the 5th French Army gained a marked and solid success, driving back with heavy loss and in disorder three German Army Corps—the 10th, the Guard, and a reserve corps. It is believed that the Commander of the 10th German Corps was among those killed. In spite of this success, however, and all the benefits which flowed from it, the general retirement to the south continued, and the German Armies, seeking persistently after the British troops, remained in practically continuous contact with our rearguards. On August 30 and 31 the British covering and delaying troops were frequently engaged, and on September 1 a very vigorous effort was made by the Germans, which brought about a sharp action in the neighbourhood of Compiégne. This action was fought principally by the 1st British Cavalry Brigade and the 4th Guards Brigade, and was entirely satisfactory to the British. The German attack, which was most strongly pressed, was not brought to a standstill until much slaughter had been inflicted upon them and until ten German guns had been captured. The brunt of this creditable affair fell upon the Guards Brigade, who lost in killed and wounded about 300 men.[5]

After this engagement our troops were no longer molested. Wednesday, September 2, was the first quiet day they had had since the battle of Mons, on August 23. During the whole of this period marching and fighting had been continuous, and in the whole period the British casualties had amounted, according to the latest estimates, to about 15,000 officers and men. The fighting having been in open order upon a wide front, with repeated retirements, has led to a large number of officers and men, and even small parties, missing their way and getting separated, and it is known that a very considerable number of those now included

[4]Actually called the 6th Army.

[5]In fact, however, it was the 1st Middlesex (19th Infantry Brigade attached to 4th Division) who captured the guns at Néry, the Guards being miles away at Villiers Cotterets.

> in the total will rejoin the colours safely. These losses, though heavy in so small a force, have in no wise affected the spirit of the troops. They do not amount to a third of the losses inflicted by the British force upon the enemy, and the sacrifice required of the Army has not been out of proportion to its military achievements. In all, drafts amounting to 19,000 men have reached our Army or are approaching them on the line of communications, and advantage is being taken of the five quiet days that have passed since the action of September 1 to fill up the gaps and refit and consolidate the units.
>
> The British Army is now south of the Marne and is in line with the French forces on the right and left. *The latest information about the enemy is that they are neglecting Paris and are marching in a south-easterly direction towards the Marne and towards the left and centre of the French line.*[6] The 1st German Army is reported to be between La Ferté sous Jouarre and Essises Viffort. The 2nd German Army, after taking Rheims,[7] has advanced to Chateau-Thierry and to the east of that place. The 4th German Army is reported to be marching south on the west of the Argonne between Suippes and Ville sur Tourbe. All these points were reached by the Germans on September 3. The 7th German Army has been repulsed by a French Corps near D'Einville. *It would therefore appear that the enveloping movement upon the Anglo-French left flank has been abandoned by the Germans, either because it is no longer practicable to continue such a great extension or because the alternative of a direct attack upon the Allied line is preferred.*[6] Whether this change of plan by the Germans is voluntary or whether it has been enforced upon them by the strategic situation and the great strength of the Allied Armies in their front, will be revealed by the course of events.
>
> There is no doubt whatever that our men have established a personal ascendancy over the Germans, and that they are conscious of the fact that with anything like even numbers the result would not be doubtful.

At this time I knew, of course, that another supreme battle was impending. My principal fear was that the French would turn too soon and make their new effort before the German thrust had reached its full extension. I was glad therefore to learn on September 3 that the French Government were quitting Paris, as it showed a resolve to treat the capital just as if it were an ordinary tactical feature to be fought round or through as might be convenient in a purely military sense. It also showed a determination to continue the war whatever might happen to Paris. We were now at the thirty-fifth day of mobilization. The Germans must be strung out in their pursuit and far ahead of supplies, munitions and drafts. The great mass of Paris with its circle of forts must either, like a breakwater, divide the oncoming German waves, or by compelling them to pass wholly to the east of it serve as a secure flank for the French.

And at this culminating moment the Russian pressure began to produce substantial effects. Honour must ever be done to the Tsar and Russian nation for the noble ardour

[6] The italics are new.

[7] The Third German Army took Rheims and were bombarded in the town by the Second Army.

and loyalty with which they hurled themselves into the war. A purely Russian treatment of their military problem would have led the Russian armies into immediate withdrawals from their frontiers until the whole of their vast mobilization was completed. Instead of this, they added to a forward mobilization an impetuous advance not only against Austria but into Germany. The flower of the Russian army was soon to be cut down in enormous and fearful battles in East Prussia. But the results of their invasion were gathered at the decisive point. The nerve of the German Headquarters failed. On August 25 two army corps and a cavalry division of the German right were withdrawn from France. On August 31 Lord Kitchener was able to telegraph to Sir John French: 'Thirty-two trains of German troops were yesterday reported moving from the western field to meet the Russians.'[8]

What had happened in the East? The Russians had invaded East Prussia with their two converging northern armies, one under Rennenkampf marching from Wilna along the Baltic shore, the other under Samsonov striking upwards from Warsaw. The defence of East Prussia had been confided to General von Prittwitz, who with an army of about 5½ corps had to meet a double attack of two armies each the equal of his own. Prittwitz had advanced to arrest Rennenkampf near the eastern frontier and on August 20 began to fight the battle of Gumbinnen. The day was indecisive although the superior qualities of the Germans were apparent. In the evening Prittwitz, alarmed by the advance of the Warsaw army, which threatened his line of retreat, broke off the battle of Gumbinnen and telephoned to Moltke at the German main headquarters at Luxemburg that in the face of the overpowering Russian masses he must retreat to the Vistula, and that in view of the low state of the river he could not even guarantee to hold this line. His agitated manner emphasized his grave tidings. Moltke when he hung up the receiver determined there and then to supersede him. Telegrams were dispatched to a Major-General named Ludendorff, a High Staff Officer, who had distinguished himself in the capture of Liège, and to General von Hindenburg, a retired commander of massive qualities, to defend the German hearths and homes in East Prussia. Moltke further urged the Austrian Commander-in-chief, Conrad von Hötzendorff, to hasten the offensive of the Austrian Army in order to relieve the perilous situation in East Prussia. Hötzendorff thereupon, with many misgivings and without his whole strength, advanced to meet the vast tide of Russian invasion and was defeated a week later in the 200-mile battle called Lemberg. Ludendorff and Hindenburg hastened to East Prussia, where they found the situation largely restored by the unerring decisions of Prittwitz's brilliant Staff Officer, General Hoffman. They arrived to find all the movements in progress which five days later were to result in the awful battle of Tannenberg.

* * * * *

The night of August 25 brought a solid assurance of victory to the German High Command. From every part of the immense battle front in the West the news was good. Everywhere the French had failed in their advances or were retreating. It was at

---

[8]Official History of the War, Appendix 22, p. 473.

this moment that Moltke felt able to cope with the anxieties which had oppressed him since, five days earlier, he had received Prittwitz's panic-stricken telephone message about Gumbinnen. Believing that the decision in France had been reached and that the supreme clash of arms was now bound speedily to end in favour of Germany, Moltke turned his eyes eastward. All Germany was in uproar about the invasion of East Prussia. The Emperor was indignant at this violation of 'our lovely Masurian Lakes.' Now is the time to send reinforcements to the east. Tappen, Head of the Operations Branch, is told to make plans for transferring thither *six army corps* from the west, two from each of the right, centre and left. However it is better not to promise more than you can give. Four of these corps are at the moment closely engaged in action or pursuit. There are only two which seem immediately available. These two are upon the wheeling German right. In the profound design of the German war plans these two corps had been reserved for the siege of Namur and they had crossed the Belgian frontier banked up behind Billow's advancing army. But now there was no siege of Namur; it had fallen almost at the first salvos of the heavy howitzers. It was already in German hands, and the two corps which were to have made the siege were, so it seemed, free. Give *them* anyhow to Ludendorff at Marienburg; the others can go later.

So Tappen clears the line, and Ludendorff on the eve of Tannenberg, a prey to all its measureless uncertainties, is offered immediately two of the best German corps, including one regular Guards division. Such an offer was a temptation to any general. It was a peculiar temptation to a man of Ludendorff's temperament; but curiously enough a temptation against which his high intellectuality and commanding view afforded him adequate protection. Although he was fighting in East Prussia for everything he cared for, including (not negligible) his own power and importance, he still retained his trained view of the general situation. Of course, he said, he would like to have the corps, but they could not arrive in time for the impending battle in the East, and anyhow the situation in the West ought not to be endangered on his account. Several notable deeds have been inscribed upon Ludendorff's record which have faded or even been expunged: here is one which will endure a long time. However, the decision is Moltke's, and the two corps situated at the very thong of the German right-handed stroke, placed in the exact position where they could have followed so easily the marches of the armies and advanced to fill any gap which might open between them, are already being entrained with magnificent German efficiency for their 700-mile journey to the Vistula.

During the whole of the next week everything continued to go well with Germany. All her armies in France strode forward on the heels of the retreating French and British as fast as men could march; and from the East arrived the dazzling news of Tannenberg. The Emperor was in what the German Staff has described as a 'shout hurrah mood.' Sure that not only victory but escape from war was in his grasp, he urged on his commanders who in their turn halloaed their troops. But Moltke's outlook seems to have undergone a change. The stubborn and unexpected French resistance of Lanrezac's army at Guise, the bloody repulse which the Bavarians had received when they in their turn attacked the French fortress lines before Nancy, the fact that Kluck had found himself in contact with an unexpectedly substantial British army which, though retiring before his masses, had at Mons, Le Cateau, Néry and Villers-Cotterets not only inflicted much slaughter, but produced a formidable military impression on the German General Staff mind—all these added to the increasing distance of the German columns from their rail-heads, mingled a dark and broadening streak of misgivings with the general rejoicings. Are these enemy armies really defeated? asked the anxious Chief of the German General Staff. 'Is the battle over?' 'Where are the prisoners? Where are the captured guns? Where is the disorganization?' In fact, as August ticked out its last crimson minutes, the most anxious man in Germany was the man who knew the most.

Meanwhile what of Joffre? We have no record of the reactions produced in the minds of the so-called 'Young Turks.' who formed his *entourage*, and walled him in from the principal commanders, of the perfect failure and frustration of all their plans. But we do know that Joffre preserved a calm, impassive and resolute demeanour and rested for a while like George II at the battle of Dettingen, '*sans peur et sans avis*.' Obviously something must be done to stem the enveloping German right wheel. Accordingly on the 25th when the results of the battles of the frontier were apparent, the following 'Instruction No. 2' was issued from G.Q.G.[9]: 'It having proved impossible to execute the offensive manœuvre projected, further operations will be arranged in such a manner as to constitute on our left by the junction of the Fourth and Fifth Armies, the British Army, and new forces drawn from the east, a mass capable of resuming the offensive, while the other armies restrain the efforts of the enemy for the present.' In pursuance of this a new French army, the Sixth, under General Maunoury, an officer of high quality, soon afterwards to be blinded by a bullet, began during the last five days to form around Amiens. The troops composing it were transported swiftly by railway from the eastern fortress line where the armies of Dubail, Castelnau and we must in justice add Sarreil, had begun for the first time to discover and reveal the power of modern weapons when used from trenches.

But now observe the intrusion of politics into the military sphere. Hitherto Joffre and his circle have had that unfettered discretion which great captains have only enjoyed when they were kings or emperors. But the crash on the frontiers has given a dismal stimulus to the civil power. On this same 25th August the French Minister of War, Messimy, himself a military man but turned politician, sent an officer to Joffre's headquarters with the following order: 'If victory does not crown the success of our armies and if these armies are reduced to retreat, an army of at least three active corps should be directed upon the entrenched camp of Paris to secure its protection.' M. Messimy gave in the war abundant proofs of courage and decision both as Deputy and soldier; but in this case he had behind him a far greater figure. In fact it is the purpose of this account to suggest that in General Galliéni, newly appointed Military Governor of Paris and holding commission as 'contingent successor' (*successeur éventuel*) to General Joffre, will be found the saviour of France.

[9]Grand Quartier Général.

The 'Young Turks' were disgusted at this intervention, and we may suppose that they took care that the emergence of Gallièni, the potential successor, at the head of important forces in the capital city was not lost upon General Joffre. But the order was imperative. Messimy, about to be replaced almost in a few hours by a new minister, wielded a constitutional authority the traditions of which were founded by the Jacobin Committee of Public Safety in the ferocious days of 1793. So Joffre and his Staff had to find the troops, and where were they to be procured? No more can be taken from the eastern fortress lines. Assuredly none can be withdrawn from the line of armies retreating from the north. Well, there is this army of Maunoury's which we should have liked to assemble on the left flank, a mixed lot—some shattered regulars, some reserve divisions mauled in their first unsuccessful action! If we have to lock up an army in Paris, if the Government insist upon it, theirs shall be the responsibility and these shall be the troops! However, no sooner had Maunoury's army begun to gather round Amiens than it was forced to conform to the general retirement. The blind force of events decreed that it should be directed on Paris, there to become the sword of Gallièni.

* * * * *

I may now be permitted to descend to a small scale of events, and to refer to an incident which has caused both stir and controversy.

By August 27 the Cabinet had formed the opinion that great friction had arisen between Sir John French and General Lanrezac and also between the British and French Headquarters. Actually the difference was with General Lanrezac, who Sir John French considered had not given him due notice of his intention to retire after the battle on the 22nd and 23rd. We were concerned with the apparent intention of the British Army to retire and refit behind the French left. Their losses so far reported to us did not exceed 10,000 men. We could not measure the exhaustion of the troops nor the extent of the disorganization inseparable from continued fighting and retreating. We accordingly decided to send Lord Kitchener at once to see the British and French Commanders-in-Chief and make sure that nothing that Britain could do should be left undone.[10] If Lord Kitchener had gone in plain clothes no difficulty would have arisen, but his appearance in Paris in the uniform of a Field-Marshal senior to the Commander-in-Chief at that dark and critical moment, wounded and disconcerted Sir John French deeply and not unnaturally. I laboured my utmost to put this right and to make it clear that the Cabinet and not Lord Kitchener were responsible.

ADMIRALTY.

September 4, 1914.

Mr. Churchill to Sir John French.

I have wanted so much to write to you and yet not to bother you with reading letters. Still, I suppose there are moments when you can find the leisure to read a

[10]The correspondence on this subject is printed in the Official History of the War, Appendix 22 p. 471.

few lines from a friend. The Cabinet was bewildered by your telegram proposing to retire from the line, coming on the top of a casualty list of 6,000, and your reports as to the good spirit of the troops. We feared that you and Joffre might have quarrelled, or that something had happened to the Army of which we had not been informed. In these circumstances telegraphing was useless, and a personal consultation was indispensable if further misunderstandings were to be avoided.

I am sure it would be wise to have some good officer on your staff like, say, Major Swinton, who could without troubling you unduly, give us a clear and complete impression of what is taking place day by day. Our only wish is to sustain and support you. We are at a point where losses will only rouse still further the spirit of the nation, provided they are incurred, as yours have been, in brilliant and successful action. But we ought to be kept in a position to form a true and connected impression of the course of events.

For my own part, I am only anxious that you shall be sustained and reinforced in every way, and I look forward confidently to seeing you ere long at the head of a quarter of a million men, and in the spring of half a million.

I enclose you a paper which I wrote three years ago, which seems to have been borne out by the course of events, and which I hope will continue to be confirmed.

In case any further difficulties arise, and you think I can be of any use, you have only to send for me, and subject to the naval situation I could reach you very quickly by motor-car or aeroplane.

It is hard sitting here day after day with so many friends engaged. The resolution of the nation is splendid. It is a different country to the one you left….

God guard you and prosper our arms.

FRANCE,
September 6, 1914.

Sir John French to Mr. Churchill.

Thank you very much for your kind and encouraging letter. It was a keen pleasure to hear from you and to read your words.

I have had a terribly anxious time and the troops have suffered severely, but they are simply *glorious*!

I think you have heard me say that I would be ready to take on any enemy in Europe half as strong again. I say that more than ever *now*! I can't find words to say all I think of them.

There has been some extraordinary misunderstanding at home as to my relations with General Joffre, the French C.-in-C. We have been on the very best terms all through, and he has spoken most kindly of the help he has received from us. I can't understand what brought Kitchener to Paris. I am writing to you as one of my greatest friends and I know you'll let me write freely and privately. His visit was really most unfortunate. He took me away from the front to visit him in Paris on a very critical day when I should have been directing the operation most carefully, and I tell you between ourselves *strictly* that when I returned to my Headquarters I found a very critical situation existing (8 p.m.!) and authoritative orders and directions badly needed. It was the day when the Guards and a Cavalry Brigade were so heavily engaged.

I do beg of you, my dear Friend, to add one more to all the many great kindnesses you have done me and *stop this interference* with field operations.

In reply I sent further explanations which, aided as they were by victory, proved acceptable.

General Headquarters,
British Forces,

September 10, 1914.

Sir John French to Mr. Churchill.

Thank you, my dear Friend, with all my heart for your truly kind reply to my letter, and also for your previous letter of the 4th. I fear I was a little unreasonable about K. and his visit, but we have been through a hard time and perhaps my temper isn't made any better by it! However, as usual, you have poured balm into my wounds—although they may have been only imaginary—and I am deeply grateful.

Since I wrote to you last the whole atmosphere has changed and for 5 solid days we have been pursuing instead of pursued, and the Germans have had simply *hell*. This very day we have captured several hundred, cut off a whole lot of transport and got 10 or 12 guns—and the ground is strewn with dead and wounded Germans. Something like this happened yesterday and the day before. But this is nothing to what they have lost in front of the 5th and 6th French armies, which have been much more strongly opposed. They are indeed fairly on the run and we are following hard.

What a wonderful forecast you made in 1911. I don't remember the paper, but it has turned out almost as you said. I have shown it to a few of my Staff.

I was afraid of Joffre's strategy at first and thought he ought to have taken the offensive much sooner, but he was quite right.

* * * * *

I felt it vitally important to my whole structure of thought on this war problem to see for myself with my own eyes what was passing at the front and what were the conditions of this new war, and to have personal contact with Sir John French. Reflection and imagination can only build truly when they are checked point by point by direct impressions of reality. I believed myself sufficiently instructed to derive an immense refreshment of judgment from personal investigation without incurring the opposite danger of a distorted view through particular experiences. But it was not until the armies came to a standstill along the line of the Aisne, that I felt justified in asking Lord Kitchener to allow me to accept the repeated invitations of Sir John French. He gladly gave his permission and I started the next morning. On September 16 the Duke of Westminster drove me from Calais to the British Headquarters at La Fère-en-Tardenois. We made a fairly wide detour as we had no exact information as to where the flanks of the moving armies actually lay, and it was not until nightfall that we fell in with the left flank of the British line. Sir John had all his arrangements ready made for me, and the next day between daylight and dark I was able to traverse the entire British artillery front from the edge of the Craonne Plateau on the right to the outskirts of Soissons on the left. I met everybody I wanted to meet and saw everything that could be seen without unnecessary danger. I lunched with 'The Greys,' then commanded by that fine soldier, Colonel Bulkeley-Johnson. I had a long talk with Sir Henry Rawlinson on a haystack from which we could observe the fire of the French artillery near Soissons. I saw for the first time what then seemed the prodigy of a British aeroplane threading its way among the smoke-puffs of searching shells. I saw the big black German shells, 'the coal boxes' and 'Jack Johnsons' as they were then called, bursting in Paissy village or among our patient, impassive batteries on the ridge. I climbed to a wooded height beneath which the death-haunted bridge across the Aisne was visible. When darkness fell I saw the horizon lighted with the quick flashing of the cannonade. Such scenes were afterwards to become commonplace: but their first aspect was thrilling. I dined with the young officers of the Headquarters Staff and met there, for the last time, alas, my brilliant, gallant friend, Hugh Dawnay. Early next morning I opened with Sir John French the principal business I had to discuss, namely, the advantage of disengaging the British Army from its position on the Aisne and its transportation to its natural station on the sea flank in contact with the Navy. I found the Field-Marshal in the most complete accord, and I undertook to lay his views before Lord Kitchener and the Prime Minister, who I knew would welcome such a development. I started home immediately and reached London the next morning.

Contact with the Army was always a great encouragement to every one who visited France. In the field, in spite of the newly-dug graves and hurrying ambulances, there was not the same sense of tragedy as hung around our windows in Whitehall. But I could not share the universal optimism of the Staff. It was firmly believed and loudly declared on every side that if all available reinforcements in officers and men were sent to the Army without delay, the war would be finished by Christmas. Fierce were the reproaches that the War Office were withholding vitally needed officers, instructors and material for the purpose of training vast armies that would never be ready in time. I combated these views to the best of my ability, being fully convinced of Lord Kitchener's commanding foresight and wisdom in resisting the temptation to meet the famine of the moment by devouring the seed-corn of the future. I repeated the memorable words he had used to the Cabinet that 'The British Empire must participate in the land war on the greatest scale and that in no other way could victory be won.' Taking a complete survey, I consider now that this prudent withholding from the Army in the field in the face of every appeal and demand, the key-men who alone could make the new armies, was the greatest of the services which Lord Kitchener rendered to the nation at this time, and it was a service which no one of lesser authority than he could have performed.

CHAPTER XIII
ON THE OCEANS

> 'Coastwise—cross-seas—round the world and back again,
> Where the flaw shall head us or the full Trade suits—
> Plain-sail—storm-sail—lay your board and tack again—
> And that's the way we'll pay Paddy Doyle for his boots!'
>
> Rudyard Kipling, *The Merchantmen*.

Expeditions against the German Colonies—The Imperial Reinforcements—The Admiralty at Full Strain—General Situation in the Outer Seas—The Price of Concentration at Home—The *Königsberg* and the *Emden* in the Indian Ocean—The Convoy System—General Situation in the Pacific—British Dispositions—Japan Declares War on Germany—Overwhelming Forces of the Allies—Difficulty of their Task—Fox and Geese—Problem of Admiral von Spee—Limitations on his Action—Plight of Cruisers without Bases—Tell-tale Coal—The Admiralty Problem—The Capture of Samoa—The great Australasian Convoy—The Capture of New Guinea—Depredations of the *Emden*—Concentration against the *Emden*—Public Dissatisfaction on Admiralty Statement—Sailing of the Australasian Convoy to Colombo—The Canadians Cross the Atlantic—First Imperial Concentration Complete.

On an August morning, behold the curious sight of a British Cabinet of respectable Liberal politicians sitting down deliberately and with malice aforethought to plan the seizure of the German colonies in every part of the world! A month before, with what horror and disgust would most of those present have averted their minds from such ideas! But our sea communications depended largely upon the prompt denial of these bases or refuges to the German cruisers; and further, with Belgium already largely overrun by the German armies, everyone felt that we must lose no time in taking hostages for her eventual liberation. Accordingly, with maps and pencils, the whole world was surveyed, six separate expeditions were approved in principle and remitted to the Staffs for study and execution. An enterprising Captain[1] had already on the outbreak of war invaded the German colony of Togoland. We now proposed, in conjunction with the French, to attack the Cameroons—a much more serious undertaking. General Botha had already declared his intention of invading German South-West Africa. The New Zealand and Australian

[1]Captain F. C. Bryant.

Governments wished at once to seize Samoa and the German possessions in the Pacific. An Anglo-Indian expedition was authorized for the attack of German East Africa. The Staff work in preparation for the military side of this last expedition was by no means perfect, and resulted in a serious rebuff. The transportation of the expeditionary forces simultaneously in all these different directions while the seas were still scoured by the German cruisers threw another set of responsibilities upon the Admiralty.

From the middle of September onwards we began to be at our fullest strain. The great map of the world which covered one whole wall of the War Room now presented a remarkable appearance. As many as twenty separate enterprises and undertakings dependent entirely upon sea-power were proceeding simultaneously in different parts of the globe.[2] Apart from the expeditions set forth above, the enormous business of convoying from all parts of the Empire the troops needed for France, and of replacing them in some cases with Territorials from home, lay heavy upon us. It was soon to be augmented.

It had been easy to set on foot the organization of the three Naval Brigades and other Divisional troops for the Royal Naval Division; but at a very early stage I found the creation of the artillery beyond any resources of which I could dispose. We could, and did, order a hundred field-guns in the United States, but the training, mounting and equipping of the artillerymen could not and ought not to be undertaken apart from the main preparation of the Army. My military staff officer, Major Ollivant, at this stage had a very good idea which provoked immediately far-reaching consequences. He advised me to ask Lord Kitchener for a dozen British batteries from India to form the artillery of the Royal Naval Division, letting India have Territorial batteries in exchange. I put this to Lord Kitchener the same afternoon. He seemed tremendously struck by the idea. What would the Cabinet say? he asked. If the Government of India refused, could the Cabinet overrule them? Would they? Would I support him in the matter? And so on. I had to leave that night for the North to visit the Fleet, which was lying in Loch Ewe, on the west coast of Scotland. Forty-eight hours later, when I returned, I visited Lord Kitchener and asked him how matters were progressing. He beamed with delight. 'Not only,' he said, 'am I going to take twelve batteries, but thirty-one; and not only am I going to take batteries, I am going to take battalions. I am going to take thirty-nine battalions: I am going to send them Territorial divisions instead—three Territorial divisions. You must get the transports ready at once.' After we had gloated over this prospect of succouring our struggling front, I observed that I could now count on the twelve batteries for the Royal Naval Division. 'Not one,' he said. 'I am going to take them all myself'; and he rubbed his hands together with every sign of glee. So the Naval Division was left again in the cold and had to go forward as infantry only.

This new development involved a heavy addition to our convoy work, and the situation in the Indian and Pacific Oceans must now be examined by the reader.

---

[2]See maps on pages 210–13.

When war began the Germans had the following cruisers in foreign stations: *Scharnhorst*, *Gneisenau*, *Emden*, *Nürnberg*, *Leipzig* (China); *Königsberg* (East Africa and Indian Ocean); *Dresden*, *Karlsruhe* (West Indies). All these ships were fast and modern, and every one of them did us serious injury before they were destroyed. There were also several gunboats: *Geier*, *Planet*, *Komet*, *Nusa* and *Eber*, none of which could be ignored. In addition, we expected that the Germans would try to send to sea upwards of forty fast armed merchantmen to prey on commerce. Our arrangements were, however, as has been narrated, successful in preventing all but five from leaving harbour. Of these five the largest, the *Kaiser Wilhelm der Grosse*, was sunk by the *Highflyer* (Captain Buller) on August 26; the *Cap Trafalgar* was sunk on September 14 by the British armed merchant cruiser *Carmania* (Captain Noel Grant) after a brilliant action between these two naked ships; and the three others took refuge and were interned in neutral harbours some months later. Our dispositions for preventing a cruiser and commerce-raider attack upon our trade were from the outset very largely successful, and in the few months with which this volume deals, every one of the enemy ships was reduced to complete inactivity, sunk or pinned in port.

Nevertheless, it is a fair criticism that we ought to have had more fast cruisers in foreign waters, and in particular that we ought to have matched every one of the German cruisers with a faster ship as it was our intention to do.[3] The *Karlsruhe* in the West Indies gave a chance to our hunting vessels at the outbreak of war, and the *Königsberg* in the Indian Ocean was sighted a few days earlier. But our ships were not fast enough to bring the former to action or keep in close contact with the latter till war was declared. As will be seen, nearly every one of these German cruisers took its prey before being caught, not only of merchant ships but of ships of war. The *Scharnhorst* and *Gneisenau* sank the *Monmouth* and *Good Hope*, the *Königsberg* surprised and destroyed the *Pegasus*, and the *Emden* sank the Russian cruiser *Zemchug* and the French destroyer *Mousquet*. Certainly they did their duty well.

The keynote of all the Admiralty dispositions at the outbreak of war was to be as strong as possible in home waters in order to fight a decisive battle with the whole German Navy. To this end the foreign stations were cut down to the absolute minimum necessary to face the individual ships abroad in each theatre. The Fleet was weak in fast light cruisers and the whole of my administration had been occupied in building as many of them as possible. None of the *Arethusas* had, however, yet reached the Fleet. We therefore grudged every light cruiser removed from home waters, feeling that the Fleet would be tactically incomplete without its sea cavalry. The principle of first things first, and of concentrating in a decisive theatre against the enemy's main power, had governed everything, and had led to delay in meeting an important and well-recognized subsidiary requirement. The inconvenience in other parts of the globe had to be faced. It was serious.

---

[3]See Memorandum on Trade Protection, Appendix C.

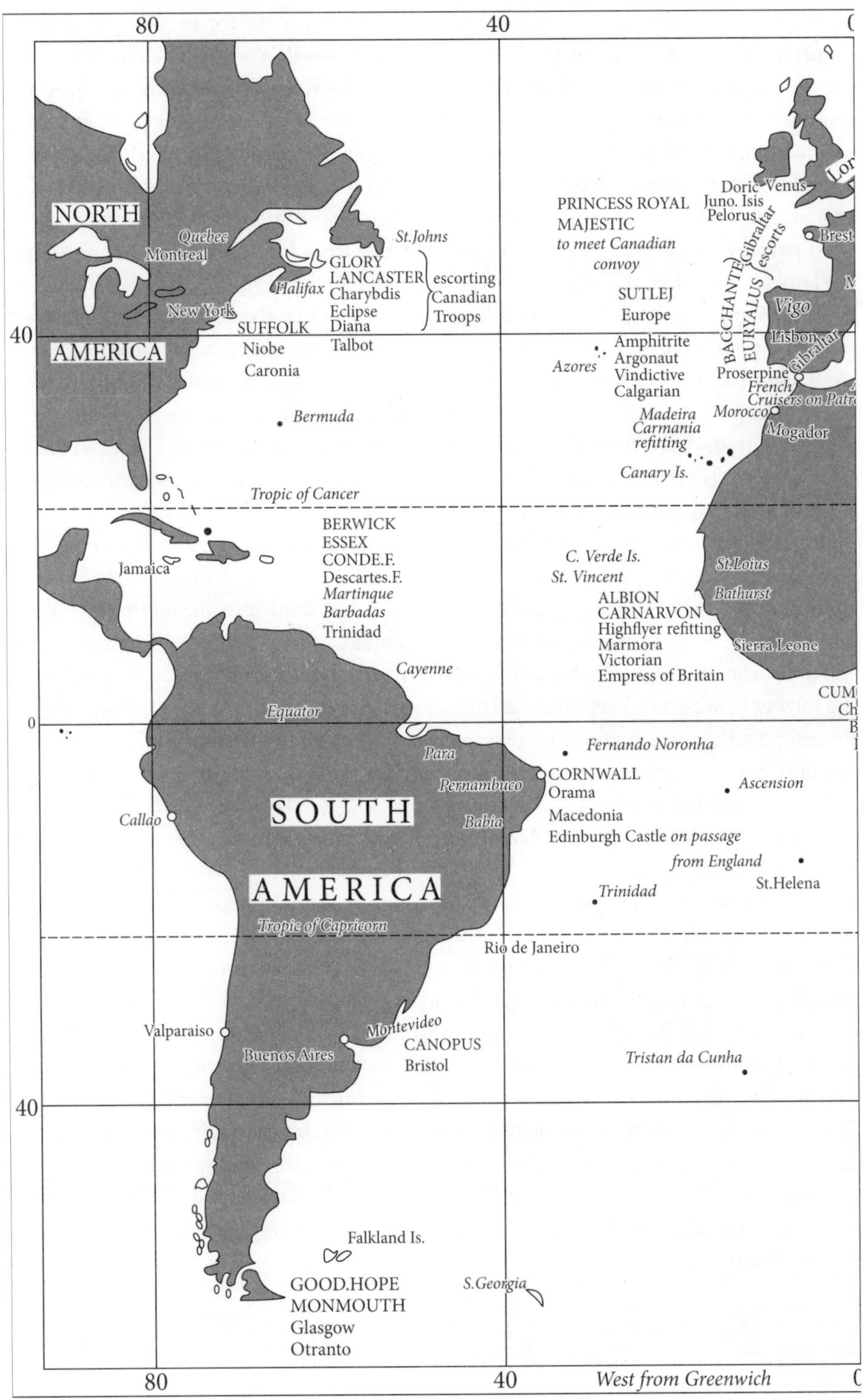
80
40
NORTH
AMERICA
Quebec
Montreal
New York
Halifax
St.Johns
GLORY
LANCASTER
Charybdis
Eclipse
Diana
Talbot
escorting
Canadian
Troops
SUFFOLK
Niobe
Caronia
Bermuda
PRINCESS ROYAL
MAJESTIC
to meet Canadian
convoy
SUTLEJ
Europe
Doric Venus
Juno. Isis
Pelorus
Gibraltar escorts
BACCHANTE
EURYALUS
Brest
Vigo
Lisbon
Gibraltar
Azores
Amphitrite
Argonaut
Vindictive
Calgarian
Proserpine
French
Cruisers on Patr
Madeira
Carmania
refitting
Morocco
Mogador
Canary Is.
Tropic of Cancer
Jamaica
BERWICK
ESSEX
CONDE.F.
Descartes.F.
Martinique
Barbadas
Trinidad
C. Verde Is.
St. Vincent
ALBION
CARNARVON
Highflyer refitting
Marmora
Victorian
Empress of Britain
St.Loius
Bathurst
Sierra Leone
Cayenne
Equator
0
Para
Fernando Noronha
Pernambuco
CORNWALL
Orama
Macedonia
Edinburgh Castle on passage
from England
Ascension
Callao
SOUTH
AMERICA
Babia
Trinidad
St.Helena
Tropic of Capricorn
Rio de Janeiro
Valparaiso
Buenos Aires
Montevideo
CANOPUS
Bristol
Tristan da Cunha
Falkland Is.
GOOD.HOPE
MONMOUTH
Glasgow
Otranto
S.Georgia
West from Greenwich

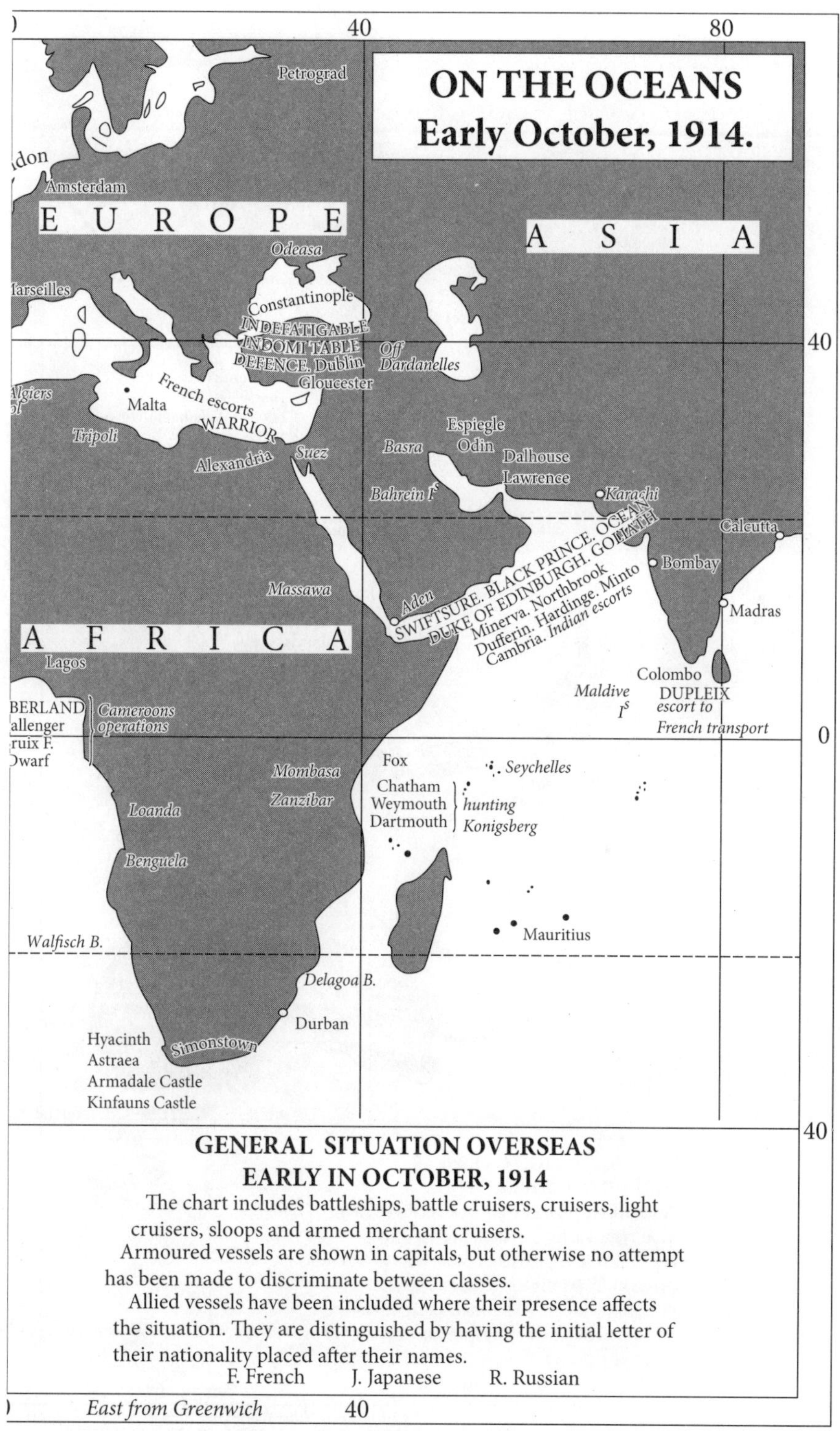
ON THE OCEANS
Early October, 1914.
40
80
Petrograd
Amsterdam
EUROPE
ASIA
Odeasa
Constantinople
INDEFATIGABLE
INDOMITABLE
DEFENCE. Dublin
Gloucester
Off Dardanelles
French escorts
Malta
WARRIOR
Tripoli
Alexandria
Suez
Basra
Espiegle
Odin
Dalhouse
Lawrence
Bahrein I^s
Karachi
SWIFTSURE. BLACK PRINCE. OCEAN
DUKE OF EDINBURGH. GOLIATH
Minerva. Northbrook
Dufferin. Hardinge. Minto
Cambria. Indian escorts
Calcutta
Bombay
Madras
Aden
Massawa
AFRICA
Lagos
Colombo
Maldive I^s
DUPLEIX
escort to
French transport
Cameroons operations
Fox
Seychelles
Chatham
Weymouth
Dartmouth
hunting
Konigsberg
Mombasa
Zanzibar
Loanda
Benguela
Mauritius
Walfisch B.
Delagoa B.
Durban
Simonstown
Hyacinth
Astraea
Armadale Castle
Kinfauns Castle
0
40
GENERAL SITUATION OVERSEAS
EARLY IN OCTOBER, 1914
The chart includes battleships, battle cruisers, cruisers, light cruisers, sloops and armed merchant cruisers.
Armoured vessels are shown in capitals, but otherwise no attempt has been made to discriminate between classes.
Allied vessels have been included where their presence affects the situation. They are distinguished by having the initial letter of their nationality placed after their names.
F. French J. Japanese R. Russian
East from Greenwich

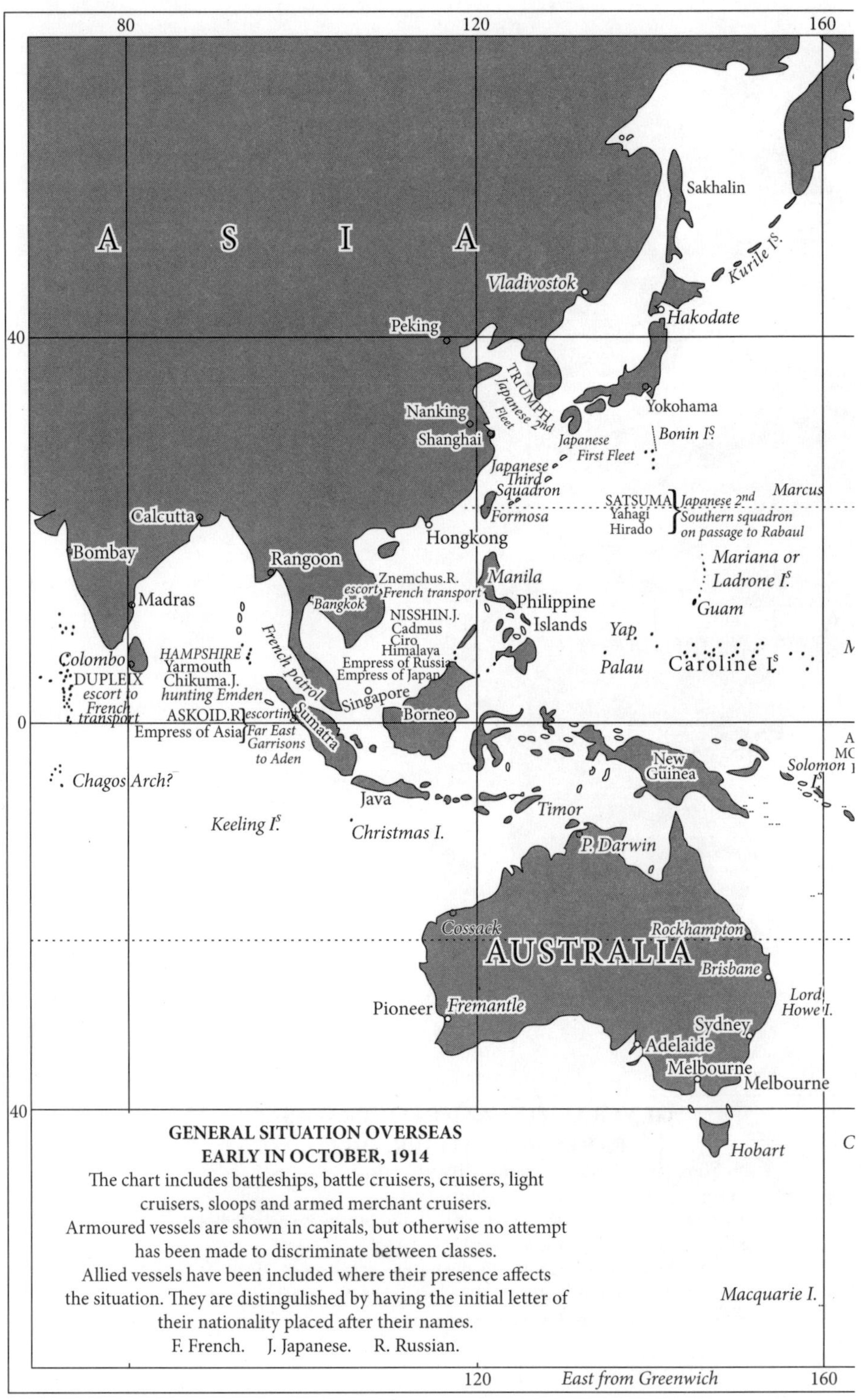

GENERAL SITUATION OVERSEAS
EARLY IN OCTOBER, 1914

The chart includes battleships, battle cruisers, cruisers, light cruisers, sloops and armed merchant cruisers.
Armoured vessels are shown in capitals, but otherwise no attempt has been made to discriminate between classes.
Allied vessels have been included where their presence affects the situation. They are distingulished by having the initial letter of their nationality placed after their names.
F. French. J. Japanese. R. Russian.

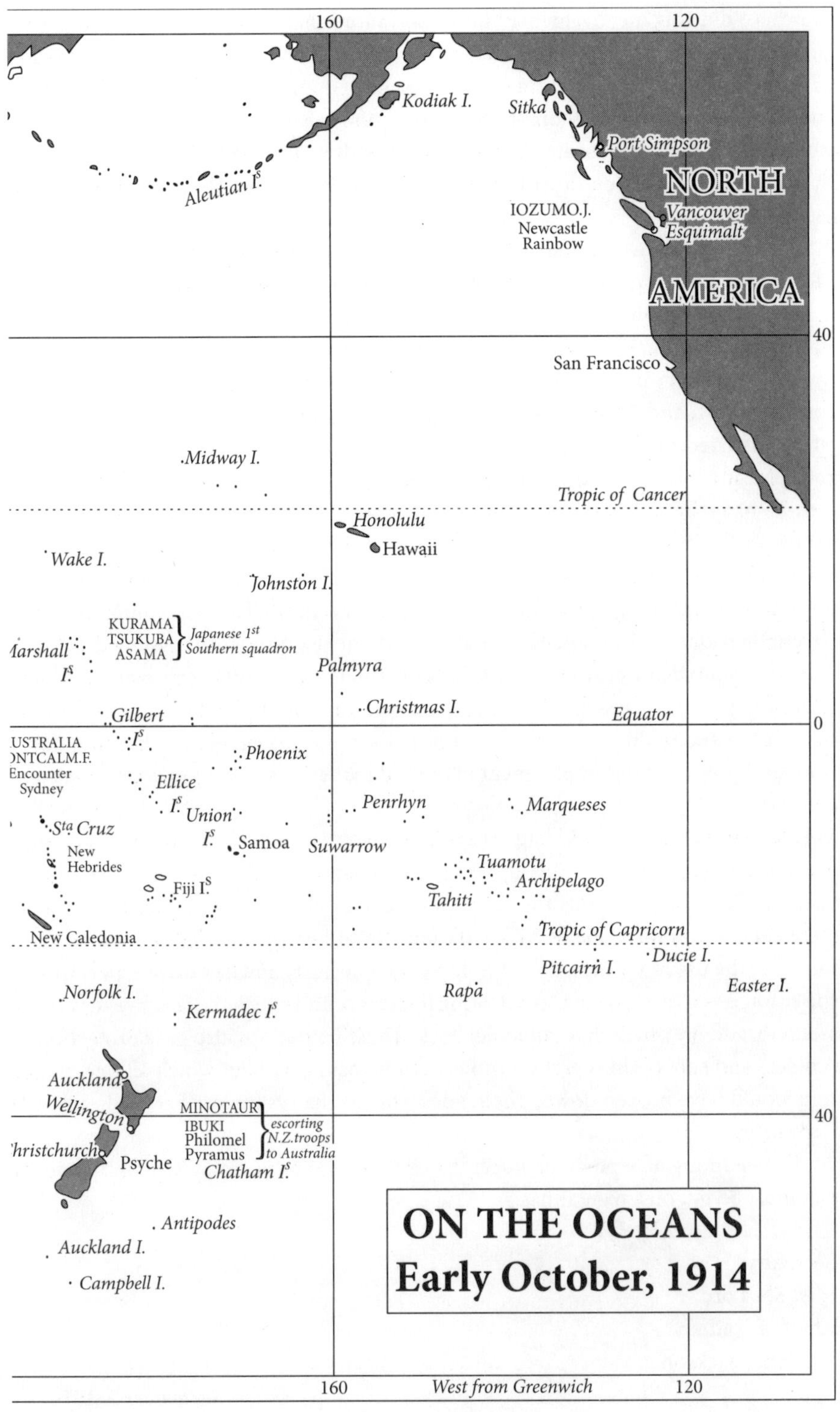
160
120
Kodiak I.
Sitka
Port Simpson
NORTH
AMERICA
Aleutian Is.
IOZUMO.J.
Newcastle
Rainbow
Vancouver
Esquimalt
40
San Francisco
Midway I.
Tropic of Cancer
Honolulu
Hawaii
Wake I.
Johnston I.
KURAMA
TSUKUBA
ASAMA
Japanese 1st Southern squadron
Marshall Is.
Palmyra
Christmas I.
Gilbert Is.
Equator
0
Phoenix
Encounter
Sydney
Ellice Is.
Union Is.
Penrhyn
Marquesas
Sta Cruz
Samoa
Suwarrow
New Hebrides
Tuamotu Archipelago
Fiji Is.
Tahiti
New Caledonia
Tropic of Capricorn
Ducie I.
Pitcairn I.
Rapa
Easter I.
Norfolk I.
Kermadec Is.
Auckland
Wellington
MINOTAUR
IBUKI
Philomel
Pyramus
escorting N.Z.troops to Australia
Christchurch
Psyche
Chatham Is.
Antipodes
Auckland I.
Campbell I.
ON THE OCEANS
Early October, 1914
West from Greenwich

Nowhere did this inconvenience show itself more than in the Indian Ocean. After being sighted and making off on July 31, the *Königsberg* became a serious preoccupation in all movements of troops and trade. Another fast German cruiser, the *Emden*, which on the outbreak of war was on the China Station, also appeared in the middle of September in Indian waters, and being handled with enterprise and audacity began to inflict numerous and serious losses upon our mercantile marine. These events produced consequences.

By the end of August we had already collected the bulk of the 7th Division from all the fortresses and garrisons of the Empire. During September the two British Indian divisions with additional cavalry (in all nearly 50,000 men) were already crossing the Indian Ocean. On top of this came the plans for exchanging practically all the British infantry and artillery in India for Territorial batteries and battalions, and the formation of the 27th, 28th and 29th Divisions of regular troops. The New Zealand contingent must be escorted to Australia and there, with 25,000 Australians, await convoys to Europe. Meanwhile the leading troops of the Canadian Army, about 25,000 strong, had to be brought across the Atlantic. All this was of course additional to the main situation in the North Sea and to the continued flow of drafts, reinforcements and supplies across the Channel. Meanwhile the enemy's Fleet remained intact, waiting, as we might think, its moment to strike; and his cruisers continued to prey upon the seas. To strengthen our cruiser forces we had already armed and commissioned twenty-four liners as auxiliary cruisers, and had armed defensively fifty-four merchantmen. Another forty suitable vessels were in preparation. In order to lighten the strain in the Indian Ocean and to liberate our light cruisers for their proper work of hunting down the enemy, I proposed the employment of our old battleships (*Canopus* class) as escorts to convoys.

Besides employing these old battleships on convoy, we had also at the end of August sent three others abroad as rallying points for our cruisers in case a German heavy cruiser should break out: thus the *Glory* was sent to Halifax, the *Albion* to Gibraltar and the *Canopus* to the Cape de Verde station. Naval history afforded numerous good examples of the use of a protective battleship to give security and defensive superiority to a cruiser force—to serve, in fact, as a floating fortress round which the faster vessels could manœuvre, and on which they could fall back. These battleships also gave protection to the colliers and supply ships at the various oceanic bases, without which all our cruiser system would have broken down. The reader will see the system further applied as the war advances.

At the beginning of September, I decided that the whole convoy system in the Indian Ocean must be put on a regular basis.

Secretary.
First Sea Lord.
Chief of Staff.
Sir Henry Jackson.

September 5, 1914.

There is no use in our sending escorts which are weaker than the enemy's ship from which attack is to be apprehended. Armed merchant cruisers can in no case be counted on except as an additional reinforcement. Single troopships may be escorted by one war vessel, if that vessel is stronger than the *Königsberg*. No convoys of transports are to go across the Indian Ocean or Red Sea unless escorted by at least two war vessels, one of which must be stronger than the *Königsberg*. In large convoys of over six vessels a third, and in very large convoys a fourth, warship should be added. Military needs must give way to the limitations of escort. Six ships, including the *Fox*, are available; and it ought to be possible to organize fortnightly if not 12-day convoys from Bombay.

Commander-in-Chief, East Indies, should be directed to submit, by telegraph, a scheme for such convoys. All transports which may want convoy must be held over till the next is ready.

W. S. C.

Secretary.
First Sea Lord.
Chief of Staff.

September 15, 1914.

In order to accelerate the despatch of the third Division from India to France, and the seven battalions to German East Africa, it is proposed that the transports now conveying the Territorial Division to Egypt shall go on to Bombay. It has also been decided to exchange thirty-one batteries of [British] Indian regular artillery for service in Europe with an equal number of Territorial batteries which are to embark shortly from home. The ships carrying the Territorial batteries will also go on to Bombay and be available as additional transport.

Please concert these measures with the War Office. It is most important that these double convoys each way should hit off our fortnightly escorts which are the governing consideration.

Pray let me have a scheme showing how all this movement can be fitted in with the greatest speed and smoothness.

W. S. C.

Secretary.
First Sea Lord.
Chief of Staff.
Sir Henry Jackson.

September 18, 1914.

In addition to the 2 Divisions now coming from India and the expedition for German East Africa, we must expect the following:—

(*a*) A third Indian Division.

(*b*) 31 batteries of field artillery from India, to be exchanged for an equal amount of Territorial artillery from home.

(*c*) 39 battalions of British infantry from India, to be exchanged for an equal number of Territorial battalions from home.

(*d*) As many more Indian troops as India in these circumstances finds it convenient to despatch.

(*e*) Reinforcements to make good wastage of Indian troops in the field.

These later movements are not all finally settled and approved, but it is certain that from now till Christmas we shall require to maintain regular fortnightly convoys. We cannot delay till then the work of hunting down *Königsberg* and *Emden* by our own fast cruisers, nor can we keep these vessels employed indefinitely on duties for which they are unsuited. It is necessary that 3 old battleships, including *Ocean* from Gibraltar, should proceed at once to the East Indies Station to relieve, as they arrive, first *Dartmouth* and *Chatham*, and next *Black Prince*. *Minerva* should go on to India with the transports she is now escorting to Egypt, and the East Indies convoy force should be as follows:—

SUEZ: 2 *Majestics*[4] and *Minerva*.
BOMBAY: 1 *Majestic*, *Swiftsure*, and *Fox*.

These escorts should sail every fortnight to exchange transports at the rendezvous 500 miles east of Aden. Modern ships would be released for other duties as these came on the spot.

(2) In the Mediterranean the French should be asked to supply 4 old battleships and 2 old armoured cruisers for convoy duty between Marseilles and Port Said, and asked to arrange fortnightly sailings via Malta to fit in with the Indian convoy service. We will escort all transports from England to Malta at times which will enable the French convoys to take them up *en route*.

(3) The force at the Dardanelles must be raised to a strength sufficient to fight the Turco-German fleet. As soon, therefore, as the French escort becomes available, *Indomitable* should join *Indefatigable*. *Defence* should also be ordered there from Malta. *Weymouth* should come home. The four destroyers from the Canal should rejoin their flotilla at the Dardanelles.

(4) In view of the above, I agree that *Fox* should remain with the Indian convoy and that *Dartmouth* should take the three transports to Mombasa, afterwards hunting *Königsberg*.

(5) The whole of this should be co-ordinated and worked out into a regular time-table of sailings, to which the military must adhere, sending more or less transports, according to their convenience. It must be clearly understood that no intermediate sailings are possible.

W. S. C.

[4] The old battleships in question were actually 'Canopuses'—the class above 'Majesties.'

The position in the Pacific was also complicated.

When I went to the Admiralty at the end of 1911, arrangements were made to form the China squadron of the *Defence*, the *Minotaur*, and an armoured cruiser of the County class. These two first-named ships were in themselves a very satisfactory disposition against the powerful German armoured cruisers *Scharnhorst* and *Gneisenau*. They were approximately equal to the Germans in modernity, size and speed, but of heavier metal, firing a broadside of 2,520 pounds as against 1,725 pounds of their rivals.

But as time passed and the pressure upon us grew more severe, we had in 1913 to bring one of these ships (*Defence*) back to the Mediterranean. In order to fill the gap with the least possible inroad upon our home strength, Prince Louis being First Sea Lord, we devised a frugal scheme by which the *Triumph*—one of the two battleships which had been built for Chili, and bought from her to prevent their falling into Russian hands at the outbreak of the Russo-Japanese War—was made to serve as a depôt ship manned on mobilization from the crews of the river gunboats on the Yangtse and the West River. Her sister (the *Swiftsure*) shortly afterwards became the flagship in the East Indies. These two ships had the good speed for battleships of their date of 20.1 knots. They carried four 10-inch and no less than fourteen 7.5-inch guns. They were not heavily armoured, and according to our ideas they were a compromise between the battleship and the armoured cruiser. Differing in conception at many points from the standard types of the Royal Navy, these vessels did not fit homogeneously into any of our battle squadrons, and were conveniently employed on special duties. Without the *Triumph*, Admiral Jerram's squadron (*Minotaur* and *Hampshire* with the light cruiser *Yarmouth*) would, on the outbreak of war, have had little or no margin, though the *Minotaur* was the strongest of all our armoured cruisers. But once the *Triumph* was mobilized, our superiority, except in speed, was overwhelming, and we could afford to see how greater matters went at home before deciding whether to reinforce the China station or not.

In the first hours of the crisis, my thoughts had turned to the China station. As early as July 28 I proposed to the First Sea Lord the discreet mobilization of the *Triumph* and the concentration of the China Squadron upon her; and this was accordingly effected in good time. Five thousand miles to the southward was the Australian squadron, consisting of the battle-cruiser *Australia*, and the two excellent modern light cruisers *Sydney* and *Melbourne*. The *Australia* by herself could, of course, defeat the *Scharnhorst* and *Gneisenau*, though by running different ways one of the pair could have escaped destruction. Our last look round the oceans before the fateful signal, left us therefore in no immediate anxiety about the Pacific.

On the outbreak of war the French armoured cruisers *Montcalm* and *Dupleix* and the Russian light cruisers *Askold* and *Zemchug*, in the Far East, were placed under British command, thus sensibly increasing our predominance. A few days later an event of the greatest importance occurred. The attitude of Japan towards Germany suddenly became one of fierce menace. No clause in the Anglo-Japanese Treaty entitled us to invoke the assistance of Japan. But it became evident before the war had lasted a week that the Japanese nation had not forgotten the circumstances and influences under which they had been forced, at the end of the Chinese War, to quit Port Arthur. They now showed themselves

WARSHIPS IN THE WESTERN PACIFIC[1]

AUGUST TO OCTOBER, 1914

	German	British		Japanese[2]	French	Russian
Battle-cruisers		*Australia*		*Ibuki*		
Battleships		Triumph				
Armoured Cruisers	*Scharnhorst*	*Minotaur*			*Montcalm*	
	Gneisenau	*Hampshire*			*Dupleix*	
Fast Light Cruisers	*Emden*	*Yarmouth*		*Chikuma*		
	Nürnberg	*Melbourne*				
		Sydney	*Philomel*			
Older Light Cruisers		*Encounter*	*Pyramus*			*Askold*
		Pioneer	*Psyche*			*Zemchug*

Ships on lined patrolling beats not available for offensive action:–

	German	British		Japanese	French	Russian
Armed Merchant Cruisers . .	*Prince Eitel*	*Empress of Asia*				
	Friedrich	*Empress of Japan*				
	Cormoran	*Empress of Russia*				
		Himalaya				
Gunboats	*Geier*	*Cadmus*			*Kersaint*	
		Clio			*Zélée*	

[1] The underlining denotes approximately the comparative values of the units.
[2] Only those ships of the Japanese Navy who took part in the operations are included.

resolved to extirpate all German authority and interests in the Far East. On the 15th, Japan addressed an ultimatum to Germany demanding within seven days the unconditional surrender of the German naval base Tsing Tau [Kiaochow], couching this demand in the very phrases in which nineteen years before they had been summoned to leave Port Arthur at the instance of Germany. In reply the German Emperor commanded his servants to resist to the end; and here, as almost in every other place where Germans found themselves isolated in the face of overwhelming force, he was obeyed with constancy.

The entry of Japan into the war enabled us to use our China squadron to better advantage in other theatres. The *Newcastle* was ordered across the Pacific, where our two old sloops (the *Algerine* and *Shearwater*) were in jeopardy from the German light cruiser *Leipzig*. The *Triumph* was sent to participate with a small British contingent in the Japanese attack upon the fortress of Tsing Tau. General arrangements were made by the British and Japanese Admiralties whereby responsibility for the whole of the Northern Pacific, except the Canadian Coast, was assumed by Japan.

The table sets forth the rival forces in the Western Pacific at the outbreak of war. Even without the ships employed by Japan or the great Japanese reserves which lay behind them, the superior strength of the Allies was overwhelming. But the game the two sides had to play was by no means as unequal as it looked. It was indeed the old game of Fox and Geese. The two powerful German cruisers *Scharnhorst* and *Gneisenau*, with their two light cruisers, formed a modern squadron fast and formidable in character. Our battle-cruiser *Australia* could catch them and could fight them single-handed. The *Minotaur* and the *Hampshire* could just catch them and, as we held, could fight them with good prospects of success; but it would be a hard-fought action. If the *Triumph* were added to *Minotaur* and *Hampshire*, there was no risk at all in the fight but almost insuperable difficulty in bringing the enemy to action. Among the light cruisers, the *Yarmouth*, *Melbourne*, *Sydney* and the Japanese *Chikuma* could both catch and kill *Emden* or *Nürnberg*. Of our older light cruisers, *Fox* and *Encounter* could have fought *Emden* or *Nürnberg* with a chance of killing or at least of crippling them before being killed: but neither was fast enough to catch them. Our remaining cruisers could only be used in combination with stronger vessels. With our forces aided by two French and two Russian ships and by the Japanese to the extent which will be described, the Admiralty had to protect all the expeditions, convoys and trade in the Pacific. To wit—

The New Zealand convoy to Australia.

The Australian and New Zealand convoy from Australia to Europe.

The convoy of the British Far Eastern garrisons to Europe.

The convoy of Indian troops to relieve our Far Eastern garrisons.

The expedition to Samoa.

The expedition to New Guinea.

All these were in addition to the general trade, which continued uninterruptedly.

Admiral von Spee, the German Commander in the Pacific, had therefore no lack of objectives. He had only to hide and to strike.

The vastness of the Pacific and its multitude of islands offered him their shelter, and, once he had vanished, who should say where he would reappear? On the other hand, there were considerable checks on his action and a limit, certain though indefinite, to the life of his squadron. With the blockade of Tsing Tau he was cut from his only base on that side of the world. He had no means of docking his ships or executing any serious repairs, whether necessitated by battle or steaming. The wear and tear on modern ships is considerable, and difficulties multiply with every month out of dock. To steam at full speed or at high speed for any length of time on any quest was to use up his life rapidly. He was a cut flower in a vase; fair to see, yet bound to die, and to die very soon if the water was not constantly renewed. Moreover, the process of getting coal was one of extraordinary difficulty and peril. The extensive organization of the Admiralty kept the closest watch in every port on every ton of coal and every likely collier. The purchase of coal and the movement of a collier were tell-tale traces which might well lay the pursuers on his track. His own safety and his power to embarrass us alike depended upon the uncertainty of his movements. But this uncertainty might be betrayed at any moment by the movement of colliers or by the interception of wireless messages. Yet how could colliers be brought to the necessary rendezvous without wireless messages? There existed in the Pacific only five German wireless stations, Yap, Apia, Nauru, Rabaul, Angaur, all of which were destroyed by us within two months of the outbreak of war. After that there remained only the wireless on board the German ships, with which it was very dangerous to breathe a word into the ether. Such was the situation of Admiral von Spee.

The problem of the Admiralty was also delicate and complex. All our enterprises lay simultaneously under the shadow of a serious potential danger. You could make scare schemes which showed that von Spee might turn up with his whole squadron almost anywhere. On the other hand, we could not possibly be strong enough every day everywhere to meet him. We had, therefore, either to balance probabilities and run risks, or reduce our movements and affairs to very narrow limits. Absolute security meant something very like absolute paralysis; yet fierce would have been the outcry attendant either upon stagnation or disaster. We decided deliberately to carry on our affairs and to take the risk. After all, the oceans were as wide for us as for von Spee. The map of the world in the Admiralty War Room measured nearly 20 feet by 30. Being a seaman's map, its centre was filled by the greatest mass of water on the globe: the enormous areas of the Pacific filling upwards of 300 square feet. On this map the head of an ordinary veil-pin represented the full view to be obtained from the masts of a ship on a clear day. There was certainly plenty of room for ships to miss one another.

As has been stated, the British China Squadron mobilized and concentrated at Hong-Kong, and the Australian Navy at Sydney. Admiral von Spee was at Ponape in the Caroline Islands when Great Britain declared war upon Germany. From Hong-Kong and Sydney to Ponape the distances were each about 2,750 miles. Although Japan had not yet entered the war, the German Admiral did not attempt to return to Kiaochau, as this might have involved immediate battle with the British China Squadron. He proceeded only as far as the Ladrone Islands (German), where the *Emden* from Kiaochau, escorting his supply ships, met him on August 12. He sent the *Emden* into the Indian Ocean to prey on commerce and turned himself eastward towards the Marshall Islands. On August 22 he detached the *Nürnberg* to Honolulu to obtain information and send messages, to cut the cable between Canada and New Zealand, and to rejoin him at Christmas Island on September 8. Here he was in the very centre of the Pacific.

The Admiralty knew nothing of these movements beyond a report that he was coaling at the Caroline Islands on August 9. Thereafter he vanished completely from our view. We could know nothing for certain. The theory of the Admiralty Staff, however, endorsed by Admiral Sir Henry Jackson, who was making a special and profound study of this theatre, was that he would go to the Marshall Islands and thereafter would most probably work across to the west coast of South America, or double the Horn on his way back to Europe. This theory, and the intricate reasoning by which it was supported, proved to be correct. In the main, though we could by no means trust ourselves to it and always expected unpleasant surprises, it was our dominant hypothesis. It is on this basis that the operations in the Pacific should be studied.

As early as August 2 the New Zealand Government—ever in the van of the Empire—had convinced themselves that war was inevitable, and had already made proposals for raising forces and striking at the enemy. The Operations Division of the War Staff proposed in consequence the capture of Samoa and the destruction of the wireless station there; and this was recommended to me by the First Sea Lord and the Chief of the Staff as a feasible operation. By August 8 New Zealand telegraphed that if a naval escort could be furnished the expedition to attack Samoa could start on August 11. The Staff concurred in this, holding that the *Gneisenau* and *Scharnhorst* were adequately covered by the Australian squadron. I assented the same day. It was arranged that the expedition should meet the battle-cruiser *Australia* and the French cruiser *Montcalm* at or on the way to Noumea.

Another expedition from Australia to attack German New Guinea had also been organized by the Government of the Commonwealth. The uncertainty about the *Scharnhorst* and *Gneisenau* invested all movements in those waters with a certain hazardous delicacy. It was thought, however, that the light cruisers *Melbourne*[5] and *Sydney* could convoy the Commonwealth New Guinea expedition northward, keeping inside the Barrier Reef, and that before they came out into open waters the New Guinea convoy could be joined by *Australia* and *Montcalm*, who would by then have completed the escort of the New Zealand expedition to Samoa. We thought it above all things important that these expeditions, once they had landed and taken possession of the German colonies, should be self-sufficing, and that no weak warships should be left in the harbours to support them. Any such vessels, apart from the difficulty of sparing them, would be an easy prey for the two large German cruisers.

Samoa was occupied on August 30. The wireless station at Nauru was destroyed on September 10. The Australian contingent was picked up by the battle-cruiser *Australia* September 9 and arrived at Rabaul safely two days later.

[5]*Encounter* went instead of *Melbourne*.

We had now to provide for the Australian convoy to Europe which was due to leave Sydney on September 27 for Port Adelaide, where they would be joined by the New Zealand contingent and its own escort as well as by the 'Australian Fleet' (*Australia, Sydney and Melbourne*) as soon as they were free from the New Guinea expedition. Our original proposal for the escort of the Australian Army was, therefore, *Australia*, *Sydney* and *Melbourne*, with the small cruisers from New Zealand. To cover the Commonwealth during the absence of all her Fleet, it was arranged that the *Minotaur*, together with the Japanese *Ibuki* and *Chikuma*, should come south to New Britain Islands.

In the middle of September the New Zealand contingent was due to sail for Adelaide. The *Australia* and her consorts were still delayed in New Guinea, where some delay was caused by the German resistance. Great anxiety was felt in New Zealand at the prospect of throwing their contingent across to Australia with no better escort than the two P class cruisers. They pointed out the dangers from the *Scharnhorst* and *Gneisenau*, which on September 14 had been reported off Samoa. The Admiralty view was that it was most improbable the *Scharnhorst* and *Gneisenau* could know of the contemplated New Zealand expedition, still less of the date of its sailing; that in order to deliver an attack in New Zealand waters they would have to steam far from their coaling bases north of the Equator, and would indeed have to be accompanied by their colliers, greatly reducing their speed and hampering their movements. In these circumstances the Admiralty foresaw but little danger to the New Zealand convoy in the first part of their voyage, were unable to provide further protection for this stage, and expressed the opinion that the risk should be accepted. To this decision the New Zealand Government bowed on September 21, and it was settled that the New Zealand convoy should sail on the 25th. Meanwhile, however, renewed exploits by the *Emden* in the Bay of Bengal created a natural feeling of alarm in the mind of the New Zealand and Australian public; and without prejudice to our original view, we decided to make arrangements to remove these apprehensions.

On the 24th, news arrived that the New Guinea expedition had successfully overcome all opposition, and we then determined on the following change of plans, viz. *Minotaur* and *Ibuki* to go to Wellington and escort the New Zealanders to Adelaide, while *Australia* and *Montcalm*, after convoying the auxiliaries and weak warships back from New Guinea to within the shelter of the Barrier Reef, should hunt for the *Scharnhorst* and *Gneisenau* in the Marshall Islands, whither it seemed probable they were proceeding. This decision altered the composition of the escort of the Australian convoy, and their protection across the Pacific and Indian Oceans was to an important extent confided to a vessel which flew the war flag of Japan. This historic fact should be an additional bond of goodwill among the friendly and allied nations who dwell in the Pacific.

Meanwhile the depredations of the *Emden* in the Bay of Bengal continued. On the 22nd she appeared off Madras, bombarded the Burma Company's oil tanks, and threw a few shells into the town before she was driven off by the batteries. This episode, following on the disturbance of the Calcutta-Colombo trade route and the numerous and almost daily sinkings of merchant ships in the Bay of Bengal, created widespread alarm, and on October 1 I sent the following minute to the First Sea Lord, proposing, *inter alia*, a concentration on a large scale in Indian waters against the *Emden*. This concentration would comprise *Hampshire*, *Yarmouth*, *Sydney*, *Melbourne*, *Chikuma* (Japan), *Zemchug* and *Askold* (Russian), *Psyche*, *Pyramus* and *Philomel*—a total of ten—and was capable of being fully effective in about a month.

Secretary. *October* 1, 1914.
Chief of Staff.
First Sea Lord.

Three transports, empty but fitted for carrying cavalry, are delayed in Calcutta through fear of *Emden*. This involves delaying transport of artillery and part of a cavalry division from Bombay. The Cabinet took a serious view, and pressed for special convoy. Have you any ship? I should be very sorry to interrupt the offensive operations against *Emden* for the sake of convoying three empty transports. I was inclined to recommend that the three should put to sea at night with lights out and steer wide of the track. It is 100 to 1 that they would get round safely, and a 1,000 to 1 that two out of the three would get round safely. Let me have your proposals at once. It is clear that the transports have got to go.[6]

* * * * *

Now that *Scharnhorst* and *Gneisenau* have been located in the Society Islands there is no need for *Melbourne* and *Sydney* to remain in Australasian waters. *Sydney* should immediately be ordered to join *Hampshire*, *Yarmouth* and *Chikuma* in the *Emden* hunt, and *Melbourne* should come there with the Australasian convoy. As soon as *Zemchug* and *Askold* have finished with their convoy, they should return and join *Hampshire*. This will give seven ships searching for *Emden* and avoid the necessity of moving one of the three Light Cruisers now hunting *Königsberg*. Numbers are everything, and the extirpation of these pests is a most important object.

What is the use of *Psyche*, *Pyramus* and *Philomel* in New Zealand waters after the convoy has started? There is nothing but the *Scharnhorst* and *Gneisenau* to be considered, and they are sufficiently dealt with by:—

(1) *Australia.Montcalm*.

(2) First Japanese Squadron.

(3) Second Japanese Squadron.

On the other hand, these three vessels, together with *Pioneer*, would be good for searching for *Emden* in company with the faster and more powerful ships. I propose, therefore, that they should accompany the Australian and New Zealand convoys home to Indian waters, and should then join up with the seven Cruisers which will then be under *Hampshire* in hunting *Emden*, making a total of ten vessels available a month from now. The necessary arrangements to enable them,

[6]They went without escort and without mishap.

in spite of their limited fuel capacity, to get to Colombo can easily be made. In the event of *Emden* being captured before this concentration is complete, all these vessels should be sent to assist in the hunt for *Königsberg*, or, conversely, if *Königsberg* is caught, the three Light Cruisers should turn over to the *Emden*. It is no use stirring about the oceans with two or three ships. When we have got Cruiser sweeps of 8 or 10 vessels ten or fifteen miles apart there will be some good prospect of utilizing information as to the whereabouts of the *Emden* in such a way as to bring her to action. Such large and decisive measures are much the cheapest and most satisfactory in the end.

W. S. C.

And again on October 15:—

'*Sydney* should escort Australians and thereafter hunt *Emden*.'

This shot as will presently be seen went home.

* * * * *

The press and the public were not in a position to understand all that the Admiralty were doing nor to appreciate the general results achieved. All they saw at this time was that a few German cruisers were apparently doing whatever they chose upon the oceans and sinking British merchantmen day after day. A great deal of discontent began to make itself heard and felt. I therefore prepared a note for publication in the hopes of placating our critics.

October 24, 1914.

The Secretary of the Admiralty makes the following statement in regard to the capture and destruction of British merchant ships by German warships:—

Eight or nine German cruisers are believed to be at large in the Atlantic, the Pacific, and the Indian Oceans. Searching for these vessels and working in concert under the various Commanders-in-Chief are upwards of 70 British (including Australian), Japanese, French, and Russian cruisers, not including auxiliary cruisers. Among these are a number of the fastest British cruisers. The vast expanses of sea and ocean and the many thousand islands of the archipelagos offer an almost infinite choice of movement to the enemy's ships. In spite of every effort to cut off their coal supply, it has hitherto been maintained by one means or another in the face of increasing difficulties.

The discovery and destruction of these few enemy cruisers is therefore largely a matter of time, patience, and good luck. The public should have confidence that the Commanders-in-Chief and the experienced captains serving under them are doing all that is possible and taking the best steps to bring the enemy to action. They have so far been also occupied in very serious and important convoy duty, but this work has somewhat lessened and the number of searching cruisers is continually augmented.

Meanwhile, merchant ships must observe Admiralty instructions, which it is obviously impossible to specify, and use all the precautions which have been suggested. On routes where these instructions have been followed, they have so far proved very effective. On the other hand, where they have been disregarded captures have been made. The same vastness of sea which has so far enabled the German cruisers to avoid capture will protect the trade.

The only alternative to the methods now adopted would be the marshalling of merchantmen in regular convoys at stated intervals. So far it has not been thought necessary to hamper trade by enforcing such a system. The percentage of loss is much less than was reckoned on before the war. Out of 4,000 British ships engaged in foreign trade only 39 have been sunk by the enemy, or just under 1 per cent. in all.

The rate of insurance for cargoes, which on the outbreak of war was fixed at 5 guineas per cent., has now been reduced to 2 guineas per cent. without injury to the solvency of the fund. For hulls, as apart from cargoes, the insurance has also been considerably reduced. Between 8,000 and 9,000 foreign voyages have been undertaken to and from United Kingdom ports, less than five per thousand of which have been interfered with, and of these losses a large number have been caused by merchant vessels taking everything for granted and proceeding without precautions as if there were no war.

On the other hand, the German oversea trade has practically ceased to exist. Nearly all their fast ships which could have been used as auxiliary cruisers were promptly penned into neutral harbours or have taken refuge in their own. Among the comparatively few German ships which have put to sea, 133 have been captured, or nearly four times the number of those lost by the very large British mercantile marine.

In these circumstances, there is no occasion for anxiety and no excuse for complaint. On the contrary, the more fully the facts concerning our oversea trade and its protection by the Royal Navy can be disclosed, and the more attentively they are studied, the greater will be the confidence and satisfaction with which the situation can be viewed.

The various changes of plan necessary to meet the natural anxieties of the New Zealand Government entailed a delay of three weeks in the sailing of the Australian convoy. This, Lord Kitchener declared, made no difference, as they could continue their indispensable training equally well in Australia. By October 25, when the convoy was about to sail, the rebellion in South Africa introduced another disturbing element. It was decided by the Cabinet on that date to make arrangements for the Australian and New Zealand Army Corps to come via the Cape instead of via the Suez Canal, so as to be available in South Africa if need be. Alternative arrangements of a complicated nature were therefore prepared. On the 30th, however, in view of later advices from South Africa, it was arranged for the whole convoy to proceed together to Colombo and for the decision about the last part of the route to be delayed until then. The convoy started on November

1 under the escort of the *Minotaur, Ibuki, Melbourne* and *Sydney*. Before they reached Colombo the *Sydney* found her quarry and the Australian and New Zealand Army Corps was more needed in Egypt than at the Cape. But this will appear in its proper place.

* * * * *

It remained to carry the Canadian Army across the Atlantic. Upwards of 25,000 volunteers of a very high individual quality, partially trained in Valcartier camp, were embarked in the St. Lawrence in a convoy of thirty-one ships, to which were added two ships carrying the Newfoundland contingent and a British battalion from Bermuda. Rear-Admiral Wemyss with a squadron of light cruisers was entrusted with the actual duties of escort, but the essential protection of the convoy was secured by far more distant and powerful agencies. All the Cruiser Squadrons of the Grand Fleet were spread in two lines between the coasts of Norway and Scotland to guard against a sortie by the German fast vessels, and the Grand Fleet itself remained at sea in their support to the northward. The North American Squadron under Rear-Admiral Hornby covered the German merchant cruisers which were lurking in New York Harbour. Two old battleships, the *Glory* and the *Majestic*, were ordered to meet the convoy at a rendezvous well off the beaten track, and Admiral Hornby himself in the *Lancaster* accompanied them the first portion of the route. Lastly, the *Princess Royal* was detached from the Grand Fleet to meet the convoy in mid-Atlantic and thus guard against any German battle-cruiser which might conceivably have slipped through the wide areas patrolled by Sir John Jellicoe. The movements of the *Princess Royal* were kept secret from everybody, and even the Canadian Government, in spite of their natural anxiety, were denied this reassurance.

The convoy sailed on October 3 and ten days later safely approached the mouth of the English Channel. The intention had been to disembark the Canadian troops at Portsmouth, where all arrangements had been made for them. But on the very day they were due to arrive, a German submarine was reported off Cherbourg and another was sighted off the Isle of Wight by the Portsmouth Defence Flotilla. On this we insisted, whatever the military inconvenience, on turning the whole convoy into Plymouth. During October 14 this armada bearing the first flower of the martial spirit of Canada was safely berthed in Plymouth Sound.

With this event all the initial movements in the Imperial concentration had been completed. They had comprised the transportation of the equivalent of 5 divisions from India to Europe and their replacement by 3 divisions of Territorials from England; the collection of the 7th and 8th divisions from all the garrisons and fortresses of the British Empire with consequential replacements from home and from India; the transportation of approximately two divisions from Canada to England; and lastly—though this was not finished till December—that of approximately two divisions from Australia and New Zealand to Egypt. The effect of this concentration was to add a reinforcement of 5 British regular divisions (7th, 8th, 27th, 28th and 29th) and 2 Anglo-Indian divisions to the regular forces immediately available to support the 6 regular divisions with which we had begun the war, raising our Army in France by the end of November to approximately

13 divisions of highly trained long-service troops. In addition the 4 Canadian and Australian divisions were completing their training in England and Egypt, and were held to be in a more advanced state of preparation than the 10 divisions of Territorials which remained in England or the 24 divisions of the New Army which Lord Kitchener was raising. The whole business of transportation by sea while all the enemy's cruisers were still at large had been conducted without accident of any kind or without the loss of a single ship or a single life.

CHAPTER XIV
IN THE NARROW SEAS

'The surly drums beat terrible afar,
With all the dreadful music of the war.'

Broome, 'The Seat of War in Flanders.' 1710.

Action of August 28 in the Heligoland Bight—Fate of the German Light Cruisers—Paralysis of German Naval Enterprise—The Ostend Demonstration—The Royal Naval Air Service—The Zeppelin Menace and the 'Hornets'—The Air Situation at the Outbreak of War—Offence the true Defence—Beginning of the Dunkirk Guerrilla—Samson's Aeroplanes—The Armoured Cars—First dawn of the 'Tank' idea—Defences of Dunkirk and Calais—The Omnibus Brigade—An Embarrassing Responsibility—The Sinking of the *Aboukir*, *Hogue* and *Cressy*.

I now have to chronicle a brilliant episode which came at a most timely moment and throughout which we enjoyed the best of good luck. My insistent desire to develop a minor offensive against the Germans in the Heligoland Bight led to conferences with Commodore Tyrwhitt, who commanded the light cruisers and destroyers of 'The Harwich Striking Force,' and Commodore Keyes, the head of the Submarine Service also stationed at Harwich. On August 23 Commodore Keyes called personally upon me at the Admiralty with a proposal for 'a well-organized drive commencing before dawn from inshore close to the enemy's coast.' On the 24th I presided at a meeting in my room between him and Commodore Tyrwhitt and the First Sea Lord and the Chief of the Staff.

The plan which the two Commodores then outlined was at once simple and daring. Since the first hours of the war our submarines had prowled about in the Heligoland Bight. They had now accumulated during a period of three weeks accurate information about the dispositions of the enemy. They knew that he was in the habit of keeping a flotilla of destroyers attended by a couple of small cruisers, cruising and patrolling each night to the North of Heligoland, and that these were accustomed to be relieved shortly after daylight by a second flotilla which worked on a much less extended beat. They proposed to take two flotillas of our best destroyers and two light cruisers from Harwich by night and reach just before dawn a point inside the Northern Coast of the Heligoland Bight not far from the island of Sylt. From this point they would make a left-handed scoop inshore, falling upon and chasing back the outcoming flotilla if they met it, and then would all turn together in a long line abreast Westward towards home to meet and if possible destroy the incoming German flotilla. Six British submarines in two divisions would take part in the operation so as to attack the German heavy ships should they come out, and two battle-cruisers (the *Invincible* and *New Zealand*) then stationed at the Humber would act as support.

Such was in short the plan proposed by these officers and approved by the First Sea Lord. Action was fixed for the 28th. As soon as Sir John Jellicoe was informed of these intentions, he offered to send in further support three battle-cruisers and six light cruisers. He did more. He sent Sir David Beatty. The result was a success which far exceeded the hopes of the Admiralty, and produced results of a far-reaching character upon the whole of the naval war.

At dawn on the 28th, Admiral Tyrwhitt's flotillas, led by the *Arethusa* and *Fearless*, reached their point of attack and, in the words of Admiral Scheer, 'broke into the Heligoland Bight.' The enemy was taken by surprise. The weather near the land was increasingly misty. The Heligoland batteries came into action, but without effect. The German battleships and battle-cruisers could not cross the bar of the outer Jade owing to the tide till 1 p.m. Only the German light cruisers on patrol or close at hand in the Elbe or the Ems could come to the aid of their flotillas. A confused, dispersed and prolonged series of combats ensued between the flotillas and light cruisers and continued until after four o'clock in the afternoon. During all this time the British light forces were rampaging about the enemy's most intimate and jealously guarded waters.

Very little, however, turned out as had been planned. Owing to a mischance, arising primarily from a fault in Admiralty staff work, the message apprising Commodores Keyes and Tyrwhitt of the presence of Admiral Beatty with his additional battle-cruisers and light cruisers, did not reach them in time; nor was Admiral Beatty aware of the areas in which the British submarines were working. Several awkward embarrassments followed from this and might easily have led to disastrous mistakes. However, fortune was steady, and the initial surprise together with the resolute offensive carried us safely through. The German light cruisers precipitately proceeding to the assistance of their flotillas and animated by the hopes of cutting off our own, ran into the British battle-cruisers. Admiral Beatty, in spite not only of the risk of mines and submarines, but also—for all he could know—of meeting superior forces, had with extraordinary audacity led his squadron far into the Bight. Two enemy cruisers (the *Ariadne* and the *Köln*) were smashed to pieces by the enormous shells of the *Lion* and the *Princess Royal*; a third (the *Mainz*) was sunk by the light cruisers and destroyers. Three others (the *Frauenlob*, *Strassburg* and the *Stettin*) limped home with many casualties. One German destroyer was sunk. The rest in the confusion and light mist escaped, though several were injured.

The good news trickled into the Admiralty during the day, but for some time we were very anxious about the *Arethusa*. A feedpipe had been smashed by a shell and her steaming power was reduced to seven or eight knots. However, she returned unmolested to the Thames.

Not a single British ship was sunk or, indeed, seriously injured; and our casualties did not exceed thirty-five killed and about forty wounded, in spite of the fact that, in the words of the German Lieutenant Tholens, 'The English ships made the greatest efforts to pick up the survivors.'[1] Two hundred and twenty-four Germans, many desperately wounded, were rescued in circumstances of much danger by Commodore Keyes on the destroyer *Lurcher*, and brought to England. Considerably more than a thousand Germans, including the Flotilla Admiral and the Destroyer Commodore, perished. A son of Admiral von Tirpitz was among the prisoners. Much more important, however, than these material gains was the effect produced upon the morale of the enemy. The Germans knew nothing of our defective Staff work and of the risks we had run. All they saw was that the British did not hesitate to hazard their greatest vessels as well as their light craft in the most daring offensive action and had escaped apparently unscathed. They felt as we should have felt had German destroyers broken into the Solent and their battle-cruisers penetrated as far as the Nab. The results of this action were far-reaching. Henceforward the weight of British naval prestige lay heavy across all German sea enterprise. Upon the Emperor the impression produced was decisive. Thus Scheer (*Germany's High Sea Fleet in the World War*, p. 57): 'The restrictions imposed on the Battle Fleet were adhered to.' And still more explicit, von Tirpitz (*Memories vol II*, p. 357): '. . . August 28th, a day fateful, both in its after-effects and incidental results, for the work of our navy. . . . The Emperor did not want losses of this sort. . . . Orders were issued by the Emperor. . . after an audience to Pohl, to which I as usual was not summoned, to restrict the initiative of the Commander-in-Chief of the North Sea Fleet: the loss of ships was to be avoided, fleet sallies and any greater undertakings must be approved by His Majesty in advance,' etc. On von Tirpitz protesting against 'this muzzling policy'. . . 'there sprang up from that day forth an estrangement between the Emperor and myself, which steadily increased.'

The German Navy was indeed 'muzzled.' Except for furtive movements by individual submarines and minelayers not a dog stirred from August till November. Meanwhile our strength, both offensive afloat and defensive in our harbours, was steadily and rapidly increasing.

The news of this naval action reached the French and British armies in the dark hour before the dawn of victory and was everywhere published to the retreating troops.[2]

* * * * *

As the German armies pressed forward towards Paris they turned the back of their right shoulder increasingly towards the sea. The Belgian Army making a sortie from Antwerp struck towards the German lines of communication and endeavoured to hamper and delay the great advance. In order to help the Belgians and to take some pressure off our own hard-pressed Army, the Admiralty, in consultation with Lord Kitchener, attempted to make a diversion. A brigade of Marines was disembarked, covered by warships (August 26), at Ostend in the hopes that it would attract the attention of the enemy and give him the impression that larger forces would follow from the sea.

---

[1]Admiral Scheer, p. 52.

[2]See also Appendix E, First Lord's Minutes.

Telegram to Belgian Government.

August 25, 1914.

In order to delay southward German advance and to create diversion favourable to the forward movement of the Belgian Army, Admiralty wish to send a brigade of Marines, 3,000 strong, to Ostend at daylight, 26th, covered by battleships and cruisers accompanied by an aeroplane squadron. This brigade will push out reconnaissances to Bruges, Thourout, and Dixmude, and will remain at Ostend to cover the disembarkation of a larger force should circumstances render that desirable. Do you agree? If so, please send the necessary instructions to your local authorities. Publicity is useful in this case. The impression to be produced is that a considerable British army is landing.

Orders to General Aston.

August 25, 1914.

1. At daylight to-morrow, if circumstances allow, you will disembark such portions of your brigade as have arrived at Ostend and occupy the town. You will push out reconnaissances of cyclists to Bruges, Thourout, and Dixmude. You will establish yourself at Ostend, forming an entrenched picket line around the town in such a way as to enable you to cover the debarkation of a Division of the Army. A squadron of aeroplanes will reach you before noon, having previously made an aerial reconnaissance of the country within 30 miles of Ostend. The aeroplanes will be placed under your orders.

2. The object of this movement is to create a diversion, favourable to the Belgians, who are advancing from Antwerp, and to threaten the western flank of the German southward advance. It should therefore be ostentatious. You should not advance inland from Ostend without further orders, but some enterprise may be permitted to the patrols. Information about the enemy will be supplied you personally at the Admiralty.

The object in view would be fully attained if a considerable force of the enemy were attracted to the coast. You will be re-embarked as soon as this is accomplished.

To give further publicity I announced in the House of Commons that a British force had begun landing at Ostend. The Marines remained on shore for the best part of a week and were then withdrawn. The old battleships and cruisers which covered them were no doubt in more danger from submarines than we thought at the time, but no mishap occurred; nor was there any loss ashore or afloat. There was no means at the time of knowing whether this petty operation exercised any appreciable influence on German movements. We now know that it was certainly a factor. The Head of the Operations

Branch of the German General Staff in his narrative shows that the news of this landing reached Main Headquarters on August 30. He says:—

> 'One day countless British troops were said to have landed at Ostend and to be marching on Antwerp; on another that there were about to be great sorties from Antwerp. Even landings of Russian troops, 80,000 men, at Ostend were mentioned. At Ostend a great entrenched camp for the English was in preparation.'

General Dupont, the French Director of Military Intelligence, goes much further and ranks the Belgian sortie as a culminating element in the German decision to make a general retreat, taken on September 10.[3] But this is clearly an exaggeration.

* * * * *

An unbroken chain of events drew the Admiralty again to the Belgian Coast; and to explain this a digression is necessary.

Before the war the British air force was divided into the Royal Flying Corps and the Royal Naval Air Service, the former of which were to be concerned with aeroplanes and the latter with hydroaeroplanes, or seaplanes as I christened them for short. The War Office claimed on behalf of the Royal Flying Corps complete and sole responsibility for the aerial defence of Great Britain. But owing to the difficulties of getting money, they were unable to make any provision for this responsibility, every aeroplane they had being earmarked for the Expeditionary Force. Seeing this and finding myself able to procure funds by various shifts and devices, I began in 1912 and 1913 to form under the Royal Naval Air Service flights of aeroplanes as well as of seaplanes for the aerial protection of our naval harbours, oil tanks and vulnerable points, and also for a general strengthening of our exiguous and inadequate aviation. In consequence I had in my own hand on the eve of the war fifty efficient naval machines, or about one-third of the number in possession of the Army. The War Office viewed this development with disfavour, and claimed that they alone should be charged with the responsibility for home defence. When asked how they proposed to discharge this duty, they admitted sorrowfully that they had not got the machines and could not get the money. They adhered however to the principle.

When the war began the situation foreseen arose. The whole of the military aeroplanes went to France at once with the Expeditionary Force, and not a single squadron or even an effective machine remained to guard British vulnerable points from German aerial attack. The Admiralty was, however, found provided with a respectable force of its own which immediately took over the protection of our dockyards and patrolled our shores in connection with the coast watch.

As the Germans overran Belgium and all the Channel ports were exposed, the danger of air attacks upon Great Britain became most serious and real. Zeppelins had already cruised over Antwerp, and it was known that London was in range of the Zeppelin sheds at Düsseldorf and Cologne. To meet this danger there was nothing except the

---

[3]Dupont, *Haut Commandement Allemand en 1914*, p. 92.

naval aeroplanes the Admiralty had been able to scrape and smuggle together. On September 3 Lord Kitchener asked me in Cabinet whether I would accept, on behalf of the Admiralty, the responsibility for the aerial defence of Great Britain, as the War Office had no means of discharging it. I thereupon undertook to do what was possible with the wholly inadequate resources which were available. There were neither anti-aircraft guns nor searchlights, and though a few improvisations had been made, nearly a year must elapse before the efficient supplies necessary could be forthcoming. Meanwhile at any moment half a dozen Zeppelins might arrive to bomb London or, what was more serious, Chatham, Woolwich or Portsmouth.

I rated the Zeppelin much lower as a weapon of war than almost any one else. I believed that this enormous bladder of combustible and explosive gas would prove to be easily destructible. I was sure the fighting aeroplane, rising lightly laden from its own base, armed with incendiary bullets, would harry, rout and burn these gaseous monsters. I had proclaimed this opinion to the House of Commons in 1913, using the often-quoted simile of the hornets.

I therefore did everything in my power in the years before the war to restrict expenditure upon airships and to concentrate our narrow and stinted resources upon aeroplanes. I confined the naval construction of airships to purely experimental limits, and in April, 1915, when the slow progress and inferior quality of our only rigid experimental airship were manifest, I gave orders that it should be scrapped, the plant broken up and the labour and material devoted to increasing the output of aeroplanes. Had I had my way, no airships would have been built by Great Britain during the war (except the little 'Blimps' for teasing submarines). After I left the Admiralty this policy was reversed, and forty millions of money were squandered by successive Boards in building British Zeppelins, not one of which on any occasion ever rendered any effective fighting service. Meanwhile the alternative policy of equipping the Fleet with aerial observation by flying aeroplanes off warships or off properly constructed carriers, lagged pitifully, with the result that at the Battle of Jutland we had no British airships and only one aeroplane in the air.

The hornet theory, at one time so fiercely derided, was, of course, ultimately vindicated by the war. Zeppelins were clawed down in flames from the sky over both land and sea by aeroplanes until they did not dare to come any more. The aeroplane was the means by which the Zeppelin menace was destroyed, and it was virtually the only means, apart from weather and their own weakness, by which Zeppelins were ever destroyed.

However, although my thought was perfectly sound in principle and the policy following from it was unquestionably right, we were not in a position at the beginning of the war to produce effective results. Aeroplane engines were not powerful enough to reach the great heights needed for the attack of Zeppelins in the short time available. Night flying had only just been born; the location of aircraft by sound was unknown; the network of telephones and observation points was non-existent. And here was the danger, certainly real and not easy to measure, literally on top of us.

It was easy to order the necessary guns, searchlights, etc., and set on foot the organization which should produce and employ them. But it was no use sitting down and waiting for a year while these preparations were completing. Only offensive action could help us. I decided immediately to strike, by bombing from aeroplanes, at the Zeppelin sheds wherever these gigantic structures could be found in Germany, and secondly, to prevent the erection of any new Zeppelin sheds in the conquered parts of Belgium or France. Here again the policy was right. Our resources were, however, feeble and slender. Compared to the terrific developments at the end of the war, they were puny. Still, they were all we had, and all that our knowledge of aviation at that time could bestow. Deficiencies in material had to be made good by daring. All honour to the naval airmen, the pioneers of the aerial offensive, who planned and executed in these early months the desperate flights over hostile territory in an element then scarcely known, which resulted in the raids on Düsseldorf and Cologne on the Rhine, Friedrichshaven on Lake Constance, and Cuxhaven in the Heligoland Bight. Altogether in the first twelve months of the war six Zeppelins were destroyed in the air or in their sheds by the offensive action of a handful of British naval airmen; and few were destroyed by any other agency except accident.

In order to strike at the Zeppelin sheds in Germany and to prevent the erection of new ones in Belgium, it was necessary to start from as near the enemy's line as possible. Extracts from my own minutes, principally to Captain Sueter, the energetic Director of the Air Division, gives as good an account as any other.

Director of Air Division. *September* 1, 1914.
Chief of Staff.

The largest possible force of naval aeroplanes should be stationed in Calais or Dunkirk. Reports have been received, and it is also extremely probable, that the Germans will attempt to attack London and other places by Zeppelin airships, of which it is said a considerable number exist. The close proximity of the French coast to England renders such an attack thoroughly feasible. The proper defence is a thorough and continual search of the country for 70 to 100 miles inland with a view to marking down any temporary airship bases, or airships replenishing before starting to attack. Should such airships be located they should be immediately attacked. Commander Samson, with Major Gerrard as second in command, will be entrusted with this duty; and the Director of Air Division will take all steps to supply them with the necessary pilots, aeroplanes and equipment.

Secretary. *September* 3, 1914.
Director of Air Division.
Third Sea Lord.

Aerial searchlights must immediately be got ready for use in conjunction with the aerial guns. Propose me without delay the quickest means of meeting this need, with estimates of time and money. At least thirty or forty aerial searchlights are required. 'Vernon'[4] should co-operate. Drastic and energetic action is required.

[4]The Naval torpedo school centre.

2. Let me have a return on one sheet of paper showing all anti-aircraft guns, regular or improvised, available afloat and ashore, at the present time; and what deliveries may be expected in the next two months. Let me have also any suggestions for increasing their number. No one can doubt that aerial attack upon England must be a feature of the near future.

Secretary. *September* 5, 1914.
First Sea Lord.
Third Sea Lord.
Chief of Staff.
Director of Naval Ordnance.
Director of Air Division.

There can be no question of defending London by artillery against aerial attack. It is quite impossible to cover so vast an area; and if London, why not every other city? Defence against aircraft by guns is limited absolutely to points of military value. . .

Far more important than London are the vulnerable points in the Medway and at Dover and Portsmouth. Oil-tanks, powerhouses, lock-gates, magazines, airship sheds, all require to have their aerial guns increased in number. Portsmouth in particular requires attention now that enemy's territory has come so near.

Aerial searchlights must be provided in connection with every group of guns. . . .

But, after all, the great defence against aerial menace is to attack the enemy's aircraft as near as possible to their point of departure. Director of Air Division has already received directions on this. The principle is as follows:—

(*a*) A strong oversea force of aeroplanes to deny the French and Belgian coasts to the enemy's aircraft, and to attack all Zeppelins and air bases or temporary air bases which it may be sought to establish, and which are in reach.

(*b*) We must be in constant telegraphic and telephonic communication with the oversea aeroplane squadrons. We must maintain an intercepting force of aeroplanes and airships at some convenient point within range of a line drawn from Dover to London, and local defence flights at Eastchurch and Calshot.

(*c*) A squadron of aeroplanes will be established at Hendon, also in telephonic communication with the other stations, for the purpose of attacking enemy aircraft which may attempt to molest London. Landing grounds must be prepared in all the parks; railings must be removed, and the area marked out by a large white circle by day and by a good system of lighting at night. It is indispensable that airmen of the Hendon flight should be able to fly by night, and their machines must be fitted with the necessary lights and instruments.

Agreeably with the above, instructions must be prepared for the guidance of the Police, Fire Brigade, and civil population under aerial bombardment. This will have to be sustained with composure. Arrangements must be concerted with the Home Office and the Office of Works for the extinction of lights upon a well-conceived plan, for the clearance and illumination in the parks, in order that the defending aeroplanes can have freedom of action, etc.

The whole of the points dealt with in this minute are to be elaborated and put into precise detail this afternoon by a Committee composed as follows:—

Third Sea Lord (in the Chair).
Director of Air Division.
Director of Naval Ordnance.
And a representative of the War Office from either the Master General of the Ordnance or Home Defence Department.

I expect to receive not later than to-morrow a definite programme for action within the lines of this minute.

The whole matter is of the highest urgency.

Secretary. *September* 5, 1914.
First Sea Lord.
Director of Air Division.

In order to discharge adequately the responsibilities which we have assumed for the aerial defence of England, it is necessary that we should maintain an aerial control over the area approximately 100 miles radius from Dunkirk. To do this, we must support the aeroplanes which are stationed on the French coast with sufficient armed motor cars and personnel to enable advanced subsidiary aeroplane bases to be established 30, 40 and 50 miles inland.

According to all accounts received, the Germans, in so far as they have penetrated this region, have done it simply by bluff. Small parties of Uhlans, taking advantage of the terror inspired by their atrocities in Belgium, have made their way freely about the country, and have imposed themselves upon the population. We require, in the first instance, 200 or 300 men with 50 or 60 motor-cars, who can support and defend our advanced aerial bases. I should propose to draw these by suitable volunteers from the Marine Brigade. They should be placed under the orders of Commander Samson, and should operate from Dunkirk. It will be necessary first to obtain permission from the French authorities. This, after consultation with Lord Kitchener, I am taking steps to do. We ought to be able to make it quite impossible for parties of 15 or 20 Uhlans to make their way with safety through this area. During the next week the Germans will presume on their immunity, and will be found in occupation of numbers of places where they cannot possibly maintain any effective force. The advantage of an aeroplane reconnaissance is that the approach of any serious body of troops can be discovered while it is still at least two days' march away. There ought, therefore, to be no difficulty in chopping these small parties of the enemy without our force getting into any trouble.

Propose me plans for immediate action on these lines in detail.

Secretary. *October* 2, 1914.
Director of Naval Ordnance.
Director of the Air Division.

> The experiments with regard to projectiles for use against aircraft must be worked out on the most generous scale, eight or ten different lines being pursued simultaneously, the necessary funds being provided. It is perfectly useless in time of war to go through successively the whole series of experiments appropriate to peace-time administration. Let me have a report on the projectiles available. We must have means of attacking Zeppelins, not only with shells from guns, but with incendiary bullets or grenades from aeroplanes.

The needs and activities of the naval aeroplanes in the neighbourhood of Dunkirk led directly to the development of the armoured car, and the armoured car led directly to the birth of the tank, which was in essence only an armoured car capable of crossing trenches. Almost immediately after the German inroad into Belgium, I received accounts of the remarkable work done by a Belgian motor-car, hastily equipped with armour and a machine gun, in shooting down and driving back the numerous Uhlans with which the enemy were seeking to overrun the country. Commander Samson was prompt to realize and seize the advantage of armoured cars for the purpose of protecting his aeroplane operations and also on their own account. In view of the reports received from him and other sources, I gave, during the latter part of August and September, successive orders for the formation of armoured-car squadrons under the Admiralty; and as all this arose out of the aeroplane squadron stationed at Dunkirk, the formation of the armoured-car squadrons was entrusted to Commodore Sueter. In this task this officer displayed great energy, and in a very short time no less than seven or eight squadrons were called into being, based on the purchase of all the Rolls-Royce cars that were available and rapidly improvised armour protection.

The first few cars had scarcely begun to show their advantages in Commander Samson's guerrilla from Dunkirk when the difficulty which ultimately led to the creation of the 'Tank' manifested itself. The German cavalry sought to protect themselves against the attack of the armoured cars by digging trenches across the road. To meet this, I gave the following directions:—

> Colonel Ollivant. *September* 23, 1914.
> Director of Air Division.
> Royal Naval Division Administration.
>
> It is most important that the motor transport and armed motorcars should be provided to a certain extent with cars carrying the means of bridging small cuts in the road and an arrangement of planks capable of bridging a ten- or twelve-feet span quickly and easily should be carried with every ten or twelve machines. A proportion of tools should also be supplied.
>
> Let me have proposals at once.[5]

---

[5]The first design of the Tank, made at my request by Admiral Bacon in September, 1914, carried a bridge in front, which, on arriving at a trench, it dropped, passed over, and automatically raised behind it.

Other conditions, however, swept down upon us very quickly, and by the middle of October, after the events to be narrated in the next chapters, the trench lines on both sides reached the sea and became continuous over the whole front. Thus at the moment when the new armoured-car force was coming into effective existence at much expense and on a considerable scale, it was confronted with an obstacle and a military situation which rendered its employment practically impossible. The conclusion was forced naturally and obviously upon me, and no doubt upon others, that if the armoured car on which so much money and labour had been spent, could not move *round* the enemy's trenches and operate against an open flank of his army, some method should be devised which would enable it to traverse and pass *over* the trenches themselves. This subject will, however, be dealt with in its proper place.

The air was the first cause that took us to Dunkirk. The armoured car was the child of the air; and the Tank its grandchild.

But besides all this the undefended condition of the Channel ports against any serious effort by the enemy inspired the Admiralty with lively alarm. The danger of the Germans taking Dunkirk, Calais and Boulogne stared us in the face for many anxious weeks. On September 3 I minuted to the First Sea Lord:—

> 'With the Germans along the French coast, modified dispositions will become necessary. The danger from aerial attack must not be underrated. The possibility of the Germans taking very heavy guns to Calais after taking the town, and getting submarines down from the Elbe to operate from Calais as a base, should also be considered. We could of course, stop any surface craft, but submarines might slip through secretly and be a great nuisance when once established.'

On September 10 I went to Dunkirk myself and was to some extent reassured. I made the following note at the time for the information of those concerned:—

September 11, 1914.

> The First Lord visited Dunkirk and Calais on the 10th instant, and conferred with the Governors of both places.
>
> Dunkirk is being defended on a considerable scale, and has already developed substantial strength. Lines of defence are constructed on a radius of 4 to 6 miles approximately from the enceinte of the town, which are armed by over 400 pieces of artillery and held by 18,000 men. These works which are strongly executed can be further protected by large inundations both of fresh and salt water. The fresh water inundations are now accumulating; the salt can be turned on at any time in two days. The place should certainly require a siege in form to reduce it, and it is getting stronger every week. The First Lord promised the assistance of warships if required to cover the flanks. The anchorage at Dunkirk gives sufficient water for the *Majestic* class, and is certainly close to the shore. The high sandhills would require the fire to be indirect, but otherwise there would be no difficulty. There is nothing to cause disquietude in the measures taken for the defence of Dunkirk.

> It seems probable that they are sufficient to make it not worth while for the enemy to undertake the reduction of the fortress.
>
> Calais is simply an enceinte rather larger in extent than that of Dunkirk, and protected by a few well-executed outlying field-works. All that can be said about Calais is that it could not be taken by a *coup de main*. It is garrisoned by 7,000 troops, but it could certainly not be counted on to hold out for more than a few days against a determined attack.

On September 16 Marshal Joffre telegraphed to Lord Kitchener asking whether a Brigade of Marines could not be sent to Dunkirk to reinforce the garrison and to confuse the enemy with the idea of British as well as French forces being in this area. Lord Kitchener asked me whether the Admiralty would help in this matter. I agreed to send the brigade if he would also send some Yeomanry Cavalry for its local protection. He sent a regiment. I was thus led, though by no means unwillingly, into accepting a series of minor responsibilities of a very direct and personal kind, which made inroads both upon my time and thought and might well—though I claim they did not—have obscured my general view. I formed a small administration to handle the business, in which Colonel Ollivant[6] was the moving spirit. On his suggestion we took fifty motor omnibuses from the London streets so as to make our Marines as mobile as possible, and very soon we had British detachments ostentatiously displaying themselves in Ypres, Lille, Tournai and Douai. Many risks were run by those engaged in these petty operations, first under General Aston and subsequently when his health had failed, under General Paris. No mishap occurred either to the Marines or to the Yeomanry. They played their part in the general scheme without loss or misadventure. It was, however, with sincere relief that a month later, on the arrival of the leading troops of Sir John French's Army in the neighbourhood, I transferred these detachments to the Commander-in-Chief, and divested myself of anxieties which though subsidiary were burdensome.

Looking back with after-knowledge and increasing years, I seem to have been too ready to undertake tasks which were hazardous or even forlorn. Taking over responsibility for the air defence of Great Britain when resources were practically non-existent and formidable air attacks imminent, was from a personal point of view 'some love but little policy.' The same is true of the Dunkirk guerrilla. Still more is it true of the attempt to prolong the defence of Antwerp which will be related in the next chapter. I could with perfect propriety, indeed with unanswerable reasons, have in every one of these cases left the burden to others. I believed, however, that the special knowledge which I possessed, and the great and flexible authority which I wielded in this time of improvisation, would enable me to offer less unsatisfactory solutions of these problems

[6]An officer of the General Staff who had been attached, at my request in 1913, to the Admiralty War Staff in order to promote an effective *liaison* between the two staffs. This very gifted officer rendered us invaluable service. He died prematurely after the hardships of the war, throughout the whole of which he served with distinction in situations of responsibility and danger.

than could be furnished in the emergency by others in less commanding positions. I could at that time give directions over a very large and intricate field of urgent and swiftly changing business, which were acted upon immediately by a great variety of authorities who otherwise would have had no common connecting centre. So I acted for the best, with confidence in the loyalty of my colleagues, in the goodwill of the public, and, above all, in my own judgment which I seemed to see confirmed from day to day by many remarkable events.

* * * * *

This chapter, which began with good luck and success, must end, however, with misfortune. The original War Orders had been devised to meet the situation on the outbreak of hostilities. They placed the pieces on the board in what we believed to be the best array, and left their future disposition to be modified by experience. Under these orders the 7th Cruiser Squadron in the Third Fleet, consisting of the old cruisers of the *Bacchante* class (*Bacchante*, *Euryalus* (flagship), *Cressy*, *Aboukir*, *Hogue*), was based on the Nore 'in order to ensure the presence of armoured ships in the southern approaches of the North Sea and eastern entrance to the Channel, and to support the 1st and 3rd Flotillas operating in that area from Harwich.' The object of these flotillas was 'to keep the area south of the 54th parallel clear of enemy torpedo craft and minelayers.' The Cruiser Force was 'to support them in the execution of these duties and also, with the flotillas, to keep a close watch over enemy war vessels and transports in order that their movement may be reported at the earliest moment.'

This very necessary patrol had accordingly been maintained day after day without incident of any kind happening, and we had now been six weeks at war. In war all repetitions are perilous. You can do many things with impunity if you do not keep on doing them over and over again.

It was no part of my duty to deal with the routine movements of the Fleet and its squadrons, but only to exercise a general supervision. I kept my eyes and ears open for every indication that would be useful, and I had many and various sources of information. On September 17, during my visit to the Grand Fleet, I heard an expression used by an officer which instantly arrested my attention. He spoke of 'the live-bait squadron.' I demanded what was meant, and was told that the expression referred to these old cruisers patrolling the narrow waters in apparently unbroken peace. I thereupon reviewed the whole position in this area. I discussed it with Commodore Tyrwhitt and with Commodore Keyes. The next morning I addressed the following minute to the First Sea Lord:—

Secretary. *September* 18, 1914.
First Sea Lord.

The force available for operations in the narrow seas should be capable of minor action without the need of bringing down the Grand Fleet. To this end it should have effective support either by two or three battle-cruisers or battleships of the Second Fleet working from Sheerness. This is the most efficiently air and destroyer

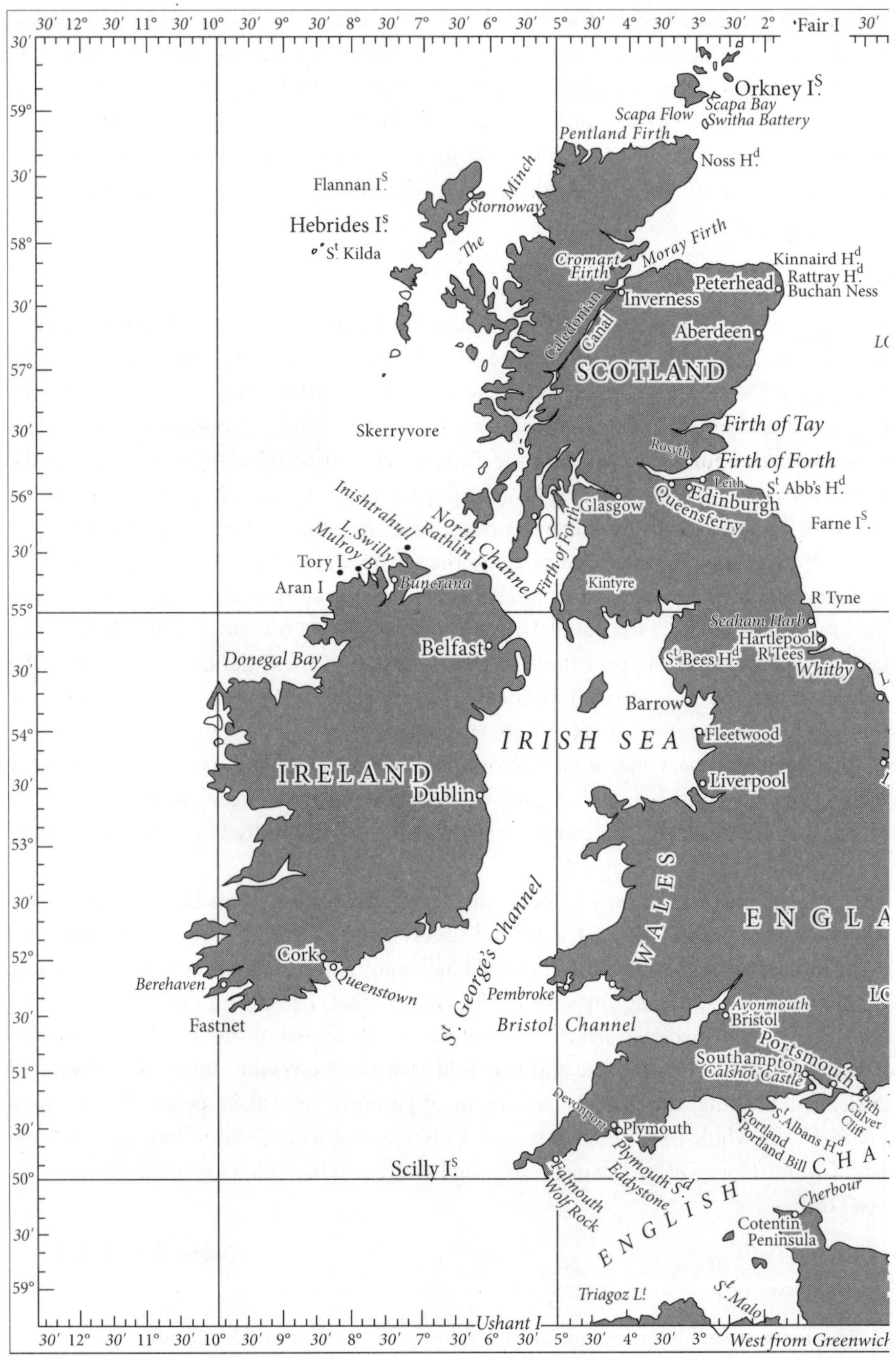
Fair I
Orkney I^s.
Scapa Bay
Scapa Flow
Switha Battery
Pentland Firth
Noss H^d.
Flannan I^s.
Stornoway
The Minch
Hebrides I^s.
S^t. Kilda
Moray Firth
Cromarty Firth
Kinnaird H^d.
Rattray H^d.
Buchan Ness
Peterhead
Inverness
Caledonian Canal
Aberdeen
SCOTLAND
Firth of Tay
Skerryvore
Rosyth
Firth of Forth
Leith
S^t. Abb's H^d.
Edinburgh
Queensferry
Glasgow
Farne I^s.
Inishtrahull
North Channel
Rathlin I.
L. Swilly
Mulroy B.
Tory I
Aran I
Buncrana
Firth of Forth
Kintyre
R Tyne
Seaham Harb
Hartlepool
Belfast
Donegal Bay
S^t. Bees H^d.
R Tees
Whitby
Barrow
Fleetwood
IRISH SEA
IRELAND
Dublin
Liverpool
WALES
ENGLA
St. George's Channel
Cork
Queenstown
Berehaven
Pembroke
Avonmouth
Bristol
Fastnet
Bristol Channel
Portsmouth
Southampton
Calshot Castle
Devonport
Plymouth
St. Albans H^d
Portland
Portland Bill
Culver Cliff
Scilly I^s.
Plymouth S^d
Eddystone
Falmouth
Wolf Rock
ENGLISH CHA
Cherbour
Cotentin Peninsula
Triagoz L^t
S^t. Malo
Ushant I
West from Greenwich

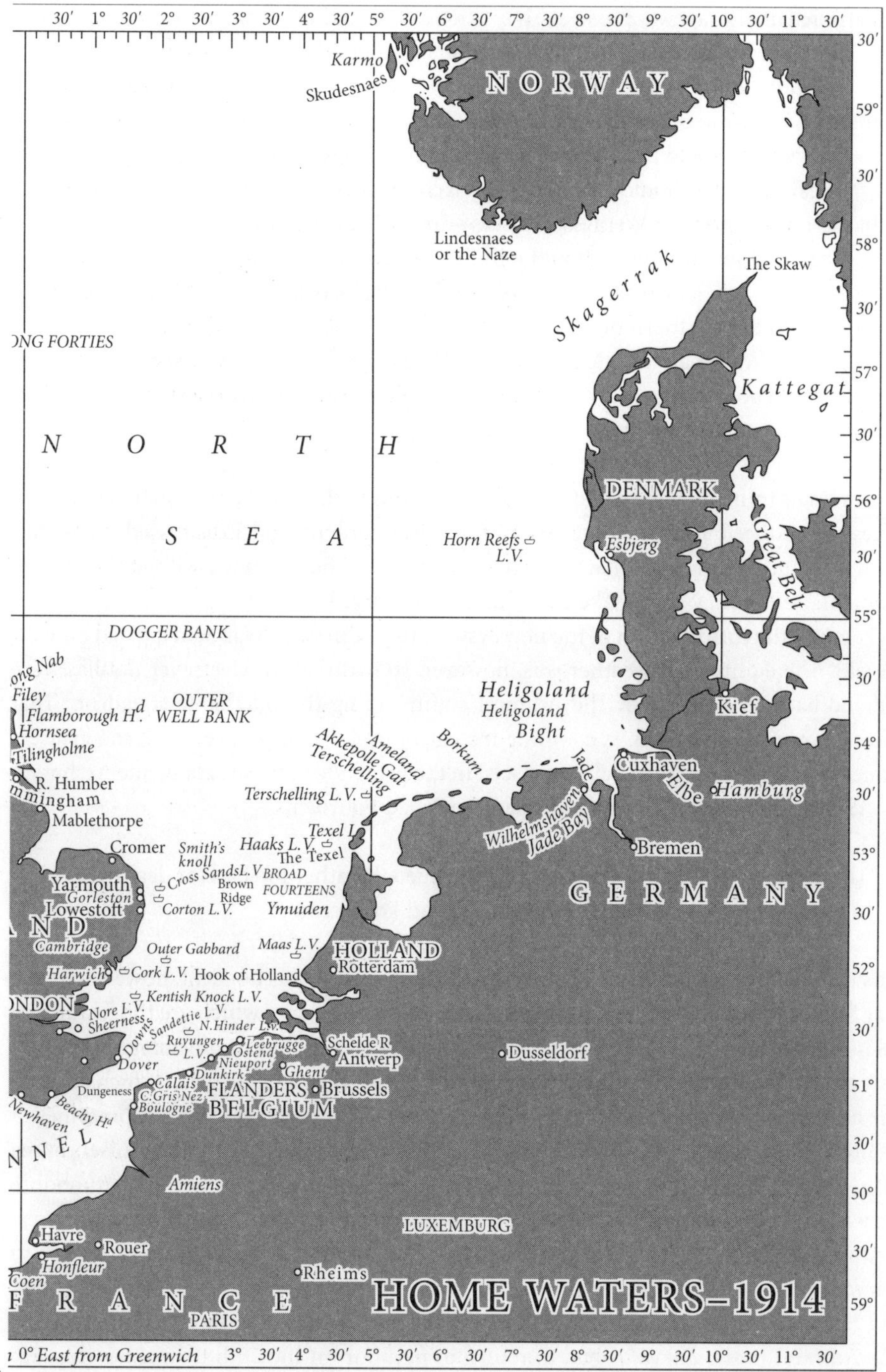
Karmo
Skudesnaes
NORWAY
Lindesnaes
or the Naze
The Skaw
Skagerrak
Kattegat
DENMARK
Esbjerg
Great Belt
Horn Reefs L.V.
NORTH SEA
DOGGER BANK
Filey
Flamborough Hd
OUTER WELL BANK
Hornsea
Tilingholme
R. Humber
Mablethorpe
Heligoland
Heligoland Bight
Kief
Ameland
Akkepolle Gat
Terschelling
Borkum
Jade
Cuxhaven
Elbe
Hamburg
Terschelling L.V.
Wilhelmshaven
Jade Bay
Bremen
Texel L
Haaks L.V.
The Texel
Cromer
Smith's knoll
Cross Sands L.V
BROAD FOURTEENS
Brown Ridge
Yarmouth
Gorleston
Lowestoft
Corton L.V.
Ymuiden
GERMANY
Cambridge
Outer Gabbard
Maas L.V.
HOLLAND
Rotterdam
Harwich
Cork L.V.
Hook of Holland
Kentish Knock L.V.
Nore L.V.
Sheerness
Downs
Sandettie L.V.
N.Hinder L.V.
Ruyungen L.V.
Leebrugge
Ostend
Nieuport
Schelde R
Antwerp
Dusseldorf
Dover
Dunkirk
Ghent
Dungeness
Calais
C.Gris Nez
Boulogne
FLANDERS
Brussels
BELGIUM
Newhaven
Beachy Hd
Amiens
LUXEMBURG
Havre
Rouer
Honfleur
Coen
Rheims
FRANCE
PARIS
HOME WATERS–1914
0° East from Greenwich

> patrolled anchorage we possess. They can lie behind the boom, and can always be at sea when we intend a raid. Battle-cruisers are much to be preferred.
>
> The *Bacchantes* ought not to continue on this beat. The risk to such ships is not justified by any services they can render. The narrow seas, being the nearest point to the enemy, should be kept by a small number of good modern ships.
>
> The *Bacchantes* should go to the western entrance of the Channel and set Bethell's battleships—and later Wemyss' cruisers—free for convoy and other duties.
>
> The first four *Arethusas* should join the flotillas of the narrow seas.
>
> I see no sufficient reason to exchange these flotillas now that they know their work, with the northern ones.
>
> As the "M" boats are delivered they should be formed into a separate half-flotilla and go north to work with the Grand Fleet. The *King Alfred* should pay off and be thoroughly repaired.

Prince Louis immediately agreed and gave directions to the Chief of the Staff to make the necessary redistribution of forces. With this I was content, and I dismissed the matter from my mind, being sure that the orders given would be complied with at the earliest moment. Before they could take effect, disaster occurred.

Pending the introduction of the new system, the Admiralty War Staff carried on with the old. The equinoctial weather was, however, so bad that the destroyer flotillas were ordered back to harbour by the Admiral commanding the *Bacchante* squadron. That officer, however, proposed to continue his patrol in the Dogger area with the cruisers alone. The Admiralty War Staff acquiesced in the principle of these arrangements, but on the 19th instructed him to watch instead the Broad Fourteens:—

> 'The Dogger Bank patrol need not be continued. Weather too bad for destroyers to go to sea. Arrange for cruisers to watch Broad Fourteens.'

This routine message did not of course come before me. It was not sent, however, by the War Staff without proper consideration. In the short steep seas which are the features of gales in these narrow waters, a submarine would be at a serious disadvantage and could only observe with extreme difficulty and imperfection. The rough weather which drove in our destroyers was believed to be an important protection against enemy submarines.

Both Admiral and Admiralty, therefore, were in agreement to leave the cruisers at sea without their flotilla. If the weather moderated, it was intended that one of Commodore Tyrwhitt's flotillas should join them there on the morning of the 20th. The sea, however, continued so high on the 20th that the flotilla, led by the *Fearless*, had to turn back to Harwich. Thus all through the 19th, 20th and 21st the three cruisers, *Aboukir*, *Cressy* and *Hogue*, were left to maintain the watch in the narrow waters without a flotilla screen. The Admiral in the *Euryalus* had to return to harbour on the 20th to coal his ship. He left the squadron in command of the senior captain after enjoining special precautions. There was no more reason to expect that they would be attacked at this time than at any other. On the contrary, rumours of German activity to the northward had brought the whole Grand Fleet out in a southerly sweep down to the line between Flamborough Head and the Horn Reef. Nor was there any connection between the orders to these cruisers and the movement of the Marine Brigade from Dover to Dunkirk which took place on the 20th. The cruisers were simply fulfilling their ordinary task, which from frequent repetition had already become dangerous and for which they were not in any case well suited.

As soon as the weather began to abate on the 21st, Commodore Tyrwhitt started off again for the Broad Fourteens with eight destroyers, and was already well on his way when the morning of the 22nd broke. As the sea subsided, the danger from submarines revived. The three cruisers however instead of going to meet their destroyers, steamed slowly northward without zigzagging and at under ten knots, as no doubt they had often done before. Meanwhile a single German submarine, becoming more venturesome every day, was prowling southward down the Dutch Coast. At 6.30 a.m., shortly after daylight, the *Aboukir* was struck by a torpedo. In twenty-five minutes this old vessel capsized. Some of her boats were smashed by the explosion, and hundreds of men were swimming in the water or clinging to wreckage. Both her consorts had hurried with chivalrous simplicity to the aid of the sinking ship. Both came to a dead standstill within a few hundred yards of her and lowered all their boats to rescue the survivors. In this posture they in their turn were both sunk, first the *Hogue* and then the *Cressy*, by the same submarine. Out of over 2,200 men on board these three ships, only 800 were saved, and more than 1,400 perished. The ships themselves were of no great value: they were among the oldest cruisers of the Third Fleet and contributed in no appreciable way to our vital margins. But like all Third Fleet ships, they were almost entirely manned with reservists, most of whom were married men; and they carried also young cadets from Osborne posted for safety to ships which it was thought would not be engaged in the great battles. This cruel loss of life, although small compared to what the Army was enduring, constituted the first serious forfeit exacted from the Navy in the war. It greatly stimulated and encouraged the enterprise of the German submarines. The commander of the fatal boat (Lieutenant Weddigen) was exultingly proclaimed as a national hero. Certainly the destruction with his own fingers of fourteen hundred persons was an episode of a peculiar character in human history. But, as it happened, he did not live long to enjoy his sombre fame. A storm of criticism was directed at the Admiralty, and naturally it was focused on me. 'Here was an instance of the disaster which followed from the interference of a civilian Minister in naval operations and the over-riding of the judgment of skilful and experienced Admirals.' The writer[7] of a small but venomous brochure which was industriously circulated in influential circles in London did not hesitate to make this charge in the most direct form,[8] and it was repeated in countless

[7]Mr. Thomas Gibson Bowles.

[8]'The loss on September 22,' wrote Mr. Gibson Bowles, 'of the *Aboukir*, the *Cressy* and the *Hogue*, with 1,459 officers and men killed, occurred because, despite the warnings of admirals, commodores and captains, Mr. Churchill refused, until it was too late, to recall them from a patrol so carried on as to make them certain to fall victims to the torpedoes of an active enemy.'

innuendoes throughout the British Press. I did not, however, think it possible to make any explanation or reply.

I caused the most searching inquiries to be made in the Admiralty into the responsibility for this tragic event. The necessary Court of Inquiry was convened. The Court found that the responsibility for the position of the cruisers on that day was attributable to the Admiralty War Staff telegram of the 19th which has been already quoted. The First Sea Lord held that this was a reflection upon the Admiralty by a subordinate Court; but it seemed to me that the criticism was just and that it should stand. It was, however, by no means exhaustive. One would expect senior officers in command of cruiser squadrons to judge for themselves the danger of their task, and especially of its constant repetition; and while obeying any orders they received, to represent an unsatisfactory situation plainly to the Admiralty instead of going on day after day, and week after week, until superior authority intervened or something lamentable happened. One would expect also that ordinary precautions would be observed in the tactical conduct of squadrons. Moreover, although the impulse which prompted the *Hogue* and *Cressy* to go to the rescue of their comrades in the sinking *Aboukir* was one of generous humanity, they could hardly have done anything more unwise or more likely to add to the loss of life. They should at once have steamed away in opposite directions, lowering boats at the first opportunity.

I remitted all these matters to Lord Fisher when two months later he arrived at the Admiralty; but he laconically replied that 'most of the officers concerned were on half pay, that they had better remain there, and that no useful purpose would be served by further action.'

CHAPTER XV

ANTWERP

'If Hopes were dupes, Fears may be liars,
  It may be in yon smoke conceal'd,
Your comrades chase e'en now the fliers,
  And but for you, possess the field.

For while the tired waves vainly breaking
  Seem here no painful inch to gain,
Far back, through creeks and inlets making,
  Comes silent flooding in the main.'

Clough.

The Battle of the Marne—The Race for the Sea—Antwerp the True Flank—Admiralty Concern about Antwerp—The Neutrality of the Scheldt—Opening of the Siege of Antwerp, September 28—Lord Kitchener's Plans—Belgian Decision to Evacuate Antwerp—Conference at Lord Kitchener's House, Midnight, October 2—British Ministers urge further Resistance—My Mission to Antwerp—French Aid Promised—The Situation in Antwerp, October 3—Proposals to the Belgian and British Governments—Progress of the German Attack—Strange Contrasts—Acceptance of Proposals by British and Belgian Governments—Chances of Success—Relief Approaching—Fighting of October 5—The Belgian Night Attack Fails—The Front broken in, October 6—Arrival of the British Naval Brigades—Arrival of Sir Henry Rawlinson—Decisions of British and Belgian Council of War, Night of October 6—The Personal Aspect—Five Days Gained.

As the German armies rolled southwards Paris loomed before them like an enormous breakwater. The enemy capital was not only the heart of France, it was also the largest fortress in the world. It was the centre of an intricate spider's web of railways. Masses of troops could debouch in almost unlimited numbers in any direction upon passers-by. No one could count on entering it without a formal siege, the German cannon for which were at this moment deploying before Antwerp. To advance upon both sides of Paris, the Germans had not the troops; to enter Paris, they had not at this moment the guns. What then remained? They must march between Paris and Verdun—which exerted a similar influence—and guarding their flanks from both these fortresses push on to the destruction of the French field armies. Surely also this was the classical tradition?

Had not Moltke—not this one but the great Moltke, now dead a quarter of a century—proclaimed 'Direction: Paris! Objective: the enemy's field armies!'[1]

At noon on August 31 a Captain Lepic sent to reconnoitre with his squadron reported from Gournay-sur-Aronde that the interminable columns of Kluck's First Army were turning south-east towards Compiègne instead of continuing their march on Paris. This news was confirmed the next day both by British and French aviators. By nightfall on the 2nd General Maunoury's Sixth Army, which had now arrived in the northern environs of Paris, reported that there were no German troops west of the line Senlis-Paris. It was upon these indications, confirmed again by British aviators on the 3rd, that Gallièni acted.

Assuredly no human brain had conceived the design, nor had human hand set the pieces on the board. Several separate and discrepant series of events had flowed together. First, the man Gallièni is on the spot. Fixed in his fortress, he could not move towards the battle; so the mighty battle has been made to come to him. Second—the weapon has been placed in his hands—the army of Maunoury. It was given him for one purpose, the defence of Paris; he will use it for another—a decisive manœuvre in the field. It was given him against the wish of Joffre. It will prove the means of Joffre's salvation. Third, the Opportunity: Kluck, swinging forward in hot pursuit of, as he believed, the routed British and demoralized French, will present his whole right flank and rear as he passes Paris to Gallièni with Maunoury in his hand. Observe, not one of these factors would have counted without the other two. All are interdependent; all are here, and all are here now.

Gallièni realized the position in a flash. 'I dare not believe it,' he exclaimed; 'it is too good to be true.' But it is true. Confirmation arrives hour by hour. He vibrates with enthusiasm. Instantly on the 3rd, he orders the army of Maunoury to positions on the north-east of Paris, which in 48 hours will enable them on the 5th to strike Kluck and with him the whole advancing line of German armies behind their right shoulder-blade. But this is not enough. What can one army—hastily improvised—do by itself amid events on such a scale? He must secure the British; he must animate Joffre. At half-past eight on the evening of the 3rd he wrote requesting Joffre's authority for the movement, which he has already ordered Maunoury's army to make, and urging a general offensive by all the French armies between Paris and Verdun simultaneously with his attack.

Joffre and Great Headquarters had arrived that day at Bar-sur-Aube. The numerous bureaux composing the elaborate staff machine had been on the move for two days and were now installing themselves at a new centre. We must not suppose that Joffre and his assistants have not been thinking about things. It was evident to any trained observer that if the fortresses of Verdun and Paris were strongly defended by mobile armies, the German invasion would bulge forward into a wide crescent between these two points; and that this would give an opportunity for a general French attack. Somehow, somewhere, sometime, Joffre and his Staff intended this. In principle they and Gallièni were agreed. From the beginning of the retreat he had said, 'I will attack when my two wings have an

[1]See map on page 254.

enveloping position.' But the How, the Where, and the When. These were the rubs; and on these vital matters it is certain that not only no resolve or design had been formed, but that important orders had been issued inconsistent with such a plan.

Gallièni's messenger reached Bar-sur-Aube on the night of the 3rd, and all the next morning while Maunoury's army was marching into its preparatory stations Gallièni waited in acute anxiety. In the afternoon of the 4th he set off by motor car to Melun to ask Sir John French for British co-operation. Remember that this man had had Joffre under his command in Madagascar and that he is his formally designated successor. He is not thinking only of the local situation around Paris. He thinks for France and he behaves with the spontaneous confidence of genius in action. But French is out with his troops. Murray, Chief of his Staff, receives the Governor of Paris. The interview is lengthy and somewhat bleak.

It was an unpropitious moment for a subordinate French General to propose a new and desperate battle to the British command. On September 2 Sir John French had written to Joffre offering, if the French would turn and fight a general battle on the Marne, to throw in the British Army and put all things to the proof; and Joffre had written back, 'I do not think it possible to contemplate at this moment (*actuellement*) a general operation on the Marne with the whole of our forces.' And the British leader who had braced himself for a supreme ordeal with his small, weary and shot-torn army had been chilled. By a swift reaction, remembering all that had passed since the battle of Mons began, he had reached precipitately, but not inexcusably, the conclusion that the French had lost heart and did not feel themselves capable of regaining the offensive—at any rate for some time to come. So far, his allies had produced nothing but repulse, defeat and retreat. All their plans, in so far as he was informed of them, seemed to have failed. He knew that the Government was quitting Paris for Bordeaux. He saw that the rearmost lines of places mentioned in Joffre's Instruction No. 2 as the limits of the retreat were far behind the positions he occupied at the moment. He could not exclude, from his mind, on the morrow of his offer being declined, the possibility of a general collapse of French resistance. Indeed it was evident that the Germans, by the very fact of disdaining Paris, sought nothing less than the destruction of the French armies. Had he been in the German Headquarters, he would have learned that at this moment Moltke looked confidently forward to driving the French masses either into Switzerland or, if Rupprecht could break through between Nancy and Toul, on to the back of their own eastern fortress line, thus swiftly compelling a universal surrender. If he had been admitted to the secrets of the French Headquarters, he would have learned that Joffre had proposed to declare Paris an open town and to surrender it to the first German troops who arrived; that he had simultaneously sent orders to General Sarrail to abandon Verdun; and that only Messimy's intrusion and Sarrail's stubbornness had prevented both these catastrophes from being already accomplished facts. One really cannot blame Sir Archibald Murray on the knowledge that he had, and in the absence of his Chief, from viewing with scepticism the ardent and admittedly unauthorized projects of the Governor of Paris. However he promised provisionally to stop the southward movement of the British Army and to face about on a certain rather rearward line.

Meanwhile, early on the 4th, Joffre at Bar-sur-Aube had received Gallièni's letter of the night before. All the morning he pondered upon it. Then at noon he authorized Gallièni by telegram to use the army of Maunoury as he had proposed, but with the express condition that it should not attack north, but south of the Marne. A little later he telegraphed to Franchet d'Espérey, now commanding the Fifth French Army, asking him when he could be ready to take part in a general offensive. Franchet replied at 4 p.m. on the 4th that he could attack on the morning of the 6th. This answer reached Joffre between 5 and 6 o'clock. But for the next three hours he did nothing. He took no decision; he sent no orders.

Gallièni arrived back in Paris from Melun shortly before 8 o'clock. He had been absent from his Headquarters for five hours, and meanwhile Joffre's reply to his letter had arrived. He was disturbed by the Commander-in-Chief's express condition that the army of Maunoury should not attack north but only south of the Marne. Other disconcerting news reached him. He heard by telegram from Sir Henry Wilson (Murray's assistant) that the British Army was continuing its retreat; and soon after he received from Colonel Huguet, the French *liaison* officer at the British Headquarters, Sir John French's reply to his proposals: 'Prefer on account of continual changes of the situation to re-study it before deciding on further operations.'

It was now 9 o'clock. Apparently nothing was happening. All the armies would before dawn resume their retreat. So far as he knew, he had received nothing but the permission to make an isolated flank attack with Maunoury's Army. Gallièni went to the telephone. He called up Joffre. The Commander-in-Chief came. The two men talked. As the Commander-in-Chief of the French armies circulating his orders through the official channels, Joffre towered above Gallièni; but now, almost in personal contact, Gallièni and his old subordinate spoke at least as equals; and Joffre, to his honour, rising above jealousies and formalities, felt the strong, clear guidance of his valiant comrade. He agreed that Gallièni should attack *north* of the Marne on the 5th, and returning to his circle of officers, ordered the general battle for the 6th. Unfortunately his hesitation and previous delays bred others. We can see from the times quoted how long these vital orders take to prepare and encipher for telegraph, and decipher on arrival. It was nearly midnight before they were dispatched. They were in fact outstripped by duplicates carried by officers in motor cars. Foch, being nearest, received his orders at 1.30 a.m. But neither Franchet nor Sir John French learned of the great decision until after 3 a.m., when their armies had already begun a further day's march to the south.

Nevertheless the die is now cast. The famous order of the day is sent out; and from Verdun to Paris the electrifying right-about-turn points a million bayonets and 1,000 cannon upon the invading hosts. The Battle of the Marne has begun.

One must suppose upon the whole that the Marne was the greatest battle ever fought in the world. The elemental forces which there met in grapple and collision of course far exceeded anything that has ever happened. It is also true that the Marne decided the World War. Half a dozen other cardinal crises have left their gaunt monuments along the road of tribulation which the nations trod; and it may well be argued that any of these might in part at least have reversed the decision of the Marne. The Allies might have been beaten on other occasions, and Germany might have emerged from the World War upon a victorious peace. If in 1917 the French Army had succumbed, if the British Navy had not strangled the submarine, if the United States had not entered the war, students of to-day and to-morrow would bend over different history books and different maps. But never after the Marne had Germany a chance of absolute triumph. Never again was there the possibility of all the claims of her proud militarism receiving complete vindication. Never again could the domination of scientific force have achieved its lasting establishment. Deep changes took place in the world and among warring powers in the terrible years that followed. The nations fought desperately, but they fought in a different atmosphere and on a lower plane. The carnage and the cannonade increased; but never were the moral or the military issues at the same pitch of intensity. By the end of 1915 England was a great warlike power, and the whole British Empire was roused and marshalling its strength. By the end of 1916 Germany was deeply conscious of her weakness. In 1917 the United States had been drawn into the conflict. It is obvious that the British Empire and the United States could in the long run have crushed Germany, even if France had been completely subjugated. But the battle of the Marne might have ended the war in six weeks; and the Kaiser and his twenty kinglets and their feudal aristocracy might have founded for many generations the legend of invincible military force.

We must remember that on September 3 the Emperor William II and the German General Staff knew that they were victorious in the East and had every reason to believe that within a week they would capture or destroy all the armies that withstood them in the West. On the 10th, according to wide report, Moltke informed his master with rugged truth that 'Germany had lost the war.' Evidently an immense transformation took place. Something of enormous and mysterious potency had worked its will, and the question which will puzzle posterity as much as it astonished those who lived through the deluge, is—what?

At the time nobody worried about the causes. Everyone facing the new perils of the hour or the week, was concerned only with the result. The German invasion of France was stopped. 'The avalanche of fire and steel' was not only brought to a standstill, but hurled backwards. The obsession of German invincibility was dispersed. There would be time for all the world to go to war—time even for the most peaceful and unprepared countries to turn themselves into arsenals and barracks. Surely that was enough. All bent their backs or their heads to the toil of war; and in the instructed circles of the allies none, and in those of the Germans few, doubted which way the final issue would go. Never again need we contemplate the entire surrender of the French Army before any other armies were afoot to take its place. At the very worst there would be parley, negotiation, barter, compromise, and a haggled peace.

* * * * *

Since the war laborious studies have been set in train, and an enormous mass of publications, official, non-official and counter-official, has been produced. These have together assembled a multitudinous array of facts. But there are so many facts adduced and some few vitally important facts withheld, and such disputations over the one or the other, that half a dozen explanatory theories may well be championed; and the world, harassed with paying the bill, has been content to rest on the solid assurance that the French beat the Germans at the battle of the Marne.

The French official history carries its discreet narration down to midnight on September 5. According to this account, with little generosity to Gallièni, the battle of the Marne does not begin till the 6th, and in the presence of this event the French military historians are mute. From the evening of September 5 till January, 1915, their pages are blank. Obviously the controversies of rival schools of professional opinion, fierce disputes about facts and their valuations, respect for the feelings of illustrious men, have induced the chroniclers to leave this climax of their tale till time has wrought its smoothing work.

So far as we may judge from the French account of the preliminaries, they consider the battle as having reached from Paris to Verdun. The German account, on the other hand, in harmony with their own schemes, comprehends it as extending from Paris right round the corner of Verdun to the Vosges Mountains. The Germans consider that all their seven armies were engaged at the Marne; the French that only five of theirs and the British Army were comprised in the battle. We have to contemplate on either view the collision of thirteen or fourteen armies, each containing the adult male population of a very large city, and all consuming food, material, ammunition, treasure and life at a prodigious rate per hour. We have to remember also that the French and British are armies whose springs are compressed back on their reserves and supplies; and that the German armies have hurried on far beyond their rearward organization and their railheads. The French have perfect communications sideways and otherwise; the Germans have not yet restored the broken roads and bridges over which their rapid advance had been made. The French are upon interior lines; the Germans are stretched round the fortified Verdun corner. It was upon this basis that the battle began.

It was less like a battle than any other ever fought. Comparatively few were killed or wounded. No great recognizable feat of arms, no shock proportionate to the event can be discerned. Along a front of more than 200 miles weary, war-ravaged troops were in a loose-desperate contact; then all of a sudden one side sustained the impression that it was the weaker, and that it had had the worst of it. But what was the mechanical causation which induced this overpowering psychologial reaction? I can only try to burnish a few links of a chain that is still partly buried.

The popular conception of the battle of the Marne as a wild counter-rush of France upon Germany, as a leopard spring at the throat of the invaders, as an onslaught carried forward on the wings of passion and ecstasy, is in singular contrast to the truth. It took some time to turn round the French armies retreating between Verdun and Paris. These ponderous bodies could only effectually reverse their motion after a substantial number of hours and even days. No sooner had the French turned about and begun to advance, than they met the pursuing Germans advancing towards them. Most prudently they stopped at once and fired upon the Germans, and the Germans withered before their fire. It is the Battle of the Frontiers fought the other way round. No longer the French advance madly to the strains of the Marseillaise while the German invaders stop and shoot them down with machine guns and artillery; the conditions are reversed. It is the Germans who try to advance and feel for the first time the frightful power of the French artillery. If only the French had done this at the frontiers; if only they had used modern firearms upon hostile flesh and blood at the outset, how different the picture of the world might look to-day!

The battle of the Marne was won when Joffre had finished his conversation with Gallièni on the night of September 4. Although the French armies had been defeated, had suffered grievous losses and had retreated day after day, they were still an enormous, unbeaten, fighting force of a very high order. Although the British had retreated with great rapidity and had lost 15,000 men, the soldiers knew they had fought double their numbers and had inflicted far heavier casualties upon the German masses. Drafts and reinforcements had reached them, and they were at the moment of the turn certainly stronger than they had ever been. Although the Germans had 78 divisions on their western front compared to 55 French and British, this superiority was not enough for the supreme objective which they had in view. The Schlieffen plan, the 'receipt for victory,' had prescribed 97 divisions against France alone, and of these 71 were to execute the great offensive wheel through Belgium. Moltke had 19 fewer divisions in the west and 16 fewer in the great offensive wheel. From these again he had withdrawn 2 army corps (4 divisions) to send to the eastern front. He had not thought it worth while to attempt to stop or delay the transport of the British Expeditionary Force across the Channel. According to the German naval history 'the chief of the General Staff personally replied that the Navy should not allow the operations that it would have otherwise carried out to be interfered with on this account. It would even be of advantage if the armies in the west could settle with the 160,000 English at the same time as with the French and Belgians.' Thus when Joffre's decision was taken the balance had already turned strongly in favour of the allies.

Contrary to the French official narrative, the battle began on the 5th when Maunoury's Army came into action on the Ourcq. Let us hasten thither.

General von Kluck's army is marching south and passes Paris in sight of the Eiffel Tower. One of his five corps is acting as flank guard. Bright and cloudless skies! Suddenly about one o'clock the flank corps begins to brush against French troops advancing upon it from Paris. In order to test the strength of their assailants, the Germans attack. At once a violent action flares out and spreads. The French appear in ever-growing strength; the flank guard is beaten. The corps retreats seven miles with heavy losses. The attack from Paris grows and lengthens with more and more weight behind it. Night comes on. The defeated General, hoping to retrieve his fortunes with the morning, sends no word to Kluck. But a German aviator has noticed the conflict far below and the unexpected position of the fighting lines and his report goes to the Army Headquarters. It is not till nearly midnight that Kluck is informed that the shield on which he had counted has been shivered. Then, and not till then did he remember Moltke's orders, namely that in the main advance to drive the French into Switzerland, the armies of Kluck and Bülow

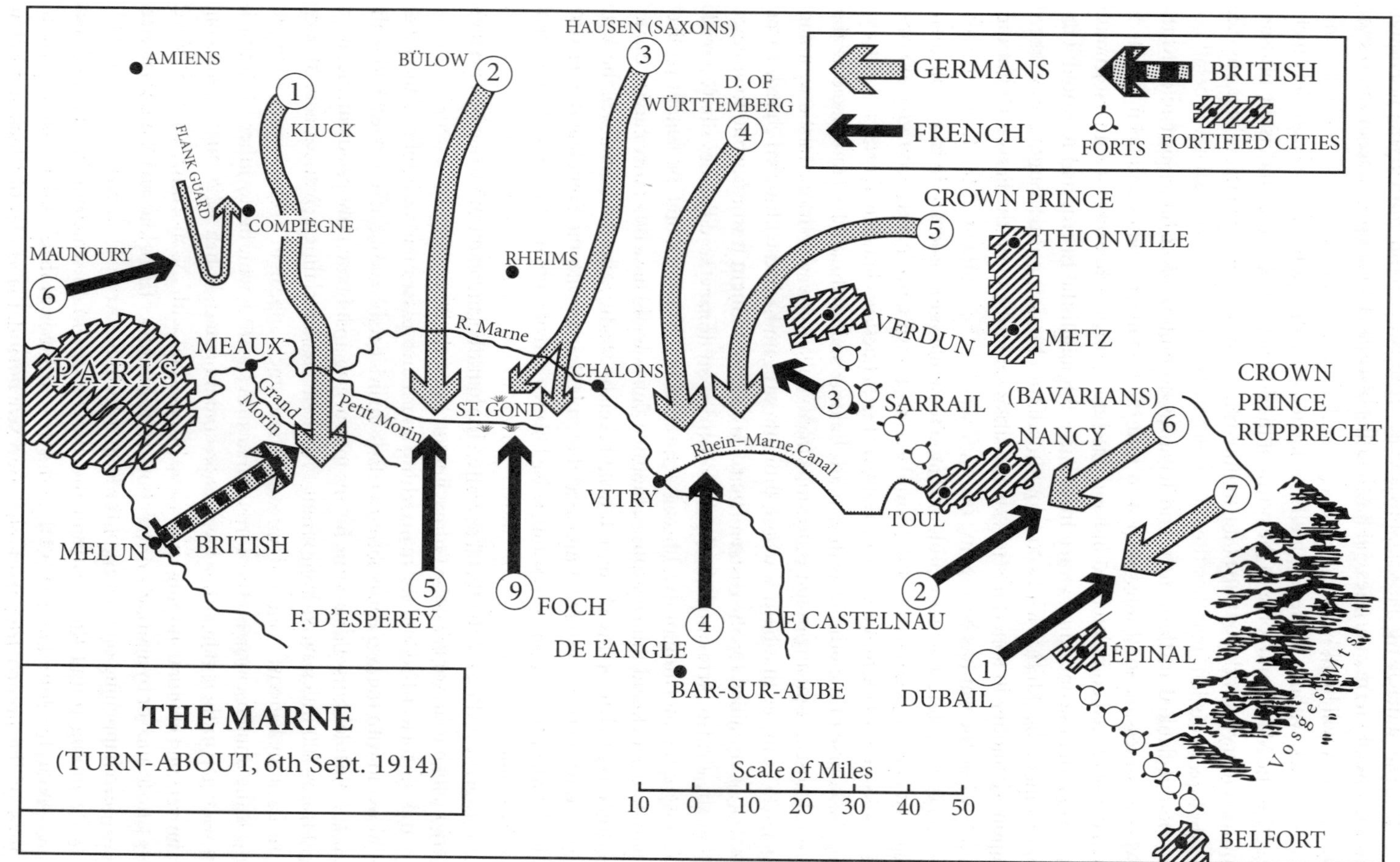

GERMANS
BRITISH
FRENCH
FORTS
FORTIFIED CITIES
AMIENS
1 KLUCK
2 BÜLOW
3 HAUSEN (SAXONS)
4 D. OF WÜRTTEMBERG
FLANK GUARD
COMPIÈGNE
6 MAUNOURY
RHEIMS
5 CROWN PRINCE
THIONVILLE
VERDUN
METZ
PARIS
MEAUX
R. Marne
CHALONS
Grand Morin
Petit Morin
ST. GOND
3 SARRAIL
(BAVARIANS) 6
CROWN PRINCE RUPPRECHT
NANCY
Rhein–Marne Canal
VITRY
TOUL
7
MELUN
BRITISH
5 F. D'ESPEREY
9 FOCH
4 DE L'ANGLE
2 DE CASTELNAU
ÉPINAL
1 DUBAIL
BAR-SUR-AUBE
Vosges Mts
THE MARNE
(TURN-ABOUT, 6th Sept. 1914)
Scale of Miles
10 0 10 20 30 40 50
BELFORT

should form a defensive flank against attacks from Paris. So far from giving protection to the line of German armies, he has had his own flank torn open; and in four hours another day will break!

So Kluck without more ado pulls back the two corps of his centre, and bids them recross the Marne and form to the north of his defeated flank guard; and as the pressure of Maunoury's attack continues during the 6th, he next takes the last of his army, the two corps of his left, marches them 60 miles in 48 hours, resolved whatever befall not to be out-flanked in the north, and have his communications cut. So here is Kluck who was pressing southward so fast to find the remains of the defeated English, now suddenly turned completely round and drawing up his whole army facing west to ward off Maunoury's continuing attack from Paris. But all this takes time and it is not till the morning of the 9th that Kluck has got himself into his new position and is ready to fall upon Maunoury in superior strength and drive him back upon the Paris fortifications. Meanwhile the war has been going on.

Next in the line to Kluck is Bülow. He too remembers his orders to form a flank guard against Paris. Moreover, the withdrawal of Kluck's army corps has left his right in the air. So Bülow pivots on his centre. His right arm goes back, his left arm comes forward, and in the course of the 6th, 7th, 8th and 9th he draws himself up in position facing Paris, and almost at right angles to his previous front. But anyone who looks at the diagram on page 257 can see that both Kluck and Bülow have now exposed their left hands to the attack of any allied forces who may be advancing upon them from the south. We know that the British Army and the Fifth French Army (Franchet d'Espérey) have turned about on the morning of the 5th and are advancing. This was only the beginning. Not only had Kluck and Bülow exposed their left flanks to the attack of powerful forces, but a hideous gap had opened between them. A gap of over 30 miles, and practically nothing to fill it with except cavalry! A great mass of cavalry indeed, two cavalry corps, the corps of Marwitz provided by Kluck and of Richthofen provided by Bülow—still only cavalry and without a common commander! An awful gap merely skinned over! We may imagine the feelings of the German Main Headquarters in Luxemburg as this apparition gradually but inexorably resolved itself upon the map. 'If we only had a couple of corps marching forward behind the main front, here is their place and this is their hour.' 'What did we do with the two corps that were to have besieged Namur?' 'Ah! yes, we sent them to the Vistula! So we did! How far have they got?' 'They are now disembarking from 80 trains 700 miles away.' Well might the Kaiser have exclaimed, 'Moltke, Moltke, give me back my legions!'

If the immense organisms of modern armies standing in a row together find there is a wide gap in their ranks, and have no reserves to come up and fill it, they cannot edge towards one another sideways like companies or battalions. They can only close the gap by an advance or by a retreat. Which is it to be? To answer this question we must see what has been happening on the rest of the long battle line.

Beginning round the corner at the extreme left of the German invasion, Prince Rupprecht has found he cannot pierce the front between Toul and Epinal. The heavy guns of the French fortresses, the prepared positions and the obstinate armies of

Dubail and Castelnau have, with much slaughter, stopped him and his Bavarians. He has been dragging the heavy cannon out of Metz; but it takes a long time to move them. Now they are called for elsewhere. Rupprecht therefore reports on September 8 that he cannot break through the Trouée des Charmes and that he is in fact at a standstill. North-east of Verdun Sarrail faces the Army of the German Crown Prince. Here again the guns of the fortress strike heavy blows. The Crown Prince's columns skirting Verdun at a respectful distance are mauled and hampered. Next come the armies of the Duke of Wurtemberg and General von Hausen. These are confronted respectively by the army of de Langle de Cary and around the marshes of St. Gond by the army of General Foch.

Throughout the centre the fighting was confused, obscure, and to say the least, indecisive. On the left of Bülow's army (with which was now associated nearly half of Hausen's) an attempt was made to advance against Foch with a desperate, gigantic bayonet attack at dawn. The Germans claim that this assault was successful. The outposts and advance troops of one of Foch's army corps were certainly driven back; but the main line of the French field artillery intact continued its devastating fire. Every one remembers Foch's staccato phrases: 'My flanks are turned; my centre gives way; I attack!'

Three German armies had tried to advance directly against the French and had failed. The French wisely and though hardly with a conscious decision abstaining from their own onslaught, had been content to shoot them down. Broadly speaking, the armies of the German Crown Prince, the Duke of Wurtemberg and General von Hausen were by September 8 at a complete standstill in front of those of Sarrail, de L'Angle and Foch. The centres of the French and German fronts were leaning up against each other in complete equipoise. We are witnessing the birth throes of trench warfare.

But what meanwhile has been happening to the gap? We must not forget the gap. It is still open, thirty miles of it between the two armies of the German right. Into this gap are now marching steadily the British Army together with the left of the Fifth French Army (Franchet's). On they march, these 5 British divisions preceded by 5 brigades of their own cavalry and a French cavalry division. They go on marching. The German aeroplanes see five dark 15-mile-long caterpillars eating up the white roads. They report 'heavy British masses advancing.' And what was there to stop them? Only one corps of cavalry now, the other has been called away by Bülow; 6 battalions of Jäger, and—a long way back—one rather battered infantry division. There is no possibility of such forces stopping or indeed delaying the march of a professional army of 120,000 men. There are three rivers or streams to cross; four wooded ridges of ground to be cleared. But nothing can prevent this wedge from being driven into the gap. With every hour and every mile of its advance the strategic embarrassments of Bülow and Kluck increased. Nothing had happened so far. The German cavalry and Jäger were being driven back before aggressive British rifle-using cavalry, backed by swiftly gathering bayonets and cannon. But in the whole four days the British lost under 2,000 men. The effects were not tactical; they were strategic.

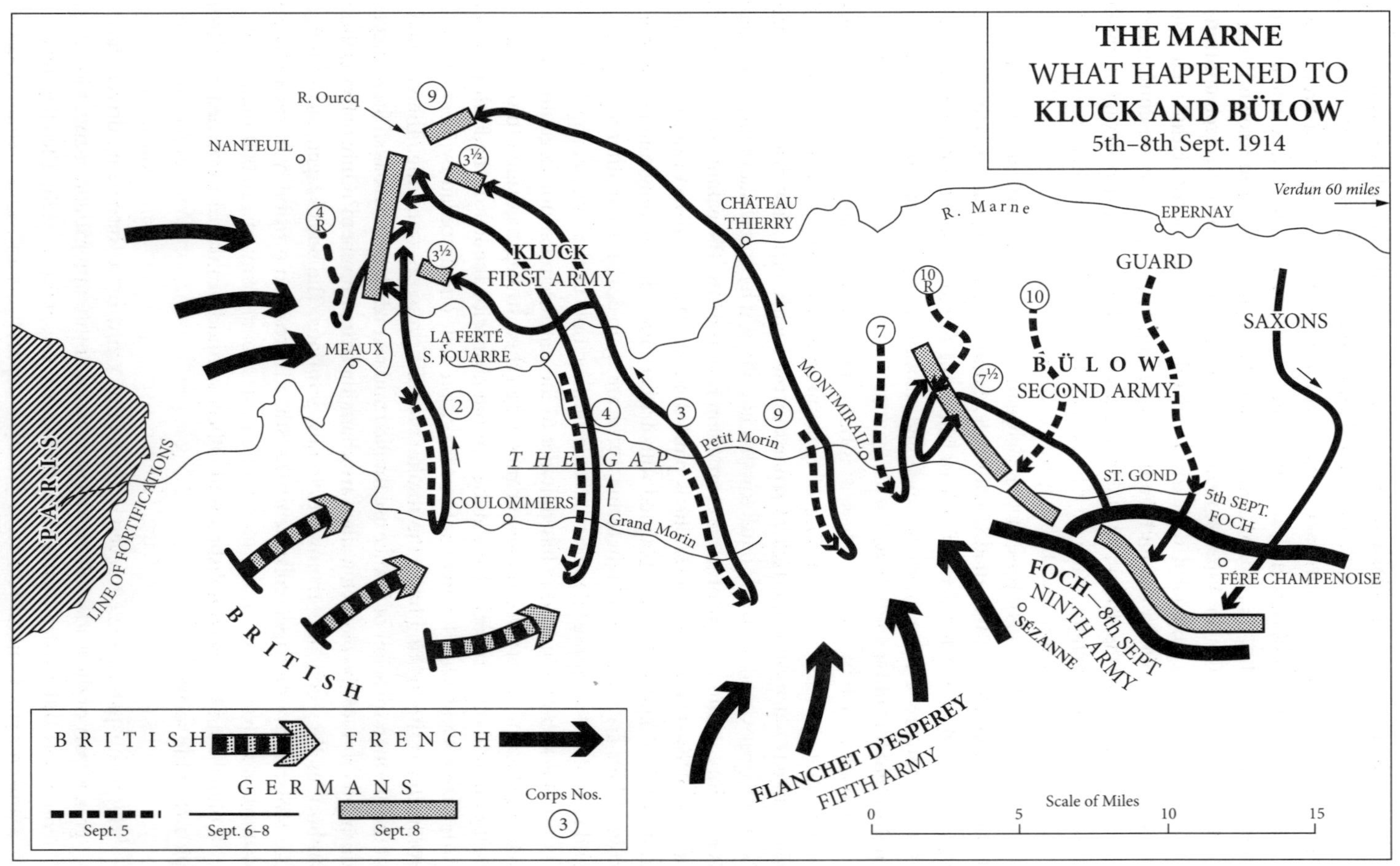
THE MARNE
WHAT HAPPENED TO
KLUCK AND BÜLOW
5th–8th Sept. 1914
R. Ourcq
NANTEUIL
MEAUX
LA FERTÉ
S. JOUARRE
KLUCK
FIRST ARMY
CHÂTEAU
THIERRY
R. Marne
EPERNAY
Verdun 60 miles
GUARD
SAXONS
BÜLOW
SECOND ARMY
MONTMIRAIL
Petit Morin
THE GAP
COULOMMIERS
Grand Morin
ST. GOND
5th SEPT.
FOCH
FÈRE CHAMPENOISE
FOCH—8th SEPT
NINTH ARMY
SÉZANNE
FLANCHET D'ESPEREY
FIFTH ARMY
PARIS
LINE OF FORTIFICATIONS
BRITISH
BRITISH
FRENCH
GERMANS
Sept. 5
Sept. 6–8
Sept. 8
Corps Nos.
Scale of Miles
0
5
10
15

No human genius planned that the British Army should advance into this gap. A series of tumultuous events had cast them into this position in the line. When they advanced, there was the gap in front of them. On the whole front it was the line of least resistance. Along it they bored and punched, and it led into the strategic vitals of the German right wing. High destiny, blind fate regulated the none too vigorous, but nevertheless decisive movements of this British Army. It marches on, wondering what has happened to the monster which had pursued it with whip and yell since Mons. Bülow finds his right flank being rolled back by the Fifth French Army, and himself cut off continually from his right-hand comrade, Kluck, by the British advance. Kluck, just as he has got himself into a fine position to fight Maunoury, finds his left and all the rear of his left, hopelessly compromised and exposed.

All these developments present themselves in the first instance upon the maps at Bülow's and Kluck's headquarters, loaded with a hundred details concerning the supplies, the safety and even the escape of at least one-third of the whole of both their armies. And the sum of these disquietudes, unwillingly disclosed item by item, reveals its terrors to the highest centre of authority.

We must now transport ourselves, as is our privilege, to the Emperor's headquarters at Luxemburg. Time: the morning of September 8. The magnates there assembled were already alarmed at the lack of reports of the hourly victories to which they had become accustomed. Instead comes Rupprecht's tale that he is at a standstill. Next there is brought a captured copy of Joffre's battle orders of the 5th. The whole French Army is attacking! The Crown Prince says he is pinned down. 'We can make only contemptible advances,' he reports. 'We are plagued with artillery fire. The infantry simply get under cover. There are no means of advancing. What are we to do?' The Dukes of Wurtemberg and Hausen tell the same tale in similar terms, varied only by the bayonet attack episode. As for Bülow and Kluck, one has only got to look at the map. One does not need to read the tactical reports from these armies, when their strategic torture is disclosed, by aeroplane and other reports. Here at the summit in spacious rooms, in an atmosphere of order, salutes and heel-clicking, far from the cannonade and desperate, squalid, glorious confusion of the fighting lines, the resultants of the pressures upon the immense body of the German invasion of France are totalled and recorded, as if by a Wall Street ticker during a crash of the market. Values are changing from minute to minute. The highest authorities are reconciling themselves to new positions. The booming hopes of the 3rd are replaced by the paper collapse of the 8th. It is the same story in terms of blood instead of scrip.

Colonel Bauer, an accomplished Staff Officer of middle rank, has furnished us with a picture of the scene.

> 'Desperate panics seized severely the entire army, or to be more correct the greater part of the leaders. It looked at its worst at the supreme command. Moltke completely collapsed. He sat with a pallid face gazing at the map, dead to all feeling, a broken man. General von Stein (Moltke's deputy) certainly said "We must not lose our heads," but he did not take charge. He was himself without confidence

> and gave expression to his feelings by saying "We cannot tell how things will go." Tappen (head of the Operations Section of whom we have heard before) was as calm as ever and did not consider that the failure was altogether his fault; nor was it, for he did not lose his nerve. But he did nothing. "We younger people could not get a hearing." '
>
> Thus Bauer!

Everything now converged upon Moltke. Who was Moltke? He was the shadow of a great name; he was the nephew of the old Field Marshal and had been his aide-de-camp. He was an ordinary man, rather a courtier; a man about the Palace agreeable to the Emperor in the palmy days of peace. The sort of man who does not make too much trouble with a Sovereign, who knows how to suppress his own personality—what there is of it; a good, harmless, respectable, ordinary man. And on to this ill-fated being crashes the brutal, remorseless, centripetal impingement of tides and impulsions under which the greatest captains of history might have blenched!

There is hardly any doubt what he should have done. A simple message to all the German armies to be imparted to every division, 'If you cannot advance, hold on, dig in, yield not a scrap of conquered territory; *vestigia nulla retrorsum*,' might well have stabilized the situation. At this time, however, only the British Army knew (from the Boer War) the power of modern weapons on the defensive. The French were just enjoying their first exultant experience of it. None of the military men on the other side yet knew that as a matter of fact a 30-mile gap in a front of 200 is only a trap for the attackers who enter into it. Almost instantly it becomes not a victory but a dangerous salient, a bulge subject to crossfire and counter-attack from both flanks, the worst place in the world for a further offensive.

The officers of the German General Staff formed a close corporation and confraternity, and bore the same relation to the German Army and its leaders, as the Jesuits of the seventeenth and eighteenth centuries bore to the priests and cardinals of the Roman Catholic Church. They spoke their own language, they had their own special affiliations, they moved men and things with the higher intelligence which comes from knowledge and organization. To one of these officers, Colonel Hentsch, the head of the Intelligence, about midday September 8, Moltke imparted his views or mood. Both men are now dead. Neither has left a record of the conversation. We only know what followed from it. Colonel Hentsch got in his long grey car and went along the whole line of the Armies, stopping at each of their headquarters and finally reached Bülow's headquarters about dark. He saw his brother Staff Officer of that army. He wrestled with him long. It was agreed between them that if the British Army was actually found to be across the Marne in force and advancing into the gap between Bülow and Kluck, Bülow should retreat to the Aisne in conformity with all the other German armies of the right and centre. Hentsch spared a few moments for a civil chat with old Bülow. The conversation, we are told, was pessimistic. He slept the night at Bülow's headquarters. He started at 7 o'clock the next morning, and the old man not being called till 9, he talked again with the General Staff Officer. It is clear that by this time—the reports

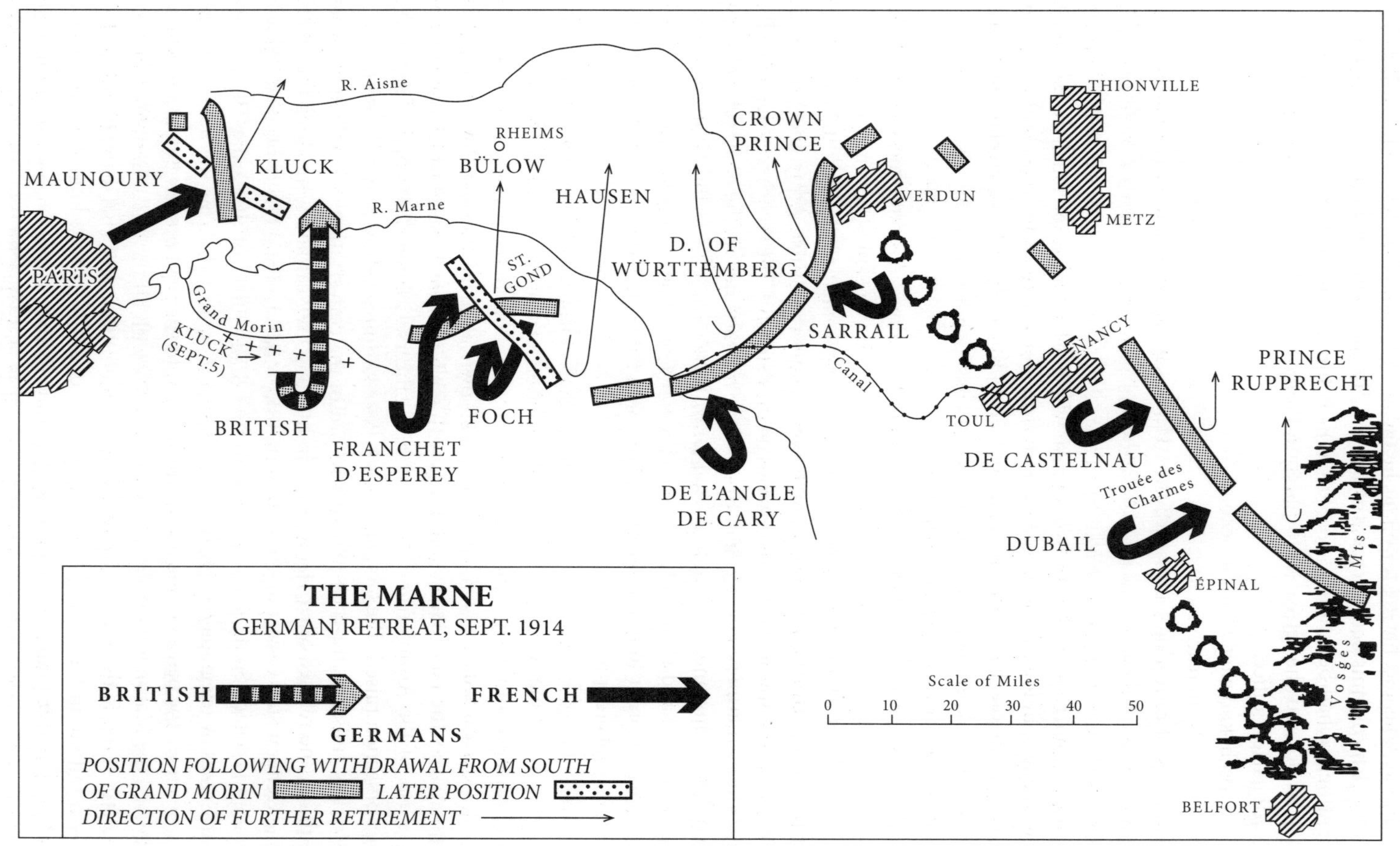
R. Aisne
RHEIMS
MAUNOURY
KLUCK
BÜLOW
HAUSEN
CROWN PRINCE
THIONVILLE
VERDUN
METZ
R. Marne
D. OF WÜRTTEMBERG
ST. GOND
PARIS
Grand Morin
KLUCK (SEPT.5)
SARRAIL
NANCY
PRINCE RUPPRECHT
Canal
TOUL
BRITISH
FOCH
FRANCHET D'ESPEREY
DE CASTELNAU
DE L'ANGLE DE CARY
Trouée des Charmes
DUBAIL
Mts.
ÉPINAL
Vosges
THE MARNE
GERMAN RETREAT, SEPT. 1914
BRITISH
FRENCH
GERMANS
POSITION FOLLOWING WITHDRAWAL FROM SOUTH OF GRAND MORIN
LATER POSITION
DIRECTION OF FURTHER RETIREMENT
Scale of Miles
0
10
20
30
40
50
BELFORT

of the previous day having been considered—there was no doubt about the heads of the British columns being across the Marne. Therefore the conditions established the night before had been fulfilled. Bülow 'on his own initiative,' as directed by his Staff Officer, ordered the retreat of the Second Army when in due course he entered his Headquarters' office.

Hentsch, knowing what the Second Army was doing, proceeded on his way. He had some difficulty in reaching Kluck. He had to cross the grisly gap and his car was blocked by masses of retreating German cavalry. He was involved in a 'panic,' as he describes it, following a British aeroplane raid. It was not till after noon that he reached Kluck's headquarters. Here again he dealt only with the Staff Officer. He never saw Kluck at all. He told von Kühl, Kluck's Chief of Staff, that as the English were now known to be advancing into the gap, Bülow's army would be retreating. But according to Hentsch, Kühl, some two hours before, had issued an order for retreat. Kühl, who is still alive and has written a massive book, admits that such an order had been telephoned by his subordinate (now dead), but that this subordinate had misconceived what he had intended. He declares that Hentsch gave him a positive order to withdraw Kluck's army to the Aisne, and seeks to lay the whole burden upon him.

At the inquiry into this celebrated episode ordered by Ludendorff in 1917 Colonel Hentsch was exonerated. It was found that his mission from Moltke was in short to see if a retreat was necessary, and if so to co-ordinate the retrograde movements of the five German armies. For this he had been given plenary authority in the name of the Supreme Command. And he had been given it only by word of mouth! But the duel between Kühl and Hentsch has been continued by Kühl over his adversary's grave. He declares the order to retreat was positive. It is however to be noted that he did not ask for this vital order in writing and that he did not tell Kluck about it till several hours had passed.

However it may be, Hentsch, a peripatetic focus of defeat, traversed and retraversed the entire line of the German armies. On the outward journey he gathered evil tidings, and as he returned he issued fateful orders. He used the powers confided to him to order successively the First, Second, Third, Fourth and Fifth German armies to retreat upon the line of the Aisne or in general conformity with that line. Only at one point was any objection raised. The German Crown Prince, who has been so mocked at, received Moltke's emissary in person. Confronted with an order to retreat, he demanded it in writing, and refused otherwise to obey. All Hentsch's directions had been verbal as from one General Staff Officer to another. Here was the first Commander with whom he had come in contact. So he said 'he would have a formal order sent from Luxemburg.' And sent it was by telegraph the next day.

So ended the battle of the Marne. Until a retreat began, the only Ally army which had crossed the Marne was the British. In fact we may say that along the whole front from Verdun to Paris the French did not advance at all in the battle of the Marne. Some of them indeed on the left of Foch and the right of Franchet actually retreated. The only Ally army which advanced continually was the British. They advanced northwards in the four days September 5–8 more than 40 miles. But lest the reader should think this an assertion of national vainglory, let me hasten to repeat *first* that at the moment when the British Army was turned round, it had farther to go than the others before it came into contact; and *secondly* that when it met the enemy it found in the main only a cavalry screen covering the fatal gap. Nevertheless the fact remains that it probed its way into the German liver.

Thus, by a succession of unforeseeable and uncontrolled events was decided almost at its beginning the fate of the war on land, and little else was left but four years of senseless slaughter. Whether General von Moltke actually said to the Emperor, 'Majesty, we have lost the war,' we do not know. We know anyhow that with a prescience greater in political than in military affairs, he wrote to his wife on the night of the 9th, 'Things have not gone well. The fighting east of Paris has not gone in our favour, *and we shall have to pay for the damage we have done*.'

From the moment when the German hopes of destroying the French armies by a general battle and thus of ending the war at a single stroke had definitely failed, all the secondary and incidental objectives which hitherto they had rightly discarded became of immense consequence. As passion declined, material things resumed their values. The struggle of *armies* and *nations* having failed to reach a decision, *places* recovered their significance, and geography rather than psychology began to rule the lines of war. Paris now unattainable, the Channel Ports—Dunkirk, Calais and Boulogne—still naked, and lastly Antwerp, all reappeared in the field of values like submerged rocks when the tidal wave recedes.

The second phase of the war now opened. The French, having heaved the Germans back from the Marne to the Aisne, and finding themselves unable to drive them further by frontal attacks, continually reached out their left hand in the hopes of outflanking their opponents. The race for the sea began. The French began to pass their troops from right to left. Castelnau's army, marching behind the front from Nancy, crashed into battle in Picardy, striving to turn the German right, and was itself outreached on its left. Foch's army, corps after corps, hurried by road and rail to prolong the fighting front in Artois; but round the left of this again lapped the numerous German cavalry divisions of von der Marwitz—swoop and counter-swoop. On both sides every man and every gun were hurled as they arrived into the conflict, and the unceasing cannonade drew ever northwards and westwards—ever towards the sea.

Where would the grappling armies strike blue water? At what point on the coast? Which would turn the other's flank? Would it be north or south of Dunkirk? Or of Gravelines or Calais or Boulogne? Nay, southward still, was Abbeville even attainable? All was committed to the shock of an ever-moving battle. But as the highest goal, the one safe inexpugnable flank for the Allies, the most advanced, the most daring, the most precious—worth all the rest, guarding all the rest—gleamed Antwerp, could Antwerp but hold out.

Antwerp was not only the sole stronghold of the Belgian nation: it was also the true left flank of the Allied front in the west. It guarded the whole line of the Channel ports. It threatened the flanks and rear of the German armies in France. It was the gateway from which a British army might emerge at any moment upon their sensitive and even vital communications. No German advance to the sea-coast, upon Ostend, upon Dunkirk, upon Calais and Boulogne, seemed possible while Antwerp was unconquered.[2]

My own feeling at the outbreak of the war had been that if the right things were done, Antwerp ought to hold out for two or even three months, that is to say, until we knew the result of the main collision of the armies on all the fronts—French, Russian, Austrian. I rested my thought on Metz and Paris in 1870–71, Plevna in 1878, Port Arthur in 1904. The fall of Namur unsettled these foundations. Still Antwerp, even apart from its permanent fortifications, was a place of great strength, fortified by rivers and inundations, and defended by all that was best in the Belgian nation and by practically its whole Field Army.

I was from the beginning very anxious to do everything that could be done out of our slender resources to aid the Belgian King and nation to maintain their stronghold, and such small items as the Admiralty could spare in guns and ammunition were freely sent. The reports which we received from Antwerp and the telegrams of the Belgian Government already at the beginning of September began to cause me deep concern. So also did the question of the Scheldt, whose free navigation both for troops and munitions seemed vital to the Belgian people.

I thought that Antwerp should be made to play its part in the first phase of the war by keeping as many German troops as possible out of the great battle. If the Belgian Army defending the city could be strengthened by British troops, not only would the defence be invigorated, but the Germans would be continually apprehensive of a British inroad upon them from this direction, the deadliness of which Lord Roberts's strategic instinct had so clearly appreciated. It was true that we had no troops in England fit to manœuvre in the field against the enemy. But the defence of the fortified lines of Antwerp was a task in which British Territorial troops might well have played their part. Accordingly on September 7 I sent a memorandum to the Prime Minister, Sir Edward Grey and Lord Kitchener emphasizing the importance of Antwerp, particularly from the naval standpoint:—

> 'The Admiralty view the sustained and effective defence of Antwerp as a matter of high consequence. It preserves the life of the Belgian nation: it safeguards a strategic point which, if captured, would be of the utmost menace.'

In order to save Antwerp, two things were necessary: first, effective defence of the fortress line; and second, free uninterrupted communication with the sea. The first was tolerably well provided for by the Belgian Army which could easily be reinforced by British Territorial troops. But the second essential, the free communication with the sea, was a larger matter, and in it were involved our relations with the Dutch. I proposed that we should request the Dutch Government to give a free passage up the Scheldt to Antwerp for whatever troops and supplies were needed. I pointed out further that it was impossible to try to supply an army at Antwerp by Ostend and Ghent; that the appeal

[2]See map on pages 266–7.

which the Belgians were then making to us to send 25,000 troops to co-operate with an equal number of Belgian troops for the purpose of keeping open the line Antwerp–St. Nicholas–Ghent–Bruges–Ostend, was a counsel of despair. To quote again from my memorandum:—

> 'It involves practically a flank position for a line of supply protected by forces large enough to be hit hard and perfectly powerless against any determined German attack which it is thought worth while to deliver. At any moment a punch up from Brussels by a German division or larger force would rupture the line, and drive the troops trying to hold it to be disarmed on neutral Dutch territory or into the sea.'

I dwelt on the disadvantages to the Allies of a neutrality which kept the Rhine open for Germany and closed the Scheldt to Antwerp.

As these questions are still of some delicacy I have thought it better to summarize rather than reprint my memorandum. But I draw the reader's attention to the date—September 7.

I still think that strong representations to the Dutch Government might well have induced them to grant this relief to Antwerp and the Belgian nation in their agony. The original guarantee of Belgian neutrality was given to the Government of the Netherlands, and it would have been a natural and legitimate demand that they should put no needless obstacle in the way of its fulfilment. The sympathies of Holland for the sufferings of Belgium were naturally restrained by the fear of sharing her fate. But a neutral Holland was of far more use to Germany than a hostile, a conquered, or even an allied Holland. Once Holland was attacked by or allied to Germany we could close the Rhine, and if we were in alliance with Holland, the Texel and other Dutch islands of enormous strategic importance would become available for the forward action of the British Navy. We should in fact have that oversea base without which a British naval offensive was impossible. I do not therefore believe that if Holland had agreed to open the Scheldt for the succour of Antwerp, Germany would have declared war upon her. There would have been a long argument about interpretations of neutrality in which the Germans, after their behaviour, would have started at a great disadvantage. I still think that if Holland could have said to Germany 'the English are threatening us with a blockade of the Rhine if we do not open the Scheldt,' Germany would have accepted the lesser of two evils.

The Foreign Secretary did not, however, feel able to put this grave issue to the Dutch Government. Neither did Lord Kitchener wish to use the British Territorial Divisions in the manner proposed, and while adhering to my own opinion I certainly do not blame him. He would not send any Territorials into Antwerp, nor was anything effective done by the Allies for the city during the whole of September. From the moment when German Main Headquarters had extricated and reformed their armies after the failure at the Marne, the capture of Antwerp became most urgently necessary to them. Accordingly on the afternoon of September 9, as is now known, the German Emperor was moved to order the capture of that city. Nothing was apparent to the Allies until the 28th. The Belgian and German troops remained in contact along the fortress line without any serious siege or assaulting operations developing. But on the 28th the Germans suddenly opened fire upon the forts of the Antwerp exterior lines with 17-inch howitzers hurling projectiles of over a ton.

Almost immediately the Belgian Government gave signs of justified alarm. British intelligence reports indicated that the Germans were seriously undertaking the siege of Antwerp, that their operations were not intended as a demonstration to keep the Belgian troops occupied or to protect the lines of communication. Information had come from Brussels that the Emperor had ordered the capture of the town, that this might cost thousands of lives, but that the order must be obeyed. Large bodies of German reserve troops were also reported assembling near Liège. In view of all these reports it was evident that the role of our small British force of marines, omnibuses, armoured cars, aeroplanes, etc., operating from Dunkirk was exhausted. They had no longer to deal with Uhlan patrols or raiding parties of the enemy. Large hostile forces were approaching the coastal area, and the imposture whereby we had remained in occupation of Lille and Tournai could be sustained no longer.

Lord Kitchener was disquieted by the opening of the bombardment upon the Antwerp forts. He immediately sent (on September 29) a Staff Officer, Colonel Dallas, into the city to report direct to him on the situation. On the evening of October 1 this officer reported that—

> 'The Belgian War Minister considered the situation very grave. Did not think that resistance to the German attack could be maintained by defensive measures only within the fortress. That the only way to save Antwerp from falling was by a diversion from outside on the German left flank. That the French had offered a division and that he looked forward to co-operation by an English force also if that could be arranged.'

The Minister had also said—

> 'That a Belgian cavalry division and some volunteers, and possibly two divisions of the Belgian Field Army, would be able to assist in the operation which would be most effective in the neighbourhood of Ghent.'

The Commander of the Antwerp fortress also considered the situation grave, and while Colonel Dallas was with him a message arrived to say that Fort Ste. Catherine had fallen, that the German troops had pressed forward between it and the adjoining work, and had occupied the Belgian infantry trenches at this point.

Colonel Dallas further reported that according to the Belgian Headquarters the German Army in Belgium comprised—'Siege army, consisting of the 3rd Reserve Army Corps, 1 division of marines, 1 Ersatz reserve division, 1 brigade of *Landsturm*, 2 regiments of pioneers, 1 regiment of siege artillery.' And that 'The troops of the Military Government of Brussels consist of a weak *Landwehr* brigade and some Bavarian *Landsturm*, number unknown.'

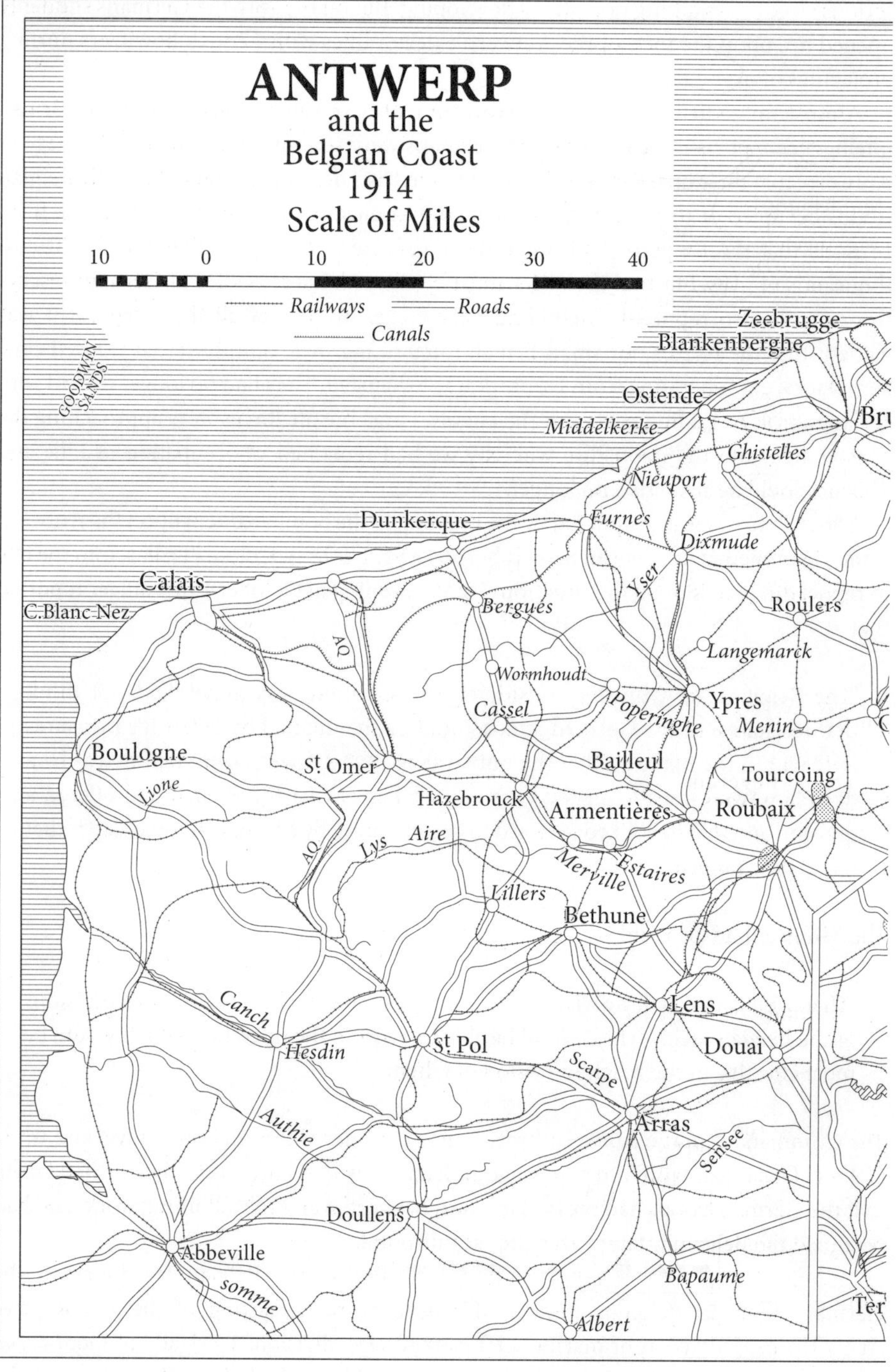
ANTWERP
and the
Belgian Coast
1914
Scale of Miles
10
0
10
20
30
40
Railways
Roads
Canals
GOODWIN SANDS
Zeebrugge
Blankenberghe
Ostende
Middelkerke
Ghistelles
Nieuport
Dunkerque
Furnes
Dixmude
Yser
Calais
C.Blanc-Nez
Bergues
Roulers
AQ
Langemarck
Wormhoudt
Poperinghe
Ypres
Cassel
Menin
Boulogne
St Omer
Bailleul
Tourcoing
Liane
Hazebrouck
Armentières
Roubaix
Lys
Aire
AQ
Merville
Estaires
Lillers
Bethune
Canch
Lens
Hesdin
St Pol
Douai
Scarpe
Authie
Arras
Sensee
Doullens
Abbeville
Bapaume
somme
Albert

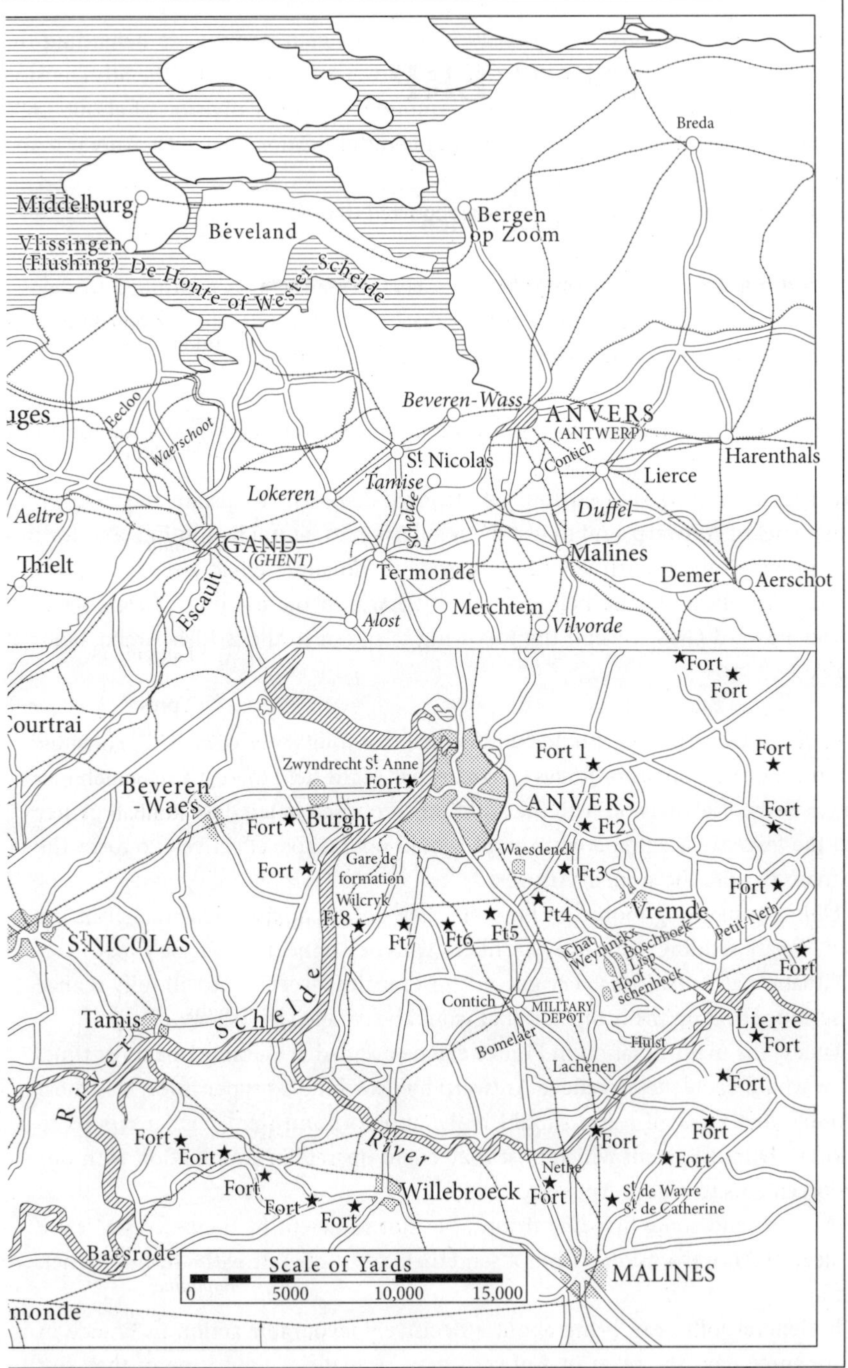
Breda
Middelburg
Bergen op Zoom
Beveland
Vlissingen (Flushing)
De Honte of Wester Schelde
Beveren-Wass
ANVERS (ANTWERP)
Harenthals
Eecloo
Waerschoot
St Nicolas
Contich
Lierce
Tamise
Lokeren
Aeltre
Scheldt
Duffel
GAND (GHENT)
Malines
Thielt
Escault
Termonde
Demer
Aerschot
Merchtem
Alost
Vilvorde
Courtrai
Fort
Fort 1
Zwyndrecht St Anne
Beveren -Waes
Burght
ANVERS
Ft2
Waesdenck
Ft3
Gare de formation
Wilcryk
Vremde
Ft4
Ft8
Ft7
Ft6
Ft5
Petit-Neth
S.t NICOLAS
Chat. Weyninrkx
Boschhoek
Lisp
Hoof schenhock
Contich
MILITARY DEPOT
Tamis
River Schelde
Bomelaer
Lierre
Hulst
Lachenen
River
Nethe
Willebroeck
St de Wavre
St de Catherine
Baesrode
Scale of Yards
0
5000
10,000
15,000
MALINES
monde

The Belgian Field Army was about 80,000 strong, in addition to which there were some 70,000 fortress troops. Four divisions of the Belgian Army were defending the southern portion of the outer perimeter of the Antwerp defences, with the 5th Division in reserve, and one weak division was at Termonde. A cavalry division of about 3,600 sabres was south-west of Termonde guarding communications between Antwerp and the coast. Ghent was held by some volunteers.

On the night of October 1, Sir F. Villiers reported that—

> 'On southern section of the outer line of forts German attacks continued to-day, and in the afternoon the enemy's troops disabled fort Wavre Ste. Catherine and adjoining works, and occupied Belgian trenches at this point.'

The Belgian troops were, however, still holding out on the Belgian side of the River Nethe.

Lord Kitchener now showed himself strongly disposed to sustain the defence or effect the relief of Antwerp, and to use the regular forces he still had in England for this purpose provided the French would co-operate eventually. He had already dispatched guns and staff officers to the beleaguered city. Early in the evening of October 2 he moved Sir Edward Grey to send the following telegram to the British Ambassador at Bordeaux:—

> 'The French Government should be informed that military advisers here consider that in view of the superior forces Germany has in the field there, the dispatch of a French Territorial division with the additions proposed in ten days' time, together with the force we are prepared to send, would not be able effectively to force the Germans to raise the siege of Antwerp.
>
> 'Unless something more can be done they do not advise the dispatch of the force. We are sending some heavy artillery with personnel to assist Belgians.
>
> 'Situation at Antwerp is very grave, and French Government will fully realize the serious effect on the campaign that would be entailed by its loss.
>
> 'Unless the main situation in France can be decided favourably in a short time, which would enable us to relieve Antwerp by detaching a proper force, it is most desirable that General Joffre should make an effort and send regular troops to region of Dunkirk, from which post they could operate in conjunction with our reinforcements to relieve Antwerp.
>
> 'We can send some first-line troops, but not sufficient by themselves to raise the siege of Antwerp, and we cannot send them to co-operate with any but French regulars.
>
> 'If General Joffre can bring about a decisively favourable action in France in two or three days the relief of Antwerp may be made the outcome of that, but if not, unless he now sends some regular troops the loss of Antwerp must be contemplated.'

All he was able to send to Antwerp was the following:—

> 'Be very careful not to raise hopes of British and French forces arriving quickly to relieve Antwerp. The matter has not been decided, as the Territorial division offered by France in ten days' time would, in my opinion, be quite incapable of doing anything towards changing the situation at Antwerp. I have represented this. Unless a change is made, I consider it would be useless to put in our little force against the very superior German forces in the field round Antwerp.'

He then entered in some detail upon the few guns he was sending, giving particular directions about the use of the two 9.2's.

Up to this point I had not been brought into the affair in any way. I read, of course, all the telegrams almost as soon as they were received or dispatched by Lord Kitchener, and followed the situation constantly. I warmly approved the efforts which Lord Kitchener was making to provide or obtain succour for Antwerp, and I shared to the full his anxieties. I saw him every day. But I had no personal responsibility, nor was I directly concerned. My impression at this time was that the situation at Antwerp was serious but not immediately critical; that the place would certainly hold out for a fortnight more; and that meanwhile Lord Kitchener's exertions or the influence of the main battle in France would bring relief. So much was this the case that I proposed to be absent from the Admiralty for about eighteen hours on the 2nd–3rd October.

I had planned to visit Dunkirk on October 3 on business connected with the Marine Brigade and other details sent there at General Joffre's request. At 11 o'clock on the night of the 2nd I was some twenty miles out of London on my way to Dover when the special train in which I was travelling suddenly stopped, and without explanation returned to Victoria Station. I was told on arrival I was to go immediately to Lord Kitchener's house in Carlton Gardens. Here I found shortly before midnight besides Lord Kitchener, Sir Edward Grey, the First Sea Lord, and Sir William Tyrrell of the Foreign Office. They showed me the following telegram from our Minister, Sir Francis Villiers, sent from Antwerp at 8.20 p.m. and received in London at 10 p.m. on October 2:—

> 'The Government have decided to leave to-morrow for Ostend, acting on advice unanimously given by Superior Council of War in presence of the King. The King with field army will withdraw, commencing with advanced guard to-morrow in the direction of Ghent to protect coast-line, and eventually, it is hoped, to co-operate with the Allied armies. The Queen will also leave.
>
> 'It is said that town will hold out for five or six days, but it seems most unlikely that when the Court and Government are gone resistance will be so much prolonged.
>
> 'Decision taken very suddenly this afternoon is result of increasingly critical situation. I have seen both Prime Minister and Minister for Foreign Affairs, who maintain that no other course was possible, in view of danger that the King's Government and field army will be caught here.'

I saw that my colleagues had received this news, which they had already been discussing for half an hour, with consternation. The rapidity with which the situation had degenerated was utterly unexpected. That the great fortress and city of Antwerp with its triple line of forts and inundations, defended by the whole Belgian Field Army (a force certainly equal in numbers to all the German troops in that neighbourhood), should collapse in perhaps forty-eight hours seemed to all of us not only terrible but incomprehensible. That this should happen while preparations were in progress both in France and England for the relief or succour of the city, while considerable forces of fresh and good troops undoubtedly stood available on both sides of the Channel, and before General Joffre had even been able to reply to Lord Kitchener's telegram, was too hard to bear. We looked at each other in bewilderment and distress. What could have happened in the last few hours to make the Belgians despair? Our last telegram from Colonel Dallas, received that afternoon, had said: 'Situation unchanged during night and Germans have not made further progress. Great slaughter of Germans reported and corresponding encouragement to Belgians, who are about to undertake counter-attack in neighbourhood of Fort Ste. Catherine.' And now a message at 10 p.m. announced immediate evacuation and impending fall!

Those who in years to come look back upon the first convulsions of this frightful epoch will find it easy with after knowledge and garnered experience to pass sagacious judgments on all that was done or left undone. There is always a strong case for doing nothing, especially for doing nothing yourself. But to the small group of Ministers who met that midnight in Lord Kitchener's house, the duty of making sure that Antwerp was not cast away without good cause while the means of saving it might well be at hand was clear. I urged strongly that we should not give in without a struggle: and we decided unitedly upon the following telegram to Sir F. Villiers:—

October 3, 1914, 12.45 a.m.

> 'The importance of Antwerp being held justifies a further effort till the course of the main battle in France is determined. We are trying to send you help from the main army, and, if this were possible, would add reinforcements from here. Meanwhile a brigade of Marines will reach you to-morrow to sustain the defence. We urge you to make one further struggle to hold out. Even a few days may make the difference. We hope Government will find it possible to remain and field army to continue operations.'

On the other hand, the danger of urging the Belgian Government to hold out against their considered judgment without a full knowledge of the local situation was present in every mind, and even if the forces for the relieving army were to come into view, there was much to be arranged and decided before precise dates and definite assurances could be given. We were confronted with the hard choice of having either to take decisions of far-reaching importance in the utmost haste and with imperfect information, or on the other hand tamely to let Antwerp fall.

In these circumstances, it was a natural decision that some one in authority who knew the general situation should travel swiftly into the city and there ascertain what could be done on either side. As I was already due at Dunkirk the next morning, the task was confided to me: Lord Kitchener expressed a decided wish that I should go; the First Sea Lord consented to accept sole responsibility in my absence. It was then about half-past one in the morning. I went at once to Victoria Station, got into my train which was waiting, and started again for Dover. A few minutes before I left, Lord Kitchener received the answer to his telegram of the 2nd from the British Ambassador in Bordeaux. Sir Francis Bertie said that before he could carry out the instructions sent him about Antwerp, he had received a letter from the French Foreign Minister stating that with the shortest delay possible two Territorial Divisions, complete with artillery and cavalry, would be sent to Ostend for the relief of the fortress. This was to be without prejudice to what the French Government expected to do very soon in respect of 'a contemplated combined movement, French, British and Belgian, on the extreme left of General Joffre's armies which indirectly would have the effect of causing German troops in the neighbourhood of Antwerp to retreat, and so effect its relief.' The French Government, he said, could not go back on their decision to employ Territorials. The French Foreign Minister declared that the Territorials were good troops, better in some respects than some of the Regulars, and that they were sending two divisions complete, with artillery and cavalry, instead of one. Sir Francis Bertie added that the French Government had received reports from its Attaché in Antwerp stating that 'though the military situation there was not good, it could not be regarded as really bad. The Germans had suffered severe losses in the attacks which they had made on some of the outer works. Those attacks had not been simultaneous, which fact indicated that the Germans were not in great force, had only a limited siege train and not more than two Army Corps before Antwerp.'

Meanwhile a telegram was also sent (1.15 a.m., October 3) by Sir Edward Grey to the Belgian Government saying that I would arrive on the morning of the 3rd.

> 'It is hoped that the First Lord of the Admiralty, who is fully acquainted with our views, may have the honour of an audience with the King before a final decision as to the departure of the Government is taken.'

On this the Belgian Council of War, sitting at dawn on the 3rd, suspended the order for the evacuation of the city.

> 'I communicated at once with Minister of War,' telegraphed Sir F. Villiers, October 3, 6.37 a.m. 'He summoned a meeting of Ministers, who, after deliberation, informed me that, awaiting arrival of First Lord, they had decided to postpone departure. Audience with King for Mr. Churchill will be arranged for at as early an hour as possible.'

* * * * *

Lord Kitchener now threw himself into the task of concentrating and organizing a relieving Army. He telegraphed at 9.40 a.m. on October 3 asking the French War Minister to make all preparations to send the proposed two divisions with cavalry and artillery complete as soon as possible and to let him know how soon they could be dispatched.

He was asked in reply whether he would prefer one Territorial Division with a complete brigade of *Fusiliers Marins*. He replied that he preferred the two divisions, and that the question of time was of the greatest importance and urgency. He was told, however, that it had been decided to send the *Fusiliers Marins* after all. He replied that whichever was most convenient to the French should be sent, so long as it was sent with the least delay possible. He telegraphed to his Staff Officer in Antwerp, Colonel Dallas, at 2.15 p.m., October 3:—

> 'What force in your opinion would suffice? Give full details of what troops are most required to deal with the situation in co-operation with the Belgian Field Army.
>
> 'The French Government say they will send two divisions with full complement of cavalry and artillery, but I do not yet know when they will be available. If a corps of our troops, under Sir John French, together with the 7th Division and cavalry division from here, [were] concentrated at Lille in order to attack the right flank of the main German Army and drive it back, would this action, if accomplished in about four or five days, in your opinion, relieve the situation at Antwerp quickly enough to prevent the fall of the place, or must any troops employed to relieve Antwerp be sent there via Zeebrugge, and, if so, can you give me approximately the longest time we can have to get troops there, so that I can inform the French Government?'

At 7.35 on the same afternoon the composition of the French contingent was received from the British Ambassador:—

> '87th Territorial Division from Havre, under General Roy, consisting of 12 battalions of infantry, 2 groups of artillery (90 millimetre guns), 2 squadrons of reserve cavalry (Dragoons), now being formed at Dunkirk, 1 engineer company, headquarters and staff and usual services attached to a division.
>
> 'The Fusiliers Marins brigade, under command of Rear-Admiral Ronarc'h, will be composed of two regiments of Fusiliers Marins (6,000), 86 mitrailleuses manned by seamen (260), 1 regiment of Zouaves (2,000). Total of contingent about 23,000 men.
>
> 'The Havre division will embark there on 5th October, and should be landed at Dunkirk 7th October.
>
> 'The Fusiliers Marins brigade will be sent to Dunkirk by land instead of by sea. It will arrive at Dunkirk at about same time as the Territorial division, namely, 7th October.'

* * * * *

I did not reach Antwerp till after 3 p.m., and after consulting with Colonel Dallas I was visited by the Belgian Prime Minister. Monsieur de Broqueville was a man of exceptional vigour and clarity both of mind and speech. He had been called to the helm of the Belgian

State at the moment of the decision not to submit to wrongful aggression. He explained to me the situation with precision. General Deguise, the Commander of the fortress, added his comments. The outer forts were falling one by one. Five or six shells from the enormous German howitzers were sufficient to smash them to their foundations, to destroy their defenders even in the deepest casemates, and to wreck the platforms of the guns. Now the forts of the inner line were being similarly attacked, and there was no conceivable means of preventing their destruction one after another at the rate of about a fort a day. The army was tired and dispirited through having been left so long entirely upon its own resources without ever a sign of the Allies for whom they had risked so much. Material of every kind—guns, ammunition, searchlights, telephones, entrenching materials—was scanty. The water supply of the city had been cut off. There were many rumours of German sympathisers in its large population of 400,000. At any moment the front might be broken in under the heavy artillery attack which was then in progress. But this was only half the danger. The life and honour of the Belgian nation did not depend on Antwerp, but on its army. To lose Antwerp was disastrous; to lose the army as well was fatal. The Scheldt was barred by a severe interpretation of neutrality. The only line of retreat was by a dangerous flank march parallel to the Dutch frontier and the sea-coast. Two Belgian divisions and the cavalry division were staving off the Germans from this only remaining line of retreat. But the pressure was increasing and the line of the Dendre was no longer intact. If Ghent fell before the Belgian Army made good its retreat, nothing would be saved from the ruin.

In these circumstances they had decided first to withdraw to what was called the entrenched camp on the left bank of the Scheldt, that is to say, towards their right; and, secondly, in the same direction through Ghent towards the left flank of the Allied armies. These orders had been suspended in consequence of the telegram from the British Government.

I then exposed Lord Kitchener's plan and stated the numbers of the French and British troops already available for the assistance of the Belgian Army. I emphasized the importance of holding the city and delaying the Germans as long as possible without compromising the retreat of the army. I pointed out that the issue of the battle for the seaward flank still hung in the balance, and that the main armies were drawing nearer to Belgium every day. I asked whether the relieving forces mentioned, if actually sent, would influence their decision. They replied that this was a new situation; that had this help been forthcoming earlier, events might have taken a different course. Even now, if their line of retreat were safeguarded by the arrival of Allied troops in the neighbourhood of Ghent, they were prepared to continue the resistance. I thereupon drew up, with their approval and agreement, the following telegram to Lord Kitchener:—

Antwerp, October 3, 1914, 6.53 p.m. (*received* 9.45 p.m.)

'Subject to confirmation on both sides, I have made following arrangement with M. de Broqueville, Prime Minister:—

'Every preparation to be made by Belgian Government now for a resistance of at least ten days, and every step taken with utmost energy. Within three days we are to state definitely whether we can launch big field operation for their relief or not, and when it will probably take effect. If we cannot give them a satisfactory assurance of substantial assistance within three days, they are to be quite free to abandon defence if they think fit. In this case, should they wish to clear out with field army, we (although not able to launch the big operation) are to help their field army to get away by sending covering troops to Ghent or other points on line of retreat. Thus, anything they will have lost in time by going on defending Antwerp with all their strength will be made up to them as far as possible by help on their way out.

'Further, we will meanwhile help their local defence in all minor ways, such as guns, marines, naval brigades, etc.

I have put the terms high to avoid at all costs our undertaking anything we could not perform, and also to avoid hurry in our saying what troops we can spare for big operations. You will be able, as your telegram No. 7 (to Colonel Dallas) indicates, to do much better than this, and to give decided promise within three days, but the vital thing is that Belgian Government and army should forthwith hurl themselves with revived energy into the defence.

'Attack is being harshly pressed at this moment, and half measures would be useless, but Prime Minister informs me that they are confident they can hold out for three days, pretty sure they can hold out for six, and will try ten.

'This arrangement, if adopted, will give time necessary for problem to be solved calmly.

'Two thousand marines are arriving this evening.

'I am remaining here till to-morrow.

'I have read this telegram to Belgian Prime Minister, who says that we are in full agreement, subject to ratification by Council of Ministers which is now being held.

'If you clinch these propositions, pray give the following order to the Admiralty: Send at once both naval brigades, minus recruits, via Dunkirk, into Antwerp, with five days' rations and 2,000,000 rounds of ammunition, but without tents or much impedimenta.

'When can they arrive?'

I had been met on arrival by Admiral Oliver, the Director of the Naval Intelligence Division. This officer had been sent by the Admiralty on September 29 to see what could be done to disable the large quantity of merchant shipping which lay in the Scheldt, so that if the city fell it could not be used by the Germans for embarking troops to invade England. He was a great stand-by in this time of stress. Night and day he laboured on the ships. With the assistance only of a Belgian sapper officer, four privates and a Belgian boy scout, he inserted explosive charges between the cylinders of thirty-eight large vessels, and by this means ruptured the propelling machinery so that not one of them was fit to go down the Scheldt during the whole of the German occupation.

While waiting for the reply from London that afternoon and also the next morning, I went out and examined the front: a leafy enclosed country, absolutely flat; a crescent of peering German kite balloons; a continuous bombardment; scarcely anything in the nature of an infantry attack; wearied and disheartened defenders. It was extremely difficult to get a clear view and so understand what kind of fighting was actually going on. We were, however, at length able to reach the actual inundations beyond which the enemy was posted. Entrenching here was impossible for either side, owing to the water met with at a foot's depth. The Belgian pickets crouched behind bushes. There was at that moment no rifle fire, but many shells traversed the air overhead on their way to the Belgian lines.

Although the artillery fire of the Germans at Antwerp was at no time comparable to the great bombardments afterwards endured on the Western Front, it was certainly severe. The Belgian trenches were broad and shallow, and gave hardly any protection to their worn-out and in many cases inexperienced troops. As we walked back from the edge of these inundations along a stone-paved highroad, it was a formidable sight to see on either hand the heavy shells bursting in salvoes of threes and fours with dense black smoke near or actually inside these scanty shelters in which the supporting troops were kneeling in fairly close order. Every prominent building—château, tower or windmill—was constantly under fire; shrapnel burst along the roadway, and half a mile to the left a wooded enclosure was speckled with white puffs. Two or three days at least would be required to make sound breastworks or properly constructed and drained trenches or rifle pits. Till then it must be mainly an affair of hedges and of houses; and the ineffective trenches were merely shell traps.

Antwerp presented a case, till the Great War unknown, of an attacking force marching methodically without regular siege operations through a permanent fortress line behind advancing curtains of artillery fire. Fort after fort was wrecked by the two or three monster howitzers; and line after line of shallow trenches was cleared by the fire of field-guns. And following gingerly upon these iron footprints, German infantry, weak in numbers, raw in training, inferior in quality, wormed and waddled their way forward into 'the second strongest fortress in Europe.'

As the fire of the German guns drew ever nearer to the city, and the shells began to fall each day upon new areas, the streams of country folk escaping from their ruined homes trickled pitifully along the roads, interspersed with stragglers and wounded. Antwerp itself preserved a singular calm. The sunlit streets were filled with people listening moodily to the distant firing. The famous spires and galleries of this ancient seat of wealth and culture, the spacious warehouses along the Scheldt, the splendid hotels 'with every modern convenience,' the general air of life, prosperity and civilization created an impression of serene security wholly contradicted by the underlying facts. It was a city in a trance.

The Marines did not arrive until the morning of the 4th, and went immediately into the line. When I visited them the same evening they were already engaged with the Germans in the outskirts of Lierre. Here, for the first time, I saw German soldiers creeping forward from house to house or darting across the street. The Marines fired with machine-guns from a balcony. The flashes of the rifles and the streams of flame pulsating from the mouth of the machine-guns, lit up a warlike scene amid crashing reverberations and the whistle of bullets.

Twenty minutes in a motor-car, and we were back in the warmth and light of one of the best hotels in Europe, with its perfectly appointed tables and attentive servants all proceeding as usual!

* * * * *

The reply of the British Government reached me on the morning of the 4th, and I sent it at once to Monsieur de Broqueville.

Lord Kitchener to First Lord.

Am arranging Expeditionary Force for relief of Antwerp as follows:—

British Force.

7th Division, 18,000 men, 63 guns, under General Capper. Cavalry Division, 4,000 men, 12 guns, under General Byng, to arrive at Zeebrugge 6th and 7th October. Naval detachment, 8,000 men already there, under General Aston, also Naval and Military heavy guns and detachments already sent. Headquarter Staff will be subsequently notified.

French Force.

Territorial Division, 15,000 men, proper complement of guns and 2 squadrons, General Roy, to arrive Ostend 6th to 9th October. Fusiliers Marins Brigade, 8,000 men, under Rear-Admiral Ronarc'h. Grand total, 53,000 men. Numbers are approximately correct.

Also one from Prince Louis, 10.30 a.m.:—

'The Naval Brigades will embark at Dover at 4 p.m. for Dunkirk, where they should arrive between 7 or 8 o'clock. Provisions and ammunition as indicated in your telegram.'

Monsieur de Broqueville replied:—

Anvers, le 4 *octobre*, 1914.

J'ai l'honneur de vous confirmer notre accord sur les points envisagés tantôt.

Comme je vous l'ai dit dès notre première conversation, nous entendons, coûte que coûte, conserver Anvers. C'est pour nous un devoir national de premier ordre.

Je tiens à vous répéter aussi que, si nous avons été sérieusement affectés de ne pas voir nos puissants garants répondre plus tôt à nos demandes de secours, notre volonté de lutter jusqu' à la mort n'a pas été affaiblie un seul instant. L'appui des 9,000 fusiliers de marine envoyés par votre Gouvernement hier et demain est pour la conservation de la place d'Anvers un appui précieux.

Plus précieux encore est l'envoi de la 7e division, appuyée par la 3e division de cavalerie.

Il serait d'extrême importance que ces troupes soient dirigées sur Gand avec le maximum de célérité: les heures ont en ce moment une exceptionnelle valeur.

Les hautes autorités militaires et le Gouvernement tout entier, consultés par moi, acceptent avec une véritable satisfaction l'entente qui s'est établie entre nous.

Le Gouvernement a appris avec un sentiment de véritable gratitude que, s'il venait à être fait prisonnier, le Gouvernement de la Grande-Bretagne ne traiterait pas sans son assentiment des questions intéressant le sort de la Belgique au moment où se négociera la paix.

Je me félicite tout particulièrement des relations si sympathiques que je viens d'avoir avec l'éminent homme d'Etat envoyé ici par la grande nation si hautement appréciée et aimée par la Belgique.

The matter had now passed into the region of pure action. Could Antwerp resist the enemy's attack long enough to enable the French and British relieving force to come to her aid? Secondly, if this succeeded, could nine or ten Allied divisions at Antwerp and Ghent hold the Germans in check until the left wing of the main armies, advancing daily from the south, could join hands with them? In that case the Allied lines in the west might be drawn through Antwerp, Ghent and Lille. All this turned on a few days, and even on a few hours.

Judged by the number of troops available on both sides, the chances of the Allies appeared good. On paper they were nearly twice as strong as the enemy. But the Belgian Army had been left without aid or comfort too long. The daily destruction of their trusted forts, the harsh and unceasing bombardment of a vastly superior artillery, their apprehensions for their line of retreat, the cruel losses and buffetings they had suffered since the beginning of the war, had destroyed their confidence and exhausted their strength.

The prime and vital need was to maintain the defence of Antwerp against the unceasing artillery attack to which its whole southern front was exposed. The position behind the river was capable of being made a strong one. It was, potentially, stronger in many respects than the line of the Yser, along which a fortnight later this same Belgian Army, in spite of further losses and discouragements, was to make a most stubborn and glorious defence. But despondency in the face of an apparently irresistible artillery, and the sense of isolation, struck a deadly chill.

Meanwhile, however, help was hurrying forward. The Marines were already in the line. Armoured trains with naval guns and British bluejackets came into action on the morning of the 4th. The two Naval Brigades reached Dunkirk that night, and were due to enter Antwerp on the evening of the 5th. At the special request of the Belgian Staff they were to be interspersed with Belgian divisions to impart the encouragement and assurance that succour was at hand.

The British 7th Division and 3rd Cavalry Division, carried daringly across the water upon personal orders from Prince Louis in the teeth of submarines, began to disembark at Ostend and Zeebrugge from the morning of the 6th onward. The French division was embarking at Havre. Admiral Ronarc'h and his 8,000 Fusiliers Marins were already entrained for Dunkirk. If only Antwerp could hold out. . . .

Meanwhile, also, it must be remembered, Sir John French was secretly withdrawing the British Army from the Aisne and moving round behind the French front to the neighbourhood of St. Omer with the intention of striking at Lille and beating in the German right. Every day that large German forces were detained in front of Antwerp helped and covered the detrainment and deployment of his army and increased its chances of success. But every day became graver also the peril to the Belgian Army of being cut off if, after all, the Germans should be the victors in the main battle.

The anxieties and uncertainties of this tremendous situation had to be supported by the Belgian chiefs in addition to those of the actual German attack battering on the crumbling Antwerp front and its exhausted defenders. That they were borne with constancy and coolness, that the defence was prolonged for five momentous days, and that although the Antwerp front was broken in before effective help could arrive, the Belgian Field Army was safely extricated, was a memorable achievement.

The attitude of the King and Queen through these tense and tragic days was magnificent. The impression of the grave, calm soldier King presiding at Council, sustaining his troops and commanders, preserving an unconquerable majesty amid the ruin of his kingdom, will never pass from my mind.

Meanwhile Lord Kitchener and Prince Louis continued to give the necessary orders from London.

I now found myself suddenly, unexpectedly and deeply involved in a tremendous and hideously critical local situation which might well continue for some time. I had also assumed a very direct responsibility for exposing the city to bombardment and for bringing into it the inexperienced, partially equipped and partially trained battalions of the Royal Naval Division. I felt it my duty to see the matter through. On the other hand, it was not right to leave the Admiralty without an occupant. I therefore telegraphed on the 4th to the Prime Minister offering to take formal military charge of the British forces in Antwerp and tendering my resignation of the office of First Lord of the Admiralty. This offer was not accepted. I have since learned that Lord Kitchener wrote proposing that it should be, and wished to give me the necessary military rank. But other views prevailed: and I certainly have no reason for regret that they did so. I was informed that Sir Henry Rawlinson was being sent to the city and was requested to do my best until he arrived.

October 5 was a day of continuous fighting. The situation fluctuated from hour to hour. I print the telegrams of this day in their sequence:—

I telegraphed to Lord Kitchener:—

10.18 a.m., *October* 5.

'Line of the Nethe is intact. Marine Brigade holding important sector north-west of Lierre, has been briskly engaged during the night, with about seventy casualties so far. It seems not unlikely that the German attack will be directed on this point, as passage of river is easier there. I am making sure that they are properly supported by detachment of artillery. General Paris is doing very well.

'Later. Infantry attack indicated now appears to be developing.'

12.22 p.m.

'It is my duty to remain here and continue my direction of affairs unless relieved by some person of consequence, in view of the situation and developing German attack. Prospects will not be unfavourable if we can hold out for next three days. We have a good deal of ground to sell, if it is well disputed, even if Nethe River is forced.'

4.45 p.m.

Lord Kitchener to First Lord:—

'I expect Rawlinson will reach Antwerp to-day. It is most necessary that Belgians should not give way before the forces now on the sea arrive for their support. You know date of arrival of troops at Ostend and Zeebrugge. I cannot accelerate anything owing to difficulties of navigation. Prince Louis is doing all he can. Are any of the guns we sent in action? Our 9.2 on line to Lierre ought to be useful. I hope Belgians realize the importance of holding Termonde so that relieving force may act promptly on the German left flank. The arrival of our troops should be kept very secret; by moving at night a surprise might be possible in the early morning.'

4.45 p.m.

First Lord to Lord Kitchener:—

'Attack has been pressed. Marines have stood well, with some loss, but, on their right a regiment has fallen back under shell fire, and some German infantry to west of Lierre are across Nethe. General Paris has ordered four Belgian battalions and his reserve battalion to join another Belgian brigade to drive them back and reoccupy positions. This is now in progress. Every effort is being made to gain time. At 9 p.m. to-night I am to attend Council of Ministers. I can get no news of time of arrival of naval brigades. They will be wanted to-morrow for certain.'

7 p.m.

Lord Kitchener to First Lord:—

'I hear the Marine Fusilier Brigade had not arrived as expected at Dunkirk to-day by train. I have in consequence telegraphed to French Government as follows:—

'"As the Marine Fusilier Brigade is moving by train, and their arrival at Antwerp is urgently required, please ask Minister of War to continue their journey by train to Antwerp."

'You might, I think, inform Belgian authorities, so as to have facilities for this force of 8,000 to proceed to wherever you think they would be most usefully employed without stopping at Ostend, and if they have not passed Dunkirk they might be warned of their destination.'

6.46 p.m.

First Lord to Lord Kitchener:—

'We now hold all our positions along the Nethe, our counterattack having been successful. Germans will probably throw bridges in night at Lierre. On outskirts of Lierre we are in contact with Germans. I have just returned from advanced trenches and find marines cheerful and well dug in.

'General Paris does not think that he has lost more than 150 men killed and wounded.

'I presume you keep Sir John French informed.'

7.15 p.m.

Admiralty to First Lord:—

'Sir H. Rawlinson just leaving Dunkirk for Antwerp via Bruges, where he stays to-night. Dunkirk reports naval brigades arrive Antwerp 1 a.m. Tuesday. First six transports, containing 10,000 troops, 2,000 horses, should arrive Zeebrugge from 4 a.m. onwards; 9,000 troops, 2,500 horses, arrive partly at Ostend, mainly at Zeebrugge. Wednesday morning; 2,500 cavalry, 2,500 horses, arrive partly Ostend, partly Zeebrugge, Thursday morning.'

8.45 p.m.

Lord Kitchener to Colonel Dallas:—

'You have been appointed as General Staff Officer on Expeditionary Force. Warn everybody to keep movement of troops absolutely secret. Try and bring off a complete or partial surprise on enemy's left; for this purpose movements of troops from sea-coast should be as much as possible at night. Am sending flying squadron, which will, I hope, protect troops from too inquisitive enemy's aircraft. Sir Henry Rawlinson has been appointed to chief command and will shortly arrive Antwerp.

'All movements going as arranged.'

In the evening I went to General Paris' Headquarters on the Lierre road for the purpose of putting him in command of the other two Naval Brigades about to arrive. The fire along this road was now heavier. Shrapnel burst overhead as I got out of the car and struck down a man at my feet. As we discussed around the cottage table, the whole house thudded and shook from minute to minute with the near explosions of shells whose flashes lit the window panes. In such circumstances was it that General Paris received from the representative of the Admiralty the command of the Royal Naval Division which he was destined to hold with so much honour until he fell grievously wounded in his trenches after three years' war. This was the most important military command exercised in the great war by an officer of the Royal Marines.

The general result of the fighting on the 5th raised our hopes. The counter-attack by one British and nine Belgian battalions drove the enemy back. All the positions that had been lost were regained, and the line of the Nethe was almost re-established. At midnight at the Belgian Headquarters General Deguise received in my presence by telephone a favourable report from every single sector. The enemy had, however, succeeded in maintaining a foothold across the river, and it seemed certain they would throw bridges in the night. General Deguise therefore resolved to make a further counter-attack under the cover of darkness in the hope of driving the enemy altogether across the river. At 1 a.m. I telegraphed as follows:—

Antwerp, *October* 6, 1 a.m.

First Lord to Lord Kitchener and Sir E. Grey:—

'All well. All positions are held along the Nethe. I hope you will not decide finally on plan of operations till I can give you my views. I have met Ministers in Council, who resolved to fight it out here, whatever happens.

'No 9.2's have arrived yet, even at Ostend.'

It was 2 o'clock before I went to bed. I had been moving, thinking and acting with very brief intervals for nearly four days in Council and at the front in circumstances of undefined but very onerous responsibility. Certainly the situation seemed improved. The line of the Nethe was practically intact and the front unbroken. The Naval Brigades, already a day behind my hopes, were arriving in the morning. By land and sea troops were hastening forward. All the various personalities and powers were now looking the same way and working for the same object. France and Britain, the Admiralty and the War Office, the Belgian Government and the Belgian Command were all facing in the same direction. Rawlinson would arrive to-morrow, and my task would be concluded. But what would the morrow bring forth? I was now very tired, and slept soundly for some hours.

All through the night the fighting was continual, but no definite reports were available up till about 9 o'clock. At the Belgian Headquarters I was told that the Belgian night attack had miscarried, that the Germans were counter-attacking strongly, that the Belgian troops were very tired and the situation along the Nethe obscure. General Paris and the Marine Brigade were also heavily engaged. The Naval Brigades had arrived and detrained and were now marching to their assigned positions in the line. But where was the line? It was one thing to put these partially trained and ill-equipped troops into a trench line, and quite another to involve them in the manœuvres of a moving action. Solidly dug in with their rifles and plenty of ammunition, these ardent, determined men would not be easily dislodged. But they were not capable of manœuvre. It seemed to me that they should take up an intermediate position until we knew what was happening on the front. General Paris was involved in close fighting with his brigade, and had not been able to take over command of the whole force. It was necessary therefore for me to give personal directions. I motored to the Belgian Headquarters, told General Deguise that these new troops must have fixed positions to fight in, and would be wasted if flung in piecemeal. I proposed to stop them about four miles short of their original destination as a support and rallying line for the Belgian troops who were falling back. He agreed that this was wise and right, and 1 went myself to see that the orders were carried out.

The moment one left the city gates the streams of wounded and of fugitives betokened heavy and adverse fighting. Shells from the enemy's field artillery were falling frequently on roads and villages which yesterday were beyond his range. We were by no means sure at what point the flow of refugees would end and the wave of pursuers begin. However, by about midday the three Naval and Marine Brigades were drawn up with the Belgian reserves astride of the Antwerp-Lierre road on the line Contich-Vremde.

In this position we awaited the next development and expected to be almost immediately attacked. The Germans to our relief did not molest the retirement of the three Belgian divisions. They waited to gather strength and to bring up and use again the remorseless artillery upon which they were mainly relying. As no German infantry appeared and no heavy bombardment began, the Naval Brigades moved forward in their turn and took up positions nearer to where the enemy had halted. I remained in the line on the Lierre road. Here at about 5 o'clock Sir Henry Rawlinson joined me.

The General took, as might be expected, a robust view of the situation, and was by no means disposed to give up the quarrel either on the Antwerp front or on the line of communications, which were already being more severely pressed. In fact I found in this officer, whom I had known for many years, that innate, instinctive revolt against acquiescing in the will of the enemy which is an invaluable quality in military men. These sentiments were also shared by Colonel Bridges, former British military attaché in Belgium, who had arrived from Sir John French. At 7 o'clock a Council of War was held in the Palace under the presidency of the King. We affirmed the readiness and ability of the British Government to execute punctually and fully the engagements into which we had entered two days earlier. But the Belgian chiefs were convinced that even if the Antwerp front along the line of the Nethe could be restored, the danger to their communications had become so great that they must without delay resume the movement of their army to the left bank of the Scheldt, which had been interrupted three days previously. Here they conceived themselves able to join hands with any Anglo-French relieving force while at the same time securing their own retreat on Ghent, which they had already on September 4 reinforced by a brigade. It was not for us to contest their view, and events have shown that they were right. The arrangements set out in the following telegram were made:—

Antwerp, October 6, 10.37 p.m.

First Lord to Lord Kitchener:—

'Germans attacked our position along the Nethe early this morning. Belgian troops on the right of Marine brigade were overpowered. General retirement with some loss was effected to a lightly entrenched position on the line Contich-Vremde, where enemy are not for the moment pressing. Germans will be enabled to bombard city to-morrow owing to lost ground. In view of this and of complete exhaustion and imminent demoralization of Belgian Army, Rawlinson, who has arrived, has, with my full agreement and that of Belgian General Staff, ordered a general retirement to inner line of forts. The three naval brigades will hold intervals between forts and be supported by about a dozen Belgian battalions. On this line, which is very strong against infantry attack, our troops can certainly hold out as long as the city will endure bombardment. Had naval brigades arrived 24 hours earlier, we could probably have held line of the Nethe. They have not been engaged, and marines have not lost more than 200 men.

'This evening Rawlinson and I attended a council of war presided over by the King. We suggested an attempt to re-establish Anglo-Belgian forces on line of the Nethe by employing 7th Division in a counter-attack in 48 hours' time, but they had all clearly made up their minds that their army was not in a fit condition to co-operate in any offensive movement. Accordingly we have arranged with them:—

'(1) That while the town endures bombardment General Paris with naval division and Belgian support will defend inner line forts to the utmost.

'(2) That the rest of the Belgian Field Army shall be immediately withdrawn across the Scheldt to what they call the entrenched camp of the left bank. This area is protected by the Scheldt, various forts and entrenchments, and large inundations, and here they hope to find time to recover and re-form. From this position they will aid to the best of their ability any relieving movement which may be possible from the west.

'(3) Rawlinson will organize relieving force at Ghent and Bruges and prepare to move forward as soon as possible.

'But I shall hope to-morrow to convince you that it should be strengthened for the operation.

'We are all agreed that in the circumstances there is no other course open.

'I return with Rawlinson to-night to Bruges, and early to-morrow morning shall be in London.

'Aviation park and heavy guns will be moved from Antwerp.'

General Rawlinson and I left the city together that night, and after an anxious drive over roads luckily infested by nothing worse than rumour, I boarded the *Attentive* at Ostend and returned to England.

So far as the personal aspect of this story is concerned, I cannot feel that I deserve the reproaches and foolish fictions which have been so long freely and ignorantly heaped upon me. I could not foresee that the mission I undertook would keep me away from the Admiralty for more than forty-eight hours, or that I should find myself involved in another set of special responsibilities outside the duties of the office which I held. No doubt had I been ten years older, I should have hesitated long before accepting so unpromising a task. But the events occurred in the order I have described; and at each stage the action which I took seemed right, natural and even inevitable. Throughout I was held in the grip of emergencies and of realities which transcended considerations of praise or blame.[3]

But, after all, it is by the results and as a whole that the episode will be judged; and these as will be shown were certainly advantageous to the Allied cause.

After the departure of the Belgian Field Army the further defence of the remaining lines of Antwerp was left to the fortress troops, the 2nd Belgian Division, and the three British Naval Brigades, who held on their front the equivalent of more than five complete German divisions, to wit: the 5th Reserve, 6th Reserve, 4th Ersatz and Marine Division, and the 26th, 37th, and 1st Bavarian Landwehr Brigades.

At midnight on the 7th the Germans, having advanced their artillery, began to bombard the city and the forts of the inner line. The forts melted under the fire, and a great proportion of the civil population fled through the night, lighted by conflagrations, over the bridges of the Scheldt to the open country, along the roads towards Ghent or into Holland. The enemy's attack was pressed continuously, and the enceinte of the city was considered to be untenable by the evening of the 8th. The Belgian Division and the British Naval Brigades evacuated Antwerp that night, crossed the Scheldt safely, and began their retreat by road and rail on Ghent and Ostend. Two naval airmen,[4] as a Parthian shot, blew up after long flights a Zeppelin in its shed at Düsseldorf and bombed the railway station at Cologne. German patrols, after many precautions, entered Antwerp towards evening on the 9th, and on the 10th the stouthearted Governor, who had retired to one of the surviving forts, capitulated.

The resistance of the city had been prolonged by five days.

---

[3]But see Lord Esher: 'One night he (Kitchener) was in bed asleep, when Mr. Churchill, then First Lord of the Admiralty, bursting into the room, pleaded for the War Minister's permission to leave at once for Antwerp. In spite of the late hour, Sir Edward Grey arrived in the middle of the discussion, and while he was engaging Lord Kitchener's attention, Mr. Churchill slipped away. He was next heard of when a telegram from Antwerp was put into Lord K.'s hands, in which his impetuous colleague asked bravely to be allowed to resign his great office, to be given command of a Naval Brigade, and pleading that reinforcements should be hurried out to those "forlorn and lonely men," as he called them, who were vainly trying to hold on to the Antwerp lines. Lord K. was not upset, but he was not unmoved, etc. . . .'—*The Tragedy of Lord Kitchener*, p. 67.

It is remarkable that Lord Esher should be so much astray; for during the war I showed him the text of the telegrams printed in this chapter and now made public for the first time. We must conclude that an uncontrollable fondness for fiction forbade him to forsake it for fact. Such constancy is a defect in an historian.

W.S.C

[4]Commanders Marix and Spenser-Grey.

CHAPTER XVI
THE CHANNEL PORTS

'This battle fares like to the morning's war,
When dying clouds contend with growing light;
What time the shepherd, blowing of his nails,
Can neither call it perfect day, nor night.
Nor sways it this way, like a mighty sea
Forc'd by the tide to combat with the wind;
Nor sways it that way, like the self-same sea
Forc'd to retire by fury of the wind:
Sometime, the flood prevails, and then, the wind:
Now, one the better; then, another, best;
Both tugging to be victors, breast to breast,
Yet neither conqueror, nor conquerèd:
So is the equal poise of this fell war.'

King Henry VI (Part III).

The Purpose of the Antwerp Effort—The Belgian Army effects its Retreat—Loss and Gain—Ten Precious Days—Onslaught of the German Reinforcements—The Struggle for the Channel Ports—Labours of the Admiralty—Achievements of the Transport Department—Correspondence with Sir John French—General Joffre requests Naval Support—Admiral Hood's Operations on the Belgian Coast—Commodore Tyrwhitt destroys the German Torpedo Boats—The German Armies reach Salt Water—Beginning of the Battle of the Yser—The Inshore Squadron—'One Flank the Germans cannot turn'—Further Correspondence with Sir John French—The Crisis of the Battle—The German Advance Stemmed—Effect of Antwerp on the Main Decision.

The object of prolonging the defence of Antwerp was, as has been explained, to give time for the French and British Armies to rest their left upon that fortress and hold the Germans from the seaboard along a line Antwerp–Ghent–Lille. This depended not only upon the local operations but on the result of the series of outflanking battles which marked the race for the sea. A decisive victory gained by the French in the neighbourhood of Peronne, or by the British beyond Armentières and towards Lille, would have opened all this prospect. High French authorities have concluded that a more rapid and therefore no doubt more daring transference of force from the right and centre of the French front to its left, 'looking sixty kilometres ahead instead of twenty-five,' and generally a more vigorous attempt to outflank the Germans following immediately upon the victory of the

Marne and the arrest of the armies at the Aisne, might well have shouldered the Germans not only away from the sea, but even out of a large part of occupied France. In the event, however, and with the forces employed, the French and British did not succeed in turning the enemy's flank. The battles at Albert, La Bassée and Armentières produced no decisive result; Peronne and Lille could not be reached and the fighting lines continued simply to prolong themselves to the north-west. The retention of Antwerp would have rewarded the victory of the main armies with a prize of the utmost value. Its extended resistance diminished the consequences of their failure. Everything at Antwerp had depended on a victory to the southward. And this victory had been denied. Nevertheless, as will now be shown, the effort was fruitful in a remarkable degree.

The fall of Antwerp released the besieging army. A marine division marched into the city on the 10th.[1] The rest of the German divisions were already streaming south and west in hot pursuit, and hoped for interception of the Belgian Army. But a surprise awaited them.

On the night of the 9th the German forces who had crossed the Dendre river had come in contact with French Fusiliers Marins at Melle and Meirelbeke, and during the 10th they found themselves in presence of British regular troops of unknown strength, whose patrols were feeling their way forward from Ghent to meet them. The 7th Division and the 3rd Cavalry Division had come upon the scene in accordance with the fourth condition of the Anglo-Belgian agreement of October 4. The British, French and Belgian forces from Ghent thus threatened the left frank of any serious German cutting-off movement northwards to the Dutch frontier.

Uncertain of the size of the army by which they were confronted, and mystified by the indefinite possibilities of landings from the sea, the Germans paused to collect their strength. They knew that the bulk of the British Army had already left the Aisne. Where was it? Where would it reappear? What were these British regulars, who stood so confidently in their path? On the 12th when they considered themselves strong enough to advance upon Ghent, the whole of the Belgian Field Army had passed the dangerous points in safety, only one single squadron being intercepted. Of this complicated operation the victorious Germans became spectators.

Only weak parties of Germans ventured beyond Lokeren during the night of the 9th–10th to molest the retreat of the Antwerp troops. The 2nd Belgian Division and two out of the three Naval Brigades, came through intact. But the railway and other arrangements for the rear brigade were misunderstood, and about two and a half battalions of very tired troops, who through the miscarriage of an order had lost some hours, were led across the Dutch frontier in circumstances on which only those who know their difficulties are entitled to form a judgment.

If the Belgian Field Army had begun its withdrawal on October 3, as originally intended, it could probably have got safely without aid to Ghent and beyond. But the fortress troops, numbering many thousands, to whom it had been throughout resolved

[1]It was perhaps an unconscious recognition of the naval significance of Antwerp that all three great Powers—Germany, France and Britain—used in its attack and defence Naval Brigades formed since the outbreak of war.

to confide the last defence of Antwerp, must in any case have been driven into surrender to the invader or internment in Holland once the Field Army had gone. The prolongation of the defence and the delay in the departure of the Field Army neither bettered nor worsened their fortunes. They, therefore, do not enter into any calculation of the loss and gain attendant on the attempted operation of relief. So far as actual results are concerned, the damage caused by the bombardment of the city, which was not extensive, and the internment of two and a half British Naval battalions, on the one hand, must be weighed against the gain of five days in the resistance and the influence exercised on subsequent events by the 7th Division and 3rd Cavalry Division on the other.

At the time the British Government decided to send help to Antwerp the total German field force in Northern Belgium had been correctly estimated at four or five divisions. But before the city capitulated and while the British troops were still at Ghent, there began to manifest itself that tremendous unexpected development of German force which from the moment of Antwerp's fall was launched against the Allied left and aimed at Calais.

Besides the liberated Siege Army and the troops which had threatened the Antwerp communications, no fewer than four fresh Army Corps (XXIInd, XXIIIrd, XXVIth and XXVIIth), newly formed in Germany and concentrating in Belgium, were already at hand. And in front of this formidable army there stood from October 10 to October 21 only the wearied Belgians, the Fusiliers Marins, and the British 3rd Cavalry and 7th Divisions. The caution of the German advance may perhaps have been induced by their uncertainty as to the whereabouts and intentions of the British Army, and their fear that it might be launched against their right from the sea flank. But, however explained, the fact remains, and to it we owe the victory of the Yser and Ever-Glorious Ypres.

A simple examination of dates will reveal the magnitude of the peril which the Allied cause escaped. Antwerp fell twenty-four hours after the last division of the Belgian Field Army left the city. Had this taken place on October 3rd or 4th, the city would have surrendered on the 4th or 5th. No British 4th Corps[2] or Fusiliers Marins would have been at Ghent to cover the Belgian retreat. But assuming that the Belgian Army had made this good unaided, the same marches would have carried them *and their German pursuers* to the Yser by the 10th. There would have been nothing at all in front of Ypres. Sir John French could not come into action north of Armentières till the 15th. His detrainments at St. Omer, etc., were not completed till the 19th. Sir Douglas Haig with the 1st Corps could not come into line north of Ypres till about the 21st. Had the German Siege Army been released on the 5th, and, followed by their great reinforcements already available, advanced at once, nothing could have saved Dunkirk, and perhaps Calais and Boulogne. The loss of Dunkirk was certain and that of both Calais and Boulogne probable. Ten days were wanted, and ten days were won.

* * * * *

We had now without respite to meet the great German drive against the Channel ports. The six divisions released from the siege of Antwerp, and the eight new divisions, whose

---

[2]Rawlinson's Force was so styled.

apparition had been so unexpected to the British and French Staffs, rolled southward in a double-banked wave. The Belgian Army trooped back in a melancholy procession along the sea-shore to the Yser. General Rawlinson, with the 7th Division and the 3rd Cavalry Division, extricating himself skilfully from large German forces—how great was not then known—and lingering at each point to the last minute without becoming seriously engaged, found himself by October 15 in the neighbourhood of a place called Ypres.[3] Meanwhile Sir John French, detraining at St. Omer, and hopefully believing that he was turning the German right, struck through Armentières towards Lille, and sent imperative orders to Rawlinson, over whose head the storm was about to break, to advance in conformity and seize Menin. The French forces intended for the relief of Antwerp and the beginnings of larger French reinforcements endeavoured to close the gap between Rawlinson and the Belgians. The dykes were opened and large inundations began to appear. In this manner was formed a thin, new, loosely organized, yet continuous allied front from the neighbourhood of La Bassée to the sea at the mouth of the Yser; and upon this front, which grew up and fixed itself at every point in and by the actual collision of hostile forces, was now to be fought the third great battle in the West.

These events involved the Admiralty at many points. The position of Rawlinson's troops in the presence of vastly superior forces was precarious, and for some days we stood ready to re-embark them. We laboured to salve everything possible from the Belgian wreck. The Royal Naval Division must be brought back to refit, reorganize and resume its interrupted training. The Admiralty details—aeroplanes, armoured trains, armoured cars, motor omnibus transport, etc.—with which I had been endeavouring during the previous weeks to conceal our nakedness in the vital coastal area, could now be merged in the arriving British armies.

It would not have been possible to deal with these complications—themselves only one subsidiary part of our task—unless Prince Louis and I, working in complete accord, had had the power to give orders covering the whole business which were unquestioningly obeyed. Yet some of the orders which I was forced to give to the Admiralty Transport Department left me with misgivings that we were asking more than they could do. Fortunately, a few weeks before, I had taken the step of appointing in the place of the retired Admiral who usually directed this cardinal machine, the young civilian Assistant Director of Transports, whose abilities in conference and on paper were distinguished. Often in these weeks and in the succeeding months I had to turn to Mr. Graeme Thomson's department with hard and complex demands. Never did they fail. October 10 was the climax of their strain. I cannot do better than quote the minute I wrote at the time:—

October 10, 1914.

Secretary.
First Sea Lord.
Director of Transports and others concerned.

---

[3]The heavy losses of the 7th Division have often been attributed to their attempt to relieve Antwerp. In fact, however, these losses did not begin until after they had joined the main army.

1. Between 5,000 and 6,000 men of the R.N. Division are assembling at Ostend. They will not be ready to embark until to-morrow, the 11th. The whole of these, including Marines, should sail after dark on the 11th for Dover and proceed to the camp at Deal, all previous orders to the contrary being cancelled.

2. 1,500 Belgian recruits and volunteers are at Ostend and are to be embarked at once for Cherbourg, the French authorities being informed by telegram.

3. The transportation of the 11,000 Belgian recruits and reservists at Dunkirk to Cherbourg is to continue without intermission as rapidly as possible. The Belgians will be rationed by the Admiralty while on board ship, and the Belgians at Dunkirk will be rationed from the supplies of the R.N. Division until embarked.

4. All transports are to leave Zeebrugge at once, and all transports, other than those employed above, which are not accommodated in safe shelter at Ostend, are to leave in both cases for convenient British ports.

5. Enough transports to embark the 7th Division and the 3rd Cavalry Division are to be kept in immediate readiness, with steam up, for the next forty-eight hours, in Ostend, Dunkirk, Dover, and the Thames. It is unlikely, having regard to the military situation, that any re-embarkation will be required, but we must be continually prepared for it, and should an emergency arise, both Zeebrugge and Ostend must be used, notwithstanding any risks. Flotilla dispositions to be arranged accordingly. General Rawlinson to be informed that we are holding these ships in readiness, and that he should communicate direct with the Admiralty by telephone if at any moment the situation renders his re-embarkation likely. We are assuming that he could give us twelve hours' notice, within which time the transports could be counted upon.

6. All Marines and R.N. Division details at Dunkirk are to be re-embarked and brought back via Dover to Deal.

7. Colonel Osmaston's Marine Artillery are to remain at Dunkirk for the present.

8. The armoured trains and naval ratings working them, and all available aeroplanes and armed motor-cars, except those now at Dunkirk under the command of Commander Samson, are placed under the orders of General Rawlinson.

9. The three monitors are to be held in readiness, with steam up, to cover a re-embarkation at Ostend or Zeebrugge, should it become necessary. General Rawlinson is to be told to telephone or telegraph if at any time he thinks such naval protection will be required.

10. The Transport Department will provide whatever ships are necessary to carry the stores, ammunition and *matèriel* of the Belgian field army. The transports standing by for the 7th Division and the 3rd Cavalry Division are a prior claim on our resources. But as there is no doubt that we can meet the two, the Transport

Department is to get into direct telephonic communication with the Belgian authorities and arrange forthwith for the beginning of the embarkation of these stores. For the embarkation of stores, as apart from troops, Zeebrugge may be used equally with Ostend.

11. 8,000 to 10,000 Belgian wounded are to be evacuated from Ostend to England as speedily as possible. The Transport Department is to make proposals and preparations for their movement, while at the same time the necessary arrangements for their reception in this country are being concerted by the medical authorities.

12. All motor transports of the R.N. Division, excluding armed and other motor-cars under Commander Samson actually employed, are to be collected at Dunkirk under Colonel Dumble, who is to reorganize them as quickly as possible, and will receive further instructions on that subject. W. S. C.

It was with a feeling of relief and of admiration that I saw all these immense demands smoothly and punctually complied with.

While in Antwerp I had been in constant communication with Sir John French both through Colonel Bridges and by aeroplane. On October 5 he had written, 'Thank you so much for writing so fully and clearly to me from Antwerp. If the place is to be saved you have saved it by your prompt action. As a matter of principle I hate putting mobile troops *inside* a fortress, but in this case it is very likely that the *appearance* of a large force inside the place may have a great moral effect. But the situation ought to be most carefully watched. . . .' The Field-Marshal proceeded to complain of the exclusion by Lord Kitchener of the forces under General Rawlinson from the main British army. What would happen if and when he joined up with them? Other points of difference arose between the Commander-in-Chief and the Secretary of State. 'I shall do the best I can,' the former continued, 'to bring relief to the place at the earliest possible moment and am arranging to concentrate in the North as quickly as circumstances will allow. The Germans are pushing out their flank defence towards the West and South West. . . .' He expressed a wish that we could meet.

I replied to this on October 11 when the fate of Antwerp was already decided. Using my old and intimate friendship with the Field-Marshal, I laboured as always, to smooth the differences between him and Lord Kitchener.

I consider that Kitchener has been thoroughly loyal to you, and has done and is doing everything in human power to support you. It would be disastrous to the cause and ruinous to all if there were any breakdown in true comradeship between you and Kitchener. Military staffs always tend to make mischief between principals, and try to set their caps at each other.

The fall of Antwerp was a great and untimely injury to the Allied cause. I do not agree with the policy which abandoned it;[4] and I fear you will now have the army

[4]i.e., The absence of a greater French effort.

which was before Antwerp to meet almost immediately. But I care for nothing but the future in war. I clear my heart of all useless reflections and sterile controversies. It is vain to look backwards, and I turn my gaze with hope to the re-entry of the British army into the decisive centre of the struggle and pray for the victory.

I am arranging the omnibuses and armoured cars for you as quickly as possible. Rawlinson has got a very good naval armoured train which I have attached to him, but which you had better take over when he joins up.

The destruction of the Zeppelin and its shed was a gallant feat of arms.

Naval affairs at the moment imperatively keep me here—Alas! I hope you will not allow Joffre to deprive you of Dunkirk as your advanced base and fortified camp. In view of embarkation facilities Calais or Boulogne ought to be entrenched too—so that you have both. But we all feel Dunkirk is the right place, and belongs to you.

The wave of [German] reinforcements from the East, and the slow development of the Russian pressure, makes the situation rather grim just now.

I hope greatly to see you soon. Only five hours from your lines!

I earnestly trust the day goes well. But anyhow we will compel the end to do so.

You will want the big army I expect before your task is finished.

On October 16 General Joffre telegraphed to Lord Kitchener as follows:—

'Now that the operations extend up to the coast of the North Sea between Ostend and the advanced defences of Dunkirk, it would be important for the two Allied Navies to participate in these operations by supporting our left wing and acting with long-range guns on the German right wing. The Commander of the Naval Forces would then act in concert with General Foch through the Governor of Dunkirk.'

This duty we instantly accepted.

First Lord to Sir John French.

October 17, 1914.

Monitors were delayed by weather, but will be in position from daylight 18th; meanwhile eight destroyers should have arrived on the flank between 4 and 5 p.m. 17th, and two scout cruisers an hour later. They have been told to communicate with Colonel Bridges on the quays of Nieuport.

We are sending two battleships mounting eight 12-inch guns to Dunkirk roadstead to-morrow to cover the fortress and its coast approaches.

We set to work forthwith to support the Allied left flank. I entrusted this operation, which required an officer of first quality, to Admiral Hood, till then my Naval Secretary. He was now appointed to the Dover Command, while I took in his stead Admiral Oliver. On the 18th the three ex-Brazilian monitors, renamed *Humber*, *Mersey* and *Severn*, escorted by four destroyers, arrived at Dunkirk and the memorable series of naval operations on the Belgian Coast began.

There was no difficulty in finding plenty of ships of different classes to cover the flank of the army. Besides the three monitors, a large proportion of the destroyers from Dover were readily available. There were many old battleships, and these at certain states of the tide could get into suitable positions for bombarding. In addition there was the Scout class, seven of which were available, all happily newly rearmed with the very best 4-inch guns. But Admiralty reserves of ammunition had been based upon the needs of purely naval actions, which are few and far between, and not many of which all ships survive. Bombarding the German positions on the Belgian Coast week after week, and possibly for months, made demands upon our stores of a totally different character. We had to pick ships primarily for the class of ammunition they fired; ships that could use up old ammunition and ships whose value was so small that we could afford to spend all their ammunition. As October wore on we scoured the dockyards for every little vessel that carried a gun of any kind. Even the smallest gunnery tenders, 250-ton gunboats forty years old, were pressed into service, and in one way or another the fire was continuously maintained.

It was evident that these operations would have to be carried on under unceasing submarine attack. Moreover, we had to be prepared for a sudden dash by German cruisers and destroyers. We trusted to Commodore Tyrwhitt with the Harwich Striking Force either to protect us from this or to exact retribution on the return journey. On the 17th the Germans, torn between the will to wound and the fear to strike, broke all the commandments of the text-books by sending a feeble force of four small destroyers from the Ems down the Dutch Coast. They were almost immediately destroyed by the Commodore, the British ships engaged being the light cruiser *Undaunted* and the destroyers *Lance, Lennox, Legion and Loyal.*

From the middle of October onwards the German hosts could look upon salt water. First Zeebrugge was occupied, then Ostend, then mile by mile the sand-dunes and golf courses and gay villas of that pleasure coast were devoured by invading war. In his first contact with the new element the land monster committed several imprudences. Apparently contemptuous of the power of ships' guns, he deployed batteries of artillery on the open beach, and opened fire on our Scouts and destroyers. These experiments were not repeated. A Swedish writer, Dr. Sven Hedin, at that time with the German armies, belauding them and bowing obsequiously before what he had convinced himself was world-conquering power, has described a scene in the restaurant of the best Ostend hotel. The room was crowded with hungry officers of the invading army, just marched in, all sitting down to excellent fare.

> 'A destroyer had just detached itself from the rest and was making at full speed for Ostend, parallel with the coast, as close as possible to the shore. Presently another destroyer appeared, following in the wake of the first. What could they want, these ruffians? Strong language was heard—it was a piece of consummate impudence to come steaming right under our noses like this. Evidently they were

> reconnoitring—but what insolence, they must have known that we had occupied Ostend! Aha! they suspect that there are submarines and destroyers in the inner harbour, and want to see whether they can detect anything from outside! . . . Astounding insolence. Two small German guns are hurried up. "Are they going to shoot?" I asked. "Oh yes, they are going to shoot all right." . . . The first shot rang out. . . . Directly the German shots had been fired, the two destroyers swung round to port and at the same moment opened fire. Their guns seemed to flash out straight at us.' . . .

The results were instantaneous. The restaurant, which had been' one of the most elegant in Europe,' was blasted into a smoking shambles of ruin and death.

In this manner the German Army and the British Navy first came into contact with one another.

Here are a few of our messages at that time:—

October 17, 1914, 1.2 p.m.

Admiralty to Rear-Admiral Hood, Dover.

Most important to send the scouts at once and some destroyers to Dunkirk to work along the coast to Nieuport to support the Belgian left, now being attacked by the Germans; also monitors as soon as weather permits. Acknowledge.

7.20 p.m.

Admiralty to Rear-Admiral Hood, H.M.S. 'Attentive.'

Belgian Army is on line River Yser left bank, from Nieuport to Dixmud, with advanced posts on E. bank at Lombartzyde Rattevalle and Mannekensvere.

King is at La Panne, the last village on French coast.

The rôle of ships is as follows:—

Firstly, to prevent any disembarkation of German troops between Nieuport and La Panne and to South-West.

Secondly, to fire against enemy, which are advancing on Nieuport.

8.20 p.m.

Admiralty to Commodore Tyrwhitt, H.M.S. 'Maidstone,' Harwich.

The first German attempt to send destroyers down the Broad Fourteens being so successfully defeated may cause a larger number to be sent next time: be ready to meet them. We are sending scouts and destroyers to support the Belgian left at Nieuport.

Two battleships are leaving Portland to-night for Dover, four more destroyers are being sent to escort them. Therefore, if you can spare four destroyers, send them temporarily for Dover patrol to arrive at daylight.

October 19.

Rear-Admiral Hood to Admiralty.

Engagement continues at Nieuport. I believe that naval bombardment has done harm to enemy.

6-inch ammunition is urgently required for monitors, and must be sent as soon as possible, otherwise they will be useless. . . .

October 21, 10.55 p.m.

Rear-Admiral Hood to Admiralty.

Fired to-day 11 hours continuously, could see no improvement in situation. Patrolling coast every night. Monitors expended 600 6-inch shells daily. In *Foresight* alone 1,100 shells fired to-day, and even then unable to comply with all demands.

October 22.

Rear-Admiral Hood, Dunkirk, to First Lord.

I have returned for a few hours to Dunkirk, at the request of Colonel Bridges, to confer on future movements.

I have enough ships.

Firing has been less to-day.

In the event of a sudden northerly gale, the monitors and *Bustard* would be lost. This is a justifiable risk if they are doing valuable work, and is much less than submarine risk.

22/10/14.

Communiqué.

On the 18th instant requests for naval assistance were made to the Admiralty by the Allied Commanders. In consequence a naval flotilla, mounting a large number of powerful long-range guns, came into action at daybreak on the 19th off the Belgian Coast, supporting the left of the Belgian Army and firing against the right of the German attack, which they were by their position able to enfilade. The Germans replied by shells from their heavy guns, but owing to the superior range of the British Marine Artillery practically no damage has been done. The three monitors, which were building in British ports for Brazil and were acquired on the outbreak of war, have proved particularly well suited to this class of operation. A heavy bombardment of the German flank has been maintained without intermission since the morning of the 19th and is being continued to-day. Observation is arranged from the shore by means of naval balloons, and all reports indicate that substantial losses have been inflicted upon the enemy and that the fire is well directed and effective against his batteries and heavy guns. Yesterday a heavy explosion, probably of an ammunition wagon, followed upon a naval shot. The naval losses have so far been very small considering the damage done and the important assistance rendered to the Belgian left flank. All reports received by the

Admiralty show the courage and determination with which the Belgian Army, animated by the King in person, is defending the last few miles of Belgian soil. The naval operations are under the command of Rear-Admiral the Hon. Horace L. A. Hood, C.B., M.V.O., D.S.O.

October 23, 1.5 a.m.

Admiralty to Rear-Admiral Hood.

From First Lord.

Vital to sustain Belgian Army with effective Naval Artillery support to-morrow.

Arrange details with Bridges.

Am sending Gunnery School tenders to Dunkirk; draw upon them as you need.

Recognize importance to Navy of dominating Belgian Coast; make the most of your opportunity.

October 23.

Rear-Admiral Hood to First Lord.

Thanks for message. All going well.

Will bombard Ostend. Belgian Headquarters granted permission.

Am quite satisfied that our firing has done good.

24/10/14.

Communiqué.

All yesterday the monitors and other vessels of the British bombarding flotilla fired on the German right, which they searched thoroughly and effectively in concert with the operations of the Belgian Army. All German attacks on Nieuport were repulsed. Much damage was done to the enemy by naval fire which enfilades the German line, and enemy's prisoners taken yesterday and the day before testify to the heavy losses they have suffered from this cause. Fire was also opened in the afternoon on the German batteries near Ostend. Admiral Hood now has a fine flotilla of vessels very suitable for this work and at the same time not of great naval value. During the day our ships were persistently attacked by an enemy's submarine, and torpedoes were fired without success at *Wildfire* and *Myrmidon*. Other British vessels again attacked the submarine. The naval aeroplanes and balloons aided in the direction of the fire. The weather continued fine and favourable. No loss was sustained by the flotillas yesterday.

October 26, 12.21 a.m.

Rear-Admiral Hood to Admiralty.

Am off Nieuport. All well here. Have not succeeded so well to-day owing to long range of German batteries, which are not yet located by me. Aeroplanes reconnoitre the place when weather permits, and, if located, shall attack batteries with guns I can muster. Portion of shell on board here proves bigger guns.

Noon.

Admiralty to Senior Naval Officer, Dover.

Urgent. Order *Venerable*[5] to raise steam at once ready to proceed to support Allied left off Nieuport. Report how soon she can be ready to proceed.

Four destroyers must accompany her.

October 27, 11.30 p.m.

First Lord to Rear-Admiral Hood.

Certainly go on, husband ammunition till good targets show, but risks must be run and Allies' left must be supported without fail by the Navy. You have all done very well, and on land the line has been maintained. Keep it up.

October 28, 1.37 a.m.

Rear-Admiral Hood to Admiralty.

The Belgian authorities begged me to fire more rapidly. Deliberate firing will not produce more results as it is unmarked. I understand that 48 hours of clinging to Nieuport may achieve decisive results. If I am to order the firing to be deliberate, I shall not be able to do what the Belgian army requires.

October 28, 4.34 p.m.

Rear-Admiral Hood to Admiralty.

Have continued bombardment against increasing opposition. Captain of *Falcon* and five men killed and several wounded. *Wildfire* hit on the water line and sent in for repairs. *Brilliant* one killed and several wounded. *Rinaldo* eight wounded.... Submarine sighted—all destroyers now chasing [her]. *Venerable* has just grounded on sandbank out of gunfire. Tide rising, fine weather. She will be off in half an hour.

October 29, 1 a.m.

First Lord to Rear-Admiral Hood.

Save ammunition where possible, but don't lose any chance of hitting the enemy. Give your ships the following message: 'The inshore flotilla and squadron have played an appreciable part in the great battle now proceeding. You have shown the Germans that there is one flank they cannot turn.'

You have full discretion to go ahead.

---

[5]A battleship.

Meanwhile the British Army was heavily engaged. Sir John French wrote to me October 21:—

> I began this letter two days ago. I had to stop in the middle of a sentence and hadn't a single minute to go on with it. We have been hard pressed the last two days. The enemy has received considerable reinforcements and a big battle has been raging all along our front from a point 10 miles North of Ypres to La Bassée, which is W.S.W. of Lille. We have given way now and then in places and recovered the ground again—and on the whole have lost nothing (except, unfortunately, men and officers!) although the enemy has attacked with the utmost vigour.
>
> I have been all along the line, but the ground is so flat and the buildings so numerous that it is impossible to see much of the infantry work. I have this moment got a wire from the 1st Corps that they have captured 350 prisoners this afternoon. . . .

He ended by some very friendly expressions about Kitchener and my part in clearing up misunderstandings; also with some kind words about Antwerp.

26/10/14

Mr. Churchill to Sir John French.

(Private and Secret.)

I am touched and honoured by the kindness of your letter written from the field of Armentières. It was a disappointment to have to give up my visit, but the press of events here was decisive.

Antwerp was a bitter blow to me, and some aspects of it have given a handle to my enemies, and perhaps for a time reduced my power to be useful. From minute to minute one does not know that some fine ship will not be blown up by mine or submarine.[6] Great good fortune has attended us so far. Out of twenty-five submarine attacks only five have been effective, and only on ships of no value. But every reconnaissance ordered, carries with it the risk of a disproportionate loss. And if an atmosphere of distrust and malice is created—as is deliberately and laboriously being done—an unlucky incident might produce a most unpleasant state of feeling.... However, I am resolved not to be drawn by any impatience from those carefully considered plans of the naval war which I revealed to you in July, which are the result of three years' study, and with which Jellicoe is in the fullest accord. These plans will not produce any feat of *éclat*, but they will keep England safe and prosperous, and enable her in good time to put in the field an army which will definitely and finally turn the scale.

Kitchener is strangely alarmed about invasion, and on the C.I.D.[7] we have witnessed an absolute reversal of roles—the W.O.[8] declaring the country not safe and an invasion of 250,000 a possibility, and the Admiralty reassuring them, or

---

[6]A curious coincidence or foreboding. Almost at that moment the *Audacious* was moving to her doom.

[7]Committee of Imperial Defence.

[8]War Office.

trying to. You know how carefully I have examined that position, and how I have never minimized the risks. But now that we are face to face with realities, I am not alarmed, and my policy is that you should be reinforced by any effective division that can be formed and maintained; and that the Navy will prevent any invasion of a serious character. The Prime Minister is solid as a rock; but waves of nervousness pass over others, and may result in some retardation of your reinforcements.

We are making extraordinary efforts to grapple with the submarine menace which tends to drive our great ships so far away, and during November we shall, I believe, have got the better of it, and have secured all our anchorages by network and other means. Then we shall be able to give a greater assurance to those who need it.

But my dear friend, I do trust you realize how damnable it will be if the enemy settles down for the winter along lines which comprise Calais, Dunkirk or Ostend. There will be continual alarms and greatly added difficulties. We must have him off the Belgian Coast, even if we cannot recover Antwerp.

I am getting old ships with the heaviest guns ready, protected by barges with nets against submarines, so as to dispute the whole seaboard with him. On the 31st instant *Revenge*, four 13½-inch guns, will come into action if required, and I have a regular fleet of monitors and 'bomb-ketches' now organized which they all say has hit the Germans hard, and is getting stronger every day.

If you could again passage off to the left, I could give you overwhelming support from the sea, and there you will have a flank which certainly they cannot turn.

You have on your front gained a fine success in hurling back the whole weight of the German right. All your messages are so good—cool, resolute and informing. They will make a good page of military history. My heart is with you in the army.

Sir John French to Mr. Churchill.

October 28.

Your letters are always a great help and strength to me. Thank you indeed for the last one. I wish you would try and take a less gloomy view of what those people chatter about. What *does* it matter. . . . I tried hard to retain a hold on the Belgians and with them to operate alone on the northern flank; but the French sent Foch and a *Mission*. As the Belgians were practically the guests of France, using their territory and Calais as a base, I had no alternative but to gracefully 'submit.'

I am, however, on the very best terms with Foch, who is doing splendid work. . . .

He added—

The fighting is still severe—I've been at two points of the line to-day—but it is certainly slackening.

The Germans will never get further west.

This is only a hurried line written in the watches of the night.

No words written after the event can convey half so truthful or half so vivid an impression as these unstudied letters and brief operative telegrams flashing to and fro. Reading them again I feel once more the battle going on, the exhausted Belgians clinging desperately to the last few miles of soil left to their nation, their dauntless King and Queen amid the shells at Furnes; the French troops hastening up, but only in driblets; the heroic *Fusiliers Marins* holding Dixmude till not a fifth were left alive; our little ships barking away along the coast with the submarines stabbing at them from underneath and heavier metal opening on them every day from the shore; inundations slowly growing, a shield of merciful water rising inch by inch, hour by hour, between the fainting Belgian line and the cruel monster who had come upon them; and all the time our own men fighting against appalling odds, ten days, twenty days, thirty days, from Ypres to Armentières; nothing to send anyone, not a man, not a musket. Each night Colonel Bridges spoke to me on the telephone from the Belgian Headquarters at Furnes. Each night we felt it might be the last time he would speak from that address. It was only very gradually towards the end of October that one began to feel that the French and Belgian troops were getting a firm grip of the line of the Yser, and that Sir John French could write, 'The Germans will never get further west.' But three more weeks of agony ensued before the decision at Ypres finally declared itself in favour of the British Army.

* * * * *

We are, I feel, entitled to treat the Antwerp episode as an integral and vital part of this tremendous battle for the Channel Ports. If we had not made our belated effort to prolong its defence, the whole aftercourse of events would have been different, and could hardly have been better. But for the time gained at Antwerp and the arrival in such a forward situation of the British and French forces assigned so hurriedly for its relief, the impulsion of the Allied Armies towards the sea—already less than was required—must have been sensibly weakened. The great collision and battle with the German right would have taken place all the same. Perhaps the same result would have been achieved. But where? Where would the line have been drawn when the armies settled down into trenches from which they were not appreciably displaced for more than four years? At the very best the water defences, Gravelines–St. Omer–Aire, would have been secured. Dunkirk and its fine harbour would have become another nest of submarines to prey on our communications in the Channel; and Calais would have been exposed to a constant bombardment. The complications of these evils—the least that could be expected—must have reacted formidably upon the whole subsequent fortunes of the Allied Armies in France.

If this be true—and history must pronounce—the men who were responsible for the succour of Antwerp will have no reason to be ashamed of their effort. Hazard and uncertainty pervade all operations of war. It is idle to pretend that Lord Kitchener or anyone else foresaw all the consequences that flowed from the decisions of October 4. The event was very different from both hopes and expectations. But rarely in the Great War were more important results achieved by forces so limited and for losses so small, as those which rewarded this almost forlorn enterprise; nor is there in modern times, a more remarkable example of the flexibility, the celerity, and the baffling nature of that amphibious power which Britain alone wields, but which she has so often neglected.

CHAPTER XVII
THE GRAND FLEET AND THE SUBMARINE ALARM: OCTOBER AND NOVEMBER, 1914

'Silence is the secret of war.'

Prior.

The Grand Fleet and the Submarine Alarm—The Harbour Peril—Antisubmarine Defences—Unwarranted Reproaches—Correspondence with Sir John Jellicoe—Telegrams—Sir David Beatty's Letter of October 17—Exertions of the Admiralty—Decisions of November 2—The Loss of the *Audacious*—Suppression of the News—The Hard Days of October and November, 1914—Public and Political Unrest—'What is the Navy doing?'—Retirement of Prince Louis of Battenberg—The Return of Lord Fisher—Fisher and Wilson—Rear-Admiral Oliver becomes Chief of the Staff—The New Admiralty War Group—The Perpetual Clock—The Port and Starboard Lights.

All the anxieties recorded in the last chapter faded before our preoccupations about the Fleet. Indeed, the alarums and excursions on the Belgian Coast were at times almost a relief compared to the stress of our prime responsibilities. Everything depended upon the Fleet, and during these same months of October and November the Fleet was disquieted about the very foundations of its being. There lay the mighty ships; every man, from stoker to Admiral, was ready to die at his duty at any moment; no personal or individual fear found foothold. Still, at the summit from which we watched, one could feel a new and heart-shaking sensation. The Grand Fleet was uneasy. She could not find a resting-place except at sea. Conceive it, the *ne plus ultra*, the one ultimate sanction of our existence, the supreme engine which no one had dared to brave, whose authority encircled the globe—no longer sure of itself. The idea had got round—'*the German submarines were coming after them into the harbours*.'

On the South Coast no one would have minded. You could go inside the Portland breakwater and literally shut the door. On the East Coast no such absolutely sealed harbour existed. But Scapa was believed to be protected by its currents from submarine attack. Destroyers no doubt could attack it—if they cared to run the very serious risk of the long daylight passage, to and fro, across the North Sea: but no one, we had believed, could take a submarine *submerged* through the intricate and swirling channels. Now, all of a sudden, the Grand Fleet began to see submarines in Scapa Flow. Two or three times the alarm was raised. The climax came on October 17. Guns were fired, destroyers thrashed the waters, and the whole gigantic Armada put to sea in haste and dudgeon.

Of course there never was a German submarine in Scapa. None during the whole war achieved the terrors of the passage. One was destroyed in the outer approaches towards the end of November in circumstances which remained a mystery to the enemy. At the very end of the war in November, 1918, after the mutiny of the German fleet, a German submarine manned entirely by officers seeking to save their honour, perished in a final desperate effort. Thus none ever penetrated the lair of the Grand Fleet. But nevertheless the mere apprehension of submarines attacking the sleeping ships on which all else reposed, was sufficient in the winter of 1914 to destroy that sense of security which every Fleet demands when in its own war harbours.

Up till the end of September, 1914, no one seriously contemplated hostile submarines in time of war entering the war harbours of either side and attacking the ships at anchor. To achieve this the submarine would have to face all the immense difficulties of making its way up an estuary or inlet amid shoal water and intricate navigation, submerged all the time and with only an occasional glimpse through the periscope; secondly, while doing this, to avoid all the patrolling craft which for many miles kept watch and ward on the approaches; thirdly, to brave the unknown and unknowable terrors of mines and obstructions of all sorts, with which it must be assumed the channels would become increasingly infested. It was thought that these deterrents would prove effectual. Looking back on the events in the light of after-knowledge, we can see now that this assumption was correct. There is no recorded instance of a German submarine having penetrated into any British war harbour. The British submarine service was certainly not inferior in enterprise to the Germans, and from the very first hours of the War our boats were in the Heligoland Bight; but no British submarine officer attempted actually to penetrate a German war harbour or run actually into the mouths of the Elbe, the Jade, the Weser or the Ems. The nearest approaches to such an enterprise were the numerous passages of the Dardanelles made by the British submarines, beginning at the end of December with the heroic exploits of Commander Holbrook. For these feats the submarines were able to start only a few miles from the mouth of the Dardanelles and, diving along a very deep channel over two miles wide, succeeded again and again in entering the Sea of Marmora. This was not comparable to penetrating a British war harbour or river-mouth; and it did not occur until experience of the war capabilities of submarines had much increased.

During August and September the Admiralty made most strenuous efforts to increase the protection of our bases in Scotland and upon the East Coast by mounting guns, by posting guardships, by placing, obstructions, by preparing booms, by laying torpedo nets. But the danger against which these defences were designed in those months, was primarily not the submarine, but a regular attack by enemy destroyers on the fleet or squadrons at anchor, or, secondly, a raid by cruisers upon bases in the temporary absence of the fleet. It was not until the middle or end of September that increasing knowledge and evidences of the power of the largest submarines under war conditions, fostered the idea that the German submarines might actually enter our northern war harbours at the Forth, at Cromarty, and at Scapa Flow. Once this idea took root, it became a grave preoccupation. Precautions taken against a rush of torpedo boats, were clearly insufficient to stop a vessel which might dive under booms and past protecting guns.

Reproach has been levelled at the Admiralty for not having accurately measured this danger before the war and taken proper precautions against it. It would have been very difficult, even had the danger been foreseen, to find out under peace conditions what actually would or would not stop a submarine. No one in peace time could have ordered a submarine crew to run such awful risks. It would have been a matter of enormous expense to create a vast system of booms with deep nets and other obstructions for the defence of all our northern harbours. 1 should have had the very greatest difficulty in coming to the Cabinet and Parliament with such a demand during 1913 and 1914. Not only was every penny of naval expenditure challenged, but this particular expenditure would have been clearly of a most alarmist character, would have been taken to indicate the imminence of war, and would have been stigmatized as a provocation to the only Power to whom it could have relation. Still, if the Sea Lords and the Naval Staff had recommended solidly and as a matter of prime importance the provision of these great obstructive works in the Humber, at the Forth, at Cromarty, and at Scapa, it would have been my duty to go forward. But no such recommendation was made to me or pressed upon me by the naval experts in the years preceding the War, no doubt for the reasons which I have described, namely, that they did not think the danger had yet assumed a sufficiently practical form to justify such extraordinary measures. It certainly does not lie with anyone who was a member of the then Board of Admiralty to level such reproaches.

Sir John Jellicoe's book, although no doubt not intended for such a purpose, has been made a foundation for several reflections upon our pre-war arrangements in this respect. He recounts the dangers to which his Fleet was subjected; but had he, either as Controller or Second Sea Lord, foreseen these dangers, he would of course have warned his colleagues and his chief. It is clear therefore that if the Admiralty is to be criticized in this respect, it would be unfair to cite him as an authority.

Moreover, this submarine danger was one which did not in fact materialize at the outbreak of war. Six months later the position was different. The enterprise and the skill of submarine commanders had greatly grown, and all sorts of possibilities never previously envisaged came successively into view. But by that time the submarines had to face a very different set of obstructions. By the time they were convinced of the possibility, the possibility had disappeared.

It seemed real enough, however, in the month of October, 1914. The booms and obstructions which were everywhere being improvised were not complete or only partially in position, while the danger had begun to take full shape in the minds both of the Fleet and of the Admiralty. There was nothing to be done but to await the completion of the booms and obstructions, and meanwhile to keep the Fleet as far as possible out of harm's way. It really only felt safe when it was at sea. There, steaming in the broad waters, the Grand Fleet was herself again; but this involved a great strain on officers, men and machinery and a large consumption of fuel.

On September 30 Sir John Jellicoe wrote to me on the general Fleet position. He pointed out that Germany had got a lead over us in oversea submarines, that we always expected that the preliminary stages of a modern naval war would be a battle of the small craft, and that the question of keeping heavy ships out of the North Sea altogether, until the small craft menace had been reduced, had been frequently discussed. He thought it suicidal to forego our advantageous position in big ships by risking them in waters infested by submarines. He was of opinion that the submarine had a very limited sphere of action, could not hurt our oversea commerce (at that time this was in the main true), nor could they help their own ships to get in. He proposed therefore to use the Battle Fleet far to the North, spread to intercept trade. We had not nearly sufficient cruisers to form the double line that was really necessary to stop all ships during the short days and long nights. It was perfectly easy, he said, to run through the line at night, as its approximate positions soon got known and could not be much varied. But with the Battle Fleet helping in waters free from the submarine danger, one could make much more certain. This however, entailed giving up the idea of southerly Battle Fleet movements. He suggested that the French submarines as well as our own should be employed on the probable paths of the German submarines. He emphasized the importance of fitting a number of our trawlers with wireless installations. He desired me to show this letter to the First Sea Lord and to know whether we were in agreement with his views, whether steps would be taken to establish a trawler patrol, and whether the idea of utilizing the Grand Fleet effectively to shut up the Northern entrance to the North Sea was approved. He concluded by urging the hastening of the submarine defences for Scapa.

In reply I wrote, on the day of my return from Antwerp:—

October 8, 1914.

> I am in full agreement with your letter. No change in principle is required in the naval policy to which we have steadily adhered since 1911. The main point is to secure the safety of the British Fleet during the long and indefinite period of waiting for a general action. The phase in which raids up to 10,000 or 20,000 men were dangerous or would have had an object has passed. A very considerable, though no doubt incomplete, watch over the Heligoland debouches is being maintained by our oversea submarines. It is not necessary, as manœuvre experience had suggested, to traverse the waters of the North Sea with the Battle Fleet with any degree of frequency. Such movements should only be undertaken for some definite, grave and primary purpose. Occasional sweeps by cruisers in different directions, and avoiding anything like routine patrolling, are all that is necessary in present circumstances. In order to secure the greatest amount of rest and security for the Fleet, and the maintenance of the highest efficiency both of the steaming and fighting of its ships, you are justified in using occasional anchorages even more remote than Scapa and Loch Ewe; but on this you should make proposals officially. You need not fear that by these withdrawals you will miss a chance of bringing the German Battle Fleet to action. If that ever comes out it will be with some definite tactical object—for instance, to cover the landing of an invading force, to break the line of blockade to the northward in order to let loose battle-cruisers on to the

trade routes, or simply for the purpose of obtaining a naval decision by fighting a battle. In the first two of these cases you would have the time to come round and meet or intercept them before their operation was completed; in the third instance, their wishes would be the same as yours.

The Committee of Imperial Defence have again considered the question of invasion in the light of the experience of the first two months of the war. The War Office have pointed out that although no troops can be spared by Germany in the present active state of the land war on all frontiers, it is possible that in the winter a deadlock may arise in both the Eastern and Western theatres, when the Germans might find it possible or useful to create a diversion by attempting to throw a regular invading army across the North Sea. In the Admiralty opinion the difficulties of such a task have been in no wise diminished by anything we have learnt since the war began. We think it is useless to discuss such matters in general terms, and we are sure that a detailed study of a concrete plan of landing, say, 150,000 men will prove fatal to such ideas. In this connection it must be remembered that the war has shown the absolute reliance of the Germans upon their artillery, without which they would cease to be formidable. The landing of great quantities of artillery and the maintenance of an ammunition supply, are operations which, even if every other part of the enemy's plan had succeeded, could not be maintained without giving ample time for the intervention of your Fleet in decisive force. Further, if the Germans could spare 150,000 of their best troops for the invasion of England during a deadlock, a similar number would be released from our side, and it is obvious that even pushing this argument to its most extreme conclusion, we could transport our men back across the Channel with the command of the sea much more swiftly and surely than the Germans could bring theirs across the much wider distances of the North Sea in the face of a greatly superior naval force. All that would have resulted from the success of this most perilous operation on the part of Germany, would be to transfer the fighting of a certain number of Army Corps from the Continent to the British islands, under circumstances unfavourable in the extreme to the Germans, and favourable in every way to our troops; with the certainty that the Germans could not be reinforced, while we could be reinforced to almost any extent, and that unless the Germans were immediately successful before their ammunition was expended, the whole force to the last man must be killed or made prisoners of war. I therefore see no reason why this contingency, any more than that of raids, should force the Battle Fleet to keep a station of danger during the winter months. The power of the superior Fleet is exerted with equal effect over the longer distances, and in fact pervades all the waters of the world.

With regard to anchorages you have only to make your proposals and we will do our best to equip with anti-submarine nets, lights, and guns the places which you may wish to use. It is of importance that these should be varied, absolute safety lying much more in the uncertainty attending the movements of the Grand Fleet than in any passive or fixed defence of any particular place. We must not be led into frittering away resources by keeping half a dozen anchorages in a state

> of semi-defence, and so far as possible we must organize a movable defence of guard-ships, trawlers, patrolling yachts, minesweepers, destroyers with towing charges, and seaplanes, which can move while the Fleet is at sea and prepare the new resting-place for its reception.
>
> The employment of a portion or occasionally of the whole of the Battle Fleet, to supplement the Northern Blockade from time to time is a matter on which you must be the judge. A large part of your time must necessarily be spent cruising at sea, and this being so the cruising should be made as useful as possible. Here, again, anything in the nature of routine or regular stations would be dangerous, and would, after a while, draw upon you, even in remote northern waters, the danger of submarine attack.
>
> The enemy in my judgment pursues a wise policy in declining battle. By remaining in harbour he secures for Germany the command of the Baltic, with all that that implies, both in threatening the Russian flank and protecting the German Coast, and in drawing supplies from Sweden and Norway. This is an immense advantage to the Germans, and is the best use to which in present circumstances they can turn their Fleet. It is to secure the eventual command of the Baltic that British naval operations must tend. I have already pointed out, in the papers which I showed you, the three alternative conditions[1] [the defeat of the German Fleet: the breaking of the Kiel Canal: or the effective blocking in of the Heligoland Bight] under which this would be possible, and I hope that proceeding on the assumption that one of these conditions exists you will make a study of the actual method by which the entrance to the Baltic could be effected when the time arrives.

These general conclusions governed our policy during the next few months. But as October wore on our anxieties were steadily aggravated. The tension grew. Telegrams and letters tell their own tale.

October 15.

First Lord to Sir John Jellicoe.

> Personal. You are invited to give your opinion secretly on every aspect of the Naval situation at home and abroad and we welcome warmly any scheme you may put forward.
>
> Your proposals about mining are being attentively considered.
>
> The general aspect of the war is grim.
>
> The Russian pressure is not what we expected, and another avalanche of [German] reinforcements is approaching the western theatre.

On October 17 Sir John Jellicoe telegraphed that a German submarine had been reported entering Scapa at 5 p.m. the previous day. Although he thought the report false, he took

[1]This will be discussed in the Second Part. The alternatives are only now inserted here by me to explain the context.

the whole Fleet to sea forthwith. He appealed urgently for submarine obstructions as he had 'no safe base at present, and the only way to coal ships is to shift the coaling anchorages constantly which seriously dislocates the organization of supply.' On the 18th he stated that Scapa Flow could not be used till the Submarine Defence was placed. On the 19th he asked the Admiralty whether he should risk the submarine menace at Scapa Flow or move the Fleet to remote bases on the west coast of Scotland or Ireland' more than 300 miles from the Pentland Firth.' He added, 'It cannot be stated with absolute certainty that submarines were inside Scapa Flow, although Captain D, 4th Destroyer Flotilla, is positive H.M.S. *Swift* was fired at inside. I am of opinion that it is not difficult to get inside at slack water.'

Another very serious warning reached me almost simultaneously:—

Sir David Beatty to First Lord.

H.M.S. *Lion*,

October 17, 1914.

(Private).

I take the opportunity of an officer going to London in charge of signal books, to write you of what goes on. I have written you before, or rather to Hood for you. I think it is right that you should know how things generally affect the Fleet. I trust that you will take this as it is written, in fact I know you will, as being written with only one idea of service to the country. I write as I do because I know that the plain truth at times such as these is the only thing worth hearing, and because you are the one and only man who can save the situation. Even at such times, official documents, requisitions and demands, are of little value; they are met at once I admit, but without understanding the time value of all that lies behind them.

At present we feel that we are working up for a catastrophe of a very large character. The feeling is gradually possessing the Fleet that all is not right somewhere. The menace of mines and submarines is proving larger every day, and adequate means to meet or combat them are not forthcoming, and we are gradually being pushed out of the North Sea, and off our own particular perch. How does this arise? By the very apparent fact that we have no Base where we can with *any* degree of safety lie for coaling, replenishing, and refitting and repairing, after two and a half months of war. This spells trouble. It is a perfectly simple and easy matter to equip Scapa Flow, Cromarty, and Rosyth, so that vessels can lie there undisturbed to do all they want, and for as long as they want, provided material and men are forthcoming. The one place that has put up any kind of defence against the submarine is Cromarty, and that is because at Cromarty there happens to be a *man* who grapples with things as they are, i.e., Commander Munro,[2] and because they

[2]This energetic and practical officer, whom I had employed during the previous eighteen months to supervise the fortification of Cromarty, had already designed a type of anti-submarine boom which he was actually installing at Cromarty.

have trained artillerymen to man their guns. That was one of the best day's work you ever did when you insisted on taking the defences there in hand. At Rosyth it appeared to me in September when there, that to deny access to submarines and destroyers was a fairly simple task; it was an awkward place to get into, but when once in, it ought to be, and could be, very easily made a safe asylum for vessels in need of rest, repair, fuel, etc. At Scapa, something has been done towards blocking the many entrances, but that is all. I am sure that all the brain and intellect at the Admiralty could devise a scheme or method of defence which would make the anchorage practically safe, and which could be done in a fortnight. No *seaman* can dispute that these three bases could have been made *absolutely* safe from submarine attack during the two and a half months that the war has been in progress. As it is, we have been lulled into a sense of false security, because we have not been attacked before; but I can assure you that it has literally been recognized by all that it was only a question of time when we should have this sense rudely shattered....

The situation as it is, we have no place to lay our heads. We are at Loch na Keal, Isle of Mull. My picket boats are at the entrance, the nets are out and the men are at the guns, waiting for coal which has run low, but ready to move at a moment's notice. Other squadrons are in the same plight. We have been running now hard since 28th July; small defects are creeping up which we haven't time to take in hand. Forty-eight hours is our spell in harbour with steam ready to move at four hours' notice, coaling on an average 1,400 tons a time; night defence stations. The men can stand it, but the machine can't, and we must have a place where we can stop for from four or five days every now and then to give the engineers a chance. Such a place does not exist, so the question arises, how long can we go on, for I fear very much, not for long, as the need for small repairs is becoming insistent.

The remedy is to fix upon a base and make it impervious to submarine attack; as I have pointed out I am firmly convinced this can be done....

You might be told that this idea of making the entrances secure is chimerical. This is not so; and I will guarantee that if the Fleet was instructed to defend the entrances to the ports named, and was provided with the material, they could and would devise not one but several methods which would satisfy most requirements, and which would keep out submarines. If the Fleet cannot spare the time and labour, turn it over to Commander Munro and give him a free hand and what labour he requires, and he will do it in a fortnight.

I think you know me well enough to know that I do not shout without cause. The Fleet's tail is still well over the back. We hate running away from our base and the effect is appreciable. We are not enjoying ourselves. But the morale is high and confidence higher. I would not write thus if I did not know that you with your quick grasp of detail and imagination would make something out of it.

Meanwhile, however, the Admiralty, particularly the First and Fourth Sea Lords, had been labouring since the end of September to devise and make the necessary protective structures. By dint of extraordinary exertions the first instalment of these was already approaching completion, and on October 20 Prince Louis was in a position to telegraph to the Commander-in-Chief:—

The defences for Scapa will leave Dockyards on 24th October.

In the meantime Admiralty approve Battle Squadrons remaining on the West Coast and if you prefer they can proceed as far as Berehaven.

In order to prevent being dogged by submarines a false course should be steered until a sufficient offing is made.

Battle-Cruisers and Cruisers will have to remain north to cover exits from North Sea. Cromarty appears to be a safe base for some of them.

October 23, 2 a.m.

Admiralty to Sir John Jellicoe.

From First Lord.

Private and Personal. Every effort will be made to secure you rest and safety in Scapa and adjacent anchorages. Net defence hastened utmost, will be strengthened by successive lines earliest. If you desire, Cabinet will I think agree declare area 30 miles east Kinnaird Head to 30 miles north Shetlands and down to 30 miles South of Hebrides prohibited to all ships not specially licensed by Admiralty or you.

All vessels whatever Flag should be dealt with in this area as you desire.

I wish to make absolute sanctuary for you there. I also propose proclaiming all Scotland north of Caledonian Canal including all Islands and Inverness prohibited area; you can do what you think necessary for safety of Fleet.

Use your powers under Defence of Realm Act and ask for anything you want in men, money or material. You must have a safe resting place: tell me how I can help you.

Sir John Jellicoe replied with suggestions for closing certain areas, and for the placing of obstructions and contact mines.

October 24, 1914.

Secretary.
First Sea Lord.
Third Sea Lord.
Fourth Sea Lord.
Naval Secretary.

Every nerve must be strained to reconcile the Fleet to Scapa. Successive lines of submarine defences should be prepared, reinforced by Electric Contact mines as proposed by the Commander-in-Chief. Nothing should stand in the way of the equipment of this anchorage with every possible means of security. The First Lord and the First Sea Lord will receive a report of progress every third day until the work is completed and the Commander-in-Chief satisfied.

W. S. C.

On receipt of Sir John Jellicoe's memorandum I convened all the authorities and after prolonged discussion issued the following directions, which since they show the variety of problems affecting the Grand Fleet at this juncture may be printed *in extenso* for those interested in details:—

Decisions of November 2, 1914.[3]

Secretary and all concerned.

1. The Fourth Sea Lord will give directions for 48 trawlers armed with guns, and 3 yachts fitted with guns and wireless, to be collected from the various trawler patrols and placed at the disposal of the Commander-in-Chief, Grand Fleet. These trawlers, etc., are to be at Scapa Flow, reporting to Admiral Colville there, by the 5th November.

2. Third Sea Lord will report what rafts and barges there are which could be fitted with torpedo nets to afford protection to ships from submarine attack, and when they can be ready.

3. Chief of the Staff will direct the Admiral of Patrols to provide 12 additional destroyers from the patrol flotillas to repair at once to Scapa Flow and join the Flag of the Commander-in-Chief.

4. Twelve armed merchant cruisers of small size have been ordered to strengthen the Northern patrol. It is necessary that these should join the Grand Fleet within a week, and any circumstances likely to cause delay must be immediately brought to notice of First Sea Lord.

5. The Naval Secretary and the Secretary have informed the Commander-in-Chief of his powers under the Defence of the Realm Act, when the area to the north of the Caledonian Canal, including all islands and the town of Inverness, has been proclaimed a prohibited area within the meaning of the Act. The Secretary will draft a letter forthwith to the War Office, asking for the proclamation as from the 3rd November, of the whole of this area.

6. The warning as to the closing of the North Sea, issued to-night by the Admiralty, is to be studied by departments concerned. The Additional Civil Lord should deal with questions arising out of it affecting trade and fishery interests in this country. Captain Webb should consider its working from the point of view of commerce; he will also consider what additional measures must be taken to increase the Examination Service on account of the increased traffic in the Channel which will result from the warning, consulting Chief of the Staff as may be necessary for military security. The Additional Civil Lord should also deal with the subject from the point of view of existing arrangements as to contraband.

[3]I have slightly abridged this minute.

7. The War Office should be asked immediately to develop for the Navy a system of lookouts on commanding points around the coast in the prohibited area in the North of Scotland and on the islands, connected as far as possible by telephone, in order that the movements of suspicious vessels, and also intelligence collected from the land, may be constantly reported. Admiral Coast Guards and Reserves will co-operate.

8. The censorship of postal and telegraph offices in the prohibited area, and the exclusion of all alien-born postal servants, and the services of a sufficient detective force at points used by the Fleet, must be undertaken forthwith. Secretary will propose the necessary measures in consultation with the War and Home Offices.

10. Fourth Sea Lord and Naval Secretary will take the necessary steps to provide, with the minimum delay, heavy booms for Scapa and Loch Ewe, as asked for by the Commander-in-Chief.

11. The Assistant Director of Torpedoes will arrange to send lines of Electric Contact mines during the next 10 days to Scapa Flow, to be disposed of under the orders of the Commander-in-Chief, Grand Fleet.

12. A bi-weekly report is to be made to the First Lord and First Sea Lord of the actual progress to date of all works now under construction for the protection of harbours against submarine and torpedo attack, and all unexpected circumstances which tend to delay the work are to be reported as they occur.

13. The Chief of the Staff will report on the general question of adding to the number of mines in our minefield.

14. A second light cruiser squadron for the patrol of the North Sea is approved. It will be formed by dividing the existing light cruiser squadron and adding *Sapphire* and *Blanche* from the 3rd Battle Squadron. The Chief of the Staff to make detailed proposals. Naval Secretary to propose a Commodore.

15. Eight light-draught, seaworthy vessels for fleet sweepers have been taken up and should be completed with all speed.

16. The Director of the Air Division should, in consultation with the Commander-in-Chief, establish an additional temporary seaplane station at some convenient point on the Scottish coast facing the Hebrides, for the better patrol and reconnaissance of that area.

17. A general order should be issued to the Fleet that no cruiser or larger vessel is to stop for the purpose of boarding or challenging any merchant ship. This work is to be invariably performed by auxiliary merchant cruisers, torpedo craft, and trawlers. Cruisers and larger vessels, wishing to turn back merchant ships, should fire a shot across their bows and make signals.

18. The Chief of the Staff should draft the necessary order to the patrolling lines of cruisers to turn back merchant ships, from the 5th November onwards, from the danger area. The orders should be submitted before being sent.

19. The reconstitution of the battle-cruisers into two squadrons:—

(1) *Tiger, Princess Royal, Lion*;
(2) *New Zealand, Inflexible, Invincible*; is authorized.

22. Sir John Jellicoe's proposal in regard to the entry of defended ports and the unsuitability of the proposed arrangements are to be reported on by the War Staff, and submitted to the Board for adoption.

24. Third Sea Lord and Fourth Sea Lord should report whether it is possible to postpone the lining of destroyers during the next two months, as Commander-in-Chief states that they cannot be spared from duty.

25. The Assistant Director of Torpedoes will report upon the need of establishing W.T. stations at St. Kilda and the other places in question. Only small installations are required.

26. The docking of ships at Home ports and partial refit, one at a time, may be permitted, beginning from the end of this month.

27. A report should be furnished on the state of the 3rd Battle Squadron repair ship.

28. Steps are to be taken to increase the pumping power of the *Orion* class and later types by adding a bilge suction to the main circulating pumps. A report should be furnished by Third Sea Lord as to what this involves in time and money.

W. S. C.

* * * * *

The Commander-in-Chief, in accordance with the Admiralty authorization, withdrew at the end of October to the north coast of Ireland for a few days' rest and gunnery practice. By extraordinary ill-luck, the arrival of the Fleet off Loch Swilly coincided with the visit of a German minelayer to those waters. The minelayer had no idea of catching the Fleet or that British warships would be in those waters. Her objective was the Liverpool trade route, but the shot aimed at a crow brought down an eagle.

On October 27th Prince Louis hurried into my room with the grave news that the *Audacious* had been struck by mine or torpedo North of Loch Swilly, and that it was feared she was sinking. In the afternoon the Commander-in-Chief telegraphed urging that every endeavour should be made to keep the event from being published; and that night, in reporting that the *Audacious* had sunk, he repeated his hope that the loss could be kept secret. I saw great difficulties in this, but promised to bring the matter before the Cabinet. Meanwhile I telegraphed to the Commander-in-Chief, October 28th, 12.30 a.m.:—

> 'I am sure you will not be at all discouraged by *Audacious* episode. We have been very fortunate to come through three months of war without the loss of a capital ship. I expected three or four by this time, and it is due to your unfailing vigilance and skill that all has gone so well. The Army too has held its own along the whole line, though with at least 14,000 killed and wounded. Quite soon the harbours will be made comfortable for you. Mind you ask for all you want.'

Measured by military standards, the *Audacious* was the first serious loss we had sustained. She was one of those vital units in which we never were at that time more than six or seven to the good, and upon which all strategic calculations were based both by friend and foe. When I brought the question of keeping her loss secret before the Cabinet, there was a considerable division of opinion. It was urged that public confidence would be destroyed if it were thought that we were concealing losses, that it was bound to leak out almost immediately, and that the Germans probably knew already. To this I replied that there was no reason why the Germans should not be left to collect their own information for themselves, that the moment they knew the *Audacious* was sunk they would proclaim it, and that then we could quite easily explain to the public why it was we had preserved secrecy. I cited the effective concealment by Japan of the loss of the battleship *Yashima* off Port Arthur in 1904. If Sir John French had lost an Army Corps, every effort would be made to conceal it from the enemy. Why then should the Navy be denied a similar freedom? Lord Kitchener strongly supported me; and our views were eventually accepted by the Cabinet.

The Press were asked by the Admiralty to abstain from making any reference to the event. Some newspapers complied with an ill grace. It was represented that hundreds of people knew already, including all the passengers of the liner *Olympic* which had passed the sinking vessel; that German spies in England would certainly convey the news to Germany in a few days, and that, anyhow, long accounts of the sinking with actual photographs would be dispatched by the next mail to the United States, whence the news would be immediately telegraphed to Germany. We, however, remained obdurate, watching the German Press very carefully for the slightest indication that they knew. Meanwhile it was thought clever by certain newspapers to write articles and paragraphs in which the word 'audacious' was frequently introduced, while I was much blamed. I found it necessary to issue a secret appeal, which, aided by the loyal efforts of the Newspaper Press committee, certainly had some effect. In the upshot it took more than five weeks before the German Admiralty learned that the *Audacious* had been sunk, and even then they were by no means convinced that they were not the victims of rumour.

Says Admiral Scheer:—

> 'The English succeeded in keeping secret for a considerable time the loss of this great battleship, a loss which was a substantial success for our efforts at

> equalization. . . . The behaviour of the English was inspired at all points by consideration for what would serve their military purpose.... In the case of the *Audacious* we can but approve the English attitude of not revealing a weakness to the enemy, because accurate information about the other side's strength has a decisive effect on the decisions taken.'

I do not remember any period when the weight of the War seemed to press more heavily on me than these months of October and November, 1914. In August one was expecting the great sea battle and the first great battles on land; but our course was obvious, and, when taken, we had only to wait for decisions. All September was dominated by the victory of the Marne. But in October and November the beast was at us again. The sense of grappling with and being overpowered by a monster of appalling and apparently inexhaustible strength on land and a whole array of constant, gnawing anxieties about the safety of the Fleet from submarine attack at sea and in its harbours, oppressed my mind. Not an hour passed without the possibility of some disaster or other in some part of the world. Not a day without the necessity of running risks.

My own position was already to some extent impaired. The loss of the three cruisers had been freely attributed to my personal interference. I was accused of having overridden the advice of the Sea Lords and of having wantonly sent the squadron to its doom. Antwerp became a cause of fierce reproach. One might almost have thought I had brought about the fall of the city by my meddling. The employment of such untrained men as the Naval Brigades was generally censured. The internment in Holland of three of their battalions was spoken of as a great disaster entirely due to my inexcusable folly. One unhappy phrase—true enough in thought—about 'Digging rats out of holes,' which had slipped from my tongue in a weary speech at Liverpool, was fastened upon and pilloried. These were the only subjects with which my name was connected in the newspapers. My work at the Admiralty—such as it was—was hidden from the public. No Parliamentary attack gave me an opportunity of defending myself. In spite of being accustomed to years of abuse, I could not but feel the adverse and hostile currents that flowed about me. One began to perceive that they might easily lead to a practical result. Luckily there was not much time for such reflections.

The Admiralty had entered upon the War with commanding claims on public confidence. The coincidence of the test mobilization with the European crisis, was generally attributed to profound design. The falsification one after another of the gloomy predictions that we should be taken unawares, that the German commerce destroyers would scour the seas, and that our own shipping, trade and food would be endangered, was recognized with widespread relief. The safe transportation of the Army to France and the successful action in the Heligoland Bight were acclaimed as fine achievements. But with the first few incidents of misfortune a different note prevailed in circles which were vocal. The loss of the three cruisers marked a turning-point in the attitude of those who in the evil times of war are able to monopolize the expression of public opinion. As the expectation of an imminent great sea battle faded, the complaint began to be heard, 'What is the Navy doing?' It was perhaps inevitable that there should be a sense of disappointment as week succeeded week and the tremendous engine of British naval power seemed to be neither seen nor heard. There was a general opinion that we should have begun by attacking and destroying the German Fleet. Vain to point to the ceaseless stream of troops and supplies to France, or to the worldwide trade of Britain proceeding almost without hindrance. Impossible, in the hearing of the enemy, to explain the intricate movement of reinforcements or expeditions escorted across every ocean from every part of the Empire, or to unfold the reasons which rendered it impossible to bring the German Fleet to battle. There was our little Army fighting for its life, and playing to British eyes almost as large a part as all the armies of France; and meanwhile our great Navy—the strongest in the world—lay apparently in an inertia diversified only by occasional mishap.

Eaten bread is soon forgotten. Dangers which are warded off by effective precautions and foresight are never even remembered. Thus it happened that the Admiralty was inconsiderately judged in this opening phase. To me, who saw the perils against which we had prepared and over which we had triumphed, and who felt a sense of profound thankfulness for the past and absolute confidence for the future, these manifestations of discontent seemed due only to lack of understanding and to impatience pardonable in the general stress of the times. But they were none the less disquieting. Nor was it easy to deal with them. The questions could not be argued out in public or in Parliament. No formal indictment was ever preferred; nor could one have been fully answered without injury to national interests. We had to endure all this carping in silence. A certain proportion of losses at sea was inevitable month by month; and in each case it was easy to assert that some one had blundered. In most cases, indeed, this was true. With a thousand ships upon the sea and a thousand hazards, real or potential, every day to menace them, accidents and mistakes were bound to happen. How many were made for which no forfeit was claimed by Fortune! There was never an hour when risks against which no provision could be made were not being run by scores of vessels, or when problems of novelty and difficulty were not being set to sea captains, scarcely any of whom had ever been tried in war. Was it wonderful that we fell occasionally into error, or even into loss? 'Another naval disaster. Five hundred men drowned. What are the Admiralty doing?' While all the time the armies reeled about in the confusion of the mighty battles, and scores of thousands were sent, often needlessly or mistakenly, to their deaths: while all the time every British operation of war and trade on the seas proceeded without appreciable hindrance.

This censorious mood produced a serious development in the case of Prince Louis. In the first flush of our successful mobilization and entry upon the war, no comment had been made upon his parentage. But now the gossip of the clubs and of the streets began to produce a stream of letters, signed and anonymous, protesting in every variety of method and often in violent terms against one of Teutonic birth filling the vital position of First Sea Lord. This was cruel; but it was not unnatural, and I saw with anxiety and distress the growth of very widespread misgiving. I gathered also from occasional remarks which he made that this atmosphere was becoming apparent to the First Sea Lord. He was thus coming to be placed in the invidious position of having to take great responsibilities and risks day by day without that support in public confidence to which he was absolutely entitled, and with the certainty that accidents would occur from time to time. I was therefore not surprised when, towards the end of October, Prince Louis asked to be relieved of his burden. The uncomplaining dignity with which he made this sacrifice and accepted self-effacement as a requital for the great and faithful service he had rendered to the British nation and to the Royal Navy was worthy of a sailor and a Prince. The correspondence which passed between us has already been made public, but is here inserted for completeness.[4] I had now to look for a successor, and my mind had already turned in one direction and in one direction alone.

Lord Fisher used to come occasionally to the Admiralty, and I watched him narrowly to judge his physical strength and mental alertness. There seemed no doubt about either. On one occasion, when inveighing against some one whom he thought obstructive,

---

October 28, 1914.

[4]DEAR MR. CHURCHILL,—

I have lately been driven to the painful conclusion that at this juncture my birth and parentage have the effect of impairing in some respects my usefulness on the Board of Admiralty. In these circumstances I feel it to be my duty, as a loyal subject of His Majesty, to resign the office of First Sea Lord, hoping thereby to facilitate the task of the administration of the great Service, to which I have devoted my life, and to ease the burden laid on H.M. Ministers.

I am,

Yours very truly,

LOUIS BATTENBERG,

Admiral.

October 29, 1914.

MY DEAR PRINCE LOUIS,—

This is no ordinary war, but a struggle between nations for life and death. It raises passions between races of the most terrible kind. It effaces the old landmarks and frontiers of our civilization. I cannot further oppose the wish, you have during the last few weeks expressed to me, to be released from the burden of responsibility which you have borne thus far with so much honour and success.

The anxieties and toils which rest upon the naval administration of our country are in themselves enough to try a man's spirit; and when to them are added the ineradicable difficulties of which you speak, I could not at this juncture in fairness ask you to support them.

The Navy of to-day, and still more the Navy of to-morrow, bears the imprint of your work. The enormous impending influx of capital ships, the score of thirty-knot cruisers, the destroyers and submarines unequalled in modern construction which are coming now to hand, are the results of labours which we have had in common, and in which the Board of Admiralty owes so much to your aid.

The first step which secured the timely concentration of the Fleet was taken by you.

I must express publicly my deep indebtedness to you, and the pain I feel at the severance of our three years' official association. In all the circumstances you are right in your decision. The spirit in which you have acted is the same in which Prince Maurice of Battenberg has given his life to our cause and in which your gallant son is now serving in the Fleet.

I beg you to accept my profound respect and that of our colleages on the Board.

I remain,

Yours very sincerely,

WINSTON S. CHURCHILL.

he became so convulsed with fury that it seemed that every nerve and blood-vessel in his body would be ruptured. However, they stood the strain magnificently, and he left me with the impression of a terrific engine of mental and physical power burning and throbbing in that aged frame. I was never in the least afraid of working with him, and I thought I knew him so well, and had held an equal relationship and superior constitutional authority so long, that we could come through any difficulty together. I therefore sounded him in conversation without committing myself, and soon saw that he was fiercely eager to lay his grasp on power, and was strongly inspired with the sense of a message to deliver and a mission to perform. I therefore determined to act without delay. I sought the Prime Minister and submitted to him the arguments which led me to the conclusion that Fisher should return, and that I could work with no one else. I also spoke of Sir Arthur Wilson as his principal coadjutor. I was well aware that there would be strong, natural and legitimate, opposition in many quarters to Fisher's appointment, but having formed my own conviction I was determined not to remain at the Admiralty unless I could do justice to it. So in the end, for good or for ill, I had my way.

October 30.

First Lord to Sir John Jellicoe.

Prince Louis has resigned on grounds of parentage, to my deep regret. The King has approved Lord Fisher as First Sea Lord. He will assume office to-morrow afternoon. I expect Sir Arthur Wilson will be associated with Admiralty for special duties. Loss of *Audacious* has nothing to do with these events. There will be no change in Naval War policy as set out in your war orders. Please telegraph whether you think Grand Fleet could prudently take four or five days' rest in Portland Harbour.

October 30.

Sir John Jellicoe to First Lord.

Secret and personal.

I have made present base secure against submarine attack and think it better to remain here than go to Portland.

I propose to send out our squadrons one at a time next week to fire at rocks off coast of Ireland, as target practice is very necessary and towing targets is difficult in present weather and possibly unsafe.

The decision to recall Lord Fisher to the Admiralty was very important. He was, as has been here contended, the most distinguished British Naval officer since Nelson. The originality of his mind and the spontaneity of his nature freed him from conventionalities of all kinds. His genius was deep and true. Above all, he was in harmony with the vast size of events. Like them, he was built upon a titanic scale.

But he was seventy-four years of age. As in a great castle which has long contended with time, the mighty central mass of the donjon towered up intact and seemingly everlasting.

But the outworks and the battlements had fallen away, and its imperious ruler dwelt only in the special apartments and corridors with which he had a lifelong familiarity. Had he and his comrade, Sir Arthur Wilson, been born ten years later, the British naval direction at the outbreak of the Great War would have reached its highest state of perfection, both at the Admiralty and afloat. The new figures which the struggle was producing—Beatty, Keyes, Tyrwhitt—had not yet attained the authority which would have made them acceptable to the Navy in the highest situations. Fisher and Wilson had outlived their contemporaries and towered above the naval generation which had followed them. It was to these two great old men and weather-beaten sea-dogs, who for more than half a century had braved the battle and the breeze, and were Captains afloat when I was in my cradle, that the professional conduct of the naval war was now to be confided.

It was clear, however, to me, who knew both these Admirals-of-the-Fleet quite well and had had many opportunities in the previous three years of hearing and reading their views, that the day-to-day organization of our Staff machinery would have to be altered. This necessitated a change in the Chief of the War Staff. In Admiral Sturdee the Navy had a sea officer of keen intelligence and great practical ability—a man who could handle and fight his ship or his squadron with the utmost skill and resolution. But he was not a man with whom Lord Fisher could have worked satisfactorily at the supreme executive centre. Happily, there was no difficulty in agreeing upon his successor.

Since Antwerp, Admiral Oliver had been my Naval Secretary. During the year before the War he had been Director of Naval Intelligence. In this capacity I had had to rely continually upon him, as upon Captain Thomas Jackson before him, for all the facts and figures upon which the controversy about British and German naval strength depended. His accuracy in detail and power of continuous and tenacious mental toil were extraordinary. He combined with capacious knowledge an unusual precision of mind and clarity of statement. His credentials as a sea officer were unimpeachable. He had been Navigating Commander to Sir Arthur Wilson, and every one in the Navy knew the story of how in the 1901 Naval manœuvres these two had taken the Channel Fleet from off Rathlin's Island at the North of Ireland through the Irish Channel to the Scillies in thick mist without sighting land or lights, and without being inclined to make a single remark to each other. On the third day the mist lifting suddenly revealed the Scilly Islands to the astonished Fleet, which had already dropped anchor in the roads.

I was very glad when Lord Fisher proposed to me that he should be made Chief of the Staff, and when he offered also to give me in exchange, for my Private Office, his own personal assistant, Commodore De Bartolomé. Everything thus started fair. We reformed the War Group, which met at least once each day, as follows: First Lord, First Sea Lord, Sir Arthur Wilson, Admiral Oliver and Commodore De Bartolomé (the last named representing the younger school of sea officers), together with the invaluable Secretary, Sir Graham Greene. Sir Henry Jackson was also frequently summoned, but not so continuously as to impose an accountable responsibility upon him.

Lord Fisher's age and the great strain to which he was now to be subjected made it necessary for him to lead a very careful life. He usually retired to rest shortly after 8 o'clock, awaking refreshed between four and five, or even earlier. In these morning hours he gave his greatest effort, transacting an immense quantity of business, writing innumerable letters and forming his resolutions for the day. Indeed, his methods corresponded closely to the maxims of the poet Blake: 'Think in the morning; act in the noon; eat in the evening; sleep in the night.' But I never heard him use this quotation. As the afternoon approached the formidable energy of the morning gradually declined, and with the shades of night the old Admiral's giant strength was often visibly exhausted. Still, judged from the point of view of physical and mental vigour alone, it was a wonderful effort, and one which filled me, who watched him so closely, with admiration and, I will add, reassurance.

I altered my routine somewhat to fit in with that of the First Sea Lord. I slept usually an hour later in the morning, being called at eight instead of seven, and I slept again, if possible, for an hour after luncheon. This enabled me to work continuously till one or two in the morning without feeling in any way fatigued. We thus constituted an almost unsleeping watch throughout the day and night. In fact, as Fisher put it, 'very nearly a perpetual clock.' Telegrams came in at the Admiralty at all hours of the day and night, and there was scarcely an hour when an immediate decision could not be given, if necessary, by one or the other of us always awake.

This arrangement was also convenient from the point of view of business. The First Lord completed everything with which he was concerned before going to bed, and three hours later the First Sea Lord addressed himself to the whole budget, and I, awaking at eight, received his dawn output. I had not previously seen the pulse of the Admiralty beat so strong and regular.

We made the agreement between ourselves that neither of us should take any important action without consulting the other, unless previous accord had been reached. To this agreement we both scrupulously adhered. We had thus formed, for the first time, an overwhelmingly strong control and central authority over the whole course of the naval war, and were in a position to make our will prevail throughout the fleets and all branches of the naval administration, as well as to hold our own against all outside interference. I had for a long time been accustomed to write my minutes in red ink. Fisher habitually used a green pencil. To quote his words, 'it was the port and starboard lights.' As long as the port and starboard lights shone together, all went well. We had established a combination which, while it remained unbroken, could not have been overthrown by intrigue at home or the foe on the sea.

CHAPTER XVIII
CORONEL AND THE FALKLANDS: OCTOBER, NOVEMBER AND DECEMBER, 1914

'Ill fared it then with Roderick Dhu,
That on the field his targe he threw,
Whose brazen studs and tough bull hide
Had Death so often dashed aside.
For train'd abroad his arms to wield
FitzJames's blade was sword and shield.'

Scott, 'The Lady of the Lake,' Canto V, xv.

The Mystery of Admiral von Spee—First Threat to South American Waters—His Apparition at Samoa—His Second Disappearance—Renewed Threat to South America—Rear-Admiral Cradock Ordered to Concentrate—The Relative Forces—Importance of the Battleship *Canopus*—The First Combination against Admiral von Spee—Rear-Admiral Cradock's Disquieting Telegram—His Cruise up the Chilean Coast without the *Canopus*—Certain News of the Enemy's Arrival—Admiralty Measures—News of the Action off Coronel—The Meeting of the Squadrons—The British Attack the Germans—Destruction of the *Good Hope* and *Monmouth*—Escape of the *Glasgow*—Reflections upon the Admiralty Examined—An Explanation of Rear-Admiral Cradock's Action—The Alternatives Open to the German Squadron—Second Combination against Admiral von Spee—Battle-cruisers *Invincible* and *Inflexible* Ordered to South America—Arrangements with the Japanese Admiralty—Development of the Second Combination—British Naval Resources at their Utmost Strain—*Konigsberg* Blockaded and the *Emden* Sunk—Relief in the Indian Ocean—Accelerated Dispatch of the Battle-Cruisers—What Admiral von Spee Found at the Falklands—News of the Battle and of Victory—The Action—Total Destruction of the German Squadron—End of the German Cruiser Warfare—End of the Great Strain.

As has already been described, Admiral von Spee, the German Commander-in-Chief in the Far East, sailed from Tsingtau (Kiauchow),[1] in the last week of June, with the *Scharnhorst* and *Gneisenau*, and on August 5, immediately after the British declaration of war, these two powerful ships were reported as being near the Solomon Islands.

[1]Throughout this chapter the map on pages 334–5 and the table of ships on page 349 will be found useful.

They were subsequently reported at New Guinea on August 7, and coaling at the Caroline Islands on the 9th. After this they vanished into the immense Pacific with its innumerable islands, and no one could tell where they would reappear. As the days succeeded one another and grew into weeks, our concern on their account extended and multiplied. Taking the Caroline Islands as the centre, we could draw daily widening circles, touching ever more numerous points where they might suddenly spring into action. These circles were varied according as the Germans were credited with proceeding at most economical speed, at three-quarter speed, or at full speed; and the speed at which they would be likely to steam depended upon the nature of the potential objective which in each case might attract them.

We have seen how the mystery of their whereabouts affected the movements of the New Zealand and Australian convoys, and what very anxious decisions were forced upon us. We have seen how the uncertainty brooded over the little expedition from New Zealand to Samoa: how glad we were when it arrived safely and seized the island: how prompt we were—providentially prompt—to snatch every vessel away from the roadstead of Samoa the moment the troops and stores were landed. When at length more than five weeks had passed without any sign of their presence, we took a complete review of the whole situation. All probabilities now pointed to their going to the Magellan Straits or to the West Coast of South America. The Australian convoy was now provided with superior escort. Not a British vessel could be found in the anchorage at Samoa. The old battleships were already on their way to guard the convoys in the Indian Ocean. There was nowhere where they could do so much harm as in the Straits of Magellan. Moreover, we thought we had indications of German coaling arrangements on the Chilean Coast. There were rumours of a fuelling base in the Magellan Straits, for which diligent search was being made. There was certainly German trade still moving along the Western Coast of South America.

Accordingly, on September 14, the Admiralty sent the following telegram to Rear-Admiral Cradock, who commanded on the South American Station:—

Admiralty to Rear-Admiral Cradock, H.M.S. 'Good Hope.'

September 14, 5.50 p.m.

The Germans are resuming trade on West Coast of South America, and *Scharnhorst* and *Gneisenau* may very probably arrive on that coast or in Magellan Straits.

Concentrate a squadron strong enough to meet *Scharnhorst* and *Gneisenau*, making Falkland Islands your coaling base, and leaving sufficient force to deal with *Dresden* and *Karlsruhe*.

Defence is joining you from Mediterranean, and *Canopus* is now *en route* to Abrolhos.[2] You should keep at least one County class and *Canopus* with your flagship until *Defence* joins.

---

[2]The rocks of Abrolhos off the Brazilian Coast were our secret coaling base in these waters.

When you have superior force, you should at once search Magellan Straits with squadron, keeping in readiness to return and cover the River Plate, or, according to information, search as far as Valparaiso northwards, destroy the German cruisers, and break up the German trade.

You should search anchorage in neighbourhood of Egg Harbour and Golfo Nuevo....[3]

Two days later all uncertainties, and with them our anxieties, vanished, and news was received that both *Scharnhorst* and *Gneisenau* had appeared off Samoa on September 14. There was nothing for them to hurt there. The empty roadstead mocked their power. The British flag flew on shore, and a New Zealand garrison far too strong for any landing party snarled at them from behind defences. Thus informed of the fate of their colony, the German cruisers put to sea after firing a few shells at the Government establishments.

A week later, the 22nd, they were at Papeete, which they bombarded, destroying half the town and sinking the little French gunboat *Zélée* which was in harbour. They left the same morning, steering on a Northerly course. We did not hear of this till the 30th. Then once again silence descended on the vast recesses of the Pacific.

We could now begin drawing our circles again from the beginning, and at any rate for several weeks we need not worry about these ships. Accordingly the Admiralty telegraphed to Admiral Cradock, on September 16, telling him the new situation and that he need not now concentrate his cruisers, but could proceed at once to attack German trade in the Straits of Magellan and on the Chilean coast.

Nothing more happened for a fortnight. On October 4, wireless signals from the *Scharnhorst* were heard by Suva wireless station, and also at Wellington, New Zealand. From this it appeared that the two vessels were on the way between the Marquesas Islands and Easter Island. Evidently the South American plan was in their mind. We passed our information to Admiral Cradock with the following telegram:—

Admiralty to Rear-Admiral Cradock. (October 5.)

It appears from information received that *Gneisenau* and *Scharnhorst* are working across to South America. *Dresden* may be scouting for them. You must be prepared to meet them in company. *Canopus* should accompany *Glasgow, Monmouth* and *Otranto*, and should search and protect trade in combination.

On the 8th (received 12th) Admiral Cradock replied as follows:—

'Without alarming, respectfully suggest that, in event of the enemy's heavy cruisers and others concentrating West Coast of South America, it is necessary to have a British force on each coast strong enough to bring them to action.

'For, otherwise, should the concentrated British force sent from South-East Coast be evaded in the Pacific, which is not impossible, (? and) thereby (? get)

[3]Details relating to colliers, supply ships and mails have been omitted, unless of significance to the account.

behind the enemy, the latter could destroy Falkland, English Bank, and Abrolhos coaling bases in turn with little to stop them, and with British ships unable to follow up owing to want of coal, enemy might possibly reach West Indies.'

And on the same day (received 11th) he reported evidences of the presence of the *Dresden* in South American waters:—

'Following intelligence *re Scharnhorst* and *Gneisenau* has been received. Evidence found by *Good Hope* revisiting Orange Bay on 7th October that *Dresden* had been there 11th September, and there are indications that *Scharnhorst* and *Gneisenau* may be joined by *Nürnberg*, *Dresden*, and *Leipzig*. I intend to concentrate at Falkland Islands and avoid division of forces. I have ordered *Canopus* to proceed there, and *Monmouth*, *Glasgow* and *Otranto* not to go father north than Valparaiso until German cruisers are located again. . . .

'With reference to Admiralty telegram No. 74, does *Defence* join my command?'

This was an important telegram. It showed a strong probability that the enemy was concentrating with the intention to fight. In these circumstances we must clearly concentrate too. I now looked at the Staff telegram of October 5, and thought it was not sufficiently explicit on the vital point, viz., concentration for battle. In order that there should be no mistake, I wrote across the back of Admiral Cradock's telegram received on October 12, the following minute:—

First Sea Lord.

In these circumstances it would be best for the British ships to keep within supporting distance of one another, whether in the Straits or near the Falklands, and to postpone the cruise along the West Coast until the present uncertainty about *Scharnhorst-Gneisenau* is cleared up.

They and not the trade are our quarry for the moment. Above all, we must not miss them.

W. S. C.

The First Sea Lord the same evening added the word 'Settled.'

On October 14, I discussed the whole situation which was developing with the First Sea Lord, and in accordance with my usual practice I sent him a minute after the conversation of what I understood was decided between us.

First Sea Lord.

I understood from our conversation that the dispositions you proposed for the South Pacific and South Atlantic were as follows:—

(1) Cradock to concentrate at the Falklands *Canopus*, *Monmouth*, *Good Hope* and *Otranto*.

(2) To send *Glasgow* round to look for *Leipzig* and attack, and protect trade on the West Coast of South America as far north as Valparaiso.

(3) *Defence* to join *Carnarvon* in forming a new combat squadron on the great trade route from Rio.

(4) *Albion* to join the flag of C.-in-C. Cape for the protection of the Luderitz Bay expedition.

These arrangements have my full approval.

Will you direct the Chief of the Staff to have a statement prepared showing the dates by which these dispositions will be completed, and the earliest date at which *Scharnhorst* and *Gneisenau* could arrive in the respective spheres.

I presume Admiral Cradock is fully aware of the possibility of *Scharnhorst* and *Gneisenau* arriving on or after the 17th instant in his neighbourhood; and that if not strong enough to attack, he will do his utmost to shadow them, pending the arrival of reinforcements.

The following telegram was sent to Admiral Cradock at the same time:—

October 14.

Admiralty to Rear-Admiral Cradock.

Concur in your concentration of *Canopus*, *Good Hope*, *Glasgow*, *Monmouth*, *Otranto*, for combined operation.

We have ordered Stoddart in *Carnarvon* to Montevideo as Senior Naval Officer north of that place.

Have ordered *Defence* to join *Carnarvon*.

He will also have under his orders *Cornwall*, *Bristol*, *Orama* and *Macedonia*.

Essex is to remain in West Indies.

On the 18th Admiral Cradock telegraphed:—

'I consider it possible that *Karlsruhe* has been driven West, and is to join the other five. I trust circumstances will enable me to force an action, but fear that strategically, owing to *Canopus*, the speed of my squadron cannot exceed 12 knots.'

Thus it is clear that up to this date the Admiral fully intended to keep concentrated on the *Canopus*, even though his squadron speed should be reduced to 12 knots. Officially the *Canopus* could steam from 16 to 17 knots. Actually in the operations she steamed 15½.

Let us now examine the situation which was developing.[4] The *Scharnhorst* and the *Gneisenau* were drawing near the South Coast of America. On the way they might be met by the light cruisers *Leipzig*, *Dresden* and *Nürnberg*. The squadron which might thus be formed would be entirely composed of fast modern ships. The two large cruisers

[4]The table of ships on page 349 will be found useful.

were powerful vessels. They carried each eight 8-inch guns arranged in pairs on the upper deck, six of which were capable of firing on either beam. Both ships being on permanent foreign service were fully manned with the highest class of German crews; and they had in fact only recently distinguished themselves as among the best shooting ships of the whole German Navy. Against these two vessels and their attendant light cruisers, Admiral Cradock had the *Good Hope* and the *Monmouth*. The *Good Hope* was a fine old ship from the Third Fleet with a 9.2-inch gun at either end and a battery of sixteen 6-inch guns amidships. She had exceptionally good speed (23 knots) for a vessel of her date. Her crew consisted mainly of reservists, and though she had good gunlayers she could not be expected to compare in gunnery efficiency with the best manned ships either in the British or German Navies. The *Monmouth* was one of the numerous County class against which Fisher had so often inveighed—a large ship with good speed but light armour, and carrying nothing heavier that a battery of fourteen 6-inch guns, of which nine could fire on the beam. These two British armoured cruisers had little chance in an action against the *Scharnhorst* and *Gneisenau*. No gallantry or devotion could make amends for the disparity in strength, to say nothing of gunnery. If brought to battle only the greatest good fortune could save them from destruction. It was for this reason that the moment the Admiralty began to apprehend the possibility of the arrival of the *Scharnhorst* and *Gneisenau* on the South American station, we sent a capital ship to reinforce Admiral Cradock. Our first intention had been to send the *Indomitable* from the Dardanelles, and at one time she had already reached Gibraltar on her way to South America when increasing tension with Turkey forced her to return to the Dardanelles. As we did not conceive ourselves able to spare a single battle-cruiser from the Grand Fleet at that time, there was nothing for it but to send an old battleship; and by the end of September the *Canopus* was already steaming from Abrolhos rocks through the South Atlantic.

With the *Canopus*, Admiral Cradock's squadron was safe. The *Scharnhorst* and *Gneisenau* would never have ventured to come within decisive range of her four 12-inch guns. To do so would have been to subject themselves to very serious damage without any prospect of success. The old battleship, with her heavy armour and artillery, was in fact a citadel around which all our cruisers in those waters could find absolute security. It was for this reason that the Admiralty had telegraphed on September 14: 'Keep at least *Canopus* and one County class with your flagship'; and again, on October 5: '*Canopus* should accompany *Glasgow*, *Monmouth* and *Otranto*.' It was for this reason that I was glad to read Admiral Cradock's telegram: 'Have ordered *Canopus* to Falkland Islands, where I intend to concentrate and avoid division of forces,' on which I minuted: 'In these circumstances it would be best for the British ships to keep within supporting distance of one another, whether in the Straits or near the Falklands'; and it was for this same reason that the Admiralty telegraphed on October 14: 'Concur in your concentration of *Good Hope*, *Canopus*, *Monmouth*, *Glasgow*, *Otranto* for combined operation. . . .'

It was quite true that the speed of the *Canopus* was in fact only fifteen and a half knots, and that as long as our cruisers had to take her about with them they could not hope to catch the Germans. All the *Canopus* could do was to prevent the Germans catching and killing them. But that would not be the end of the story; it would only be its beginning. When the Germans reached the South American coast after their long voyage across the Pacific, they would have to coal and take in supplies: they were bound to try to find some place where colliers could meet them, and where they could refit and revictual. The moment they were located, either by one of our light cruisers or reported from the shore, uncertainty of their whereabouts was at an end. We could instantly concentrate upon them from many quarters. The Japanese battleship *Hizen* and cruiser *Idzumo*, with the British light cruiser *Newcastle*, were moving southward across the Northern Pacific towards the coast of South America—a force also not capable of catching the *Scharnhorst* and *Gneisenau*, but too strong to be attacked by them. On the East Coast of South America was Rear-Admiral Stoddart's squadron with the powerful modern armoured cruiser *Defence*, with two more County class cruisers, *Carnarvon* (7.5-inch guns) and *Cornwall*, the light cruiser *Bristol*, and the armed merchant cruisers *Macedonia* and *Orama*. All these ships could be moved by a single order into a common concentration against the German squadron the moment we knew where they were; and meanwhile, so long as he kept within supporting distance of the *Canopus*, Admiral Cradock could have cruised safely up the Chilean coast, keeping the Germans on the move and always falling back on his battleship if they attempted to attack him. The *Good Hope* and *Monmouth* steaming together were scarcely inferior in designed speed to the *Scharnhorst* and *Gneisenau*, and these last had been long at sea. Admiral Cradock could, therefore, have kept on observing the Germans, disturbing them, provoking them and drawing them on to the *Canopus*. Moreover, in the *Glasgow* he had a light cruiser which was much superior in speed to the *Scharnhorst* and *Gneisenau*, and superior both in strength and speed to any one of the German light cruisers concerned.

I cannot therefore accept for the Admiralty any share in the responsibility for what followed. The first rule of war is to concentrate superior strength for decisive action and to avoid division of forces or engaging in detail. The Admiral showed by his telegrams that he clearly appreciated this. The Admiralty orders explicitly approved his assertion of these elementary principles. We were not, therefore, anxious about the safety of Admiral Cradock's squadron. A more important and critical situation would arise, if in cruising up the West Coast of South America with his concentrated force Admiral Cradock missed the Germans altogether, and if they passed to the southward of him through the Straits of Magellan or round the Horn, refuelling there in some secret bay, and so came on to the great trade route from Rio. Here they would find Admiral Stoddart, whose squadron when concentrated, though somewhat faster and stronger than the Germans, had not much to spare in either respect. It was for this reason that I had deprecated in my minute of October 12 Admiral Cradock's movement up the West Coast and would have been glad to see him remaining near the Straits of Magellan, where he could either bar the path of the *Scharnhorst* and the *Gneisenau*, or manœuvre to join forces with Admiral Stoddart. However, I rested content with the decisions conveyed in the Admiralty telegram of October 14, and awaited events.

Suddenly, on October 27, there arrived a telegram from Admiral Cradock which threw me into perplexity:—

Rear-Admiral Cradock to Admiralty.

Good Hope. 26th October, 7 p.m. At sea.

> Admiralty telegram received 7th October. With reference to orders to search for enemy and our great desire for early success, I consider that owing to slow speed of *Canopus* it is impossible to find and destroy enemy's squadron.
>
> Have therefore ordered *Defence* to join me after calling for orders at Montevideo.
>
> Shall employ *Canopus* on necessary work of convoying colliers.

We were then in the throes of the change in the office of First Sea Lord, and I was gravely preoccupied with the circumstances and oppositions attending the appointment of Lord Fisher. But for this fact I am sure I should have reacted much more violently against the ominous sentence: 'Shall employ *Canopus* on necessary work of convoying colliers.' As it was I minuted to the Naval Secretary (Admiral Oliver) as follows:—

> 'This telegram is very obscure, and I do not understand what Admiral Cradock intends and wishes.'

I was reassured by his reply on October 29:—

> 'The situation on the West Coast seems safe. If *Gneisenau* and *Scharnhorst* have gone north they will meet eventually *Idzumo*, *Newcastle*, and *Hizen* moving south, and will be forced south on *Glasgow* and *Monmouth* who have good speed and can keep touch and draw them south on to *Good Hope* and *Canopus*, who should keep within supporting distance of each other.'

The half fear which had begun to grow in my mind that perhaps the Admiral would go and fight without the *Canopus*, which I thought was so improbable that I did not put it on paper, was allayed. It would, of course, be possible for him to manœuvre forty or fifty miles ahead of the *Canopus* and still close her before fighting. To send the *Defence* to join Admiral Cradock would have left Admiral Stoddart in a hopeless inferiority. Indeed, in a few hours arrived Admiral Stoddart's protest of October 29:—

> 'I have received orders from Admiral Cradock to send *Defence* to Montevideo to coal, obtain charts, and to await further orders.
>
> 'Submit I may be given two fast cruisers in place of *Defence*, as I do not consider force at my disposal sufficient. . . .'

The Admiralty Staff had, however, already replied in accordance with all our decisions:—

Admiralty to Rear-Admiral Cradock.

(Sent October 28, 1914, 6.45 p.m.)

Defence is to remain on East Coast under orders of Stoddart.

This will leave sufficient force on each side in case the hostile cruisers appear there on the trade routes.

There is no ship available for the Cape Horn vicinity.

Japanese battleship *Hizen* shortly expected on North American coast; she will join with Japanese *Idzumo* and *Newcastle* and move south towards Galapagos.

But neither this nor any further message reached Admiral Cradock. He had taken his own decision. Without waiting for the *Defence*, even if we had been able to send her, and leaving the *Canopus* behind to guard the colliers, he was already steaming up the Chilean coast. But though he left the inexpugnable *Canopus* behind because she was too slow, he took with him the helpless armed merchant cruiser *Otranto*, which was scarcely any faster. He was thus ill-fitted either to fight or run.

He telegraphed to us from off Vallenar at 4 p.m. on October 27 (received November 1, 4.33 a.m.):—

'Have received your telegram 105. Have seized German mails. *Monmouth*, *Good Hope* and *Otranto* coaling at Vallenar. *Glasgow* patrolling vicinity of Coronel to intercept German shipping rejoining flag later on. I intend to proceed northward secretly with squadron after coaling and to keep out of sight of land. Until further notice continue telegraphing to Montevideo.'

And at noon on October 29 (received November 1 7.40 a.m.):—

'Until further notice mails for Rear-Admiral Cradock, *Good Hope*, *Canopus*, *Monmouth*, *Glasgow*, *Otranto*, should be forwarded to Valparaiso.'

The inclusion of the *Canopus* in the middle of the latter message seemed to indicate the Admiral's intention to work in combination with the *Canopus* even if not actually concentrated. These were the last messages received from him.

On October 30 Lord Fisher became First Sea Lord. As soon as he entered the Admiralty I took him to the War Room and went over with him on the great map the positions and tasks of every vessel in our immense organization. It took more than two hours. The critical point was clearly in South American waters. Speaking of Admiral Cradock's position, I said, 'You don't suppose he would try to fight them without the *Canopus*?' He did not give any decided reply.

Early on November 3 we got our first certain news of the Germans.

Consul-General, Valparaiso, to Admiralty. (Sent 5.20 p.m., *2nd November. Received* 3.10 a.m., *3rd November.*)

Master of Chilean merchant vessel reports that on 1st November 1 p.m. he was stopped by *Nürnberg* 5 miles off Cape Carranza about 62 miles north of Talcahuano. Officers remained on board 45 minutes. Two other German cruisers lay west about 5 and 10 miles respectively. Master believes one of these was *Scharnhorst*. On 26th October, 1 p.m. *Leipzig* called at Mas-a-Fuera having crew 456 and 10 guns, 18 days out from Galapagos. She was accompanied by another cruiser name unknown. They bought oxen and left same day. On 29th October unknown warship was seen in lat. 33 south, long. 74 west, steaming towards Coquimbo.

Here at last was the vital message for which the Admiralty Staff had waited so long. Admiral von Spee's squadron was definitely located on the West Coast of South America. He had not slipped past Admiral Cradock round the Horn as had been possible. For the moment Admiral Stoddart was perfectly safe. With the long Peninsula of South America between him and the *Scharnhorst* and *Gneisenau*, there was no longer any need for him to keep the *Defence*. She could join Cradock for what we must hope would be an early battle. After surveying the new situation we telegraphed to Admiral Stoddart as follows:—

(*Sent* 6.20 p.m., *3rd November.*)

Defence to proceed with all possible dispatch to join Admiral Cradock on West Coast of America. Acknowledge.

This telegram was initialled by Admiral Sturdee, Lord Fisher and myself. We telegraphed at the same time to the Japanese Admiralty:—

Scharnhorst, *Gneisenau*, *Nürnberg*, *Leipzig*, *Dresden* have been located near Valparaiso coaling and provisioning. This squadron is presumably concentrated for some serious operation. We are concentrating *Glasgow*, *Good Hope*, *Canopus*, *Monmouth* and *Defence* on the S.W. coast of South America, hoping to bring them to battle. . . . We hope that the Japanese Admiralty may now find it possible to move some of their squadrons eastward in order to intercept the German squadron and prevent its return to Asiatic or Australian waters. . . . We indicate our views in order to obtain yours and to concert common action.

We also telegraphed to Admiral Cradock once more reiterating the instructions about the *Canopus:—*

(*Sent* 6.55 p.m. *3rd November.*)

Defence has been ordered to join your flag with all dispatch. *Glasgow* should find or keep in touch with the enemy. You should keep touch with *Glasgow* concentrating

> the rest of your squadron including *Canopus*. It is important you should effect your junction with *Defence* at earliest possible moment subject to keeping touch with *Glasgow* and enemy. Enemy supposes you at Corcovados Bay. Acknowledge.

But we were already talking to the void.

When I opened my boxes at 7 o'clock on the morning of November 4, I read the following telegram:—

Maclean, Valparaiso, to Admiralty. (Sent November 3, 1914, 6.10 p.m.)

> Have just learnt from Chilean Admiral that German Admiral states that on Sunday at sunset, in thick and wicked weather, his ships met *Good Hope*, *Glasgow*, *Monmouth* and *Otranto*. Action was joined, and *Monmouth* turned over and sank after about an hour's fighting.
>
> *Good Hope*, *Glasgow* and *Otranto* drew off into darkness.
>
> *Good Hope* was on fire, an explosion was heard, and she is believed to have sunk.
>
> *Gneisenau*, *Scharnhorst* and *Nürnberg* were among the German ships engaged.

The story of what had happened, so far as it ever can be known, is now familiar; it is fully set out in the official history, and need only be summarized here. Arrived on the Chilean coast, having refuelled at a lonely island, and hearing that the British light cruiser *Glasgow* was at Coronel, Admiral von Spee determined to make an attempt to cut her off, and with this intention steamed southward on November 1 with his whole squadron. By good fortune the *Glasgow* left harbour before it was too late. Almost at the same moment, Admiral Cradock began his sweep northward, hoping to catch the *Leipzig*, whose wireless had been heard repeatedly by the *Glasgow*. He was rejoined by the *Glasgow* at half-past two, and the whole squadron proceeded northward abreast about fifteen miles apart. At about half-past four the smoke of several vessels was seen to the northward, and in another quarter of an hour the *Glasgow* was able to identify the *Scharnhorst*, *Gneisenau* and a German light cruiser. The *Canopus* was nearly 300 miles away. Was there still time to refuse action? Undoubtedly there was. The *Good Hope* and *Monmouth* had normal speeds of 23 knots and 22.4 respectively and could certainly steam 21 knots in company that day. The *Glasgow* could steam over 25. The *Scharnhorst* and *Gneisenau* had nominal speeds of 23.2 and 23.5; but they had been long in southern seas and out of dock. On the knowledge he possessed at that moment Admiral Cradock would have been liberal in allowing them 22 knots. Rough weather would reduce speeds equally on both sides. Had he turned at once and by standing out to sea offered a stern chase to the enemy, he could only be overhauled one knot each hour. When the enemy was sighted by the *Glasgow* at 4.45, the nearest armoured ships were about 20 miles apart. There were scarcely two hours to sundown and less than three to darkness.

But the *Otranto* was a possible complication. She could only steam 18 knots, and against the head sea during the action she did in fact only steam 15 knots. As this weak, slow ship had been for some unexplained reason sent on ahead with the *Glasgow*, she was at the moment of sighting the enemy only 17 miles distant. Assuming that Admiral von Spee could steam 22 knots, less 3 for the head sea, i.e. 19, he would overhaul the *Otranto* 4 knots an hour. On this he might have brought her under long-range fire as darkness closed in. To that extent she reduced the speed of the British squadron and diminished their chances of safety. This may have weighed with Admiral Cradock.

We now know, of course, that in spite of being cumbered with the *Otranto* he could, as it happened, easily and certainly have declined action had he attempted to do so. At the moment of being sighted, Admiral von Spee had only steam for 14 knots, and had to light two more boilers to realize his full speed. Further, his ships were dispersed. To concentrate and gain speed took an hour and a half off the brief daylight during which the British ships would actually have been increasing their distance. Moreover, in the chase and battle of the Falklands the greatest speed ever developed by the *Scharnhorst* and *Gneisenau* did not exceed 20 knots in favourable weather. There is therefore no doubt he could have got away untouched.

But nothing was farther from the mind of Admiral Cradock. He instantly decided to attack. As soon as the *Glasgow* had sighted the enemy, she had turned back towards the flagship, preceded by the *Monmouth* and the *Otranto* all returning at full speed. But Admiral Cradock at 5.10 ordered the squadron to concentrate, not on his flagship the *Good Hope*, the farthest ship from the enemy, but on the *Glasgow*, which though retreating rapidly was still the nearest. At 6.18 he signalled to the distant *Canopus:* 'I am now going to attack enemy.' The decision to fight sealed his fate, and more than that the fate of the squadron.

To quote the log of the *Glasgow*, 'The British Squadron turned to port four points together towards the enemy with a view to closing them and forcing them to action before sunset, which if successful would have put them at a great disadvantage owing to the British squadron being between the enemy and the sun.' The German Admiral easily evaded this manœuvre by turning away towards the land and keeping at a range of at least 18,000 yards. Both squadrons were now steaming southward on slightly converging courses—the British to seaward with the setting sun behind them, and the Germans nearer the land. And now began the saddest naval action in the war. Of the officers and men in both the squadrons that faced each other in these stormy seas so far from home, nine out of ten were doomed to perish. The British were to die that night: the Germans a month later. At 7 o'clock the sun sank beneath the horizon, and the German Admiral, no longer dazzled by its rays, opened fire. The British ships were silhouetted against the after-glow, while the Germans were hardly visible against the dark background of the Chilean coast. A complete reversal of advantage had taken place. The sea was high, and the main deck 6-inch guns both of the *Monmouth* and of the *Good Hope* must have been much affected by the dashing spray. The German batteries, all mounted in modern fashion on the upper deck, suffered no corresponding disadvantage from the rough weather. The unequal contest lasted less than an hour. One of the earliest German salvos probably disabled the *Good Hope's* forward 9.2-inch gun, which was not fired throughout the action. Both she and the *Monmouth* were soon on fire. Darkness came on and the sea increased in violence till the *Good Hope*, after a great explosion, became only a glowing speck which was presently extinguished; and the *Monmouth*, absolutely helpless but refusing to surrender, was destroyed by the *Nürnberg*, and foundered, like her consort, with her flag still flying. The *Otranto*, an unarmoured merchantman, quite incapable of taking part in the action, rightly held her distance and disappeared into the gloom. Only the little *Glasgow*, which miraculously escaped fatal damage among the heavy salvos, continued the action until she was left alone in darkness on the stormy seas. There were no survivors from the two British ships: all perished, from Admiral to seaman. The Germans had no loss of life.

Quoth the *Glasgow* in her subsequent report:—

> '. . . Throughout the engagement the conduct of officers and men was entirely admirable. Perfect discipline and coolness prevailed under trying circumstances of receiving considerable volume of fire without being able to make adequate return. The men behaved exactly as though at battle practice; there were no signs of wild fire, and when the target was invisible the gunlayers ceased firing of their own accord. Spirit of officers and ship's company of *Glasgow* is entirely unimpaired by serious reverse in which they took part, and that the ship may be quickly restored to a condition in which she can take part in further operations against the same enemy is the unanimous wish of us all.'

This as it happened they were not to be denied.

Surveying this tragic episode in the light of after knowledge, the official historian has blamed the Admiralty on various grounds: first, for dividing the available force into two inadequate squadrons under Admiral Cradock and Admiral Stoddart; secondly for a lack of explicitness in the wording of the Staff telegrams. I cannot admit that the first charge is in any way justified. It would, of course, have been much simpler to have concentrated the squadrons of Admiral Cradock and Admiral Stoddart in the Straits of Magellan and awaited events. But until we knew for certain that the German cruisers were coming to South America, there was a great disadvantage in denuding the main trade route from Rio of all protection. Suppose we had done this and Admiral von Spee had remained, as he could easily have done, for many weeks at Easter Island, or anywhere else in the Pacific, the whole of the Plate trade would then, for all we knew, have been at the mercy of the *Karlsruhe* or of any other German commerce destroyer. At least six different courses were open to von Spee, and we had, while our resources were at the fullest strain, to meet every one of them. Suppose for instance he had gone northward to the Panama Canal and, passing swiftly through, had entered the West Indies: of what use would be our concentration in the Straits of Magellan? The reasoning and state of mind which would have led to such a concentration would have involved a virtual suspension of our enterprises all over the world. We could not afford to do that. We decided deliberately in October to carry on our protection of trade in every theatre in spite of the menace of the unlocated *Scharnhorst* and *Gneisenau*, and to do this by means of squadrons which, though they would not be homogeneous in speed and class, were in every case if held together capable of fighting the enemy with good prospects of success. This was true of

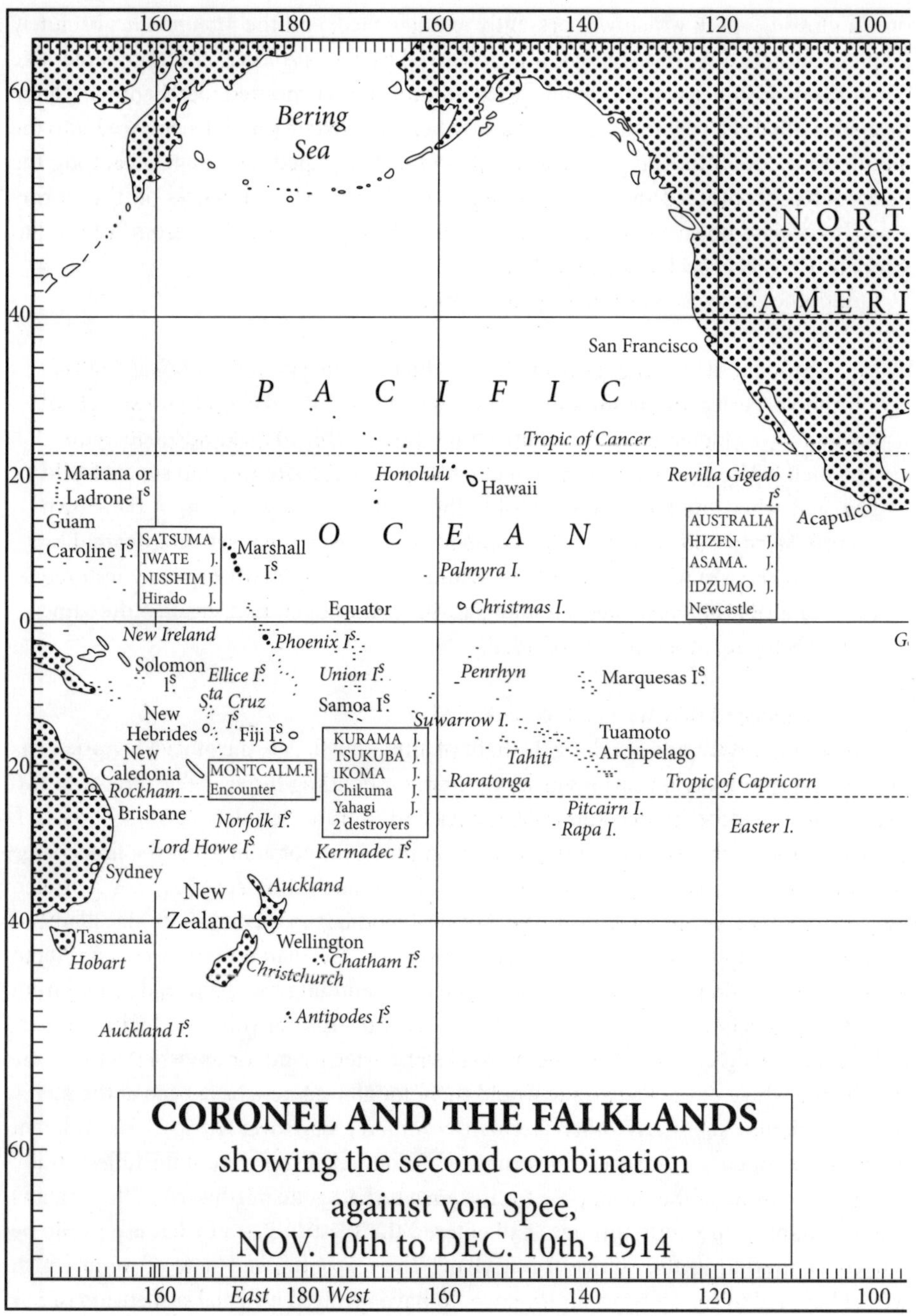

CORONEL AND THE FALKLANDS
showing the second combination against von Spee,
NOV. 10th to DEC. 10th, 1914

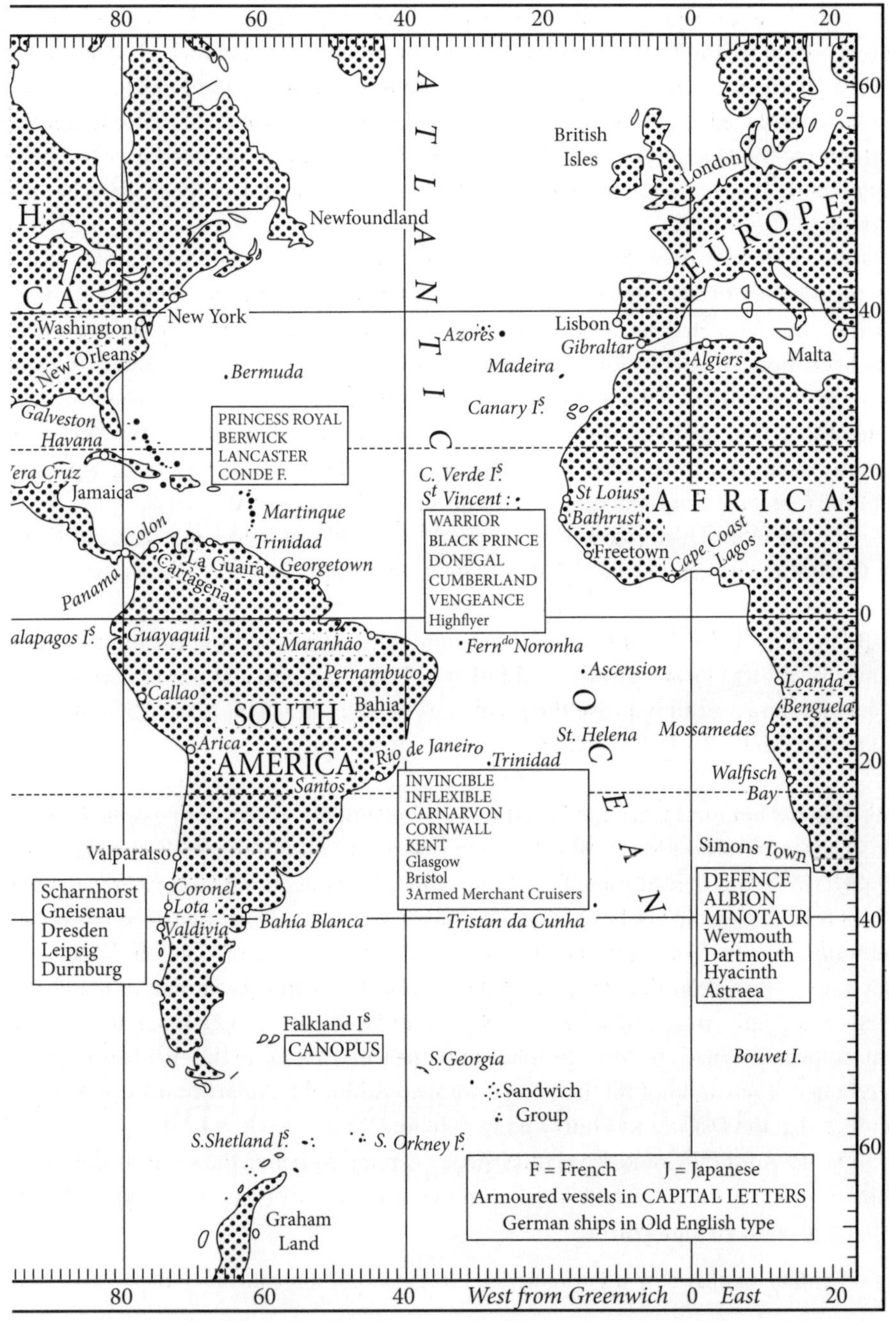
British Isles
London
EUROPE
Newfoundland
ATLANTIC
OCEAN
New York
Washington
New Orleans
Galveston
Havana
Vera Cruz
Jamaica
Bermuda
PRINCESS ROYAL
BERWICK
LANCASTER
CONDE F.
Azores
Madeira
Canary Is
Lisbon
Gibraltar
Algiers
Malta
C. Verde Is
St Vincent
WARRIOR
BLACK PRINCE
DONEGAL
CUMBERLAND
VENGEANCE
Highflyer
St Loius
Bathrust
Freetown
AFRICA
Cape Coast
Lagos
Martinque
Trinidad
Colon
La Guaira
Cartagena
Georgetown
Panama
Galapagos Is
Guayaquil
Maranhão
Pernambuco
Ferndo Noronha
Ascension
Callao
SOUTH AMERICA
Bahia
Arica
Rio de Janeiro
Santos
Trinidad
St. Helena
Mossamedes
Loanda
Benguela
Walfisch Bay
INVINCIBLE
INFLEXIBLE
CARNARVON
CORNWALL
KENT
Glasgow
Bristol
3Armed Merchant Cruisers
Simons Town
Valparaiso
Scharnhorst
Gneisenau
Dresden
Leipsig
Durnburg
Coronel
Lota
Valdivia
Bahía Blanca
Tristan da Cunha
DEFENCE
ALBION
MINOTAUR
Weymouth
Dartmouth
Hyacinth
Astraea
Falkland Is
CANOPUS
S.Georgia
Sandwich Group
Bouvet I.
S.Shetland Is
S. Orkney Is
Graham Land
F = French J = Japanese
Armoured vessels in CAPITAL LETTERS
German ships in Old English type
West from Greenwich 0 East

the Anglo-Japanese squadron. It was true of the escort of the Australian convoy. It was true of Admiral Stoddart. Most of all was it true of Admiral Cradock. The last word in such an argument was surely spoken by Admiral von Spee. 'The English,' he wrote the day after the battle, 'have here another ship like the *Monmouth*; and also it seems a battleship of the *Queen* type, with 12-inch guns. Against this last-named we can hardly do anything. If they had kept their forces together we should, I suppose, have got the worse of it.'

So far as the clarity of the Staff telegrams is concerned, no doubt here another ship like the *Monmouth*; and also it seems a battleciently precise, and this fault ran through much of the Naval Staff work in those early days; but on the main point nothing could have been more emphatic, nor, indeed, should any emphasis have been needed. It ought not to be necessary to tell an experienced Admiral to keep concentrated and not to be brought to action in circumstances of great disadvantage by superior forces. Still, even this was done, and in telegram after telegram the importance of not being separated from the *Canopus*, especially sent him for his protection, was emphasized.

Lastly, the official historian has represented the new decision to reinforce Cradock by the *Defence* as a reversal by Lord Fisher of the mistaken policy hitherto pursued.

> 'By the time it (Admiral Cradock's telegram of 31st) reached the Admiralty the new Board was installed with Lord Fisher as First Sea Lord, and one of their first acts was an effort to improve the precarious position in which Admiral Cradock found himself. The *Defence* was immediately ordered to join him.'[5]

This is unjust both to Prince Louis and to Admiral Sturdee. It was not possible to order the superior concentration until the enemy had been located, and such concentration would have been ordered by any Board the moment the uncertainty was cleared up. The official historian would not have fallen into this error in a work distinguished for its care and industry, if he had mentioned the telegram from the Consul-General, Valparaiso, which was received on the morning of the 3rd, or if he had noticed that although the position in South American waters was known to Lord Fisher on October 30, no fresh dispositions were made or could be made until the whereabouts of the enemy was clearly ascertained. Then and not till then could we strip Admiral Stoddart or inform Admiral Cradock that the *Defence* was hurrying to join him.

So far as Admiral Cradock is concerned, I cannot do better than repeat the words which I wrote at the time and which commanded the recorded assent both of Lord Fisher and of Sir Arthur Wilson.

> *Draft of an answer to a Parliamentary question not subsequently put.*
>
> SIR,—As I have already said, I did not think it convenient to go into this matter, but since it is pressed I will state that the *Canopus* was sent from St. Vincent to join Admiral Cradock's flag on September 4th, as soon as the possibility of the

[5]*Official History of the War: Naval Operations*, Vol. I, p. 344.

> arrival of the *Scharnhorst* and *Gneisenau* on the West Coast of South America could be taken into account. On October 12th Admiral Cradock telegraphed to the Admiralty that the indications showed the possibility of *Dresden*, *Leipzig* and *Nürnberg* joining *Scharnhorst* and *Gneisenau*; and that he had ordered *Canopus* to Falkland Islands, where he intended to concentrate and avoid division of forces; and on October 14th the Admiralty approved specifically by telegram Admiral Cradock's proposed concentration of *Good Hope*, *Monmouth*, *Canopus*, *Glasgow* and *Otranto* for combined operations. The squadron thus formed was amply strong enough to defeat the enemy if attacked by them. It was not fast enough to force an engagement; but in view of the uncertainty as to which part of the world the enemy's squadron would appear in, it was not possible at that time to provide another strong fast ship at that particular point.
>
> Admiral Cradock was an experienced and fearless officer, and we are of opinion that feeling that he could not bring the enemy immediately to action as long as he kept with the *Canopus*, he decided to attack them with his fast ships alone, in the belief that even if he himself were destroyed in the action, he would inflict damage upon them which in the circumstances would be irreparable and lead to their certain subsequent destruction. This was not an unreasonable hope; and though the Admiralty have no responsibility for Admiral Cradock's decision they consider that it was inspired by the highest devotion, and in harmony with the spirit and traditions of the British Navy.

We had now to meet the new situation. Our combinations, such as they were, were completely ruptured, and Admiral von Spee, now in temporary command of South American waters, possessed a wide choice of alternatives. He might turn back into the Pacific, and repeat the mystery tactics which had been so baffling to us. He might steam northward up the West Coast of South America and make for the Panama Canal. In this case he would run a chance of being brought to battle by the Anglo-Japanese Squadron which was moving southward. But of course he might not fall in with them, or, if he did, he could avoid battle owing to his superior speed. He might come round to the East Coast and interrupt the main trade route. If he did this he must be prepared to fight Admiral Stoddart; but this would be a very even and hazardous combat. Admiral Stoddart had against the two armoured German ships three armoured ships, of which the *Defence*, a later and a better ship than either of the Germans, mounted four 9.2-inch and ten 7.5-inch guns, and was one of our most powerful armoured-cruiser class. Lastly, he might cross the Atlantic, possibly raiding the Falkland Islands on his way, and arrive unexpectedly on the South African coast. Here he would find the Union Government's expedition against the German colony in full progress and his arrival would have been most unwelcome. General Botha and General Smuts, having suppressed the rebellion, were about to resume in a critical atmosphere their attack upon German South-West Africa, and a stream of transports would soon be flowing with the expedition and its supplies from Cape Town to Luderitz Bay. Subsequently or alternatively to this intrusion, Admiral von Spee might steam up the African coast and strike at the whole of the shipping of the expedition to the Cameroons, which was quite without means of defending itself against him.

All these unpleasant possibilities had to be faced by us. We had to prepare again at each of many points against a sudden blow; and, great as were our resources, the strain upon them became enormous. The first step was to restore the situation in South American waters. This would certainly take a month. My minute of inquiry to the Chief of the Staff, written an hour after I had read the first news of the disaster, will show the possibilities which existed. It will be seen that in this grave need my mind immediately turned to wresting a battle-cruiser from the Grand Fleet which, joined with the *Defence*, *Carnarvon*, *Cornwall* and *Kent*, would give Admiral Stoddart an overwhelming superiority.

4/11/14.

Director of Operations Division.

1. How far is it, and how long would it take *Dartmouth* and *Weymouth* to reach Punta Arenas, Rio, or Abrolhos respectively, if they started this afternoon with all dispatch?

2. How long would it take—
   - (*a*) KENT to reach Rio and Abrolhos?
   - (*b*) *Australia* (1) without, and (2) with *Montcalm* to reach Galapagos via Makada Islands, and also *Idzumo* and *Newcastle* to reach them?
   - (*c*) The Japanese 2nd Southern Squadron to replace *Australia* at Fiji?
   - (*d*) *Defence*, CARNARVON and CORNWALL respectively to reach Punta Arenas?
   - (*e*) INVINCIBLE to reach Abrolhos, Rio, Punta Arenas?
   - (*f*) *Hizen* and *Asama* to reach Galapagos or Esquimalt?[6]

W. S. C.

But I found Lord Fisher in a bolder mood. He would take two battle-cruisers from the Grand Fleet for the South American station. More than that, and much more questionable, he would take a third—the *Princess Royal*—for Halifax and later for the West Indies in case von Spee came through the Panama Canal. There never was any doubt what ought to be sent. The question was what could be spared. We measured up our strength in Home Waters anxiously, observing that the *Tiger* was about to join the 1st Battle-Cruiser Squadron, that the new battleships *Benbow*, *Emperor of India* and *Queen Elizabeth* were practically ready. We sent forthwith the following order to the Commander-in-Chief:—

(*November* 4, 1914, 12.40 p.m.)

Order *Invincible* and *Inflexible* to fill up with coal at once and proceed to Berehaven with all dispatch. They are urgently needed for foreign service. Admiral and Flag-Captain *Invincible* to transfer to *New Zealand*. Captain *New Zealand* to

[6]All the ships in small capitals fought eventually in the battle of the Falkland Islands.

> *Invincible. Tiger* has been ordered to join you with all dispatch. Give her necessary orders.

I also telegraphed personally to Sir John Jellicoe as follows:—

> (*November* 5, 12.5 a.m.)
>
> From all reports received through German sources, we fear Cradock has been caught or has engaged with only *Monmouth* and *Good Hope* armoured ships against *Scharnhorst* and *Gneisenau*. Probably both British vessels sunk. Position of *Canopus* critical and fate of *Glasgow* and *Otranto* uncertain.
>
> Proximity of concentrated German squadron of 5 good ships will threaten gravely main trade route Rio to London. Essential recover control.
>
> First Sea Lord requires *Invincible* and *Inflexible* for this purpose.
>
> Sturdee goes Commander-in-Chief, South Atlantic and Pacific.
>
> Oliver, Chief of Staff. Bartolomé, Naval Secretary.

Apparently we had not at this stage decided finally to send the *Princess Royal.* Sir John Jellicoe rose to the occasion and parted with his two battle-cruisers without a word. They were ordered to steam by the West Coast to Devonport to fit themselves for their southern voyage. Our plans for the second clutch at von Spee were now conceived as follows[7]:—

(1) Should he break across the Pacific, he would be dealt with by the very superior Japanese 1st Southern Squadron, based on Suva to cover Australia and New Zealand, and composed as follows:—*Kurama* (battleship), *Tsukuba* and *Ikoma* (battle-cruisers), *Chikuma* and *Yahagi* (light cruisers). At Suva also were the *Montcalm* and *Encounter.* Another strong Japanese squadron (four ships) was based on the Caroline Islands.

(2) To meet him, should he proceed up the West Coast of South America, an Anglo-Japanese Squadron, comprising *Australia* (from Fiji), *Hizen*, *Idzumo*, *Newcastle*, was to be formed off the North American Coast.

(3) Should he come round on to the East Coast, *Defence*, *Carnarvon*, *Cornwall*, *Kent* were ordered to concentrate off Montevideo, together with *Canopus*, *Glasgow* and *Bristol*, and not seek action till joined by *Invincible* and *Inflexible*, thereafter sending the *Defence* to South Africa.

(4) Should he approach the Cape station, he would be awaited by *Defence* and also *Minotaur* (released from the Australian convoy, after we knew of von Spee's arrival in South American waters), together with the old battleship *Albion*, and *Weymouth*, *Dartmouth*, *Astrœa* and *Hyacinth*, light cruisers: the Union Expedition being postponed for 14 days.

(5) Should he come through the Panama Canal, he would meet the *Princess Royal*, as well as the *Berwick* and *Lancaster*, of the West Indian Squadron, and the French *Condé*.

---

[7]Here the reader should certainly look at the map on pages 334–5, which deals directly with this situation.

(6) Cameroons were warned to be ready to take their shipping up the river beyond his reach.

(7) Should he endeavour to work homewards across the South Atlantic, he would come into the area of a new squadron under Admiral de Robeck to be formed near the Cape de Verde Islands, comprising the old battleship *Vengeance*, the strong armoured cruisers *Warrior* and *Black Prince* and the *Donegal*, *Highflyer*, and later *Cumberland*.

Thus to compass the destruction of five warships, only two of which were armoured, it was necessary to employ nearly thirty, including twenty-one armoured ships, the most part of superior metal, and this took no account of the powerful Japanese Squadrons, and of French ships or of armed merchant cruisers, the last-named effective for scouting.

I telegraphed to the Japanese Admiralty as follows:—

British Admiralty to Japanese Admiralty.

November 5, 1914.

In consequence of unsuccessful action off Chili and definite location of German squadron, we have ordered concentration off Montevideo of *Defence*, *Kent*, *Carnarvon* and *Cornwall*. These will be joined with all dispatch by *Invincible* and *Inflexible* battle-cruisers from England, and *Dartmouth* light cruiser from East Africa, and remainder of defeated squadron from Chili. This assures the South Atlantic situation. We now desire assistance of Japan in making equally thorough arrangements on Pacific side. We propose for your consideration and friendly advice the following:—*Newcastle* and *Idzumo* to go south in company to San Clemente Island off San Diego, California, there to meet *Hizen* from Honolulu. Meanwhile *Asama* will be able to effect internment or destruction of *Geier*. We also propose to move *Australia* battle-cruiser from Fiji to Fanning Island. By the time these moves are complete, probably by November 17, we may know more of *Scharnhorst* and *Gneisenau* movements and a further concentration of *Australia* and *Asama* with *Hizen*, *Idzumo* and *Newcastle* will be possible either at San Clemente or further to the south, further movements depending on the enemy.

We should also like a Japanese squadron to advance to Fiji to take the place of the *Australia*, and so guard Australia and New Zealand in case the Germans return.

With regard to the Indian Ocean and Western Pacific, it is now known that *Emden* is the only enemy ship at large. We therefore hope that the Japanese squadrons and vessels not involved in the eastward movement will draw westward into the vicinity of Sumatra and the Dutch East Indies in order to block every exit and deny every place of shelter up to the 90th meridian of east longitude.

British Admiralty are combining in Indian waters in search of *Emden* the following light cruisers:—*Weymouth*, *Gloucester*, *Yarmouth*, *Melbourne*, *Sydney*, and the armoured cruiser *Hampshire* and Russian cruiser *Askold*. These ships will be ready by the middle of November. Thus by concerted action between the Allied fleets the *Emden* should be speedily run down.

Japanese Admiralty to British Admiralty. November 7, 1914.

Secret and Private.

Japanese Admiralty give their consent generally to strategical scheme proposed and beg to withdraw the proposal of November 6, put forward through Admiral Oguri to the British War Staff. Measures will be taken in vicinity of Sumatra and Dutch East Indies as asked. First Southern Squadron will be dispatched to Fiji, but Japanese Admiralty think that it may be necessary for them to extend their sphere of operations to the Marquesas Islands. With reference to the movements of the *Hizen* and *Asama*, Japanese Admiralty will carry out your wishes as far as possible, bearing in mind necessity of watching the *Geier* until her (? disposition) is settled, but the *Hizen* will be dispatched at once.

With reference to the *Hizen*, *Asama* and *Idzumo*, Japanese Admiralty request British Admiralty to make arrangements necessary for their supply of coal, etc.

Meanwhile it had been necessary to provide, as far as possible, for the safety of the surviving ships of Admiral Cradock's squadron and to move the reinforcing ships.

Admiralty to H.M.S. 'Kent.'

(*November* 4, 1914.)

Urgent. Proceed to the Abrolhos Rocks with all dispatch and communicate via Rio. It is intended you shall join Admiral Stoddart's squadron.

Admiralty to Rear-Admiral Stoddart, 'Carnarvon.'

(*November* 4, 1914.)

In view of reported sinking of *Good Hope* and *Monmouth* by *Scharnhorst* and *Gneisenau* off Coronel, November 1, armoured ships on S.E. Coast America must concentrate at once. *Carnarvon*, *Cornwall* should join *Defence* off Montevideo. *Canopus*, *Glasgow*, *Otranto* have been ordered if possible to join you there. *Kent* from Sierra Leone also has been ordered to join your flag via Abrolhos. Endeavour to get into communication with them. Enemy will most likely come on to the Rio trade route. Reinforcements will meet you shortly from England.

Acknowledge.

From Admiralty to 'Canopus.'

(*November* 4, 1914.)

In view of reported sinking of *Good Hope* and *Monmouth* by *Scharnhorst* and *Gneisenau* on 1st November you should make the best of your way to join *Defence* near Montevideo. Keep wide of track to avoid being brought to action by superior force.

If attacked, however, Admiralty is confident ship will in all circumstances be fought to the last as imperative to damage enemy whatever may be consequences.

Admiralty to 'Glasgow,' Otranto'

(*November* 4, 1914.)

You should make the best of your way to join *Defence* near Montevideo. Keep wide of track to avoid being brought to action by superior force.

Admiralty to Governor, Falkland Islands.

(*November* 5, 1914.)

German cruiser raid may take place. All Admiralty colliers should be concealed in unfrequented harbours. Be ready to destroy supplies useful to enemy and hide codes effectively on enemy ships being sighted. Acknowledge.

In a few days we learned that her continuous fast steaming had led to boiler troubles in the *Canopus*, and we had to direct her to the Falklands.

Admiralty to 'Canopus.'

(*November* 9, 1914, 3.10 a.m.)

You are to remain in Stanley Harbour. Moor the ship so that the entrance is commanded by your guns. Extemporize mines outside entrance. Send down your topmasts and be prepared for bombardment from outside the harbour. Stimulate the Governor to organize all local forces and make determined defence. Arrange observation stations on shore, by which your fire on ships outside can be directed Land guns or use boats' torpedoes to sink a blocking ship before she reaches the Narrows. No objection to your grounding ship to obtain a good berth.

Should *Glasgow* be able to get sufficient start of enemy to avoid capture, send her on to the River Plate; if not, moor her inside *Canopus*.

Repair your defects and wait orders.[8]

The strain upon British naval resources in the outer seas, apart from the main theatre of naval operations, was now at its maximum and may be partially appreciated from the following approximate enumerations:—

Combination against von Spee, 30 ships.

In search of the *Emden* and *Königsberg*, 8 ships.

[8]All the above telegrams had to be sent by various routes and most were repeated by several routes, as of course we could not communicate direct across these great distances. But I omit the procedure to simplify the account.

General protection of trade by vessels other than the above, 40 ships.

Convoy duty in the Indian Ocean, 8 ships.

Blockade of the Turco-German Fleet at the Dardanelles, 3 ships.

Defence of Egypt, 2 ships.

Miscellaneous minor tasks, 11 ships.

Total, 102 ships of all classes.

We literally could not lay our hands on another vessel of any sort or kind which could be made to play any useful part. But we were soon to have relief.

Already on October 30 news had reached us that the *Königsberg* had been discovered hiding in the Rufigi River in German East Africa, and it was instantly possible to mark her down with two ships of equal value and liberate the others. On November 9 far finer news arrived. The reader will remember for what purposes the *Sydney* and *Melbourne* had been attached to the great Australian convoy which was now crossing the Indian Ocean. On the 8th, the *Sydney*, cruising ahead of the convoy, took in a message from the wireless station at Cocos Island that a strange ship was entering the Bay. Thereafter, silence from Cocos Island. Thereupon the large cruiser *Ibuki* increased her speed, displayed the war flag of Japan and demanded permission from the British Officer in command of the convoy to pursue and attack the enemy. But the convoy could not divest itself of this powerful protection, and the coveted task was accorded to the *Sydney*. At 9 o'clock she sighted the *Emden* and the first sea fight in the history of the Australian Navy began. It could have only one ending. In a hundred minutes the *Emden* was stranded, a flaming mass of twisted metal, and the whole of the Indian Ocean was absolutely safe and free.

In consideration of all the harm this ship had done us without offending against humanity or the laws of sea war as we conceived them, we telegraphed:—

Admiralty to Commander-in-Chief, China.

November 11, 1914.

Captain, officers and crew of *Emden* appear to be entitled to all the honours of war. Unless you know of any reason to the contrary, Captain and officers should be permitted to retain swords.

These martial courtesies were, however, churlishly repaid.

The clearance of the Indian Ocean liberated all those vessels which had been searching for the *Emden* and the *Königsberg*. Nothing could now harm the Australian convoy. Most of its escort vanished. The *Emden* and the *Königsberg* were accounted for, and von Spee was on the other side of the globe. The *Minotaur* had already been ordered with all speed to the Cape. All the other vessels went through the Red Sea into the Mediterranean, where their presence was very welcome in view of the impending Turkish invasion of Egypt.

Meanwhile the *Invincible* and *Inflexible* had reached Devonport. We had decided that Admiral Sturdee on vacating the position of Chief of the Staff should hoist his flag in the *Invincible*, should take command on the South American station, and should assume general control of all the operations against von Spee. We were in the highest impatience to get him and his ships away. Once vessels fall into dockyard hands, a hundred needs manifest themselves.

On November 9, when Lord Fisher was in my room, the following message was put on my table:—

> 'The Admiral Superintendent, Devonport, reports that the earliest possible date for completion of *Invincible* and *Inflexible* is midnight 13th November.'

I immediately expressed great discontent with the dockyard delays and asked, 'Shall I give him a prog?' or words to that effect. Fisher took up the telegram. As soon as he saw it he exclaimed. 'Friday the thirteenth. What a day to choose!' I then wrote and signed the following order, which as it was the direct cause of the Battle of the Falklands may be reproduced in facsimile[9]:—

> ADMIRALTY TO C.-IN-C., DEVONPORT. Ships are to sail Wednesday 11th. They are needed for war service and dockyard arrangements must be made to conform. If necessary dockyard men should be sent away in the ships to return as opportunity may offer. You are held responsible for the speedy despatch of these ships in a thoroughly efficient condition. Acknowledge.
>
> (Signed) W. S. C.

The ships sailed accordingly and in the nick of time. They coaled on November 26 at Abrolhos, where they joined and absorbed Admiral Stoddart's squadron (*Carnarvon*, *Cornwall*, *Kent*, *Glasgow*, *Bristol* and *Orama*) and dispatched *Defence* to the Cape, and without ever coming in sight of land or using their wireless they reached Port Stanley, Falkland Islands, on the night of December 7. Here they found the *Canopus* in the lagoon prepared to defend herself and the colony in accordance with the Admiralty instructions. They immediately began to coal.

* * * * *

After his victory at Coronel, Admiral von Spee comported himself with the dignity of a brave gentleman. He put aside the fervent acclamations of the German colony of Valparaiso, and spoke no word of triumph over the dead. He was under no delusion as to his own danger. He said of the flowers which were presented to him, 'They will do for my funeral.' Generally, his behaviour would lead us to suppose that the inability of the Germans to pick up any British survivors was not due to want of humanity; and this view has been accepted by the British Navy.

---

[9]See opposite page.

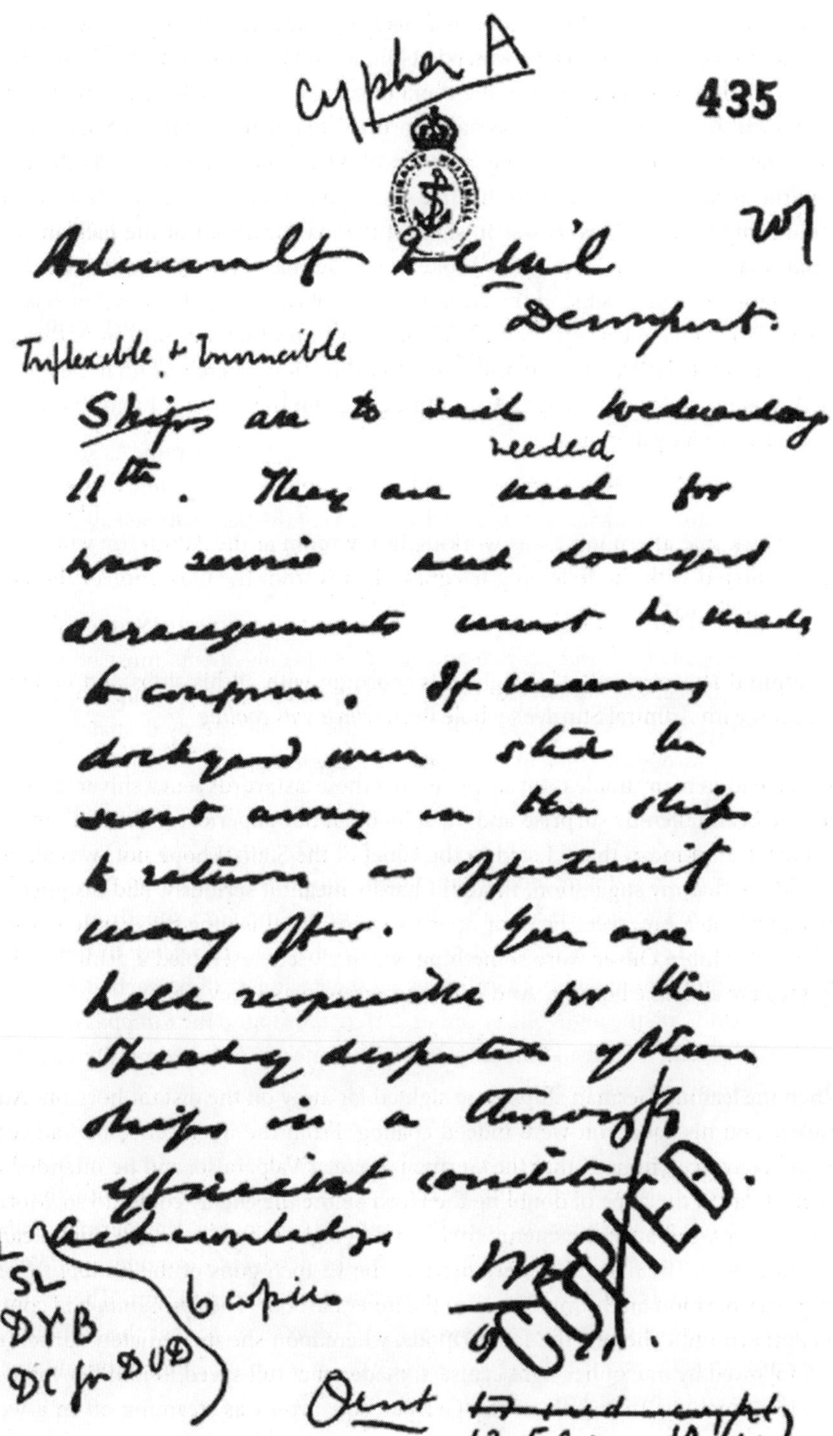

Cypher A

435

207

Admiralty to C in C

Devonport.

Inflexible & Invincible

Ships are to sail Wednesday 11th. They are ~~used~~ needed for war service and dockyard arrangements must be made to conform. If necessary dockyard men should be sent away in the ships to return as opportunity may offer. You are held responsible for the speedy despatch of these ships in a thoroughly efficient condition.

Acknowledge

[illegible]

1L
1SL
DYB
DC for DOD

6 copies

COPIED.

Sent ~~[illegible]~~ 12 5 a.m. 10/11

Facsimile of Order leading to the Battle of the Falklands

After a few days at Valparaiso he and his ships vanished again into the blue. We do not know what were the reasons which led him to raid the Falkland Islands, nor what his further plans would have been in the event of success. Presumably he hoped to destroy this unfortified British coaling base and so make his own position in South American waters less precarious. At any rate, at noon on December 6 he set off to the eastward from the Straits of Magellan with his five ships; and about 8 o'clock on December 8 his leading ship (the *Gneisenau*) was in sight of the main harbour of the Falklands. A few minutes later a terrible apparition broke upon German eyes. Rising from behind the promontory, sharply visible in the clear air, were a pair of tripod masts. One glance was enough. They meant certain death.[10] The day was beautifully fine and from the tops the horizon extended thirty or forty miles in every direction. There was no hope for victory. There was no chance of escape. A month before, another Admiral and his sailors had suffered a similar experience.

* * * * *

At 5 o'clock that afternoon I was working in my room at the Admiralty when Admiral Oliver entered with the following telegram. It was from the Governor of the Falkland Islands and ran as follows:—

> 'Admiral Spee arrived at daylight this morning with all his ships and is now in action with Admiral Sturdee's whole fleet, *which was coaling*.'

We had had so many unpleasant surprises that these last words sent a shiver up my spine. Had we been taken by surprise and, in spite of all our superiority, mauled, unready, at anchor? 'Can it mean that?' I said to the Chief of the Staff. 'I hope not,' was all he said. I could see that my suggestion, though I hardly meant it seriously, had disquieted him. Two hours later, however, the door opened again, and this time the countenance of the stern and sombre Oliver wore something which closely resembled a grin. 'It's all right, sir; they are all at the bottom.' And with one exception so they were.

* * * * *

When the leading German ships were sighted far away on the distant horizon, Admiral Sturdee and his squadron were indeed coaling. From the intelligence he had received he had convinced himself that the Germans were at Valparaiso, and he intended to sail the next day in the hope of doubling the Horn before the enemy could do so. More than two hours passed after the enemy first came in sight before he could raise steam and get under way. The first shots were fired by the 12-inch guns of the *Canopus* from her stationary position on the mudbanks of the inner harbour. The *Gneisenau* had continued to approach until she saw the fatal tripods, whereupon she immediately turned round and, followed by one of her light cruisers, made off at full speed to join her main body. In a few moments the whole of the German squadron was steaming off in a westerly

[10]Only Dreadnoughts had tripods.

direction with all possible speed. At 10 o'clock, the *Kent*, *Carnarvon* and *Glasgow* having already sailed, Admiral Sturdee came out of the harbour in the *Invincible*, followed by the *Inflexible* and *Cornwall*; while the light cruisers, one of whom (the *Bristol*) had her engines actually opened up, hurried on after as fast as possible.

The whole five ships of the German squadron were now visible, hull down on the horizon about fifteen miles away. The order was given for general chase, but later on, having the day before him, the Admiral regulated the speeds, the battle-cruisers maintaining only about 20 knots. This, however, was quite sufficient to overhaul the Germans, who after their long sojourn in the Pacific without docking were not able to steam more than 18 knots in company. Even so, the *Leipzig* began to lag behind, and shortly before 1 o'clock, the *Inflexible* opened fire upon her at 16,000 yards. Confronted with having his ships devoured one by one, von Spee took a decision which was certainly in accordance with the best traditions of the sea. Signalling to his light cruisers to make their escape to the South American coast, he turned with the *Scharnhorst* and *Gneisenau* to face his pursuers. The action which followed was on the British side uneventful. The German Admiral endeavoured more than once to close to ranges at which his powerful secondary armament of 5.9's could play their part. The British held off just far enough to make this fire ineffective, and pounded their enemy with their 12-inch guns. At this long range, however, it took a considerable time and much ammunition to achieve the destruction of the German cruisers. The *Scharnhorst*, with the Admiral and all hands, sank at 4.17 p.m., her last signal to her consort being to save herself. *Gneisenau* continued to fight against hopeless odds with the utmost fortitude until about 6 o'clock when, being in a completely disabled condition, she opened her sea-cocks and vanished, with her flag still flying, beneath the icy waters of the ocean. The British ships rushing to the spot and lowering every available boat were able only to save 200 Germans, many of whom died the next day from the shock of the cold water. When both the *Scharnhorst* and *Gneisenau* had sunk, the *Inflexible* had only thirty and the *Invincible* only twenty-two rounds left for each of their 12-inch guns.

Meanwhile the other British cruisers had each selected one of the flying German light vessels, and a series of chases ensued. The *Kent* (Captain Allen) overtook and sunk the *Nürnberg* by an effort of steaming which surpassed all previous records and even, it is stated, her designed speed. The *Nürnberg* refused to surrender, and as she foundered by the head, the victors could see a group of men on her uplifted stern waving to the last the German flag. The *Leipzig* was finished off by the *Glasgow* and the *Cornwall*. The *Dresden* alone for the time made good her escape. She was hunted down and destroyed three months later in the roadstead of Mas-a-Fuera.

Thus came to an end the German cruiser warfare in the outer seas. With the exception of the *Karlsruhe*, of which nothing had been heard for some time and which we now know was sunk by an internal explosion on November 4, and the *Dresden* soon to be hunted down, no German ships of war remained on any of the oceans of the world. It had taken four months from the beginning of the war to achieve this result. Its consequences were far-reaching, and affected simultaneously our position in every part of the globe. The strain was everywhere relaxed. All our enterprises, whether of war or commerce, proceeded in every theatre without the slightest hindrance. Within twenty-four hours orders were sent to a score of British ships to return to Home waters. For the first time we saw ourselves possessed of immense surpluses of ships of certain classes, of trained men and of naval supplies of all kinds, and were in a position to use them to the best advantage. The public, though gratified by the annihilating character of the victory, was quite unconscious of its immense importance to the whole naval situation.

CORONEL AND THE FALKLANDS

SHIPS DIRECTLY INVOLVED

Approximate Figure of Comparative Power	Name	Effective Speed: Knots	Guns	Approximate Figure of Comparative Power	Name	Effective Speed: Knots	Guns
	BATTLE CRUISERS						
5	INVINCIBLE	24	8 12-inch				
5	INFLEXIBLE	24	8 12-inch				
	BATTLESHIP						
4	CANOPUS	15½	4 12-inch 12 6-inch				
	CRUISERS						
3	DEFENCE	22	4 9.2-inch 10 7.5-inch	2½	SCHARNHORST	22	8 8.2-inch 6 5.9-inch
2	GOOD HOPE	21½	2 9.2-inch 16 6-inch	2½	GNEISENAU	22	8 8.2-inch 6 5.9-inch
1½	CARNARVON	21	4 7.5-inch 6 6-inch				
1	MONMOUTH	21	14 6-inch				
1	KENT	21½	14 6-inch				
1	CORNWALL	21	14 6-inch				
	LIGHT CRUISERS						
	GLASGOW	21	2 6-inch 10 4-inch		LEIPZIG	21	10 4.1-inch
					NÜRNBERG	22	10 4.1-inch
	BRISTOL	21	4 6-inch 10 4-inch		DRESDEN	22	10 4.1-inch
	ARMED MERCHANT CRUISERS						
	MACEDONIA	17					
	OTRANTO	16	4 4.7-inch				

NOTE—The figures of comparative value are only intended to enable the reader to follow the account. As broad classifications they are true, but they can only be taken as approximate.

CHAPTER XIX
WITH FISHER AT THE ADMIRALTY: NOVEMBER AND DECEMBER, 1914

'. . . that pale, that white-faced shore,
Whose foot spurns back the ocean's roaring tides,
. . . .
That water-walled bulwark, still secure
And confident from foreign purposes.'

King John, Act II, Sc. I1.

German Dreadnoughts off Yarmouth—What does it mean?—Anti-climax—Inroads upon the Grand Fleet—The Drain of Refits—Sir John Jellicoe's Protests—Admiralty and Commander-in-Chief—The Dreadnought Margin—The Third Battle Squadron to Rosyth—The Admiralty Insist on their View—The Destroyer Distribution—A Real Difficulty—A Wearing Discussion—The Actual Facts of Relative Strength—British Readiness to Accept Battle—The Attempted Seaplane Raid on Cuxhaven—The Grand Fleet Sweeps South—The Invasion Alarm—Moon and Tides—Further Intervention on the Belgian Coast—Immense Relief of the Falklands Victory—Lord Fisher's View—Correspondence between us—Lord Fisher and Admiral Sturdee—Admiral Oliver's Foresight—Growing Power of the Fleet—New Construction—Submarines—Fisher's Great Impulse—The Battle-Cruisers *Repulse* and *Renown*—Monitors—The Great Programme—Full Speed Ahead.

Lord Fisher had barely taken up his duties in the Admiralty, when an incident occurred which seemed to indicate the ending of the period of German inactivity in the North Sea which had succeeded the action of August 28 in the Heligoland Bight. Early in the morning of November 3, the unusual signal was made to the Admiralty that several German battle-cruisers or battleships had been sighted off Gorleston on the Norfolk coast by the mine-sweeping gun-boat *Halcyon* and that she was engaged with them. Almost immediately afterwards heavy shells were reported to be bursting in the water and on the beach near Yarmouth. The First Sea Lord and I reached the War Room from our bedrooms in a few minutes. The question was, What did it mean? It seemed quite certain that German battle-cruisers would not be sent to throw shells at an open town like Yarmouth. Obviously this was a demonstration to divert the British Fleet from something else which was going to happen—was already perhaps happening. Was it a

German raid into the Channel, or a serious attempt by the German Navy to intervene upon the Belgian coast while the land battle was still raging? Was it a descent on the British coast at Sunderland or Blyth? We had no means of judging. The last thing it seemed possible to believe was that first-class units of the German Fleet would have been sent across the North Sea simply in order to disturb the fisher-folk, of Yarmouth. By other signals our destroyers, *Leopard* and *Lively*, who were patrolling in the neighbourhood of Yarmouth, also reported that they were engaged, and added that they were proceeding to attack the enemy. Where were our main forces? The Commander-in-Chief was for the first time in the war at the Admiralty, whither he had been summoned to confer with the new First Sea Lord. The Grand Fleet was at Lough Swilly in the North of Ireland. The 3rd Battle Squadron was steaming through the Irish Channel. No part of the Grand Fleet was nearer than Beatty and his battle-cruisers: and these were as far off as Cromarty. Whatever happened, we could not fight a general action with our main Fleet till late on the following day. Meanwhile the Harwich Striking Force, the Dover flotillas, Admiral Hood's forces off the Belgian coast and Admiral Burney's Channel Fleet must do the best they could. If the German demonstration off Yarmouth was the prelude or concomitant to a serious attempt to break into the Channel, the very greatest naval events would follow. The contingency, as the reader is aware, had always been faced, and we were well aware that we should have to wait for our revenge till the next day. Meanwhile there was nothing to be done but to put all the fleets and flotillas on guard and in motion with the double object of resisting to the utmost a German attack to the southward and intercepting as speedily as possible from the North the return of the enemy. Several hours of tension passed; and then gradually it became clear that the German battle-cruisers were returning home at full speed, and that nothing else was apparently happening; and the incredible conclusion forced itself upon us that the German Admiralty had had no other purpose in hand than this silly demonstration off Yarmouth beach.

This anticlimax was fatiguing. The experience of bracing ourselves to the most tremendous events, and then finding nothing happen, was one which we were compelled more than once to undergo at the Admiralty.

* * * * *

The new First Sea Lord was even more sure of the superiority of the British line of battle over the enemy than I was, and in this his views contrasted very sharply with those of the Commander-in-Chief. In full agreement with Sir Arthur Wilson, he proposed on his assumption of office to bring the Third Battle Squadron (the *King Edwards*) down to Portland to increase our security against a German incursion into the Channel; and he moved the Fifth Battle Squadron (the *Formidables*) with the two *Lord Nelsons* to Sheerness to provide battleship support for the Harwich Striking Force, and to give an additional security against raid or invasion. These movements were no sooner determined than news of the Battle of Coronel was received (November 4), and we were forced to make far more serious inroads upon Sir John Jellicoe's command. The battle-cruisers *Inflexible* and *Invincible* were sent as described to the Falklands: and Lord Fisher, as we have seen, demanded the *Princess Royal* for the Atlantic.

This last order produced continuous protests from Sir John Jellicoe, and led to an interchange of telegrams and letters in which the Commander-in-Chief dwelt upon every aspect of his dangers and weakness and the Admiralty, while insisting on their decision, endeavoured to reassure and placate him.

Our Dreadnought margin in home waters at the outbreak of war had been just sufficient. Every ship was ready and in good order. We did not feel that we could spare one. But after the first two months we were compelled to send ships one at a time from each Battle Squadron down to their home ports on the South Coast for refit. A regular system of refits, as was foreseen, had to be instituted. This involved the permanent absence of two or three of the most important vessels from the Grand Fleet. The enemy, on the other hand, lying in his main base, could always in theory be credited with having all his ships available at his selected moment for battle. Before, however, the drain of refits came upon us we had succeeded in reinforcing the Fleet by five fine ships, so that we began the war at our maximum possible strength and always, except for the briefest intervals, held or improved on that number.

The requirements of the Commander-in-Chief were, however, hard to meet. The strategy on which we were all agreed, involved keeping the Grand Fleet in distant northern waters and required very large forces of destroyers and other light craft for its local security, and for its service in battle. On the other hand, while no properly defended war harbour had yet been created capable of holding the entire fleet, various other bases had to be effectively guarded and patrolled, for which separate flotillas must be supplied. If at any time from any cause, two or three ships were absent from the Grand Fleet for a week or two, the Commander-in-Chief drew severe comparisons between the German Fleet and his own. He was a master of this kind of argument. From his own side he deducted any ship which had any defect, however temporary, however small—even defects which would not have prevented her from taking her place in the line in an emergency. He sometimes also deducted two or three of the most powerful battleships in the world which had newly joined his command because they were not trained up to the full level of efficiency of the others, and these were absolutely blotted out as if they were of no value whatever.[1] He next proceeded to deal with the enemy. He always credited them with several ships more than we now know they had, or were then thought likely to have. In October 1914, he gave credence to a suggestion that the four German Dreadnoughts of the *König* class had been completely re-armed with 14-inch guns. In 1915 the size of these guns had advanced to 15-inch. I was on both occasions compelled to set up expert committees to demolish these baseless suppositions. Unable to deny that the British line of battle could fire a broadside double in weight to that of the Germans, he developed a skilful argument to prove that this advantage was more than counteracted by other disadvantages arising from the superior displacement of contemporary German ships. He dwelt on this even at a period when his fleet had been reinforced by seven or eight additional units of enormous power without any corresponding accession to the enemy's strength.

---

[1] *The Grand Fleet*, by Sir John Jellicoe p. 31.

One must admit, nevertheless, that the withdrawal of the *Princess Royal* inflicted a very serious injury upon the Battle Cruiser Squadron, and that Sir David Beatty might have had to fight an action without any margin of superiority during her absence. In this matter, however, Lord Fisher entered the lists in person.

First Sea Lord to Commander-in-Chief.

Personal.

November 12, 1914.

I want to make it clear to you what the *Scharnhorst* Squadron means as regards our dispositions.

1. We have not heard of them since November 4.
2. They may adopt the following courses:—
   (*a*) Go through Panama Canal, smash our West Indian Fleet and release all the armed German liners from New York—hence the *Princess Royal.*
   (*b*) Go to south-east coast of America and stop our vital food supplies—hence the two *Invincibles.*
   (*c*) Go to the Cape and raid the Army base at Walfish Bay—hence the *Minotaur* to reinforce *Albion.*
   (*d*) Go to Duala and relieve the Germans, destroying our ships and military expedition—hence the *Warrior, Black Prince* and three *Edgar Quinet.*

I hope to send Bartolomé to you to-morrow with information which is too secret to be written or telegraphed.

The secret information pointed to the possibility of the Germans endeavouring to slip one or two of their battle-cruisers into the Atlantic to help the return to Germany of the *Scharnhorst* and *Gneisenau* and incidentally to release all their fast liners in New York. Lord Fisher became vehemently impressed with this idea, and certainly the period was one of extreme strategic tension when some enterprise by the enemy seemed especially to be expected.

Admiralty to Commander-in-Chief.

November 13, 1914.

Since war began you have gained two Dreadnoughts on balance, and will have by 20th twenty-seven superior units to twenty. We intend *Princess Royal* to rejoin you as soon as *Scharnhorst* is dealt with.

During the next month you should suspend sending ships away for refit, doing the best you can at Scapa. If notwithstanding the above you feel the need of reinforcements we should propose to meet you by stationing the eight *King Edwards* at Rosyth, where they would be well placed to join you for general action or to attack an invading force.

> This would avoid necessity for stationing cruisers there for the present.
> If you agree the eight *King Edwards* will be ordered to sail to-night.

The Commander-in-Chief in reply asserted that the twenty-seven units quoted included three ships, two of which had never fired a gun and the third was only partially trained. He deprecated the Third Battle Squadron being stationed at Rosyth, as without being covered by cruisers or sea-going destroyers, it would run a great risk from mines and submarines outside the limits of the port defence. He suggested that it was preferable to keep them at Cromarty closely adjacent to the main base where they would be covered by the cruisers of the Grand Fleet and by the Destroyer Flotilla stationed at Cromarty.

The Admiralty, however, insisted on the Third Battle Squadron being stationed at Rosyth.

Admiralty to Commander-in-Chief.

November 16, 1914.

> . . . The importance of preventing the enemy from making a serious attack on our coast and getting away without being engaged makes it imperative to have a force nearer the probable points of attack than either Scapa Flow or Cromarty, which are practically the same distance off. The coast has been so denuded of destroyers for the sake of strengthening the force with you (amounting now to seventy-one destroyers) that there is only a skeleton force of patrol vessels available on the East Coast, amounting to three Scouts, twenty-three Destroyers, twelve Torpedo Boats, between the Naze and St. Abbs Head, a distance of 300 miles. In these circumstances we are reluctantly compelled to decide on the *King Edwards* and the Third Cruiser Squadron going to Rosyth, and you should detach half a flotilla of the seventy-one destroyers at Scapa Flow to act with them. We are sending you a carefully compiled table of comparative strength of your Fleet and the German High Sea Fleet, which makes it clear that without the Third Battle Squadron you have such a preponderance of gun power that with equal gunnery efficiency a successful result is ensured. . . .
>
> The Admiralty have in mind the importance of getting back the *Princess Royal* as soon as the situation admits. Your proposals as to mining have been carefully considered, but the work done by our submarines in the Bight has been of such importance that it is undesirable to add to their dangers by laying mines whose positions must be very uncertain. The Germans have no difficulty in sweeping any channel they wish when they want to bring any of their ships out, and do so daily. It would be very difficult for us to lay fresh lines in any channels they sweep on account of the dangers to the minelayers from our own mines.

This and preceding telegrams expressed the deliberate views of the First Sea Lord and Sir Arthur Wilson, and I was in the fullest agreement with them.[2]

---

[2]See Appendix D.

The Commander-in-Chief, however, urged that the 71 destroyers mentioned by the Admiralty included 10 which were absent refitting, and pointed out with justice that the 40 destroyers of the Harwich flotillas had been omitted from those at the disposition of the Admiralty. He asked particularly for reconsideration of the order to detach half a flotilla with the Third Battle Squadron. Without these additional 12 destroyers he stated that the safety of the Dreadnought Battle Fleet was seriously endangered; a submarine attack on Scapa Flow was quite feasible and 'as I am directed to use this base, I trust I shall not be held responsible for any disaster that may occur.' He concluded by pointing out that the relative strength of the High Sea Fleet and the Grand Fleet could not be decided without reference to the cruiser and destroyer strength of the two fleets: his comparative weakness in these essentials counterbalanced, he declared, any battleship superiority he possessed and made him anxious to be concentrated.

Admiralty to Commander-in-Chief.

November 17, 1914.

We have carefully reviewed the position and given fullest consideration to your wishes. We are confident that your fleet with its cruisers and flotillas is strong enough for the definite task entrusted to it. In view of the grave needs we have to meet elsewhere we cannot reinforce you at present, nor alter our dispositions.

The 3rd Battle Squadron, 3rd Cruiser Squadron and eight destroyers should proceed to Rosyth as ordered. You have, of course, full discretion to move your Fleet in any way necessary to provide for its safety and enable you to meet the enemy, and are not tied to Scapa. Every effort is being made to accelerate the completion of the submarine defences.

The destroyer question was one of real difficulty. Although we had more than double the seagoing strength of the German flotillas, we had so much to guard, that we could not provide a superior force kept always intact in the hand of the Commander-in-Chief for a great Fleet action. 'I know perfectly well,' wrote Sir John Jellicoe on December 4 to Lord Fisher, 'that the First and Third Flotillas [from Harwich] will not join me in time.' . . . The Germans, he declared, would have eight flotillas comprising 88 torpedo boat destroyers, all of which would certainly be ready at the selected moment. 'They have five torpedoes each: total 440 torpedoes—*unless I can strike at them first*.' He himself might, he claimed, fall as low as 32 or even 28 destroyers. 'You know,' he added, 'the difficulty and objections to turning away from the enemy in a Fleet action: but with such a menace I am bound to do it, unless my own torpedo boat destroyers can stop or neutralize the movement.' There was no doubt that all the Commander-in-Chief's thought fitted together into one consistent whole and was the result of profound study and reflection. Lord Fisher, however, remained obdurate. 'I think we have to stand fast,' he wrote to me, enclosing Sir John Jellicoe's letter. 'The Tyrwhitt mob and our oversea submarines are our sole aggressive force in the South.' He proposed however to put one of the Harwich flotillas in the Humber. 'We wait your return before action[3]—Humber and Harwich each 290 miles from Heligoland—but the complete flotilla at the Humber is very much nearer Jellicoe, and so a salve to him in reply to enclosed. As A. K. Wilson observed a moment ago, both he and I would probably have written exactly the same letter as Jellicoe, *trying to get all we could*! Yours till death, F.'

This was a wearing discussion, and no one can blame the Commander-in-Chief for expressing his anxieties and endeavouring to keep his command up to the highest strength. I always tried to sustain him in every possible way. His powerful orderly brain, his exact and comprehensive knowledge, enabled him to develop and perfect in this first year of the war the mighty organization of the Grand Fleet. He bore with constancy the many troubles and perplexities of the early months. His fine sailor-like qualities made him always ready night or day to take his whole gigantic Fleet to sea, and he was never so happy as when he was at sea. Even when I did not share his outlook, I sympathized with his trials. The opinions of Lord Fisher at this period upon the margin of strength required for the Grand Fleet were, as will be seen, in sharp contrast with those he expressed at a later period during the operations at the Dardanelles. Personally, I always considered our line of battle amply superior; nor did I believe the Germans would be able to bring out at a given moment all the 88 torpedo boats with which Sir John Jellicoe always credited them. We now know the actual forces which the enemy assembled on December 16 of this same year, on the occasion when the whole High Sea Fleet made almost the most ambitious sortie into the North Sea which its history records. There were 13 Dreadnought battleships and 4 battle-cruisers, total 17 Dreadnoughts instead of the 20 which were completed and which the Admiralty counted as available; and 53 torpedo boats in place of the Commander-in-Chief's 88. Against this Sir John Jellicoe had (until refits were re-opened at the end of November) 27 superior units (subject to what he says about them); and as many of the 71 destroyers as were fit for sea on any given day. The Germans also took to sea on December 16 a squadron of 8 pre-Dreadnoughts, and against this our Third Battle Squadron, which had been rightly restored to the Grand Fleet, was a proper and superior provision. This balance of strength represents the period of our greatest strain in Home waters and all over the world.

At this, as at all other times, the Admiralty would have welcomed a general battle. An attack by seaplanes launched from carrying ships upon the Zeppelin sheds near Cuxhaven, was planned by us for November 22. On the 20th we telegraphed to Sir John Jellicoe:—

> 'Our reliable German information and also our telegram No. 338 to you shows, firstly, concentration of German cruisers, battle-cruisers and battleships in Weser and Elbe; and secondly, disposal of their submarines to hunt in the Shetlands and English Channel. In these favourable circumstances the aerial attack on Cuxhaven Zeppelin sheds, which we had previously planned and considered desirable in

---

[3] I was in France for thirty-six hours.—W.S.C.

itself, might easily bring on a considerable action in which your battle-cruisers and the Grand Fleet might take part without undue risk from German submarines.

'We suggest for your consideration Tyrwhitt and aeroplanes attacking on Monday at daybreak, with you supporting him from the northward with whatever force is necessary, if the enemy respond to the challenge. Further, if it should prove, as some reliable information indicates, that the enemy is preparing an offensive raid or sortie himself, our movement would bring on a collision at the outset unexpected and disconcerting to him.'

The Commander-in-Chief, after some discussion, preferred Tuesday daybreak for the attack, as the longer notice would enable him to finish certain repairing work. The Admiralty plans were altered accordingly. We telegraphed on the 21st:—

'We consider the present a good occasion for a sweep southward by the Grand Fleet. The seaplane attack is incidental and subsidiary, though very desirable in itself. It may bring on an action now that the German Fleet is concentrated near Wilhelmshaven, and their cruisers and battle-cruisers are active. It will frustrate any offensive movement they may intend, as reported.... Tuesday, 24th, at 5.30 a.m., will be the time.'

No result was, however, achieved. Sir John Jellicoe brought the Battle Fleet down into the centre of the North Sea about 180 miles from Heligoland, with the battle-cruisers about 40 miles nearer. But in the weather prevailing the seaplanes could hardly get off the water; and the Germans remained unaware of our movements and without any plans of their own. The episode shows however the underlying confidence of the Admiralty and of the Commander-in-Chief in the strength of the Grand Fleet even during this time of strain.

To add to the distractions of this hard month of November, 1914, an invasion scare took a firm hold of the military and naval authorities. It was argued by the War Office that the lull on the fighting fronts would enable the Germans to spare large numbers of good troops—250,000 if necessary—for the invasion of Great Britain. Lord Kitchener directed all defensive preparations to be made, and Lord Fisher threw himself into the task with gusto. Although, as the reader is aware, I was sceptical on this subject, I felt that the precautions were justifiable, and would at any rate add interest to the life of our coast and Home defence forces. I therefore allowed myself to succumb to the suppressed excitement which grew throughout the highest circles, and did my utmost to aid and speed our preparations. We stationed as described the 3rd Battle Squadron at the Forth, brought the 2nd Fleet to the Thames, disposed the old *Majestic* battleships in the various harbours along the East Coast, arranged block ships to be sunk, and laid mines to be exploded, at the proper time in the mouths of our undefended harbours; while the whole coastal watch, military, aerial and marine, throbbed with activity. The Army arrangements were complicated by the fact that some of the divisions which were sufficiently trained to be used to repel the invaders, had lent their rifles to those that were undergoing training, and these rifles had to be collected and redistributed as a part of the procedure prescribed for the supreme emergency. To such expedients were we reduced! However, the Germans remained absolutely quiescent; the tides and moon, which for some days before November 20 were exceptionally favourable to nocturnal landings, ceased to present these conditions, and the sense of some great impending event gradually faded from our minds.

Lord Fisher to Mr. Churchill.

7 a.m., November 21, 1914.

An angel's sleep! In Heaven from 9 till now!

It WAS kind of you not to wake me with Grey's credible witness!

Let us entreat and urge Kitchener to send a hundred thousand men AT ONCE to Flanders, and warn Joffre not to be 'two divisions too few and two days too late!' Kitchener's balance of 160,000 men will amply suffice and the 'Ides of March' have passed! The waning moon and dawning tide [dawn high-tide] will not recur till days following December 10. *Do write to him accordingly, or shall I?*

It has been a splendid 'dress rehearsal,' tell him, and very reassuring—his mass of men and his mobile guns! We MUST press him to send 100,000 men to Flanders. . . .

On November 20 General Joffre asked for further naval co-operation on the Belgian coast.

'General Foch,' he stated, 'reports that for some little time the French or English ships have no longer been participating in the action of our forces in the neighbourhood of Nieuport. On account of very violent bombardment by the enemy in this region, it would be advantageous if the ships could attack the numerous German batteries established to the east of the mouth of the Yser. I should be glad if you would notify the Ministry of Marine, and the Admiralty, of this situation, in order to obtain a more active co-operation on the part of the squadron between Nieuport and Ostend.'

We were able to send the old battleship *Revenge*, whose guns had been specially re-mounted for long range fire, and several smaller vessels under Admiral Hood, and the naval bombardment of the German right was effectively resumed. 'The conditions on the coast,' Hood, however, reported on the 22nd, 'are quite different from what they were during the first few days. To-day there was a heavy fire from guns I could not locate or damage. No troops are ever visible. The inundation has stopped their movement.'

To the situation of strain and effort which gripped us during November came the welcome relief of the victory at the Falklands. Lord Fisher received it with a moderated satisfaction.

'We cannot,' he wrote to me on December 10, 'but be overjoyed at the *Monmouth* and *Good Hope* being avenged! But let us be self-restrained—*not too exultant!—till we know details! Perhaps their guns never reached us!* (We had so few casualties!) We know THEIR gunnery was excellent! Their THIRD salvo murdered Cradock! So it may have been like shooting pheasants: the pheasants not shooting back! Not too much glory for us, only great satisfaction. Not a battle for a Poet Laureate! *Let us wait and hear before we crow!* Then again, it may be a wonder why the cruisers escaped—if they have escaped—I hope not, for we had such a preponderating force—such numbers! (*How the Glasgow must have enjoyed it!*) Anyhow, don't let us encourage ourselves in too many joy messages till we know more.'

But I made haste to ascribe to him all the credit that was his due.

December 10.

This was your show and your luck.

I should only have sent one Greyhound[4] and *Defence*. This would have done the trick.

But it was a niggling coup. Your *flair* was quite true. Let us have some more victories together, and confound all our foes abroad—and (don't forget) at home.

This delighted the Admiral, and in his reply (December 11) he threw a friendly light upon other fields of activity than those with which this chapter has been concerned.

'Your letter *pleasant*! There is another *quite lovely scheme*! *I* am to be praised so as to get "swelled head" and think myself ignored by you, and to be in your shoes! It is all too sweet for words! It is palpably transparent! I was told of this yesterday! It really *is curious* why they so hate you! I think I told you what G.—– said, that though he abhorred me, yet… I have splendid friends in the Tory camp!'

A cause of difference, however, soon arose between us. The First Sea Lord was displeased with Sir Doveton Sturdee for not having succeeded in destroying the German light cruiser *Dresden* with the rest, and he searchingly criticized that Admiral's dispositions after the action. He wished to leave Admiral Sturdee in South American waters till the *Dresden* was hunted down. As it was imperative that the *Invincible* and *Inflexible* should come home at once, such a decision would have entailed transferring Admiral Sturdee's flag to the *Carnarvon*, and leaving him with a command scarcely suited to his rank and standing, and woefully out of harmony with his recent achievement. I was obliged to veto this proposal, and Lord Fisher was for some time much vexed at my decision.

The First Sea Lord also made the disquieting suggestion that the Germans might slip a battle-cruiser like the *Derfflinger* through our blockade in the long winter nights and fall upon the returning *Invincible* and *Inflexible*, who had fired away three-quarters of their ammunition. I was greatly disturbed at this, and hastened to the Chief of the Staff. But Admiral Oliver was not often found improvident. He had already several weeks

[4]Battle-cruiser.

before sent the battleship *Vengeance* with a quarter outfit for both vessels to St. Vincent, where it awaited them.

* * * * *

In spite of their anxieties, November and December were months of rapidly growing power to the Navy. The variety and scope of Admiralty business extended continually, and the number of important directions to be given increased every week. The reader who is further interested should study in the Appendix the selection of First Lord's Minutes which I have thought it worth while to print.[5] From these original documents, conceived under the pressure of events, a truer idea can be formed of what was passing than from much description.

In no part of our work did Lord Fisher and I act together in greater harmony than in the realm of new construction.

The first task of the Admiralty in naval construction on the outbreak of war was to accelerate the completion of all the warships which were building in Great Britain, and according to the schemes we had had prepared before the war, extreme priority was to be assigned to vessels which could be finished within six months. On this basis we proceeded during the first three months. When it became clear that the war would not be ended one way or the other by the first main decisions on land, and that the sea battle was indefinitely deferred, I extended this original period, and we adopted the principle 'Everything that can be finished in 1915, and nothing that can't.'

This brought very large numbers of vessels into the accelerated class and, of course, opened the way for a considerable new construction of submarines, destroyers and even light cruisers. There had already been ordered when Lord Fisher arrived at the Admiralty a score of new destroyers and submarines, in addition to all the pre-war vessels under accelerated construction.

The yards were therefore full of work, and care was needed not to impede current construction by new orders. Lord Fisher, however, brought a very great surge of impulse to this sphere of our activities. It was a moment when megalomania was a virtue. Some progress had already been made on two of the British battleships of the programme of 1914–1915. The First Sea Lord at once demanded to make them into battle-cruisers, sacrificing two more guns in each in order to get the immense speed for which he thirsted. I agreed to this, although it involved some delay; and the *Repulse* and the *Renown* were redesigned accordingly.

The construction of submarines was more urgent. I was not alarmed about the immediate position, although all sorts of rumours were afoot.

Naval Intelligence Division.

November 7, 1914.

With reference to your report of yesterday, apparently attaching credence to a statement that from 100 to 200 small submarines have been manufactured secretly

[5]Appendix E.

in Germany, have you considered how many trained officers and personnel this important flotilla would require? What evidence is there at your disposal to show that the Germans have trained this number of submarine captains and officers? I have always understood that their flotilla of submarines before the war did not exceed 27. There is no personnel that requires more careful training than the submarine personnel. All the experience of our officers shows that a submarine depends for its effectiveness mainly upon its captain. The function of the Intelligence Division is not merely to collect and pass on the Munchausen tales of spies and untrustworthy agents, but carefully to sift and scrutinize the intelligence they receive, and in putting it forward to indicate the degree of probability which attaches to it. It appears to me impossible that any large addition to the German submarine force can be made for many months to come. Even if the difficulties of material were overcome those of personnel would impose an absolute limit. It is very likely that a few small portable submarines have been prepared for coast work.

W. S. C.

But the future already contained its menaces. I greeted Fisher on his arrival with the following minutes, the first two of which were addressed to his predecessor:—

Secretary.
Third Sea Lord.

October 13, 1914.

Please state exactly what is the total submarine programme now sanctioned by the Cabinet or under construction in the various yards. What measures can be adopted for increasing the number of submarines? Is it possible to let further contracts for submarines on a fifteen months' basis? It is indispensable that the whole possible plant for submarine construction should be kept at the fullest pressure night and day.

W. S. C.

Secretary.
First Sea Lord.
Naval Secretary.

October 28, 1914.

Please propose without delay, the largest possible programme of submarine boats to be delivered in from 12 to 24 months from the present time. You should assume for this purpose that you have control of all sources of manufacture required for submarines, that there is no objection to using Vickers' drawings, and that steam engines may be used to supplement oil engines. You should exert every effort of ingenuity and organization to secure the utmost possible delivery. As soon as your proposals are ready, which should be in the next few days, they can be considered at a conference of the Sea Lords. The Cabinet must be satisfied that the absolute maximum output is being worked to in submarines. We may be sure that Germany is doing this.

Third Sea Lord's department must therefore act with the utmost vigour, and not be deterred by the kind of difficulties which hamper action in time of peace.

W. S. C.

Secretary.
First Sea Lord.
Third Sea Lord.

October 30, 1914.

More important than the deliveries of battleships is the acceleration of light cruisers and submarines. With regard to light cruisers, it ought not to take more than one year to construct *Castor*, *Inconstant*, *Cambria* and *Canterbury*. What is the present position of these ships? Have they been begun yet? Proposals should be made which secure their delivery before the end of 1915.

2. Proposals should also be made to accelerate *Royalist*, *Cleopatra*, *Champion*, and *Carysfort*, *Conquest*, and *Calliope*, so as to obtain deliveries in February. This will only be possible by working night and day in three 8-hour shifts on all these vessels, arranging with other firms not concerned in their construction to lend the necessary men.

3. All the 'M' Class destroyers to be delivered in August, 1915, should be pushed forward into April and May. There is surely no reason why this cannot be done. Firms who will undertake to complete their vessels by this date could be immediately given another order for a repeat ship, so that there would be no fear of dislocation of their business. Let me have proposals on this.

4. Submarines F2, F3, G6, G8, G15, G9, G7, G10 to G13, and G1 to G5, all ought to be delivered before the end of 1915. There is an extraordinary gap after G4, when for 6 months we do not receive a single new submarine, and in 12 months we only receive 2. This is shocking, and must be bridged at all costs.

Pray let me have further proposals after such conferences as may be necessary with the firms concerned.

W. S. C.

Lord Fisher hurled himself into this business with explosive energy. He summoned around him all the naval constructors and shipbuilding firms in Britain, and in four or five glorious days, every minute of which was pure delight to him, he presented me with schemes for a far greater construction of submarines, destroyers and small craft than I or any of my advisers had ever deemed possible. Mr. Schwab was at that time passing through England on his return to the United States. We invited him to the Admiralty; and he undertook to build twenty-four submarines—twelve in Canada and twelve in the

United States—the bulk of which were to be completed in the hitherto incredibly short period of six months. I arranged a system of heavy bonuses for early delivery. These large negotiations were completed and the subsequent work was carried out with wonderful thoroughness and punctuality by the immense organization of the Bethlehem Steel Company. One evening, as Lord Fisher, Mr. Schwab and I sat round the octagonal table in the Admiralty, after a long discussion on the submarine contracts, we asked Mr. Schwab, 'Have you got anything else that will be of use to us?' He thereupon told us that he had four turrets carrying two 14-inch guns each which had almost been completed for the Greek battleship *Salamis* then building in Germany for Greece. We set our hearts on these; and I had an idea. The reader will remember the three small monitors building for Brazil, which although no one could see any use for them at the time, I had decided to take over at the outbreak of war. The operations on the Belgian Coast had shown their value. I suggested to Lord Fisher that we should buy these 14-inch turrets and build monitors to carry them. The Admiral was delighted with the plan, and in a few hours he was closeted with his constructors designing the vessels. In all our correspondence we referred to them as the *Styx* class.

Secretary.
First Sea Lord.

December 11, 1914.

We ought without delay to order more 'Styx' class for heavy in-shore work. There are, for instance, the four reserve 13.5-inch guns of the *Audacious*, which should certainly be mounted in new monitors. It should also be possible to draw from the reserve of 15-inch guns, and to make in a short time 15-inch or 18-inch howitzers. We require now to make ships which can be built in 6 or 7 months at the outside, and which can certainly go close in shore and attack the German Fleet in its harbours. These are special vessels built for a definite war operation, and we must look to them in default of a general action for giving us the power of forcing a naval decision at the latest in the autumn of 1915.

Our thought is proceeding independently on the same lines. I propose, as a basis of discussion, that in addition to the 4 Schwab monitors, we prepare 8 more at a cost of not more than £700,000 apiece. These vessels should be armed either with 13.5-inch or 15-inch guns, two or four in each as convenient. Or, alternatively, they should be armed with four 18-inch howitzers in separate cupolas sunk low on their heavily-armoured turtle backs. They should draw 8 feet at most, and be propelled entirely by internal combustion at a speed not exceeding 10 knots; no funnels; three or four alternative telescopic masts for fire observation; strong crinolines 20 feet away all round to make them immune from mine or torpedo, etc. . . .

W. S. C.

We soon embarked on an extensive scheme of monitor building.

Besides making four monitors to carry the American 14-inch gun turrets, we took two spare 15-inch gun turrets which had been prepared for two of the furthest-off new battleships (now converted into battle-cruisers), and eight 12-inch gun turrets out of four 'Majestics,' which we laid up; and with these and the American guns we armed no less than fourteen monitors, namely, two with two 15-inch guns, four with two 14-inch guns, and eight with two 12-inch guns apiece. Lord Fisher then went on and pulled the 9.2-inch guns out of the old 'Edgars' and mounted them in fourteen small monitors, drawing 6 feet 6 inches of water; and ten 6-inch guns[6] were mounted in still smaller monitors drawing 5 feet 11 inches. We also built later on twelve large river gunboats capable of being transported by rail for service on the Danube, if we ever got there, and twelve small river gunboats, or baby monitors, for service on the Tigris and the Euphrates. The bulk of the large monitors were constructed in Belfast with extraordinary celerity by Harland & Wolff and their sturdy ardent men. We also prepared 240 lighters with steel shields and internal combustion engines for landing troops under fire.

Thus in the autumn of 1914, under various programmes culminating in the great Fisher impetus, we set on foot the following enormous Fleet, all due to complete by the end of 1915:—

Battleships and Battle-cruisers of the greatest power	7
Light cruisers	12
Destroyers of the largest class and leaders	65
Oversea submarines	40
Coastal submarines	22
Monitors—	
Heavy	18
Medium	14
Light	5
Sloops and smaller anti-submarine vessels	107
Motor launches	60
Ex-lighters with internal combustion engines	240

This tremendous new Navy, for it was nothing less, was a providential aid to the Admiralty when more than two years later the real German submarine attack began. Its creation on such a scale is one of the greatest services which the nation has owed to the genius and energy of Lord Fisher. Probably Fisher in all his long life never had a more joyous experience than this great effort of new construction. No man knew better than he how to put war thought into a ship. Shipbuilding had been the greatest passion of his life. Here were all the yards of Britain at his disposal and every Treasury barrier broken down.

Of the battle-cruisers *Repulse* and *Renown*, and still more of the light battle-cruisers *Courageous*, *Furious* and *Glorious*, to which I consented four months later in circumstances which will be narrated in their place, it must be said that they were an old man's children. Although possessing many marvellous qualities never hitherto

[6]Two had had to be removed from each of the five 'Queen Elizabeths,' owing to spray interference: total—10.

combined in a ship of war, they were light in the bone; and the Navy always considered them wanting in the structural strength and armour which the new conditions of war more than ever required. None the less, their parent loved them dearly and always rallied with the utmost vehemence when any slur was cast upon their qualities.

I presided over all this process in November and December with the greatest admiration for the First Sea Lord, but with some misgivings on the score of expense. I was not yet satisfied that the war would be prolonged beyond 1915, and I did not wish to draw away from the armies men or material which might be needed in their service. Not until April, 1915, when the failure of Russia as a decisive factor became final, did I authorize a further extension of view to December 31, 1916, and agree to plans for additional new construction being made within that limit. Meanwhile I endeavoured to satisfy Lord Fisher as best I could. I pointed out to him repeatedly that from some points of view a ship finished twelve months before the end of the war was worth twelve times as much as a ship finished one month before its end, and urged continuously that vessels nearest completion must in no way suffer. He was, however, very difficult to feed. In a day he would sketch the design of a capital ship. In a week he would devour a programme and come back asking for more. A tit-bit like an 18-inch experimental gun which I suggested he should make, was snapped up the moment it was mentioned. 'I will put it in a light cruiser and drive her 40-knots,' he cried. 'Hit how you like, when you like, where you like.' This was his theme; but what about his doctrine 'Armour is vision'? However, I backed him up all I could. He was far more often right than wrong, and his drive and life-force made the Admiralty quiver like one of his great ships at its highest speed.

CHAPTER XX
THE BOMBARDMENT OF SCARBOROUGH AND HARTLEPOOL: DECEMBER 16, 1914

'All comes out even at the end of the day, and all comes out still more even when all the days are over.'

—Voltaire.

Naval Intelligence—The Captured German Signal Book—Directional Wireless—Sir Arthur Wilson's Task—His Conclusions of December 14—Orders to the Fleets—December 16: Bombardment of Scarborough and Hartlepool—Favourable Position of the British Forces—The Visibility Fails—Groping in the Mist—The German High Sea Fleet at Sea—Disappointment—A Forlorn Hope—What had Happened—The Dawn Situation—A Fateful Hour—Flight of the German Fleet—The British Sweep to the West—The Brush with the Enemy's Light Cruisers—Mischance—von Hipper dodges to the North—Escape of the German Battle-Cruisers—The Admiralty Communiqué—Public Discontent.

Our Intelligence service has won and deserved world-wide fame. More than perhaps any other Power, we were successful in the war in penetrating the intentions of the enemy. Again and again the forecasts both of the military and of the naval Intelligence Staffs were vindicated to the wonder of friends and the chagrin of foes. The three successive chiefs of the Naval Intelligence Division, Captain Thomas Jackson, Rear-Admiral Oliver, and lastly, Captain Reginald Hall, were all men of mark in the service, and continuously built and extended an efficient and profound organization. There were others—a brilliant confederacy—whose names even now are better wrapt in mystery. Our information about German naval movements was principally obtained (1) from the reports of secret agents in neutral and enemy countries and particularly in Germany, (2) from the reports of our submarines, which lay far up in the Heligoland Bight in perilous vigilance, and (3) from a special study we had made of the German wireless. In this we were for a time aided by great good luck.

At the beginning of September, 1914, the German light cruiser *Magdeburg* was wrecked in the Baltic. The body of a drowned German under-officer was picked up by the Russians a few hours later, and clasped in his bosom by arms rigid in death, were the cypher and signal books of the German Navy and the minutely squared maps of the North Sea and Heligoland Bight. On September 6 the Russian Naval Attaché came to see me. He had received a message from Petrograd telling him what had happened, and that the Russian Admiralty with the aid of the cypher and signal books had been able to decode portions at least of the German naval messages. The Russians felt that as the leading naval Power, the British Admiralty ought to have these books and charts. If we would send a vessel to Alexandrov, the Russian officers in charge of the books would-bring them to England. We lost no time in sending a ship, and late on an October afternoon Prince Louis and I received from the hands of our loyal allies these sea-stained priceless documents. We set on foot at once an organization for the study of the German wireless and for the translating of the messages when taken in. At the head of the organization was placed Sir Alfred Ewing, the Director of Naval Education, whose services to the Admiralty in this and other matters were of the first order. The work was of great complexity, as of course the cypher is only one element in the means of preserving the secrecy of a message. But gradually during the beginning of November our officers succeeded in translating intelligible portions of various German naval messages. They were mostly of a routine character. 'One of our torpedo boats will be running out into square 7T at 8 p.m.,' etc. But a careful collection of these scraps provided a body of information from which the enemy's arrangements in the Heligoland Bight could be understood with a fair degree of accuracy. The Germans, however, repeatedly changed their codes and keys and it was only occasionally and for fitful periods that we were able to penetrate them. As the war went on they became increasingly suspicious and devised measures which were completely baffling. While, however, this source of information lasted, it was obviously of the very greatest value.

The German official history shows itself at last well-informed upon this subject (*Germany's High Sea Fleet* by Reinhard Scheer, p. 194): 'Even if doubt were to exist that the British Admiralty were in possession of the whole secret cyphering system of the German Fleet, it has been cleared away by the reliable news from Petrograd, that after the stranding of the *Magdeburg* off Odensholm the secret papers of that ship, which had been thrown overboard, were picked up by the Russians and communicated to their Allies.'

Lastly, largely through the foresight of Admiral Oliver, we had begun setting up directional stations in August, 1914. We thus carried to an unrivalled and indeed unapproached degree of perfection our means of fixing the position and, by successive positions, the course of any enemy ship that used its wireless installation.

'The English,' says Scheer (*Germany's High Sea Fleet*, p. 73), 'received news through their "directional stations" which they already had in use, but which were only introduced by us at a much later period.... In possessing them the English had a very great advantage in the conduct of the war, as they were thus able to obtain quite accurate information of the locality of the enemy as soon as any wireless signals were sent by him. In the case of a large fleet, whose separate units are stationed far apart and communication between them is essential, an absolute cessation of all wireless intercourse would be fatal to any enterprise.'

But between collecting and weighing information, and drawing the true moral therefrom, there is very often an unbridged gap. Signals have been made, the wireless note of a particular ship is heard, lights are to be shown on certain channels at certain hours, ships are in movement, sweeping vessels are active, channels are buoyed, lock-gates are opened—what does it all mean? At first sight it all appears to be only ordinary routine. Yet taking the items together may lead to a tremendous revelation. Suffice it to say that all these indications, from whatever sources they emanated, were the subject of a special study by Sir Arthur Wilson, and he had the solemn duty of advising our War Group upon them.

The silence of the North Sea remained unbroken until the afternoon of Monday, December 14. At about 7 o'clock Sir Arthur Wilson came to my room and asked for an immediate meeting with the First Sea Lord and the Chief of Staff. It took only a few minutes to gather them. He then explained that his examination of the available intelligence about the enemy indicated the probability of an impending movement which would involve their battle-cruisers and perhaps—though of this there was no positive evidence—have an offensive character against our coasts. The German High Sea Fleet, he stated definitely, appeared not to be involved. The indications were obscure and uncertain. There were gaps in the argument. But the conclusion reached after hearing Sir Arthur Wilson was that we should act as if we knew that our assumptions and suppositions were true. It was decided not to move the whole Grand Fleet. A great deal of cruising had been imposed on the Fleet owing to the unprotected state of Scapa, and it was desirable to save wear and tear of machinery and condensers as much as possible. Moreover, the risks of accident, submarine and mine, which were incurred every time that immense organization was sent to sea, imposed a certain deterrent upon its use except when clearly necessary.

This decision, from which the Commander-in-Chief did not dissent, was, in the light of subsequent events, much to be regretted. But it must be remembered that the information on which the Admiralty was acting, had never yet been tested; that it seemed highly speculative in character, and that for whatever it was worth, it excluded the presence at sea of the German High Sea Fleet. Orders were therefore given immediately for the battle-cruisers and the 2nd Battle Squadron, with a light cruiser squadron and a flotilla of destroyers, to raise steam and to proceed to sea at such hours and at such speeds as to enable them to be in an intercepting position at daylight the next morning. Orders were sent to Commodore Tyrwhitt's Harwich Force to be at sea off Yarmouth, and to Commodore Keyes to place our eight available oversea submarines in a position off Terschelling to guard against a southward raid. The coastal forces were also put upon the alert.[1]

Admiralty to Commander-in-Chief.

December 14, 1914. *Sent* 9.30 p.m.

Good information just received shows German 1st Cruiser Squadron with Destroyers leave Jade River on Tuesday morning early and return on Wednesday

---

[1]See map on pages 376–7.

night. It is apparent from the information that the Battleships are very unlikely to come out.

The enemy force will have time to reach our coast.

Send at once leaving to-night the Battle Cruiser Squadron and Light Cruiser Squadron, supported by a Battle Squadron preferably the Second.

At daylight on Wednesday morning they should be at some point where they can make sure of intercepting the enemy on his return.

Tyrwhitt with his Light Cruisers and Destroyers will try to get in touch with enemy off British coast and shadow him keeping Admiral informed.

From our information the German 1st Cruiser Squadron consists of 4 Battle-Cruisers and 5 Light Cruisers and there will possibly be three flotillas of Destroyers.

Acknowledge.

Admiralty to Commodore 'T' Harwich.

December 15, 1914. *Sent* 2.5 p.m.

There is good probability of German Battle-Cruisers, Cruisers and Destroyers being off our coast to-morrow about daybreak.

One M. Class Destroyer is to patrol vicinity of North Hinder Lightship from midnight until 9 a.m. A second M Class Destroyer is to patrol a line extending 15 miles south magnetic from a position lat. 53° 0′ N., long. 3° 5′ E. from midnight until 9 a.m.

The duty of these Destroyers is to look out for and report the enemy and trust to their speed to escape.

If the weather is too bad, they are to return to Harwich. Report their names.

The 1st and 3rd Flotillas with all available Light Cruisers are to be under way off Yarmouth before daylight to-morrow ready to move to any place where the enemy may be reported from, whether it is to the northward or southward.

Their duty is to get touch with the enemy, follow him and report his position to the Vice-Admiral 2nd Battle Squadron and Vice-Admiral 1st Battle Cruiser Squadron.

The 2nd Battle Squadron, 1st Battle Cruiser Squadron, 3rd Cruiser Squadron and Light Cruiser Squadron will be in a position in N. lat. 54° 10′ E. long. 3° 0′ at 7.30 a.m. ready to cut off retreat of enemy.

Should an engagement result your Flotillas and Light Cruisers must endeavour to join our Fleet and deal with enemy Destroyers.

If the weather is too bad for Destroyers use Light Cruisers only and send Destroyers back. Acknowledge.

All measures having been taken on the chance of their being necessary, we awaited during thirty-six hours the events of Wednesday morning with a doubting but expectant curiosity. On the morning of December 16 at about half-past eight I was in my bath, when the door opened and an officer came hurrying in from the War Room with a naval signal which I grasped with dripping hand. 'German battle-cruisers bombarding Hartlepool.' I jumped out of the bath with exclamations. Sympathy for Hartlepool was mingled with what Mr. George Wyndham once called 'the anodyne of contemplated retaliation.' Pulling on clothes over a damp body, I ran downstairs to the War Room. The First Sea Lord had just arrived from his house next door. Oliver, who invariably slept in the War Room and hardly ever left it by day, was marking the positions on the map. Telegrams from all the naval stations along the coast affected by the attack, and intercepts from our ships in the vicinity speaking to each other, came pouring in two and three to the minute. The Admiralty also spread the tidings and kept the Fleets and flotillas continuously informed of all we knew.

Everything was now sent to sea or set in motion. The 3rd Battle Squadron (*King Edwards*) from the Forth was ordered to prevent the enemy escaping to the Northward. As a further precaution (though, unless the Germans were driven far to the North, this could hardly be effective in time), the Grand Fleet itself was after all brought out. Commodore Tyrwhitt and his cruisers and destroyers of the Harwich Striking Force were directed to join Sir George Warrender, who commanded the Second Battle Squadron, and was the senior Admiral with the intercepting force. The weather was, however, too rough for the destroyers, and only the light cruisers could proceed. Lastly, later in the day Commodore Keyes, who was in the *Lurcher*—one of our latest destroyers and had also with him the destroyer *Firedrake*—was told to take his submarines from his preliminary station off Terschelling into the Heligoland Bight and try to catch the enemy returning.

The bombardment of open towns was still new to us at that time. But, after all, what did that matter now? The war map showed the German battle-cruisers identified one by one within gunshot of the Yorkshire coast, while 150 miles to eastward *between them and Germany*, cutting mathematically their line of retreat, steamed in the exact positions intended, four British battle-cruisers and six of the most powerful battleships in the world forming the 2nd Battle Squadron. Attended and preceded by their cruiser squadrons and flotilla, this fleet of our newest and fastest ships all armed with the heaviest gun then afloat, could in fair weather cover and watch effectively a front of nearly 100 miles. In the positions in which dawn revealed the antagonists, only one thing could enable the Germans to escape annihilation at the hands of an overwhelmingly superior force. And while the great shells crashed into the little houses of Hartlepool and Scarborough, carrying their cruel message of pain and destruction to unsuspecting English homes, only one anxiety dominated the thoughts of the Admiralty War Room.

The word 'Visibility' assumed a sinister significance. At present it was quite good enough. Both Warrender and Beatty had horizons of nearly ten miles: near the coast fighting was actually in progress at 7,000 yards. There was nothing untoward in the weather indications. At 9 a.m. the German bombardment ceased, and their ships were soon out of sight of land, no doubt on their homeward voyage. We went on tenter-hooks to breakfast. To have this tremendous prize—the German battle-cruiser squadron whose loss would fatally mutilate the whole German Navy and could never be repaired—actually within our claws, and to have the event all turn upon a veil of mist, was a racking ordeal. Meanwhile telegraph and telephone were pouring the distress of Hartlepool and Scarborough to all parts of the Kingdom, and by half-past ten, when the War Committee of the Cabinet met, news magnified by rumour had produced excitement. I was immediately asked how such a thing was possible. 'What was the Navy doing, and what were they going to do?' In reply I produced the chart which showed the respective positions at the moment of the British and German naval forces, and I explained that subject to moderate visibility we hoped that collision would take place about noon. These disclosures fell upon all with a sense of awe, and the Committee adjourned till the afternoon.

At 10.30 the Admiralty learned that the enemy was leaving our coasts and apprised Admiral Warrender accordingly.

> 'Enemy is probably returning towards Heligoland. You should keep outside minefield and steer so as to cut him off.'

But now already ominous telegrams began to arrive. Warrender soon had horizons of only 7,000 yards; Beatty of only 6,000; some of the light cruisers nearer to the coast already mentioned 5,000; and later on 4,000 was signalled. Meanwhile no contact. Noon passed, and then 1 o'clock. The weather got steadily worse. It was evident that the mist curtains were falling over the North Sea. 3,000 yards visibility, 2,000 yards visibility were reported by ships speaking to each other. The solemn faces of Fisher and Wilson betrayed no emotion, but one felt the fire burning within. I tried to do other work, but it was not much good. Obscure messages were heard from our fleet. Evidently they were very close to the enemy, groping for him in a mist which allowed vessels to be distinguished only within 2,000 yards. We heard Warrender order his priceless ships to steam through the located German minefield off the Yorkshire coast apparently in an endeavour to close with something just out of sight, just beyond his finger-tips. Then all of a sudden we heard Rear-Admiral Goodenough with the light cruisers report that he had opened fire upon a German light cruiser at 3,000 yards. Hope flared up. Once contact was established, would it not drag all other events in its train? The prospect of a confused battle at close range had no terrors for the Admiralty. They had only one fear—lest the enemy should escape. Even the proposed movement of the 2nd Battle Squadron through the minefield was received in utter silence.

About half-past one Sir Arthur Wilson said 'They seem to be getting away from us.' But now occurred a new development of a formidable kind. At 1.50 we learned that the High Sea Fleet was at sea. Up till noon this great Fleet had not spoken. Once she had spoken and the necessary calculations had been made, which took some time, we could both recognize and locate her. She had already in fact advanced far into the North Sea. The apparition of the German Fleet, which as we then supposed was advancing to the support of the German battle-cruisers, entirely altered the balance of strength. Our ten great ships steaming together with their light squadrons and flotillas, were not only the strongest but the fastest naval force in the world. No equal German force existed which could at once overtake and overcome them. On the other hand, they were not capable of meeting the High Sea Fleet. The German battle-cruisers were still separated from their fleet by 150 miles, but it seemed to us that a running action begun with the German battle-cruisers, might in the thick weather then prevailing conceivably lead to a surprise encounter with the main naval power of the enemy. This was certainly not the wish of the Admiralty. We instantly warned our squadrons.

Admiralty to 2nd Battle Squadron and 1st Battle Cruiser Squadron.

Sent 1.50 p.m.

(Urgent.)

High Sea Fleet is out and was in latitude 54° 38′ N. longitude 5° 55′ E.[2] at 0.30 p.m. to-day, so do not go too far to Eastward.

These sinister possibilities soon faded like our earlier hopes. The High Sea Fleet was not, as we imagined, coming out, but had long been out and was now retiring.

At 3 o'clock I went over and told the War Committee what was passing; but with what a heavy heart did I cross again that Horse Guards Parade. I returned to the Admiralty. The War Group had re-assembled around the octagonal table in my room. The shades of a winter's evening had already fallen. Sir Arthur Wilson then said, in his most ordinary manner, 'Well, there you are, they have got away. They must be about here by now,' and he pointed to the chart on which the Chief of the Staff was marking the positions every fifteen minutes. It was evident that the Germans had eluded our intercepting force, and that even their light cruisers with whom we had been in contact had also escaped in the mist. Said Admiral Warrender in his subsequent report, 'They came out of one rainstorm and disappeared in another.'

It was now nearly 8 o'clock.

Was it then all over? I inquired about our submarines. They had already been collected by Commodore Keyes from their first position and were now moving on to the German line of retreat. But whether the enemy's course would come within their limited range was a matter of luck. Sir Arthur Wilson then said, 'There is only one chance now. Keyes with the *Lurcher* and *Firedrake*, is with the submarines. He could probably make certain of attacking the German battle-cruiser squadron at it enters the Bight to-night. He may torpedo one or even two.' It seemed indeed a forlorn hope to send these two frail destroyers with their brave Commodore and faithful crews, far from home, close to the enemy's coast, utterly unsupported, into the jaws of this powerful German force with its protecting vessels and flotillas. There was a long silence. We all knew Keyes well. Then someone said, 'It is sending him to his death.' Someone else said. 'He would be the last man to wish us to consider that.' There was another long pause. However, Sir Arthur Wilson had already written the following message:—

8.12 p.m.

[2]i.e. about 80 miles West of Heligoland.

> 'We think Heligoland and Amrun lights will be lit when ships are going in. Your destroyers might get a chance to attack about 2 a.m. or later on the line given you.'

The First Sea Lord nodded assent. The Chief of the Staff took it, got up heavily and quitted the room. Then we turned to the ordinary business of the day and also to the decision of what could be told to the public about the event.

Two days later when I received Admiral Keyes in my room at the Admiralty, I said, 'We sent you a terrible message the other night. I hardly expected to see you again.' 'It *was* terrible,' he said, 'not getting it till I was nearly home. I waited three hours in the hopes of such an order, and I very nearly did it on my own responsibility,' and he proceeded to reproach himself without need.[3]

* * * * *

So far I have described this episode of December 16 exactly as it appeared from the War Room of the Admiralty, and as we understood it at the time. But let us now see in essentials what had happened.[4] No one could tell at what point on our shores the German attack would fall; and with 500 miles of coast studded with possible objectives to guard, there could be no certain solution. The orders issued by the Commander-in-Chief, however, and the dawn position selected, ably comprehended the design of the enemy. In pursuance of these orders the 2nd Battle Squadron (6 ships) and the Battle Cruiser Squadron (4 ships), together with the 3rd Cruiser Squadron, a Squadron of Light Cruisers and a flotilla, steaming down from Scapa, Cromarty and the Forth, arrived at about 5.30 in the morning of the 16th, two hours and a half before daybreak, at the Southern edge of the Dogger Bank. Here in the very centre of the North Sea, almost on a line drawn from Hartlepool to Heligoland, the advanced screen of British destroyers became engaged with German destroyers and light cruisers, and when daylight came they sighted a large German cruiser identified as the *Roon*.[5] Fighting ensued, some of our destroyers were hit, and the Germans retreated to the Eastward. Thereupon Admiral Beatty with his battle-cruisers began to chase the *Roon*. From this pursuit he was recalled by the news which reached him and Admiral Warrender from the Admiralty about 9 a.m., that the German battle-cruisers were bombarding Hartlepool and later Scarborough. All the British ships at once turned to the Westward and steamed abreast in a long line

[3]It must be explained that in these days the wireless communication with destroyers and still more submarines was not as perfect as it became later on. The *Firedrake* had therefore been stationed in the morning midway between the submarines and Harwich to pass on messages. She had late in the afternoon, after the orders to take the submarines into the Bight had reached her, rejoined Commodore Keyes and the link was for the time being, broken.

[4]The whole of this operation is described in minute detail in the official British Naval History, and should be studied with the excellent charts by those who are interested in its technical aspect. So complicated is the full story that the lay reader cannot see the wood for the trees. I have endeavoured to render intelligible the broad effects.—W.S.C.

[5]See map on pages 376–7, 'The Dawn Situation.'

towards the British coast and the German battle-cruisers, whose interception appeared highly probable.

During the war we were puzzled to understand what the *Roon* and the German light forces were doing on the edge of the Dogger Bank at this hour in the morning. It was an ill-assorted force to be in so exposed a position, and it was not a force, or in a position, which could be of any help to the German cruisers raiding the British coasts. Now we know the answer. The *Roon* and her cruisers and destroyers were part of the advanced screen of the German High Sea Fleet who were out in full force, three squadrons strong, with all their attendant vessels and numerous flotillas. Admiral von Ingenohl in command of the High Sea Fleet had sailed from Cuxhaven after darkness had fallen on the evening of the 15th (between 4 and 5 p.m.) and before dawn on the 16th was pushing boldly out towards the Dogger Bank in support of his battle-cruisers who, under Admiral von Hipper, were already approaching the British shores. Had von Ingenohl continued on his course, as was his intention, his scouts would between 8 and 9 o'clock, in the clear weather of that morning in this part of the North Sea, have come in sight of the British battle-cruisers and the 2nd Battle Squadron coming down from the North. A meeting was almost certain. What would have happened? Admiral von Tirpitz proclaims that this was the one heaven-sent never-recurring opportunity for a battle with the odds enormously in German favour. 'On December 16,' he wrote a few weeks later, 'Ingenohl had the fate of Germany in the palm of his hand. I boil with inward emotion whenever I think of it.' We will examine this claim later. Let us first follow the event.

Admiral von Ingenohl had already strained his instructions by going so far to sea. An appeal by him against the 'Muzzling Order,' which the Emperor had issued after the action of the Heligoland Bight (August 28), had recently encountered a rebuff. 'The Fleet must be held back and avoid actions which might lead to heavy losses.' Such had been the latest *ukase*. And here was the Fleet right out in the middle of the North Sea in the darkness of a December dawn. Suddenly the flashes of guns, English destroyers reported in action with the cruisers of his screen, the screen retiring, the destroyers pursuing—and still two hours before daylight. Von Ingenohl conceived himself in danger of a torpedo attack in darkness. At about 5.30 therefore he turned his whole Fleet about and steamed off South-Eastward, and shortly after 6 o'clock, increasingly disquieted by his hampering instructions, but knowing no more of the presence of our squadrons than they of him, he, in the justly chosen words of the British official historian, 'fairly turned tail and made for home, leaving his raiding force in the air.' Even so, at 6 o'clock the two Fleets were only about 50 miles apart and their light forces in contact! Says Scheer, who was in command of the German 2nd Squadron (*Germany's High Sea Fleet*, p. 71), 'Our premature turning on to an East-South-East course had robbed us of the opportunity of meeting certain divisions of the enemy according to the prearranged plan, which is now seen to have been correct.'

There was, however, no compulsion upon Admirals Warrender and Beatty to fight such an action. Their squadrons were moving properly protected by their screen of cruisers and destroyers. In this part of the sea and at this hour the weather was quite clear. They would have known what forces they were in presence of, before they could

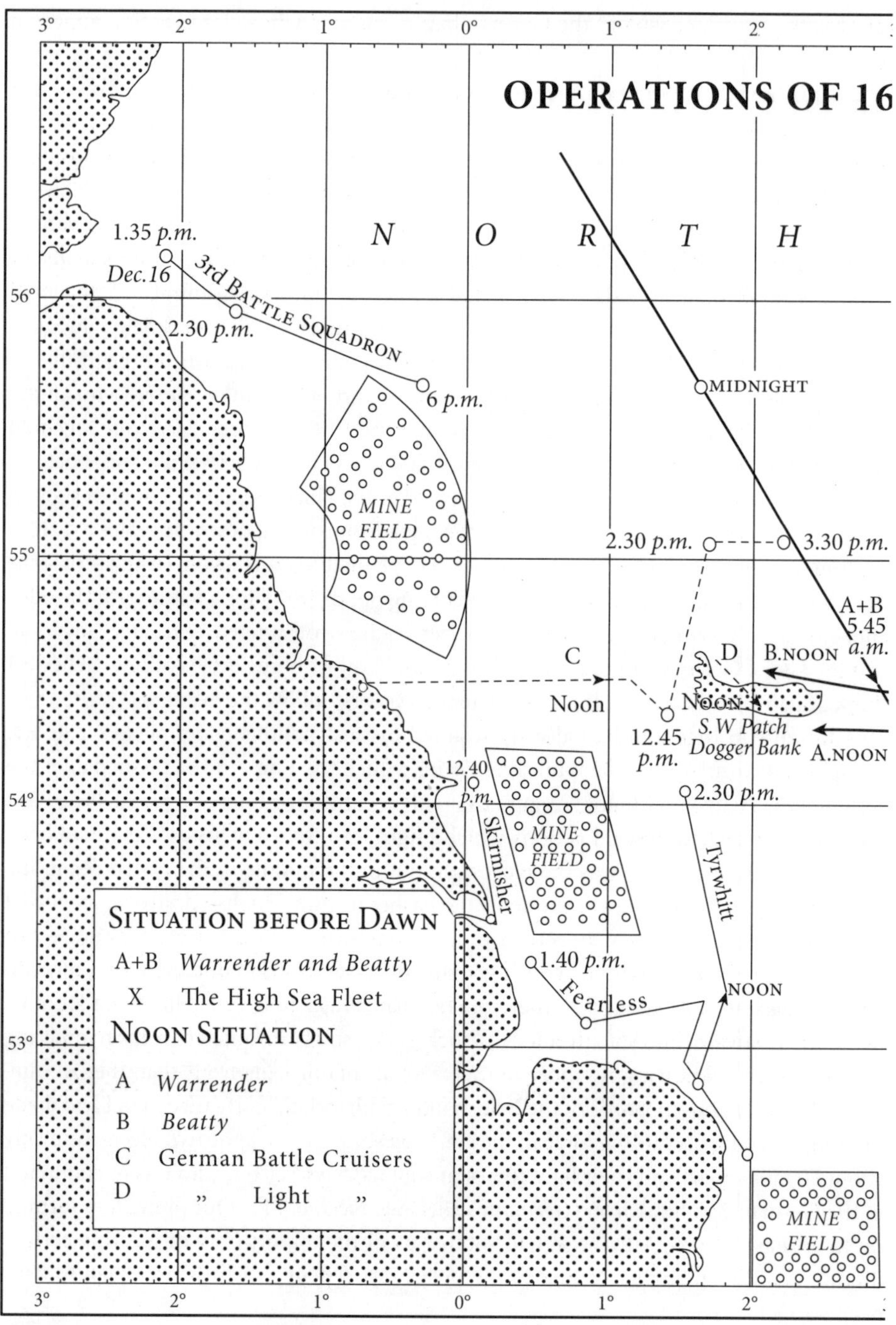
OPERATIONS OF 16
N O R T H
1.35 p.m.
Dec.16
3rd Battle Squadron
2.30 p.m.
6 p.m.
MIDNIGHT
MINE FIELD
2.30 p.m.
3.30 p.m.
A+B
5.45
a.m.
C
D
B.NOON
Noon
Noon
12.45
p.m.
S.W Patch
Dogger Bank
A.NOON
12.40
p.m.
2.30 p.m.
Skirmisher
MINE FIELD
Tyrwhitt
1.40 p.m.
Fearless
NOON
MINE FIELD
Situation before Dawn
A+B Warrender and Beatty
X The High Sea Fleet
Noon Situation
A Warrender
B Beatty
C German Battle Cruisers
D " Light "
3°
2°
1°
0°
1°
2°
56°
55°
54°
53°

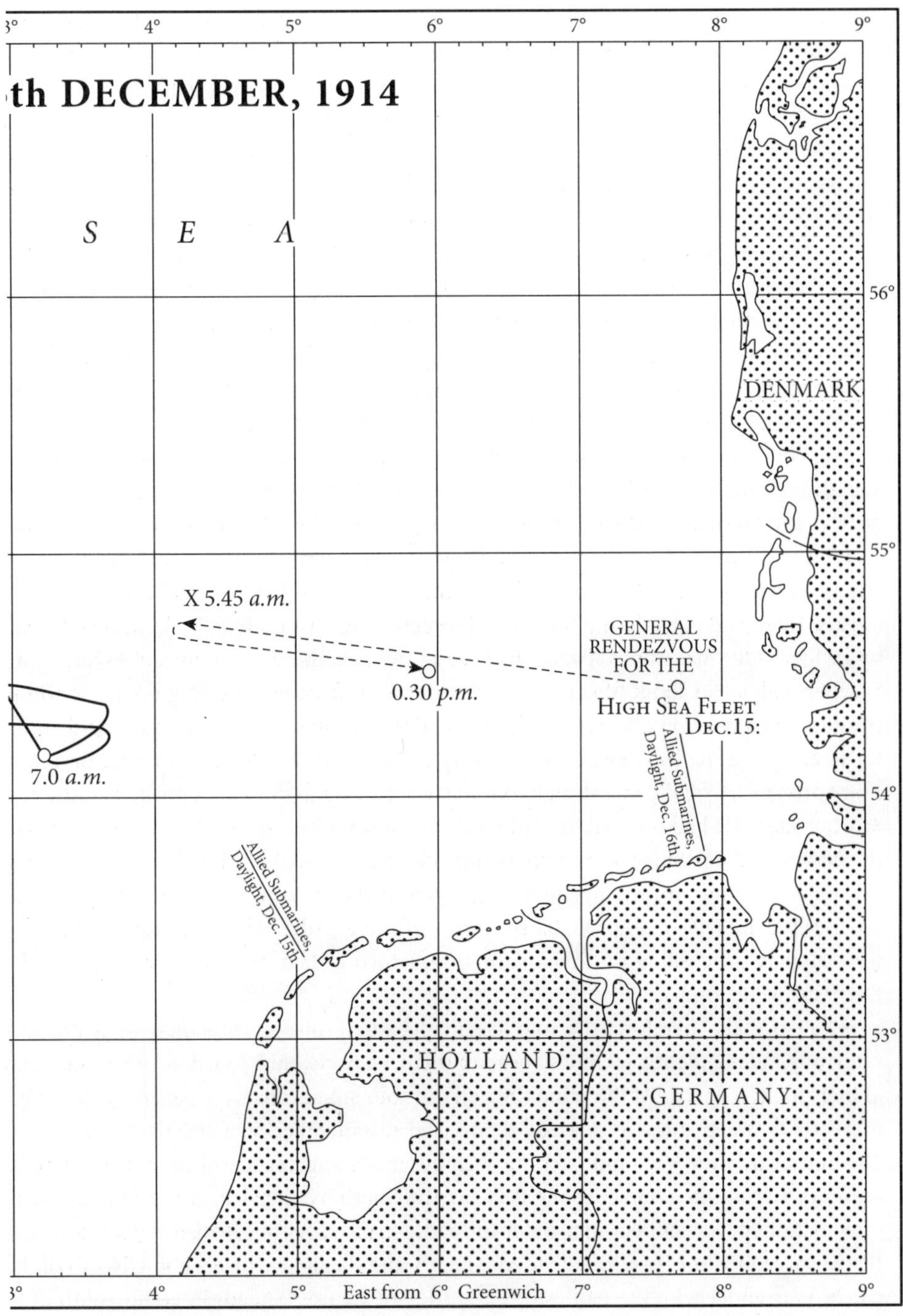
th DECEMBER, 1914
S E A
DENMARK
X 5.45 a.m.
GENERAL
RENDEZVOUS
FOR THE
HIGH SEA FLEET
DEC.15:
0.30 p.m.
7.0 a.m.
Allied Submarines,
Daylight, Dec. 16th
Allied Submarines,
Daylight, Dec. 15th
HOLLAND
GERMANY
3° 4° 5° 6° 7° 8° 9°
56°
55°
54°
53°
East from Greenwich

become seriously engaged. There would not have been any justification for trying to fight the High Sea Fleet of twenty battleships, with six battleships and four battle-cruisers, even though these comprised our most powerful vessels. Nor was there any need. The British 2nd Battle Squadron could steam in company at 20 knots, or could escape with Forced Draught at 21, and only six of von Ingenohl's ships could equal that speed. As for the battle-cruisers, nothing could catch them. The safety of this force acting detached from the main British Fleet was inherent in its speed. Admirals Warrender and Beatty could therefore have refused battle with the German Fleet, and it would certainly have been their duty to do so. Still, having regard to the large numbers of destroyers at sea with the German Fleet and the chances of darkness and weather, the situation at this juncture, as we now know it to have been, gives cause for profound reflection. That it never materialized unfavourably was the reward of previous audacity. The sixteenth of December lay under the safe-guard of the twenty-eighth of August.

We now enter upon the second phase of this extraordinary day. All four British squadrons with their flotilla between 9 and 10 o'clock were steaming towards the British coasts. The German raiding cruisers, having finished their bombardments, were now seeking to return home with the utmost speed. There were two large minefields which had been laid earlier in the war by the Germans off the Yorkshire coast, and we, having located them and considering them as a protection against raiding, had improved them by laying additional mines. Between these minefields there was opposite Whitby and Scarborough a gap about fifteen miles wide. Sir John Jellicoe, reflecting upon the whole position from the *Iron Duke* from afar, formed the opinion that the enemy would either try to escape to the Northward by steaming up our coast inside the minefield or, much more probably, would come straight out Eastward through the gap opposite Whitby and Scarborough. He had ordered the 3rd Battle Squadron from the Forth to close the gap to the Northward and this was rapidly being effected. At 10.10 he signalled to Sir George Warrender telling him the position of the gap in the minefields opposite Whitby and adding 'Enemy will in all probability come out there.' Admirals Warrender and Beatty were already proceeding on this assumption, which in fact correctly divined what the Germans were doing.

At 11 o'clock, therefore, the four German battle-cruisers, with their light cruisers returning independently 60 miles ahead of them, were steaming due East for Heligoland at their highest speed. At the same time all our four squadrons were steaming due West in a broad sweep directly towards them. The distance between the fleets was about 100 miles, and they were approaching each other at an aggregate speed of over 40 miles an hour. Across the course of our fleet lay the South-West patch of the Dogger Bank on which there was not enough water for battle-cruisers, either British or German. The British sweeping line therefore divided—Beatty and the light cruisers going North of the patch, Warrender with the battleships and the 3rd Cruiser Squadron going South of it. This involved a certain detour and delay in our advance. The weather, moreover, became very bad. The mist descended and the sea ran high. The German light cruisers were now sighted by our Light Cruiser Squadron scouting ahead of Beatty through the driving mist and rainstorms. The *Southampton*, the most Southerly light cruiser, opened fire and was answered by the enemy. Hopes on board the *Lion* rose. Just at the place and just at the moment when they might expect it, was the enemy's cruiser screen. Clearly the main body was behind them: probably it was not far behind. But now Mischance intervened.

The other three British light cruisers, seeing the *Southampton* engaged to the Southward, turned in that direction to join in the fight and the *Birmingham* opened fire. This was not in accordance with the wishes of Admiral Beatty, who wished to keep his scouts in front of him at the time when he must expect to be closely approaching the enemy's battle-cruisers, and when the danger of missing them was so great. He therefore ordered his light cruisers to return to their stations. The signal, instead of being directed by name to the two vessels who were not engaged, was made general to the Light Cruiser Squadron, and acting on this order the *Southampton* and *Birmingham* both broke off their action with the German cruiser and resumed their places in the line. The German light cruisers turned off to the Southward and vanished in the mist. Contact with them was thus lost.

Meanwhile, however, the battle-cruisers on both sides continued rapidly to approach each other. At 12.15 Admiral von Hipper warned by his light cruisers that an enemy force was immediately in front of him, also turned slightly and to the South-East. Admiral Beatty continued on his course till 12.30. At this moment the two battle-cruiser forces were only 25 miles apart and still rapidly closing.[6] But now again Mischance! The German light cruisers, deflected away to the Southward from Beatty, came into contact with the 3rd Cruiser Squadron in front of Warrender. Fire again was opened and returned, and again the enemy cruisers were lost in the thick mist. They reported to von Hipper that on this path also was a blocking force. Thereupon at 12.45 he made 'a three-quarters left about turn' (if I may employ a cavalry term), and dodged off due North. This by itself would not have saved him. Had Admiral Beatty held on his original course for another quarter of an hour, an action at decisive ranges must have begun before 1 o'clock. But observe what had happened.

At 12.30 Admiral Beatty had received a signal from Sir George Warrender at the moment of the second contact with the German light cruisers, 'Enemy cruisers and destroyers in sight.' He therefore concluded that the German battle-cruisers had slipped past him to the Southward, and acting in addition on the sound principle of keeping between the enemy and the enemy's home at all costs, he too whipped round and steamed back on his course, i.e., Eastward, for three-quarters of an hour. At 1.15, hearing that the enemy battle-cruisers had turned North, he too turned North; but contact was never re-established. Von Hipper succeeded in escaping round the Northern flank of our squadrons. His light cruisers, so thick was the weather, made their way through the 3rd Cruiser Squadron, passing for a few moments actually in sight of Warrender's battleships.

Thus ended this heart-shaking game of Blind Man's Buff.

It remains only to mention the action of our British submarines. By 3.30 Commodore Keyes had collected four of his boats from their station submerged off Terschelling,

---

[6]See map on pages 376–7, 'The Noon Situation.'

and in accordance with Admiralty orders was making for the Heligoland Bight. Eventually he succeeded in placing three boats on the Southern side of Heligoland and one on the Northern. This solitary boat, under Commander Nasmith, on the morning of the 17th found itself in the middle of von Hipper's squadron and flotillas returning from their raid and fired two torpedoes at battle-cruisers under very difficult conditions and without effect.

Such was the episode of the Scarborough and Hartlepool raids. All that we could tell the public was contained in the following communiqué which was issued in the morning papers of December 17:—

> *Admiralty, December* 16, 9.20 p.m.
>
> This morning a German cruiser force made a demonstration upon the Yorkshire coast, in the course of which they shelled Hartlepool, Whitby, and Scarborough.
>
> A number of their fastest ships were employed for this purpose, and they remained about an hour on the coast. They were engaged by the patrol vessels on the spot.
>
> As soon as the presence of the enemy was reported, a British patrolling squadron endeavoured to cut them off. On being sighted by British vessels the Germans retired at full speed, and, favoured by the mist, succeeded in making good their escape.
>
> The losses on both sides are small, but full reports have not yet been received.
>
> The Admiralty take the opportunity of pointing out that demonstrations of this character against unfortified towns or commercial ports, though not difficult to accomplish provided that a certain amount of risk is accepted, are devoid of military significance.
>
> They may cause some loss of life among the civil population and some damage to private property, which is much to be regretted; but they must not in any circumstances be allowed to modify the general naval policy which is being pursued.

Naturally there was much indignation at the failure of the Navy to prevent, or at least to avenge, such an attack upon our shores. What was the Admiralty doing? Were they all asleep? Although the bombarded towns, in which nearly five hundred civilians had been killed and wounded, supported their ordeal with fortitude, dissatisfaction was widespread. However, we could not say a word in explanation. We had to bear in silence the censures of our countrymen. We could never admit for fear of compromising our secret information where our squadrons were, or how near the German raiding cruisers had been to their destruction. One comfort we had. The indications upon which we had acted had been confirmed by events. The sources of information upon which we relied were evidently trustworthy. Next time we might at least have average visibility. But would there be a next time? The German Admiral must have known that he was very near to powerful British ships, but which they were, or where they were, or how near he was, might be a mystery. Would it not also be a mystery how they came to be there? On the other hand, the exultation of Germany at the hated English towns being actually made to feel for the first time the real lash of war might encourage a second attempt. Even the indignation of our own newspapers had a value for this purpose. One could only hope for the best. Meanwhile British naval plans and secrets remained wrapped in impenetrable silence.

CHAPTER XXI
TURKEY AND THE BALKANS

'Now mark me well—it is provided in the essence of things, that from any fruition of success, no matter what, shall come forth something to make a greater struggle necessary.'

—Walt Whitman, *The Open Road.*

Britain and Turkey—My Correspondence with Djavid, 1911—Effect of Requisitioning the Turkish Battleships—Nominal Transfer of the *Goeben* and the *Breslau* to Turkey—General Situation in the Balkans—Bulgaria the Dominant Factor—Venizelos Offers a Greek Alliance—Reasons against Acceptance—My Letter to Mr. Noel Buxton—Menacing Attitude of Turkey—Possibilities of a Greek Military Attack upon Gallipoli—Difficulties of Greek Intervention—Search for an Army—Withdrawal of the British Naval Mission in Constantinople—Letter to Sir Edward Grey of September 23—Alternative Considerations—Secret Turco-German Treaty of August 2—The Turco-German Attack on Russia—Ultimatum to Turkey and Declaration of War—The Bombardment of the Dardanelles Forts of November 3—Impending Turkish Attack upon Egypt—Naval Concentration in the Canal—Repulse of the Turkish Attack—Arrival of the Australians in Egypt—The Prelude to the Dardanelles—General Survey of the War—The Great Strain—The Sudden Relief—The End of the Beginning.

It is now necessary to describe the circumstances attending the entry of Turkey into the war. In Turkey, as in Greece and all the Balkan States except Serbia, there were two violently conflicting parties—pro-German and pro-Entente. The assiduous courting of Turkey by Germany and the condonation of her most atrocious actions had given the Germans great advantages at Constantinople. In addition the profound instinct of the Turk was to be on the opposite side to his historic and tremendous enemy, Russia. Britain, on the other hand, took no trouble to counteract these formidable tendencies. Large sections of the British Press and public denounced the Turk, often with justice, in unmeasured terms, and no foreign policy based on special relations with Turkey could have stood for a day in a Liberal House of Commons. Notwithstanding all this, British influence in Turkey rested on foundations so deep and ancient, and the impression produced upon the Turkish mind by her obviously disinterested course of action was so strong, that at any rate up till the beginning of 1914 she would have welcomed a British alliance. This was the wish not only of the old Turks but of the young Turks. When in the summer of

1909 I had visited Constantinople, I made the acquaintance of the Young Turk leaders and passed several days in the company of Djavid, Talaat and Halil. I also met at the German Manœuvres of 1910 Enver Pasha, with whom I established amicable relations. All these men seemed animated by a sincere desire to help their country to reform and revive, and I could not help feeling much sympathy for them in their difficulties.

In 1911, after Turkey had been attacked by Italy and her Tripoli Province seized, I received the following letter from Djavid Bey written on behalf of his friends on the then all-powerful Committee of Union and Progress:—

Djavid Bey to Mr. Churchill.

October 29, 1911.

My belief in your sincere friendship for Turkey and the Young Turks leads me to speak of a very important matter to-day.

After the Constitution in Turkey those that believed in the beginning of a close friendship between England and Turkey saw with regret the misunderstanding that prevented it. I need not speak of its different causes here. Only the true friends of England in Turkey never ceased from trying to remove it. The actual circumstances appear to be a good occasion for success. The attack of one of the Triple Alliance Powers on our territory has turned the public opinion greatly against the Triplice. The pro-English statesmen in Turkey and pro-Turkish statesmen in England could profit of this occasion.

Knowing and believing you to occupy an important and influential position among our friends in England, I will beg you to join our efforts using your influence in bringing out this friendship. Has the time arrived for a permanent alliance between the two countries? On what basis could it be attempted? Will you please write me your personal views on the matter? They will be considered entirely personal and unofficial. But I will consider myself happy if we can prepare a possible ground for official purposes.

I commended this matter promptly to Sir Edward Grey, but the danger of estranging Italy—apart from domestic and political considerations—made it impossible for him to authorize me to say more than the following:—

Mr. Churchill to Djavid Bey.

Admiralty, November 19, 1911.

It is a great pleasure to me to receive your letter, the importance of which I fully recognize. So far as the present lamentable struggle is concerned, we have definitely declared our neutrality; and it is not to be expected that we shall alter a policy so gravely decided. My answer therefore to your question must be that at the present time we cannot enter upon new political relations. In the future the enormous interests which unite the two great Mussulman Powers should keep us in touch.

> That is our wish; the feeling of British public opinion, as you will have seen from recent manifestations of it, opposes no barrier to that wish, if only the Turkish Government will not alienate it by reverting to the oppressive methods of the old regime or seeking to disturb the British status quo as it now exists; and you and your friends, whom I remember to have met with so much pleasure, should bear in mind that England, almost alone among European States, seeks no territorial expansion, and that alone among them she retains the supremacy of the sea. We earnestly desire to revive and maintain our old friendship with Turkey, which while we retain that supremacy should be a friendship of value.
>
> I must apologize for the delay in answering your letter, which was due to the importance of its nature.

In the years which followed, the Young Turks looked towards Germany, and here they were very powerfully swayed by their military instincts and training. They rightly regarded Germany as the leading military Power: many of them had received their military education in Berlin, and they were spellbound by the splendour and authority of Prussian organization. They saw the Russian giant ever growing to the east and to the north. And if England stood aloof, where else could Turkey find protection except through the German sword? I do not see what else we could have expected. Therefore, from the very beginning of the war I hoped for nothing from Turkey and apprehended much.

The Ottoman Empire was in 1914 already moribund. Italy, using sea power, had invaded and annexed Tripoli in 1909, and a desultory warfare was still proceeding in the interior of this province, when the Balkan States in 1912 drew the sword upon their ancient conqueror and tyrant. Important provinces and many islands were ceded by the defeated Turkish Empire in the Treaty of London, and the division of the spoils became a new cause of bloodshed among the Balkan victors. Rich prizes still remained in European Turkey to tempt the ambition or satisfy the claims of Roumania, Bulgaria, Serbia and Greece; and through all Constantinople glittered as the supreme goal. But imminent as were the dangers of the Turkish Empire from the vengeance and ambition of the Balkan States, nothing could supplant in the Turkish mind the fear of Russia. Russia was in contact with Turkey by land and water along a thousand-mile frontier which stretched from the western shores of the Black Sea to the Caspian. England, France and Italy (Sardinia) in the Crimean War, the exceptional power of England under Disraeli in 1878, had preserved the Turkish Empire from ruin and Constantinople from conquest. Although before the Balkan Allies quarrelled among themselves, the Bulgarians had marched to the gates of Constantinople from the West, the sense of peril from the North still outweighed all else in Turkish thoughts.

To this was added the antagonism of the Arab race in the Yemen, the Hedjas, Palestine, Syria, Mosul, and Iraq. The population of Kurdistan and the widely distributed Armenian race were estranged. From every quarter the nations and races who for five or six hundred years had waged war against the Turkish Empire or had suffered the fate of Turkish captives, turned their gaze in a measureless hatred and hunger upon the dying Empire from which they had endured so much so long. The hour of retribution and restoration was at hand; and the only doubt was how long could the busily spun webs of European diplomacy, and particularly of English diplomacy, postpone the final reckoning. The imminent collapse of the Turkish Empire like the progressive decay and disruption of the Austrian Empire, arising from forces beyond human control, had loosened the whole foundations of Eastern and South-Eastern Europe. Change—violent, vast, incalculable, but irresistible and near, brooded over the hearths and institutions of 120 millions of people.

It was at this hour and on this scene that Germany had launched her army to the invasion of France through Belgium, and all other quarrels had re-aligned themselves in accordance with the supreme struggle. What was to happen to scandalous, crumbling, decrepit and penniless Turkey in this earthquake?

She received what seemed to British eyes the most favourable offer ever made to any government in history. She was guaranteed at the price merely of maintaining her neutrality the absolute integrity of all her dominions. She was guaranteed this upon the authority not only of her friends, France and Britain, but on that of her enemy, Russia. The guarantee of France and England would have protected Turkey from the Balkan States, and especially Greece; the guarantee of Russia suspended to indefinite periods the overhanging menace from the North. The influence of Britain could largely allay and certainly postpone the long rising movement of the Arabs. Never, thought the Allies, was a fairer proposition made to a weaker and more imperilled State.

But there was another side to the picture. Within the decaying fabric of the Turkish Empire and beneath the surface of its political affairs lay fierce, purposeful forces both in men and ideas. The disaster of the first Balkan War created from these elements a concealed, slow-burning fire of strange intensity unrealized by all the Embassies along the shores of the Bosphorus—all save one. 'During this time' (the years before the Great War), wrote a profoundly informed Turk in 1915, 'the whole future of the Turkish people was examined by Committees down to the smallest details.'[1]

The Pan-Turk Committee accepted the Anglo-Russian Convention of 1907 as a definite alliance between the Power who had been Turkey's strongest and most disinterested supporter and friend with the Power who was her ancient and inexorable enemy. They therefore looked elsewhere for help in the general European war which they were convinced was approaching. Their plan, which seemed in 1913 merely visionary, was based upon the recreation of Turkey on a solely Turkish human foundation: to wit, the Turkish peasantry of Anatolia. It contemplated as a national ideal the uniting of the Moslem areas of Caucasia, the Persian province of Azerbaijan, and the Turkish Trans-Caspian provinces of Russia (the homeland of the Turkish race) with the Turks of the Anatolian peninsula; and the extension of Turkey into the Caspian Basin. It included the rejection of theocratic government; a radical change of relationship between Church and State; the diversion of the 'Pious Foundations'; endowments to the secular needs of the State, and a rigorous disciplining of the professional religious classes. It included also

[1] *Turkish and Pan-Turkish Ideals*, by 'Tekin Alp.' First published in German. 1915.

the startling economic, social and literary changes which have recently been achieved in Turkey. Mustapha Kemal has in fact executed a plan decided upon, and to which he may well have been a party, fifteen years ago. The centre point of all the Pan-Turk schemes was the use of Germany to rid Turkey of the Russian danger. Marschall von Bieberstein, for so many years German Ambassador at Constantinople, nursed these hidden fires with skilful hands.

Pan-Turkish schemes might have remained in dreamland but for the fact that in a fateful hour there stood almost at the head of Turkey a man of action. A would-be Turkish Napoleon, in whose veins surged warrior blood, by his individual will, vanity and fraud was destined to launch the Turkish Empire upon its most audacious adventure. Enver, the German-trained but Turkish-hearted subaltern, had 'thrown his cap over the fence' (to quote himself) as the signal for the Young Turk Revolution in 1909. Together with his handful of Young Turk friends forming the committee of Union and Progress, he had bravely faced all the gathering foes. When Italy had seized Tripoli, it was in the deserts of Tripoli that Enver had fought; when the armies of Balkan Allies were at the lines of Chatalja, it was Enver who had never despaired. 'Adrianople,' said Mr. Asquith, then Prime Minister in 1912, 'will never be restored to Turkey.' But Enver entered Adrianople within a month, and Adrianople is Turkish to-day. The outbreak of the Great War saw Enver with his associate, Talaat, and his skilful and incorruptible Finance Minister, Djavid, in control of Turkish affairs. Above them, an imposing façade, were the Sultan and the Grand Vizier: but these men and their adherents were the unquestioned governing power, and of them Enver in all action was the explosive force.

The Turkish leaders rated the might of Russia for the rough and tumble of a general war far lower than did the Western allies of the Czar. They were convinced that the Germanic group would win the war on land, that Russia would be severely mauled and that a revolution would follow. Turkey would secure in the moment of a German victory gains in territory and population in the Caucasus which would at least ward off the Russian danger for several generations. In the long preliminary discussions Germany promised Turkey territorial satisfaction in the Caucasus in the event of a victory by the Central Powers. This promise was decisive upon Turkish policy.

The policy of the Pan-Turks in every sphere of Turkish life and their territorial ambitions were embodied in a definite war plan. This plan required as its foundation the Turkish command of the Black Sea. Whenever the Great War should come—as come they were sure it must—and Russia was at grips with Germany and Austria, the Pan-Turks intended to invade and conquer the Caucasus. The control of the sea route from Constantinople to Trebizond was indispensable to an advance from Trebizond to Erzerum. Hence Turkey must have a navy. Popular subscriptions opened in 1911 and 1912 throughout Anatolia, and even throughout Islam, provided the money for the building for Turkey in Great Britain of two dreadnoughts. The arrival of one at least of these battleships at Constantinople was the peg upon which the whole Turkish war plan hung. The supreme question in July, 1914, among the Turkish leaders was: Would the ships arrive in time? Obviously the margin was small. The first Turkish dreadnought, the *Reshadieh*, was due for completion in July; the second, a few weeks later. Already Turkish agents in Russian territory round Olti, Ardahan and Kars were busy arranging for the hoarding of corn crops by the Moslem Turkish peasantry who formed the bulk of the population, in order to make possible the advance of the Turkish columns down the valley of the Chorukh and against the Russian rear. On July 27 a secret defensive and offensive alliance between Germany and Turkey against Russia was proposed by Turkey, accepted forthwith by Germany, and signed on August 2. The mobilization of the Turkish army was ordered on July 31.

But now came a surprise. England suddenly assumed an attitude of definite resistance to Germany. The British fleets had put to sea in battle order. On July 28 I requisitioned both the Turkish dreadnoughts for the Royal Navy. I took this action solely for British naval purposes. The addition of the two Turkish dreadnoughts to the British Fleet seemed vital to national safety. No one in the Admiralty, nor so far as I know in England, had any knowledge of the Turkish designs or of the part these ships were to play in them. We builded better than we knew. I was later in the year criticized in some quarters for having requisitioned the Turkish ships. The rage and disappointment excited thereby throughout Turkey was said to have turned the scale and provoked Turkey into war against us. We now know the inner explanation of this disappointment. The requisitioning of these ships, so far from making Turkey an enemy, nearly made her an Ally.

I did my best, with the approval of the Cabinet, to allay the legitimate heartburnings of the Turkish Ministry of Marine. These efforts were seconded by Admiral Limpus, the Head of the British Naval Mission to Turkey, whose relations with the Turks were extremely good and whose mission had won much esteem.

But there still remained to the Turks one hope: the *Goeben*. This fast German battle-cruiser was as has been described in the western Mediterranean under peace time orders to refit at Pola in the Adriatic. She was in herself sufficient to dominate the Russian squadron in the Black Sea. Would the Germans send the *Goeben* back to Constantinople? Would she get there? It was at this moment that the news of the British ultimatum to Germany, carrying with it the certainty of the British declaration of war, reached Constantinople. The Turkish realists had never counted on such an event. It transformed the naval situation in the Mediterranean. Could the *Goeben* escape the numerous British flotillas and cruiser squadrons and the three more powerful though less speedy British battle-cruisers which lay between her and the sea? When on the night of August 3 Enver learned that the *Goeben* was under orders to escape up the Adriatic to Pola, his anxiety knew no bounds. He immediately sought the Russian military attaché, General Leontev, and casting all previous schemes to the wind, including the agreement he had signed with Germany the day before, proposed to this astonished officer an alliance between Turkey and Russia on various conditions, including Turkish compensations in Western Thrace. Whether the Germans realized that they would never be forgiven by the Pan-Turks unless the *Goeben* made an effort to reach Constantinople, or whether it was already part of their war plan, fresh orders to go to Constantinople were at this moment (August 3) being sent by Admiral Tirpitz to the *Goeben* then about to coal at Messina; and after events which are well known she reached the Dardanelles about 5 o'clock on the afternoon of August 10 and was after some parley admitted to the Sea of Marmora. The following minutes tell their own tale:—

Sir Edward Grey.

August 12, 1914.

Goeben and *Breslau*.

In all the circumstances, the Admiralty agree that the sale or transfer of these two vessels to the Turkish flag should be allowed, provided that the transference is *bona fide* and permanent. The essential condition to insist on is that all the German officers and men of the crews of both ships must, without exception, be at once repatriated to Germany under parole, not to serve again during the war. We cannot agree to any exceptions being made, whether of officers or skilled ratings or of the ordinary crew. The British Embassy, assisted if necessary by the English Naval Mission, should assure themselves that all the Germans leave at once, and that the ships are definitely handed over to the Turkish Navy. In these circumstances, the Admiralty would allow the [British] Naval Mission to remain, as requested by the Grand Vizier. The Turks could also be informed that after the war is over, we should be quite ready in principle, and as far as we can now foresee, to transfer one or both of the two ships we have requisitioned to their flag, and that we are quite ready to negotiate with them at the present time in regard to payment of the sums due to Turkey.

W. S. C.

Sir Edward Grey.

August 17, 1914.

The situation about *Goeben* and *Breslau* is extremely unsatisfactory. Their sale to Turkey is probably itself a breach of neutrality. The vital condition of the repatriation of the German complements down to the last man has not taken place; probably the whole of the German crews are still on board, and it is admitted that 'experts are to be retained.' Meanwhile, the British Naval Mission has been banished from the Turkish ships committed to their charge, and forbidden to go on board the two ex-Germans. As long as the *Goeben* and *Breslau* remain in this condition, and until we know that the whole of the German crews are definitely repatriated, we have to keep two British [battle] cruisers, which are urgently needed elsewhere, waiting with other vessels outside the Dardanelles. This is a situation which cannot continue indefinitely.

W. S. C.

Enver's confidence was now restored, for the command of the Black Sea rested potentially with the Turks. But the certain hostility of Great Britain was serious, in view of her naval supremacy and the undefended conditions of the Dardanelles. Moreover Italy had unexpectedly separated herself from the Triple Alliance. It might therefore perhaps be prudent for Turkey to see how the impending great battles on land, and especially those upon the Russian front, were decided. Meanwhile the mobilization of the Turkish Army could proceed unostentatiously and be justified as a precautionary measure. Thus there followed a period lasting for about three months of Turkish hesitation and delay, having the effect of consummate duplicity. I can recall no great sphere of policy about which the British Government was less completely informed than the Turkish. It is strange to read the telegrams we received through all channels from Constantinople during this period in the light of our present knowledge. But all the Allies, now encouraged by the friendly assurances of the Grand Vizier and the respectable-effete section of the Cabinet, now indignant at the refusal to intern and disarm the *Goeben* and generally mystified by many contradictory voices, believed that Turkey had no policy and might still be won or lost. This period was ended when Enver in November, acting as the agent of all the Pan-Turk forces, delivered the unprovoked attack by the *Goeben* and the Turkish Fleet upon the Russian Black Sea ports, and thus plunged Turkey brutally into the war.

* * * * *

The Turkish position could only be judged in relation to the general situation in the Balkans; and this could not be understood unless the dominant facts of pre-war Balkan history were continually borne in mind. The first Balkan war saw Bulgaria triumphantly bearing the brunt of the attack on Turkey. While her armies were advancing on Constantinople against the best troops of the Turkish Empire, the Greeks and Serbians were overrunning the comparatively weakly-held regions of Thrace and Macedonia. The Bulgarians, having fought the greatest battles and sustained by far the heaviest losses, found themselves finally checked before Constantinople, and, turning round, beheld almost the whole of the conquered territory in the hands of their Allies. The destination of this territory had been regulated before the war by treaty between the four belligerent minor States. Adrianople had not however surrendered, and in obedience to the treaty the Serbians came to the aid of the Bulgarian forces, and played a prominent part in the capture of that fortress. Both the Serbians and the Greeks utilized the argument that the war had been prolonged through the need of reducing Adrianople as a ground for claiming to repudiate in important particulars the pre-war treaty, and meanwhile they retained occupation of all the conquered districts in their possession. The Bulgarians were quick to repay this claim with violence. They attacked the Greeks and Serbians, were defeated by the more numerous armies of these two Powers, and in the moment of extreme weakness and defeat were invaded from the other side by Roumania, who, having taken no part in the conflict, had intact armies to strike with. At the same time the Turks advanced in Thrace, and led by Enver Pasha recaptured Adrianople. Thus the end of the second Balkan war saw Bulgaria stripped not only of almost all her share of the territory conquered from the Turks (and this entirely divided between Greece and Serbia), but even her native province of the Dobroudja had been wrested from her by Roumania. The terrible cruelties and atrocities which had been perpetrated on both sides in the internecine struggle that followed the expulsion of the Turks had left a river of blood between the Greeks and Serbians on the one hand and the Bulgarians on the other.

It is possible that no nation ever contemplated its fortunes with more profound and desperate resolve than the Bulgarians at this juncture. All their sacrifices had been useless and worse than useless. All the fruits of their conquests had gone to aggrandise their rivals. They had been, as they considered, stabbed in the back and blackmailed by Roumania, to whom they had given no provocation of any kind. They saw the great Powers, England in the van, forbid the return of the Turk to Adrianople without offering the slightest attempt to make their words good. They saw not only Salonika, but even Kavala, seized by the Greeks. They saw large districts inhabited largely by the Bulgarian race newly liberated from the Turks pass under the yoke—to them scarcely less odious—of Serbians and Greeks. It was in these circumstances that the Bulgarian army, in the words of King Ferdinand, 'furled its standards' and retired to wait for better days.

This warlike and powerful Bulgaria, with its scheming King and its valiant peasant armies brooding over what seemed to them intolerable wrongs, was the dominant factor in the Balkans in 1914 and 1915.

* * * * *

On August 19, 1914, Monsieur Venizelos, then Prime Minister of Greece, with the approval which he had, astonishing to relate, obtained of King Constantine, formally placed at the disposal of the Entente powers all the naval and military resources of Greece from the moment when they might be required. He added that this offer was made in a special sense to Great Britain with whose interests those of Greece were indissolubly bound. The resources of Greece, he said, were small, but she could dispose of 250,000 troops, and her navy and her ports might be of some use. This magnanimous offer, made as it was while all was so uncertain, and even before the main battle in France had been joined, greatly attracted me. No doubt on the one hand it was a serious thing to run the risk of adding Turkey to our enemies. On the other hand, the Greek Army and Navy were solid factors; and a combination of the Greek armies and fleet with the British Mediterranean squadron offered a means of settling the difficulties of the Dardanelles in a most prompt and effective manner. The Gallipoli Peninsula was then only weakly occupied by Turkish troops, and the Greek General Staff were known to be ready with well-thought-out plans for its seizure. Moreover, it seemed to me that anyhow Turkey was drifting into war with us. Her conduct in regard to the *Goeben* and *Breslau* continued openly fraudulent. The presence of these two vessels themselves in German hands in the Sea of Marmora offered a means of putting decisive pressure on the neutrality party in Constantinople. If we were not going to secure honest Turkish neutrality, then let us, in the alternative, get the Christian States of the Balkans on our side. Could we not get them on our side? Could we not make a Balkan confederation of Serbia, Greece, Bulgaria and Roumania? Whatever happened, we ought not to fall between two stools.

Sir Edward Grey, however, after very anxious consideration, moved the Cabinet to decline Monsieur Venizelos' proposal, as he feared, no doubt with weighty reasons, that an alliance with Greece meant immediate war with Turkey and possibly Bulgaria. He feared that it might jeopardize Greece without our being able to protect her. He was anxious above all things not to foster a Greek enterprise against Constantinople in such a way as to give offence to Russia. And, lastly, he hoped that Sir Louis Mallet, who was in close and intimate relations with the Grand Vizier and the leaders of the Turkish neutrality party in Constantinople, would after all be able to keep the peace. Certainly nothing could exceed the skill and perseverance with which the British Ambassador laboured. It followed from this that we should maintain the very handsome offer we had made in common with France and Russia at the outbreak of the war to guarantee the integrity of the Turkish Empire in return for her faithful neutrality. I naturally conformed to the Cabinet decision, but with increasing misgivings. I still continued to work and hope for a Balkan confederation. I gave the following letter, of which the Foreign Secretary approved, to Mr. Noel Buxton, who was starting for a propaganda tour in the Balkans. Of course in view of our decision about Turkey, it could refer only to the common interests of these States against Austria.

August 31, 1914.

It is of the utmost importance to the future prosperity of the Balkan States that they should act together. This is the hour when the metal can be cast into the mould. It is only by reclaiming from Austria territories which belong naturally to the Balkan races that the means can be provided to satisfy the legitimate needs and aspirations of all the Balkan States. Without taking Austrian territory, there is no way by which any Balkan State can expand except by internecine war. But the application of the principle of nationality to the Southern Provinces of Austria will produce results so advantageous to the Balkan States that the memory and the consequences of former quarrels could be assuaged for ever.

The creation of a Balkan Confederation comprising Bulgaria, Serbia, Roumania, Montenegro and Greece, strong enough to play an effective part in the destinies of Europe, must be the common dream of all their peoples. The result of this war is not doubtful. Sooner or later, Germany will be starved and beaten. Austria will be resolved into its component parts. England has always won in the end; and Russia is unconquerable. England has been the friend of every Christian State in the Balkans during all their years of struggle and suffering. She has no interests of her own to seek in the Balkan Peninsula. But with her wealth and power she will promote and aid every step which is taken to build up a strong union of the Christian peoples, like that which triumphed in the first Balkan War. By acting together in unity and good faith the Balkan States can now play a decisive part, and gain advantages which may never again be offered. By disunion they will simply condemn themselves to tear each other's throats without profit or reward, and left to themselves will play an utterly futile part in the destinies of the world.

I want you to make your friends in Greece and in Bulgaria realize the brilliant but fleeting opportunity which now presents itself, and to assure them that England's might and perseverance will not be withheld from any righteous effort to secure the strength and union of the Balkan peoples.

In the early days of September it seemed highly probable that Turkey, under the influence of the German advance on Paris, would make war upon us and upon Greece whatever we did. I began immediately to prepare for the event.

Mr. Churchill to General Sir Charles Douglas, Chief of the Imperial General Staff.

September 1, 1914.

Secret.

I arranged with Lord Kitchener yesterday that two officers from Admiralty should meet two officers from the Director of Military Operations Department of the War Office to-day to examine and work out a plan for the seizure by means of a Greek army of adequate strength of the Gallipoli peninsula, with a view to admitting a British Fleet to the Sea of Marmora.

In his absence I would ask you to give the necessary directions, as the matter is urgent, and Turkey may make war on us at any moment.

The meeting can take place either here or at the War Office as soon as you can arrange with our Chief of Staff. I will myself explain verbally to the Committee the subject on which his Majesty's Government desire information.

The Director of Military Operations, General Callwell, replied on the 3rd, on behalf of the General Staff, that the operation of seizing the Gallipoli peninsula would be an extremely difficult one. Sixty thousand men would be required, thirty thousand of whom should be landed in the first instance, should gain as much ground as possible, should prepare landing stages, and hold their own for a week while the transports returned to Greece for the second thirty thousand. On this basis the operation was considered feasible. These estimates were not excessive, and the Greeks could certainly provide a considerably larger force if necessary.

Thereupon I telegraphed, with the approval of the Foreign Office, to Rear-Admiral Mark Kerr, the head of our naval mission to Greece, as follows:—

September 4.

In event of war with Turkey, with England and Greece as Allies, Admiralty consider it essential, as a Staff precaution, that the question of the right war policy to be followed should be examined, in consultation with Greek General and Naval Staff, leaving political probabilities to be decided by respective Governments.

Admiralty give you permission to do this, should you be approached by the Greek Government. In principle, the Admiralty views are as follows:

In order to provide unquestionable and decisive superiority over the German and Turkish vessels, the Greek Fleet would be offered, as reinforcements, a squadron and flotilla, and the whole of the combined Fleets would be placed under your command, with the *Indomitable* as your Flagship. Should circumstances demand it, you would be reinforced with any class of vessel necessary and to any extent.

> In order that the right and obvious method of attack upon Turkey (viz. by striking immediately at the heart) may be carried out, the Greek Army would, under superiority of sea predominance, have to seize the Gallipoli Peninsula, thus opening the Dardanelles and enabling the Anglo-Greek Fleet, in the Sea of Marmora, to fight and sink the Turco-German ships, and from there the whole situation can be dominated, in combination with the Black Sea Fleet of the Russians and their military forces.
>
> The Admiralty desire that, in consultation with you, the Greek Naval and Military Experts should immediately examine this enterprise, and that you should report fully by telegraph to the Admiralty what are the general views of the Greek Government upon it, and what, in their opinion, would be the force required to carry it out, assuming that safe transportation is assured. Should we provide the necessary transports, or in what time and to what extent could Greece do so? Have they any alternative suggestions?

The Rear-Admiral's reply reached me through the Foreign Office on the 9th.

> The Greek General Staff have been consulted on the subject of your telegram, and I agree with them in their opinion that, if Bulgaria does not attack Greece, the latter can take Gallipoli with force at their disposal. Greece will not trust Bulgaria unless she at the same time attacks Turkey with all her force. They will not accept Bulgaria's guarantee to remain neutral.
>
> Subject to above conditions, plan for taking Dardanelles Straits is ready.
>
> Greece can provide necessary transports for troops. A British squadron of two battle cruisers, one armoured cruiser, three light cruisers and flotilla of destroyers will be needed to assist. General Staff and myself originally formulated this plan, but operation has become greater since Turkey has mobilized and obtained German ships.

He mentioned as an alternative the region of Alexandretta.

On September 6 Monsieur Venizelos told our Minister in Athens that he was not afraid of a single-handed attack from Turkey by land as the Greek General Staff were confident of being able to deal with it. The Greek Government had received from Sofia positive assurances of definite neutrality, but did not trust them. They would, however, be satisfied with a formal protest by the Bulgarian Government against a violation of Bulgarian territory by Turkish troops proceeding to attack Greece. If, however, Bulgaria joined Turkey while Serbia was occupied with Austria, the situation would be critical. On this I pointed out to the Foreign Secretary on the same date that a Russian Army Corps could easily be brought from Archangel, from Vladivostock, or with Japanese consent from Port Arthur to attack the Gallipoli Peninsula. 'The price to be paid in taking Gallipoli would no doubt be heavy, but there would be no more war with Turkey. A good army of 50,000 men and sea power—that is the end of the Turkish menace.'

But it was easier to look for armies than to find them. Sir Edward Grey replied by sending me a telegram that had been received that very morning from Petrograd stating that in view of the very large number of German troops which were being transferred from the Western to the Eastern theatre, Russia was calling up every available man from Asia and the Caucasus, and was only leaving one Army Corps in the latter. Greece would therefore, according to the Petrograd telegram, have to bear the brunt of the war single-handed unless she could placate Bulgaria by territorial concessions. He added on the back of my note, 'You will see from the telegram from St. Petersburg that Russia can give no help against Turkey. I do not like the prospect in the Mediterranean at all, unless there is some turn of the tide in France.'

It is only by faithful study of this problem that its immense difficulties are portrayed. Lest it should be thought that I underrated the gravity of a war with Turkey, it must be remembered that I had convinced myself that Turkey would attack us sooner or later, and that I was also proceeding on the belief that the German invasion of France would be brought to a standstill. Both these assumptions proved true. I do not claim that my view was the wisest, but only to expose it to historical judgment. The policy emerging from such a view would of course at this juncture have offered Cyprus to Greece in compensation for her offering Kavala to Bulgaria. It would have put the most extreme pressure on Serbia to make concessions to Bulgaria in Monastir. Whether these measures would have succeeded at this time I do not pronounce.

By September 9 the behaviour of the Turks about the *Goeben* and the *Breslau* had become so openly defiant that it became necessary to withdraw the British Naval Mission, who were exposed to daily insolences at the hands of the Germans and of the Turkish war party. It was my intention to appoint the head of the mission, Rear-Admiral Limpus, to command the squadron watching the Dardanelles, and orders were sent definitely to that effect. This project was not, however, pursued, it being thought that it would be unduly provocative to employ on this station the very officer who had just ceased to be the teacher of the Turkish Fleet. No doubt this was a weighty argument, but in bowing to it we lost the advantages of having at this fateful spot the Admiral who of all others knew the Turks, and knew the Dardanelles with all its possibilities. It was a small link in a long chain. Delay was caused and I had to make fresh arrangements.

On September 21, I telegraphed to Vice-Admiral Carden, who was in charge of the Malta Dockyard:—

> Assume command of the squadron off Dardanelles. Your sole duty is to sink *Goeben* and *Breslau*, no matter what flag they fly, if they come out of Dardanelles. We are not at war with Turkey but the German Admiral Souchon is now Commander-in-Chief Turkish Navy and Germans are controlling and largely manning it. Turks have been told that any Turkish ships which come out with *Goeben* and *Breslau* will be equally attacked by us. You are authorized to act accordingly without further declaration or parley. You must deal at your discretion with any minor Turkish war vessel which may come out alone from Dardanelles, either ordering her back or

allowing her to proceed as you may think fit, remembering that we do not want to pick a quarrel with Turkey unless her hostile intention is clear.

Indomitable will be diverted from convoy off Crete and ordered to join your squadron. French Commander-in-Chief has been requested to send 2 battleships of *Patrie* class to reinforce your flag.

The victory of the Marne, although afterwards discounted by adverse events, checked the developments in the Near East. Turkey was steadied for the moment, and her attitude towards Greece became less menacing. This however produced a corresponding cooling at Athens about joining in the European war. From the middle of September the conditions throughout the Balkans had declined again from crisis into suspense. They remained however fundamentally vicious.

I continued increasingly to press as opportunity served for a policy of uniting the Balkan States without reference to what might happen in Turkey.

On September 23, I wrote to Sir Edward Grey as follows:—

September 23, 1914.

Mr. Churchill to Sir Edward Grey.

I must write you a line about Turkey. . . . We are suffering very seriously from Turkish hostility. Our whole Mediterranean Fleet is tied to the Dardanelles. We are daily trying to buy Turkish neutrality by promises and concessions. Meanwhile the German grip on Turkey tightens, and all preparations for war go steadily forward. But all this would in itself be of minor consequence but for the fact that in our attempt to placate Turkey we are crippling our policy in the Balkans. I am not suggesting that we should take aggressive action against Turkey or declare war on her ourselves, but we ought from now to make our arrangements with the Balkan States particularly Bulgaria, without regard to the interests or integrity of Turkey. The Bulgarians ought to regain the Turkish territory they lost in the second Balkan War, and we ought to tell them that if they join with Roumania, Greece, and Serbia in the attack upon Austria and Germany, the Allied Powers will see that they get this territory at the peace. We always said that Adrianople should never fall back into Turkish hands, and the strongest possible remonstrances were addressed to the Porte by you at the time. There is therefore nothing wrong or inconsistent in our adopting this position. If we win the war, we shall be quite strong enough to secure this territory for Bulgaria, and Turkey's conduct to us with repeated breaches of neutrality would release us from any need of considering her European interests. Like you, I sympathize deeply with Mallet in the futile and thankless task on which he is engaged. I do not know what the result will be, but I am sure it is not worth while sacrificing the bold and decisive alternative of throwing in our lot frankly with the Christian States of the Balkans to get the kind of neutrality which the Turks have been giving us, and for which we are even asked to pay and be grateful. The whole tone of the telegrams from Roumania and Bulgaria is hopeful. I do most earnestly beg you not to be diverted from the highway of sound policy in this part

> of the world, both during the war and at the settlement, by wanderings into the labyrinth of Turkish duplicity and intrigue. All I am asking is that the interests and integrity of Turkey shall no longer be considered by you in any efforts which are made to secure common action among the Christian Balkan States.

Judged in afterlight these views can hardly be contested. I have never swerved from them; but the reader should understand the other arguments by which the Cabinet was ruled. The loyal desire not to spread the war to regions still uncursed; the dangers in India of a British quarrel with Turkey; our awful military weakness in 1914; Lord Kitchener's expressed wish to keep the East as quiet as possible till the two Indian Divisions were safely through the Suez Canal; the difficulties of winning the support of Greece, and particularly of King Constantine, without exciting the suspicion and jealousies of Russia about Constantinople; and, lastly, the doubts—admittedly substantial—whether Bulgaria and King Ferdinand could ever, in the absence of substantial military successes in the main theatres or strong local intervention by Allied forces in the Balkans, be detached from the Teutonic system.

When I talked these questions over at the time with Sir Edward Grey it was upon this last argument that he was most inclined to dwell. 'Until Bulgaria believes that Germany is not going to win the war, she will not be moved by any promises of other people's territory which we may make her.' The swift overrunning of Northern France by the German armies, the withdrawal of the French Government to Bordeaux, the fall of Antwerp, the tremendous victories of Hindenburg over the Russians, were events all of which dominated the Bulgarian equally with the Turkish mind. England, without an army, with not a soldier to spare, without even a rifle to send, with only her Navy and her money, counted for little in the Near East. Russian claims to Constantinople directly crossed the ambitions both of King Ferdinand and of King Constantine. In all the Balkans only one *clairvoyant* eye, only the genius of Venizelos, discerned the fundamental moral issues of the struggle, measured justly the relative powers of the mighty combatants, and appraised at their true value both the victories of the German Army, and the Sea Power under which were slowly gathering the latent but inexhaustible resources of the British Empire.

So the Allies continued to wait and hope at Constantinople, and the days slipped swiftly by.

Not till long after did we learn the blasting secret which would have destroyed all British and Russian doubts. Already in the crisis of July the leaders of the Young Turk party had been in vital negotiation with the Germans, and on August 2 an alliance had been signed between Germany and Turkey. Thus all this time we were deceived. Whether anything that it was in our power to do could have averted the evils must always remain a disputed question; but that the evils were not averted is certain. In the end we had all the evils of both courses and the advantages of no course. We were forced into a war with Turkey which ultimately became of enormous magnitude. Greece was thrown into inextricable confusion. Serbia was overrun. Bulgaria, joining hands with her recent enemies the Turks, became our foe. And Roumania, when she finally came in isolated upon the allied side, suffered the direst vengeance at German hands. A more fearful series of tragedies has scarcely ever darkened the melancholy page of history.

It must not be thought that the action of Turkey was inspired solely by treachery and duplicity. Two parties were struggling for mastery in the capital, but in view of the Treaty of Alliance which had been signed on August 2, there could have been no doubt about the final outcome. Moreover, in the *Goeben* and *Breslau*, to say nothing of the Turkish Fleet, Enver Pasha and the war party had the means to force the Turkish Government to adhere to the covenants which they had entered into on her behalf. By the middle of October we learnt that Turkish preparations to invade Egypt were actually being made. We learned also from a secret source, that the Austrian Ambassador at Constantinople had received solemn assurances from Enver that Turkey would enter the war against the Entente at an early date. At the end of October, our outposts beyond the Suez Canal had to be withdrawn in face of gathering Turkish forces; and finally, about October 27, the *Breslau*, with the Turkish cruiser *Hamidieh* and a division of destroyers, followed by the *Goeben*, steamed into the Black Sea, and on the 29th and 30th bombarded the Russian fortress of Sevastopol, sank a Russian transport, raided the harbour of Odessa, torpedoed a gunboat, and, lastly, practically destroyed Novorossisk, its oil tanks and all the shipping in the port.

On this the Russian Ambassador at Constantinople immediately demanded his passports; and the British Foreign Office at 8.15 p.m. on October 30, after reciting its many griefs against the Turks, especially their invasion of the Sinai Peninsula and their misconduct about the *Goeben*, sent an ultimatum requiring repudiation of these acts and the dismissal of the German Military and Naval Missions within 12 hours. The Admiralty conformed to this decision by telegraphing to all Admirals concerned as follows:—

(*October* 31, 1914. 12.35 a.m.)

> Orders sent Ambassador Constantinople 8.15 p.m. October 30 to present ultimatum to Turkey expiring at end of 12 hours. Do not yourself commence hostilities without further orders.
>
> *Add to Vice-Admiral Carden (Indefatigable).*
>
> You may therefore expect Embassy to be leaving very shortly.

Russia declared war on Turkey at the expiry of the ultimatum; and the British and French Ambassadors, in company with their Russian colleague, left Constantinople on November 1—the same day on which at the other end of the world the battle of Coronel was being fought. Naval orders to commence hostilities were sent, in concert with the Foreign Office, in conformity with the expiry of the ultimatum.

Admiralty to all ships.

October 31, 1914. (*sent* 5.5 p.m.)

> Commence hostilities at once against Turkey. Acknowledge.

On November 1 two of our destroyers, entering the Gulf of Smyrna, destroyed a large armed Turkish yacht which was lying by the jetty carrying mines; and late that same day Admiral Carden was instructed to bombard the outer Dardanelles forts at long range on the earliest suitable occasion. This bombardment was carried out on the morning of November 3. The two British battle-cruisers, firing from a range beyond that of the Turkish guns, shelled the batteries on the European side at Sedd-el-Bahr and Cape Helles. The French battleships fired at the Asiatic batteries at Kum Kali and Orkanieh. About eighty rounds were fired altogether, resulting in considerable damage to the Turkish forts, and in several hundred casualties to the Turks and Germans who manned them.

The reasons for this demonstration have been greatly canvassed. They were simple though not important. A British squadron had for months been waiting outside the Dardanelles. War had been declared with Turkey. It was natural that fire should be opened upon the enemy as it would be on the fronts of hostile armies. It was necessary to know accurately the effective ranges of the Turkish guns and the conditions under which the entrance to the blockaded port could be approached. It has been stated that this bombardment was an imprudent act, as it was bound to put the Turks on their guard and lead them to strengthen their defences. That the organization of the defences of the Straits should be improved steadily from the declaration of war was inevitable. To what extent this process was stimulated by the bombardment is a matter of conjecture. When, three and a half months later (February 19, 1915), Admiral Carden again bombarded these same forts, the Gallipoli Peninsula was however totally unprepared for defence, and was still weakly occupied; and small parties of Marines were able to make their way unopposed into the shattered forts and a considerable distance beyond them.

We had now to provide against the impending Turkish attack upon Egypt. The First Cruiser Squadron, comprising the *Black Prince*, *Duke of Edinburgh* and *Warrior*, had been either employed on escort duties at sea or on guard at Alexandria or Port Said. Even before the news of Coronel had reached us, the increasing strain upon our resources had made it necessary to replace these fine ships by older smaller vessels. They were now urgently required to form a combat squadron near the Cap de Verde Islands as part of the second general combination against von Spee. They were also promised to the Commander-in-Chief for the Grand Fleet at the earliest possible moment thereafter. We should have been hard pressed in these circumstances to find a new and satisfactory naval force for the defence of the Canal against the now imminent Turkish attack. The discovery and blocking in of the *Königsberg* on October 31 liberated two out of the three vessels searching for her. But this was not enough. The destruction of the *Emden* on November 9 was an event of a very different order. It afforded us immediate relief, and relief exactly where we required it. The Indian Ocean was now clear. The battleship *Swiftsure* from the Fast Indian station was at once ordered to the Canal. Of the fast cruisers that had been searching for the *Emden*, the *Gloucester*, *Melbourne*, *Sydney*, *Hampshire* and *Yarmouth* were immediately brought homewards through the Red Sea into the Mediterranean. I felt that the Commander-in-Chief in the East Indies must come himself to the new scene of danger.

Admiralty to Commander-in-Chief, East Indies.

November 14, 1914.

Naval operations in the Red Sea and Egypt cannot be directed from India. Your presence in Egypt is imperative. You should rejoin your flagship *Swiftsure* at Port Said by the quickest route at once. *Gloucester* can take you if she has not already sailed. Telegraph what date you expect to arrive at Suez. On arrival you should consult with General Officer Commanding, Egypt, and work hand in hand with him and with the British authorities…. The following ships will be at your disposal in the Red Sea: *Swiftsure, Minerva, Doris, Proserpine*… and eight torpedo-boats from Malta. Measures are also being taken to organize armed launches and improvised gunboats for use in the Canal. Telegraph whether you feel able to discharge the other duties of your command, namely convoy and Persian Gulf operations, at the same time, or what temporary arrangements you suggest during your absence in Egyptian waters.

A few days earlier I had minuted:—

November 18, 1914.

First Sea Lord.
Chief of Staff.

I cannot agree to this. It would be a great waste of a valuable ship. Considerably more than a week has passed since I minuted that *Askold* should be ordered to the Mediterranean. There or in Egyptian waters this Russian ship will have a chance of fighting against Turkey. To send her off to Hong-Kong is an altogether purposeless errand. Her stores should go on with the mines or in another vessel which keeps company with the mines from Vladivostock. No convoy is necessary; but if it were, the *Clio* or *Cadmus*, or some little vessel like them, could be used. The whole Japanese Navy is in the Pacific and Indian Oceans. They would quite willingly find a convoy for the mines and the *Askold* stores. The whole area of the sea, from the coast of Chili to the coast of Mozambique, has been cleared of the enemy. But for vague rumours of a possible armed merchantman at large, there is not the slightest menace. We must profit from this situation to the full while it lasts, and this can only be done by moving every ship that is of any use promptly into waters where they are required. No one knows how many ships we shall want in Egypt when the Turkish invasion begins. There may also be massacres of Christians in the coast towns of Levant which will require vessels for immediate action there. All the ships out of the Indian Ocean that can play an effective part ought to be hurried home. The cruisers ought to steam at least 18 knots. Nearly all these ships have lost three or four precious days since the destruction of the *Emden* was known.

W. S. C.

These directions were complied with. I searched the oceans for every available ship. During the second and third weeks of November the *Swiftsure* and the squadron and flotilla mentioned above, together with the French *Requin* and the Russian *Askold*, entered the Canal for the defence of Egypt. The Turkish attack proved however to be only of a tentative character. Finding themselves confronted with troops and ships, they withdrew after feeble efforts into the Eastern deserts to gather further strength.

All this time the great Australasian convoy, carrying the Australian and New Zealand Army Corps, 'A.N.Z.A.C.,' had been steaming steadily towards France across the Pacific and Indian Oceans. Preparations had been made if necessary to divert them to Cape Town. But before the convoy reached Colombo, General Botha and General Smuts had suppressed the rebellion in South Africa. The Australians and New Zealanders therefore continued their voyage to Europe under the escort of the *Ibuki* and the *Hampshire*. By the end of November their transports were entering the Canal. As the Turkish invasion of Egypt was still threatening, the need of resolute and trustworthy troops in Egypt was great, and on the first day of December Lord Kitchener, in the fateful unfolding of events, began to disembark the whole Australian and New Zealand Force at Suez for the double purpose of completing their training and defending the line of the Canal.

* * * * *

At this point we may leave the Turkish situation for a time. The German grip was strengthening every day on Turkey. The distresses of her peoples and the improvement of her military organization were advancing together. Under the guns of the *Goeben* and *Breslau*, doubt, division and scarcity, dwelt in Constantinople. Outside the Straits the British squadron maintained its silent watch. Greece, perplexed at the attitude of Britain, distracted by the quarrels of Venizelos and King Constantine, had fallen far from the high resolve of August. Serbia stoutly contended with the Austrian armies. Roumania and Bulgaria brooded on the past and watched each other with intent regard. In Egypt the training of the Australian and New Zealand Army Corps perfected itself week by week.

Thus, as this act in the stupendous world drama comes to its close, we see already the scene being set and the actors assembling for the next. From the uttermost ends of the earth ships and soldiers are approaching or gathering in the Eastern Mediterranean in fulfilment of a destiny as yet not understood by mortal man. The clearance of the Germans from the oceans liberated the Fleets, the arrival of the Anzacs in Egypt created the nucleus of the Army needed to attack the heart of the Turkish Empire. The deadlock on the Western Front, where all was now frozen into winter trenches, afforded at once a breathing space and large possibility of further troops. While Australian battalions trampled the crisp sand of the Egyptian desert in tireless evolutions, and Commander Holbrook in his valiant submarine dived under the minefields of Chanak and sank a Turkish transport in the throat of the Dardanelles, far away in the basins of Portsmouth the dockyard men were toiling night and day to mount the fifteen-inch guns and turrets of the *Queen Elizabeth*. As yet all was unconscious, inchoate, purposeless, uncombined. Any one of a score of chances might have given, might still give, an entirely different direction to the event. No plan has been made, no resolve taken. But new ideas are astir, new possibilities are coming into view, new forces are at hand, and with them there marches towards us a new peril of the first magnitude. Russia, mighty steam-roller, hope of suffering France and prostrate Belgium—Russia is failing. Her armies are grappling with Hindenburg and Ludendorff, and behind their brave battle fronts already the awful signs of weakness, of deficiency, of disorganization, are apparent to anxious Cabinets and Councils. Winter has come and locked all Russia in its grip. No contact with her Allies, no help from them, is possible. The ice blocks the White Sea. The Germans hold the Baltic. The Turks have barred the Dardanelles. It needs but a cry from Russia for help, to make vital what is now void, and to make purposeful what is now meaningless. But as yet no cry has come.

* * * * *

I cannot close without taking a more general survey of the naval war.

The reader has now followed through six chapters the steady increase of strain upon Admiralty resources which marked in every theatre the months of September, October and November, 1914. He must understand that, although for the purposes of the narrative it is necessary to deal in separate chapters with each separate set of strains and crises, many of the events were proceeding simultaneously in all theatres at once, and the consequent strains were cumulative and reciprocally reacting on one another, with the result that during November an extraordinary pitch of intensity was reached which could not well be prolonged and could not possibly have been exceeded.

It is worth while to review the whole situation. First, the transport of troops and supplies to France was unceasing and vital to our Army. On the top of all this came the operations on the Belgian Coast, the approach of the enemy to the Channel ports, and the long-drawn crisis of the great battle of Ypres-Yser. Secondly, all the enemy's cruisers were still alive, and a number of hostile armed merchantmen were free in the outer seas, each threatening an indefinite number of points and areas and requiring from five to ten times their numbers to search for them and protect traffic while they were at large. At the same time the great convoys of troops from India, from Canada, from Australia, and the collection of the British regular garrisons from all parts of the world were proceeding; and no less than six separate expeditions, viz., Samoa, New Guinea. German East Africa, Togoland, the Cameroons and German South-West Africa, were in progress or at a critical stage. Upon this was thrust the outbreak of war with Turkey, the attack upon the Suez Canal, and the operations in the Persian Gulf.

To meet these fierce obligations we had to draw no less than three decisive units from the Grand Fleet. This Fleet, which at the outset of the war was in perfect order, was already requiring refits by rotation, with consequent reduction of available strength. Meanwhile, the submarine menace had declared itself in a serious form, and was moreover exaggerated in our minds. Although the most vehement efforts were being made to give security to our fleets in their Northern harbours, these measures took many weeks during which anxiety was continual. Behind all stood the German Fleet, aware, as we must suppose, of the strain to which we were being subjected, and potentially ready at any moment to challenge the supreme decision. With the long nights of winter, the absence of all regular troops from the country, the then inadequate training of the

Territorial Force and the embryonic condition of the new Kitchener armies, the fear of invasion revived; and, although we rejected it in theory, nevertheless we were bound to take in practice a whole series of precautionary measures. It was a formidable time. More than once the thought occurred that the Admiralty would be forced to contract their responsibilities and abandon to their fate for a time some important interests, in order that those which were vital might be secured. In the event we just got through. It may be claimed that during these months we met every single call that was made upon us, guarded every sea, carried every expedition, brought every convoy safely in, discharged all our obligations both to the Army in France and to the Belgians, and all the time maintained such a disposition of our main forces that we should never have declined battle had the enemy ventured to offer it.

Then suddenly all over the world the tension was relaxed. One after another the German cruisers and commerce destroyers were blocked in or hunted down. The great convoys arrived. The Expeditions were safely landed. Ocean after ocean became clear. The boom defences of our harbours were completed. A score of measures for coping with the submarine were set on foot. Large reinforcements of new ships of the highest quality and of every class began to join the Fleet. The attack on the Suez Canal was stemmed. The rebellion in South Africa was quelled. The dangers of invasion, if such there were, diminished every day with the increasing efficiency of the Territorials and the New Armies. The great battle for the Channel ports ended in decisive and ever glorious victory. And finally with the Battle of the Falkland Islands the clearance of the oceans was complete, and soon, except in the land-locked Baltic and Black Seas and in the defended area of the Heligoland Bight, the German flag had ceased to fly on any vessel in any quarter of the world.[2]

As December passed, a sense of indescribable relief stole over the Admiralty. We had made the great transition from peace to war without disaster, almost without mishap. All the perils which had haunted us before the war, and against which we had prepared, had been warded off or surmounted or had never come to pass. There had been no surprise. The Fleet was ready. The Army had reached the decisive battlefield in time and was satisfactorily maintained. The Mine danger had been overcome. We thought we had the measure of the submarine, and so indeed we had for nearly two years to come. All the enemy's plans for commerce destruction and all our alarms about them had come to nought. British and allied commerce proceeded without hesitation throughout the world; the trade and food of Britain were secured; the war insurance dropped to one per cent. A feeling of profound thankfulness filled our hearts as this first Christmas of the war approached; and of absolute confidence in final victory.

The mighty enemy, with all the advantages of preparation and design, had delivered his onslaught and had everywhere been brought to a standstill. It was our turn now. The initiative had passed to Britain—the Great Amphibian. The time and the means were at our command. It was for us to say where we would strike and when. The strength of the Grand Fleet was, as we believed, ample; and in addition the whole of those numerous

---

[2]The *Dresden* and two armed merchant cruisers were alive for a few weeks more, but in complete inactivity.

squadrons which hitherto had been spread over the outer seas now formed a surplus fleet capable of intervening in the supreme struggle without in any way compromising the foundation of our naval power.

But these realizations were only permissible as the prelude to fresh and still more intense exertions. It would indeed be shameful, so it seemed at least to me, for the Admiralty to rest contented with the accomplishment of the first and most hazardous stage of its task and to relax into a supine contemplation of regained securities and dangers overcome. Now was the time to make our weight tell, perhaps decisively, but certainly most heavily, in the struggle of the armies. Now was the time to fasten an offensive upon the Germans, unexpected and unforeseeable, to present them with a succession of surprising situations leading on from crisis to crisis and from blow to blow till their downfall was achieved.

Moreover, these same Germans were, of all the enemies in the world, the most to be dreaded when pursuing their own plans; the most easily disconcerted when forced to conform to the plans of their antagonist. To leave a German leisure to evolve his vast, patient, accurate designs, to make his slow, thorough, infinitely far-seeing preparations, was to court a terrible danger. To throw him out of his stride, to baffle his studious mind, to break his self-confidence, to cow his spirit, to rupture his schemes by unexpected action, was surely the path not only of glory but of prudence.

* * * * *

Here then ends the first phase of the naval war. The first part of the British task is done both by land and sea. Paris and the Channel Ports are saved, and the oceans are cleared. It is certain that the whole strength of the British Empire can be turned into war power and brought to bear upon the enemy. There is no chance of France being struck down, before the British Empire is ready; there is no chance of the British Empire itself being paralysed, before its full force can be applied to the struggle. The supreme initiative passes from the Teutonic Powers to the Allies. Resources, almost measureless and of indescribable variety in ships, in men, in munitions and devices of war, will now flow month by month steadily into our hands. What shall we do with them? Strategic alternatives on the greatest scale and of the highest order present themselves to our choice. Which shall we choose? Shall we use our reinforced fleets and great new armies of 1915, either to turn the Teutonic right in the Baltic or their left in the Black Sea and the Balkans? Or shall we hurl our manhood against sandbags, wire and concrete in frontal attack upon the German fortified lines in France? Shall we by a supreme effort make direct contact with our Russian ally or leave her in a dangerous isolation? Shall we by decisive action, in hopes of shortening the conflict, marshal and draw in the small nations in the North and in the South who now stand outside it? Or shall we plod steadily forward at what lies immediately in our front? Shall our armies toil only in the mud of Flanders, or shall we break new ground? Shall our fleets remain contented with the grand and solid results they have won, or shall they ward off future perils by a new inexhaustible audacity?

The answers to these momentous questions will appear as this tale is carried forward to a further stage.

APPENDIX A
MEMORANDUM BY THE FIRST LORD ON NAVAL STAFF TRAINING AND DEVELOPMENT

(A.)—*Military Education and War Staff Training.*

1. It is necessary to draw a distinction between the measures required to secure a general diffusion of military knowledge among naval officers and the definite processes by which Staff Officers are to be trained. The first may be called 'Military Education,' and the second 'War Staff Training.' They require to be treated separately, and not mixed together as in the report of the Committee. Both must again be distinguished from all questions of administration, of material, and of non-military education and training. The *application* of fighting power can thus be separated from its *development*. We are not now concerned with the forging of the weapon, but only with its use.

Military Education.

2. As early as possible in his service the mind of the young officer must be turned to the broad principles of war by sea and land. His interest must be awakened. He must be put in touch with the right books, and must be made to feel the importance of the military aspect of his profession. The existing curriculum at Dartmouth and on the cruiser is already too full; and until the officer has reached the rank of Lieutenant I see no immediate opportunity of adding to his instruction. But thereafter his 'Military Education' should be provided for in two ways. First: Every Lieutenant should go through a military course of (say) two months during the first four years of his service. The course to be prepared by the Training Division of the War Staff; aim, thoroughness in a simple and strictly limited sphere. The course to conclude by a standard examination to test only what the pupil remembers of his instruction. It would be preferable to hold the courses at Greenwich continuously. Thus a good scheme of instruction adapted to the class of officers and the limits of time will develop and uniformity will be established; and young officers will be accustomed to associate Greenwich with the study of war.

All specialist officers, submarine and air service officers included, must go through this course.

In exceptional circumstances, where exigencies of service do not allow, extension to within the first six years may be granted.

The course will be obligatory on officers now under two years' service as Lieutenant. There should be four courses a year; the first to begin October, 1914. It should be voluntary for officers now over two years' service as Lieutenant.

(Let me have calculations about numbers which can be handled during the first five courses; and make proposals for giving effect to the above scheme in detail.)

No grading as Assistant War Staff Officers will result from this course, and no certificate will be given or letters printed after an officer's name. It is a pure matter of routine, and a necessary qualification of all future naval officers. The college authorities will, however, keep a register of officers, and report upon their general aptitudes for staff work and tactical subjects. This will be of use later in considering claims to compete for entry into the War College.

Secondly, as soon as practicable (if possible, next time) an examination should be held for entry into the War College for the War Staff Course. This examination should be competitive. It will be open to all Commanders and Lieutenant-Commanders, or Lieutenants who will be Lieutenant-Commanders before the course is completed, whose names are submitted by the Flag Officers under whom they are serving and who are approved as candidates by the Admiralty. A proportion of vacancies will be assigned to each rank. The results will be published. The object of this examination will be to test ability for staff work. In the first instance the tests will have to be of a simple character, but gradually, as the military education of the naval officer develops, they can be stiffened and extended. The examination will be conducted by the War College according to principles prescribed by the War Training Division. Intending candidates will be notified three months in advance of the subjects in which they should prepare themselves.

When an officer is successful in the competition, but owing to foreign service or other exigency cannot at once attend the War Course, he may be allowed to take a vacancy next time.

Captains of Ships and War Staff Officers afloat will aid officers to prepare themselves for this examination.

War Staff Training.

3. The successful candidates will enter the War College at Greenwich as residents for War Staff training. This course must for the present be limited to one year, but later it should be extended to eighteen months. As an examination will be held every six months, there will at the beginning be two batches under instruction, rising later to three. This will give the necessary numbers at the College. The period of this course, provided the officer gives satisfaction, should, in my opinion, count as sea service.

On completing the course, the officers who have qualified may be placed upon the War Staff List, with the approval of the Admiralty, as at present, and will then be available for staff employment.

(B.)—*Development of the Admiralty War Staff.*

1. Two years have passed since this body was instituted, and both the progress made in the Admiralty and the acceptance of the idea by the Fleet justify a further advance.

Three main questions have arisen:—

(1) The creation of a Trade Division.

(2) The preparation of Manuals and direction of training generally.

(3) The detachment of the Mobilization Department from the War Staff.

I have come to the conclusion that the first essential is the creation of a War Training Division, under a Director, and equal in importance to the Operations and Intelligence Divisions. This division will be charged with the theoretical direction and co-ordination of all tactical and strategical exercises and instruction whether in the Fleets or at the Colleges. It will, of course, have nothing to do with the education which fits a cadet to become a naval officer, or with the training of Specialists of any kind, or with the training which fits a boy to become an able seaman. All this is in the Administrative sphere and belongs to the Second Sea Lord. The War Training Division is concerned only with what the naval officer learns about war, what tactical use the gunnery and torpedo experts make of their weapons, and what exercises are prescribed for the Fleets and Squadrons.

2. Nothing in the work of this division will relieve Flag Officers from their present duties and responsibilities in the training of their commands. But henceforward they will work on regularly explored and considered lines, and within limits which are the result of collective thought and experience; and henceforward continuity and uniformity will be preserved by a central direction and co-ordination, which gathers up and authorizes the established conclusions, without restricting reasonable initiative. It is no answer to the advocates of such a Division, to say that war training is given by the Commanders-in-chief at sea, and that war training is in the department of the First Sea Lord. The Commanders-in-chief change repeatedly, and with them their personal instruction changes, very often without leaving a trace behind. The First Sea Lord cannot possibly prepare manuals of tactical and strategic instruction. This work can only be done by a regular department permanently at work.

3. I propose, therefore, in principle to constitute without delay a War Training Division of the Admiralty War Staff. This division will be organized under a Director (D.T.D., short for D.N.T.D.) in three sections, denominated respectively *x*, *y*, and *z*.

The following will be the main distribution of duties:—

(x) Manuals and Exercises.

Preparation and revision of all Training Books and Manuals (other than technical or administrative) including Signal Books in their tactical aspect.
Preparation of manœuvre schemes.
Report and criticism of manœuvres.
Record and criticism of tactical and strategic exercises.
Advice upon the initiation of experiments (other than technical or administrative), upon the organization of units, upon War Establishments, and upon the tactical aspects of New Construction.
Distribution of War Staff publications.

(y) War Colleges: Examinations and Courses.

Supervision of War Colleges and all war educational arrangements.
Examinations and courses in tactical and strategic subjects.
Libraries.

(z) Historical.

The staff of this new division will be formed in part by reductions from the Mobilization and Operations Divisions (some of which latter's work is taken over); and in part by an addition to the Estimates for which Treasury sanction will be required. As a set-off against this there is the economy of reducing an Admiral by bringing the War College to Greenwich.

Nine or ten officers (some of whom can be retired officers) should suffice with the necessary clerks and writers.

Let me have proposals on these lines with estimates.

4. *The Operations Division* will have been to some extent relieved by the formation of the War Training Division. It must, however, be augmented by the addition of a new section (the Manning Department) dealing with War Mobilization, which will be explained later; and, secondly, by the new Trade Defence Section. This latter is clearly only a part of the Operations sphere. It is grouped with Operations because the defence of trade is essentially an offensive operation against the enemy's armed ships.

The Operations Division will, therefore, be organized in four sections—*(a)*, *(b)*, *(c)*, and *(d)*—as follows:—

(*a*) *War Plans.*
  Distribution of the Fleet.
  Schemes of attack of all kinds.
  Joint naval and military action.
  C.I.D. work.
  War Room.

(*b*) *Coast Defence.*
  Plans for the employment of
    Patrol Flotillas.
    Air Craft at the Naval Air Stations.
    Coastal submarines.
  Organization of Signal and Wireless Stations.
  Examination Service.
  Distribution of Intelligence along the coast.
  Joint naval and military action in coast defence.
  Home Ports Defence Committee.
  Overseas Defence Committee.

(*c*) *Trade Defence.*
  All arrangements for the direction of trade in time of war.
  All naval questions connected with food supply.

Armed merchantmen.
Distribution of warships for the control of the trade routes.
International law.
All relations with the Mercantile Marine.

(*d*) *War Mobilization.*
Supervision of the arrangements of the Manning Department for the mobilization of the Fleet.
Advice upon the complements of ships.

Attention is drawn to the minute of the Secretary on the proposed issue of charts and returns to the Trade Division. This necessity is not proved. The staff of the new section must be reconsidered accordingly.

5. *The Intelligence Division* requires little change, but should, in principle, be divided into three sections, as follows:—

(*l*) Potentially hostile countries.
(*m*) Friendly countries.
(*n*) Neutral countries.

Section *(l)* is to be charged with the new duty of preparing war plans for the hostile countries separately or in combination against us alone or allied, showing both—

(1) What they will probably do against us.
(2) What would be the worst they could do against us. From time to time war games will be played between the Intelligence and Operations Divisions.

Section *(m)* will likewise report on the needs and dangers of the friendly countries and study the measures best adapted to strengthen them in peace and war.

These new duties open to the Intelligence Division a large creative and imaginative sphere, and offer opportunities for the highest tactical and strategic ability.

6. *The Mobilization Division* is not well named. Mobilization is a small and infrequent part of the duties of this division. Mobilization is, indeed, a comparatively unimportant feature in our naval system, all the more powerful vessels being constantly in full commission, and the Second Fleet requiring only to be 'completed.' The day-to-day provision of complements for ships commissioning, and the intricate arrangements connected therewith, constitute the staple of the work of this Department.

Further, its duties are almost entirely administrative, and administration is foreign to the sphere of the War Staff.

I therefore propose that the Mobilization Division shall be separated from the War Staff, and shall be called the '*Manning Department*.'

A section of the Manning Department will, however, be formed to deal with War Mobilization, and this section will work under the D.M.D., but in close association with the new Training Division of the War Staff.

Thus the whole administrative work connected with the manning of the Fleet will be left intact under the Second Sea Lord, while, at the same time, the War Staff will have included in its circle everything necessary to its reflective and organizing duties. I await definite proposals to give effect to this.

7. It is important that every officer serving in the War Staff should look for recommendation for advancement from the Chief of the Staff. I propose, therefore, that the Chief of the Staff should be allotted a proportion of recommendations as if he were a Flag Officer in independent command, and should make them to my Naval Secretary in the usual way for the half-yearly promotions. The Chief of the Staff will also initiate all recommendations for War Staff appointments and appointments to the Naval War College, and all lists of officers for war courses of all kinds will be proposed by him and submitted through the First Sea Lord to me.

The record books in the Private Office will be sufficient for general purposes, but a *Staff Register* should be formed for recording the War Staff capacities and services of officers whether at the

Admiralty, the Colleges, or afloat, and a copy of this register will be kept written up to date in the Private Office.

It may be found necessary to add an officer to the personal staff of the Chief of the Staff.

8. I attach a skeleton chart of the new organization. (*See page 410.*)

9. I add the following general observations. The divisions of the War Staff though separate are parts of one united organization. Each discharges its own functions in association with the others. They are not to do each other's work. The Operations Division is not, for instance, to collect its own data. It is to accept them from the Intelligence Division. The Training Division is to accept the conclusions of the Operations Division and propose the Fleet for their execution. But there must also be unity and free intercourse between the three Directors. In order to promote and ensure this, the Chief of the Staff will be enjoined to hold every month a formal Staff meeting with his three Directors and any of their subordinates who may be required for the discussion of Staff questions, and the agenda and minutes of these meetings will be submitted through the First Sea Lord to the First Lord.

(C)—*The Operations Staff Afloat.*

I agree with the proposals of the Second Sea Lord as concurred in and amended by the First Sea Lord. This organization observes the principle of a clear division between the thinking and administrative branches.

The Captain for administration should bear the title of Flag Captain. The Captain of the ship should simply be styled 'The Captain.'

The extra officers for the Intelligence and Operations 'Groups' (Divisions is too large a word and already taken) can be found from the War Training Division of the Admiralty War Staff which will cease to exist on mobilization. They should go afloat whenever large manœuvres are in progress, and should be appropriated by name to their posts in war. The Commander-in-Chief should have no one on his staff in war that he does not know and has not worked with.

It is desirable that the Commander-in-Chief's staff when formed should work out strategic and tactical exercises together at the War College, Portsmouth, or if possible at Greenwich, at least once a year, apart from actual manœuvres afloat, in order that each may know his exact function.

The approved form of the Fleet Flagship Staff is as follows:—

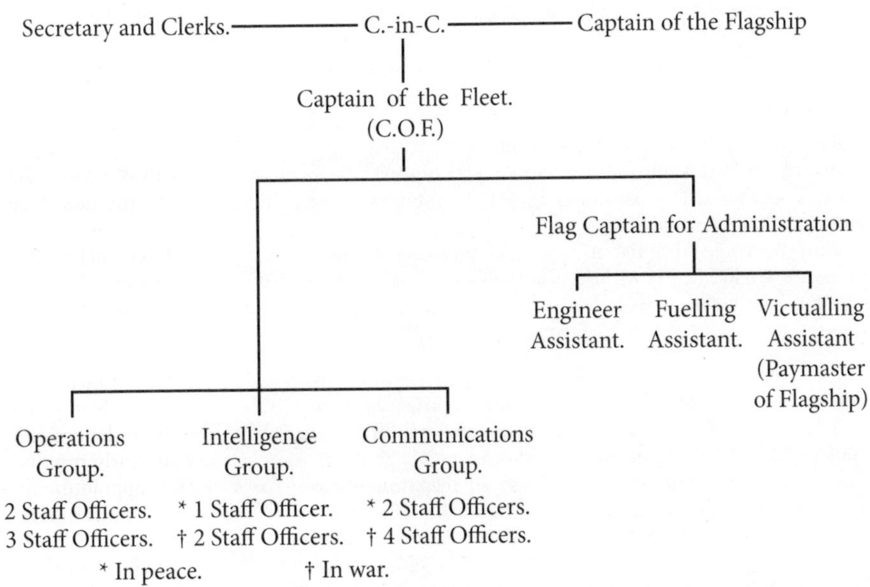

I approve also the Second Sea Lord's proposals for the staffs of Squadron Flagships.

SKELETON CHART OF ADMIRALTY WAR STAFF ORGANIZATION.

New additions in heavy type.

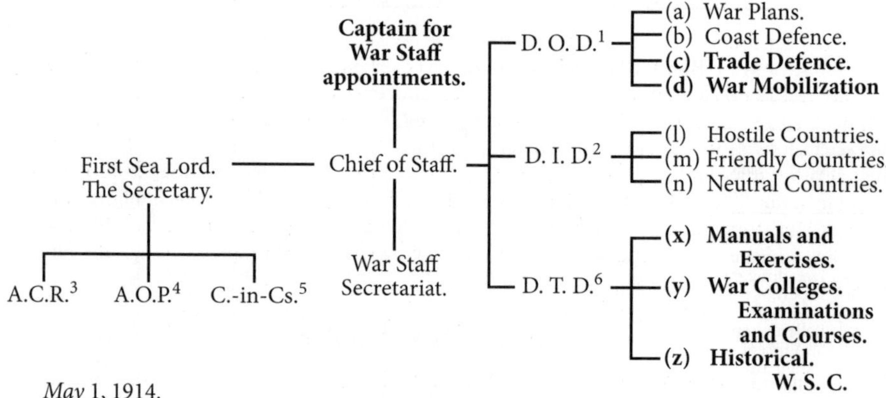

W. S. C.

May 1, 1914.

[1] Director of Operations Division.
[2] Director of Intelligence Division.
[3] Admiral of Coastguards and Reserves.
[4] Admiral of Patrols.
[5] Commanders-in-Chief.
[6] Director of Training Division.

APPENDIX B
TABLES OF FLEET STRENGTH

BRITISH DREADNOUGHT STRENGTH, 1914

Consecutive No.	Ship.	Launched.	Displacement	Speed (designed).	Armour belt (max.).	Armament (excluding guns below 12 prs.).	Weight of broadside primary guns.
	BATTLESHIPS BUILT						
			tons.	knots	In.		lb.
1	Lord Nelson	1906	16,500	18.5	12	4—12 in., 10—9.2 in., 24—12 prs.	5,300
2	Agamemnon	1906					
3	Dreadnought	1906	17,900	20.9	11	10—12 in., 24—12 prs.	6,800
4	Superb	1907					
5	Temeraire	1907	18,600	20.75	10	10—12 in., 16—4 in.	6,800
6	Bellerophon	1907					
7	St. Vincent	1908					
8	Vanguard	1909	19,250	21	10	10—12 in., 20—4 in.	6,800
9	Collingwood	1908					
10	Neptune	1909	19,900	21	10	10—12 in., 16—4 in.	8,500
11	Colossus	1910	20,000	21	11	10—12 in., 16—4 in.	8,500
12	Hercules	1910					
13	Orion	1910					
14	Thunderer	1911					
15	Monarch	1911	22,500	21	12	10—13.5 in., 16—4 in.	12,500
16	Conqueror	1911					
17	King George V	1911					
18	Centurion	1911	23,000	21	12	10—13.5 in., 16—4 in.	14,000
19	Ajax	1912					
20	Audacious	1912					
21	Iron Duke	1912	25,000	21	12	10—13.5 in., 12—6 in., 2—3 in.	14,000
22	Marlborough	1912					
	BUILDING						
23	Benbow	1913	25,000	21	12	10—13.5 in., 12—6 in., 2—3 in.	14,000
24	Emperor of India	1913					
25	Queen Elizabeth	1913					
26	Warspite	1913					
27	Valiant	—	27,500	25	13	8—15 in., 16—6 in., 2—3 in.	15,360
28	Barham	—					
29	Malaya	—					
30	Resolution	—					
31	Ramillies	—					
32	Revenge	—	25,750	21	13	8—15 in., 16—6 in., 4—3 in.	15,360
33	Royal Sovereign	—					
34	Royal Oak	—					
	SHIPS BUILDING IN GREAT BRITAIN FOR FOREIGN POWERS AND REQUISITIONED FOR THE ROYAL NAVY						
35	Agincourt	—	27,500	22	9	14—12 in., 12—6 in., 8—3 in., 2—3 in. A.A.C.	12,900
36	Erin	—	23,000	21	12	10—13.5 in., 16—6 in., 2—3 in. A.A.C.	14,800
37	Canada	—	28,000	23	9	10—14 in., 12—6 in., 2—3 in. A.A.C.	16,560
	BATTLE CRUISERS						
1	Invincible	1907					
2	Inflexible	1907	17,250	26	7	8—12 in., 16—4 in.	6,800
3	Indomitable	1907					
4	Indefatigable	1909	18,750	25	7	8—12 in., 16—4 in.	6,800
5	Lion	1910	26,350	28	9	8—13.5 in., 16—4 in.	10,000
6	Australia	1911	18,800	25	7	8—12 in., 16—4 in.	6,800
7	New Zealand	1911					
8	Princess Royal	1911	26,350	28	9	8—13.5 in., 16—4 in.	11,200
9	Queen Mary	1912	27,000	28	9	8—13.5 in., 16—4 in.	11,200
	BUILDING						
10	Tiger	1913	28,000	28	9	8—13.5 in., 12—6 in.	11,200

GERMAN DREADNOUGHT STRENGTH, 1914

Consecutive No.	Ship.	Launched.	Displacement	Speed (designed).	Armour belt (max.).	Armament (excluding guns below 12 prs.).	Weight of broadside primary guns.
	BATTLESHIPS BUILT						
			tons	knots.	in.		lb.
1	Nassau	1908					
2	Westfalen	1908					
3	Rheinland	1908	18,600	19	11.81	12—11 in., 12—5.9 in., 16—3.4 in.	5,376
4	Posen	1908					
5	Ostfriesland	1909					
6	Helgoland	1909					
7	Thuringen	1909	22,440	20.5	11.81	12—12 in., 14—5.9 in., 14—3.4 in.	7,232
8	Oldenburg	1910					
9	Kaiser	1911					
10	Friedrich der Grosse	1911					
11	Kaiserin	1911	22,310	21	13.78	10—12 in., 14—5.9 in., 12—3.4 in., 4—13 prs.	9,040
12	Prinzregent Luitpold	1912					
13	König Albert	1912					
14	Grosser Kurfürst	1912					
15	König	1912	25,390	22 ?	?	10—12 in., 14—5.9 in., 12—3.4 in., 4—13 prs.	9,040
16	Markgraf	1913					
	BUILDING						
17	Kronprinz	1914	25,390	22 ?	?	10—12 in., 14—5.9 in., 12—3.4 in., 4—13 prs.	9,040
19	Ersatz Wörth	—					
19	T	—	28,050 ?	22 ?	?	8—15 in., 16—5.9 in.	15,360 ?
20	Ersatz Kaiser Friedrich III	—					
	BATTLE CRUISERS						
1	Blücher	1908	15,550	25	6	12—8.2 in., 8—5.9 in., 16—3.4 in.	2,204
2	Von der Tann	1909	18,700	25	6	8—11 in., 10—5.9 in., 16—3.4 in.	5,376
3	Moltke	1910	22,640	27	11	10—11 in., 12—5.9 in., 12—3.4 in.	6,720
4	Goeben	1911					
5	Seydlitz	1912	24,640	27	11	10—11 in., 12—5.9 in., 12—3.4 in.	6,720
6	Derfflinger	1913	28,000	27	7	8—12 in., 12—5.9 in., 12—3.4 in.	7,232
	BUILDING						
7	Lützow	1913	28,000	27	7	8—12 in., 12—5.9 in., 32—3.4 in.	7,232
8	Ersatz Hertha	Edg.					

BRITISH AND GERMAN FLEETS IN HOME WATERS AT THE OUTBREAK OF WAR

BRITISH.

Grand Fleet.

Iron Duke (10—13.5 inch), Fleet Flagship.

1st Battle Squadron.

1 Iron Duke (10—13.5 inch).
2 Colossus
1 Neptune
3 St. Vincents
1 Bellerophon } 10—12 inch.

2nd Battle Squadron.

4 King George V
4 Orions } 10—13.5 inch.

3rd Battle Squadron.

8 King Edward VII (4—12 inch; 4—9.2 inch).

4th Battle Squadron.

1 Dreadnought
2 Bellerophons } 10—12 inch.
1 Agincourt (14—12 inch).
(One Light Crusier attached to each Battle Squadron.

1st Battle Cruiser Squadron.

3 Lions (8—13.5 inch).
1 New Zealand (8—12 inch).

2nd Cruiser Squadron.

1 Shannon (4—9.2 inch; 10—7.5 inch).
3 Achilles (6—9.2 inch; 4—7.5 inch).

3rd Cruiser Squadron.

4 Antrims (4—7.5 inch; 6—6 inch).

1st Light Cruiser Squadron.

3 Birminghams (9—6 inch).
1 Southampton
1 Falmouth } 8—6 inch.
1 Bristol (2—6 inch; 10—4 inch)

Destroyer Flotillas.

2 Flotillas, each of 20 vessels, with Light Cruiser Active and Flotilla Leader Swift.

Harwich Force.

1 Amethyst (12—4 inch).
2 Amphions (12—4 inch).
35 Destroyers.

GERMAN

High Seas Fleet.

Friedrich der Grosse (10—12 inch), Fleet Flagship.

1st Battle Squadron.

4 Helgolands (12—12 inch).
4 Nassaus (12—11 inch).

2nd Battle Squadron.

10 Preussens (4—11 inch).

3rd Battle Squadron.

4 Kaisers (10—12 inch).

Cruiser Squadron.
Battle Cruisers.

2 Moltke (10—11 inch).
1 Von der Tann (8—11 inch).
1 Derfflinger (8—12 inch).
1 Blücher (12—8.2 inch).

Light Cruisers.

1 Rostock
2 Strassburgs
3 Mainz } 12—4.1 inch.

Destroyer Flotillas.

7 Flotillas, each of 11 vessels.

BRITISH AND GERMAN FLEETS IN HOME WATERS AT THE OUTBREAK OF WAR

BRITISH—*continued*

Channel Fleet.

5th Battle Squadron.

8 Formidables (4—12 inch).

6th Battle Squadron.

2 Lord Nelsons (4—12 inch; 10—9.2 inch).
5 Duncans } 4—12 inch.
1 Glory }

7th Battle Squadron.

4 Majestics (4—12 inch).

8th Battle Squadron.

1 Majestic (4—12 inch).
5 Glory
4 Light Cruisers were attached to the Battle Squadrons.

7th Cruiser Squadron.

5 Cressys (2—9.2 inch; 12—6 inch).

12th Cruiser Squadron.

3 Talbots (11—6 inch).
1 Charybdis (2—6 inch; 8—4.7 inch) (patrolling west end of Channel),

Dover Patrol.

2 Light Cruisers.
22 Destroyers.

11th Cruiser Squadron.

5 Talbots (11—6 inch) (on the coast of Ireland).

10th Cruiser Squadron.

8 Crescents (Northern Patrol).

Patrol Flotillas on East Coast.

3 Light Cruisers.
48 Destroyers.
24 Torpedo Boats.

Submarines.

65, organized in 8 Flotillas, 7 Flotillas for Coast Defence, 1 for Overseas Operations.

GERMAN—*continued*

Other Vessels in Home Waters.

Battleships.

5 Wittelsbachs.
5 Kaiser Class (old) (5—9.4 inch).
2 Brandenburgs (6—11 inch).

Cruisers

2 Roons (4—8.2 inch; 10—5.9 inch).
2 Prinz Adalbert (4—8.2 inch); 10—5.9 inch).
1 Prinz Heinrich (2—9.4 inch); 10—5.9 inch).

Light Cruisers.

12 Vessels, with armaments of 10 or 12—4.1 inch guns.

Destroyers.

67 available for coast patrol, service in Baltic, etc.

Submarines.

27 serviceable.

APPENDIX C
MEMORANDUM BY THE FIRST LORD ON TRADE PROTECTION ON AND AFTER THE OUTBREAK OF WAR

Written August 23, 1913, *Revised April*, 1914.

1. The first security for British merchant ships must be the superiority of the British Navy which should enable us to cover in peace, and hunt down and bring to battle in war, every enemy's warship which attempts to keep the seas. A policy of vigorous offence against the enemy's warships wherever stationed, will give immediately far greater protection to British traders than large numbers of vessels scattered sparsely about in an attitude of weak and defensive expectancy. This should be enjoined as the first duty of all British warships. Enemy's cruisers cannot live in the oceans for any length of time. They cannot coal at sea with any certainty. They cannot make many prizes without much steaming; and in these days of W.T. their whereabouts will be constantly reported. If British cruisers of superior speed are hunting them, they cannot do much harm before they are brought to action. Very few German Town Class cruisers are assigned to foreign stations for this work. If others are detached from the North Sea, and get out safely, we shall be able to detach a larger proportion of the similar British cruisers which have been hitherto opposing them there. They cannot afford to send away many without crippling their battle fleet.

2. As for enemy's armed merchantmen or merchantmen converted into cruisers for commerce destruction, the only answer to that is to have an equal number of British merchant vessels plying on the trade routes armed and commissioned to engage them when met with. The whole of this threat is very shadowy. Whether the German vessels have their guns on board is extremely doubtful. Not a scrap of evidence has been forthcoming during the last year and a half in spite of every effort to procure it. How are they to be converted on the high seas? Where are they to get rid of their passengers? Are they to take hundreds of non-combatants with them on what the stronger naval Power may well treat as a piratical enterprise? Where are they to coal? To say that we have to maintain a large cruiser fleet to deal with this danger appears extravagant in the highest degree. All that is needed is to arm a similar number of British merchant vessels of the right speed and make arrangements to commission these for their own defence and that of other British ships in their neighbourhood and on their route. The presence of these vessels plying always in considerable numbers along the regular trade routes will from the very outset of the war, and however suddenly it may begin, provide a constant and immediate counter to enemy armed merchantmen, and probably deter them from any injurious action.

3. But the best safeguard for the maintenance of British trade in war is the large number of merchant ships engaged in trading, and the immense number of harbours in the United Kingdom they can approach by ocean routes. This makes any serious interruption by enemy's commerce destroyers impossible. We must rely on numbers and averages. Provided that we can induce all these ships to put to sea and carry on their business boldly, and provided that they are warned in time and encouraged to leave the regular trade routes and travel wide of them, very few captures will be made even in the early days of the war.

4. It is no use distributing isolated cruisers about the vast ocean spaces. To produce any result from such a method would require hundreds of cruisers. The ocean is itself the best protection. We must recognize that we cannot specifically protect trade routes; we can only protect confluences.

The only safe trade routes in war are those which the enemy has not discovered and those upon which he has been exterminated. There are areas where the trade necessarily converges and narrow channels through which it must pass; and these defiles or terminals of the trade routes should be made too dangerous for enemy's commerce destroyers to approach, by employing our older cruisers in adequate force so as to create an effective sanctuary, control or catchment for our trading ships. These areas should be judiciously selected so as to husband our resources, and not with a view to finding employment for as many old cruisers as possible. It may be taken for certain that no enemy's armed merchantman unless possessed of exceptional speed will dare to approach the area where he may encounter a British cruiser. Many of our old cruisers steam 19 knots. The number of German merchantmen which steam more is not large. As for the enemy's warships and his few exceptionally fast vessels, they must be marked down and hunted by fast modern vessels which are concerned with nothing else but to bring them to action.

5. British attacks on the German trade are a comparatively unimportant feature in our operations, and British cruisers should not engage in them to the prejudice of other duties. Economic pressure will be put on Germany by the distant blockade of her shores which will cut off her trade, both export and import, as a whole. If this is effectively done it is of very little consequence to us whether individual German vessels are captured as prizes, or whether they take refuge in neutral harbours till the end of the war. It is reasonable to suppose that German merchant ships, other than those armed and commissioned for warlike purposes, will run for neutral harbours as soon as war breaks out, and that very few will attempt under the German flag to return home running the gauntlet of the numerous British fleets operating in the North Sea.

6. Protection will be afforded to British seaborne trade in time of war by the following measures:—

A. Hunting down of enemy's warships and armed vessels.

Every German cruiser stationed abroad should be covered in peace and brought to action in war by a superior vessel of superior speed, or alternatively by two equal vessels having speed advantage.

B. Organized warning of British merchant vessels.

All British armed merchantmen plying on the routes will, on receiving the warning telegram by wireless, open their secret instructions which direct them to steam along their regular route warning all unarmed British vessels met with to leave the trade route, and steam without lights at night, keeping well away from their usual course, avoiding company, and making their own way to their port of destination.

7. Similar warnings and directions adapted to each case and each route will be issued by British Consuls at all ports. These should be prepared beforehand in the fullest detail and according to a general scheme. For instance, the British Consul at Buenos Ayres should have separate instructions all ready prepared for every British ship leaving the port for the United Kingdom. These instructions will be regularly kept up to date by the Trade Division of the Admiralty War Staff. They will prescribe for each ship the general course she is to follow, the portions of the voyage she should endeavour to cover in darkness, and the areas within which she will find safety. A good wireless organization can, of course, deal at once with all vessels so fitted. Thus the unarmed trade will, in the first week of the war, be effectively scattered over immense areas of ocean.

The control and guidance of merchant traffic must, of course, vary with circumstances. There are two quite different situations to consider. The first is that which occurs at the moment of a sudden outbreak of war. We must assume that hostilities begin by surprise, and that the enemy's commerce destroyers, whether warships or armed merchantmen, will begin their attacks within a very few hours of the first warning being given. None of our Third Fleet cruisers will be on their stations. The only vessels available will be the ordinary foreign squadrons and the fast cruisers shadowing individual German warships, and these will probably not be in positions which have any special relation to the trade routes. None of the British converted auxiliary merchant cruisers will be on the routes: the only thing that will be there and that can be there are the defensive armed merchantmen. In these circumstances it seems probable that the best course would be to scatter the trade; and it is in any case essential that we should have the power to do so, and that all arrangements should be made to that end.

8. When, however, the war has been in progress for some time, and in proportion as our available force increases and we pass from a peace to a war organization, it may well be that the scattering of the trade will no longer be necessary or even desirable, except perhaps locally between special points. Trading vessels would then be told to return to their regular trade routes; and this might easily lead to drawing such commerce destroyers as then remain into areas where they could be reported, located, and destroyed, by the British cruisers.

9. The organization for the control and guidance of the trade should therefore be of so complete a character that the trade may be either dispersed about the ocean or concentrated along particular routes; or in some places dispersed and in others concentrated; and that changes from one policy to the other can be made when necessary at any time.

10. The British armed merchantmen will only be employed on a strictly limited service, namely, that of carrying food supplies to the United Kingdom. They will be forbidden to engage enemy's warships and are to surrender if overtaken by them. They will not molest or pursue unarmed ships of the enemy. They will only fire on enemy's armed merchantmen if they are themselves attacked or pursued by them.

The result of these arrangements will be that the enemy's armed merchantmen will either have to scatter in haphazard search for prizes, or run into a succession of armed British vessels plying the usual route, finding prizes few and far between on the first course, and nothing but kicks on the other.

11. C. As soon as possible after the outbreak of war a sufficient number of British merchant ships or liners of high speed, selected and prepared beforehand, will be converted into auxiliary cruisers and commissioned for the further policing of the trade routes, and incidentally or if desired to prey on enemy's commerce. These vessels will be taken over on the same or similar basis as the Cunarders. They will differ from the armed merchantmen in 'B,' in that their duties will not be limited to self-defence and warning; they will be directly employed in limiting down enemy's armed merchantmen; they may be used offensively against enemy's trade; they will not carry on their ordinary business; they will be wholly taken over by and maintained by the Admiralty; they will be officered and manned by the Royal Navy, will fly the White Ensign, and execute the orders of the Admiralty.

12. D. While we have a large supply of older cruisers, they may be employed in protecting the approaches to the principal trade terminals, and at certain special points. These cruisers will be additional to any fast modern British vessels employed on the general service of hunting down individual German cruisers. They will neglect no opportunity of engaging enemy's warships or armed merchantmen. They may be at any time withdrawn from their areas by the Admiralty for such a purpose. Only the older ships will be employed on this service; and as they wear out, control will be maintained by a smaller number of new, fast vessels employed on the general and primary service of hunting down the enemy's warships.

13. E. The last but indispensable condition of maintaining British food supplies and British trade in time of war, is that British traders should send their ships to sea, and from the very beginning of the war press forward boldly on their regular business. The question of encouraging them to do this by means of a system of State Insurance under certain restrictions to guard against fraud, is now being considered by a Sub-Committee of the C.I.D. We have expressed on behalf of the Board of Admiralty the strongest opinion in favour of the adoption of such a system, it being essential to all our arrangements that very large numbers of British vessels, undeterred by a small proportion of captures, should continue to traverse the seas under the British flag.

In exceptional cases convoys will, if necessary, be organized under escort of Third Fleet vessels. It is hoped, however, that this cumbrous and inconvenient measure will not be required.

April, 1914. W. S. C.

APPENDIX D
MINING

In order to combat the many unwise proposals which were pressed upon me at this time to squander our small stock of mines, I drew up the following paper with which I endeavoured to repel the demands from the Cabinet, the Admiralty and the Fleet. I am aware that these views will be disputed, and I shall no doubt be told that the experience of the later stages of the war has disproved them. I still believe, however, that they were sound and truly applicable to the circumstances of 1914. But I go further and declare that the reasoning held good all through 1915 and 1916. If I am reminded that as part of the life and death struggle against the German submarines in 1917, we were led into a mining policy on a scale so gigantic as dwarfed every previous scheme, and if as the result of this huge diversion of our resources a certain number of German submarines were destroyed, still I assert that these conditions would never have arisen if a proper offensive had been developed by the Royal Navy, as would have been possible at far less cost. All being said, I take my stand, as I wrote to Lord Fisher, on the *dictum* 'Mine in Haste and Sweep at Leisure.'

NOTES BY THE FIRST LORD

Mining is mainly of two kinds, ambush mining and blockade mining.

Ambush Mining.

Ambush mining depends on the whereabouts of the field remaining unknown. These mines may be scattered about in patches, or short lines in the neighbourhood of the enemy's ports or of the approaches to your own ports or landing places on the chance of enemy ships running into them. This chance is not great. The seas are very large; the area mined, even if on a great scale, very small. The chances of preserving secrecy long are not great, and most ambush minefields are soon discovered by merchant ships, or other craft of no military value, being blown up by them. On the other hand, every patch of mines soon hampers the movement of the stronger fleet. The position of the minefields cannot be accurately known. There is very often a tendency for them to drag with their anchors in tide and sea. Also ships cannot always be sure of their positions, and very often when out of sight of land, in weather unsuited to taking observations of the sun, 15, 20, or 30 miles' error in position may easily arise. The fact that you know generally where your own mines are and when you are getting near their area, but do not exactly know where they are, or exactly where you are, tends to paralyse your own movements, and might easily prevent effective action against or the interception of the enemy's fleet should it put to sea. The conclusion to be drawn is that ambush mines should be very sparingly used, chiefly in sight of land, and that not very much is to be expected from them. The general failure, so far as our present experience goes, of the German policy of ambush mining with which they opened the war, illustrates the truth of these conclusions. The only British warship, apart from the gunboat *Speedy* (which was actually engaged in fishing up mines), lost by this agency has been the *Amphion*, and she was drifted out of her course on to the very minefield whose position she knew and which she was endeavouring to avoid.

This is not by any means to decry the use of ambush mines as an immediate part of a concerted tactical combination. It is for this purpose mainly that the British Fleet mine-layers are organized. To lay mines in the course of an enemy before or during a battle, or across his homeward path if he has put to sea, may be operations of the greatest consequence and value, and it would be most unwise to deplete them of their not too extensive store of mines, which should be reserved for this purpose, and not squandered on promiscuous and haphazard uses.

One more class of ambush mines deserves to be noted. A few scattered about on trade routes and off enemy ports, if well advertised and enforced by a few ships actually blown up, may exercise a very effective deterrent on neutral commerce which may be of use to the enemy.

Blockade Mining.

It is not possible to blockade a modern fleet by mining, even on a very large scale, unless superior force is maintained in the neighbourhood of the minefield to prevent or oppose the mines being removed. In the days when Admiral Togo mined the debouches from Port Arthur the submarine did not exist, and it was possible to maintain a close and constant watch on the minefields, so that even if he was unable to stop the enemy removing the mines he knew when they were doing so, and this perhaps gave some clue to their future intentions. Even so, the Russian Fleet put to sea whenever they wanted to. It would not be possible to keep such a watch now without exposing the vessels so engaged to almost certain destruction from the enemy's submarines. Further, blockade mining is more effective the closer in it is to the enemy's ports, and therefore the watching vessels would be continually exposed not only to the attacks of the submarines, but to a greatly superior force of enemy destroyers and light cruisers. In order to maintain them against this, appropriate supports would have to be kept close at hand in proper tactical relation and brought up as the need arose, with the result that more and more ships of greater value would be drawn into the most dangerous area of the enemy's submarine activities, and considerable operations would develop in waters less suited to us and most favourable to the enemy.

But if the minefield is not watched, the enemy has no difficulty in proceeding, to sea at any time he chooses. He will soon learn the existence of the minefield, because one or two small craft will be blown up on it. In the British Fleet the regular mine-sweepers can sweep a clear channel ahead of the Fleet at a rate of 12 knots an hour through any minefield. The Germans have not used, as we have, old gunboats converted as mine-sweepers, but have built a special class of good, fast vessels. It must therefore be assumed that they could sweep a channel at least as quickly as, and probably quicker than, we could. They could therefore proceed to sea at any time if they wished to do so, and with scarcely any delay. Also, if they did not wish immediately to proceed to sea, they could sweep a channel through the minefield of which they would know the existence, and which, being in close contact with land where actual bearings could be obtained, they could follow exactly, and so have continued means of ingress and egress. We, on the other hand, would not know where this channel was, and would be prevented from approaching by the known existence of our own field. The conclusion is that it is not possible by blockade mines to stop a fleet from putting to sea, even if that were what we wanted to do.

Still less is it possible to stop the enemy's submarines from putting to sea, either by ambush mines or blockade mines. The rise and fall of the tide between high and low water makes a minefield ineffective against shallow-draft craft for half the twenty-four hours. The distance of 50 yards, which is the usual interval between mines, is five times the breadth of a submarine. By diving to 50 feet, the chance of contact with the mine is removed, and only the lesser danger of fouling the moorings remains. It is perfectly easy to sweep a channel for submarines, as for other vessels, at any time. Where there is any uncertainty about the whereabouts of a minefield, trawlers, or small merchant ships with a very few people on board, can go ahead of the submarines and pilot them out. If necessary, vessels could be specially prepared as mine-bumpers, with a kind of cow-catcher apparatus in front of them. We are experimenting with five different methods of fitting ships for mine-bumping, and shall very soon have a number of vessels which can go almost with impunity into a minefield. British submarines have frequently traversed, wittingly and unwittingly, the German minefields around Heligoland, and German submarines are probably traversing our southern mined area with indifference, and impunity, at the present time.

On the other hand, it is a curious truth that your own minefield is a greater deterrent to your own operations than to those of the enemy. You have put it down yourself, so you do not want to sweep it up. You know where it is, though not very accurately. You instinctively try to avoid the waters you have yourself fouled. Nothing has been more valuable than the searching and relentless watching maintained in the Heligoland Bight by our submarines since the beginning of the war. Its vigilance and efficiency have defeated themselves by forcing the Germans to retire actually inside their basins and canal, and thus depriving our submarines of any targets. It would be a great pity to hamper them in their work and expose them to additional dangers for the sake of such vain and illusory, precautions. The weak passive defence of mines cannot for a moment be compared as a military measure with the enterprising offensive of submarines.

The above considerations also apply to suggested schemes for shutting submarines in by a network of mines fastened together by wire. Mine-sweepers or mine-bumpers would force a channel through this as easily as through ordinary lines of mines, the only difference being that several being dragged along by the string would be exploded at the same time. Also it is evident that the limitations of this form of defence cannot be carried very far on account of the enormous quantities of material and explosives required. It would be very difficult and dangerous to lay in close proximity to the enemy's ports and fleets. The process would be slow; the losses certain, and it could in any case block only a very small portion of the 100-mile broad mouth of the Heligoland Bight. Devices of this character may, however, be useful in defending one's own harbours, and making anchorages submarine proof, where we can, by our superior strength, prevent our arrangements from being interfered with. A variety of these methods are at present in use, and are being rapidly extended and developed. The following seven principal expedients are being applied:—

(1) Sinking ships with cement or stone in such a way as to form an absolute breakwater and barrier like the mole of a harbour.

(2) Electrical contact mines strung very closely together, and capable of being made dangerous or safe by the current being switched on or off.

(3) Barges or piles, with torpedo nets attached to them.

(4) Loose wire nets of very large mesh, not fastened at either end, which clog round a submarine and entangle it.

(5) Network arrangement, with explosives attached.

(6) Network arrangements, with upright floating spars, which also entangle the submarine.

(7) Long lengths of fishing nets, particularly Portuguese tunny nets, which operate in the same way.

As the war progresses, we shall gradually improvise the torpedo-proof harbours, of which, except on our southern coast, we are now entirely destitute.

I explained to the Cabinet the quantities of mines which we had in store, and which were available in the future. The experience of the last three months seems to justify the partial and limited reliance put by the Admiralty upon mining as a method of warfare.

October, 1914. W. S. C.

APPENDIX E
FIRST LORD'S MINUTES

Formation of the Royal Naval Division

Secretary.
First Sea Lord.
Second Sea Lord.

In order to make the best possible use of the surplus naval reservists of different classes, it is proposed to constitute permanent cadres of one marine and two naval brigades. The marine brigade has already been partially formed in four battalions, aggregating 1,880 active service men. To this will be added an approximately equal number of reservists, making the total strength of the brigade 3,900, organized in four battalions of four double companies of approximately 250 men. The two naval brigades will also consist of four battalions, each, if possible, of 880 men, organized in sixteen double companies of 220. The composition of each battalion should be as follows:—

R.N.V.R.	375
R.F.R. (picked, under 30 years of age)	313
R.N.R.	190

The total numbers required for the two naval brigades would therefore be:—

R.N.V.R.	3,000
R.F .R.	2,500
R.N.R.	1,500

The marine brigade will be commanded by a Colonel, and each battalion by a Lieutenant-Colonel; each company by a Major and a Captain. The means of remedying the shortage of junior officers will be dealt with separately. About fifty new subalterns, R.M., must be entered either permanently or on a three years', or till the war stops, engagement.

Each naval brigade will be commanded by a Captain, R.N.; five of the battalions by a Commander or naval officer promoted to that rank, and three by R.N.V.R. Commanders; each company will be commanded by a Lieutenant-Commander, R.N. or R.N.V.R., or, if these are not forthcoming, by a Major, R.M. The question of making good deficiencies in these and in the marine brigade will be dealt with separately. There are, however, available 50 R.N.V.R. Lieutenants, 66 Sub-Lieutenants, and 12 Midshipmen; total, 128. About 50 more officers would be required.

The use of these brigades need not be considered until the organization has advanced sufficiently to allow of their military value to be judged.

The formation of these brigades should be completed so far as resources allow in the present week. The officers commanding the companies and battalions must be appointed forthwith. The first essential is to get the men drilling together in brigades; and the deficiencies of various ranks in the battalions can be filled up later. It may ultimately be found possible in the course of the war to build up all battalions of the marine and naval brigades to the army strength of 1,070, and the organization will readily adapt itself to this. All the men, whether sailors or marines, while training in the three brigades will be available if required for service afloat, and it must be distinctly understood that this is the paramount claim upon them; but in the meanwhile they will be left to be organized for land service.

August 16, 1914. W. S. C.

ACTION OF AUGUST 28

Secretary.
First Sea Lord.
Third Sea Lord.
Director of Naval Ordnance.

1. Let me have an estimate of how long it will take to refit for service in every particular the vessels damaged in the recent action. Careful attention should be paid to the wishes and suggestions of the officers who fought them, in order that everything possible can be done to increase their fighting efficiency.

2. The failure of the 4-inch guns in the *Arethusa* is most serious, and must be thoroughly investigated. I am informed that it arose both from the breaking of the ejector catches, of which there were no spares, and secondly from the coating of the cartridge cases, which gradually fouled the gun. At one critical moment only one 4-inch gun could fire, and but for her 6-inch guns the *Arethusa* would have been destroyed. I wish to receive a statement showing that an effective remedy has been provided.

3. Every effort should be made while the ships are refitting to give the officers and men a few days' leave. The nervous strain of a modern action is considerable, and a change of scene is required to restore poise and resiliency.

August 30, 1914. W. S. C.

Secretary.
First Sea Lord.
Chief of Staff.

1. Selections might be made from all the reports of this action, beginning with some of the submarine reconnaissance reports which the Prime Minister has repeatedly urged me to publish. All interesting matter which can be made public without detriment to the future should be collected, circulated to the Fleet, and published in the newspapers.

2. The criticism in the Commander-in-Chief's report and various references to discrepancies in the arrangements which occur in Commodore S's and other statements must all be kept absolutely secret. Mistakes are always made in war, but there is no need to weaken confidence by dwelling on them after success has been obtained. The Senior Officers concerned in the manœuvre should, however, all have the opportunity of studying the full reports in order that every effort may be made to improve arrangements in the future. Beyond this profoundly secret circle no whisper must go.

3. I am awaiting your recommendations for honours, promotions, and rewards to be accorded to the officers and men who distinguished themselves in this fortunate and skilful enterprise.

September 6, 1914. W. S. C.

SEPARATION ALLOWANCES FOR THE NAVY

Financial Secretary.

I have today obtained the assent of the Cabinet in principle to the granting of a separation allowance to the whole Navy at once. The scale should be the full Army scale less any deductions which should be made on account of higher pay and allowances the sailor may receive as compared with the soldier. These details are to be settled between the Admiralty and the Treasury. I regard the matter as one of prime importance and urgency.

It is, of course, understood that the present decision only authorizes the payment of a separation allowance during the period of active service, and that the question of what is to happen in time of peace is not prejudiced.

I wish you to take up this question in conjunction with the Accountant-General and the Naval Branch and make me your proposals in the course of tomorrow. It will be a great fillip to our sailors when this boon to them is announced to the Fleet, as I hope it may be, in the next few days. Pray press it forward by every means in your power, acting with the Treasury and calling me in where there is a hitch or difficulty.

September 4, 1914. W. S. C.

Financial Secretary.

The Cabinet decided that evidence of allotment regularly made, should decide whether the Separation Allowance should be paid or not, and that legal marriage is not indispensable. Where it is clear that the woman has been dependent on the man, and the man has recognized this tie by a regular allotment, the legality of the marriage will be assumed.

September 19, 1914. W. S. C.

ENEMY RESERVISTS

Secretary.

Please inquire who was responsible for allowing a merchant ship from Buenos Ayres with 400 German reservists on board, to pass Gibraltar and to convey them to Italian ports, whence they left to join their units. How was it that these men were not arrested and made prisoners of war when passing the Straits?

September 5, 1914. W. S. C.

LIFE-BELTS

Secretary.
First Sea Lord.
Fourth Sea Lord.
Chief of Staff.

The sinking of the *Pathfinder* shows how important it is that there should be more life-belts or life-buoys available on our ships. Many lives would have been saved in this case if such steps had been taken. I don't like the German system of going into action with life-belts on, but there certainly ought to be in the boats and on the deck of British ships something like 100 life-belts or life-buoys which could be seized and would float overboard if the vessel foundered.

Pray let me have a proposal.

September 10, 1914. W. S. C.

SUBMARINE HONOURS

Secretary.
Naval Secretary.
First Sea Lord.

Since it is difficult to choose which man in a submarine has done specially well, it is necessary that the decoration should be given to the boat, and that the men should ballot among themselves to decide who is to have it.

September 17, 1914. W. S. C.

BLOCKADE

Secretary.
First Sea Lord.
Additional Civil Lord (A.C.L.).
Chief of the Staff and others.

A standing Admiralty Committee will be formed under the presidency of the Additional Civil Lord, to be called 'The Restriction of Enemies' Supplies Committee,' composed as follows:—

One representative of the Trade Division of the War Staff.

One representative of the Foreign Office.
One representative of the Board of Trade.
Mr. Alan Burgoyne, M.P.
Mr. C. Money, M.P.

The duties of this Committee will be to examine and watch continually all means or routes by which supplies of food or raw material may reach Germany and Austria; to report weekly all importations or exportations to and from these countries coming to their knowledge; and to recommend by what methods, financial, commercial, diplomatic, and military, they may be hampered, restricted, and, if possible, stopped. Measures should, in the first instance, be recommended to secure full and accurate information from day to day of all vessels unloading cargoes which may ultimately reach Germany or Austria at neutral ports, and the port of Rotterdam especially, as well as the possibility of supplies coming through a northern part of Sweden or from Sweden itself across the Baltic, or through Norway and Denmark. Holland must be the subject of the closest study, it being clearly impossible for the British Government to allow the neutral port of Rotterdam to serve as a base of supplies to the enemy. Trustworthy agents in Holland must be obtained or dispatched thither for this purpose. Any possible importation overland through Italy or up the Adriatic must be included in the survey.

Funds will be forthcoming for any special action required.

The committee should hold its first meeting on Friday, the 14th, using a committee room at the Admiralty.

A.C.L. to nominate his own Secretary, and make all further arrangements to carry this minute into effect.

August 13, 1914. W. S. C.

MUNITIONS

Lord Kitchener.

Captain Hankey, of the Committee of Imperial Defence, has been to me with what seems rather a good idea. He suggests that Girouard should be put at the head of an emergency armament multiplication committee or department, to set on foot and develop the maximum possible output of guns, rifles, ammunition, etc. I am sure, myself, that more could be done by the firms than is being done at present. For instance, after you told me of the pressure you had put upon them and that their complete limits had been reached, our people went round and obtained undertakings from the trade to produce 700 rifles a week more, additional to all that had been ordered by you.

This is only a half-formed idea, and I pass it on to you not as a recommendation, but simply for what it is worth.

September 3, 1914. W. S. C.

UNITED STATES NEUTRALITY

Sir Edward Grey.

Please see attached. [*Not printed.*]

I should be so glad if you could see your way to making a strong stand against this. Even if we ultimately have to give way, the fact that they will have overruled our protest will, in the existing balance of public opinion in the United States, make them desirous of being helpful, or at any rate not unfriendly, on other points at issue.

Our case is clear. The Germans have announced their intention, have endeavoured on a large scale, and have partially begun, to arm merchant ships as commerce destroyers, and they even claim to carry out this process of arming and equipping in neutral harbours or on the high seas. We have been forced in consequence of this to arm a number of our ships in self-defence. In doing this we follow the undoubted law of the seas as it was practised in all the great wars of the past. We claim that by international law a merchant ship armed in her own defence, so long as she takes no aggressive action, is entitled to the full status of a peaceful trading ship. We ask that our ships so armed for this purpose shall be accorded that status in the neutral ports of the world.

We are quite willing to agree that German merchant ships similarly armed in self-defence shall be similarly treated. It is only when merchant ships are armed and commissioned as auxiliary cruisers, not for purposes of self-defence, but for those of commerce destruction, that we claim they should be treated as ships of war. And here again we ask no better treatment for ourselves than for the enemy.

We recognize the natural difficulty to a neutral State, anxious to preserve a strict impartiality, of discerning whether ships carrying the same armament are intended for offensive or defensive action. We offer that this question should be decided by a simple and practical test. If the armed merchant ship is engaged in ordinary commerce, discharging and taking a regular cargo, and embarking passengers in the usual way, she should be counted as a trader in spite of her armament. If, on the other hand, she is not engaged in commerce, is not doing the ordinary things she would do and has done in times of peace, but is either carrying special cargoes of coal and stores to belligerent cruisers on the high seas, or is travelling in ballast, or is not trafficking in her cargo in the natural way, then we say she should be treated as a ship of war, even if the Government of the State whose flag she flies declares that she is only armed and will only fight in self-defence. We must therefore hold a neutral Government impeccable if she allows a German armed merchantman, which takes a regular cargo in the ordinary way, to arm in her ports or leave them for the high seas, even if subsequently that vessel engages not merely in self-defence, but in actual aggressive attack. Neutrals who deal with ships according to the 'Cargo Test' must be held blameless by us whatever the subsequent careers of the vessels may be. The issues which remain open after these ships have put to sea can only be decided between the belligerents.

The second point that I hope you will be able to fight is: no transference after the declaration of war of enemy's ships to a neutral flag, as agreed upon in the Declaration of London. We cannot recognize such transferences, which are plainly, in the nature of things, designed to enable the transferred ship to obtain under the neutral flag an immunity from the conditions created by the war.

I would earnestly ask that both these points should be pressed now in the most direct and formal manner on Powers concerned, and particularly upon the United States, and that very great pressure should be exerted.

In this connection it may be pointed out that the United States have already allowed one or more ships, including the *Kronprinz Wilhelm*, to leave their ports armed, denuded of cargo, and cleared for action, and that to stop British ships of a self-defensive character is showing a partiality to one of the belligerents incompatible with fair and loyal neutrality. If to this is to be added the attempt which Mr. Bryan has made, by his personal intervention, to take over the Hamburg-American liners from Germany and run them under the American flag, it seems to me clear that a situation has arisen which, in the ultimate issues, ought, in some form or other, to be brought publicly before the people of the United States. I am under no illusions as to their attitude, but the forces at work there in the present circumstances are such as to make it impossible for any Government to load the dice against England, or go openly one inch beyond an even neutrality.

I venture to suggest to you that this position ought to be fought up to the point of full publicity, and by every means and influence at our disposal, before we are forced to consider the various inferior alternatives which no doubt exist.

August 19, 1914. W. S. C.

Secretary.
First Sea Lord.
Admiral Slade.
Chief of Staff.
Captain Webb.

The Cabinet decided this morning that we must abandon, under protest and as an exception, the running of defensively-armed merchantmen to American ports. We do this on the assumption that we in no way waive the principle, but in consideration of the fact that the United States are preventing a large number of German ships suitable for armament from fitting out. We must also stipulate that the guns, having been landed from these ships, shall be returned without their mountings in some other non-military vessel on which and from which they clearly cannot be used during the voyage.

Pray draft a note to the Foreign Office accordingly.

September 3, 1914. W. S. C.

THE BRITISH PATROL OFF NEW YORK

Secretary.
First Sea Lord.
Chief of Staff.
Admiral Slade.

I have felt uncomfortable about this for some time. Although it is strictly legal, it must be very galling to the Americans to see their capital port picketed in this way. Instructions should be given that the patrolling cruisers should usually keep 8 or 10 miles away, or even farther if possible, and should only close in occasionally when there is some special need. They should, above all, be careful never to infringe the 3-mile limit, and should discharge their duties with tact, remembering how greatly British interests are concerned in the maintenance of good relations with the United States. On the other hand, the closest watch should be kept on shore upon the Hamburg-American liners, and our cruisers should be given the earliest warning if these are seen to be getting up steam. It ought to be quite easy to give our cruisers full warning of any movement. The prevention of these Hamburg-American liners leaving armed and fuelled is practically the whole duty of our vessels off New York; and as long as they are in a position to discharge this they need not be too obtrusive in their other duties.

October 26, 1914. W. S. C.

ANTI-SUBMARINE MEASURES

Dover.

First Sea Lord and others.

It is intolerable that we should be told that Dover is not safe against submarine attack. It is the only military harbour we have except Portland. We *must* be able to keep ships there safely. Measures are being taken to close one of the entrances by sinking two ships. This is urgent and vital, and should be pressed forward from hour to hour without a moment's pause. The other entrance should have an anti-submarine net and gate arranged. If the boom defence has carried away it must be repaired and replaced by night-and-day exertions. Meanwhile the long barges fitted with nets which have been prepared at Dunkirk should be brought over as soon as the weather allows, and used either to block the entrance or to give net protection to ships lying inside.

November 1, 1914. W. S. C.

HIGH-EXPLOSIVE PRODUCTION

A.C.L.

You must act in this matter and refer to me only when special need arises. The points to be held in view are clear and simple:—

1. We must have effective Government control of all the explosive works, so as to attain the maximum output, and ensure our not being hampered by German influences, which are powerful and subtle in the Explosive Trust.

2. Naval interests must be properly safeguarded, and this can only be either by the Navy taking Nobels and the other two companies, or by an absolutely equal representation and control as between the two Departments [i.e. Admiralty and War Office] over the whole of the explosive factories combined. We cannot be placed in the position of being overborne by the military authorities, and having our necessary demands set aside.

3. It is, however, our duty to do everything in our power to aid in the expansion of the Army and the production of war material for the conduct of the campaign, and at a certain point only State policy can decide whether naval or military interests are to claim priority.

4. We must make a good bargain for the country; and if these people are financed by Government money to set up great new works and broaden the scale of their business, good arrangements should be made to transfer these works to the Government at the end of the war.

November 9. 1914. W. S. C.

THE DUMMY FLEET

(Most Secret.)
Secretary.
First Sea Lord.
Third Sea Lord.
Director of Naval Construction.
Naval Secretary.

It is necessary to construct without delay a dummy fleet: 10 merchant vessels, either German prizes or British ships, should be selected at once. They should be distributed among various private yards not specially burdened with warship building at the present time. They are then to be mocked up to represent particular battleships of the 1st and 2nd Battle Squadrons. The actual size need not correspond exactly, as it is notoriously difficult to judge the size of vessels at sea, and frequently even destroyers are mistaken for cruisers. We are bearing in mind particularly aerial and periscope observations, where deception is much more easy. It is not necessary that the structures should be strong enough to stand rough weather. Very little metal would be required, and practically the whole work should be executed in wood or canvas. The ships would move under their own power under favourable conditions of weather from one base to another, and even when the enemy knows that we have such a fleet its presence will tend to mystify and confuse his plans and baffle and distract the enterprise of his submarines. He will always be in doubt as to which is the real and which is the dummy fleet. An attack upon the dummy fleet can be made not less dangerous than an attack upon the real fleet by the proper use of our own submarines and destroyers with towing charges, and possibly by traps of nets and mines.

The matter is urgent. Three years ago I formed this idea, and deeply regret that I have been so long deterred from putting it into execution. The Third Sea Lord, Fourth Sea Lord, and Naval Secretary will meet today under the Third Sea Lord and formulate detailed proposals for immediate action. The utmost secrecy must be observed, and special measures taken to banish all foreigners from the districts where the mocking-up is being done. I should hope to receive the list of ships which are selected for conversion tomorrow morning, and the list of firms among whom the work will be parcelled out during the course of that day. Estimates of cost and time should also be made, but paint, canvas, and woodwork can be quickly done, and I should expect in a fortnight, or at the outside in three weeks, that 10 vessels will be actually at our tactical disposal.

October 21, 1914. W. S. C.

THE COASTAL PATROL

Secret.
First Sea Lord.

If the system of working the patrol flotillas, explained in the enclosed memorandum, has actually been enforced, it is in complete violation not only of the obvious principles of war, but of all the orders and directions issued on this subject during the last three years. The word 'distribution' applied to armed force implies the most vicious ideas. To proceed by dividing the front to be watched by the number of destroyers available for watching and working out the number of miles to the destroyers is the negation of good sense and military principle.

Ever since the Manœuvres of 1912 I have repeatedly explained the principles which should govern the working of the patrol flotillas (*see* attached papers), and these have been expounded to the C.I.D. and issued to the War Staff with the full concurrence of the First Sea Lord and the C.O.S. If there has been a departure from these principles and an adoption of the barbarous method of 'distributing' the destroyers along the whole coast in a single row like toy soldiers on the kitchen table, this shows a total lack of comprehension.

It must again be repeated:—

1. That the coast, with its cyclists, signal stations, and watchers, is the line of observation, and the only line of observation, which can certainly report the arrival of an enemy;

2. That the patrol flotillas, both of submarines and destroyers, instead of being frittered away on useless cordon and patrolling duties, should be kept concentrated and ready for action at selected sallyports along the coast, ready to proceed in force to any point where shore information shows that an enemy is attempting to land;

3. That there is to be nothing like routine or sentry-go patrolling, except at the mouths of harbours, and that from time to time occasional good bold reconnaissances 60, 70, and 80 miles out to seaward should be pushed from each sallyport by the whole of the boats available, varied occasionally by the prying scouting of a single destroyer;

4. That the prevention of mine-laying can only be done by trawlers, who must summon help from the nearest patrol centre if necessary.

It must be recognized that nothing in our dispositions prevents an enemy from approaching the British coasts with transports, and beginning a landing there, but that if the flotillas are properly handled he should be attacked within a few hours by submarines and destroyers, and that the numbers and strength of the forces against him should continually increase until long before any considerable force can be landed the enemy's transports and escort would be overwhelmed, and those who are landed hopelessly cut off. The only alternative to this policy of letting the enemy begin to land and then attacking him while his landing is in progress, is the close blockade of the Heligoland Bight. There is much to be said for and against both courses, but the intermediate course of 'distributing' a weak and thin cordon of patrols at a short distance from the coast in the hopes of putting up some defensive shield or screen is utterly futile.

The policy at present approved is to concentrate the flotillas at fixed points and keep them strong and fresh and fit for action, while relying upon the coast watch to give early and accurate information of any attack by the enemy. If this policy be adhered to strictly and simply, it will not be found impossible to spare the 12 destroyers which the Commander-in-Chief needs. It is, however, to be considered whether they could not better be taken from the two 1st Fleet Flotillas at Harwich.

November 7, 1914. W. S. C.

THE RIFLE SHORTAGE

The following course is to be adopted:—

1. As soon as the War Office are ready to hand over the 50,000 Japanese rifles, the whole of the rifles, long and short, whether used by sailors or marines, on board H.M. ships at home and abroad, will be collected and brought on shore to the Royal Naval Ordnance Depots. The Japanese rifles will be issued to all ships in their place: there will be no rifles of any sort on board H.M. ships other than Japanese.

2. From the British rifles surrendered by the Fleet, 15,000 short .303 charger loading rifles will be set aside for the Royal Naval Division, i.e., one rifle for each of 12,000 men plus 25 per cent for reserve and training. All the rifles now possessed by the Royal Naval Division will then be surrendered to the Ordnance Depots in exchange for the 15,000 short .303 British rifles aforesaid. Therefore the Royal Naval Division will have 15,000 short British .303 and no more.

3. There will then be handed over to the Army 57,800 rifles of which 9,000 will be short charger loading.

4. The 50,000 Japanese rifles will be issued to the Fleet in the following proportion:—

One rifle for each marine, and one rifle for every 5 sailors, ships on foreign service receiving one rifle for every 3 sailors. The rest of the rifles will be issued as required to trawlers and auxiliaries, and kept in the Royal Marine and Royal Naval Ordnance Depots.

The Fleet will thus be completely re-armed with the 50,000 Japanese rifles, and the Royal Naval Division with .303 short rifles ready for field service.

Let me now have calculations worked out on this basis; and draft a letter accordingly to the War Office.

November 25, 1914. W. S. C.

INDEX